When should I travel to get the best airfare?
Where do I go for answers to my travel questions?
What's the best and easiest way to plan and book my trip?

frommers.travelocity.com

Frommer's, the travel guide leader, has teamed up with **Travelocity.com**, the leader in online travel, to bring you an in-depth, easy-to-use resource designed to help you plan and book your trip online.

At **frommers.travelocity.com**, you'll find free online updates about your destination from the experts at Frommer's plus the outstanding travel planning and purchasing features of Travelocity.com. Travelocity.com provides reservations capabilities for 95 percent of all airline seats sold, more than 47,000 hotels, and over 50 car rental companies. In addition, Travelocity.com offers more than 2,000 exciting vacation and cruise packages. Travelocity.com puts you in complete control of your travel planning with these and other great features:

Expert travel guidance from Frommer's - over 150 writers reporting from around the world!

Best Fare Finder - an interactive calendar tells you when to travel to get the best airfare

Fare Watcher - we'll track airfare changes to your favorite destinations

Dream Maps - a mapping feature that suggests travel opportunities based on your budget

Shop Safe Guarantee - 24 hours a day / 7 days a week live customer service, and more!

Whether traveling on a tight budget, looking for a quick weekend getaway, or planning the trip of a lifetime, Frommer's guides and Travelocity.com will make your travel dreams a reality. You've bought the book, now book the trip!

Also available from Hungry Minds

the Unofficial Guide® to

Bed & Breakfasts and Country Inns in the Mid-Atlantic

1st Edition

Barbara Sturm

Hungry Minds, Inc.
New York, NY • Indianapolis, IN • Cleveland, OH

Please note that prices fluctuate in the course of time, and travel information changes under the impact of many factors that influence the travel industry. We therefore suggest that you write or call ahead for confirmation when making your travel plans. Every effort has been made to ensure the accuracy of information throughout this book and the contents of this publication are believed correct at the time of printing. Nevertheless, the publishers cannot accept responsibility for errors or omissions or for changes in details given in this guide or for the consequences of any reliance on the information provided by the same. Assessments of attractions and so forth are based upon the author's own experience and therefore, descriptions given in this guide necessarily contain an element of subjective opinion, which may not reflect the publisher's opinion or dictate a reader's own experience on another occasion. Readers are invited to write to the publisher with ideas, comments, and suggestions for future editions.

Published by Hungry Minds, Inc.
909 Third Avenue
New York, NY 10022

1st edition

Produced by Menasha Ridge Press
COVER DESIGN BY MICHAEL J. FREELAND
INTERIOR DESIGN BY MICHELE LASEAU
LLUSTRATIONS BY RASHELL SMITH, KARL BRANDT, BRENT SAVAGE, AND CLINT LAHNEN

ISBN 0-7654-6233-9

ISSN 1531-1589

Manufactured in the United States of America

10 9 8 7 6 5 4 3 2 1

Contents

List of Maps

About the Author and Illustrators

Barbara Sturm has produced travel articles and photography focusing on the Mid-Atlantic region for nearly three decades. Her travel journalism career has taken her throughout the United States and to 60 countries. More than 750 of her articles have been published, in outlets that include *The Washington Post, Baltimore Sun, Chicago Sun-Times, Daily News* and *Los Angeles Times,* as well as *Asia Travel Trade* and *Child Magazine.* For nearly a decade, her twice-monthly travel features have appeared in the *Asbury Park Press* and *Home News Tribune* and can now be seen on the Injersey internet site. Born in Takoma Park, Maryland, and raised in Washington, D.C., her love of travel began in childhood. After earning her BA in Cultural History from the University of Wisconsin, she studied in Perugia, Italy, and lived in Hawaii, California, Wyoming, South Carolina, Massachusetts, and New York. She currently resides in Edison, New Jersey where she enjoys the culinary efforts of her husband, George, a retired FBI Agent. They have a son, Christopher, and a frisky cairn terrier named Bullet. Her interests include golf and the Circumnavigators Club, an organization of world travelers.

Rashell Smith, Karl Brandt, Brent Savage, and **Clint Lahnen** are the talented contributing illustrators for this book. They are all part of the Indianapolis Production Services Department for Hungry Minds, Inc.

Rashell is a graduate of International Business College with a degree in Graphic Design. She is from Mays, Indiana, and loves to garden and play softball.

Karl is a Graduate of Purdue University with a degree in Computer Graphics. He lives in Indianapolis with his wife Bridget and enjoys listening to and playing music.

Brent is also a Graduate of Purdue University with a degree in Computer Graphics. He lives in Fishers, Indiana, and works part-time for the Fishers Fire Department.

Clint is a graphic artist and enjoys fishing, hockey, and golf in his spare time. He and his wife Amanda have two children, Courtney and Cooper, and reside in Pittsboro, Indiana.

Acknowledgments

Making a personal visit to more than 300 bed-and-breakfasts in a seven state area is a pleasant but complex task. It was my good fortune to find a number of people to help manage the scheduling details and/or provide transportation. During this project I traveled several thousand miles in all kinds of weather—by plane and train, but mostly by car. My heartfelt thanks go to these stalwart folks who saw to it that I got where I needed to be and showed me tourist attractions en route. They are Anne Melious, Patti Donahue, Vanessa Greene, Jeff Shipley, Heather Weber, Laurie Nichiporuk, Pat White, Pam Saperstein, Nancy Arena, Nancy Gold, Susan Cayea, Andrea Coman, Ann Cooper, Peter Carafano, Jennifer Boes, Lucinda Hampton, Denise Fegan, Dottie Sarisky, Anita Miller, Connie Yingling, Martha Steger, Mary Pat Kloenne, Cindy Harrington, Steve Shaluta, Matt Turner, and George Sturm. I am grateful for the hospitality of all bed-and-breakfast owners and innkeepers who welcomed me, graciously showed me their properties, and patiently answered my questions. My sincere thanks goes to Bob Sehlinger and Molly Merkle for their encouragement and support and to Nathan Lott for his editorial expertise.

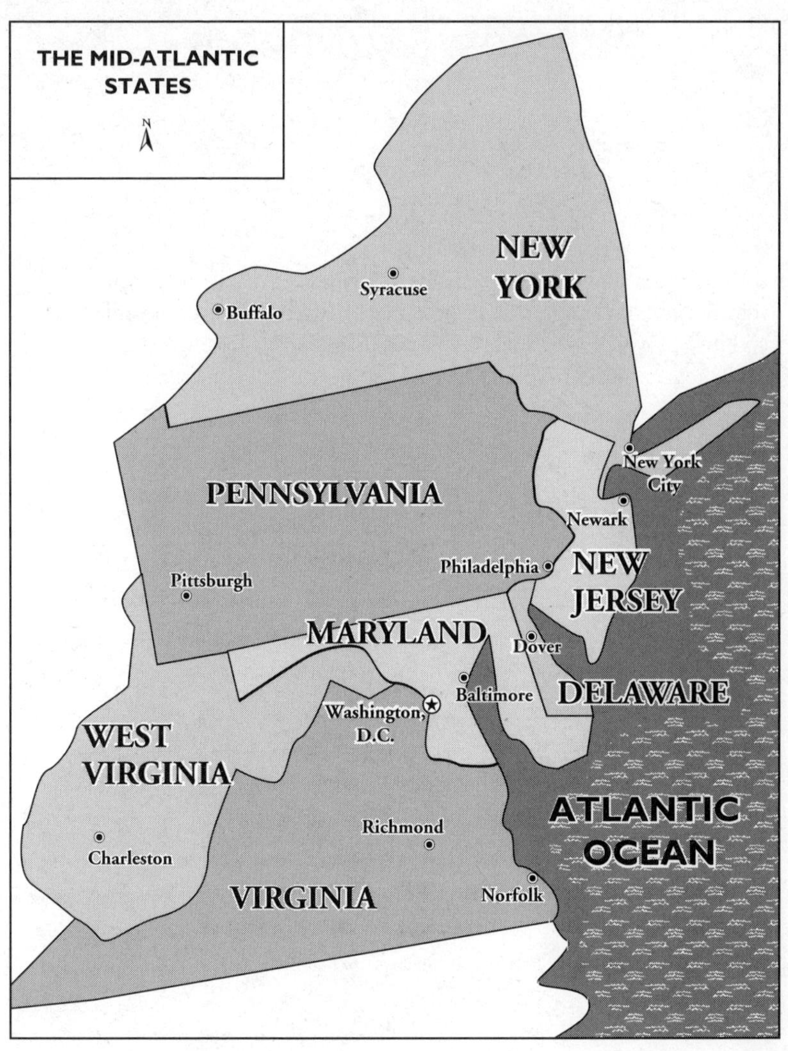
THE MID-ATLANTIC STATES
N
NEW YORK
Syracuse
Buffalo
PENNSYLVANIA
New York City
Newark
Philadelphia
NEW JERSEY
Pittsburgh
MARYLAND
Dover
Baltimore
DELAWARE
Washington, D.C.
WEST VIRGINIA
ATLANTIC OCEAN
Richmond
Charleston
Norfolk
VIRGINIA

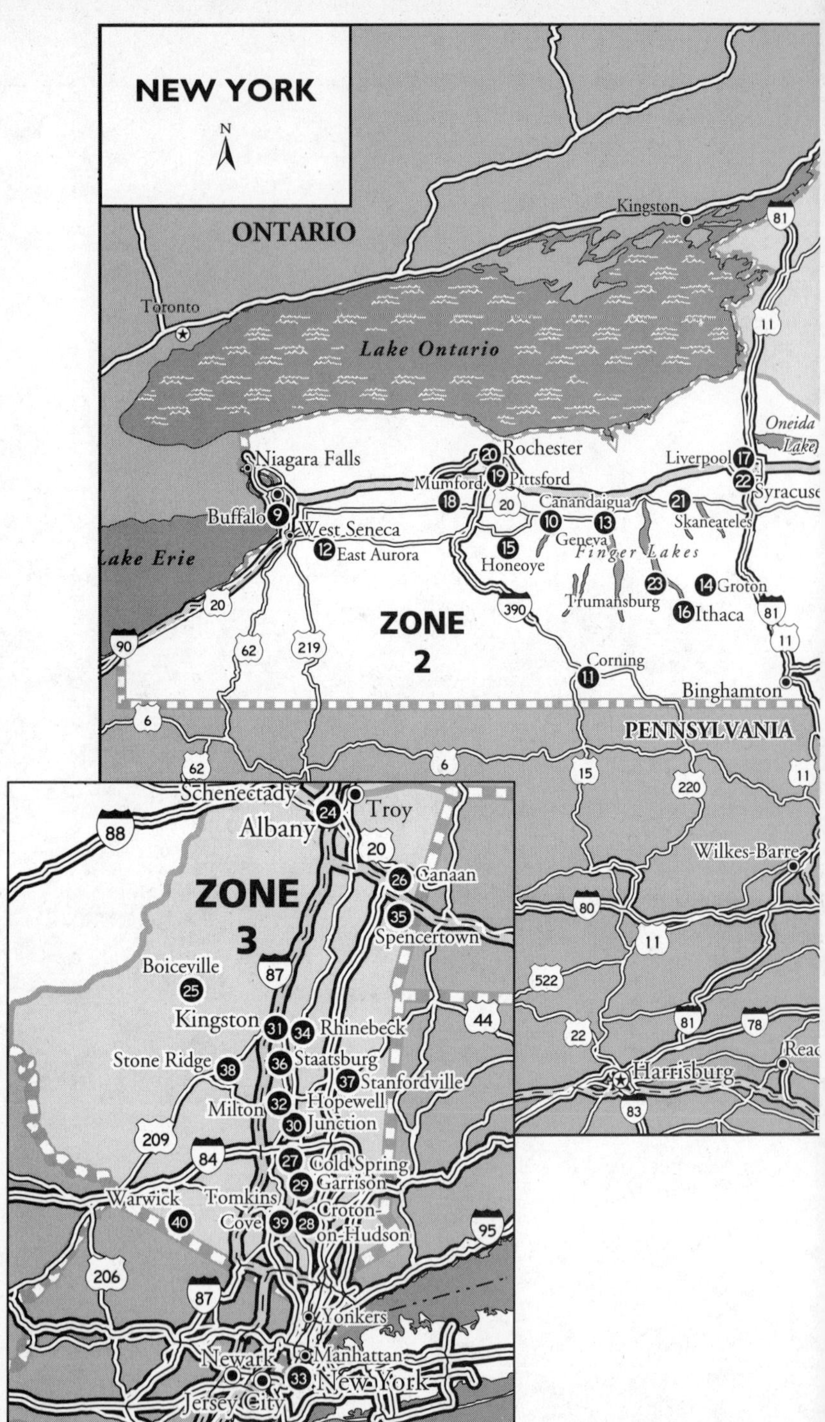
NEW YORK
N
ONTARIO
Kingston
Toronto
Lake Ontario
Oneida Lake
Niagara Falls
Rochester
Liverpool
Mumford
Pittsford
Syracuse
Canandaigua
Buffalo
West Seneca
Skaneateles
Geneva
Lake Erie
East Aurora
Finger Lakes
Honeoye
Groton
Trumansburg
Ithaca
ZONE 2
Corning
Binghamton
PENNSYLVANIA
Schenectady
Troy
Albany
Canaan
Wilkes-Barre
ZONE 3
Spencertown
Boiceville
Kingston
Rhinebeck
Stone Ridge
Staatsburg
Stanfordville
Hopewell Junction
Milton
Harrisburg
Cold Spring
Garrison
Warwick
Tomkins Cove
Croton-on-Hudson
Yonkers
Newark
Manhattan
New York
Jersey City

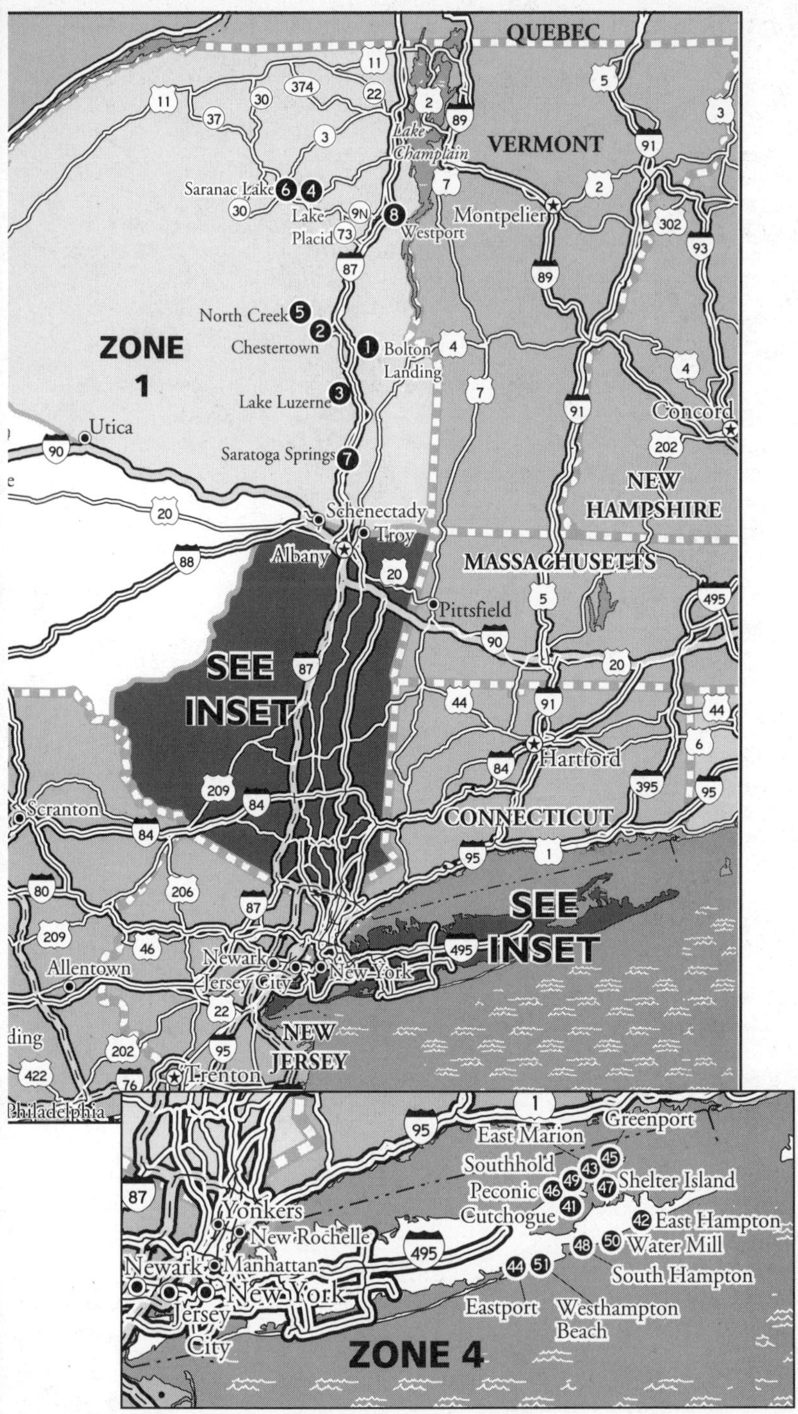

QUEBEC
VERMONT
Lake Champlain
Montpelier
Saranac Lake
Lake Placid
Westport
North Creek
Chestertown
Bolton Landing
Lake Luzerne
Saratoga Springs
ZONE 1
Utica
Schenectady
Troy
Albany
Concord
NEW HAMPSHIRE
MASSACHUSETTS
Pittsfield
SEE INSET
Hartford
CONNECTICUT
Scranton
SEE INSET
Newark
Jersey City
New York
Allentown
NEW JERSEY
Trenton
Philadelphia
Greenport
East Marion
Southhold
Shelter Island
Peconic
Cutchogue
East Hampton
Water Mill
South Hampton
Yonkers
New Rochelle
Newark
Manhattan
New York
Jersey City
Eastport
Westhampton Beach
ZONE 4

New York Properties by Zone and City

New Jersey Properties by Zone and City

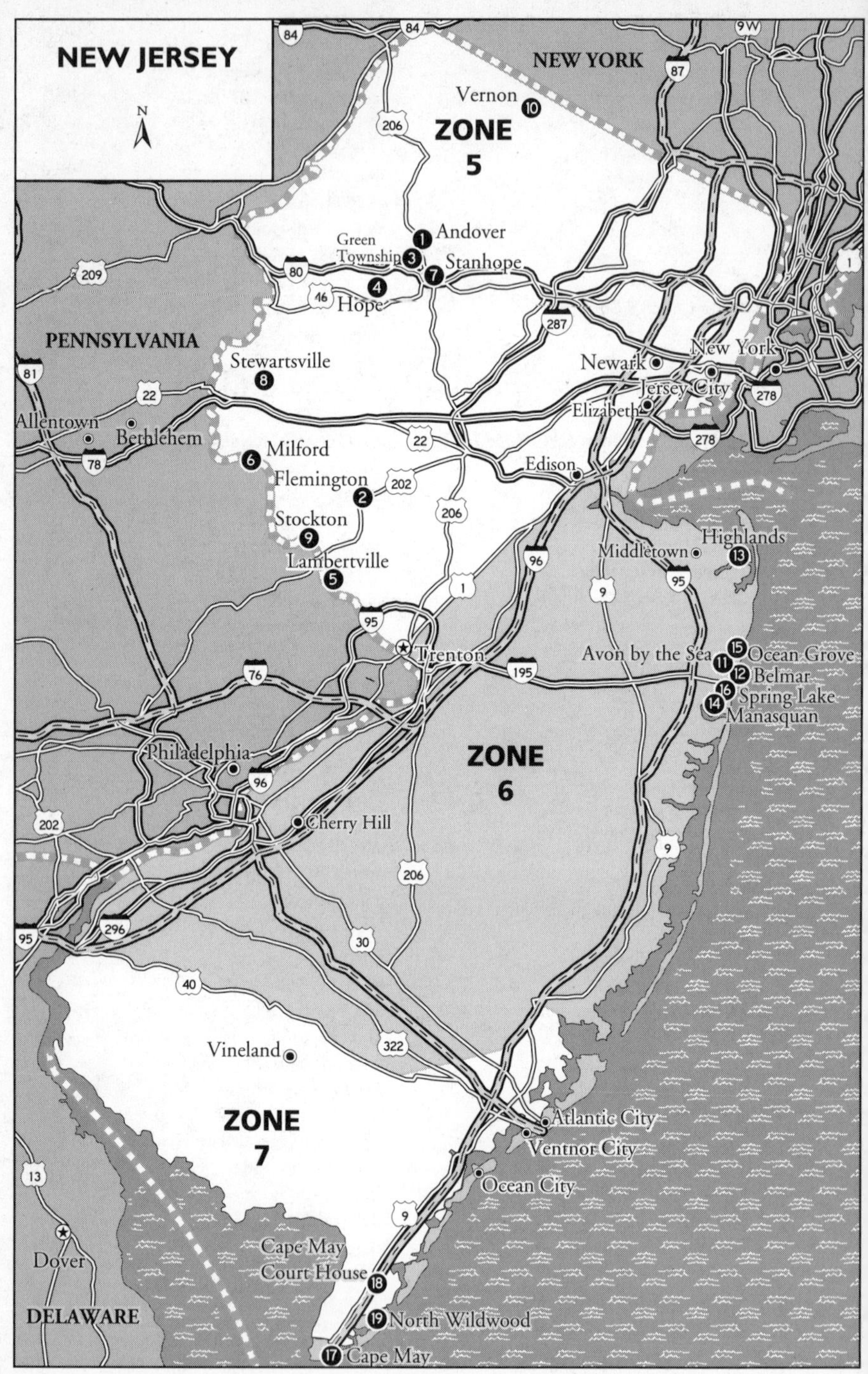
NEW JERSEY
N
NEW YORK
PENNSYLVANIA
DELAWARE
ZONE 5
ZONE 6
ZONE 7
Vernon 10
Andover 1
Green Township 3
Stanhope 7
Hope 4
Stewartsville 8
Milford 6
Flemington 2
Stockton 9
Lambertville 5
Trenton
Newark
New York
Jersey City
Elizabeth
Edison
Middletown
Highlands 13
Avon by the Sea 11
15 Ocean Grove
12 Belmar
16 Spring Lake
14 Manasquan
Allentown
Bethlehem
Philadelphia
Cherry Hill
Vineland
Atlantic City
Ventnor City
Ocean City
Cape May Court House 18
19 North Wildwood
17 Cape May
Dover
84
9W
87
206
209
80
46
287
81
22
78
202
96
95
1
9
76
195
278
30
40
322
296
13
1

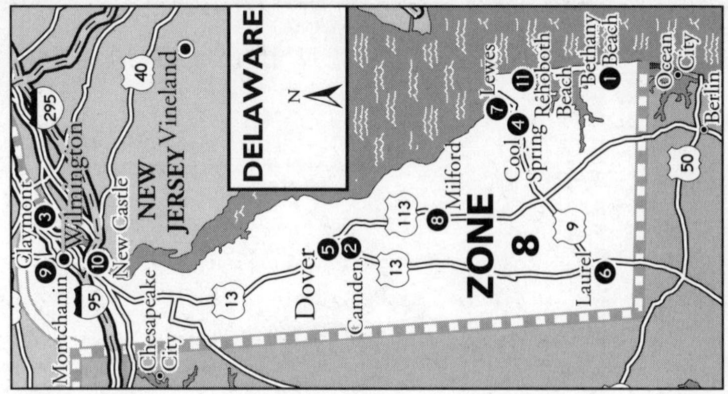

Delaware Properties by Zone and City

Pennsylvania Properties by Zone and City

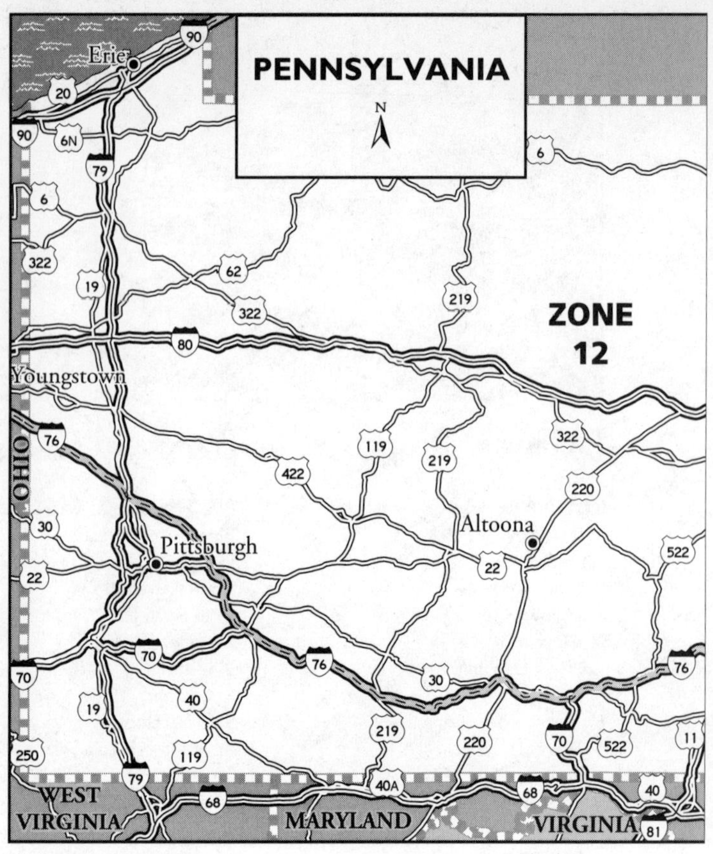

Pennsylvania Properties *(continued)*

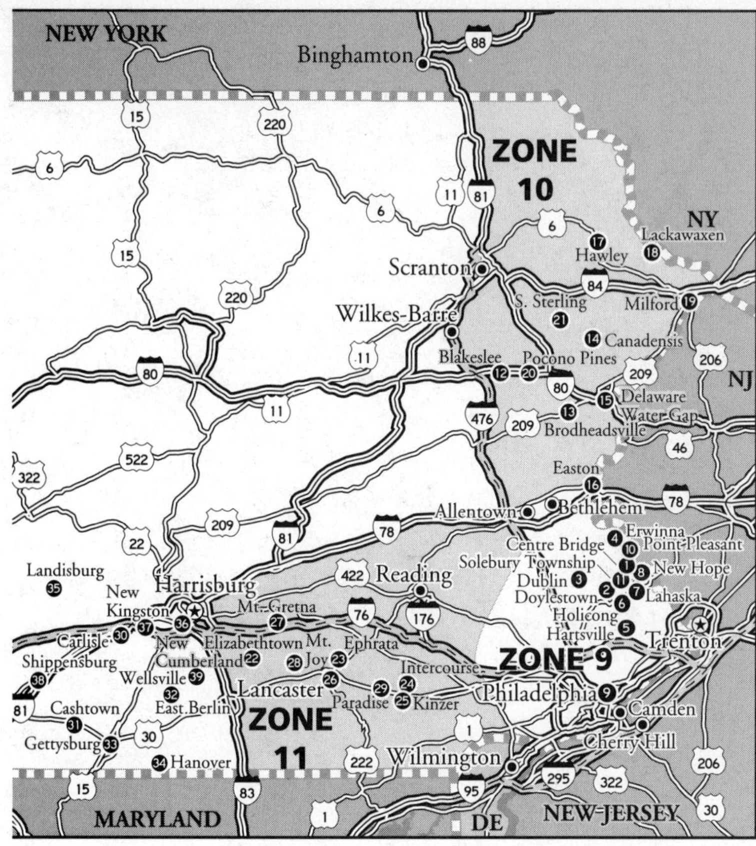
NEW YORK
Binghamton
ZONE 10
NY
Lackawaxen
Hawley
Scranton
Milford
S. Sterling
Wilkes-Barre
Canadensis
Blakeslee
Pocono Pines
NJ
Delaware Water Gap
Brodheadsville
Easton
Allentown
Bethlehem
Erwinna
Centre Bridge
Point Pleasant
Solebury Township
New Hope
Dublin
Doylestown
Lahaska
Holicong
Hartsville
Trenton
Landisburg
New Kingston
Harrisburg
Mt. Gretna
Reading
Carlisle
New Cumberland
Elizabethtown
Mt. Joy
Ephrata
Shippensburg
Wellsville
Intercourse
ZONE 9
Lancaster
Paradise
Kinzer
Philadelphia
Camden
Cashtown
East Berlin
Gettysburg
ZONE 11
Cherry Hill
Hanover
Wilmington
MARYLAND
DE
NEW JERSEY

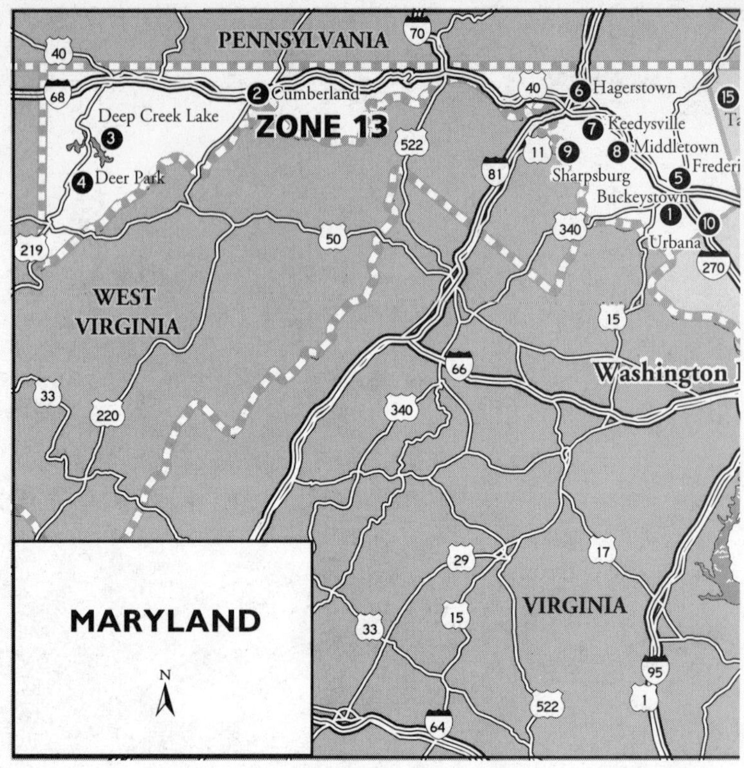

Maryland Properties by Zone and City

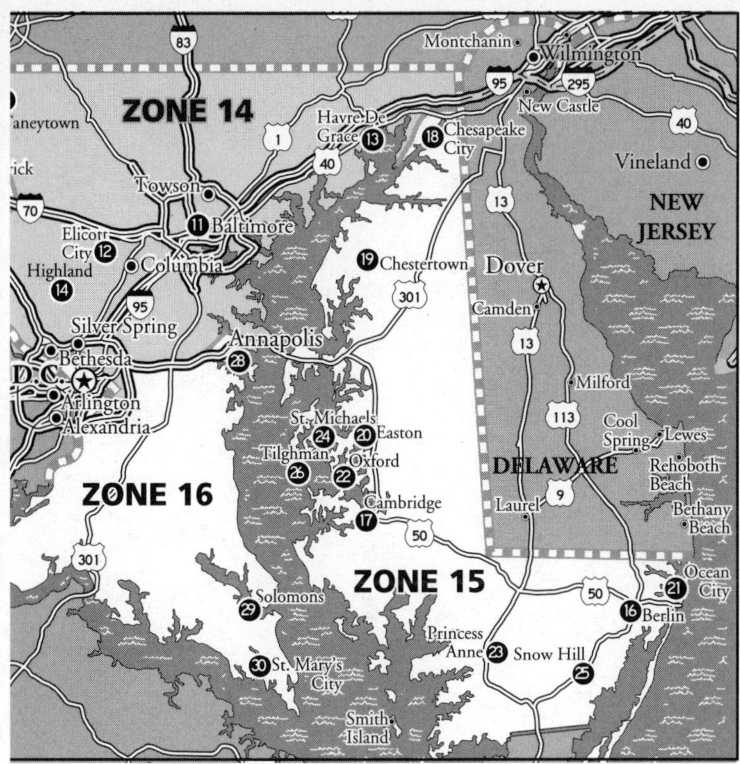

ZONE 15 *Eastern Shore*

ZONE 16 *Annapolis & Southern MD*

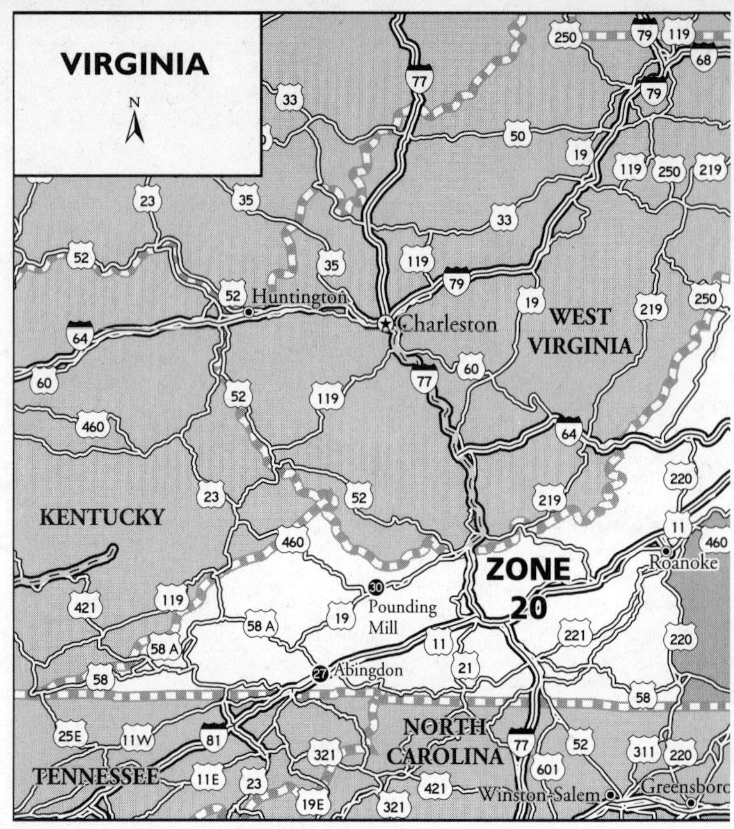

Virginia Properties by Zone and City

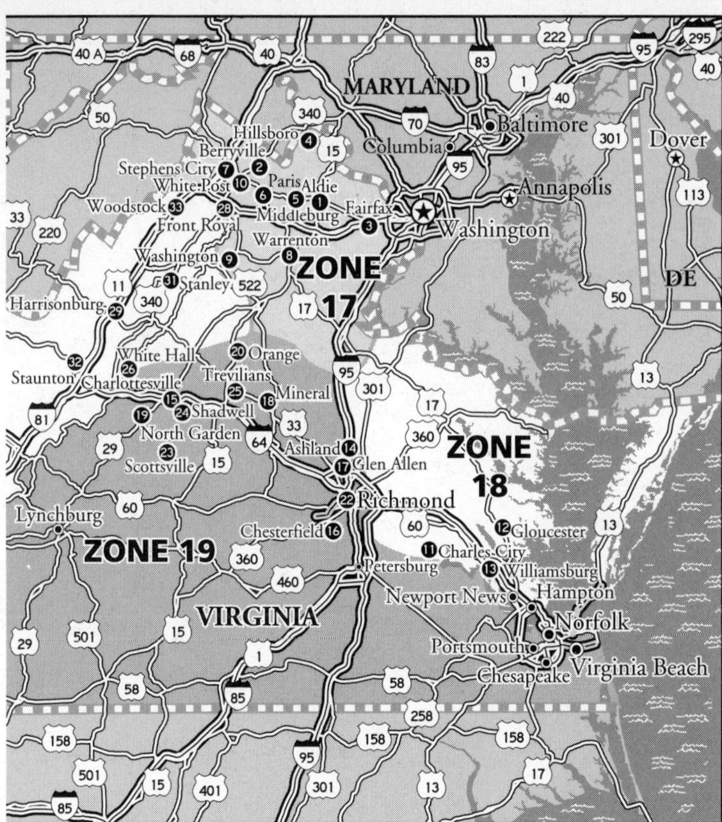
MARYLAND
Baltimore
Columbia
Dover
Annapolis
Washington
DE
Hillsboro
Berryville
Stephens City
White Post
Paris
Aldie
Woodstock
Front Royal
Middleburg
Fairfax
Warrenton
Washington
Stanley
Harrisonburg
ZONE 17
White Hall
Orange
Staunton
Charlottesville
Trevilians
Mineral
Shadwell
North Garden
Scottsville
Ashland
Glen Allen
ZONE 18
Richmond
Lynchburg
Chesterfield
Gloucester
ZONE 19
Charles City
Petersburg
Williamsburg
Newport News
Hampton
VIRGINIA
Norfolk
Portsmouth
Chesapeake
Virginia Beach

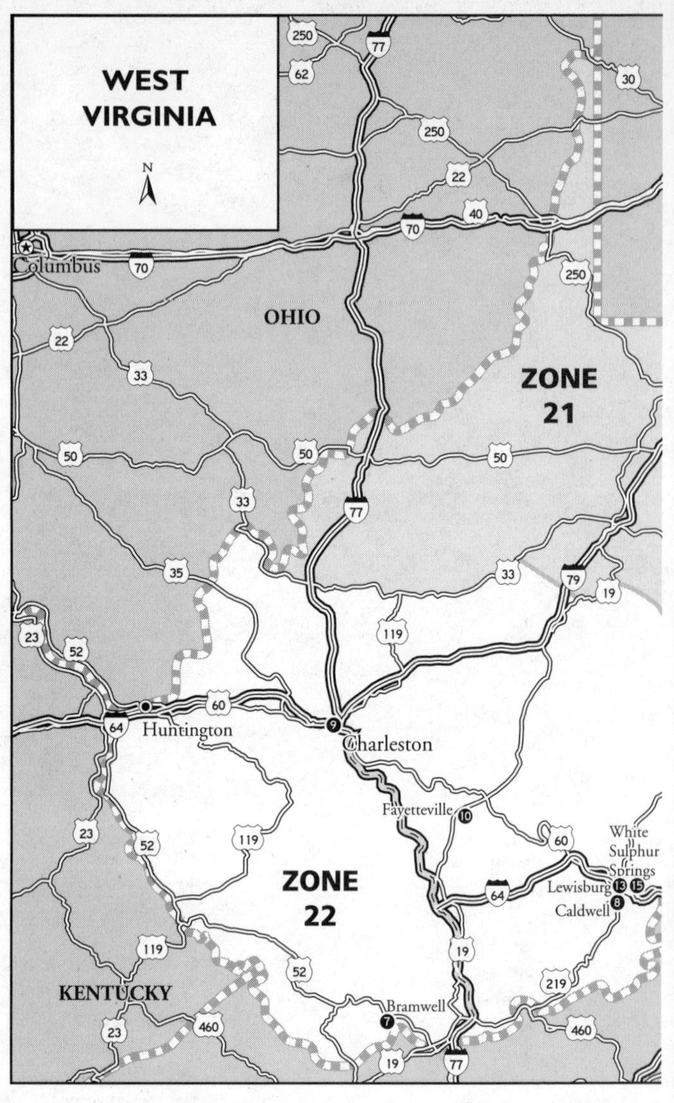

West Virginia Properties by Zone and City

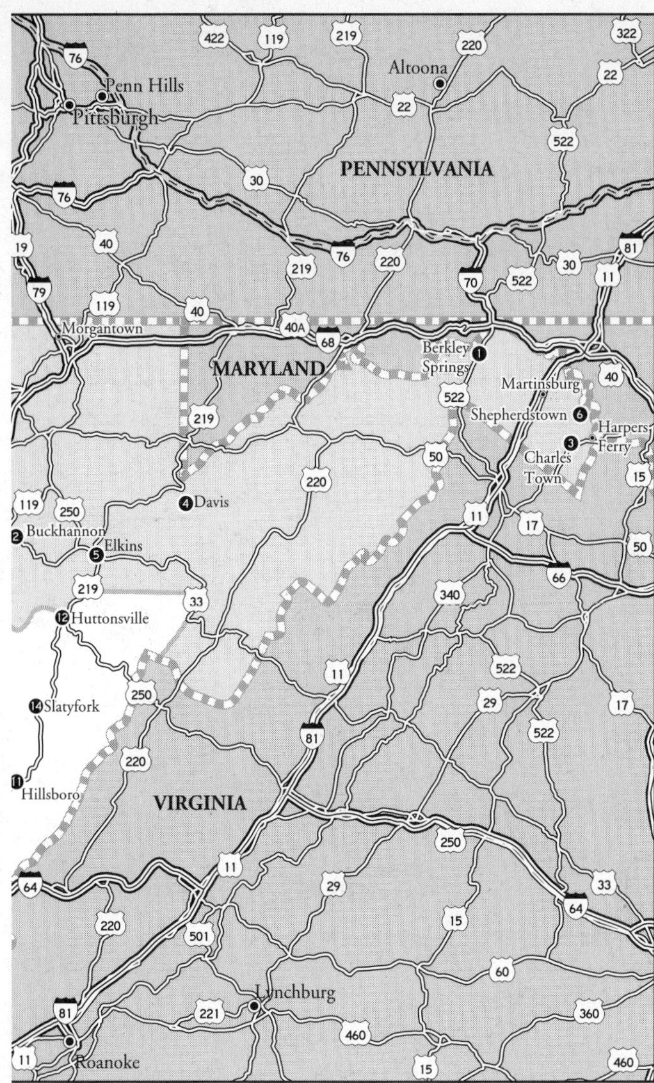

ZONE 22 ***Sothern WV***

7. Bramwell
Perry House, 350

8. Caldwell
Old Stone Manse, 351

9. Charleston
Brass Pineapple, 352

10. Fayetteville
White House, 353

11. Hillsboro
The Current, 354

12. Huttonsville
Hutton House, 355

13. Lewisburg
Lee Street, 356

14. Slatysford
Elk River Touring Center, 357

15. White Sulphur Springs
James Wylie House, 358
White Oaks, 359

The Best of the Mid-Atlantic

TOP OVERALL, *5 Stars* ★★★★★

Delaware
- Inn at Montchanin Village
- Little Creek Inn

Maryland
- Annapolis Inn
- Antrim 1844
- Blue Max Inn
- Brampton Inn
- Chanceford Hall
- Combsberry 1730
- Dr. Dodson House
- Great Oak Manor
- Inn at Antietam
- Inn at the Canal
- Lazyjack Inn
- Piper House
- Savage River Lodge
- Stone Manor

New Jersey
- Ocean Plaza
- The Queen Victoria

New York
- Dickenson House on James
- Evelyn's View
- Hobbit Hollow Farm
- Inn at Irving Place
- Inn at Stony Creek
- J. Harper Poor Cottage
- Morgan-Samuels Inn
- Onteora, The Mountain House
- Peach Grove Inn
- Silver Maple Farm
- The Point

Pennsylvania
- Battlefield Inn
- Country Log House Farm
- Doubleday Country Inn & Farm
- Inn at Fordhook Farm
- Mansion Inn
- Ravenshead
- Settlers Inn
- Sheppard Mansion
- The French Manor

Virginia
- Ashby Inn
- Bailiwick Inn
- Clifton - The Country Inn
- Goodstone Inn & Estate
- Inn at Little Washington
- Inn at Warner Hall
- Liberty Rose
- Prospect Hill Plantation

West Virginia
- Graceland

TOP OVERALL, *4.5 Stars* ★★★★½

Delaware
- Addy Sea
- Blue Heron Inn
- Blue Water House
- The Towers

Maryland
- Back Creek Inn
- Brome-Howard Inn
- Cambridge House
- Chez Amis
- Deer Park Inn
- Inn at Mitchell House
- Inn of Silent Music
- Inn on the Ocean
- Lake Pointe Inn
- Mr. Mole
- Paternal Gift Farm
- Waterloo Country Inn

New Jersey
- Carriage House
- Chestnut Hill on the Delaware
- La Maison
- Sea Crest By The Sea
- Wooden Duck

New York

1880 House
Acorn Inn
Alexander Hamilton House
Boathouse
Freddy's House
Friends Lake Inn
Glenwood House
Green Glen
Home Port
Inn on 23rd
Olde Rhinebeck Inn
Rose Inn
The Ivy Southampton
Victorian on the Bay

Pennsylvania

Doubleday Inn
EverMay-On-The-Delaware
Mountaintop Lodge
Mt. Gretna Inn
Pine Tree Farm
Twin Pine Manor

Virginia

Colonial Gardens
Mayfield Inn

West Virgina

Deerpark Country Inn
Hillbrook
Old Stone Manse

BUDGET (UNDER $75)

Delaware

William Penn
Zwaanendael Inn

Maryland

Beaver Creek House
Spencer-Silver Mansion
Turning Point Inn

New Jersey

Avon Manor Inn

New York

All Tucked Inn
Inn on the Library Lawn

Pennsylvania

Black Walnut
Country View
Doubleday Country Inn & Farm
Morning Glories
Warrington Farm

Virginia

Mayfield Inn

West Virginia

Current
Elk River Touring Center
Governor's Inn
Perry House

FARM OR RURAL SETTING

Delaware

Blue Heron Inn
Inn at Montchanin Village
Little Creek Inn
Manor at Cool Spring
Spring Garden

Maryland

Antietam Overlook Farm
Beaver Creek House
Brampton Inn
Brome-Howard Inn
Combsberry 1730
Great Oak Manor
Inn at Buckeystown
Inn at Mitchell House
Inn of Silent Music
Lazyjack Inn
Paternal Gift Farm
Piper House
Stone Manor
Turning Point Inn
Waterloo Country Inn

FARM OR RURAL SETTING *(continued)*

New Jersey
- Chimney Hill Farm
- Crossed Keys
- Stewart Inn
- Wooden Duck
- Woolverton Inn

New York
- Bird & Bottle Inn
- Freddy's House
- Genesee Country Inn
- Glenwood House
- Greenwoods
- Hobbit Hollow Farm
- Home Port
- Inn at Box Farm
- Inn at Stone Ridge
- Inn at Stony Creek
- Lakehouse Inn on Golden Pond
- Morgan-Samuels Inn
- Olde Rhinebeck Inn
- Rose Inn
- Silver Maple Farm
- Spencertown Country House
- Taughannock Farms Inn
- Victorian on the Bay
- Whistlewood Farm
- White Spring Manor

Pennsylvania
- Ash Mill Farm
- Baladerry Inn
- Barley Sheaf
- Battlefield Inn
- Black Walnut
- Blueberry Mountain Inn
- Cashtown Inn
- Chestnut Hill
- Country Gardens
- Country Log House Farm
- Country View
- Doubleday Country Inn & Farm
- Doubleday Inn
- EverMay-On-The-Delaware
- Field & Pine
- Green Acres Farm
- Hollyhedge Estate
- Inn at Fordhook Farm
- Mountaintop Lodge
- Pheasant Field
- Stone Ridge Farm
- The French Manor
- Twin Pine Manor
- Warrington Farm
- Whitehall

Virginia
- Ashby Inn
- Bellmont
- Black Horse Inn
- Buckskin Manor
- Clifton—The Country Inn
- Edgewood Plantation
- Goodstone Inn & Estate
- High Meadows Vineyard
- Inn at Sugar Hollow
- Inn at the Crossroads
- Inn at Vaucluse Spring
- Inn at Warner Hall
- Jordan Hollow Farm Inn
- L'Auberge Provencale
- Littlepage Inn
- Mayhurst Plantation
- North Bend Plantation
- Prospect Hill Plantation
- Virginia Cliffe Inn
- Willow Grove Inn

West Virginia
- Current
- Deerpark Country Inn
- Elk River Touring Center
- Hillbrook
- Old Stone Manse
- White Oaks

FAMILY ORIENTED

Delaware
- Blue Heron Inn
- Blue Water House

Maryland
- Inn at Mitchell House
- Inn at Walnut Bottom
- River House Inn
- Turning Point Inn

New Jersey
Cashelmara
Inn at the Shore
Inn on the Library Lawn
Mill House Inn
Ram's Head Inn

Pennsylvania
10-11 Clinton
Battlefield Inn
Black Walnut
Country Gardens
Country Log House Farm
Doubleday Country Inn & Farm
Green Acres Farm
Lafayette Inn
Settlers Inn
Wedgewood Collection

Virginia
Cedars
Henry Clay Inn
Inn at Meander Plantation
Inn at Narrow Passage
Jordan Hollow Farm Inn
North Bend Plantation
Virginia Cliffe Inn

West Virginia
Bright Morning Inn
Elk River Touring Center
Hutton House
James Wylie House

GROUPS AND FUNCTIONS EASILY ACCOMMODATED

Delaware
Addy Sea
Blue Heron Inn
Inn at Montchanin Village
The Towers
Zwaanendael Inn

Maryland
Antrim 1844
Atlantic Hotel
Brampton Inn
Brome-Howard Inn
Camel Cove Inn
Chanceford Hall
Combsberry 1730
Great Oak Manor
Inn at Buckeystown
Inn at Mitchell House
Inn on the Ocean
Paternal Gift Farm
River House Inn
Savage River Lodge
Stone Manor
Turning Point Inn
Waterloo Country Inn
Wayside Inn

New Jersey
Atlantic View Inn
Chimney Hill Farm
Crossed Keys
Doctors Inn
Inn at Millrace Pond
Inn at the Shore
La Maison
Nathaniel Morris Inn
Normandy Inn
Rhythm of the Sea
Wooden Duck
Woolverton Inn

New York
Batcheller Mansion Inn
Belvedere Mansion
Benn Conger Inn
Bird & Bottle Inn
Black Lion Mansion
Bykenhulle House
Evelyn's View
Friends Lake Inn
Hobbit Hollow Farm
Hudson House
Inn at Stone Ridge
Interlaken Inn
J. Harper Poor Cottage
Mill House Inn
Peach Grove Inn
Pig Hill
Porcupine
Quintessentials
Ram's Head Inn
Rose Inn
Silver Maple Farm
Spencertown Country House
Taughannock Farms Inn
Whistlewood Farm

GROUPS AND FUNCTIONS EASILY ACCOMMODATED *(continued)*

Pennsylvania

Ash Mill Farm
Barley Sheaf
Centre Bridge Inn
Cliff Park Inn & Golf Course
Doubleday Country Inn & Farm
Doubleday Inn
EverMay-On-The-Delaware
Golden Pheasant Inn
Hollyhedge Estate
Inn at Fordhook Farm
Lafayette Inn
Pheasant Field
Settlers Inn
Sheppard Mansion
The French Manor
Twin Pine Manor
West Ridge Guest House

Virginia

Ashby Inn
Bailiwick Inn
Black Horse Inn
Chester
Clifton - The Country Inn
Edgewood Plantation
Goodstone Inn & Estate
Henry Clay Inn
High Meadows Vineyard
Inn at the Crossroads
Inn at Vaucluse Spring
Inn at Warner Hall
Jordan Hollow Farm Inn
Joshua Walton House Inn
Killahevlin
L'Auberge Provencale
Littlepage Inn
Mayfield Inn
Mayhurst Plantation
North Bend Plantation
Prospect Hill Plantation
Silver Thatch Inn
Virginia Cliffe Inn

West Virginia

Current
Deerpark Country Inn
Elk River Touring Center
Hillbrook
White Oaks

HISTORIC PROPERTY

Delaware

Addy Sea
Armitage Inn
Darley Manor Inn
Inn at Montchanin Village
John Penrose Virden House
Little Creek Inn
Rose Tower
Royal Retreat
Spring Garden
The Towers
Wild Swan Inn
William Penn

Maryland

55 East
Abercrombie Badger
Annapolis Inn
Antrim 1844
Atlantic Hotel
Back Creek Inn
Beaver Creek House
Bishop's House
Blue Max Inn
Brampton Inn
Brome-Howard Inn
Cambridge House
Chanceford Hall
Chesapeake Wood Duck Inn
Chez Amis
Combsberry 1730
Currier House
Deer Park Inn
Dr. Dodson House
Five Gables Inn & Spa
Flag House
Georgian House
Glasgow Inn
Inn at Antietam
Inn at Mitchell House
Inn at the Canal
Inn at Walnut Bottom
Inn of Silent Music
Jacob Rorhbach House

Lake Pointe Inn
Lazyjack Inn
McCleery's Flat
Mr. Mole
Old Brick Inn
Parker House
Paternal Gift Farm
Piper House
River House Inn
Ship Watch Inn
Solomons Victorian Inn
Spencer-Silver Mansion
Stone Manor
Tyler Spite House
Waterloo Country Inn
Wayside Inn
White Swan Tavern
William Page Inn
Wingrove Manor

New Jersey

Ashling Cottage
Atlantic View Inn
Avon Manor Inn
Cape May
Captain Mey's
Cashelmara
Chestnut Hill on the Delaware
Chimney Hill Farm
Doctors Inn
Fairthorne
Humphrey Hughes House
Inn at Millrace Pond
Inn on Ocean
Inn-to-the-Sea
John F. Craig House
La Maison
Main Street Manor
Manor House Inn
Melrose
Nathaniel Morris Inn
Normandy Inn
Ocean Plaza
f the Sea
Sea Crest By The Sea
Seascape Manor
Spring Lake Inn
Stewart Inn
The Queen Victoria
Victoria House
Whistling Swan Inn
White Dove Cottage
Wooden Rabbit
Woolverton Inn

New York

1871 House
1880 House
Acorn Inn
Alexander Hamilton House
All Tucked Inn
Ancestor's Inn
Bartlett House
Batcheller Mansion Inn
Beau Fleuve
Belhurst Castle
Belvedere Mansion
Bird & Bottle Inn
Black Lion Mansion
Bykenhulle House
Evergreen On Pine
Freddy's House
Friends Lake Inn
Genesee Country Inn
Goose Pond Inn
Green Glen
Home Port
Hudson House
Inn at Box Farm
Inn at Irving Place
Inn at Stone Ridge
Inn at Stony Creek
Inn on 23rd
Inn on the Library Lawn
J. Harper Poor Cottage
Lamplight Inn
Mill House Inn
Morgan-Samuels Inn
Olde Rhinebeck Inn
Oliver Loud's Inn
Peach Grove Inn
Pig Hill
Porcupine
Quintessentials
Rosewood Inn
Spencertown Country House
Taughannock Farms Inn
The Ivy Southampton

HISTORIC PROPERTY *(continued)*

***New York* (continued)**

The Point
White Spring Manor
William Henry Miller Inn
Willow Hill House

Pennsylvania

10-11 Clinton
Ash Mill Farm
Baladerry Inn
Barley Sheaf
Battlefield Inn
Bechtel Mansion Inn
Cashtown Inn
Cliff Park Inn & Golf Course
Country Log House Farm
Creekside Inn
EverMay-On-The-Delaware
Farm Fortune
Field & Pine
Gaslight Inn
Golden Pheasant Inn
Green Acres Farm
Hollyhedge Estate
Inn at Fordhook Farm
Jacob's Resting Place
Lafayette Inn
Mansion Inn
Mt. Gretna Inn
Pheasant Field
Pine Tree Farm
Roebling Inn on the Delaware
Sheppard Mansion
Shippen Way Inn
Stone Ridge Farm
Tattersall Inn
Thomas Bond House
Whitehall

Virginia

200 South Street
Abingdon Boarding House
Applewood Colonial
Ashby Inn
Bailiwick Inn
Bellmont
Black Horse Inn
Buckskin Manor
Cedars
Chester
Chester House
Clifton—The Country Inn
Colonial Capital
Edgewood Plantation
Eighteen Seventeen
Emmanuel Hutzler House
Goodstone Inn & Estate
Hidden Inn
High Meadows Vineyard
Inn at Little Washington
Inn at Monticello
Inn at Narrow Passage
Inn at the Crossroads
Inn at Vaucluse Spring
Inn at Warner Hall
Joshua Walton House Inn
Killahevlin
L'Auberge Provencale
Liberty Rose
Little River Inn
Littlepage Inn
Mayfield Inn
Mayhurst Plantation
North Bend Plantation
Prospect Hill Plantation
Sampson Eagon Inn
Silver Thatch Inn
Willow Grove Inn

West Virginia

Bright Morning Inn
Carriage Inn
Current
Deerpark Country Inn
Governor's Inn
Highlawn Inn
Hutton House
James Wylie House
Old Stone Manse
Perry House
Thomas Shepherd Inn
Washington House Inn

MOUNTAIN SETTING

Maryland
Antietam Overlook Farm
Beaver Creek House
Camel Cove Inn
Deer Park Inn
Savage River Lodge

New Jersey
Alpine Haus

New York
Cove House
Friends Lake Inn
Goose Pond Inn
Interlaken Inn
Lamplight Inn
Onteora, The Mountain House
Pig Hill
Porcupine
The Point

Pennsylvania
Blueberry Mountain Inn
Mountaintop Lodge
Mt. Gretna Inn
Shepard House
The French Manor

Virginia
Ashby Inn
Inn at Little Washington
Inn at Monticello
Inn at Sugar Hollow
Jordan Hollow Farm Inn

West Virginia
Bright Morning Inn
Elk River Touring Center
Highlawn Inn
Hutton House
White Oaks

NO CREDIT CARDS ACCEPTED

Delaware
Spring Garden

Maryland
Bishop's House
Dr. Dodson House
Inn of Silent Music
Parker House

New Jersey
Chestnut Hill on the Delaware
Nathaniel Morris Inn

New York
Cove House
Freddy's House
Green Glen
Home Port
Lakehouse Inn on Golden Pond
Porcupine
Willow Hill House

Pennsylvania
Country Log House Farm
Country View

Virginia
Abingdon Boarding House

West Virginia
Perry House

PET FRIENDLY

Delaware
Little Creek Inn

Maryland
Five Gables Inn & Spa
River House Inn
Spencer-Silver Mansion
Waterloo Country Inn

New Jersey
Melrose

New York
Benn Conger Inn
Inn at Box Farm
Inn at Stone Ridge
Interlaken Inn
Mansion Hill Inn
Olde Rhinebeck Inn
The Point
Whistlewood Farm

PET FRIENDLY *(continued)*

Pennsylvania

10-11 Clinton
Blueberry Mountain Inn
Cliff Park Inn & Golf Course
Doubleday Country Inn & Farm
Golden Pheasant Inn
Green Acres Farm
Pheasant Field
Wedgewood Collection

Virginia

Chester House
High Meadows Vineyard
Jordan Hollow Farm Inn
Willow Grove Inn

West Virginia

Current
Governor's Inn
White Horse

ROMANTIC

Delaware

Addy Sea
Armitage Inn
Bay Moon
Inn at Montchanin Village
John Penrose Virden House
Little Creek Inn
The Towers

Maryland

Annapolis Inn
Antietam Overlook Farm
Antrim 1844
Blue Max Inn
Brampton Inn
Chanceford Hall
Combsberry 1730
Deer Park Inn
Dr. Dodson House
Great Oak Manor
Inn at the Canal
Inn on the Ocean
Lake Pointe Inn
Lazyjack Inn
Mr. Mole
Paternal Gift Farm
Savage River Lodge
Ship Watch Inn
Waterloo Country Inn
Wayside Inn

New Jersey

Ashling Cottage
Captain Mey's
Carriage House
Chestnut Hill on the Delaware
Crossed Keys
La Maison
Normandy Inn
Rhythm of the Sea
Sea Crest By The Sea
Seascape Manor
The Queen Victoria
Victoria House
Wooden Duck
Wooden Rabbit
Woolverton Inn

New York

1880 House
Acorn Inn
Batcheller Mansion Inn
Belvedere Mansion
Bird & Bottle Inn
Black Lion Mansion
Boathouse
Bykenhulle House
Evelyn's View
Glenwood House
Hobbit Hollow Farm
Home Port
Inn at Stony Creek
Inn New York City
J. Harper Poor Cottage
Lakehouse Inn on Golden Pond
Morgan-Samuels Inn
Peach Grove Inn
Ram's Head Inn
Rose Inn
The Ivy Southampton
The Point
Victorian on the Bay
White Spring Manor

Pennsylvania

Blueberry Mountain Inn
Doubleday Inn
EverMay-On-The-Delaware

Field & Pine
Golden Pheasant Inn
Hollyhedge Estate
Inn at Fordhook Farm
Mansion Inn
Ravenshead
Sheppard Mansion
Tattersall Inn
The French Manor
Twin Pine Manor

Virginia

Ashby Inn
Bailiwick Inn
Black Horse Inn
Clifton—The Country Inn
Colonial Gardens
Edgewood Plantation
Goodstone Inn & Estate
Inn at Little Washington
Inn at Vaucluse Spring
Inn at Warner Hall
L'Auberge Provencale
Legacy of Williamsburg
Liberty Rose
Prospect Hill Plantation
Silver Thatch Inn
Virginia Cliffe Inn

West Virginia

Deerpark Country Inn
Highlawn Inn
Hillbrook
White Oaks

RUSTIC

Maryland

Antietam Overlook Farm
Piper House
Savage River Lodge
White Swan Tavern
The Point
Whistlewood Farm

New Jersey

Alpine Haus

New York

Bird & Bottle Inn
Freddy's House
Greenwoods
Hudson House
J. Harper Poor Cottage
Olde Rhinebeck Inn
Onteora, The Mountain House
Pig Hill

Pennsylvania

Shippen Way Inn
Stone Ridge Farm

Virginia

Inn at Narrow Passage
Inn at the Crossroads
Legacy of Williamsburg
Little River Inn
Littlepage Inn
Silver Thatch Inn

West Virginia

Bright Morning Inn
Deerpark Country Inn

SOLO-ORIENTED

Delaware

Blue Water House
Darley Manor Inn
Delaware Inn
Spring Garden
William Penn

Maryland

Abercrombie Badger
Back Creek Inn
Bishop's House
Brome-Howard Inn
Cambridge House
Camel Cove Inn
Chesapeake Wood Duck Inn
Chez Amis
Combsberry 1730
Currier House
Dr. Dodson House
Five Gables Inn & Spa
Flag House
Georgian House
Inn at Antietam
Inn at Buckeystown
Inn at the Canal
Inn of Silent Music
Jacob Rorhbach House

SOLO-ORIENTED *(continued)*

***Maryland* (continued)**
- Lazyjack Inn
- McCleery's Flat
- Parker House
- Piper House
- Ship Watch Inn
- Turning Point Inn
- Wayside Inn
- William Page Inn

New Jersey
- Avon Manor Inn
- Candlelight Inn
- Cape May
- Inn at the Shore
- Inn on Ocean
- La Maison
- Main Street Manor
- Melrose
- Morning Dove
- Nathaniel Morris Inn
- Ocean Plaza
- Spring Lake Inn
- The Manse
- Victoria House
- Whistling Swan Inn
- White Dove Cottage
- Woolverton Inn

New York
- All Tucked Inn
- Ancestor's Inn
- B&B Wellington
- Beau Fleuve
- Benn Conger Inn
- Dartmouth House
- Dickenson House on James
- Freddy's House
- Genesee Country Inn
- Glenwood House
- Green Glen
- Inn at Irving Place
- Inn on 23rd
- Inn on the Library Lawn
- Lamplight Inn
- Mansion Hill Inn
- Olde Rhinebeck Inn
- Pig Hill
- Quintessentials
- Rosewood Inn
- Spencertown Country House
- Whistlewood Farm
- William Henry Miller Inn

Pennsylvania
- 10-11 Clinton
- Baladerry Inn
- Battlefield Inn
- Chestnut Hill
- Creekside Inn
- Doubleday Country Inn & Farm
- Farm Fortune
- Gaslight Inn
- Jacob's Resting Place
- Mt. Gretna Inn
- O'Flaherty's Dingeldein House
- Pine Tree Farm
- Ravenshead
- Settlers Inn
- Shepard House
- Thomas Bond House
- Wedgewood Collection
- Whitehall

Virginia
- 200 South Street
- Abingdon Boarding House
- Bellmont
- Berryville
- Buckskin Manor
- Chester
- Chester House
- Emmanuel Hutzler House
- Henry Clay Inn
- Inn at Monticello
- Inn at Sugar Hollow
- Inn at the Crossroads
- Joshua Walton House Inn Killahevlin
- Liberty RoseLittle River Inn
- Mayfield Inn
- North Bend Plantation
- Virginia Cliffe Inn
- Willow Grove Inn

West Virginia
- Brass Pineapple
- Current
- Hutton House
- Lee Street
- Old Stone Manse
- Perry House
- Washington House Inn

SMOKING OK

Delaware
Zwaanendael Inn

Maryland
Celie's Waterfront

New York
Belhurst Castle
Benn Conger Inn
Goose Pond Inn
Inn at Irving Place
Interlaken Inn
Mansion Hill Inn
Onteora, The Mountain House
White Spring Manor
Willow Hill House

Pennsylvania
Cliff Park Inn & Golf Course
Thomas Bond House

Virginia
North Bend Plantation
Prospect Hill Plantation

SWIMMING POOL

Delaware
Little Creek Inn
The Towers

Maryland
Antrim 1844
Chanceford Hall
Five Gables Inn & Spa
Great Oak Manor
Paternal Gift Farm
Tyler Spite House
Waterloo Country Inn

New Jersey
Stewart Inn
Wooden Duck

New York
1880 House
Belvedere Mansion
Bykenhulle House
Inn at Stone Ridge
J. Harper Poor Cottage
The Ivy Southampton

Pennsylvania
Blueberry Mountain Inn
Jacob's Resting Place
Pine Tree Farm
Whitehall

Virginia
Buckskin Manor
Chester
Clifton - The Country Inn
Edgewood Plantation
Goodstone Inn & Estate
Inn at Vaucluse Spring
L'Auberge Provencale
Mayfield Inn
Prospect Hill Plantation

SMALL PROPERTIES

Delaware
Blue Heron Inn
John Penrose Virden House
Manor at Cool Spring
Rose Tower
Royal Retreat
Wild Swan Inn

Maryland
55 East
Annapolis Inn
Deer Park Inn
Dr. Dodson House
Paternal Gift Farm
Piper House

New York
1880 House
Freddy's House
Home Port
Olde Rhinebeck Inn
Willow Hill House

Pennsylvania
Morning Glories
Pine Tree Farm

SMALL PROPERTIES *(continued)*

Virginia
Abingdon Boarding House
Bellmont
Berryville

West Virginia
Lee Street
Old Stone Manse

LARGE PROPERTIES

Delaware
Inn at Montchanin Village
Zwaanendael Inn

Maryland
Antrim 1844

New Jersey
The Queen Victoria

New York
Belvedere Mansion
Rose Inn

Virginia
200 South Street

WATERSIDE

Delaware
Addy Sea
Armitage Inn
Blue Heron Inn

Maryland
Back Creek Inn
Chesapeake Wood Duck Inn
Combsberry 1730
Currier House
Great Oak Manor
Inn at the Canal
Inn of Silent Music
Inn on the Ocean
Lake Pointe Inn
Lazyjack Inn
River House Inn
Ship Watch Inn
Solomons Victorian Inn
Waterloo Country Inn

New Jersey
Cashelmara
Chestnut Hill on the Delaware
Inn on Ocean
Morning Dove
Sea Crest By The Sea

New York
All Tucked Inn
Belhurst Castle
Boathouse
Evelyn's View
Genesee Country Inn
Hudson House
Inn on the Library Lawn
Lakehouse Inn on Golden Pond
Oliver Loud's Inn
Ram's Head Inn
The Point
Victorian on the Bay

Pennsylvania
Black Walnut
Chestnut Hill
EverMay-On-The-Delaware
Farm Fortune
Golden Pheasant Inn
Jacob's Resting Place
Roebling Inn on the Delaware

Virginia
Inn at Narrow Passage
Inn at Warner Hall

West Virginia
White Oaks

Introduction

How Come "Unofficial"?

The book in your hands is part of a unique travel and lifestyle guidebook series begun in 1985 with *The Unofficial Guide to Walt Disney World.* That guide, a comprehensive, behind-the-scenes, hands-on prescription for getting the most out of a complex amusement park facility, spawned a series of like titles: *The Unofficial Guide to Chicago, The Unofficial Guide to New Orleans,* and so on. Today, dozens of *Unofficial Guides* help millions of savvy readers navigate some of the world's more complex destinations and situations.

The *Unofficial Guides to Bed-and-Breakfasts and Country Inns* continue the tradition of insightful, incisive, cut-to-the-chase information, presented in an accessible, easy-to-use format. Unlike in some popular books, no property can pay to be included—those reviewed are solely our choice. And we don't simply rehash the promotional language of these establishments. We visit the good, the bad, and the quirky. We finger the linens, chat with the guests, and sample the scones. We screen hundreds of lodgings, affirming or debunking the acclaimed, discovering or rejecting the new and the obscure. In the end, we present detailed profiles of the lodgings we feel represent the best of the best, select lodgings representing a broad range of prices and styles within each geographic region.

We also include introductions for each state and zone to give you an idea of the nearby general attractions. Area maps with the properties listed by city help you pinpoint your general destination. And detailed mini-indexes help you look up properties by categories and lead you to places that best fit your needs.

With *The Unofficial Guides to Bed-and-Breakfasts and Country Inns,* we strive to help you find the perfect lodging for every trip. This guide is unofficial because we answer to no one but you.

Letters, Comments, and Questions from Readers

We expect to learn from our mistakes, as well as from the input of our readers, and to improve with each book and edition. Many of those who use the *Unofficial Guides* write to us to ask questions, make comments, or share their own discoveries and lessons learned. We appreciate all such input, both positive and critical, and encourage our readers to continue writing. Readers' comments and observations will contribute immeasurably to the improvement of revised editions of the *Unofficial Guides.*

How to Write the Author

Barbara Sturm
The Unofficial Guide to Bed-and-Breakfasts
and Country Inns in the Mid-Atlantic
P.O. Box 43673
Birmingham, AL 35243

Be an Unofficial Correspondent

Look out for new or special properties not profiled in this book. If you provide us with five new lodgings that we choose to visit and write about in the next edition, we'll credit you and send a copy when the edition is published. That's reason enough to get out and explore the Mid-Atlantic.

When you write, be sure to put your return address on your letter as well as on the envelope—they may get separated. And remember, our work takes us out of the office for long periods of research, so forgive us if our response is delayed.

What Makes It a Bed-and-Breakfast?

Comparing the stale, sterile atmosphere of most hotels and motels to the typical bed-and-breakfast experience—cozy guest room, intimate parlor, friendly hosts, fresh-baked cookies, not to mention a delicious breakfast—why stay anywhere other than a bed-and-breakfast? But this isn't a promotional piece for the bed-and-breakfast life. Bed-and-breakfasts are not hotels. Here are some of the differences:

A bed-and-breakfast or small inn, as we define it, is a small property (about 3 to 25 guest rooms, with a few exceptions) with hosts around, a distinct personality, individually decorated rooms, and breakfast included in the price (again, with a few exceptions). Many of these smaller properties have owners living right there; at others, the owners are nearby, a phone call away.

Recently, the bed-and-breakfast and small inn trade has taken off—with mixed results. This growth has taken place on both fronts: the low and high ends. As bed-and-breakfasts gain popularity, anyone with a spare bedroom can pop an ad in the Yellow Pages for "Billy's Bedroom B&B." These enterprises generally lack professionalism, don't keep regular hours or days of operation, are often unlicensed, and were avoided in this guide.

On the other end of the spectrum are luxury premises with more amenities than the finest hotels. Whether historic homes or lodgings built to be bed-and-breakfasts or inns, interiors are posh, baths are private and en suite, and breakfasts are gourmet affairs. In-room whirlpool tubs and fireplaces are the norm, and extras range from in-room refrigerators (perhaps stocked with champagne) to complimentary high tea to free use of state-of-the-art recreational equipment to . . . the list goes on! (One longtime innkeeper, whose historic home was tidily and humbly maintained by hours of elbow grease and common sense, dubbed this new state of affairs "the amenities war.")

The result is an industry in which a simple homestay bed-and-breakfast with a shared bath and common rooms can be a budget experience, while a new, upscale bed-and-breakfast can be the luxury venue of a lifetime.

Who Stays at Bed-and-Breakfasts?

American travelers are finally catching on to what Europeans have known for a long time. Maybe it's a backlash against a cookie-cutter, strip-mall landscape, or a longing for a past that maybe never was, and for an idealized, short-term interaction with others. Maybe it's a need for simple pleasures in a world over-the-top with theme parks and high-tech wonders. Who can say for sure?

The bed-and-breakfast trade has grown so large that it includes niches catering to virtually every need: some bed-and-breakfasts and small inns are equipped to help travelers conduct business, others provide turndown service and fresh flowers by the honeymooners' canopied bed, and still others offer amenities for reunions or conferences. Whatever your needs, there is a bed-and-breakfast or small inn tailored to your expectations. The challenge, and one this guide was designed to help you meet, is sifting through the choices until you find the perfect place.

Romantics

More and more, properties are establishing at least one room or suite with fireplace, whirlpool, canopied king, and the trappings of romance. Theme rooms can also be especially fun for fantasizing. Always check out the privacy factor. Sometimes a property that caters to families has a carriage house in the back or a top-floor room away from the others. If an inn allows children under 16, don't be surprised if it's noisy; look for ones that are for older children or adults only.

Families

Face it, Moms and Dads: rumpled surroundings will sometimes have to be accepted where children are welcome. You may have to give up pristine decor and breakfast tea served in bone china for the relaxed, informal mood, but on the upside, you won't have to worry as much about Anna or Sam knocking over the Wedgwood collection on the sideboard.

When an establishment says "Yes" to kids, that usually means a really kid-friendly place. Check the age restrictions. If your children are underaged but well-behaved, let the host know; often they will make exceptions. (But be sure it's true—other guests are counting on it.) On the flip side, honeymooners or other folks who might prefer common areas free of crayons, and breakfasts without sugar-frosted confetti, may want to look elsewhere.

Many bed-and-breakfasts with cottages, cabins or accommodations that really separate guests are perfect for families with trouble-free infants and well-behaved kids. This gives parents with good intentions an alternative to "sweating-it-out" in case easy-going Cindy decides to break a tooth and cries through the night.

Generally, bed-and-breakfasts are not ideal for high-action kids. But if your children enjoy games, puzzles, books, a chance for quiet pleasures, and meeting others; if they don't need TVs; and if they can be counted on to be thoughtful and follow instructions ("whisper before 9 a.m.," "don't put your feet on the table"), you and your kids can have a wonderful experience together—and so can the rest of the guests.

Business Travelers

For individual business travelers, bed-and-breakfasts and small inns are becoming much more savvy at anticipating your needs, but in differing degrees. While phone lines and data ports are fairly common, they vary from one bed-and-breakfast to another. Some say they offer data ports when in fact they have two phone jacks in every room but only one phone line servicing the entire property. This can be fine for a three-room inn in the off-season, but if you're trying to conduct business, look for properties with private lines and/or dedicated data ports. If in doubt, ask. Rooms are often available with desks, but these also vary, particularly in surface area and quality of lighting. If this is an important feature, ask for specifics and make sure you secure a room with a desk when you reserve.

Some establishments even offer couriers, secretarial support, and laundry services. And for business travelers who don't have time to take advantage of a leisurely and sumptuous breakfast, hosts often provide an early-morning alternative, sometimes continental, sometimes full.

Finally, there are intangibles to consider. After the sterile atmosphere of the trade show, meeting hall, or boardroom, a small inn with a host and a plate of cookies and a personal dinner recommendation can be nice to come home to.

The atmosphere is also a plus for business meetings or seminars: The relaxed surroundings are quite conducive to easygoing give and take. During the week when guest rooms are often available, some bed-and-breakfasts and small inns are usually eager to host business groups. Discounts are often included and special services such as catering and equipment are offered if you rent the entire property. But forget weekends; these properties are still tourist oriented.

Independents

If you are on your own, small lodgings are ideal. Look for a place with single rates, and even if a special rate isn't listed, you can often negotiate a small discount. If you want some interaction, just sit in the parlor, lounge, or common rooms, and talk to people before meals. Most of the time if you're friendly and interested, you'll get an invite to join someone at a table. You could talk to the innkeepers about this even before you arrive, and they might fix you up with friendly folks. (And if you are traveling with others, invite a single to join you.) As for breakfast, communal tables are perfect for singles. Note our profiles to choose properties with that in mind.

Groups

Whether you are part of a wedding, reunion, or just a group of people who want to travel together, an inn or bed-and-breakfast is a delightful place to stay. The atmosphere is special, your needs are taken care of in a personal way, the grounds are most often spacious and lovely, and in the evening you can all retire in close proximity. It's especially fun when you take over the whole place—so you may want to choose an especially small property if that's your goal.

Those with Special Needs

Look in our profiles for mention of disabled facilities or access. Then call for details to determine just how extensive the accessibility is. Remember also that some of these houses are quite old, and owners of a small bed-and-breakfast will not have a team of accessibility experts on retainer, so be specific with your questions. If doorways must be a certain width to accommodate a wheelchair or walker, know how many inches before you call; if stairs are difficult for Great Aunt Mary Ann, don't neglect to find out how many are present outside, as well as inside. And if a property that seems otherwise special doesn't seem to have facilities, perhaps you can patch things together, such as a room on the first floor. Realistically, though, some historic properties were built with many stairs and are situated on hilltops or in rural terrain, so you will have to choose very carefully.

If you suffer from allergies or aversions, talk this over when you book. A good innkeeper will make every attempt to accommodate you. As for food, if you request a special meal and give enough notice, you can often get what you like. That's one of the joys of a small, personalized property.

You and Your Hosts

Hosts are the heart of your small inn or bed-and-breakfast experience and color all aspects of the stay. They can make or break a property, and sometimes an unassuming place will be the most memorable of all because of the care and warmth of the hosts. Typically, they are well versed in navigating the area and can be a wealth of "insider information" on restaurants, sight-seeing, and the like.

While many—most, in these guides—hosts live on the premises, they often have designed or remodeled their building so that their living quarters are separate. Guests often have their own living room, den, parlor, and sitting room; you may be sharing with other guests, but not so much with your hosts. The degree of interaction between host families and guests varies greatly; we try to give a feel for the extremes in the introduction to each profile. In most cases, hosts are accessible but not intrusive; they will swing through the common areas and chat a bit, but are sensitive to guests' need for privacy. Sometimes hosts are in another building altogether; in the other extreme, you intimately share living space with your hosts. This intimate, old-style bed-and-breakfast arrangement is called a "homestay." We try to note this.

In short, most bed-and-breakfast hosts are quite gracious in accommodating travelers' needs, and many are underpinning their unique small lodging with policies and amenities from hotel-style lodgings. But bed-and-breakfasts and small inns are not the Sheraton, and being cognizant of the differences can make your experience more pleasant.

Planning Your Visit

When You Choose

If you're not sure where you want to travel, browse through our listings. Maybe something in an introduction or a description of a property will spark your interest.

If you know you are going to a certain location, note the properties in that zone, and then read the entries. You can also call for brochures or take a further look at websites, especially to see rooms or to book directly.

We've provided a listing of some useful websites below; state- and zone-specific websites follow their respective introductions.

WEBSITES

bbchannel.com
bbinternet.com
bbonline.com
bnbcity.com
bnbinns.com
epicurious.com
getawayguides.com
innbook.com
inns.com
innsandouts.com
innsnorthamerica.com
johansens.com

relaischateaux.fr/[name of inn]	travel.com/accom/bb/usa	travelguide.com
trip.com	triple1.com	virtualcities.com

When You Book

Small properties usually require booking on your own. Some travel agents will help, but they may charge a fee, because many small properties don't give travel agents commissions. The fastest, easiest ways to book are through the Internet or a reservation service, but if you have special needs or questions, we suggest contacting properties directly to get exactly what you want.

Ask about any special needs or requirements, and make sure your requests are clear. Most of these properties are not designed for people in wheelchairs, so be sure to ask ahead of time if you need that accessibility. Specify what's important to you—privacy, king-size bed, fireplace, tub versus shower, view or first-floor access. A host won't necessarily know what you want, so make sure you decide what is important—writing it down will help you remember. Note the room you want by name, or ask for the "best" room if you're not sure. Remember to ask about parking conditions—does the property have off-street parking or will you have to find a place on the street? And if air-conditioning is a must for you, always inquire—some bed-and-breakfasts do not have it.

Verify prices, conditions, and any factors or amenities that are important to you. The best time to call is in the early afternoon, before new guests arrive for the day and when hosts have the most free time. Book as soon as possible; for weekends and holidays, preferred properties could be filled a year or more in advance.

A Word about Negotiating Rates

Negotiating a good rate can be more straightforward at a bed-and-breakfast than at a hotel. For starters, the person on the other end of the line will probably be the owner and will have the authority to offer you a discount. Second, the bed-and-breakfast owner has a smaller number of rooms and guests to keep track of than a hotel manager and won't have to do a lot of checking to know whether something is available. Also, because the number of rooms is small, each room is more important. In a bed-and-breakfast with four rooms, the rental of each room increases the occupancy rate by 25%.

To get the best rate, just ask. If the owner expects a full house, you'll probably get a direct and honest "no deal." On the other hand, if there are rooms and you are sensitive about price, chances are you'll get a break. In either event, be polite and don't make unreasonable requests. If you are overbearing or contentious on the phone, the proprietor may suddenly discover no rooms available.

Some Considerations

Like snowflakes, no two bed-and-breakfasts are alike. Some are housed in historic homes or other buildings (churches, schoolhouses, miner's hotels, and more). Some are humble and cozy, some are grand and opulent. Some are all in one building, while others are scattered amongst individual, free-standing units. Some offer a breakfast over which you'll want to linger for hours, others…well, others make a darn good muffin. Bed-and-breakfasts are less predictable than hotels and motels but can be much more interesting. A few bed-and-breakfast aficionados have discovered that "interesting" sometimes comes at a price. This guide takes the "scary" out of "interesting" and presents only places that meet a certain standard of cleanliness, predictability, and amenities. However, there are certain questions and issues common to bed-and-breakfasts and small inns that first-time visitors should consider:

Choosing Your Room

Check out your room before lugging your luggage (not having elevators is usually part of the charm). This is standard procedure at small properties and saves time and trouble should you prefer another room. When a guest room has an open door, it usually means the proud innkeeper wants you to peek. You may just find a room that you like better than the one you are assigned, and it may be available, so ask.

Bathrooms

Americans are picky about their potties. While the traditional bed-and-breakfast set-up involved several bedrooms sharing a bath, this is becoming less common. Even venerable Victorians are being remodeled to include private baths. In fact, many bed-and-breakfasts offer ultra-luxurious bath facilities, including whirlpool tubs, dual vanities, and so forth. Our advice is not to reject shared bath facilities out of hand, as these can be excellent values. Do check the bedroom-to-bath ratio, however. Two rooms sharing a bath can be excellent; three or more can be problematic with a full house.

Security

Many bed-and-breakfasts have property locks and room locks as sophisticated as hotels and motels. Others do not. For the most part, inns with three stars or more have quality locks throughout the premises. (Many with lower rankings do as well.) Even with locks, it is common to have to ask innkeepers for keys. Very often, bed-and-breakfasts will leave the key in the room or in the door if you choose to use one. Beyond locks, most bed-and-breakfasts provide an additional measure of security in that they are small properties, generally in a residential district, and typically with live-in hosts on the premises. Single female travelers might take comfort in coming "home" to a facility like this as opposed to a 150-room hotel with a cardlock system but God-knows-what lurking in the elevator.

Privacy

At a hotel, you can take your key and hole up in solitude for the duration of your stay. It's a little harder at a bed-and-breakfast, especially if you take part in a family-style breakfast (although many inns offer the option of an early continental breakfast if you're pressed for time or feeling antisocial, and some offer en suite breakfast service—these options are noted in the profiles). Most bed-and-breakfast hosts we've met are very sensitive to guests' needs for privacy and seem to have a knack for being as helpful or as unobtrusive as you wish. If privacy is hard to achieve at a given property, we've noted that in the profile.

Autonomy

Most bed-and-breakfasts provide a key to the front door and/or an unlocked front door certain hours of the day. While you might be staying in a family-style atmosphere, you are seldom subject to rules such as a curfew. (A few properties request that guests be in by a specific time; these policies are noted and rare.) Some places have "quiet hours," usually from about 10 or 11 p.m. until about 7 a.m. Such policies tend to be in place when properties lack sufficient sound insulation and are noted in the profile. Generally, higher ratings tend to correspond with better sound insulation.

What the Ratings Mean

We have organized this book so that you can get a quick idea of each property by checking out the ratings, reading the information at the beginning of each entry and then, if you're interested, reading the more detailed overview of each property. Obviously ratings are subjective, and people of good faith (and good taste) can and do differ. But you'll get a good, relative idea, and the ability to quickly compare properties.

Overall Rating The overall ratings are represented by stars, which range in number from one to five and represent our opinion of the quality of the property as a whole. It corresponds something like this:

★★★★★	The Best	★★½	Fair
★★★★½	Excellent	★★	Not so good
★★★★	Very Good	★½	Barely Acceptable
★★★½	Good	★	Unnacceptable
★★★	Good enough		

The overall rating for the bed-and-breakfast or small inn experience takes into account all factors of the property, including guest rooms and public rooms, food, facilities, grounds, maintenance, hosts, and something we'll call "specialness," for lack of a better phrase. Many times it involves the personalities and personal touches of the hosts.

Some properties have fairly equal star levels for all of these things, but most have some qualities that are better than others. Also, large, ambitious properties that serve dinner would tend to have a slightly higher star rating for the same level of qualities than a smaller property (the difference, say, between a great novel and a great short story; the larger it is the harder it is to pull off, hence the greater the appreciation). Yet a small property can earn five stars with a huge dose of "specialness."

Overall ratings and room quality ratings do not always correspond. While guest rooms may be spectacular, the rest of the inn may be average, or vice versa. Generally, though, we've found through the years that a property is usually consistently good or bad throughout.

Room Quality Rating The quality ratings, also given on a five-star scale, represent our opinion of the quality of the guest rooms and bathrooms only. For the room quality ratings we factored in view, size, closet space, bedding, seating, desks, lighting, soundproofing, comfort, style, privacy, decor, "taste," and other intangibles. A really great private bathroom with a claw-foot tub and antique table might bring up the rating of an otherwise average room. Conversely, poor maintenance or lack of good lighting will lower the rating of a spacious, well-decorated room. Sometimes a few rooms are really special while others are standard, and we have averaged these where possible. It's difficult to codify this, but all factors are weighed, and the ratings seem to come up easily.

Value Rating The value ratings—also expressed using a one-to-five -star scale—are a combination of the overall and room quality ratings, divided by the cost of an average guest room. They are an indication rather than a scientific formulation—a general idea of value for money. If getting a good deal means the most to you, choose a property by looking at the value rating. Otherwise, the overall and room quality ratings are better indicators of a satisfying experience. A five-star value, A room quality, overall five-star inn or bed-and-breakfast would be ideal, but most often, you'll find a three-star value, and you are getting your money's worth. If a wonderful property is fairly priced, it may only get a three-star value rating, but you still might prefer the experience to an average property that gets a five-star value rating.

Price Our price range is the lowest-priced room to the highest-priced room in regular season. The range does not usually include specially priced times such as holidays and low season. The room rate is based on double occupancy and assumes breakfast is included. It does not assume that other meals are included in the rate. However, be sure to check the inn's Food & Drink category. Lodgings where MAP, which stands for the hotel industry's standard Modified American Plan, is applicable offer breakfast and dinner in the room rate. Unless specifically noted, prices quoted in the profiles do not include gratuities or state and local taxes, which can be fairly steep. Gratuities are optional; use your own discretion. Prices change constantly, so check before booking.

The Profiles Clarified

The bulk of information about properties is straightforward, but much of it is in abbreviated style, so the following clarifications may help. They are arranged in the order they appear in the profile format.

Many of the properties in this book have similar names; for example, Victoria House is in Spring Lake, New Jersey, while The Queen Victoria is in Cape May, New Jersey. Town names, too, can be strikingly similar. Make sure you don't confuse properties or town names when selecting an inn.

Location

First, check the map for location. Our directions are designed to give you a general idea of the property's location. For more complete directions, call the property or check its Web site.

Building

This category denotes the design and architecture of the building. Many of the properties in the *Unofficial Guides* are historically and architecturally interesting. Here are a few architectural terms you may want to brush up on, in no particular order: Colonial, Craftsman, Queen Anne, Princess Anne, Cape Cod, Hand-hewn Log, Foursquare, Art Deco, Georgian, Victorian, Arts and Crafts, Ranch, Farmhouse, Gabled, Boarding House, Miner's Hotel, Teepee, Duncan Phyfe accessories, Sandstone, Timber Sided, Bunkhouse, Carriage House, Chalet, William Morris wallpaper, Sheepherder's Wagon, Eastlake, Greek Revival, Edwardian, claw-foot tub, pedestal sink, and many more. The more you know the jargon, the better you can select the property you want.

Food & Drink

For food and drink, we offer a taste of the inn or bed-and-breakfast, so to speak. Most properties go all out to fill you up at breakfast, so that you could easily skip lunch (factor that into the value). In some areas, however, the tourist board regulates that properties can only serve a continental breakfast without a hot dish. Note whether we state "gourmet breakfast," if that experience is paramount. In most cases, a bed-and-breakfast breakfast—even a continental—tends to include more homemade items, greater selection, and greater care in presentation.

In this category, what we call "specialties" are really typical dishes, which may not always be served, but should give you a good idea of the cuisine. Very few bed-and-breakfasts and inns do not include the breakfast in the price. However, it is almost always offered as an option.

Many inns and bed-and-breakfasts offer afternoon tea, snacks, sherry, or pre-dinner wine and after-dinner desert. Note that if an inn offers meals to the public as well as guests, the atmosphere becomes less personal. Also, if MAP is noted in this category, it means the inn offers meals other than breakfast as part of the room rate.

Some inns provide alcoholic beverages to guests, some forbid consumption of alcohol—either extreme is noted in the inn's profile. The norm is that alcohol consumption is a private matter, and guests may bring and consume their own, if they do so respectfully. Glassware is generally provided. Bed-and-breakfasts are not well suited to drunkenness and partying.

A diet and a bed-and-breakfast or small inn go together about as well as a haystack and a lighted match. Come prepared to eat. Some bed-and-breakfasts will serve dinner on request, and we included that info when it was available.

Most bed-and-breakfasts are sensitive to dietary needs and preferences but need to be warned of this in advance. When you make your reservation, be sure to explain if you are diabetic, wheat- or dairy-intolerant, vegetarian/vegan, or otherwise restricted. Many proprietors pride themselves on accommodating difficult diets.

Recreation

We do not usually spell out whether the activities noted in the format are on-site. With some exceptions, assume that golf, tennis, fishing, canoeing, skiing, and the like are not on-site (since these are small properties, not resorts). Assume that games and smaller recreational activities are on the property. But there are some exceptions, so ask.

Amenities & Services

These blend a bit. Generally, amenities include extras such as swimming pools and games, and services cover perks such as business support and air conditioning. Business travelers should note if any services are mentioned, and if there are public rooms, group discounts, and so forth to back them up. Almost all bed-and-breakfasts and inns can provide advice regarding touring, restaurants, and local activities; many keep maps, local menus and brochures on hand.

Deposit

Be pretty confident that you will be staying at a particular bed-and-breakfast when you make a reservation. The more popular the property, usually the more deposit you'll have to put down, and the further ahead. Many cancellation policies are very strict, and many innkeepers recommend that guests purchase travelers insurance in case there is an unforeseen circumstance. When canceling after the site's noted policy, most will still refund, less a fee, if the room is re-rented. Check back on this.

Discounts

Discounts may extend to singles, long-stay guests, kids, seniors, packages, and groups. Even though discounts may not be listed in the text, it doesn't hurt to ask, as these sorts of things can be flexible in small establishments, midweek, off-season, last-minute, and when innkeepers may want to fill their rooms. This category also includes a dollar figure for additional persons sharing a room (beyond the two included in the basic rate).

Credit Cards

For those properties that do accept credit cards (we note those that do not), we've listed credit cards accepted with the following codes:

V	VISA	MC	MasterCard
AE	American Express	D	Discover
DC	Diner's Club International	CB	Carte Blanche

Check-in/Out

As small operators, most bed-and-breakfast hosts need to know approximately when you'll be arriving. Many have check-in periods (specified in the profiles) during which the hosts or staff will be available to greet you. Most can accommodate arrival beyond their stated check-in period but need to be advised so they can arrange to be home or get a key to you. Think about it—they have to buy groceries and go to the kids' soccer games and get to doctors' appointments just like you. And they have to sleep sometime. Don't show up at 11:30 p.m. and expect a smiling bellhop—the same person who lets you in is probably going to be up at 5 or 6 a.m. slicing mushrooms for your omelet!

Check-in times are often flexible, but, as with any commercial lodging, check-out times can be critical, as the innkeeper must clean and prepare your room for incoming guests. If you need to stay longer, ask and you'll often get an extension. Sometimes a host will let you leave your bags and enjoy the common areas after check-out, as long as you vacate your room. Please take cancellation policies seriously. A "no-show" is not a cancellation! If an establishment has a seven-day, or 72-hour, or whatever cancellation policy, you are expected to call and cancel your reservation prior to that time, or you could be liable for up to the full amount of your reserved stay. After all, a four-unit bed-and-breakfast has lost 25% of its revenue if you arbitrarily decide not to show up.

Smoking

We've indicated in the inn's profile if smoking is banned outright or if it is OK to smoke outside, but ask your hosts before you light up. Be mindful, too, of how you dispose of the butts—when you flick them into a nearby shrub, it's likely that your hosts, not some sanitation team, will be plucking them out next week.

Pets

We have not mentioned most of the inn-house pets in the profiles, as this situation changes even more frequently than most items. Many properties have pets on the premises. Don't assume that because an establishment does not allow guests to bring pets that pets aren't present. Dogs and cats and birds (and horses, pigs, goats, llamas, etc.) are often around. If you foresee a problem with this, be sure to clarify "how around," before booking. If properties allow pets, we have noted this, but most do not. And if you can't bear to leave your own beloved Fido or Miss Kitty for long periods, and want to stay in an inn that does not allow them, good innkeepers often know of reputable boarding facilities nearby.

Open

Properties often claim they are open all year, but they can close at any time—at the last minute for personal reasons or if business is slow. Similarly, properties that close during parts of the year may open specially for groups. If you can get a bunch of family or friends together, it's a great way to stay at popular inns and bed-and-breakfasts that would be otherwise hard to book. And remember, in low-season things slow down, dinners may not be served, and even when some properties are "open," they may be half-closed.

An Important Note

Facts and situations change constantly in the small-lodging business. Innkeepers get divorced, prices go up, puppies arrive, chefs quit in the middle of a stew, and rooms get redecorated, upgraded, and incorporated. So use this format as a means to get a good overall idea of the property, and then inquire when you book about the specific details that matter most. Changes will definitely occur, so check to be sure.

Making the Most of Your Stay

Once you're settled in, it's a good idea to scope out the entire place, or you may not realize until too late that your favorite book was on the shelf, or that an old-fashioned swing would have swung you into the moonlight on a warm evening. If you are alone in the inn, it can feel like the property is yours (and that, in fact, is a good reason to go midweek or off-season).

Take advantage of the special charms of these lodgings: the fireplace, the piano, other guests, the gardens. What makes an inn or bed-and-breakfast experience an integral part of a trip are small moments that can become cherished memories.

Did you love it? You can perhaps duplicate in your daily life some of the touches that made the experience special, whether it was warm towels, an early weekend breakfast by candlelight, fancy snacks in the afternoon or a special recipe for stuffed French toast. Hosts usually enjoy sharing ideas and recipes. You can also make small "bed-and-breakfast" type changes at your own home that may make all of the difference in your world—a small rose in a vase, a new throw rug, a handmade quilt from a local craft fair—or really splurge and install a whirlpool tub with waterfall faucet!

These small lodgings are stress-busters, far away from sitcoms and fast food and the media mania of the day. They are cozy places to settle into and curl up with a book, or a honey, or a dream. Or, if you must, a laptop and a cell phone.

Mid-Atlantic Bed-and-Breakfasts

If George Washington were alive today, he'd be delighted to know there are so many bed-and-breakfasts and country inns where he could spend the night in the Mid-Atlantic—his old stomping grounds.

As we begin the 21st century, people seem to want to slow down, enjoy nature, and participate in the community life of small-town America in a more personal way. While some properties in this *Unofficial Guide* are in big cities like New York, Philadelphia, and Baltimore, most are in small towns or rural, off-the-beaten-track byways.

They invite you to explore and take pleasure in the grandeur of the region's terrain and the diversity of its culture. They give you access to miles of wide, beautiful Atlantic Ocean beaches in five states. They put you in touch with the fresher air of the Adirondack, Catskill, Pocono, Allegheny, Appalachian, and Blue Ridge Mountains, and the pleasures of valleys like the Hudson, Shenandoah, and Greenbrier. And, they introduce you to National Forests, where the region's hardwood trees are so visually dramatic in the fall that leaf-peeping season is the busiest of all for some innkeepers.

For water sports, the Mid-Atlantic region offers extraordinary resources, including the Chesapeake and Delaware Bays and the Potomac, Rappahannock, York, James, Delaware, Susquehanna, Monongahela, and Hudson Rivers. Its reach includes the Finger Lakes, the Barge Canal System, Lake Champlain, and the Saint Lawrence River.

Throughout the area you'll find a vast array of sporting and leisure activities, and every season has appropriate festivals and community events.

Each of the bed-and-breakfasts and small country inns profiled in this *Unofficial Guide* was chosen because it has one or more qualities that are distinctive. The mark of distinction may be beautiful antiques or unique furnishings, stellar cuisine, fireplaces in the bedrooms and common rooms, a swimming pool, proximity to historic attractions and access to good entertainment, or the building's historical and architectural significance. In some cases, it was all of the above. Whether it's a lavish mansion or a humble farmhouse, if a property delivers a very special experience it can earn a top rating here.

This guidebook contains facts, but it's full of stories, as well—at least the beginnings of stories. You'll meet talented innkeepers from many different backgrounds who like to decorate, cook, plan activities, share local history, tell humorous stories, explain their hobbies, or create special occasions. The best innkeepers make a conscious effort to nurture thought, please the eye, and boost the spirits—and do it all with joy and a sense of humor.

Innkeepers tell us that they went into this business for a variety of reasons, including empty nest syndrome, early retirement, and a chance to do what they've always loved. Surprisingly, one says she did it by accident. Her husband answered the front door to find a man standing there who asked if their house was a bed-and-breakfast. "It could be, come on in," he replied and installed the unexpected guest in an upstairs bedroom. When she returned home from work that evening, he told her "there's a man asleep upstairs and tomorrow morning he'll want breakfast." It worked out so well that she quit her job and has been a full-time innkeeper ever since.

The kinds of properties we cover in this *Unofficial Guide* are diverse. We found them in a converted boathouse in upstate New York, a church in West Virginia, and an old mill in New Jersey, as well as on a Mennonite farm in Pennsylvania, a lavender plant farm in Delaware, and a horse farm in Virginia's Shenandoah Valley. Several of the bed-and-breakfasts have been stagecoach taverns, one is a French castle look-alike, and another is a mansion that is part of a college curriculum.

Some of the bed-and-breakfasts have interesting histories, as well—as a potato farm, workers' cottages for the Du Pont company, a tavern for barge canalers, a Catholic mass house, and even Pearl Buck's dairy farm. A few of our Mid-Atlantic properties boast prominent owners (both past and present). Among them are a William Avery Rockefeller, the inventor of plastic bags, the owner of Hellmann's Mayonnaise, Thomas Jefferson's son-in-law, a Danish sea captain, art collector Joseph Hirshhorn, a Hanover Shoe Company founder, and the Burpee Seed Company founder.

As bonus to their guests, one innkeeper offers a chance to sail the Chesapeake Bay on his yacht; another will fly the flag of your country of origin on his front porch. For some guests, the pièce de résistance may be the innkeeper at Doubleday Country Inn and Farm who will lend you a vintage baseball uniform and put you in the line-up to play nine innings on a regulation-size baseball diamond with a former All Star, World Series Champ, MVP, or Rookie of the Year on your team.

Celebrity watchers will find two properties in this guidebook that have served as film sets, and several inns that claim to have hosted famous actors. And, of course, most innkeepers collect something. We found examples of Victorian underwear, Czechoslovakian communion sets, antique hunting and fishing paraphernalia, Egyptian art, Native American art, and ceramic bedpans (displayed on the back porch).

The most common denominator in the Mid-Atlantic region is the age of the buildings. Many are over 100 years old and good examples of a specific architectural style. We met many self-styled preservationists who are passionate about saving and restoring some lovely old relic or polishing an architectural gem. Standout examples include Mayfair in Petersburg, Virginia; The Towers in Milford, Delaware; and the Black Lion Mansion in Kingston, New York.

We noticed a big push to provide private baths, and in many cases innkeepers have installed whirlpools and/or steam showers. Tour de forces in the bathroom category include two rooms in the Alexander Hamilton House in Cronton-on-Hudson, New York, and some rooms at Inn at Little Washington in Washington, Virginia.

Some innkeepers in this *Unofficial Guide* took full-time or for-credit cooking courses to prepare them for running a bed-and-breakfast. Just reading the breakfast specialties we've mentioned gives an indication of the mouth-watering fare that they serve. Some properties even serve dinners, and a few allow you to cook in during your stay, if you like. Our favorite guest kitchen is at Dickenson House on James in Syracuse, New York.

Room decor counts, but tastes are subjective. Some innkeepers follow restrictive design rules, while others are more enthusiastic and free spirited in their use of color and form and choice of a theme. For sheer imagination and personal style, we liked Liberty Rose in Williamsburg, Virginia, Ravenhead in Hartsville, Pennsylvania; and Mr. Mole in Baltimore, Maryland.

Being a good concierge is especially valuable to out-of-towners who need reliable information about local activities and attractions and help in finding a good restaurant. The best can help you maximize your time and indulge your true interests. We found extra-helpful innkeepers at Inn at Vaucluse Springs in Stephens City, Virginia, and Inn at Buckeystown, Buckeystown, Maryland.

Many inns we visited have one or two pets, but only Jordan Hollow Farm in Stanley, Virginia is home to a dozen cats and invites you to adopt one to take to your room during your visit if you like.

After visiting more than 300 properties first hand, we now know that photographs on promotional websites and in brochures often don't convey the reality of an inn. Some make a property look better than it actually is, and others make a property look worse. We hope these selections will help you find meaningful differences among the many choices for bed-and-breakfast travelers in the Mid-Atlantic.

A Few of My Favorite Things about Mid-Atlantic Bed-and-Breakfasts

My list of personal favorites reflects the extraordinary variety available at Mid-Atlantic bed-and-breakfasts:

The wow factor for grandeur and scale is especially high at Combsberry 1730 in Oxford, Maryland; Great Oak Manor in Chestertown, Maryland; the Inn at Warner Hall in Gloucester, Virginia; and the art-filled Inn a Fordhook Farm in Doylestown, Pennsylvania.

Standouts for brilliant natural locations are the mountaintop Antietam Overlook Farm in Keedysville, Maryland. with its sweeping multi-state views, and Onteora, The Mountain House atop a pine-studded promontory in New York's Catskill mountains. The prettiest cultivated settings are at Hillbrook Inn in Charlestown, West Virginia, where purple and yellow iris fringe a pond full of swans, and Morgan-Samuels Inn in Canandaigua, New York, which is surrounded by flower-filled countryside that's so idyllic you won't want to leave.

Ashby Inn in Paris, Virginia, reflects the charm of a European-style village, while J. Harper Poor's Cottage in East Hampton, New York, and Abingdon Boarding House in Abingdon,Virginia, give a wonderful entree to unique small towns. Appealing choices with a cozier flavor are The Point at Saranac Lake, New York; Olde Rhinebeck Inn, a Colonial-era farmhouse in Rhinebeck, New York; and the folksy Acorn Inn in Canandaigua, New York.

For eye-popping architecture, I love the modern lines at Twin Pine Manor in Ephrata, Pennsylvania; the beachy charm of Victorian on the Bay in Eastport, New York; the old-world elegance of Sheppard Mansion in Hanover, Pennsylvania; and the distinctive Hobbit Hollow Farm in Skaneateles, New York.

For travelers emphasizing decor, vivid primary colors enliven the main floor at The Ivy in Southampton, New York, and Liberty Rose in Williamsburg, Virginia, is over the top with red plush velvets, silks, and satins. Every nook and cranny is imaginatively decorated at Mr. Mole in Baltimore.

Horse country ambience is the lure at Goodstone Inn & Estate in Middleburg, Virginia, where guests can sleep in renovated stables. At

Stone Ridge Farm in Dublin, Pennsylvania, and Silver Maple Farm in Columbia County, New York, guests can sleep in renovated barns.

To learn about history, I found two bed-and-breakfasts on Civil War battlefields. Piper House in Sharpsburg, Maryland, sits on land where the bloody Battle of Antietam took place. Doubleday Inn at Gettysburg, Pennsylvania, overlooks a ridge where Union and Confederate troops once clashed.

When in the mood for water views, I'd return to the oceanfront Addy Sea on a pristine beach in Bethany Beach, Delaware. Oliver Loud's Inn in Pittsford, New York, offers a close-up view of the Erie Canal. Golden Pheasant and Evermay-on-the-Delaware in Erwinna, Pennsylvania, are both adjacent to the Delaware Canal.

Two of the quirkiest finds are Bedrock Inn next to an active rock quarry in Pounding Mill, Virginia, and Boathouse Bed & Breakfast in Bolton Landing, New York, where the deepwater basement is used to moor boats.

My favorite guest activities are at Battlefield Inn in Gettysburg, Pennsylvania, where the host gives spirited lectures on Civil War history, and Country Log House Farm in Mount Joy, Pennsylvania, where you can ride in a tractor, pet the farm animals, gather just-laid eggs, and visit a dairy barn. Also, at Doubleday Country Inn & Farm in Landisburg, Pennsylvania, you can play nine innings with old-time baseball professionals as teammates.

Meals are generally important events at B&Bs. The candlelit four-course breakfast at The Whitehall Inn in Lahaska, Pennsylvania, is notable. The delicious chocolate chip scones and blueberry pancakes at Brampton Inn in Chestertown, Maryland, had me asking for recipes.

Gourmet picnic lunches were a highlight at Honeoye in Greenwoods, New York. Gourmet dinners are offered at Antrim 1844 in Taneytown, Maryland; The Stone Manor in Middletown, Maryland; and Little Creek Inn in Dover, Delaware. Chef Patrick O'Connell at The Inn at Little Washington in Washington, Virginia, won the 2001 James Beard Chef of the Year award. Kudos go to the kitchens at Settlers Inn in Hawley, Pennsylvania; Ashby Inn in Paris, Virginia; Prospect Hill Plantation in Trevilians, Virginia; and Clifton—The Country Inn in Shadwell, Virginia. All merit praise.

Several innkeepers showed "before" photos of extensive restoration projects. Some are experts, including Joan and Dane Wells at The Queen Victoria in Cape May, New Jersey, who generously shared their encyclopedic knowledge.

Virginia excels in historic restorations, including Mayfield Inn in Petersburg, Mayhurst Plantation in Orange, Clifton—The Country Inn in Shadwell, Prospect Hill Plantation in Trevilians, Inn at Warner Hall in

Gloucester, Inn at Vaucluse Spring in Stephens City, and Emmanuel Hutzler House on Richmond's Monument Avenue.

Restored gems in other states are the 30-room Green Glen in East Aurora, New York; the classic William Henry Miller Inn in urban Ithaca, New York; the stately Black Lion Mansion in Kingston, New York; the white-pillared Peach Grove Inn in Warwick, New York; and the elegant Mansion Inn in downtown New Hope, Pennsylvania. The woodwork-rich parlors at John Penrose Virdin House in residential Lewes, Delaware, and at The Towers in Milford, Delaware, have special appeal.

Meeting the dedicated innkeepers made the project of researching this guidebook doubly meaningful. In down-to-earth Maryland, I enjoyed a laughter-filled conversation with Carol and Captain Mike Richards at Lazyjack Inn at Tilghman Island, and with Alice Kesterson and Randy Ifft, the husband and wife team at Chanceford Hall in Snow Hill. It was hilarious to hear how a troop of jugglers lined up save heirloom crockery by tossing it out of a burning building—a story told by Mary Ioppolo at Inn at the Canal in Chesapeake City. It was inspiring to hear how Jan Russell and Mike Dreisbach spent ten years creating the extraordinary Savage River Lodge in Deep Creek Lake.

In New Jersey, Linda and Rob Castagna lit a cozy fire, served tea, and shared a lifetime of wisdom at Chestnut Hill on the Delaware in Milford. In Virginia, I remember the heartfelt hospitality of Margaret and James Clifton at Virginia Cliffe Inn in Glen Allen and the humor and sophistication of Roma and John Sherman at Ashby Inn in Paris. In New York, it was fun to dine with Tim Thuell, general manager at The Point in Saranac Lake, as he regaled dinner companions with anecdotes. In Pennsylvania, Denise Fegan and Chuck De Marco at Pheasant Field in Carlisle loaned me their car when mine broke down, and Joy Feigle at Pine Tree Farm in Doylestown shared homemade soup on a chilly winter day.

Like the hosts themselves, many owners' collections add uniquness to a propety. At the Porcupine in Saranac Lake, New York, guests find a mini-museum for baseball and sports memorabilia. Captain Mey's Inn in Cape May, New Jersey, displays Victorian-era ladies underwear in the parlor. Inn at Mitchell House in Chestertown, Maryland, hangs stuffed waterfowl from the ceiling as if in mid-flight. Most unusual, however, are the shoe forms, textile spools, porcelain bedpans and potbellied stoves at B&B Wellington in Syracuse, New York.

Whaterver its location or theme, each bed-and-breakfast in this Mid-Atlantic guidebook offers a satisfying slice of American life.

Part One

New York

New York is the largest state in the Mid-Atlantic region. You must drive 675 miles from the eastern tip of Long Island to reach the state's western boundary with Pennsylvania, and 310 miles south from the Canadian border to arrive in Manhattan.

New York is strongly identified with its cities and towns, but most of the Empire State is rural landscapes. **Niagara Falls,** at its western border, draws people from around the world to gaze at the spectacle.

Adirondacks State Park is larger than Yosemite and Yellowstone Parks and the Grand Canyon combined. A half million acres is said to be true old-growth forest, including 200,000 acres of never-been-logged hardwoods and pristine forests of pine, maple, and birch. When leaves change color in autumn, the beauty is so dazzling you must see it to believe it. The mountains are also impressive, offering challenging, non-technical climbs to amazing summit views. Of the Adirondacks 2,000 peaks, over one hundred exceed 3,000 feet. Mounts Marcy and Algonquin soar more than 5,000 feet.

New York's **Finger Lakes** occupy a 9,000-square-mile area that was gouged out during the Ice Age. All offer boating, swimming, and fishing. Many are surrounded by vineyard-covered slopes, shady ravines, and fertile farmland.

The visual grandeur of the **Hudson River Valley** has inspired fine artists and architects ever since the emergence of the school of artists that bears its name. The most dramatic scenery in the region is a 15-mile-long gorge called the **Hudson Highlands.**

As one approaches **New York City,** manmade wonders rightly become the main draw. The city is a tourist mecca for it's historical, cultural, and architectural offerings. The nearby beaches of **Long Island,** however, are legendary as a scenic escape from the hectic city. From the time railroads reached Westhampton in 1870, New Yorkers have decorated these wide, oceanfront vistas with their bronzed torsos and conspicuous wealth—one of many waves of settlement over the course of New York's history.

The Dutch were the state's first European settlers, arriving in 1624 to build outposts near present-day Albany and New York City. But, that wasn't to last. The British took over in 1664, intending to stay. Colonists fended them off in the more than 300 engagements of the Revolutionary War. Of these, 92 battles were fought in New York State, including the Battle of Saratoga, which was a major turning point in the war.

Skipping ahead a couple of centuries, historians credit the building of the Erie Canal between Albany and Buffalo as the main reason why New York City was transformed, practically overnight, into a world financial center and a premier port. The 524-mile Barge Canal System, which opened in 1825, moved produce and resources from the Great Lakes and Canada to Buffalo and Manhattan. Then, hoards of people bought tickets for the return ride to speed the settlement of the western territories.

The engineers of the nineteenth and twentieth centuries then built skyscrapers, bridges, tunnels, roads, apartments, museums, airports, reservoirs, and dams throughout the Empire State. Few places are these monuments to progress as grand and impressive as they are in New York City.

If New York State were a foreign country requiring a visa and passport, no doubt it would be at the top of everyone's list of must-visit places. As it is, it's easy to visit, and the range of all-season attractions is vast. Whether you're looking for big city excitement or quiet landscapes that calm the nerves and rest the mind, you can find both in New York State.

FOR MORE INFORMATION

New York State Department of
Econmic Development
Division of Tourism
1 Commerce Plaza
Albany, NY 12245
(800) 225-5697 or (518) 474-4116

Empire State B&B Association
(585) 396-0375; esbba.com

Zone One

Northern New York/ the Adirondacks

Welcome to New York's majestic Adirondacks, a region of such startling beauty that its deep woods may evoke memories of childhood fairy tales.

Magical things happen when urban folks come face-to-face with fresh air, aisles of snow-tinged trees, uninhibited streams glistening with ice, and a black sky littered with five-carat stars. But make sure you begin your trip with a full tank of gas. **Adirondacks State Park** comprises six million acres—one-fifth of the entire state of New York.

In winter, there are heavy snowfalls, which create opportunities to ski, toboggan, ice skate, ride horse-drawn sleighs, and join moonlit cross-country ski treks. World-class winter sports are available in **Lake Placid,** which hosted the 1932 and 1980 Winter Olympics. Ten major ski areas have, at last count, 244 downhill trails.

In summer, the Adirondacks excel as a canoeing and backpacking destination. For fishermen, the angling is excellent, with some 2,000 ponds and lakes to choose from. Hikers head for the north end of **Lake George,** where 50 miles of trails fan out from the shore.

Thomas Jefferson described Lake George as the most beautiful water he had ever seen. Even today, it's clear enough to see the bottom ten feet and more below. In Colonial times, battles were fought over local water routes between Canada and the south. The story and film *The Last of the Mohicans* is a quasi-accurate description of the struggle at nearby **Fort William Henry,** which is now restored and open for tours.

For most of the eighteenth and early nineteenth centuries, the Adirondacks region was the domain of hunters and loggers. Then, wealthy people claimed it as a woodland retreat, building grand camps and rustic-looking hotels where they installed trophy heads from hunting expeditions as well as improbable luxuries like ballrooms and bowling alleys. The **Adirondack Museum** on Blue Mountain Lake recaptures that past.

In all seasons, the modern day traveler can count on well-maintained roads. Bed-and-breakfasts are scattered over a large area, but those few that exist are a far cry from camping in the woods, boasting feathertop mattresses, in-depth wine cellars, and all the luxuries you could hope for.

FOR MORE INFORMATION

Adirondacks Regional Tourism Council
Box 2149
Plattsburgh, New York 12901
(518) 846-8016; adk.com

Adirondack Regional Chamber of Commerce
(518) 798-1761

Lake George Chamber of Commerce
(518) 668-5755

Lake Placid Visitors Bureau
(800) 447-5224; lakeplacid.com

Gore Mountain Chamber of Commerce
(518) 251-2612

BOATHOUSE, Bolton Landing

OVERALL ★★★★½ | QUALITY ★★★★ | VALUE ★★★ | PRICE $125–$325

Boating enthusiasts will love the fact that this was once the summer home of speedboat racer and gold cup winner George Reis. The dock under the property housed his speedboat, *El Lagarto,* which won three Gold Challenge Cup races in 1933, 1934, and 1935 on Lake George. You can now see the boat on display at Blue Mountain Lake Museum. The boathouse fell into disrepair but was rescued by the current owner, a banker. The unobstructed view of Lake George, with its islands and mountainous shoreline, is dramatic. Not only can you share the house for a few days, but you can walk to The Sagamore, one of the region's premier resorts offering a fitness center, golf course, tennis center, spa, and fine dining.

SETTING & FACILITIES

Location Western side of Lake George. **Near** Next to The Sagamore & adjacent to Smith's Marina; 9 mi. north of Lake George Village & 25 mi. southeast of Gore Mountain. **Building** 1916 boathouse, chimney, & columns of stone, exterior is pale gray siding, dock under the house holds 3 boats. **Grounds** 1 acre w/ hanging baskets, potted plants, & floral borders. **Public Space** Great room/DR, deck. **Food & Drink** Full breakfast w/ juice, fruit, baked goods; specialties—quiche, French toast, & pancakes. **Recreation** Golf, skiing, horseback riding, whitewater rafting, antiquing; canoe, kayak & motor boat rentals next door; Hot Air Balloon Festival, Saratoga Horse Racing, Barbershop Quartet Competition, winter carnivals. **Amenities & Services** Fax & e-mail, outdoor hot tub April–Nov., use of The Sagamore facilities, sheltered boat dock for $10–$20 per night.

ACCOMODATIONS

Units 4 guest rooms, 1 suite. **All Rooms** TV, phone, piped-in stereo music, ceiling fan. **Some Rooms** Balcony (2). **Bed & Bath** King (4), queen (1); all private baths. **Favorites** The suite—four-poster king bed, stereo, TV, private porch w/ lake & mountain view. **Comfort & Decor** The great room and dining area are combined under a high, beamed ceiling, and there are numerous windows to enjoy water views on three sides. Walls are walnut and plaster; floors are longleaf pine. A fireplace, sink-in leather sofa, and family photos give a homey look. Modest-sized guest rooms are simply decorated.

RATES, RESERVATIONS, & RESTRICTIONS

Deposit 1 night, refund w/ 14-days notice Oct.–May; 2 nights, refund w/ 30-days notice June–Sept., less $25 fee. **Discounts** None. **Credit Cards** AE, V, MC. **Check-In/Out** 2:30 p.m./11 a.m. **Smoking** No. **Pets** No. **Kids** Over age 12. **Minimum Stay** 2 nights on weekends April–Oct. & holidays. **Open** All year. **Hosts** Joe Silipigno & Patti Gramberg, Box 1576, Bolton Landing, 12814. **Phone** (518) 644-2554. **Fax** (518) 644-3065. **Email** stay@boathousebb.com. **Web** boathousebb.com.

FRIENDS LAKE INN, Chestertown

OVERALL ★★★★½ | QUALITY ★★★★ | VALUE ★★★ | PRICE $205–355 ($245-395 MAP)

The inn was built as a retreat for tanners, once Chestertown's primary industry. Local tanneries used tree bark, a by-product of the logging industry, to soften hides. The tenor of the area changed during the Prohibition Era and eventually there were six inns and several boarding houses on the lake. Horse-drawn carriages brought New Yorkers from the nearest train stop for extended summer visits. At Friends Lake, guests dressed formally to dine at assigned tables and dance to music played by a house band.

But the inn eventually fell on hard times and closed in 1969. After remaining vacant for 15 years the current innkeepers bought Friends Lake and undertook a massive renovation, returning the property to its glory days. The restaurant is a popular choice with locals. The Grand Award wine collection is extraordinary—with 23,000 bottles to choose from.

SETTING & FACILITIES

Location Overlooking Friends Lake. **Near** 23 mi. north of Lake George, 18 mi. southeast of Gore Mountain Ski area. **Building** 1864 Adirondack Lodge, restored & enlarged. **Grounds** 5 acres w/ outdoor heated swimming pool & sauna, on-site Nordic Ski Center w/ 32 mi. of groomed cross-country trails. **Public Space**: Foyer, Murphy room, 4 DR, upstairs library, billiard room. **Food & Drink** Full breakfast w/ juice, cereals, hot beverages; specialties—Belgian waffles w/ apple compote, fritatta, old-fashioned oats w/ streusel topping, & eggs any style; chocolate chip cookies on arrival; picnics avail., lunch & dinner served, award-winning wine collection. **Recreation** Swimming, canoeing, fishing, hiking, golf, cross-country & downhill skiing, whitewater rafting, antiquing; access to private beach with 3 kayaks & 2 canoes avail. **Amenities & Services** Fax & e-mail, outdoor sauna, videos, massage avail.; wine tastings, ski events, interpretative hikes, wilderness picnics; meetings (30), weddings (350).

ACCOMODATIONS

Units 17 guest rooms. **All Rooms** AC, phone, hair dryer, robes, iron & board. **Some Rooms** Wood-burning fireplace (3), ceiling fan (4), CD clock-radio (6), private entrance (3). **Bed & Bath** King (2), queen (15), four-poster (6), all featherbeds; all private baths, 6 single whirlpools, 6 double whirlpools, 2 tubs. **Favorites** River Rock—queen bed, fireplace, private balcony, Adirondack "Great Camp" furniture, cathedral ceiling, view of pond & gardens; Great Room—even grander w/ king bed, large bath w/ steam shower & whirlpool, fireplace, balcony. **Comfort & Decor** Enjoy rustic elegance with a warm country flair. The dining room has a tin ceiling and burnished chestnut and oak woodwork that glows by candlelight. Bedrooms have quilts and spreads coordinated with Waverly print wallpaper and curtains—some bold, others mellow. Many have lake views.

RATES, RESERVATIONS, & RESTRICTIONS

Deposit Check for 50%, refund w/ 14-days notice. **Discounts** AAA 10%. **Credit Cards** AE, V, MC, DC. **Check-In/Out** 2 p.m./noon. **Smoking** No. **Pets** No. **Kids** Age 12 & over. **Minimum Stay** 2 nights with some Saturday stays. **Open** All year. **Hosts** Sharon & Greg Taylor, 963 Friends Lake Rd., Chestertown, 12817. **Phone** (518) 494-4751. **Fax** (518) 494-4616. **Email** email@friendslake.com. **Web** friendslake.com.

LAMPLIGHT INN, Lake Luzerne

OVERALL ★★★★ | QUALITY ★★★★ | VALUE ★★★ | PRICE **$95–$ 229**

This is another house built for a prominent local businessman and decades later rescued from demise. The original owner was Howard Conkling, a wealthy lumberman and an eligible bachelor of his era. In 1984, Linda, a former textile artist and designer, and Gene, a former engraving manufacturer, were newlyweds when they found and fell in love with this property, buying it as a last minute decision. It's one of the few bed-and-breakfasts that offer a true disabled-access room, with wide doors, a lower sink, shower seating, etc. (That room is called Northern Exposure.) Because Gene is now a contractor, he can see to such details. Linda chooses the wall coverings, fabrics, and furnishings that show off the house's elegant turn-of-the-century beauty.

SETTING & FACILITIES

Location On a knoll at the southern edge of Adirondack Park. **Near** 0.5 block to Lake Luzerne, 1 block to Hudson River, 1 mi. south of Lake George, 16 mi. north of Saratoga Springs. **Building** 1890 Victorian Gothic w/ wraparound porch, new carriage house. **Grounds** 10 acres w/ towering white pines & flower beds. **Public Space** LR, DR, game room. **Food & Drink** Full breakfast w/ juice, fruit, home baked goods; specialties—omelets, Belgian waffles, French toast, & buttermilk pancakes. **Recreation** Swimming, kayaking & canoeing, whitewater rafting, hiking, horseback riding, golf, biking, skiing, snowmobiling, antiquing; Winter Carnival, World's Largest Garage Sale, fireworks on summer weekends, park concerts. **Amenities & Services** Fax, 1 wheelchair-access room; meetings (50).

ACCOMODATIONS

Units 17 guest rooms. **All Rooms** AC, phone, ceiling fan, teddy bear on every bed. **Some Rooms** TV (7), hair dryer (5), deck (4), fireplace (12), private entrance (1). **Bed & Bath** Jacuzzi king (3), queen (14), canopy (8); 15 private baths, 2 detached private baths, 7 tubs. **Favorites** Mountain View—5 windows brighten this corner room, w/ an iron bed, antique quilt & oak dresser, a fireplace, & tub; Rose—the original master bedroom is large & has a carved oak fireplace & queen canopy bed. **Comfort & Decor** An old-fashioned Victorian living room with 12-foot cross-beamed ceilings, parquet flooring, and a keyhole staircase banister is perked up with a Queen Anne sofa & warm wood wainscoting trim. Most furnishings are family heirlooms. Lots of sunlight and ceiling fans, lace curtains, Victorian lamps, and collections of dolls; turtle statues and teacups add personality. Guest rooms vary in quality and style.

RATES, RESERVATIONS, & RESTRICTIONS

Deposit 50%, refund w/ 14-days notice Oct.–June; you need 21-days notice July–Sept. **Discounts** AAA. **Credit Cards** AE, V, MC. **Check-In/Out** 3 p.m./11 a.m. **Smoking** No. **Pets** No. **Kids** Over age 12. **Minimum Stay** 2 or 3 nights, depending on day & season. **Open** All year, except Christmas Eve & Day. **Hosts** Linda & Gene Merlino, 231 Lake Ave., Box 70, Lake Luzerne, 12846. **Phone** (800) 262-4668 or (518) 696-5294. **Fax** (518) 696-5256. **Email** lamp@netheaven.com. **Web** lamplightinn.com.

INTERLAKEN INN, Lake Placid

OVERALL ★★★½ | QUALITY ★★★½ | VALUE ★★★ | PRICE $80–$165 ($160–$245 MAP)

Golfers have an advantage here, because Carol is knowledgeable about local courses and has the contacts to make tee times for her guests. She began running this property in 1986, after moving here with her husband from Southern California. Their son Kevin, a graduate of the Culinary Institute of America, runs the inn's kitchen, turning out such popular fare as rack of lamb, fresh fish, and black-angus filet mignon. At the moment, it seems more energy goes into the dining room than the guest rooms. Carol makes time to do decorative painting each night, and many of her pieces are displayed at the inn or are for sale in the gift shop.

SETTING & FACILITIES

Location Signal Hill residential area. **Near** 7 mi. south of Saranac Lake, 2 mi. to Olympic Ski Jumps. **Building** 1906 Adirondack Victorian Inn. **Grounds** 1 acre w/ flower gardens. **Public Space** LR, bar, breakfast porch, DR. **Food & Drink** Full breakfast w/ juice, fruit; specialties—eggs Benedict, stuffed French toast, & egg casserole w/ artichokes & cheese; 5-course dinner included w/ MAP rates, extensive wine list avail. **Recreation** Golf, tennis, hiking, boating, fishing, downhill & cross-country skiing, bobsledding, horseback riding; spa at Mirror Lake Inn; hosts can arrange tee times at 4 local golf courses. **Amenities & Services** Videos; meetings (12), weddings (40).

ACCOMODATIONS

Units 10 guest rooms, 1 suite. **All Rooms** Clock radio, sherry. **Some Rooms** AC (4), TV (1), balcony (3), ceiling fan (7). **Bed & Bath** King (4), queen (5), double (2), canopy (1); all private baths, 9 tubs. **Favorites** #8—white canopied bed, porch, small sterile bath; #20—king & twin sleigh bed, chaise, bigger bath w/ claw tub & skylight (but bedroom ceiling is cracked). **Comfort & Decor** The staff is friendly. The public rooms are pleasant with such details as walnut paneling and a tin ceiling. The innkeeper displays part of her collection of 250 Byer's Choice figurines. Bedrooms are non-descript and some are converted from sleeping porches.

RATES, RESERVATIONS, & RESTRICTIONS

Deposit 1 night, refund w/ 14-days notice less $25. **Discounts** 10% on weeklong stays. **Credit Cards** AE, V, MC. **Check-In/Out** 3 p.m./11 a.m. **Smoking** Common areas only. **Pets** Small pets OK w/ advance notice; $10 per day. **Kids** Over age 5. **Minimum Stay** 2 nights on summer, fall, & winter weekends, 3 nights on holidays. **Open** All year. **Hosts** Carol & Roy Johnson, 15 Interlaken Ave., Lake Placid, 12946. **Phone** (800) 428-4369 or (518) 523-3180. **Fax** (518) 523-0117. **Email** interlkn@northnet.org. **Web** innbook.com.

GOOSE POND INN, North Creek

OVERALL ★★★½ | QUALITY ★★★½ | VALUE ★★★ | PRICE $95–$125

Pleasing and light-hearted clutter creates a friendly, whimsical ambience at Goose Pond Inn. And, it's needed to balance the more somber St.

James Catholic cemetery located immediately next door. The only phone and television are in the living room, where Beverly displays many of her collectibles, including rows of oil lamps, homemade candles, cow art, geese art, bells, jugs, Bohemian glassware, and dolls. These innkeepers formerly lived in New Jersey, where Beverly was an operating room nurse at St. Peters' Hospital in New Brunswick. "Now I'm making beds here," she quips. She's created a cozy ambience, with lots of plants to add energy. The inn is convenient for skiers, camp parents, and couples who want to relax far away from the maddening crowds.

SETTING & FACILITIES

Location At the eastern foot of Gore Mountain. **Near** 1 mi. to Gore Mountain ski area's access road. **Building** 1894 Victorian, restored. **Grounds** 1 acre w/ pond. **Public Space** LR, DR (2), game room w/ pool table, upstairs sitting room. **Food & Drink** Full breakfast w/ juice, fruit, baked goods; specialties—brandied French toast w/ sautéed apples, Belgian waffles w/ flambéed bananas or fresh fruit, pancakes w/ seasonal fruit, & crêpes w/ rhubarb sauce. **Recreation** Skiing, snowboarding, hiking, rafting on the Hudson River, mountain biking, snowmobiling, ice climbing, antiquing, leaf peeping. **Amenities & Services** Outdoor sauna, massage avail., fax & e-mail; ski races; meetings (12).

ACCOMODATIONS

Units 4 guest rooms. **All Rooms** AC, fresh flowers or plant, hair dryer, clock. **Some Rooms** Collectibles on display. **Bed & Bath** Queen (3), double (1), twin (2); all private baths, 1 tub. **Favorites** Victorian—nice bathroom; Deco—rug beater & hat collections, nice quilt. **Comfort & Decor** Antiques and collectibles.

RATES, RESERVATIONS, & RESTRICTIONS

Deposit 50% a week in advance, refund w/ 14-days notice or if rooms are re-rented. **Discounts** Packages avail. **Credit Cards** No. **Check-In/Out** 3 p.m./11 a.m. **Smoking** Living room only. **Pets** No (3 English cockers on premises). **Kids** Age 10 & over. **Minimum Stay** 2 or 3 nights on holiday weekends & special events. **Open** All year. **Hosts** Beverly & Jim Englert, Box 273, Main St., North Creek, 12853. **Phone** (800) 806-2601 or (518) 251-3434. **Fax** (518) 251-3434. **Web** goosepondinn.com.

PORCUPINE, Saranac Lake

OVERALL ★★★★ | QUALITY ★★★★ | VALUE ★★★★ | PRICE $130–$150

There are a lot of interesting visual details attached to this big, old rambling house, which is listed on the National Register of Historic Places. It's noteworthy that early owner Thomas Bailey Aldrich was a friend of fellow writer, Mark Twain. And, some people believe that a popular book written by Aldrich entitled 'The Story of a Bad Boy' was the inspiration for Twain's novels about Tom Sawyer and Huckleberry Finn. Aldrich's influence was felt in other ways, as well. After he became editor of *The Atlantic Monthly*, the literary magazine was regarded as a touchstone for American taste in his era. The house is befitting a man of his stature—and the newly added sports memorabilia collection brings it smartly up to date.

SETTING & FACILITIES

Location On a residential street between Mounts Pisgah & Baker. **Near** Adjacent to the Saranac River, 19 mi. north of Tupper Lake, 8 mi. southwest of Lake Placid. **Building** 1903 Shingle-style w/ 6 gables, gambrel roof. **Grounds** 3.5 acres w/ lawn, woods, floral borders. **Public Space** Foyer, LR, DR, veranda. **Food & Drink** Full breakfast w/ juice, fruit, baked goods; specialties—blackberry cobbler, egg & mushroom soufflé, & a farmer's breakfast. **Recreation** Swimming, fishing, boating, hiking, skating, alpine & Nordic skiing, leaf peeping, luge & bobsled runs, rock & ice climbing, berry picking, antiquing; theater at The Pendragon, The Adirondack Museum. **Amenities & Services** Fax & e-mail; meetings (8), weddings (35).

ACCOMODATIONS

Units 5 guest rooms. **All Rooms** Clocks. **Some Rooms** Hair dryer, cure porch (2), fireplace (2). **Bed & Bath** Bed sizes vary; 3 private baths, 1 detached private bath, 3 tubs. **Favorites** Charles Room—queen bed, sitting area, fireplace, private porch, bright & cheerful. **Comfort & Decor** The cheerful public rooms are in pristine condition and offer comfy furnishings and yellow/beige walls. The living room, dining room, and hall walls are a mini-museum of baseball and sports memorabilia, including 1916 bats, rare pennants, hall of fame gloves, balls and bats, even a Ted Williams shirt. Antique fly rods, golf clubs, sleds, skis, snowshoes, and an Oglala Sioux headdress are also displayed. Guest room furnishings are eclectic.

RATES, RESERVATIONS, & RESTRICTIONS

Deposit 50%, refund w/ 7-days notice less 10%. **Discounts** No. **Credit Cards** No. **Check-In/Out** 3–9 p.m./11 a.m. **Smoking** No. **Pets** No. **Kids** No. **Minimum Stay** 2 nights on weekends. **Open** All year. **Hosts** Barbara & Jerry Connolly, 147 Park Ave., Saranac Lake, 12983. **Phone** (518) 891-5160. **Email** porcupine@northnet.org. **Web** theporcupine.com.

THE POINT, Saranac Lake

OVERALL ★★★★★ | QUALITY ★★★★★ | VALUE ★★ | PRICE **$1,000–$1,900**

You'll live like a Rockefeller—William Avery Rockefeller, to be precise—in this informal luxurious yet rustic Great Camp, which he built as a lakeside retreat. All guest rooms are splendidly rustic with views of remote

Upper Saranac Lake. The eye-popping price includes all meals, an always-open bar, carte blanche use of sports equipment and facilities, but not the 18% service charge. So, help yourself to the house champagne, enjoy lake-side picnics, and cuddle up by a wood-burning fireplace. Name any sport and you can probably arrange it, including sunset chasing and impromptu full-moon cruises on a 33-foot mahogany HackerCraft. At dinner look for celebrities or icons of finance and business. In the guest book, handwritten messages from happy campers glow with satisfaction, in spite of the price tag. Most are anniversary celebrants or returnees. And, why not? It's like attending an exclusive house party—a rare chance to savor the beauty of nature while indulging in the comforts of a five-star resort.

SETTING & FACILITIES

Location On Whitney Point, a wooded peninsula on the western shore of Upper Saranac Lake. **Near** 20 mi. west of Lake Placid, 30 mi. northeast of the Adirondack Museum. **Building** 1930–33 Adirondack Great Camp w/ main lodge & 3 guest houses. **Grounds** 10 acres w/ herb & edible flower gardens, waterfront seating & hammocks, picnic areas, 1 tennis court, 65 acres of trails. **Public Space** Great Hall, pub, deck, powder room, boathouse. **Food & Drink** Full breakfast delivered to your room or served in the Great Hall or patio; 50-item menu offers juice, fruit, homemade baked goods, beverages, & specialties including corned beef w/ poached eggs, omelet w/ goat cheese, blueberry pancakes, & oatmeal w/ dried fruit; lunch or picnic provided, afternoon tea, cocktail hour 7–8 p.m., gourmet dinner 8 p.m. w/ other guests or room service upon request. **Recreation** Swiming, tubing, water skiing, boating, lake fishing (for trout, salmon, pike, & bass; licenses avail.), tennis, mountain biking, cross-country skiing, ice skating, ice fishing, dog sledding, snowshoeing, bonfires, croquet, horseshoes; gear for the above sports is available for guest use, including boats (motor and sailboats, as well as canoes & kayaks); antiquing, golf, horseback riding, fly-fishing, & miles of hiking trails avail. nearby. **Amenities & Services** Massage, outdoor guides (fishing, hunting, & hiking), tee times arranged, pre-dinner lake cruise; TV/VCR/DVD avail. in pub, classic videos, laundry, fax & e-mail; meetings (26), weddings (26).

ACCOMODATIONS

Units 11 guest rooms. **All Rooms** Fresh flowers, fireplace, featherbed, his & hers electric blanket, flashlight, robes, ceiling fan, clock, iron & board, shoe polish, tea service, safe, wine, walking sticks, umbrellas, lake view. **Some Rooms** Soaking tubs. **Bed & Bath** King (7), queen (4), hanging beds (2), canopy (1); all privates baths, 5 large soaking tubs, 4 regular tubs. **Favorites** Trappers—a cozy hideaway w/ antique sporting equipment to evoke the outdoor life, a low ceiling, birch tree sections framing the king bed, sofas draped with ethnic blankets, lake view; Boat House—like a luxury houseboat, w/ canopied king bed, oversized sofa and chairs, deck overlooking the lake, dining area, fully stocked bar; Boat House is almost twice the price of Trappers, but only avail. in the summer. **Comfort & Decor** Sink into comfy cushions on Adirondack chairs and enjoy the rustic look of twig furniture, old iron lamps, hand-sewn bark wastebaskets and vases. Huge stone fireplaces and sitting areas with lake views are dramatic. Each guest room is uniquely outfitted. The tone is formal two nights a week, when black tie is preferred for dinner. But the rest of the time, plan to kick back, relax, and soak up the ultimate in country chic. No room keys are issued. Television and phones are available only in the main lodge.

RATES, RESERVATIONS, & RESTRICTIONS

Deposit Payment in full, refund w/ 30-days notice less $50 per room. **Discounts** No. **Credit Cards** AE, V, MC. **Check-In/Out** Before 1 p.m. to have lunch/vacate your room by noon but stay for the day if you like. **Smoking** Yes, everywhere but the main lodge. **Pets** Yes (dog beds & treats provided). **Kids** 18 and over (unless you book the entire property). **No-Nos** No tipping, no cell phones in the main lodge. **Minimum Stay** 2 nights on weekends, 3–4 nights over holidays. **Open** All year (except mid-March to mid-April). **Hosts** Christie & David Garrett; Tim Thuell, Gen. Mgr., Box 65, Saranac Lake, 12983. **Phone** (800) 255-3530 or (518) 891-5674. **Fax** (518) 891-1152. **Email** thepoint@northnet.org. **Web** pointny.com.

BATCHELLER MANSION INN, Saratoga Springs

OVERALL ★★★★ | QUALITY ★★★★½ | VALUE ★★★ | PRICE **$125–$400**

Ambassador George Batcheller's three-story white stucco house is so unique it was patented. Exterior details include a red and gray Mansard roof, dormers accented with clamshell arches, ornate bays, balustraded balconies, an Islamic-style capped minaret à la Arabian Nights, plus a portico with arches and columns. Interiors are appropriately stunning—all restored to perfection or replicated to seem authentic. You'll see a mahogany staircase with tiger maple inlay, a rococo newel post, decorative moldings, coffered ceilings, high-arched doorways, and tall recessed windows with ornamental cornices. Carved marble fireplaces and faux Impressionist art add to the glamour.

SETTING & FACILITIES

Location Commercial neighborhood. **Near** 40 mi. north of Albany, 30 mi. south of Lake George. **Building** 1873 High Victorian Gothic w/ eclectic details. **Grounds** City lot w/ small yard. **Public Space** Foyer, LR, library, DR, 2 porches. **Food & Drink** Cont'l breakfast Mon.–Fri.; full breakfast on weekends & in racing season w/ juice, fresh fruit, fresh baked good, & specialties including omelets, pancakes, eggs any style—the basics; fresh baked cookies anytime. **Recreation** Saratoga Racetrack, Saratoga Performing Arts, Saratoga State Park, National Museum of Dance, National Museum of Racing, Equine Sports Center, Skidmore College, Lake George, Gore Mountain. **Amenities & Services** Fax & e-mail, turndown service w/ chocolates; groups (50), weddings (80).

ACCOMODATIONS

Units 9 guest rooms. **All Rooms** TV, phone, robes, fridge stocked w/ Saratoga Springs water. **Some Rooms** Double whirlpool tub, private terrace, dormers. **Bed & Bath** King (2), the rest are queens, canopy (1), four-poster (3); private baths, 2 whirlpools, 2 tubs. **Favorites** Katrina Trask—lace-swathed king canopy bed, heavily tufted velvet setee w/ curved filigree frame, desk, private circular terrace, large bathroom (ideal for brides); Diamond Jim Brady—wrought-iron king bed, 19th-century settee, fireplace, pool table, double whirlpool, mirrored wall. **Comfort & Decor** The living room has a grand piano, 12-foot high windows, and faux Impressionist art. The dining room table is set with crystal, china, silver, and lace. The library features a 48-inch screen TV and comfortable seating. Second floor guest rooms are handsomely decorated. Third floor rooms have dormers and gables and are less opulent.

RATES, RESERVATIONS, & RESTRICTIONS

Deposit Credit card, refund w/ 14-days notice less 10%. **Discounts** AAA, corp. **Credit Cards** AE, V, MC. **Check-In/Out** 3 p.m./noon. **Smoking** No. **Pets** No. **Kids** Age 14 & older. **Minimum Stay** 2 nights on holidays & May–Dec. weekends; 4 nights July 25–Sept. 3 (racing season). **Open** All year. **Hosts** Bruce Levinsky, owner; Sue McCage, innkeeper, 20 Circular St., Saratoga Springs, 12866. **Phone** (800) 616-7012 or (518) 584-7012. **Fax** (518) 581-7746. **Email** mail@batchellermansioninn.com. **Web** batchellermansioninn.com.

ALL TUCKED INN , Westport

OVERALL ★★★ | QUALITY ★★★ | VALUE ★★★ | PRICE **$55–$110**

Claudia is an attorney with her own practice in Albany. Tom, a self-described history buff and golf enthusiast, was a lobbyist for 15 years prior to becoming an innkeeper here in 1992. The community has a nice, New England feel to it, offering four seasons and a chance to immerse yourself in the early history of our country. Tom says the original settler was William Gilliland, who founded several area communities, including Elizabethtown and Bessboro (now Westport), which was named for his daughter. The town's early economy was based on lumber, mining and agriculture. During the American Revolution, naval battles and military skirmishes took place on Lake Champlain, some across from this inn.

SETTING & FACILITIES

Location Across from Ballard Park, overlooking the western shore of Lake Champlain. **Near** A public marina; 45 min. to Lake Placid Olympic facilities. **Building** 1872 French country–style w/ gray siding. **Grounds** 2 acres w/ gardens. **Public Space** LR, DR, glass-enclosed porch. **Food & Drink** Full breakfast w/ juice, fresh fruit, homemade baked goods, hot beverages; specialties—stuffed French toast, fruited pancakes, & eggs any style; dinner for guests only avail. w/ advance notice ($25 per person). **Recreation** Golf, swimming, hiking, snowmobiling, ice fishing, cross-country skiing, sledding, ice skating, apple picking, trout fishing; Depot theatre, Thurs. night summer concerts, historic sites, Essex Ferry to Vermont for sightseeing, reenactments at Fort Ticondaroga. **Amenities & Services** Videos, communal VCR & fireplace, fax & e-mail; meetings (8), weddings (40).

ACCOMODATIONS

Units 9 guest rooms. **All Rooms** Ceiling fan, clock. **Some Rooms** Fireplace (3). **Bed & Bath** King (2), queen (5), double (2), four-poster (1); all private baths, 2 tubs. **Favorites** #14—two wing chairs face a fireplace; #19—ditto, plus a king bed. **Comfort & Decor** Furnishings are casual and non-descript. Stuffed animals are everywhere, adding a touch of whimsy.

RATES, RESERVATIONS, & RESTRICTIONS

Deposit 1 night or 50% for longer stays, refund w/ 14-days notice less $10. **Discounts** March madness 20% off. **Credit Cards** No. **Check-In/Out** 3 p.m./11:30 a.m. **Smoking** No. **Pets** No (2 collies on premises). **Kids** Age 6 & over. **Minimum Stay** 2 nights weekends June through Oct. **Open** All year. **Hosts** Claudia Ryan & Tom Haley, 53 S. Main St., Westport, 12993. **Phone** (888) 255-8825 or (518) 962-4400. **Fax** (518) 962-4400. **Email** haleyt@westelcom.com. **Web** alltuckedin.com.

INN ON THE LIBRARY LAWN, Westport

OVERALL ★★★½ | QUALITY ★★★ | VALUE ★★★★ | PRICE $59–$115

This inn is filled with sturdy, sensible furnishings that families traveling with children will be comfortable using. Kids activities are thoughtfully provided in the upstairs sitting area. On the main floor, the small sitting area is next to the large restaurant area, which has a liquor license and a bar. In summer, outdoor hanging planters, flower boxes, and gardens add charm. The inn plays up it's namesake location next door to the town library with a quantity of well-worn books perched on shelves, tables, and dressers throughout the inn. You're invited to pick one up and discover a classic, mystery, or juicy novel. Both innkeepers are part-time teachers, he in college microbiology and she in elementary school. Avid readers will appreciate their efforts to promote the printed word.

SETTING & FACILITIES

Location Center of town, 1 block to Lake Champlain, 1 block to train station. **Near** Fort Ticonderoga, Crown Point, Shelburne Museum, Vermont State Craft Center, Ausable Chasm, High Falls Gorge, Lake Placid Olympic Center. **Building** 1877 Italianate. **Grounds** 0.5 acre corner city lot w/ flower boxes. **Public Space** Fireplace lounge, TV room, lobby, deck, upstairs library/sitting area. **Food & Drink** Full breakfast w/ juices, fresh fruit, pastries; specialties—sticky buns, quiche, French toast, pancakes & waffles w/ maple syrup; afternoon refreshments; boxed lunches & dinners avail. w/ advance notice; guest fridge. **Recreation** Golf, fishing, hiking, summer theater, historic sites, boating (kayak, canoe, & sail); skiing at Whiteface Mountain—downhill & cross country. **Amenities & Services** Videos, fax & e-mail, rides to Westport train depot; meetings(20), weddings (30).

ACCOMODATIONS

Units 10 guest rooms. **All Rooms** AC, clock radio. **Some Rooms** TV (6). **Bed & Bath** King (1), queen (4), twin (1), double (4); all private baths, 7 tubs. **Favorites** Thackery—white four-poster bed w/ vines, quilt, wicker chairs, TV, lake view; Agatha Christie—four-poster bed, stack of mystery novels. **Comfort & Decor** A modest TV room offers cable and puzzles. Lounge furnishings are eclectic, including a gas fireplace, Oriental cabinet, screen, ginger jars, and three bay windows overlooking Lake Champlain. There's lakeview dining, as well. Guest rooms are named for authors and stocked with books written by that author.

RATES, RESERVATIONS, & RESTRICTIONS

Deposit Credit card to hold, refund w/ 14-days notice less $10. **Discounts** No. **Credit Cards** AE, V, MC. **Check-In/Out** 3 p.m./10:30 a.m. **Smoking** No. **Pets** No. **Kids** Age 5 & up. **Minimum Stay** 2 days. **Open** All year. **Hosts** Susann & Don Thompson, Box 390, Westport, 12993. **Phone** (888) 577-7748 or (518) 962-8666. **Fax** (518) 962-2007. **Email** innthompson@msn.com. **Web** theinnonthelibrarylawn.com.

Zone 2

Western New York/ Finger Lakes

Eleven elongated, finger-shaped lakes give special character to the rolling hills of central New York State. They were named for the tribes of the Iroquois Nations. Lake Senaca is the deepest (more than 600 feet) and Cayuga is the longest (40 miles).Resembling the fjords of Norway, a patchwork of fields and forest descends right to the lakes' cottage-ringed shores.

The area is too large to tour completely in a weekend. There are cities to explore, including **Ithaca,** which lives up to its description on local bumper-stickers: "Ithaca is gorges." Gorgeous gorges can be reached via short, steep walks from town. **Seneca Falls,** near the northern end of Cayuga Lake, was birthplace of the women's rights movement. An excellent museum commemorates the progress and setbacks of the American woman.

Auburn, at the northern end of Owasco Lake, is home to fine Victorian houses. **Skaneateles** is an upscale tourist town facing the Skaneateles Lake. **Geneva** at the north and **Watkins Glen Falls** at the south sandwich Seneca Lake. The latter city is known for auto racing, a state park with unusual rocks, and a series of waterfalls. Near **Canandaigua,** north of its namesake lake, you'll find small, family-operated wineries.

In **Rochester,** near Lake Ontario, you can tour the **Eastman Kodak Company** and the **George Eastman Estate**. In **Syracuse,** you can visit museums devoted to science, art, and the Erie Canal. In **Rome,** costumed interpreters reenact Colonial-era military life in the reconstructed earth-and-log **Fort Stanwix.** Nearby, you can ride on an 1840s mule-drawn packet boat along a restored section of the Erie Canal.

Then, there are land-locked cities like **Corning,** which is home to a newly-upgraded million-dollar **Corning Glass Center.** It gives you an encyclopedic look at the glass industry, from early blowing techniques to mass production, to the use of exotic glass in space travel.

Buffalo, the state's second largest city, is worth a visit to see its extraordinary architecture and the **Albright-Knox Art Gallery**. It is also the gateway to **Niagara Falls,** which spans the United States and Canadian border and remains one of the world's most famous natural wonders.

In the Finger Lakes region, a number of bed-and-breakfast owners have restored lovely older homes to preserve a bit of American history. The numerous bed-and-breakfasts in these gentle landscapes range from easy-going country inns to luxurious, upscale retreats.

FOR MORE INFORMATION

The Finger Lakes Association
309 Lake St.
Penn Yan, NY 14527
(315) 536-7488

Canandaigua Chamber of Commerce
(716) 394-4400

Greater Corning Chamber of Commerce
(607) 936-4686

Greater Buffalo CVB
(800) 283-3256

Greater East Aurora Chamber of Commerce
(716) 652-8444

Geneva Area Chamber of Commerce
(315) 789-1776

Ithaca/Tompkins County CVB
(800) 284-8422

Niagara Falls CVB
(800) 421-5223

Greater Rochester Visitors Association
(800) 677-7282

BEAU FLEUVE, Buffalo

OVERALL ★★★★ | QUALITY ★★★★ | VALUE ★★★ | PRICE $75–$125

The first known resident of Beau Fleuve was Albert J. Wright, a Buffalo stockbroker. From 1895 to the 1930s, the Abell family lived here, beginning with Colonel Charles Lee Abell, descendant of a Mayflower pilgrim, Civil War officer in the 4th New York Regiment, and bank president. The house underwent extensive renovation in the 1980s, and the current owners are preservationists. Rik is a journalism and broadcast professor at Buffalo State College, and Ramona is a retired editor of educational materials. They met in Egypt and have accessorized their public rooms with souvenirs from that country. Guest rooms are themed to reflect Buffalo's ethnic heritage—Irish, German, French, Polish, and Italian.

SETTING & FACILITIES

Location Residential area, historic district. **Near** 2.5 mi. to Peace Bridge access to Canada, 9 mi. southwest of Buffalo Airport, 16 mi. south of Niagara Falls. **Building** 1883 stick style w/ medieval half-timber & Queen Anne elements. **Grounds** Corner city lot w/ trees, shrubs. **Public Space** Parlor, great hall, DR, upstairs landing. **Food & Drink** Candlelight breakfast w/ choice of juices, fruit plate, just-baked muffins; specialities include veggie frittata, eggs Benedict or Florentine, fruited Belgian waffles, raspberry-almond waffles, & Tanzania, Peaberry, Kenyan, or Mocha Java coffee; guest fridge & snack center w/ beverages; will adjust menu for allergy & diet restrictions. **Recreation** Architecture walking tours, Frank Lloyd Wright–designed houses, Albright-Knox Art Gallery, Burchfield-Penney Art Center, historic forts, symphony, baseball, theater at Niagara-on-the-Lake; Hellenic Festival (May), Allentown Art Festival (June), Italian Festival (July), Taste of Buffalo (July). **Amenities & Services** Meetings (10).

ACCOMMODATIONS

Units 5 guest rooms. **All Rooms** AC, phone, ceiling fan, robe, clock radio/tape player, coffeemaker. **Some Rooms** TV (1), decorative fireplace (1). **Bed & Bath** King (1), queen (2), full (2), four-poster (1), brass (1), each bed has a down comforter; 1 private bath, 2 detached private baths, 1 shared bath. **Favorites** Irish—William Morris wallpaper, pale green spread, books & art reflecting Irish culture, the inn's only in-room bath. **Comfort & Decor** Common areas have Egyptian artifacts, multicolored stained glass panels, and interesting light fixtures. The signature sunflower motif is carved in the oak staircase and several glass windows. The loft is dedicated to western New York tribes of the Iroquois Nation. Accessories include a 1920s Navaho rug, sand paintings, and painted plates. Guestroom decor celebrates the heritage of early settlers in Buffalo. It's all very interesting.

RATES, RESERVATIONS, & RESTRICTIONS

Deposit Credit card, refund w/ 14-days notice less $15 fee. **Discounts** Non-profit groups, gov't, corp., extended stay. **Credit Cards** AE, V, MC, D. **Check-In/Out** 3 p.m./11 a.m. **Smoking** No. **Pets** No (cat on premises). **Kids** Yes, well-behaved. **Minimum Stay** 2 nights on summer, holiday, and autumn leaf weekends. **Open** All year. **Hosts** Ramona & Rik Whitaker, 242 Linwood Ave., Buffalo, 14209. **Phone** (800) 278-0245 or (716) 882-6116. **Fax** (716) 882-2490. **E-mail** innkeeper@beaufleuve.com. **Web** beaufleuve.com.

ACORN INN, Canandaigua

OVERALL ★★★★½ | QUALITY ★★★★½ | VALUE ★★★ | PRICE $120–$210

The Clarks originally opened this house as an antiques and rare book shop called The Acorn. Over the years, so many of their customers said "this would make a great bed-and-breakfast" that they finally succumbed to the idea in 1989. Some of their best antiques, paintings, and Oriental carpets furnish the spacious rooms. Books are everywhere. The beds are comfortable, and the breakfast is tasty. You can begin your day with a soak in the garden hot tub, reading under a shade tree by the "frog" pond, or enjoying the birds attracted to numerous feeders. Joan is a fastidious housekeeper. (One page of the information book in our room was a tutorial on how to clean up accidental spills if she wasn't immediately available.) Nevertheless, you can feel the stress melt away as you enter this Hansel and Gretel retreat.

SETTING & FACILITIES

Location On Rte. 64 in the hamlet of Bristol Center. **Near** 5 mi. north of Bristol Mountain ski resort, 8 mi. southwest of Canandaigua, 15 mi. north of Naples. **Building** 1795 Federal, former stage coach inn & tavern, brown shingle w/ red sash & trim, original windows, posts, & beams. **Grounds** 38 acres w/ extensive gardens, dry stone wall, frog pond, outdoor hot tub. **Public Space** Gathering room, DR, reception area, barn. **Food & Drink** Full country breakfast w/ juice, fresh fruit in season; specialties—French toast crème brûlée, fritatta, strata; snacks & stocked guest fridge; tea on request. **Recreation** Tennis, soccer, running track, Cummin Nature Center, hiking, skiing, biking, fishing, canoeing, excursions to wineries, historic homes, & theater; Balloon Fest (May),

Civil War. Reenactment (summer), Grape Festival (Sept.). **Amenities & Services** Videos, massage, fax & e-mail, ski & bike storage, card & board games.

ACCOMMODATIONS

Units 4 guest rooms. **All Rooms** AC, TV, fresh flowers, hair dryer, robe, clock, iron & board, fan, radio/CD player. **Some Rooms** Fireplace (2). **Bed & Bath** Queen (4), canopy (4), all with down quilts; all private baths, 1 whirlpool, 3 tubs. **Favorites** Hothkiss—canopy bed, 2 chairs,fireplace, TV & books, lots of charm, sliding glass doors to private patio facing garden & bird feeders; Bristol—blue & white check fabrics, canopy bed, reading alcove, whirlpool. **Comfort & Decor** Sturbridge Village and Colonial Williamsburg paints lend an historic look to rooms filled with period antiques and outstanding art. In a sense, the cottage-style house itself—and the garden—is a work of art. Collections include baskets and china.

RATES, RESERVATIONS, & RESTRICTIONS

Deposit Credit card, refund w/ 14-days notice less 10%. **Discounts** AAA. **Credit Cards** AE, V, MC, D. **Check-In/Out** 3–5 p.m./11 a.m. **Smoking** No. **Pets** No. **Kids** Over age 12. **Minimum Stay** 2 nights on weekends in July & Aug. **Open** All year. **Hosts** Joan & Louis Clark, 4508 Rte. 64S, Canandaigua, 14424. **Phone** (888) 245-4134 or (716) 229-2834. **Fax** (716) 229-5046. **E-mail** acorninn@rochester.rr.com. **Web** acorninn.com.

MORGAN-SAMUELS INN, Canandaigua

OVERALL ★★★★★ | QUALITY ★★★★½ | VALUE ★★★ | PRICE $109–$325

A 2,000-foot driveway leads to this stunning property, which has been carefully organized to make sure that all senses are touched—with bright flowers, pleasant sounds, flavorful foods, and tactile comforts. One previous owner was Howard Samuels, the man who invented the plastic bag and served as President Lyndon Johnson's under-Secretary of State. The other was playwright-actor Judson Morgan. The current owners say they transformed the home into a bed-and-breakfast as a way to serve people, sensing "this is what the Lord wants us to do." Each room contains a copy of "The Five Love Languages: How to Express Heartfelt Commitment to Your Mate," a guide for couples to improve their relationships.

SETTING & FACILITIES

Location On a knoll overlooking farmland & pasture. **Near** 2.5 mi. northeast of Canandaigua. **Building** 1810 stone mansion w/ 1930 additions. **Grounds** 46 acres w/ spring stream, fields of corn & hay, woods. **Public Space** Common room, library/game/TV room, glass-enclosed Victorian stone porch, DR, tea room, 3 brick patios. **Food & Drink** Early coffee, multi-course candlelit breakfast w/ elaborate fruit tray, homemade muffins & breads; specialties—buckwheat pancakes w/ berries or pecans & black capberry syrup, French toast w/ berries, herbed scrambled eggs, Canadian bacon, spiced sausage or double-smoked bacon; early evening hors d'oeuvres w/ tea & fresh-pressed cider (or bring your own wine). **Recreation** Tennis court w/ rackets & balls avail., croquet, cross-country skiing; Performing Arts Center, Steam Pageant (Aug.), Farm Days (Aug.), Grape Festival (Sept.). **Amenities & Services** Videos, massage avail., laundry, fax & e-mail.

ACCOMMODATIONS

Units 6 guest rooms. **All Rooms** AC, fireplace, hair dryer, robes, clock, radio/tape deck. **Some Rooms** Balcony (3), ceiling fan (4), private entrance (1), French doors (3). **Bed & Bath** King (4), queen (2), four-poster (1); all private baths, 4 whirlpool, 1 tub. **Favorites** Morgan suite—cedar closet, whirlpool, fridge. **Comfort & Decor** The house has 11 fireplaces and only one TV. The prettiest room is the glass-enclosed stone porch that overlooks an idyllic country setting. Space and color are organized with a sense of proportion and eye-pleasing balance. Both the decorator and the gardener deserve kudos.

RATES, RESERVATIONS, & RESTRICTIONS

Deposit Credit card, refund less 10% if re-rented. **Discounts** Corp. **Credit Cards** AE, V, MC, D. **Check-In/Out** 3 p.m./11 a.m. (vacate your room & stay until 2 p.m.). **Smoking** No. **Pets** No. **Kids** Under age 2 & over age 12. **Minimum Stay** 2 nights on weekends & holidays mid-May to mid-Nov. **Open** All year (except Dec. 24 & 25). **Hosts** Julie & John Sullivan, 2920 Smith Rd., Canandaigua, 14424. **Phone** (716) 394-9232. **Fax** (716) 394-8044. **E-mail** morgansamuelsinn@aol.com. **Web** morgansamuelsinn.com.

ROSEWOOD INN, Corning

OVERALL ★★★½ | QUALITY ★★★★ | VALUE ★★★ | PRICE **$95–$185**

Suzanne likes to dress the part of a Victorian-era lady, wearing shear, flowing gowns or dramatic black velvets, big hats, roses, and elaborate jewelry—wherever she goes. She lives out the fantasy and romance of an earlier era. She has decorated this house with hints of whimsy, including soft-sculpture dolls and a collection of 200 miniature hippos of every conceivable material. It's a far cry from a former life, when she and Stewart spent 25 years as the owners of a printing manufacturing plant in New Jersey. "Now I have a job where I can stay home and have company everyday," she says—clearly enjoying that role. Stewart's realm is the kitchen, where he wears chef whites and cooks some tasty family recipes.

SETTING & FACILITIES

Location Residential street in National Historic neighborhood. **Near** 1 block to Corning Hospital, 3 blocks south of downtown, 0.75 mi. to Corning Museum of Glass. **Building** 1917 English Tudor superimposed over 1855 Greek Revival, pink w/ London brown trim. **Grounds** City lot. **Public Space** Guest parlor, DR, porch, 2nd floor sitting area, what-not room. **Food & Drink** Full candlelight breakfast w/ juice, fruit, hot cereal, & granola, homemade breads & muffins; specialties—Stewart's Grandma's eggs, Stewart's French toast, mushroom/cheese strata w/ English-kissed corn muffins; afternoon refreshments. **Recreation** Antiquing, golf, Corning Museum of Glass, National Warplane Museum, National Soaring Museum, Rockwell Museum, art galleries, Festival of Arts (July), Carder-Steuben Glass Seminar (Sept.). **Amenities & Services** Laundry.

ACCOMMODATIONS

Units 5 guest rooms, 2 suites. **All Rooms** AC, clock. **Some Rooms** TV (2), phone (2), private entrance (2), clock/radio (2). **Bed & Bath** Queen (5), full (1), twin (2), canopy (1), four-poster (1); all private baths, 2 tubs. **Favorites** Elizabeth I—antique headboard, stained glass panels, chandelier, English art, books; Lewis Carroll—four-poster, claw tub.

Comfort & Decor Wood paneling, trim, built-in shelves, and original flooring create a dark, dramatic effect. The sitting room features Cooper rockers, a red velvet sofa, and lots of lace and doilies. A time traveler from the Victorian era would feel right at home.

RATES, RESERVATIONS, & RESTRICTIONS

Deposit One night, refund less $10 with 3-days notice, 14-days for holidays or event weekends. **Discounts** No. **Credit Cards** AE, V, MC, D, DC, CB. **Check-In/Out** 3–7 p.m./11 a.m. **Smoking** No. **Pets** No (2 pugs in residence). **Kids** Over age 12. **Minimum Stay** 2 nights on special events weekends. **Open** All year. **Hosts** Suzanne & Stewart Sanders, 134 E. First St., Corning, 14830. **Phone** (607) 9622-3253. **E-mail** info@rosewoodinn.com. **Web** rosewoodinn.com.

GREEN GLEN, East Aurora

OVERALL ★★★★½ | QUALITY ★★★★ | VALUE ★★★★ | PRICE **$80–$145**

These innkeepers opened their bed-and-breakfast in 1988 as a way to finance the restoration of this wonderful 30-room house. It's their second major renovation project, so they did it with eyes wide open. And, now their dream has come true. Formerly, Ed was an editor and reporter for newspapers in New York state, including the *Buffalo Evening News*. Martha worked for Moog, an aerospace company. They raised three children and often hosted exchange students. "We like having a houseful of people, and this has been a happy transition from both of our careers," says Ed, in his deep, sonorous voice. They work as a team, sharing hosting and kitchen chores, and maintaining two cutting gardens that yield fresh flowers for each guest room. The hospitality is heartfelt.

SETTING & FACILITIES

Location On the town's historic Main Street, 8 blocks east of Roycroft Campus. **Near** Vidler's 5 & 10 store, Toy Town Museum, Explore & More, Elbert Hubbard Roycroft Museum, Millard Fillmore House. **Building** 1892 Queen Anne w/ 1948 addition. **Grounds** 6 acres of woodland, gardens, creek. **Public Space** Smoking lounge, parlor, drawing room, DR, office area. **Food & Drink** Full breakfast w/ juice, fresh fruit, homemade muffins & breads; specialties—various omelets, frittata, waffles, pancakes. **Recreation** Jogging, biking (4 bikes avail.), golf, tennis, antiquing. **Amenities & Services** Videos.

ACCOMMODATIONS

Units 4 guest rooms. **All Rooms** AC, fresh flowers, hair dryer, radio, clock. **Some Rooms** Balcony (1). **Bed & Bath** King (1), queen (2), double (2), twin (1), four-poster (3); 3 private baths, 1 shared bath, 3 tub/showers, 1 tub. **Favorites** S.H. Peek—queen four-poster bed, private tiled/wainscoted bath, sitting area, air conditioner. **Comfort & Decor** Antiques and family heirlooms fill the spacious, high-ceilinged rooms. Televisions are available in two public rooms and books line shelves in the drawing room. Interesting mantels, wonderful woodwork, original stained glass and classic wallpaper enhance a house which already has strong bones and plenty of character.

RATES, RESERVATIONS, & RESTRICTIONS

Deposit $75, refund w/ 15-days notice less $15. **Discounts** Corp. **Credit Cards** No. **Check-In/Out** 3–7 p.m./11:30 a.m. **Smoking** One lounge only. **Pets** No. **Kids** Some.

Minimum Stay 2 nights on weekends May–Sept. **Open** All year. **Hosts** Martha & Ed Collins, 898 Main St., East Aurora, 14052. **Phone** (716) 655-2828. **E-mail** info@green-glen.com. **Web** green-glen.com.

BELHURST CASTLE, Geneva

OVERALL ★★★ | QUALITY ★★★★ | VALUE ★★★ | PRICE **$125–$315**

We included this property for its unusual architecture, stunning lakefront location, and colorful past. The land it sits on was once the site of a Seneca Indian village and home to the Council of the Six Nations of Iroquois. The most infamous person to live on this site was William Henry Bucke, who embezzled funds from London's Covent Garden Theater, married his stepmother, and came here under an assumed name. Later, Carrie Harron Collins tore down the old structure and employed 50 men for four years to build the Belhurst Castle you see today. During the 1930s, it became a speakeasy and gambling casino, and then a restaurant. Today it is listed on the National Register of Historic Places.

SETTING & FACILITIES

Location North end of Seneca Lake, 3.5 mi. southwest of downtown Geneva. **Near** Seneca Lake Wine Trail. **Building** 1885 Romanesque castle–style w/ turrets. **Grounds** 22 acres w/ lake access, dock for boats. **Public Space** 2nd floor sitting area, 6 public dining rooms. **Food & Drink** Cont'l breakfast buffet w/ fresh fruit, Danish pastries, waffles, hot beverages. **Recreation** Winery tours. **Amenities & Services** Fax & e-mail; meetings & weddings (300).

ACCOMMODATIONS

Units 12 rooms, 2 suites. **All Rooms** AC, phone TV, clock, hair dryer, iron & board, fresh flowers. **Some Rooms** VCR (4), fireplace usable Oct. 1–June 1 (4), robes (1). **Bed & Bath** King (1), queen (13), four-poster (6), canopy (1); all private baths, 1 whirlpool, some tubs. **Favorites** Tower room—spiral staircase, lake view; Dwyer—high four-poster, dining alcove in turret, wood-burning fireplace, lake view. **Comfort & Decor** Rich woods, a grand staircase, and jewel-toned stained glass windows distinguish this imposing building. When the dining rooms are full, the tone gets a bit hectic.

RATES, RESERVATIONS, & RESTRICTIONS

Deposit Last night's stay, refund w/ 7-days notice. **Discounts** No. **Credit Cards** V, MC. **Check-In/Out** 3 p.m./11 a.m. **Smoking** Yes. **Pets** No. **Kids** Allowed but not encouraged. **Minimum Stay** No. **Open** All year. **Host** Duane Reeder, Box 609, Geneva, 14456. **Phone** (315) 781-0201. **Fax** (315) 781-0201 ext. 3333. **Web** bellhurstcastle.com.

WHITE SPRING MANOR, Geneva

OVERALL ★★★½ | QUALITY ★★★★½ | VALUE ★★★ | PRICE **$65–$295**

The building looks a bit drab. But, if you want privacy and a sense of escape, White Springs Manor offers lots of advantages. Guests check in at a lakeside sister property, then drive a few minutes to this off-site manor house, where they're left alone to enjoy the peace and quiet. Rooms are unusually spacious and a 30-mile panoramic view encompasses Seneca Lake. Big beds, oversized whirlpools, and lots of fireplaces raise the comfort quotient. If you can do without an on-site innkeeper to look after your last-minute needs and provide conversation, this is a fine choice. Concierge service is a phone call away and a good restaurant is just down the road.

SETTING & FACILITIES

Location Residential farming area w/ distance view of Seneca Lake. **Near** Seneca Lake Wine Trail. **Building** 1901 Georgian Revival. **Grounds** 18 acres on a hilltop w/ terraces, lawn, pond, gazebo. **Public Space** 2 sitting areas, porch. **Food & Drink** Cont'l breakfast is served off-site at Belhurst Castle; honor bar in each room. **Recreation** Croquet, golf, tennis, fishing, sailing, boat tours, historic homes, summer theater, Sonnenberg Gardens, thoroughbred racing. **Amenities & Services** Disabled access (Smith room).

ACCOMMODATIONS

Units 10 guest rooms, 2 suites, 1 cottage. **All Rooms** AC, TV, phone, hair dryer, clock, iron & board. **Some Rooms** Fireplace (9), robes (10), VCRs. **Bed & Bath** King (8), queen (5), canopy (3), most have featherbed mattresses; all private baths, 11 whirlpools. **Favorites** Dining room—mirrored headboard, whirlpool, mauve/green decor, book shelves, sofa facing fireplace, lake, & flowering fruit trees. **Comfort & Decor** There's no on-site innkeeper, but, surrounded by farmland, you have ultimate in privacy and peace and quiet. Public areas are minimally furnished and drab with no personal touches. But, spacious guest rooms feature period antiques, reproductions, and many luxury touches.

RATES, RESERVATIONS, & RESTRICTIONS

Deposit 1 night, refund w/ 7-days notice. **Discounts** No. **Credit Cards** V, MC. **Check-In/Out** 3 p.m./11 a.m. **Smoking** Yes. **Pets** No. **Kids** Yes. **Minimum Stay** No. **Open** All year. **Hosts** Duane Reeder, Box 609, Geneva, 14456. **Phone** (315) 781-0201. **Web** bellhurstcastle.com.

BENN CONGER INN, Groton

OVERALL ★★★★ | QUALITY ★★★★½ | VALUE ★★★ | PRICE **$120–$260**

Built for a founder of the Corona Corporation, this house was once a haven for bootlegger and racketeer Dutch Schultz. It has the aura of being off the beaten path, though it's only a stone's throw from a lumber company. You can count on some great cooking by owner and self-trained chef, Peter van der Meulen, a Dutchman. Breakfasts are noteworthy, but "dinner is what we're all about," says his enthusiastic wife, Alison. Both are type-A personalities who retired from high-powered jobs in Manhattan. He was a TV producer for *Night Line* and *World News Tonight* and she was a publisher for *Conde Nast.* Both enjoy good conversation and a chance to share their knowledge of the Finger Lakes region. "Our guests know there's love that goes into what we do, and that makes a big difference," says Alison.

SETTING & FACILITIES

Location Hillside perch overlooking the village of Groton and rural Owasgo inlet. **Near** 15 mi. northeast of Ithaca, 30 mi. south of Syracuse; drive east to 3 lakes, 5 state parks.

Building 1921 Colonial Revival & 1898 Victorian next door. **Grounds** 19.5 acres w/ rolling lawn, flower-filled gardens, wildflower paths, beech grove, creek, beaver pond, gazebo, jogging & cross-country ski paths. **Public Space** Library/bar, 2 common rooms, 3 DR, conservatory, terrace, powder rooms. **Food & Drink** Five course breakfast w/ custom juices (guava, papaya, mango), fruit, batter course, & egg course; specialties—Danish aebleskiver, Genoa-style frittata, Italian corn fritters, Belgian waffles, quiche; public dining rooms feature Mediterranean cuisine and earned *Wine Spectator* Awards of Excellence. **Recreation** Hiking, biking, horseback riding, golf, tennis, hunting, fishing, antiquing, cultural activities, skiing at Greek Peak, Adirondack Trail, Groton Old Home Days (Aug.), Madison-Bouckville Antique Show (Aug.) Groton Line Dancing Championships (summer). **Amenities & Services** Videos, privileges at Groton Fitness Center, massage avail., laundry service, disabled access (1), fax & e-mail; meetings (35), weddings (125).

ACCOMMODATIONS

Units 10 guest rooms (5 in each building). **All Rooms** TV w/ digital cable, fresh flowers and/or plants, hair dryer, robe, clock/radio. **Some Rooms** Phone w/ modem (6), ceiling fan (6), private porch (6), fireplace (7), private entrance (2). **Bed & Bath** King (6), queen (4), canopy (4); all private baths, 6 whirlpool, 1 bidet. **Favorites** Dutch Schultz suite—spacious, nice fabrics. **Comfort & Decor** Period furnishings and a 17-foot mural in the dining room create a grand impression. Collections include jazz CDs and books about English royalty. Imported linens that are ironed and scented, and a library of pillows provide extra pampering. Each guest room has some whimsical item.

RATES, RESERVATIONS, & RESTRICTIONS

Deposit Credit card, refund w/ 14-days notice. **Discounts** Corp. Sun–Thurs. **Credit Cards** AE, V, MC, DC. **Check-In/Out** 2 p.m./11 a.m. **Smoking** Library/bar only. **Pets** Limited basis by interview. **Kids** Child-friendly. **Minimum Stay** No. **Open** All year. **Hosts** Alison & Peter van der Meulen, 206 W. Cortland St., Groton, 13073. **Phone** (607) 898-5817. **Fax** (607) 898-5818.

GREENWOODS, Honeoye

OVERALL ★★★★ | QUALITY ★★★★ | VALUE ★★★ | PRICE $95–$145

It was the dream of these innkeepers to trade in their fast-paced California careers for a more laid-back lifestyle. In 1999, they made it happen when they took over this turn-key bed-and-breakfast. Since it's rather remote, consider it more of a destination and relaxation point than a jumping off place for sightseeing. Nearby Honeyoe Lake offers some of the region's best fishing, and the hosts can arrange for a license. They excel in breakfasts and preparing gourmet picnic lunches for leisurely outings. Presentation is an important part of everything that comes from their kitchen, prompting many guests to grab a camera before picking up their fork. Before launching their innkeeping career both Sue and Dave studied full-time for six months at the California Culinary Academy.

SETTING & FACILITIES

Location Hilltop overlooking Honeoye Lake. **Near** Naples, Conesus Lake, Bristol Mountain winter resort; 15 mi. southwest of Canandaigua. **Building** 1990 lodge w/ main floor of pine logs, conventional siding on ground & top floors. **Grounds** 7 acres w/ 3 ponds, fountain, garden, wishing well, nature trails. **Public Space** Foyer, great room, breakfast room, upstairs library/game room, view room, butler's pantry, 3 decks. **Food & Drink** Full country breakfast w/ juice, fruit dish, homemade baked goods; specialties—strata, egg strudel, stuffed French toast; homemade cookies & afternoon beverages. **Recreation** Water sports, golf, alpine/Nordic skiing, horseback riding, antiquing, vineyards; Grange Homestead & Carriage Museum, Sonnenberg Gardens & Mansion, National War Plane Museum, Grape Festival, October Fest; fall foliage. **Amenities & Services** Videos, massage avail., fax & e-mail, picnic baskets; meetings (10), weddings (25); outdoor Jacuzzi spa, board games.

ACCOMMODATIONS

Units 5 guest rooms. **All Rooms** AC, TV & VCR, robes, iron & board. **Some Rooms** Ceiling fan (1), fireplace (2), private entrance (1). **Bed & Bath** Queen (5), canopy (2), all featherbeds w/ triple sheeting; all private baths, 5 tubs. **Favorites** Timberlake—gas fireplace, log-style canopy bed, access to deck w/ hammock, private pantry; Comstock—red/black/white decor, fireplace, partial canoe mounted on wall, nice view; Gabby—pine walls, red and white decor. **Comfort & Decor** Antiques, hooked rugs, and four rows of dried flowers hanging from the rafters create a 'down-home' feeling in the great room. Folksy displays in the breakfast room include aprons, baskets, rooster bric-a-brac and butterfly photos. You can sign up for private time in the outdoor spa.

RATES, RESERVATIONS, & RESTRICTIONS

Deposit Credit card, refund w/ 14-days notice. **Discounts** Extended stay midweek. **Credit Cards** AE, V, MC, D. **Check-In/Out** 3–7 p.m./11 a.m. **Smoking** No. **Pets** No. **Kids** Not encouraged. **Minimum Stay** None. **Open** All year. **Hosts** Sue & Dave Green, 8136 Quayle Rd., Honeoye, 14471. **Phone** (800) 914-3559 or (716) 229-2111. **Fax** (716) 229-0034. **E-mail** greenwoodsinn@aol.com. **Web** greenwoodsinn.com.

ROSE INN, Ithaca

OVERALL ★★★★½ | QUALITY ★★★★★ | VALUE ★★★ | PRICE **$125–$320**

Charles' credentials in the hospitality industry are impeccable. First, he earned his Hotel Administration degree from University of Heidelberg, Germany. Then, he was invited to supervise the opening of Cornell University's 125-room Statler Hotel, which is part of its hotel management school. He saw the potential of this property, originally purchased as a five-bedroom residence—one that just kept growing. Sherry is an interior designer "which allows her to buy nicer and more," says Charles. They created a separate conference center and restaurant. A simple chapel-shaped wooden frame is used for weddings in the garden and a spacious lawn can host huge tents for special occasions. It's upscale country chic.

SETTING & FACILITIES

Location On Rte. 34 north in farm country. **Near** 3.5 mi. east of Cayuga Lake, 10 mi. north of Ithaca. **Building** 1842 Italianate w/ cupola, 3 additions. **Grounds** 17 acres w/ formal garden, 2 ponds, fruit trees, berry bushes. **Public Space** Reception area, conservatory, 4 porches, conference center, public restaurant. **Food & Drink** Early coffee, full breakfast w/ juice, fresh muffins, fruit garnishes; specialties—German apple pancakes, eggs Benedict, bagels & lox, frittata, homemade jams; honor bar. **Recreation** Croquet, sailing, swimming, canoeing, cross-country & downhill skiing, antiquing, wineries, Corning Glass Museum, National Woman's Hall of Fame, Harriet Tubman House, William Seward Home, winemakers dinners (March), Apple Festival (Oct.). **Amenities & Services** Videos, massage avail., disabled access (1), fax & e-mail; meetings (60), weddings (200).

ACCOMMODATIONS

Units 8 guest rooms, 12 suites. **All Rooms** AC, phone, hair dryer, robes, clock/radio, iron & board, ceiling fan. **Some Rooms** TV (9), fireplace (7), private entrance (7). **Bed & Bath** King (14), queen (4), double (2), all featherbeds; all private baths, 12 double whirlpools. **Favorites** #7—four-poster, rosewood fireplace mantel, burgundy w/ wood trim decor, whirlpool, marble top French cabinet sink; #11 (honeymoon suite)—French Bombay chests, 5 windows face formal garden & fruit orchard, sunken whirlpool, wood-burning fireplace. **Comfort & Decor** The woodcraft in this house is notable, especially the circular staircase made of Honduran mahogany that took two years to build. It extends to a cupola on the roof. Floors are inlaid parquet. The spacious conservatory has high ceilings, a crystal chandelier, and elegant furnishing. The dining room has a Venetian mirror, an Italian secretary, and an Ithaca calendar clock. The emphasis is on elaborate furniture throughout—predominantly in the Empire style.

RATES, RESERVATIONS, & RESTRICTIONS

Deposit Full payment due within 7 days of reserving, refund w/ 14-days notice. **Discounts** No. **Credit Cards** AC, V, MC. **Check-In/Out** 3 p.m./11 a.m. **Smoking** No. **Pets** No (1 dog on premises, kennel nearby). **Kids** Over age 12. **Minimum Stay** 2 nights w/ Saturday stay April–Nov. **Open** All year. **Hosts** Sherry & Charles Rosemann, Box 6576, 813 Auburn Rd., Ithaca, 14851. **Phone** (607) 533-7905. **Fax** (607) 533-7908. **E-mail** info@roseinn.com. **Web** roseinn.com.

WILLIAM HENRY MILLER INN, Ithaca

OVERALL ★★★★ | QUALITY ★★★★½ | VALUE: ★★★ | PRICE $95–$155

Cornell University's first student of architecture built this house as a private home for the Stowell family. It is especially rich in such details as American chestnut woodwork, a grand staircase with an elaborate newell post, built-in cabinets, stained glass windows, and four fireplaces. For many years, town folks called it the Osborn House for the family who resided here from 1914 to 1997. The current owners renamed it, added nine bathrooms, all new plumbing and electricity, heirloom furnishings, a new kitchen, and plenty of Waverly, York, and Schumacher wallpaper. The Inn is ideally located within walking distance of Ithaca Commons, the award-winning vegetarian Moosewood restaurant, and the Kitchen Theater. It has access to the city's diverse cultural life—and to lakes, waterfalls, gorges, and walking trails that characterize the Finger Lakes region.

SETTING & FACILITIES

Location East Hill Historic District. **Near** 2 blocks to Ithaca Commons & Moosewood Restaurant, 6 uphill blocks to Cornell University, 10 blocks to Cayuga Lake, 10 min. to

Tompkins County airport. **Building** 1880 Queen Anne w/ Arts & Crafts details, carriage house. **Grounds** Corner city lot. **Public Space** Parlor, music room, DR, powder room, 2nd floor sitting area, porch. **Food & Drink** Early coffee & newspaper; full candlelight breakfast w/ juice, fruit, fresh breads; specialties—eggs Miller w/ bacon, orange French toast, artichoke frittata; afternoon tea, evening dessert, bottomless coffee pot. **Recreation** Art galleries, theater, botanical gardens, wineries, cross-country skiing, swiming, sailing, hiking, fishing (poles avail.), repelling wall at Cornell, antiqing, Ithaca Festival (June), Grassroots Festival (Aug.), Cabin Fever Festival (Feb.). **Amenities & Services** Disabled access (1), wheel chair lift, health club privileges, massage avail., laundry, iron & board, copier.

ACCOMMODATIONS

Units 8 guest rooms, 1 suite. **All Rooms** AC, TV, phone w/ dataport, hair dryer, clock radio, dimmer switches. **Some Rooms** Fireplace (1), private entrance (2), CD player (1), ceiling fan. **Bed & Bath** King (2), queen (7), twin (1), four-poster (1); all private baths, 3 whirlpools. **Favorites** Sanctuary—bright corner room overlooking church steeples, whirlpool. **Comfort & Decor** With 12-foot ceilings, the ground floor has several Victorian chandeliers, two pianos, and an Ithaca-made organ. The living room features a gas fireplace, turret alcove, built-in bookshelves, and a CD player for background music. The dining room has jewel-toned stained glass panels, a corner fireplace, and elegant cabinets. Guest rooms are spacious and comfortable.

RATES, RESERVATIONS, & RESTRICTIONS

Deposit Credit card, refund w/ 5-days notice. **Discounts** Corp. **Credit Cards** AE, V, MC, D, DC, CB. **Check-In/Out** 3 p.m./11 a.m. **Smoking** No. **Pets** No (kennels nearby). **Kids** Over age 12. **Minimum Stay** 2 nights on weekends. **Open** All year. **Hosts** Lynnette & Ken Scofield, 303 N. Aurora St., Ithaca, 14850. **Phone** (607) 256-4553. **Fax** (607) 256-0092. **E-mail** millerinn@aol.cocm. **Web** millerinn.com.

ANCESTOR'S INN, Liverpool

OVERALL ★★★★ | QUALITY ★★★★ | VALUE ★★★★ | PRICE **$75–$95**

Here's yet another lovely old house that was rescued by the energy and commitment of new owners who wanted to open a bed-and-breakfast. It was formerly a dentist's office. Mary and Dan spent seven months making major renovations before opening in October 1998. They moved walls, removed sinks, replace rotted wood, and more—doing much of the heavy lifting themselves. And, they studied their family's genealogies (his is Irish and German and hers is German). Guest rooms' names, pictures, and family trees reflect that interest, but numerous thoughtful, lighthearted touches relieve the seriousness of all those ancestors staring at you from their picture frames. With the focus on history and people from the past, guests are encouraged to swap stories about their own ancestors.

SETTING & FACILITIES

Location Residential area, 2 blocks north of Onondaga Lake & park. **Near** 5 mi. northwest of Syracuse, 7 mi. northwest of Syracuse Univ. **Building** 1869 Italianate, brick w/ yellow & green trim. **Grounds** City lot w/ garden, borders, hanging baskets. **Public Space** Parlor, ladies parlor DR, phone booth, front porch. **Food & Drink** Candlelight breakfast w/ seasonal fruit, homemade breads & pastries; specialties—egg/potato/ham/cheese casserole, feta/spinach/egg casserole, baked eggs w/ onions, herbs, tomato, cheese; afternoon tea, lemonade & picnic baskets avail. **Recreation** Boating, roller blade trails, cross-country skiing, Beaver Lake Nature Center w/ hiking trails, 2 theaters, Syracuse symphony, museums, Antique Fest (July), State Fair (Aug.). **Amenities & Services** Videos, fax; meetings (15) weddings (40).

ACCOMMODATIONS

Units 4 guest rooms. **All Rooms** AC, hair dryer, clock, ceiling fan, TV & VCR, sound machine, electric mattress pad, flash light. **Some Rooms** Room darkening shades (2). **Bed & Bath** Queen (4), sleigh (1); 2 private baths, 2 detached private baths, 2 whirlpool, 1 claw-foot tub. **Favorites** Valentine's room—red & black theme, sleigh bed, sitting area, double whirlpool; Steve & Elma's room—named for Dan's grandparents, the violet cluster Waverly wallpaper reflects their interest in gardening. **Comfort & Decor** Stenciling in the foyer creates a garden effect. The living room has ten-foot ceiling, a library alcove, Eastlake chairs, an old Emerson Victrola with wax cylinder and a mission-style grandmother's clock. Hand-painted doors add interest. There's a TV with lots of videos. Stairs to the second floor are steep.

RATES, RESERVATIONS, & RESTRICTIONS

Deposit 50%, refund w/ 7-days notice. **Discounts** Gov't, extended stay. **Credit Cards** AE, V, MC, D. **Check-In/Out** 3–8 p.m./11 a.m. **Smoking** No. **Pets** No. **Kids** Yes, by special arrangement. **Minimum Stay** 2 nights on weekends during special college events. **Open** All year. **Hosts** Mary & Dan Weidman, 215 Sycamore St., Liverpool, 13088. **Phone** (888) 866-8591 or (315) 461-1226. **E-mail** innkeeper@ancestorsinn.com. **Web** ancestorsinn.com.

GENESEE COUNTRY INN, Mumford

OVERALL ★★★½ | QUALITY ★★★★ | VALUE: ★★★ | PRICE $85–$140

This property was used as a mill for 100 years and then as a fishing lodge before being converted to a bed-and-breakfast in 1982. The innkeeper visited more than 60 inns with her late husband before renovating this building. Changes included adding ten bathrooms and two staircases. The inn's personality is defined by the use of American folk art, including period wall stenciling, hand-painted tables, fireboards, and other furnishings. Collections also encompass basket weaving and thermo, a technique for stenciling on velvet that dates from the 1800s. Special ladies weekends focus on needlework and cross-stitching projects, including instructions and high English teas. For the guys, there's catch and release sports fishing available on the property. Rumor has it that the inn is for sale.

SETTING & FACILITIES

Location Hamlet center. **Near** 1 mi. east of Genesee Country Village-Museum, 17 mi. south of Rochester. **Building** 1833 limestone mill, 3 stories, restored. **Grounds** 8.5 acres w/ stocked trout stream & 18-ft. waterfall, gardens, woods. **Public Space** LR, waterfront breakfast room, gazebo for picnics. **Food & Drink** Full candlelight breakfast w/ juice, fruit, hot breads; specialties—waffles w/ cinnamon cider sauce, omelet of the day; afternoon cheese, cookies, & tea. **Recreation** Catch & release trout fishing, museums, Letchworth State Park (20 min.), golf, tennis. **Amenities & Services** Videos, fax & e-mail; meetings (20).

ACCOMMODATIONS

Units 9 guest rooms. **All Rooms** AC, TV, phone. **Some Rooms** VCR (4), hair dryer (3), balconies (2), fireplace (3), private entrance (2). **Bed & Bath** Queen (7), double (2), canopy (3); all private baths, 5 tubs. **Favorites** Stewart room—sitting area, Laura Ashley fabrics, fireplace, tub. **Comfort & Decor** Country chic with stenciled walls.

RATES, RESERVATIONS, & RESTRICTIONS

Deposit Credit card, refund w/ 7-days notice. **Discounts** No. **Credit Cards** V, MC, D, DC. **Check-In/Out** 3–7 p.m./11:30 a.m. **Smoking** No. **Pets** No (1 cat in residence, kennel nearby). **Kids** Yes, but no high chairs, playground equipment, etc. avail. **No-Nos** Candles. **Minimum Stay** 2 nights some weekends. **Open** All year. **Host** Glenda Barcklow, Box 340, 948 George St., Mumford, 14511. **Phone** (800) 697-8297 or (716) 538-2500. **Fax** (716) 538-4565. **E-mail** room2escapeinn@aol.com. **Web** geneseecountryinn.com.

OLIVER LOUD'S INN, Pittsford

OVERALL ★★★★ | QUALITY ★★★★ | VALUE ★★★ | PRICE **$135–$155**

Oliver Loud received his first stagecoach tavern–keepers license in 1813. Then located in the town of Egypt, his tavern was a haven for both passengers and the rollicking canal builders who helped to construct the watery roads to America's west. In 1978, the building was rescued from ruin and moved to its present site by Vivienne and Andrew Wolfe. The canal has been rescued as well, thanks to a crusade by local boaters. Currently the *Emita II,* the *Sam Patch,* and the *Seneca Chief* make seasonal cruises, passing in front of the inn, but in general the canal remains underutilized. Watching the boats go by may be part of the charm of staying at this inn. But, keep in mind that the canal is 75 percent drained by late October and there's no boating until it's refilled around Mother's Day each year.

SETTING & FACILITIES

Location On the Erie Canal in Bushnell Basin, near Lock #32. **Near** 0.2 mi. from Exit 27 of Rte. 490 east, 2 mi. east of historic Pittsford village, 12 mi. east of Rochester International Airport, 35 mi. west of Finger Lakes region. **Building** 1812 Federal-style stagecoach inn, restored, signature yellow exterior, wraparound porch, part of the 5-building Richardson's Canal Village. **Grounds** 3 acres on the banks of the Erie Canal, silver poplar trees, access to canal towpath. **Public Space** Common room w/ fireplace. **Food & Drink** Welcome tray w/ fruit, cookies, mineral water; cont'l plus breakfast hamper delivered to your room in a picnic basket w/ juice, pastries, cereals; beverages avail; afternoon tea w/ cookies; Richardson's Canal House Restaurant in a separate building offers informal suppers & formal dinners Mon.–Sat. **Recreation** Hiking, biking or roller blading on the towpath, canoeing, feeding ducks, cross-country skiing, golf, tennis, the George Eastman House & the Strong Museum, Lilac Festival, LPGA golf tournament. **Amenities & Services** Boat tie-up avail., disabled access (room #3), laundry service, French & Spanish spoken, fax & e-mail.

ACCOMMODATIONS

Units 8 guest rooms. **All Rooms** AC, phone, TV, desk, hair dryer, modem line, magnifying makeup mirror, clock radio. **Some Rooms** Private entrance (1). **Bed & Bath** King (6), double (2), canopy (2), four-poster (4); all private baths. **Favorites** #4—four-poster king bed, access to private porch overlooking canal; #5—light-filled, canal view. **Comfort & Decor**. Quality reproduction furniture, Oriental rugs, silver pitchers, orchids, and artifacts are part of the common area. In winter, the fireplace is inviting, and in summer, porch rockers overlook the canal. Guest rooms have Stickley furniture, documentary wallpaper borders used by affluent families circa 1812, and mohair shawls on the bed.

RATES, RESERVATIONS, & RESTRICTIONS

Deposit Credit card, refund w/ 7-days notice. **Discounts** AAA, corp., gov. **Credit Cards** AE, V, MC. **Check-In/Out** 3 p.m/11 a.m. **Smoking** No. **Pets** No. **Kids** Age 13 & up. **Minimum Stay** None. **Open** All year. **Hosts** Vivienne Tellier, owner; Jill Way, mgr., 1474 Marsh Rd., Pittsford, 14534. **Phone** (716) 248-5200. **Fax** (716) 248-9970. **E-mail** rchi@frontiernet.net. **Web** www.frontiernet.net/~rchi.

DARTMOUTH HOUSE, Rochester

OVERALL ★★★★ | QUALITY ★★★★ | VALUE ★★★ | PRICE $120

This house was built for one of America's foremost toy designers. After raising five children here, the innkeepers opened it to guests in 1988. Elinor is a former teacher, and Bill retired from Kodak to become a professor. She is a serious collector of Depression-era glass and serves her six-course breakfasts, including flavored ice and dessert, on one of her many matching sets. Tea is served on her grandmother's tea set—"because nice things are meant to be used," she says. Elinor is a former church organist. She keeps an organ on the stair landing with earphones, so guests can play without disturbing others. Her philosophy about innkeeping? "It's important that my guests always learn something while they're here," she says.

SETTING & FACILITIES

Location Quiet residential street, 1 mi. southeast of downtown Rochester. **Near** 0.5 mi. to George Eastman Mansion, 3 mi. east of University of Rochester. **Building** 1905 English Tudor, butternut stucco w/ brown trim. **Grounds** City lot w/ small landscaped backyard. **Public Space** Library alcove, great room, DR, business area, guest pantry w/ microwave, fridge, porch. **Food & Drink** Early coffee, 6-course candlelight breakfast w/ juice, fruit, hot breads, Italian ice, dessert; specialties—blueberry blintz soufflé, French toast a l'orange, hash brown pie, banana pecan pancakes, raspberry-fudge truffle bars; bottomless chocolate chip cookie jar, popcorn, hot beverages anytime. **Recreation** Strong Museum, Rochester Museum & Science Center, Planetarium, Memorial Art Gallery, George Eastman International Museum of Photography, theater, Lilac Festival (May), Park Avenue Festival (Aug.), Clothesline Art Festival (Sept.). **Amenities & Services** Video library, massage nearby, fax & e-mail, baskets for picnics.

ACCOMODATIONS

Units 4 guest rooms. **All Rooms** AC, phone, TV & VCR, lighted makeup mirror, dataport, hair dryer, robes, iron & board, fresh plant or flowers, ceiling fan, flashlight. **Some**

Rooms Window seat. **Bed & Bath** King (2), queen (2), canopy (1); 3 private baths, 1 detached private bath, 2 claw-foot English soaking tubs. **Favorites** Queen's room—largest, blue cabbage roses; King's room—window seat to curl up with a book, soaking tub. **Comfort & Decor** The living room has a grand piano, fireplace, cozy window seats, beamed ceilings, and Arts & Crafts pocket doors. Collections include old cameras and Depression-era glass.

RATES, RESERVATIONS, & RESTRICTIONS

Deposit Credit card, refund w/ 7-days notice. **Discounts** No. **Credit Cards** AE, V, MC, D, DC. **Check-In/Out** 3–6 p.m./11 a.m.–noon. **Smoking** No. **Pets** No. **Kids** Over age 12 welcome. **Minimum Stay** Some weekends. **Open** All year, except Dec. 28–March 1. **Hosts** Elinor & Bill Klein, 215 Dartmouth St., Rochester, 14607. **Phone** (800) 724-6298 or (716) 271-7872. **Fax** Call first. **E-mail** stay@dartmouthhouse.com. **Web** dartmouthhouse.com.

HOBBIT HOLLOW FARM, Skaneateles

OVERALL ★★★★★ | QUALITY ★★★★½ | VALUE ★★★ | PRICE **$100– $270**

This distinquished-looking property is flanked by a horse barn and riding ring. Acres of green pastures and farmland stretch to the horizon, and in the entry foyer a freehand-painted, wall-sized mural echoes the magnificent setting. From the master suite, you awaken to vistas of horse pastures, white picket fences, and the sun rising over tree-fringed Skaneateles Lake. Breakfast is served in a formal dining room with a silver-plated tea service. All seems well with the universe in this idyllic setting. The only thing off-key is that some rooms are too close to the noisy road—a jarring note for light sleepers that's easily ignored if you bring ear plugs.

SETTING & FACILITIES

Location West side of Lake Skaneateles, 2 mi. south of the village on Rte. 41A south. **Near** 0.25 mi. to lake access for public boating, 5 mi. east of Auburn, 35 mi. southwest of Syracuse. **Building** 1911 Colonial Revival. **Grounds** 320 acre farm w/ trails, ponds, equestrian stables. **Public Space** Foyer, 2 LR, library, DR, 2 porches, powder room. **Food & Drink** Full farm breakfast w/ juice, fresh fruit; specialties—raspberry French toast, crab shrimp egg bake, lemon soufflé pancakes w/ raspberry sauce; afternoon wine & snacks, beverages; will adjust menu for allergies. **Recreation** Boat rides, downhill & cross-country skiing, fishing, hiking, antiquing, wineries, historic homes, museums, fall festival, boat show. **Amenities & Services** Videos, laundry, fax & e-mail avail.; meetings (10), weddings (250).

ACCOMMODATIONS

Units 5 guest rooms. **All Rooms** AC, phone, terry robes, fresh flowers, hair dryer, clock radio. **Some Rooms** Fireplace (2). **Bed & Bath** King (1), queen (3), double (1); four-poster beds (3), all have fine linens & quilts; 4 private baths, 1 private detached bath, 4 tubs. **Favorites** Master suite—a total of 20 windows, side porch w/ white wicker furniture, four-poster king bed, gas fireplace, crisp white walls with painted wood trim, large armoire, crystal lamps that reflect rainbows on unexpected surfaces; Chanticleer—spacious with farm printed fabrics, borders and art, rooster lamp, custom four-poster bed, partial lake view. **Comfort & Decor** Master-crafted period furniture and antiques look new. Accessories in the public rooms include books by J. R. Tolkien, and are mostly impersonal. Excessive road noise may bother light sleepers.

RATES, RESERVATIONS, & RESTRICTIONS

Deposit 1 night, refund w/ 10-days notice. **Discounts** Corp. **Credit Cards** AE, V, MC, D. **Check-In/Out** 3 p.m./noon. **Smoking** No. **Pets** No. **Kids** No. **Minimum Stay** None. **Open** All year. **Hosts** Noreen & Michael Falcone, owners; Joan Hughes, innkeeper, 3061 West Lake Rd., Skaneateles, 13156. **Phone** (315) 685-3426. **Fax** (315) 685-3426. **E-mail** innkeeper@hobbithollow.com. **Web** hobbithollow.com.

B&B WELLINGTON, Syracuse

OVERALL ★★★½ | QUALITY ★★★½ | VALUE ★★★ | PRICE $75–$125

Architect Ward Welling Ward designed this Arts & Crafts home, which is now both a national and New York State registered historic property. Locals tell us that today this isn't the most prosperous section of town, but the immediate block is pleasant and it's convenient for business travelers. The house is full of funky collections and conversation pieces, including a dozen porcelain bed pans, shoe lasts, an antique dental chair with tool case, old bottles, pot-bellied stoves, 65 antique lamps (all working, they claim), Wallace Nutting paintings, surveyor's tripods, and large textile spools (the latter make attractive stands for potted violets). "We're always looking for the right thing to fill the right little space," says Wendy.

SETTING & FACILITIES

Location Residential neighborhood, north side of Syracuse. **Near** 0.75 mi. east of Carousel Center, 1 mi. north of Syracuse University, 1.5 mi. north of Carrier Dome, 3 mi. south of Hancock International Airport. **Building** 1914 Tudor-style Arts & Crafts, brick & stucco. **Grounds** Urban lot w/ floral border, 52 cedar flower boxes. **Public Space** LR, DR, sunporch, 2nd floor landing, access to basement treadmill. **Food & Drink** Cont'l breakfast Mon.–Fri. w/ homemade baked goods; full breakfast Sat. & Sun.; specialties—vegetarian crustless quiche, stuffed French toast w/ macadamia nut & fruit sauce, egg & apple stratta. **Recreation** Golf, antiquing, theater, New York State Fair (Aug.–Sept.). **Amenities & Services** Videos, e-mail & fax; meetings (20), weddings (60).

ACCOMMODATIONS

Units 4 guest rooms, 1 suite. **All Rooms** AC, phone, dataport, high-speed DSL connection, TV & VCR, iron & board, clock radio, emergency light, fresh flowers. **Some Rooms** Porch (3), balcony (1), fireplace (1). **Bed & Bath** King (1), queen (4), double (1); 4 private baths, 1 detached shared bath, 4 tubs. **Favorites** Mercer—paisley fabrics, shared porch. **Comfort & Decor** A Mercer tiled fireplace and mission-style furniture by L. J. and G. Stickley are distinctive features. The living room has built-in wood shelves, attractive glass-paneled doors and windows, archways, and window seats. All guest rooms have hardwood floors with Oriental carpets. Avoid the gang suite in the basement.

RATES, RESERVATIONS, & RESTRICTIONS

Deposit 1 night, refund w/ 3-days notice. **Discounts** Military, gov't. **Credit Cards** AE, V, MC, D, DC, CB. **Check-In/Out** 3 p.m./11 a.m. **Smoking** No. **Pets** No. **Kids** Yes. **Minimum Stay** 2 nights on some weekends. **Open** All year. **Hosts** Wendy Wilber & Ray Borg, 707 Danforth St., Syracuse, 13208. **Phone** (800) 724-5006 or (315) 474-3641. **Fax** (315) 474-2557. **E-mail** innkeepers@bbwellngton.com. **Web** bbwellington.com.

DICKENSON HOUSE ON JAMES, Syracuse

OVERALL ★★★★★ | QUALITY ★★★★ | VALUE ★★★★ | PRICE **$99–$125**

A mid-life crisis prompted Ed to add the title innkeeper to his career as a consulting mechanical engineer. The living room is packed with interesting accessories and there's a story behind everything, so don't be afraid to ask. This house earns our top prize in the Mid-Atlantic for best guest kitchen. It's attractive and so well equipped that you could make a Thanksgiving dinner. A reading of guest diaries indicates that Ed is a great ambassador for Syracuse. Two doctors and one attorney wrote that they settled here thanks to Ed's enthusiasm and help getting oriented while staying at Dickenson House. A special perk is riding in the rumble seat of Ed's antique Model A.

SETTING & FACILITIES

Location Central Heights area. **Near** 1.5 mi. northeast of the Convention Center, 2 mi. north of Syracuse University, close to a major hospital, museums, & performing arts center. **Building** 1920s English Tudor Revival w/ exposed timbers, partial brick & stucco exterior, high-pitched roof, gables, & dormers. **Grounds** City lot w/ gardens. **Public Space** LR, DR, foyer, guest kitchen. **Food & Drink** Full breakfast w/ juice, fruit, homemade baked goods, cereals, hot beverages; specialties—various quiches, apple & cinnamon strata, orange/maple crusted French toast; cookies, wine, beverages, cheese, nuts, fruit avail. anytime. **Recreation** Zoo, theater, golf, antiquing. **Amenities & Services** Videos, access to tennis on clay courts, laundry, fax & e-mail, airport limo service avail.; meetings (12).

ACCOMMODATIONS

Units 4 guest rooms. **All Rooms** AC, phone, TV, clock radio, robes, internet access, iron, robes, fresh flowers, hair dryer, shawl. **Some Rooms** Ceiling fan (1). **Bed & Bath** King (1), queen (3), sleigh (1), canopy (1); 3 private baths, 1 private detached bath, 3 tubs. **Favorites** Elizabeth's Room—spacious, bright, white wicker, & lace accented with patchwork quilts, king plus a single sleigh bed, rocking chair, tub w/ skylight. **Comfort & Decor** The living room is literary themed. Conversation pieces include an old-fashioned Victrola, two antique cameras, a vintage violin, and stereoscopic photographs. The dining room is 1880s Empire style. Guest rooms are named for British poets and contain their books.

RATES, RESERVATIONS, & RESTRICTIONS

Deposit Credit card, refund w/ 2-days notice (7-days on special weekends). **Discounts** No. **Credit Cards** AE, V, MC, D. **Check-In/Out** 3 p.m./11 a.m. **Smoking** No. **Pets** No. **Kids** Call first. **Minimum Stay** No. **Open** All year. **Hosts** Pam & Ed Kopiel, 1504 James St., Syracuse, 13203. **Phone** (888) 423-4777 or (315) 423-4777. **Fax** (315) 425-1965. **E-mail** innkeeper@dickensonhouse.com. **Web** www.dreamscape.com/dickensonhouse.com.

TAUGHANNOCK FARMS INN, Trumansburg

OVERALL ★★★★ | QUALITY ★★★★ | VALUE ★★★★ | PRICE $95–$140

This was once the 600-acre country estate of Philadelphian John Jones. Most of his land was donated in the 1930s to create Taughannock Falls State Park. Some of Jones's furniture remains in the inn. One strong point is the distant lake view and nearby trails to a lovely waterfall. Susan, an Ithaca native, taught hotel management at the University of Houston for 14 years and worked for major hotels. Tom, who is from Syracuse, has worked in business administration and as the inn's pastry chef. It's handy to have a good restaurant on the premises. Romantics will enjoy the main building. Outdoors enthusiasts and families should choose a guest house.

SETTING & FACILITIES

Location Hillside overlooking Cayuga Lake, surrounded by Taughannock Falls State Park. **Near** 8 mi. north of Ithaca, 2 mi. south of Taughannock Falls. **Building** 1873 Victorian country inn, beige clapboard w/ green trim, 3 guest houses. **Grounds** 12 acres, w/ flower gardens, pond, access to Upper & Lower Gorge hiking trail. **Public Space** Bar, 2nd floor parlor, porch. **Food & Drink** Expanded cont'l breakfast w/ juice, fruit, pastries, & coffee; dinner served April–Nov., for holidays parties in Dec. **Recreation** Swimming, fishing, boating, hiking, picnics, golf. **Amenities & Services** Fax; meetings & weddings (140).

ACCOMMODATIONS

Units 13 guest rooms (5 in the main house). **All Rooms** AC, clock radio. **Some Rooms** TV (7), phone (7), private entrance (3). **Bed & Bath** King (1), queen (11), twin (1), canopy (2); 12 private baths, 1 shared bath, 9 tubs. **Favorites** North Lake—white fabrics, claw-foot tub, lake view; South Lake—canopy bed (but the bed wasn't comfortable), nice window treatment; Park View Cottage—spacious, nestled in the trees w/ a pretty walkway, a clean & crisp look, wicker seating in the alcove. **Comfort & Decor** The 1870s-era antiques in the main house look a bit staid. Furnishings in the guest houses are eclectic. New carpeting, wallpaper, and country curtains add some style.

RATES, RESERVATIONS, & RESTRICTIONS

Deposit $50, refund w/ 10-days notice less $10. **Discounts** No. **Credit Cards** AE, V, MC, D. **Check-In/Out** 3 p.m./noon. **Smoking** No. **Pets** No. **Kids** Yes. **No-Nos** Candles. **Minimum Stay** Special events weekends. **Open** April 1–Jan. 1. **Hosts** Susan & Tom Sheridan, 2030 Gorge Rd., Trumansburg, 14886. **Phone** (607) 387-7711. **Fax** (607) 387-7721. **Web** t-farms.com.

Zone 3

Catskills/ Hudson Valley/ New York City

The Hudson River School was America's first designated school of landscape painters. Today, art is everywhere in the region. As far north as **Glens Falls,** you can enjoy the **Hyde Collection,** which boasts some 24 centuries of European and American painting and sculpture, casually displayed in a Florentine Renaissance mansion.

A more modern collection enlivens the state building corridors and outdoor plazas in **Albany.** The **Empire State Collection** comprises 92 paintings and sculptures created in the 1960s and 70s—mostly by avant garde New York artists. Even the state capital is festooned with elaborate carvings and sculptures. Inside, architects installed a million-dollar staircase.

Downriver, at **Storm King Art Center** in **Mountainville,** some 120 monumental post-1945 sculptures are arranged on 200 acres of hilly terrain to create a museum where the walls are trees, and the ceiling is sky. The art is especially attractive when framed by autumn leaves or dogwood blossoms.

Artists Henri Matisse and Marc Chagall created the jewel-toned stained glass windows at **Union Church of Pocantico Hills,** a mile north of **Tarrytown.** In nearby river towns like **Rhinebeck** and **Cold Spring,** small art galleries line quaint streets.

The Hudson River Valley is also known for its grandiose estates, including the **Roosevelt Estate** in **Hyde Park,** now open to visitors. The complex includes the **Presidential Library and Museum,** which documents the life of Franklin D. Roosevelt. Nearby is the more modest cottage **Val-Kill,** where Eleanor Roosevelt lived.

Few houses on the Hudson rival the **Vanderbilt Mansion** located two miles north of Hyde Park. No expense was spared to furnish this 1898 Beaux-Arts gem. Another river-view treasure is **Montgomery Place,** which sits on 434 acres of land and houses portraits by Gilbert Stuart.

One of the area's largest estates, **Philipsburg Manor,** was a farm and trading center owned by a family of loyalists who were forced to leave the country after the Revolutionary War. It is open for tours, as are **Sunnyside,** the picturesque cottage where author Washington Irving lived and worked and **Lyndhurst,** the Gothic revival home of financier J. Gould in Tarrytown. According to legend, Gould kept 75 Saint Bernard dogs on the grounds and, in summer, cruised to work on Wall Street aboard his yacht.

Kykuit, a retreat for four generations of Rockefellers, has a commanding view of the Hudson River and elaborate terraced gardens. Governor Nelson Rockefeller installed an extraordinary collection of art and sculpture during his 19-year residency there.

Art and architecture are also important in making **New York City** a world-class destination. Most of Manhattan's architecture is relatively new. Only **Saint Paul's Chapel** and the iron fence around **Bowling Green** remain from Colonial times. And, the narrow and irregular pattern of the streets themselves in lower Manhattan remains faithful to the city's earliest maps. Street names such as Broad Street and Broadway also survive.

Manhattan's must-see sights include: **Times Square,** a ride to the top (86th floor) of the **Empire State Building** at night, **Central Park** (in daytime), a walk up Fifth or Madison Avenues from 59th to 72nd Street, the **Metropolitan Museum of Art, Lincoln Center, South Street Seaport,** and a Sunday morning church service in Harlem.

You won't find many true bed-and-breakfasts in the city, however. Most of the properties are upstate and on Long Island.

FOR MORE INFORMATION

Albany County CVB
(800) 258-3582; albany.org

Catskill Association for Tourism
(800) 697-2287; catskillregiontoday.com

Columbia County Tourism
(800) 724-1846; columbiacountyny.org

Dutchess County Tourism
(800) 445-3131; dutchesstourism.com

Historic Hudson Valley
150 White Plains Rd.
Tarrytown, NY 10591
(914) 631-8200

Historic River Towns of Westchester
(914) 232-6583; hudsonriver.com

New York City & County CVB
810 Seventh Ave.
New York, NY 10019
(800) 692-8474

Orange County Tourism
(845) 291-2136; orangetourism.org

Poughkeepsie Chamber of Commerce
(845) 454-1700

Putnam Visitors Bureau
(800) 470-4854

Rockland County Tourism
(800) 295-5723; rockland.org

Ulster County Tourism
(800) 342-5826; www.co.ulster.ny.us

Westchester County Office of Tourism
(800) 833-9282;
westchestertourism.com

MANSION HILL INN, Albany

OVERALL ★★★★ | QUALITY ★★★½ | VALUE ★★★ | PRICE $165

These hosts opened with two rooms in 1984 and grew their business to three houses. Steve, a self-taught chef, runs the friendly store-front restaurant. Themed dinners, cooking camp for kids, and cigar dinners (which he pioneered in 1991) are part of his repertoire. Maryellen, who is from Albania, was a banker until recently. Their location is great—in the shadow of Corning Tower and an easy walk to Empire State Plaza. Currently, theirs is Albany County's only quality independent small inn. Their only competition is the budget Ramada Inn and the 385-room Crown Plaza, a business hotel. Here, you won't pay extra for parking or local phone calls, and you certainly don't get a blank stare at the front desk. These folks go out of their way to provide service with a smile. It's a good choice whether you're traveling for business or pleasure.

SETTING & FACILITIES

Location Historic mansion district. **Near** State Capitol, Governor's Mansion; 8 mi. southeast of Albany International Airport. **Building** Two 1861–1912 row houses. **Grounds** 3 city lots w/ flowers, shrubs, terraced courtyard, koi pond. **Public Space** Store-front restaurant. **Food & Drink** Full breakfast w/ juice, fruit, coffee; specialties—French toast, omelets, blueberry pancakes; innkeeper's wine & cheese reception nightly; ground floor restaurant serves upscale comfort food and interesting wines. **Recreation** Golf, biking (5 bikes avail.), jogging in Washington Park, hiking on 60 mi. preserve along the Hudson River, Empire State Plaza, Nelson Rockefeller's art collection, *USS Slater*, Larkfest (May), Empire State Regatta (June). **Amenities & Services** Privileges at Steuben Athletic Club, disabled access to 1 room & restaurant, laundry equip., fax & e-mail, free local phone calls & no service charge for long distance; meetings (20), weddings (40).

ACCOMMODATIONS

Units 8 guest rooms. **All Rooms** AC, phone, dataport, hair dryer, iron & board, daily newspaper, desk. **Some Rooms** Fridge, crib. **Bed & Bath** All queen beds, down comforters; all private baths. **Favorites** #304 & #321—top floor facing courtyard, quiet, mauve & forest green decor. **Comfort & Decor** The restaurant has hardwood floors, forest green wainscoting w/ mauve trim, a chair rail, low ceilings, a brick fireplace, and floral wallpaper. The alcove booth is the most romantic. Guest rooms are pleasant and comfortable, if a bit plain. They are consistent with the feel of this working class neighborhood.

RATES, RESERVATIONS, & RESTRICTIONS

Deposit Credit card to hold, refund w/ 5-days notice. **Discounts** AAA. **Credit Cards** AE, V, MC, D. **Check-In/Out** 4 p.m./noon. **Smoking** Some rooms. **Pets** Yes (preferred in a portable kennel). **Kids** Yes. **Minimum Stay** 1 night. **Open** All year. **Hosts** Maryellen & Steve Stofelani, Jr., 115 Philip St., Albany, 12202. **Phone** (888) 299-0455 or (518) 465-2038. **Fax** (518) 434-2313. **E-mail** inn@mansionhill.com. **Web** mansionhill.com.

ONTEORA, THE MOUNTAIN HOUSE, Boiceville

OVERALL ★★★★★ | QUALITY ★★★★ | VALUE ★★★ | PRICE $240–$270

By age 50, Richard Hellmann commanded a mayonnaise empire that stretched from coast to coast. But his doctor's news was blunt: "You have six months to live—however, there's a chance you could live longer—if you retire now and move to the country." That's exactly what he did. He chose this extraordinary site to build his retreat and selected an architect who filled the rooms with windows that dramatize wide vistas of the Hudson River Valley and distant mountain peaks. It was 1930 when the Hellmanns took occupancy, and the change was so successful that Richard lived to be 94 years old. No doubt, some of this health-giving ambience can rub off on everyone who spends a night or two surrounded by these panoramic views.

SETTING & FACILITIES

Location Pine-studded promontory in the Catskills overlooking Ashokan Valley. **Near** Wilson State Park, Ashokan Reservoir, Woodstock; 20 mi.west of Kingston. **Building** 1930 Adirondack w/ additions. **Grounds** Wooded w/ floral borders, twig gazebo, fish pond, meandering paths, hiking trails. **Public Space** Foyer, great room, game room, powder rooms, glass-enclosed porch. **Food & Drink** Full breakfast w/ juice, fresh fruit, hot beverages; specialties—crêpes, eggs Hellmann, waffles. **Recreation** Hiking, biking, fishing, tubing, downhill skiing, billiards. **Amenities & Services** Sauna, videos, massage avail. at two nearby spas; meetings (40), weddings (250).

ACCOMMODATIONS

Units 5 guest rooms. **All Rooms** Simple. **Some Rooms** Fireplace (1). **Bed & Bath** Queen beds (5); all private baths, 4 whirlpools. **Favorites** Mt. Tremper has a cathedral ceiling, the best bathroom w/ skylighted whirlpool, views looking west & north. **Comfort & Decor** Dramatic mountain views that are accessible via large picture windows, decks, and outdoor seating make this property distinctive. The 20' by 30' ft. great room has a cathedral ceiling, massive stone fireplace, and comfortable furnishings. The 40' covered dining porch has Adirondack-style tree trunk columns and railings. Guest rooms are modest in size and decor, but the natural beauty of the surroundings is so compelling it raises this experience to a top rating.

RATES, RESERVATIONS, & RESTRICTIONS

Deposit 50%, refund w/ 14-days notice less $50. **Discounts** 15% for long stays. **Credit Cards** V, MC, D. **Check-In/Out** 3 p.m./11 a.m. **Smoking** Game room only. **Pets** No (dog on premises). **Kids** Over age 12. **Minimum Stay** 2 nights on weekends. **Open** All year. **Hosts** Robert McBroom & Joe Chen, 96 Piney Point Rd., Box 356, Boiceville, 12412. **Phone** (845) 657-6233. **E-mail** info@onteora.com. **Web** onteora.com.

SILVER MAPLE FARM, Canaan

OVERALL ★★★★★ | QUALITY ★★★★ | VALUE ★★★ | PRICE **$80–$295**

The innkeepers were inspired to open this attractive property after visiting a bed-and-breakfast in England's Lake District. Bill is an actor/singer/producer who has produced live theater in Los Angeles and was nominated for a Tony in 1982. Raised by his grandmother, he loves to cook and entertain. The bed-and-breakfast is a perfect way to combine his talents. Joel practiced medicine in Los Angeles for nearly three decades before moving nearer to his native New Jersey. This property will appeal to weekenders who want a quiet, bucolic retreat with contemporary overtones. A bevy of cultural attractions lie just beyond the Massachusetts border in Lenox and closer. You can explore local villages and country roads. Or, kick back with a good book, stay put, and relax.

SETTING & FACILITIES

Location Foothills of the Berkshires in Columbia County. **Near** 4.5 mi east of NYS Thruway exit 21A, 8 mi. northeast of Chatham, 11 mi. northwest of Tanglewood. **Building** White barn w/ white rail fencing. **Grounds** 10 acres w/ open fields, trees, perennial gardens, Adirondack chairs, hammock, red barn, carriage house. **Public Space** Post & beam great room, conference room, guest pantry. **Food & Drink** Full breakfast w/ fruit, homemade breads & muffins, granola; specialties—baked French toast, quiche, apple pie pancakes w/ warm maple syrup; afternoon tea & cookies. **Recreation** Tennis, golf, hiking, biking (3 avail.), swimming at Queechy Lake, skiing, sledding, snowshoeing (3 pair avail.), antiquing, summer stock, Shaker Museum, Hancock Shaker Village, Berkshire Botanical Garden, Jacob's Pillow, Tanglewood concerts (July & Aug.), Shakespeare Festival (June–Sept.). **Amenities & Services** Massage avail., outdoor whirlpool spa 8 a.m. to 9 p.m., disabled access (1), fax & e-mail, golf privileges at two country clubs; meetings (30), weddings (120).

ACCOMMODATIONS

Units 9 guest rooms, 2 suites. **All Rooms** AC, cable TV, phone, individual heat, down comforters. **Some Rooms** Ceiling fan, fridge, fireplace (2 suites), private entrance (4). **Bed & Bath** King (3), queen (6), twin (1), double (1), four-poster (1); all private baths, 2 deep soaking tubs, 6 regular tubs. **Favorites** Cottage Room—bright & airy, high queen bed, hand-painted floral mural, hillside view; The Loft—spacious suite w/ cathedral ceiling, gas fireplace, soaking tub, fridge, wraparound countryside views; Sapling—small, adequate, affordable. **Comfort & Decor** The great room features Shaker-inspired furnishings. Classical jazz music adds a contemporary feeling. Pine floors, custom-made cupboards, antique trunks, and hand-painted murals give a unique personality to each simply-furnished guest room. Room sizes vary; the most spacious are the Loft and Pines.

RATES, RESERVATIONS, & RESTRICTIONS

Deposit Credit card for 1 night, refund w/ 7-days notice. **Discounts** Corp. **Credit Cards** AE, V, MC, D. **Check-In/Out** 3–9 p.m./11 a.m. **Smoking** No. **Pets** No. **Kids** Over age 12. **Minimum Stay** 2 nights on May through Nov. weekends, 3 nights on some holidays. **Open** All year. **Hosts** Joel Weisman & Bill Hutton, Rte. 295, Canaan, 12029. **Phone** (518) 781-3600. **Fax** (518) 781-3883. **E-mail** info@silvermaplefarm.com. **Web** silvermaplefarm.com.

HUDSON HOUSE, Cold Spring

OVERALL ★★★½ | QUALITY ★★★½ | VALUE ★★★ | PRICE $140–$225

Originally named the Pacific Hotel and later the Hudson View Inn, this is one of the valley's largest riverside inns, and is said to be the second-oldest continuously operating inn in the state. And, original details remain, earning it a listing on the National Register of Historic Places. Families of West Point students fill the guest rooms on football and graduation weekends. Hospitality is the hallmark in two large dining rooms that offer casual fare and a formal menu of regional specialties, fresh seafood, Colorado rack of lamb, and veal. A distinguished wine list earned a *Wine Spectator* Award for Excellence. Cold Spring, where Civil War Parrott guns were produced, is eminently walkable, if you don't mind the uphill slant of things.

SETTING & FACILITIES

Location Banks of the Hudson River across from West Point, 65 mi. north of Manhattan. **Near** In walking distance of Cold Spring train station. **Building** 1832 Federal-style inn. **Grounds** Corner city lot. **Public Space** River Room, porch, Half Moon Tavern. **Food & Drink** Cont'l breakfast weekdays; full breakfast Sat. & Sun.; specialties—eggs, waffles, pancakes; coffee station & cookies; picnic lunches avail. **Recreation** Sailing, kayaking, hiking the Appalachian Trail, biking, antiquing, Shakespeare Festival; inn hosts live jazz on Fridays. **Amenities & Services** Fax; meetings & weddings (55).

ACCOMMODATIONS

Units 11 guest rooms, 1 suite. **All Rooms** AC, TV, phone. **Some Rooms** Balcony (6). **Bed & Bath** Queen (10), full (2); all private baths, 12 tubs. **Favorites** #14—small but cozy w/ four-poster pencil-post bed, red toile wallpaper & spread; #5—same toile pattern in black & white; #3 & 4—combine to create suite w/ balcony, stenciling & exposed beams add charm. **Comfort & Decor** Guests may use a small sitting area with a comfortable sofa and chairs in front of the fireplace, located adjacent to the tavern and two public restaurants. The front porch overlooks a waterfront park with a dramatic view of West Point across the Hudson River. Guest rooms are small and most are non-descript. River views and easy access to dining are the main attractions.

RATES, RESERVATIONS, & RESTRICTIONS

Deposit Credit card, refund w/ 14-days notice. **Discounts** No. **Credit Cards** AE,V, MC, D. **Check-In/Out** 3–9p.m./11 a.m. **Smoking** No. **Pets** No. **Kids** Yes. **Minimum Stay** 2 nights on weekends. **Open** All year. **Hosts** Regina L. & Sam Bei, 2 Main St., Cold Spring, 10516. **Phone** (845) 265-9355. **Fax** (845) 265-4532. **Web** hudsonhouseinn.com.

PIG HILL INN, Cold Spring

OVERALL ★★★½ | QUALITY ★★★½ | VALUE ★★★ | PRICE **$120–$170**

Cold Spring is a place to get in touch with the past. This inn is in the middle of town, within walking distance of the train station, restaurants, and numerous antique shops. Main Street's nineteenth century buildings are part of the National Historic District, which once housed railroad and foundary workers. The history of these modest buildings is described on Sunday afternoon walking tours mid-May through mid-November, but any time of the year is good for browsing. Garrisons Landing train station, one town away, was used in the filming of "Hello Dolly" and is now the Garrison Art Center. It's a one-mile drive to Boscobel Restoration, a mansion that captures a grander aspect of early nineteenth century Federal domestic architecture. With acres of beautiful lawns and gardens overlooking the Hudson River and West Point, Boscobel is an especially fine place for picnicking.

SETTING & FACILITIES

Location Main shopping street of village. **Near** 2 blocks from Hudson River, 5 mi. to Rte. 84 or Taconic Pkwy. **Building** 1825 Federal, brick; glass conservatory added in back. **Grounds** 2 city lots w/ backyard garden. **Public Space** LR, DR, glassed-in breakfast room. **Food & Drink** Full breakfast w/ juice, fruit, baked goods; specialties—eggs any style, pancakes, side meats. **Recreation** Hiking, sightseeing. **Amenities & Services** Fax, disabled access (1); meetings (20), weddings (50).

ACCOMMODATIONS

Units 9 guest rooms. **All Rooms** AC, fresh flowers. **Some Rooms** Fireplace (7). **Bed & Bath** King (1), queen (6), double (2), canopy (2), four-poster (1), sleigh (1); 5 private baths, 4 shared baths, 6 tubs. **Favorites** #3—bleached four-poster, blue & white decor; #4—raspberry/floral decor, round-top canopy bed; #9—brass bed, blue & yellow tones. **Comfort & Decor** The house doubles as an antique consignment shop. Almost every item is for sale, including the bed you sleep on and the dish holding your soap, and many have small price tags attached. Some antiques come as is—in need of a handyman's skills. The pig theme is played up in the living room area, with arts and crafts items ranging from banks to lamp shades. Window treatments in the guest rooms are standouts. Other decor may change, as items are sold. There's no television on the premises.

RATES, RESERVATIONS, & RESTRICTIONS

Deposit Credit card, refund w/ 15-days notice less 10%. **Discounts** No. **Credit Cards** AE, V, MC. **Check-In/Out** 2 p.m./11 a.m. **Smoking** No. **Pets** No. **Kids** Yes. **Minimum Stay** No. **Open** All year. **Hosts** Vera & Henry Keil, 73 Main St., Cold Spring, 10516. **Phone** (845) 265-9247. **Fax** (845) 265-4614. **E-mail** pighillinn@aol.com. **Web** piighillinn.com.

ALEXANDER HAMILTON HOUSE, Croton-on-Hudson

OVERALL ★★★★½ | QUALITY ★★★★ | VALUE ★★★ | PRICE $100–$250 (10% GRATUITY ADDED)

Innkeeper Barbara Notarius wrote *Open Your Own Bed & Breakfast,* now in its fourth edition. She lives up to her reputation as a grand dame of the industry. Her spacious Victorian is awash with handicrafts of the 1880s, including hair wreathes, tramp art frames, and wax floral arrangements, all of which give guests a sense of the past alongside the inn's modern amenities. She can steer guests to attractions and restaurants that suit them. She can educate guests about local history and regale them with funny stories. After nearly two decades in the business, she's still enjoys "seeing the world pass through" her living room. "I always wanted to have a big family, and now I have an enormous extended family," she says.

SETTING & FACILITIES

Location 2 blocks from village center. **Near** Tarrytown, White Plains, Kykuit, Sunnyside, Lyndhurst, Boscobel, West Point. **Building** 1889 Victorian, white w/ picket fence. **Grounds** 0.75 cliff-side acres, w/ trees, garden, swimming pool, gazebo. **Public Space** Foyer, parlor, DR, sunporch. **Food & Drink** Full breakfast w/ fruit or juice, cereal, entrée of the day; specialties—cheese, egg, & bread casserole, stuffed croissants; fresh chocolate chip cookies daily. **Recreation** Sailing,, boating, horseback riding, mountain biking, golf, hiking, apple picking, wineries, Croton Sailing School. **Amenities & Services** Massage avail., fax & e-mail, reduced rate at NY Sports Gym, closed caption TV for hearing impaired, bouquets, picnic baskets & balloons avail.; weddings/elopements (16).

ACCOMMODATIONS

Units 6 guest rooms, 2 suites. **All Rooms** AC, phone, answering machine, TV, clock radio, ceiling fan, modem port. **Some Rooms** VCR, CD player, & tape deck (2). **Bed & Bath** King (1), queen (6), double (1), reproduction iron beds (8); 6 private baths, 2 private detached baths, 2 whirlpools **Favorites** Master suite—brass bed, French armoire, art nouveaux, show-stopping English tile bath in cobalt blue; other 3rd floor suite—5 skylights, elegant burgundy bath tile. **Comfort & Decor** Spacious public rooms are filled with reproduction antiques and collectibles. Guest room decor is nice, but the bathrooms are really gorgeous. If we gave prizes for best bathrooms in the Hudson Valley region, those two on the third floor would tie for first place.

RATES, RESERVATIONS, & RESTRICTIONS

Deposit Credit card to hold, refund w/ 7-days notice, 1 night non-refundable if reservation is held longer than 3 mo. **Discounts** 7th consecutive night. **Credit Cards** AE, V, MC, DC, D. **Check-In/Out** Noon–9 p.m./11 a.m. **Smoking** No. **Pets** No. **Kids** Well-behaved children welcome. **Minimum Stay** 2 nights on weekends. **Open** All year. **Hosts** Barbara Notarius, 49 Van Wyck St., Croton-on-Hudson, 10520. **Phone** (914) 271-6737. **Fax** (914) 271-3927. **E-mail** alexhous@bestweb.net. **Web** alexanderhamiltonhouse.com.

BIRD & BOTTLE INN, Garrison

OVERALL ★★★★ | QUALITY ★★★★ | VALUE ★★★ | PRICE **$210–$240**

This famed landmark on the old Albany–New York Post Road has an international reputation as a romantic getaway. With eight fireplaces and a fine dining restaurant, it captures the essence of an old-fashioned country inn—so old, in fact, that it hosted guests decades before the Revolutionary War. The kitchen is a main draw, and a night's stay includes a $75 credit towards dinner. The chefs, whose signature dishes include rack of lamb and black bean soup, have appeared on the Food Network. Some folks will remember scenes from *Kiss Me Goodbye,* starring Sally Field and James Caan, filmed at the inn in 1982, but most have forgotten the area's role during the Revolutionary War, when Connecticut and New York troops encamped here to prevent the British from occupying the Hudson Highlands.

SETTING & FACILITIES

Location Wooded area in bucolic country setting. **Near** 4 mi. southeast of Cold Spring, 1 mi. west of Fahnestock State Park. **Building** 1761 stagecoach inn, butter yellow. **Grounds** 8 acres w/ stream, wooden bridge, gazebo, bench, chairs, 100-year-old maple trees. **Public Space** 3 dining rooms w/ wood-burning fireplaces, map room, drinking room. **Food & Drink** Full breakfast w/ juice, fresh fruit; menu of 10 entrées; specialties—eggs any style, pancakes, waffles. **Recreation** Nature walks, golf, cross-country skiing, boating, historic sites, Garrison Crafts Fair (Aug.), Artists on Location (May & Oct.). **Amenities & Services** Fax & e-mail, wine dinners; meetings (30), weddings (200).

ACCOMMODATIONS

Units 2 guest rooms, 1 suite, 1 cottage. **All Rooms** AC, clock radio, hair dryer, wood-burning fireplace. **Some Rooms** Balcony (2), private entrance (1). **Bed & Bath** Queen (3), double (1), four-poster (2), canopy (2); all private baths, 4 tubs. **Favorites** Beverly Robinson suite—fireplace, 2 comfy wing-back chairs, four-poster canopy bed, porch, understated look w/ beige & soft floral tones. **Comfort & Decor** This venerable relic of draftier times looks best in the flickering light of candles or the warm glow of a crackling fireplace. Original floors, ceiling beams, paneling, and fireplaces are accented with powder blue wainscoting and blue floral wallpaper. Waterfowl art adds interest. Tables are set with pewter chargers. In guest rooms, period furnishings transport you to times gone by.

RATES, RESERVATIONS, & RESTRICTIONS

Deposit $100 per night, refund w/ 7-days notice. **Discounts** No. **Credit Cards** AE, V, MC, D, DC. **Check-In/Out** 2 p.m. on/noon. **Smoking** No. **Pets** No. **Kids** No. **Minimum Stay** 2 nights if staying Sat. **Open** All year. **Hosts** Ira Boyar, 1123 Old Albany Post Rd., Garrison, 10524. **Phone** (800) 782-6837 or (845) 424-3000. **Fax** (845) 424-3283. **E-mail** innkeeper@birdbottle.com. **Web** birdbottle.com.

BYKENHULLE HOUSE, Hopewell Junction

OVERALL ★★★½ | QUALITY ★★★★ | VALUE ★★★ | PRICE $145–$165

The birth of this bed-and-breakfast is notable. While Florence was at work one day, a man who was lost came to their front door and asked Bill if this was a B&B. (At the time it was not.) Bill replied "it could be, come on in." When Florence got home he told her, "there's a man sleeping upstairs and tomorrow morning he'll want breakfast." It worked out so well that Florence soon retired from real estate to become a full time innkeeper. Their house, built by a prominent Dutch silversmith and listed on the National Register of Historic Places, is perfectly suited to the task. Antique shops and notable four- and five-star restaurants are minutes away. "It's a tremendous responsibility to entertain people on vacation or in their free time. I want to make it a wonderful experience for them," says Florence.

SETTING & FACILITIES

Location Residential area. **Near** 12 mi. southeast of Poughkeepsie. **Building** 1841 Georgian manor house. **Grounds** 6 acres w/ lawn, perennial flower gardens, gazebo, swimming pool. **Public Space** 2 LR, DR, sunroom. **Food & Drink** Full country breakfast w/ juice, fresh fruit & yogurt sauce, homemade baked goods; specialties—French toast, eggs Benedict, apple pancakes, crêpes. **Recreation** Visit Hyde Park (home of Franklin D. Roosevelt), Vanderbilt Mansion, Ogden Mills Estate, Culinary Institute of America, West Point; hiking, biking, fishing, antiquing, wineries, fly-fishing school; Stormville Flea Market. **Amenities & Services** Meetings (100), weddings (145).

ACCOMMODATIONS

Units 5 guest rooms. **All Rooms** AC, TV, phone. **Some Rooms** Fireplace (2) **Bed & Bath** Queen (5), four-poster (3), brass beds (2); all private baths, 2 Jacuzzis, 3 tubs. **Favorites** #5—four-poster bed, floral wallpaper & spread, wood floor w/ area rugs, 3 high windows; #3—fireplace, floral decor, tub, stuffed animal collection in antique cradle. **Comfort & Decor** Elegant crystal chandeliers set a formal tone in two living rooms accessorized with a grandfather's clock, needlepoint camelback sofa, Oriental carpet, Staffordshire lamps, Heisey glass, antiques, silk flowers, and a Teddy Bear collection. Dining room walls are covered with a floral fabric—authentic but a bit faded and water stained. Three ground-floor fireplaces add warmth. Wicker enhances a sunporch adjacent to a ballroom used for meetings and weddings. Guest rooms are more understated.

RATES, RESERVATIONS, & RESTRICTIONS

Deposit Credit card to hold, refund w/ 10-days notice, less $15 fee. **Discounts** Military. **Credit Cards** V, MC. **Check-In/Out** 2 p.m./11:30 a.m. **Smoking** No. **Pets** No. **Kids** Over age 12. **No-Nos** More than 2 persons in a room. **Minimum Stay** None.

Open All year. **Hosts** Florence & Bill Beausoleil, 21 Bykenhulle Rd., Hopewell Junction, 12533. **Phone** (845) 221-4182. **Web** www.pojonews.com/bh.

BLACK LION MANSION, Kingston

OVERALL ★★★★ | QUALITY ★★★★ | VALUE ★★★★ | PRICE **$119–$229**

The first owner of this grand, river-view mansion, cigar-manufacturer George W. Smith, spared no expense. Everything about this house is grand, beginning with the pedestaled lion's heads in the driveway, the gilded entry foyer with fireplace, oak pillars, and staircase with river-view landing. It fell into disrepair after World War II and became a run-down apartment building—until 1994 when the current owner, an Ali McGraw look-alike, bought it to save it. This is her third restoration project, and this time she kept a plasterer busy full time for 18 months just working on the ceiling and walls. The results of her mammoth undertaking are impressive—and much of it was done with her own hands. She credits her grandfather, a Swiss contractor, with "teaching me not to be afraid."

SETTING & FACILITIES

Location Hilltop overlooking Kingston & Hudson River. **Near** 2 mi. southeast of New York Thruway, Exit 19. **Building** 1880s hybrid of Victorian & Gothic w/ unpolished marble & brick exterior. **Grounds** 3.75 acres w/ front gardens & rear hillside filled w/ wildflowers. **Public Space** Entry rotunda, foyer, parlor, DR, side room, solarium, 2 porches. **Food & Drink** Full breakfast w/ juice, fruit, hot beverages; specialties—peaches & cream French toast, banana pancakes w/ pecan butter, corn cakes. **Recreation** Hiking, biking, rock climbing, antiquing, historic sites. **Amenities & Services** Fax & e-mail; meetings (50), weddings (90).

ACCOMMODATIONS

Units 6 guest rooms, 2 suites. **All Rooms** AC, TV, phone, clock. **Some Rooms** Fireplace (3), ceiling fan (1). **Bed & Bath** King (2), queen (5), double (1), 6 private baths, 2 private detached baths, 1 whirlpool, 3 tubs. **Favorites** Olive Library—Jefferson windows give access to a terrace, one wall of book-lined shelves, king bed, hunt prints, very small bath; Wisteria—fireplace, herringbone wood floor, French armoire & bed, antique side tables, beryl marble bath, marble sink, whirlpool. **Comfort & Decor** The domed and gilded entry rotunda with a mosaic floor is impressive. The huge living room offers many antiques, mirrors, plants, porcelain, statuary, and accessories from homes of the Hapsburgs in Austria. The dining room has a super-sized brass chandelier, wood fireplace with marble mantle, wainscoting, paisley wallpaper, and mosaic wood ceiling. Guest rooms have an eclectic mix of antiques and quality fabrics.

RATES, RESERVATIONS, & RESTRICTIONS

Deposit Credit card to hold, refund w/ 7-days notice. **Discounts** Corp. **Credit Cards** AE, V, MC. **Check-In/Out** 1 p.m./11:30 a.m. **Smoking** No. **Pets** No (6 cats on premises). **Kids** Yes. **Minimum Stay** 2 nights on all weekends for 2 rooms, others are 2 nights on weekends Memorial Day through Oct. only. **Open** All year. **Host** Patricia Pillsworth, 124 W. Chestnut St., Kingston, 12401. **Phone** (845) 338-0410. **Fax** (845) 331-5194. **E-mail** blacklionmansion@msn.com. **Web** theblacklionmansion.com.

EVELYN'S VIEW, Milton

OVERALL ★★★★★ | QUALITY ★★★★ | VALUE ★★★★ | PRICE **$95–$180**

This brother-and-sister team opened their family homestead as a bed-and-breakfast in 1998 and named it in honor of their mother, Evelyn. Their father built it as a country home in 1940, commuting to Manhattan to run his engineering company, whose contracts included work on the Hudson Tunnel and Panama Canal. The property, which began as seven acres, has doubled. A commercial kitchen was added in the garage to cater weddings, which are the backbone of the business from May through October. Bill, who retired from his auto repair business jokes that he's "gone from mufflers to marriages." The location, high above the river with spectacular views, access to a showcase swimming pool, and private tennis court, makes this a top pick in any season.

SETTING & FACILITIES

Location On a knoll overlooking the Hudson River & an apple orchard. **Near** 11 mi. southeast of New Paltz, 60 mi. north of Manhattan. **Building** 1870 Colonial w/ white siding, large picture windows. **Grounds** 14 acres w/ gardens, pond, trail, tennis court. **Public Space** LR, DR, solarium. **Food & Drink** Full breakfast w/ juice, fruit, muffins; specialties—French toast, eggs & bacon, pancakes; hot beverages always avail. **Recreation** Historic sites, antiquing, golf, fishing, hiking, horseback riding, skiing, river cruises, tennis on site (balls & racquets avail.). **Amenities & Services** Videos, fax & e-mail; meetings (50), weddings (250).

ACCOMMODATIONS

Units 4 guest rooms, 1 cottage. **All Rooms** AC, hair dryer. **Some Rooms** Robes (2), balcony (2), private entrance (1). **Bed & Bath** Queen (4), full (2), 3 private baths, 2 shared baths. **Favorites** Captain's View—cozy, red floral spread, porch w/ spectacular view; Carriage House—spacious, post & beam ceiling, 2 bedrooms, deck. **Comfort & Decor** Spacious Victorian living room with fireplace adjoins a flower-filled greenhouse. The dining room has hand-carved country furnishings and spectacular panoramic river views. Guest rooms have eclectic, old-fashioned charm.

RATES, RESERVATIONS, & RESTRICTIONS

Deposit Credit card, refund w/ 10-days notice. **Discounts** No. **Credit Cards** No. **Check-In/Out** 3–6 p.m./11 a.m. **Smoking** No. **Pets** No. **Kids** Carriage House only. **Minimum Stay** 2 nights on peak weekends. **Open** All year. **Hosts** Yvonne Sherman & William Stiefel, 12 Riverknoll Rd., Milton, 12547. **Phone** (845) 795-2376. **Fax** (845) 795-5650. **Web** evelynsview.com.

1871 HOUSE, New York City

OVERALL ★★★★ | QUALITY ★★★★ | VALUE ★★★ | PRICE **$165–$370**

Privacy and exclusivity with easy access to the best of urban New York City gives this property a rating boost—that and the opportunity to stay in a genuine renovated brownstone. If you're used to spacious baths and kitchens, you'll learn first hand how New Yorkers cope with such essentials squeezed into Lilliputian spaces. (The bedrooms are grander and more elegantly furnished.) The hosts' list of personal favorites in local eateries is a plus. Each guest is gifted with a CD of classical piano music—a nice gesture, which makes up for the fact that breakfast is not included and only some rooms have pantrys with coffee and tea. Also, don't be shocked when the hosts require you to sign a long list of (mostly common sense) agreements to protect their property. It's a real New York experience.

SETTING & FACILITIES

Location Upper East Side—in the 60s blocks between Park Ave. & Lexington Ave. **Near** Central Park, Madison Ave. boutiques, Bloomingdale's. **Building** 1871 brownstone townhouse, 5 stories. **Grounds** Narrow city lot, 20-feet wide by 100-feet deep. **Public Space** Foyer. **Food & Drink** Breakfast is not included, except by special arrangement; there are nifty coffee shops around the corner, including City Café & Mon Petite Café. **Recreation** Museums, art galleries, picnic & horseback riding in Central Park, carriage rides, zoo. **Amenities & Services** Fax & e-mail, access to concierge service for the tri-state area, parting gift off a classical music CD.

ACCOMMODATIONS

Units 4 guest rooms, 1 suite. **All Rooms** AC, television, pay phone. **Some Rooms** Mini-kitchen (4), wood fireplace (2), balcony (1), irons and hair dryers by request. **Bed & Bath** Queen (5), double (1), twin (2); sleigh (1); all private baths, tubs (2). **Favorites** Mission—basement accessed by steep, narrow stairs, handcrafted cherry wood furnishings, 9 lithographs of Manhattan, dining nook, small kitchen, sleeps 4; Parlor Room—iron bed, wood fireplace, street view, art, high windows w/ lace curtains, antique oak desk, side table, mirror, & miniature chair; Great Room—small bath but delightful terrace. **Comfort & Decor** An interesting mix of antiques and eye-catching, over-sized accessories gives each guest room a unique look. Quality fabrics and designer-brand items add elegance. (You may want to avoid the one bathroom that's so small you must use a handheld shower while sitting on the commode.) There's no public space, but you're in the heart of Manhattan.

RATES, RESERVATIONS, & RESTRICTIONS

Deposit 50%, balance due 30 days in advance, refund w/ 30-days notice less 25%. **Discounts** Last minute specials begin at $135. **Credit Cards** AE, V, MC. **Check-In/Out** 4 p.m./10 a.m. **Smoking** No, $200 cleaning fee for violators. **Pets** No. **Kids** Over age 12. **No-Nos** Noise between 10 p.m. & 8 a.m. **Minimum Stay** 4 nights (fewer if rooms avail.). **Open** All year. **Hosts** Lia & Warren Raum, 1871 House (exact address provided when booking), New York City, 10021. **Phone** (212) 756-8823. **Fax** (212) 588-0995. **E-mail** info@1871house.com. **Web** 1871house.com.

ABINGDON, New York City

OVERALL ★★★½ | QUALITY ★★★½ | VALUE ★★★ | PRICE $177–$222

Here's your chance to stay in a Greenwich Village townhouse. No. 13 was a mystery bookstore, then a chic Italian restaurant before Steve Austin rented it to open Brew Bar, which serves exotic coffees and pastries. He then renovated the four rooms upstairs to open a bed-and-breakfast, and eventually bought the building. Three years later, in 1998, he bought No. 21, a former storefront church and repeated the process. Steve has been a commercial photographer, property developer, hotel and restaurant manager, and caterer. He enjoys shopping at antique stores and estate sales. Neighbors now include actresses Gwyneth Paltrow on West 4th Street and Meryl Streep on West 12th Street, and celebrities like Molly Shannon and Ricki Lake come to the coffee shop. Quiet, mature adults are welcome.

SETTING & FACILITIES

Location West Greenwich Village, between W. 12th St. & Jane St. **Near** Bleeker Street, Westside promenade. **Building** 2 townhouses, same block but not adjoining. **Grounds** Narrow city lots. **Public Space** Brew Bar Coffee Shop, tiny garden. **Food & Drink** Buy your own at the downstairs coffee shop, where the menu includes everything from chai to espresso plus pecan fudge bars, fig bars, turtlebars, lemon bars, raspberry linzers, honey-raisin scones, Russian coffeecake, chocolate croissants; expect to spend around $5 per person. **Recreation** Chelsea Pier offers rock climbing, golf, basketball, swimming, & a gym; jog, bike, & roller blade on Westside promenade. **Amenities & Services** Fax, e-mail.

ACCOMMODATIONS

Units 9 guest rooms. **All Rooms** AC, cable TV, robes, alarm clock/sound machine, hair dryer, iron & board, safe, silk flowers. **Some Rooms** Ceiling fan (5), non-working fireplace (7), wet-bar/kitchenette, VCR. **Bed & Bath** King (1), queen (6), twin (2), canopy (2), four-poster (2); 5 private baths, 4 detached private baths, 6 tubs. **Favorites** Ambassador—four-poster king bed, sleeper love seat, garden view, wetbar/kitchenette, red lantern walls (a Ralph Lauren color); Sherwin—high ceilings, four-poster Shaker bed w/ canopy, damask spread, double-paneled windows, hand-painted secretary, towel warmer, chili-pepper wall color, street view. **Comfort & Decor** The only real public space is the friendly but busy Brew Bar. Narrow stairs lead to stylishly eclectic guest rooms, enhanced by exposed brick walls and some original tin ceilings. African dresses, a Turkish wall hanging, and steer skulls carry out room themes. Luxury amenities brighten the mood. Room sizes vary. In Martinque, the bed and walls are thisclose. Avoid Perrin—it's a little too funky.

RATES, RESERVATIONS, & RESTRICTIONS

Deposit Credit card to hold, refund w/ 4-days notice (10 days for holidays). **Discounts** None. **Credit Cards** AE, V, MC, D. **Check-In/Out** 2 p.m./noon. **Smoking** No. **Pets** No. **Kids** Over age 12. **No-Nos** Candles. **Minimum Stay** Usually 4 nights on weekends. **Open** All year. **Host** Steve Austin, 13 Eighth Ave., New York City, 10014. **Phone** (212) 243-5384. **Fax** (212) 807-7473. **Web** abingdonguesthouse.com.

INN AT IRVING PLACE, New York City

OVERALL ★★★★★ | QUALITY ★★★★½ | VALUE ★★★ | PRICE $325–$495

Enjoy a classic New York experience in a well-preserved neighborhood and get a taste of life in the nineteenth and early twentieth centuries—when neighbors included prominent writers such as Nathaniel West, S. J. Perlman, William Dean Howells, Herman Melville, and Stephen Crane. The building is a restoration gem with carefully preserved details recalling a private home. The amenities of a small luxury hotel add sophistication.

Among the many repeat guests are superstars and celebrities (who wish to remain unnamed). One parlor is perpetually set up for afternoon tea, which attracts local ladies-who-lunch and folks nostalgic for New York's halcyon days. The high-energy club Ci Bon, located at street level, ensures that the tone at this inn isn't all old-fashioned and sedate.

SETTING & FACILITIES

Location South of Grammercy Park between Park Ave. & 3rd St., 17th St., & 18th St. **Near** Union Square, Guggenheim Soho, Greenwich Village, Chinatown, Little Italy. **Building** Two 1836 brownstone townhouses, 3-story w/ wrought iron fence, gaslight. **Grounds** Tree-lined street, flower borders, window boxes. **Public Space** Parlor, Lady Mendl's Tea Salon, ground floor bar/restaurant. **Food & Drink** Continental breakfast w/ juice, fresh fruit, granola, bakery items, hot beverages; breakfast in bed avail.; welcome champagne, 5-course afternoon tea avail. Wed.–Sun.; room service. **Recreation** Cultural attractions, sightseeing, art galleries, movie theaters. **Amenities & Services** Massage, same-day laundry, video store nearby, fax & e-mail, *New York Times*; access to New York Sports Club & Equinox Sports Club; meetings (20), weddings (50).

ACCOMMODATIONS

Units 11 guest rooms, 1 suite. **All Rooms** AC, TV, phone w/ dataport, robes, CD clock, wet bar, non-working fireplace. **Bed & Bath** King (1), queen (11), four-poster (3), ornate headboards, Frette linens & towels, handmade silk duvet covers; all private baths w/ upscale amenities. **Favorites** Madame Wolenski—bay window used as a reading nook, king four-poster bed, remote-control AC, interesting accessories; Stanford White—3rd floor hideaway, pleasant & comfortable, spacious bathroom. **Comfort & Decor** The parlor glows with flickering light from a gas fireplace, candlelight, and fringed and leaded Victorian-era lamps. High ceilings have ornate molding. Two pocket doors have been preserved. Wood-trimmed sofa and chairs, an antique screen, and tea pots are eye-catching. Steep stairways require sturdy legs.

RATES, RESERVATIONS, & RESTRICTIONS

Deposit Credit card, refund w/ 2-days notice. **Discounts** No. **Credit Cards** AE, V, MC, DC. **Check-In/Out** 3 p.m./noon. **Smoking** Yes. **Pets** No. **Kids** Over age 12. **Minimum Stay** 2 nights on all weekends. **Open** All year. **Host** Naomi Blumenthal, owner, 56 Irving Pl., New York City, 10003. **Phone** (212) 533-4600. **Fax** (212) 533-4611. **E-mail** inn@innatirving.com. **Web** innatirving.com.

INN NEW YORK CITY, New York City

OVERALL ★★★★ | QUALITY ★★★★★ | VALUE ★★ | PRICE **$350–$575**

Famous conductors and opera stars would feel right at home at this bed-and-breakfast when they're in town performing at nearby Lincoln Center. This show-stopping stage setting, created by a mother-daughter team, is appropriate for any guests who want to experience the high style of the Waldorf yet remain anonymous in a carefully-guarded Upper West Side location. Ruth, a former antiques dealer and interior designer, stored her treasures in a New Jersey barn for nearly 12 years, before opening this Manhattan brownstone about 1985. Elyn, a graduate of the Fashion Institute of

Technology is equally creative and resourceful. You'll feel like a well-heeled New Yorker for a night or two.

SETTING & FACILITIES

Location West 70s on the Upper West Side. **Near** Lincoln Center for the Performing Arts, Museum of Natural History. **Building** Late 19th century brownstone, restored. **Grounds** City lot, 16' wide by 60' deep. **Public Space** None. **Food & Drink** Fresh fruit, juice, pastries, granola, hot beverages, cheese, bagels. **Recreation** Museums, concerts. **Amenities & Services** Fax, copier, valet service, turn-down service on request; meetings & weddings (12).

ACCOMMODATIONS

Units 4 suites on 4 levels. **All Rooms** AC, cable TV, stereo, CD/tape player, VCR, videos, phone w/ voice mail, intercom, ceiling fan, fresh flowers, hair dryer, bath pillow, shoe polisher, daily *New York Times,* dining table and chairs, fully-stocked full-service kitchen. **Some Rooms** Private entrance (1), washer-dryer (3), 2nd TV. **Bed & Bath** King (1), queen (3); all private baths, 2 whirlpool, 1 sauna. **Favorites** Opera Suite—grand piano, parquet floors, high ceiling w/ stained glass panel, chandelier, large live plants, fireplace, statuary, Chinese vases, fringed lamp shades, wall sconces, lots of tassels, elegant furnishings, French door to private terrace, long stem roses, bottle of Chardonnay; Spa Suite—king bed on platform, antique armoire, barber's chair, fireplace, stereo, lots of reading material, sauna, double Jacuzzi, bidet, glass-block windows. **Comfort & Decor** Rich in amenities and visual appeal, elegant fabrics and good lighting, the narrow rooms are laid out like railroad cars. Highlights include tin ceiling, stained glass, hall wainscotting, and nickel and crystal Victorian chandeliers.

RATES, RESERVATIONS, & RESTRICTIONS

Deposit 1 night or 25%, refund w/ 14-days notice less $50 fee. **Discounts** No. **Credit Cards** AE, V, MC. **Check-In/Out** 2 p.m./11 a.m. **Smoking** No. **Pets** No. **Kids** Yes, when appropriate. **No-Nos** Candles (owner must light fireplace). **Minimum Stay** 2 nights. **Open** All year. **Hosts** Elyn & Ruth Mensch, Inn New York City (exact address provided when booking), NewYorkCity, 10023. **Phone** (212) 580-1900. **Fax** (212) 580-4437. **Web** innnewyorkcity.com.

INN ON 23RD, New York City

OVERALL ★★★★½ | QUALITY ★★★★½ | VALUE ★★★ | PRICE **$185–$350**

Capture the feeling of having your own urban apartment. It's not the most convenient location, but at the corner, you'll find subway stops to whisk you almost anywhere in the city, plus the PATH train stop to New Jersey. In this mixed-usage commercial block, the entrance to this property looks surprisingly classy. The parlor is homey and welcoming. It adjoins a dining area and commercial kitchen where the New School for Social Research conducts cooking classes. (Their school's staff also prepares breakfast fixings for inn guests.) Annette and Ken opened this renovated townhouse in 1999, one of the city's few true bed-and-breakfasts. They are excellent hosts. You'll find lots to love about this comfortable urban hideaway.

SETTING & FACILITIES

Location Chelsea. **Near** Grammercy Park, lower Fifth Avenue, PATH trains. **Building** 1850s townhouse w/ elevator. **Grounds** City lot on busy shop-lined street. **Public Space** Living room w/ cooking demo area, library/breakfast room, elevator. **Food & Drink** Expanded cont'l breakfast w/ juice, fresh fruit, cereals, yogurt, bagels, muffins, croissants, jams, cream cheese, tea & coffee. **Recreation** Museums, art galleries, walking tours, concerts. **Amenities & Services** Disabled access, fax & e-mail.

ACCOMMODATIONS

Units 10 guest rooms, 1 suite. **All Rooms** AC, phone w/ two-line voice mail, dataport, iron & board, hair dryer, alarm clock. **Some Rooms** Coffee maker. **Bed & Bath** King (4), queen (8), canopy (1), pillow-top mattresses; all private baths, 11 tubs. **Favorites** #54, Skylight—captures the energy & creativity of Manhattan, 3 brick walls, huge skylight, 2 small glass chandeliers, couch, armoire, pedestals, writing desk, striking black & white poster-size photo of a city street scene, nice window treatments, brass king bed w/ comfortable feathertop mattress, like being in a modified loft; #51, The Suite—spacious for NYC, view of Empire State Building lighted at night, French headboard, armoire, marble-topped chest, mirrors, extra sofa bed, Victorian lamp. **Comfort & Decor** The parlor/lobby has an exposed brick wall, strong selections of art and sculpture, Victorian sofas, a wood floor with three large carpets, plants, and whimsical accessories. The second floor library has an oak bar with brass rails, hundreds of haphazardly arranged books, whimsical sculptures, a game table, and access to three daily newspapers. Guest rooms are heavily-themed, including Asian, western, French provincial, and the 1940s.

RATES, RESERVATIONS, & RESTRICTIONS

Deposit Credit card to hold, refund w/ 7-days notice. **Discounts** No. **Credit Cards** AE, V, MC. **Check-In/Out** 2–9 p.m./noon. **Smoking** No. **Pets** No. **Kids** Over age 12. **No-Nos** Lost key fee is $25. **Minimum Stay** 2 nights on weekends. **Open** All year. **Hosts** Annette & Ken Fisherman, 131 W. 23rd St., New York City, 10011. **Phone** (212) 463-0330. **Fax** (212) 464-0302. **E-mail** innon23rd@aol.com. **Web** www.bbonline.com.

OLDE RHINEBECK INN, Rhinebeck

OVERALL ★★★★½ | QUALITY ★★★★ | VALUE ★★★ | PRICE $195–$275

The house has tremendous visual appeal, thanks to original architectural details from Dutch Palatine settlers who built it three decades before the Revolutionary War. Jonna, who decided at age seven to have her own bed-and-breakfast business, says she was enveloped by the feeling this would be the place the moment she saw it. Soon after she opened her dream property, a movie production company took over the rooms to house their stars, including Brook Shields, Deborah Unger, and Jared Harris. One reason Jonna feels that the house is so comfortable and approachable is that it was home to 12 generations of the same family—now buried in the old church cemetery down the road. Newly married, she and David are energetic and savvy about how to preserve this cultural treasure and showcase it for visitors. Breakfasts are particularly enjoyable.

SETTING & FACILITIES

Location Rural road in horse country. **Near** 3 mi. south of Rhinebeck, 90 mi. north of New York City. **Building** 1745 farmhouse. **Grounds** 13 acres, pond stocked w/ bass, miniature exotic goats. **Public Space** LR, DR, stone patio. **Food & Drink** Full country breakfast w/ fruit smoothie, fresh fruit bowl, home baked goods; specialties—sweet potato frittata, stuffed French toast, pear pancakes; coffee station. **Recreation** Omega Institute for Holistic Studies, Culinary Institute of America, FDR Home & Historic Site, Vanderbilt Mansion, Montgomery Place, Old Rhinebeck Aerodome, Hudson Valley Raptor Center, Rhinebeck Performing Arts Center, wineries, antiquing, fairgrounds events, Dutchess County Fair (Aug.), Sheep & Wood Festival (Oct.). **Amenities & Services** Fax & e-mail; meetings (6).

ACCOMMODATIONS

Units 3 guest rooms. **All Rooms** AC, TV, hair dryer, robes, fresh flowers. **Some Rooms** Fridge (2), balcony (1), porch (1). **Bed & Bath** Queen (3), twin (1), canopy (1); all private baths, 1 whirlpool, 3 tubs. **Favorites** Ryefield suite—spacious, queen canopy bed, sitting room, huntsman motif. **Comfort & Decor** Wide plank floors, the patina of centuries-old buttermilk finishes, and rugged hand-hewn chestnut beams earned this home a listing on the National Register of Historic Places. Breakfasts are a delight, and locally grown anemones add color.

RATES, RESERVATIONS, & RESTRICTIONS

Deposit 50%, refund w/ 14-days notice, less $25 **Discounts** Extended stay. **Credit Cards** AE, V, MC. **Check-In/Out** 3 p.m./noon. **Smoking** No. **Pets** Small dogs, please inquire. **Kids** One room avail. **Minimum Stay** 2 nights on weekends. **Open** All year. **Hosts** Jonna Paolella & Dave Kliphon, 340 Wurtemburg Rd., Rhinebeck, 12572. **Phone** (845) 871-1745. **Fax** (845) 876-8809. **E-mail** Innkeeper@rhinebeckinn.com. **Web** rhinebeckinn.com.

WHISTLEWOOD FARM, Rhinebeck

OVERALL ★★★★½ | QUALITY ★★★★ | VALUE ★★★ | PRICE **$95–$325**

Maggie moves from wrangling horses to preparing gourmet breakfasts with the greatest ease. Her western memorabilia collection is interesting, including six-shooters, saddles, bronze horse sculptures, and a wild boar's head. It's all casually displayed, making you think you're somewhere out West—Wyoming, perhaps. Also notable is the full-wall mural in one hallway depicting Maggie's horse farm and some of her favorite horses. She's a busy lady, but she manages to find time for a chat with her guests. As one of the very first people in this area to open a bed-and-breakfast, she'll steer you towards the best places to go and the best things to do during your visit.

SETTING & FACILITIES

Location Perched on a hilltop, 6 mi. east of Taconic Pkwy. **Near** Rhinebeck Tennis Club, Rhinebeck Performing Arts Center, Mills, Roosevelt & Vanderbilt mansions. **Building** 1960 lodge & guest house. **Grounds** 25 acres, working horse farm w/ barn, paddocks, walking trail. **Public Space** LR, solarium, country kitchen, family room, front porch, decks. **Food**

& Drink Full country breakfast served on a 1904 stove w/ juice, fresh fruit, homemade baked goods; specialties—buttermilk pancakes, French toast, scrambled eggs w/ bacon or sausage; anytime coffee, beverages, cake, & homemade pie; picnic basket & dinner avail. **Recreation** Swimming, boating, canoeing, kayaking, fishing, hiking, biking, tennis, horseback riding antiquing, apple picking, pick-your-own farms, wineries, scenic boat rides, aerial dog-fight and barnstormer exhibitions on summer weekends. **Amenities & Services** Massage avail., disabled access (1), fax & e-mail; meetings (25) weddings (125).

ACCOMMODATIONS

Units 6 guest rooms. **All Rooms** AC, ceiling fan, fresh flowers, robes, hair dryer. **Some Rooms** Private patio (4), fireplace (3). **Bed & Bath** Queen four-poster (6); 5 private baths, 1 detached private bath, 3 whirlpools, 1 tub. **Favorites** Wyoming—spacious, queen four-poster plus antique twin sleigh bed, western accessories, Rockies cabin atmosphere, large canoe hangs from the rafters, sliding glass double doors open to wild-flower garden, double whirlpool; Juniper—rough pine siding, antique Indian blankets, two beds, colorful country prints, private deck faces Juniper shrubs. **Comfort & Decor** This rambling ranch house is colorful and eclectic throughout. The rustic living room has a fieldstone fireplace and cathedral ceiling with hand-hewn beams. The kitchen is a magnet for guests. Newer rooms in the carriage house are upscale.

RATES, RESERVATIONS, & RESTRICTIONS

Deposit Credit card to hold, 50% by check in advance, refund w/ 14-days notice less $20. **Discounts** 5 days or more. **Credit Cards** AE. **Check-In/Out** 2–7 p.m./11:30 a.m. **Smoking** No. **Pets** Yes, by prior arrangement, if housebroken, $15 nightly fee (3 labs on premises); horses boarded. **Kids** Over age 12. **Minimum Stay** 2 nights on weekends, 3 nights holiday weekends. **Open** All year. **Host** Maggie Myer, 52 Pells Rd., Rhinebeck, 12572. **Phone** (845) 876-6838. **Fax** (845) 876-5513. **E-mail** whistlwd @valstar.net. **Web** whistlewood.com.

SPENCERTOWN COUNTRY HOUSE, Spencertown

OVERALL ★★★★ | QUALITY ★★★★ | VALUE ★★★ | PRICE **$65–$195**

In the 1950s, the property was converted to an inn that soon gained local fame as a site for weddings and other celebrations. When Heather and John relocated from Wycoff, New Jersey and took over as innkeepers in 1996, they changed the focus to the comforts of overnight guests. Comments in their guest books indicate they've found the formula for success. "This is the perfect place to come to sit on the porch with a good book or enjoy the beautiful gardens," says one. "Wonderfully peaceful retreat—appreciated all your attention to details," says another. "Lovely and relaxing like home—only better," writes a third. It's off the beaten track, but worth the drive.

SETTING & FACILITIES

Location Country road in the Berkshire foothills. **Near** 5 mi. east of Chatham, 18 mi. southwest of Tanglewood. **Building** 1803 farmhouse, enlarged; a blend of Federal (front) & Victorian (side). **Grounds** 5 acres w/ gardens, stream, carriage barn, old silo, Adirondack chairs, picnic tables, 3- & 5-mi. walking trails. **Public Space** 2 parlors, DR, veranda. **Food & Drink** Full breakfast w/ fresh squeezed juices, homemade breads, locally-made marmalades, cereal; specialties—French Panitone toast, various fruit pancakes, cheese omelets; afternoon tea & cookies **Recreation** Hiking, biking, fishing, horseback riding, cross-country & downhill skiing, antiquing, theater, dance, music performances, board games, croquet, Chatham Fair (Sept.). **Amenities & Services** Videos, disabled access (1), fax, massage avail. at Angel Hill Wellness Center (2 mi.); meetings (10).

ACCOMMODATIONS

Units 5 guest rooms in the main house, 3 rooms & 1 suite in the carriage barn. **All Rooms** AC, hair dryer. **Some Rooms** Vermont Castings stove (1), private entrance (1), dataport, TV, VCR, fridge. **Bed & Bath** Queen (6), double (1), twin (2), four-poster (1); all private baths, 5 tubs. **Favorites** Gunda's room—periwinkle blue w/ queen bed, windows on three sides, built-in desk, nice bath; Taconic room—beige, brown, & terra cotta colors, queen bed, bath sink transformed from early 1900s dresser, adjoins all-season porch w/ Vermont cast stove & wicker chairs. **Comfort & Decor** Cleanliness is stressed in this comfortably furnished inn. Period antiques are used throughout. Original features include old wood doors and hardware, leaded glass bay windows, and wide-board pine floors. A collection of primitive American portraiture and folk art adds character.

RATES, RESERVATIONS, & RESTRICTIONS

Deposit 1 night (50% for 3 nights or more), refund w/ 7-days notice less $10. **Discounts** Off season. **Credit Cards** AE, V, MC, D. **Check-In/Out** 2 p.m./11 a.m. **Smoking** No. **Pets** No. **Kids** Under age 12 in specific rooms. **Minimum Stay** 2 nights on weekends June–Oct. & holidays weekends (3 nights some weekends). **Open** All year (except Jan.). **Hosts** Heather & John Spitzer, 1909 County Rte. 9, Spencertown, 12165. **Phone** (888) 727-9980 or (518) 392-5292. **Fax** (518) 392-7453. **E-mail** info@spencertowncntryhouse.com. **Web** spencertowncntryhouse.com.

BELVEDERE MANSION, Staatsburg

OVERALL ★★★★ | QUALITY ★★★★½ | VALUE ★★★ | PRICE $175–$350

Hudson Valley has nine mansions to visit, but here's one where you can actually stay. The white-columned house was originally a wedding gift to socialite Mary Hastings, then reborn as a fat farm from 1950 to 1986. The setting, high above the road overlooking a panoramic view of the distant Hudson River and Catskills, may be grand, but you'll feel right at home. Jewel-tone walls and crackling fireplaces in the restaurant provide a romantic backdrop for gourmet meals prepared by chef Michael Dedrick. Experienced hosts, Patricia and Nick have owned floral, landscaping, and antiques businesses, as well as a Manhattan restaurant. "This may have been a fat farm once, but we're now an indulgence center," says Patricia.

SETTING & FACILITIES

Location Hillside overlooking the Hudson River and Catskill Mountains, 90 mi. north of New York City. **Near** 3.5 mi. south of Rhinebeck, across from Dinsmore Golf Course and Southlands Riding Foundation. **Building** 1760 Neo-classic mansion, rebuilt in 1900, restored. **Grounds** 15 acres of rolling lawns, grove of 100 year-old trees, columned gazebos, pond, swimming pool, tennis court. **Public Space** LR, 2nd floor sitting area, DR, glassed-in porch, 2 gazebos. **Food & Drink** Full country breakfast w/ juice, fresh fruit platter, homemade baked goods; specialties—eggs sardou, crème brûlée oatmeal, pumpkin-pecan Belgian waffles; dinners served, French American cuisine features local produce. **Recreation** Hiking, biking, kayaking, tubing, rock climbing, cross-country skiing, horse-drawn sleigh rides, golf, wineries, antiquing, shows at Old Rhinebeck Aerodrome, pick-your-own farms; croquet, bocce, & volleyball equip. avail. at inn. **Amenities & Services** Massage avail., disabled access (1), fax & e-mail; meetings (70), weddings (180).

ACCOMMODATIONS

Units 6 guest rooms, 1 suite. **All Rooms** AC, ceiling fan, sherry. **Some Rooms** River views. **Bed & Bath** King (3), queen (4), twin (2), canopy (1); all private baths, 7 tubs. **Favorites** Astor—French Empire bed, mirrored armoire, seductive Caravaggio red walls, great views of river & mountains; Lafayette—Aubusson carpet of ecru, claret, & mossy green, pale yellow decor, mirrored armoire, gilded claw-foot slipper tub, Empire bed & fireplace, mountain & river views. **Comfort & Decor** Furnishings are reminiscent of the Gilded Age, with eighteenth-century French antiques, trompe l'oeil and cloud painted ceiling, silk and damask fabric walls, and vintage light fixtures. Mansion guest rooms feature matching antique headboards and armoires. Motel-quality rooms are available in two separate buildings on the property for $75–$175, with access to the restaurant and pool.

RATES, RESERVATIONS, & RESTRICTIONS

Deposit 50% in advance, refund w/ 14-days notice. **Discounts** Group & extended stays. **Credit Cards** AE, V, MC, D. **Check-In/Out** 3 p.m./11 a.m. **Smoking** Restaurant is cigar friendly. **Pets** No, can arrange boarding at local kennel. **Kids** Well-behaved children welcome. **Minimum Stay** 2 nights on weekends. **Open** All year. **Hosts** Patricia & Nick Rebraca, Box 758, Rhinebeck, 12572. **Phone** (845) 889-8000. **Fax** (845) 889-8811. **Web** belvederemansion.com.

LAKEHOUSE INN ON GOLDEN POND, Stanfordville

OVERALL ★★★½ | QUALITY ★★★★ | VALUE ★★ | PRICE **$295–$675**

This property photographs beautifully, but in person the house is quite ordinary. The living room is rescued from looking nondescript by accessories that include a chess set, a bonsai tree, a bird motel, an antique child's bike, glazed pottery, and two stained glass panels. The real visual draw is the small lake, reached via wood decking and steep stairs from the main house. You can see it best from bedrooms in the front of the house, and it's a plus to have a private porch overlooking the water. A big emphasis is placed on well-appointed bedrooms, where people are encouraged to express their special feelings for each other. You can row a boat, sunbathe, relax, and swim. Picnics are great, but it's a bit of a drive to the nearest romantic eatery.

SETTING & FACILITIES

Location On private lake. **Near** Wilcox State Park, Rhinebeck. **Building** 1990 cedar house and cottage. **Grounds** 22 acres, lake w/ private docks, woods, flower border and garden, hammocks. **Public Space** LR, deck w/ tables, chairs, hanging floral baskets. **Food & Drink** Cont'l breakfast served to guest rooms in covered basket w/ fruit, juice, tin of pastries, cereal; specialties—apple tartin, cheese platter w/ croissants, apple bread pudding. **Recreation** Bass fishing, boating (rowboats provided), cross-country skiing, horseback riding, golf, tennis, wineries, summer theatre, antiquing, historic mansions, apple picking. **Amenities & Services** About 50 videos in each room, massage avail., fax.

ACCOMMODATIONS

Units 7 guest rooms. **All Rooms** Jacuzzis for 2, wood-burning fireplace, private deck, color TV/VCR, CD/tape player, robes, bath pillows, mini-fridge, coffee/tea/cappuccino, private entrance. **Some Rooms** Kitchenette (1). **Bed & Bath** King (6), queen (1), four-poster (1), canopy (4), duvets; all private baths w/ whirlpools. **Favorites** Master suite—spacious, dramatic lake view, lots of amenities. **Comfort & Decor** The modest living room features an eclectic mix of antiques under a pine ceiling with rafters that creates a cottage-style mood. Guest rooms are quiet, secluded, and moderate in size.

RATES, RESERVATIONS, & RESTRICTIONS

Deposit One to two nights, refund w/ 21-days notice. **Discounts** No. **Credit Cards** No. **Check-In/Out** 3–9p.m./11 a.m. **Smoking** No. **Pets** No. **Kids** On occasion. **Minimum Stay** 2 nights on weekends, 3 nights on holiday weekends. **Open** All year. **Host** Judy Kohler, Shelley Hill Rd., Stanfordville, 12581 **Phone** (845) 266-8093. **Fax** (845) 266-4051. **E-mail** judy@lakehouseinn.com. **Web** lakehouseinn.com.

INN AT STONE RIDGE, Stone Ridge

OVERALL ★★★½ | QUALITY ★★★★ | VALUE ★★★ | PRICE **$195–$425**

Dutch settlers built this house, beginning with two rooms, and it grew like Topsy over time. Dan says his guests typically don't want to schmooze with the host—they prefer more privacy and they get it. The guests do like good food, however, and his kitchen staff is eager to provide it. Even Suzanne, a self-taught cook, participates as the pastry chef. The inn runs a cozy, rustic-style restaurant with three dining rooms and a tavern. Fireside lunches and dinners are based on a menu of regional American fare, from the Hudson Valley to the Pacific Rim and from the Santa Fe Trail to the Mississippi Delta. The ambience is lovely, especially in spring when the flowers are blooming and in fall when the leaves are ablaze.

SETTING & FACILITIES

Location Historic Old Kings Hwy. (now Rte. 209) in Rondout Valley, at the base of Mohonk Mountain. **Near** 4 mi. to Mohonk Preserve parking, 8.5 mi. south of NY State Thruway (Exit 19), 12 mi. northwest of New Paltz. **Building** 18th century Dutch Colonial w/ Federal features, fieldstone exterior w/ white wood trim, columned open porch. **Grounds** 150 acres w/ maple & spruce trees, commercial apple orchard, 2 ponds, walking trails, gardens, swimming pool, stable & carriage house. **Public Space** Game room, TV room, family room, 3 DR, bar. **Food & Drink** Full breakfast w/ juice, fruit, homemade pastries, specialties—prime rib hash, applewood smoked trout w/ walnut toast, cheese crêpes, omelets to order; full brunch on Sundays. **Recreation** Hiking, mountain biking, rock climbing, antiquing, historic sites, showshoeing, cross-country skiing, ice fishing (equip. avail. in New Paltz). **Amenities & Services** Fax & e-mail; meetings (40), weddings (200).

ACCOMMODATIONS

Units 2 guest rooms, 3 suites. **All Rooms** AC, coffee/tea service. **Some Rooms** Fireplace (2), balcony (2), TV. **Bed & Bath** King (3), queen (3), canopy (1), sleigh (1); all private baths, 1 whirlpool, 5 tubs. **Favorites** #11—has the most amenities, including king bed, antique couch & dresser, whirlpool, & dresser sink. **Comfort & Decor** Good bedding is a hallmark. Some guest rooms are oddly configured but still attractively decorated.

RATES, RESERVATIONS, & RESTRICTIONS

Deposit 25%, balance due 30 days prior to arrival, refund w/ 30-days notice. **Discounts** None. **Credit Cards** AE, V, MC, D. **Check-In/Out** 1 p.m./11 a.m. **Smoking** Tavern only. **Pets** Yes, at your own risk. **Kids** Yes. **Minimum Stay** 2 nights on holiday weekends. **Open** All year. **Hosts** Suzanne & Dan Hauspurg, Rte., 209, Box 76, Stone Ridge, 12484. **Phone** (845) 687-0736. **Fax** (845) 687-0112. **E-mail** innfuse@aol.com. **Web** innatstoneridge.com.

COVE HOUSE, Tompkins Cove

OVERALL ★★★ | QUALITY ★★★½ | VALUE ★★★ | PRICE **$70–$100**

This property is accessible via an extremely steep road, so you'll need good brakes. The owners say they were pioneers in building on this mountainside and one of the first in the area to design a home that uses passive solar energy. Over the years, power lines and a smoke stack or two were installed, and now they somewhat impair the view. But it's still noteworthy. History buffs can tour the Stony Point Battlefield and West Point Military Academy. Nature lovers can hike in the scenic woods of Bear Mountain and Harriman State Parks. And, the nearby village of Nyack is good for antiquing and lunch. Dan is a professional drummer who plays in bands and teaches music part time. But he has time to help guests organize their time wisely.

SETTING & FACILITIES

Location On Bald Mountain 350 ft. above the Hudson River. **Near** 4.5 mi. south of Bear Mountain. **Building** 1988 contemporary. **Grounds** 3 wooded acres. **Public Space** LR, dining area, solarium, deck. **Food & Drink** Full breakfast w/ juice, fruit, pastries, hot beverages; specialties—eggs in a blanket, French toast, pancakes w/ fruit, egg & cheese casserole, side meats; afternoon tea. **Recreation** Hiking, boating, horseback riding, golf, Bear Mountain zoo, board games, October Fest, Sugarloaf Crafts Center. **Amenities & Services** Laundry equip., fax & e-mail.

ACCOMMODATIONS

Units 3 guest rooms. **All Rooms** AC, TV, ceiling fan. **Some Rooms** Balcony (1), private entrance (1), hair dryer & iron (2). **Bed & Bath** Queen (1), full (2); 1 private bath, 2 shared baths. **Favorites** Queen room—skylight, ceiling fan, old trunk, only private bath, glass door opens to deck w/ spectacular valley view. **Comfort & Decor** Public area furnishings are casual and comfortable. A large Victorian dollhouse adds interest to the living room. The main focus is the view of the river. Guest rooms and beds are modest in size.

RATES, RESERVATIONS, & RESTRICTIONS

Deposit One night, refund w/ 7-days notice. **Discounts** No. **Credit Cards** No. **Check-In/Out** 3 p.m./11 a.m. **Smoking** No. **Pets** No. **Kids** Over age 12. **Minimum Stay** 2 nights on holiday weekends. **Open** All year (except Dec. and Jan.). **Hosts** Patricia & Dan Sciscente, 4 Herbert Ct., Tomkins Cove, 10986. **Phone** (845) 429-9695. **Fax** (845) 429-9695. **E-mail** dpscis@aol.com. **Web** www.pojonews.com/covehouse.

GLENWOOD HOUSE, Warwick

OVERALL ★★★★½ | QUALITY ★★★★½ | VALUE ★★★★ | PRICE $110–$295

Maybe it was the years living in Italy that gave hostess Andrea Coman her impeccable sense of style, eye for pleasing decor, and savvy about how to provide sybaritic pleasures. Whatever the source, visitors to this delightful farm setting can expect to have their weary bones and wilted spirits renewed. Those with romance in mind should book the Harvest Moon suite, where ultra-romantic touches include everything from light dimmers, candles, and background music to art and literature about love. It adds a bit of ironic fun to know that this now-upscale room was created from a former chicken coop. And, that the equally elegant Lord Byron suite next door once was a tool shed. The comforts, tasty breakfasts, and warm hospitality make this property a great find.

SETTING & FACILITIES

Location Rural country road on the Pine Island section of Warwick, 55 mi. northwest of Manhattan. **Near** 8 mi. west of Warwick, 5 mi. north of Vernon, NJ. **Building** Circa 1860 Victorian farmhouse w/ cottage. **Grounds** 2.5 acres w/ flower border, fishpond, 8-person hot tub, deck, barn. **Public Space** Library, DR, porch. **Food & Drink** Full breakfast w/ juice, fruit, baked goods; specialties—harvest apple French toast, 3 types of pancakes, eggs any style, homemade jellies. **Recreation** Golf, wineries, antiquing, biking, artist studio tour, fruit picking, boating, rafting, tubing & canoeing, hay & sleigh rides, drive-in movies, Hidden Valley Ski Area, Mountain Creek Ski Area, Mountain Creek Water Park, Sugar Loaf Art & Crafts Village. **Amenities & Services** Videos, massage avail., laundry equip., fax & e-mail; meetings (12), weddings (75).

ACCOMMODATIONS

Units 5 guest rooms (2 are in a detached cottage). **All Rooms** AC, robes, hair dryer. **Some Rooms** Gas fireplace (2), private entrance (2), TV & VCR, CD player (4), ceiling fan (1). **Bed & Bath** King (2), queen (4), canopy (3); 4 private baths, 1 private detached bath, 3 whirlpool, 1 tub. **Favorites** Harvest Moon—located in the guest cottage for privacy, cathedral ceiling, picture windows, four-poster king featherbed, double whirlpool surrounded by candles, gas fireplace, cable TV, VCR, CD player, rocking chair, books & tapes to relax by; Misty Valley—most luxurious and romantic room in the main house, pine floor, double whirlpool, Victorian oak bed w/ crocheted covers, best view. **Comfort & Decor** Filled with antiques and reproductions, the library and dining room have a casual look and comfortable feel. Furnishings are Arts & Crafts style with Native American accents. Extra care was taken to make every guest room a show stopper.

RATES, RESERVATIONS, & RESTRICTIONS

Deposit Credit card, refund w/ 7-days notice less $25 fee. **Discounts** Specials offered on website. **Credit Cards** AE, V, MC. **Check-In/Out** 3–6p.m./11 a.m. **Smoking** No. **Pets** No. **Kids** Yes. **Minimum Stay** Some weekends. **Open** All year. **Host** Andrea Coman, 49 Glenwood Rd., Pine Island, 10960. **Phone** (845) 258-5066. **Fax** (914) 258-4226. **E-mail** info@glenwoodhouse.com. **Web** glenwoodhouse.com.

INN AT STONY CREEK, Warwick

OVERALL ★★★★★ | QUALITY ★★★★½ | VALUE ★★★★ | PRICE $130

The Windy Hollow Hunt Club hunts fox on an adjacent field. A picturesque stream flows through the property. Mature trees and stone walls decorate the landscape. A sense of quiet and peacefulness pervades the neighborhood. Everything seems to be as it should. And, this sense of well-being continues inside the Stony Creek B&B, where attention to detail is key. Seeing it today, in nearly perfect condition, it's hard to imagine the house required four years of restoration. Enjoy the orchids and cut tulips. Ask about the live-in parrot and cockatoo. "I'm bored, come get me," squawked one of the exotic birds, adding a touch of humor to our visit.

SETTING & FACILITIES

Location Rural country road. **Near** 3 mi. southwest of Sugarloaf Craft Village, 5 mi. west of Warwick. **Building** 1840 Greek Revival farmhouse, restored. **Grounds** 9 acres, stone wall, stream, open fields, mountain views, walking trail, birdhouses. **Public Space** LR, DR, guest fridge, 2 porches. **Food & Drink** Full breakfast w/ juice, fresh fruit, homemade muffins; specialties—mushroom omelet in pastry puff w/ cheddar dill sauce, egg soufflé, banana walnut pancakes (or in-season fruit), fried zucchini blossom w/ maple syrup. **Recreation** Golf, wineries, antiquing, biking, artist studio tours, fruit picking, boating, rafting, tubing, canoeing, hay & sleigh rides, drive-in movies, Hidden Valley Ski Area, Mountain Creek Ski Area, Mountain Creek Water Park, Sugar Loaf Art & Crafts Village.

ACCOMMODATIONS

Units 4 guest rooms. **All Rooms** AC, TV & VCR, phone, fruit, chocolates, flowers, robes. **Some Rooms** Ceiling fan (2). **Bed & Bath** Queen (4), four-poster (3), sleigh (1); 3 private baths, 1 detached private bath, 2 tubs. **Favorites** #1 Patriot—Civil War–era antiques, four-poster bed, oak armoire; #2 Horse & Hound—Empire chest w/ mirror, 1850s side stand, four-poster bed, smaller bath. **Comfort & Decor** This is an extremely pleasant house filled with many mint-condition antiques, including 35 antique clocks. The living and dining rooms have a formal look with great attention to detail. Look for brass chandeliers, Oriental carpets, wing chairs, a marble fireplace, pocket doors, ceiling molding, tall bubble glass windows, and an antique clock collection. Guests dine at separate tables in a light-filled space with pastoral views.

RATES, RESERVATIONS, & RESTRICTIONS

Deposit 1 night, refund w/ 7-days notice less $35 fee. **Discounts** AARP. **Credit Cards** AE, V, MC. **Check-In/Out** 3–6p.m./11 a.m. **Smoking** No. **Pets** No. **Kids** Over age 12. **Minimum Stay** 1 night. **Open** All year (except Jan.). **Host** Bill Signor, 34 Spanktown Rd., Warwick, 10990. **Phone** (845) 986-3660. **E-mail** stonycreek@warwick.net. **Web** innstonycreek.com.

PEACH GROVE INN, Warwick

OVERALL ★★★★★ | QUALITY ★★★★½ | VALUE ★★★ | PRICE **$115–$145**

For most people, retirement means downsizing, but not Lucy and John. "This is the third house we've restored and each one has been progressively larger," says John, who does much of the work himself, including the wallpapering. Lucy, who was an antiques dealer, contributes her knowledge of furnishings and accessories. Together they've created the premier bed-and-breakfast in Warwick—the largest, with the most coveted location. Formerly a graphic designer specializing in toy packaging, John is also a serious tea enthusiast. He and Lucy serve elegant weekend tea parties to guests and the public. It's become "the" thing to do when in the area.

SETTING & FACILITIES

Location Busy Rte. 17A. **Near** Hickory Hill Golf Course, pick-your-own apple orchards, 2 mi. to Mt. Peter Ski area. **Building** 1850 Greek Revival w/ fluted columns. **Grounds** 1 acre surrounded by rolling farmland. **Public Space** Hall, 2 parlors, DR, back porch. **Food & Drink** Full family-style breakfast served on fine china, w/ fruit course, baked goods; specialties—cheese strata, stuffed French toast, corn pancakes, side meats; formal afternoon tea on Sat. & Sun. open to the public for $18. **Recreation** Hiking the Appalachian Trail, wineries, parks, Apple Fest, garden tours, Holly Trail, artist studio tours. **Amenities & Services** Fax & e-mail; meetings (25), weddings (120).

ACCOMMODATIONS

Units 3 guest rooms, 1 suite. **All Rooms** AC, hair dryer, ceiling fan. **Some Rooms** Fireplace (3). **Bed & Bath** Queen (2), full (2), canopy (1), four-poster (1), brass bed; all private baths. **Favorites** Isaac Wheeler—fireplace, magnolia spread, nice bath, armoire; Servants. Quarters—golden oak dresser & bed headboard, floral pattern, 3 windows, nice view of fields. **Comfort & Decor** The 11-foot ceilings, 8.5-foot doors, 8 fireplaces, and Antebellum-sized rooms recall a bygone lifestyle in an earlier, more gracious era. The hallway is remarkable for its original marbelized walls, hand-painted on plaster circa 1850. The living room has a marble fireplace and baby grand piano. Room and bath sizes vary.

RATES, RESERVATIONS, & RESTRICTIONS

Deposit 1 night, refund w/ 7-days notice. **Discounts** No. **Credit Cards** AE, V, MC. **Check-In/Out** 3:30–7:30 p.m./11:30 a.m. **Smoking** No. **Pets** No. **Kids** Over age 12 (or when renting the entire building). **Minimum Stay** No. **Open** All year. **Hosts** Lucy & John Mastropierro, 205 Rte. 17A, Warwick, 10990. **Phone** (845) 986-7411. **Fax** (845) 986-7590. **E-mail** peachgrv@warwick.net. **Web** peachgroveinn.net.

Zone 4

Long Island/ The Hamptons

Some of the best, and most popular beaches in American stretch 60 miles along the southern coast of Long Island from Moriches to Montauk.

Mid-week is the best time to visit the Hamptons. That's when locals reclaim their towns from second-home owners. You can rise early, when the sea shines iridescent and the empty beaches are tinged pink by a still distant sun, and hear nothing but the crashing of surf and the caw of gulls.

The first Hampton you come to from New York is **Westhampton Beach.** Its beaches encompass nearly three miles of dune-fringed, soft, white sand. In its picture-perfect village, located a half-mile inland, mini-flower gardens frame nearly every gift shop, clothing boutique, bakery, and ice cream parlor, and baskets of impatiens hang from wrought iron street lamps.

Southampton is the oldest village in New York and arguably the most exclusive. But, underneath the sophisticated trappings informality reigns. You can rub shoulders with locals and second-home owners at benefit cocktail parties, but the rich and famous residents stay secluded in oceanfront "cottages" behind very high hedges.

Many consider **East Hampton** to be hub of the Hamptons. Year-round, **Guild Hall** presents celebrity speakers, film festivals, and special events. Fine restaurants offer trendy menus. There's so much to do, you may not have time for the beach.

The quieter, less pricey **North Fork,** which extends 28 miles from Riverhead to Orient Point, finds new fans every year. **Atlantic Marine World** draws thousands of families to Riverhead. In season, more than a dozen vineyards are open for wine tasting.

In **Montauk,** you can tour a lighthouse commissioned by George Washington or take a whale-watching cruise. On the **North Shore** of western Long Island, the museum at **Stony Brook** houses vintage automobiles and the **Vanderbilt Mansion** captures the mood of the Gilded Age.

The list of Long Island bed-and-breakfasts is growing. Even in summer, you can find vacancies on weekends—and certainly mid-week. Consider a visit in fall, when the light is golden and Hampton beaches are at their best.

FOR MORE INFORMATION

Long Island CVB
(877) 246-5354; licvb.com

Southampton Chamber of Commerce
(631) 283-0402;
southamptonchamber.com

Greater Westhampton Chamber of Commerce
(631) 288-3337; whbcc.org

East Hampton Chamber of Commerce
631-324-0362;
easthamptonchamber.com

FREDDY'S HOUSE, Cutchogue

OVERALL ★★★★½ | QUALITY ★★★★ | VALUE ★★★★ | PRICE $125–$150

Prudence, the granddaughter of prominent local farmer John Wickham, gave up a career in nursing to continue the family's proud tradition of farming the North Fork. Dan was formerly a logger in Maryland. Freddy's House is named for J. Fred Tuthill, a neighbor who died without heirs, leaving his farm to the Wickhams. According to local lore, Freddy lived here happily with two maiden sisters, one of whom never showed her face in public after being spurned by her betrothed. The house is immaculate. A hammock in the yard beckons; paths lead to an isolated beach. It will appeal to people who enjoy peace and quiet and cherish the simple things in life.

SETTING & FACILITIES

Location 0.2 mi south of Rte. 25 in the heart of the North Fork wine district. **Near** 15 mi. east of Riverhead, 23 mi. to Atlantic Ocean beaches. **Building** 1798 Cape Cod carefully restored w/ 1880 addition, yellow siding. **Grounds** 300 acres, lawn, daisy borders, willow trees, bird feeders, cultivated farm, fruit orchards; 1700's shed, barn, & misc. buildings, dirt roads for hiking; private beach on Peconic Bay. **Public Space** Tea room. **Food & Drink** Victorian tea breakfast w/ juice, fruit, home made baked goods; specialties—ham & broccoli quiche, chilled peach soup, waffles w/ fresh fruit; often served outdoors on picnic table. **Recreation** Antiquing, wineries, beach activities, fishing, boating; bike & kayak rentals nearby. **Amenities & Services** Beach passes; family-owned produce stand; in season pick-your-own asparagus, berries, fruit, & pumpkins; autumn hayrides, corn maze.

ACCOMMODATIONS

Units 2 guest rooms. **All Rooms** Fresh flowers, alarm clock, CD player, robes, private entrance. **Some Rooms** AC (upstairs), ceiling fan (downstairs). **Bed & Bath** King (1), queen (1); private baths, 1 claw-foot tub. **Favorites** Alice's Room—large bath with antique pull toilet, tub, glass shower, wide plank floor, king bed w/ porch railing headboard, interesting oil paintings by Wickham family members. **Comfort & Decor** The parlor has a teacup wallpaper border, lace curtains, simple heirloom furniture and antiques. Moldings and paint colors are original. In the small guest rooms photos of Freddy's two unmarried sisters, art, old hats, handmade curtains, dust ruffles, and pillows add personality.

RATES, RESERVATIONS, & RESTRICTIONS

Deposit 1 night, refund w/ 14-days notice or if rebooked. **Discounts** None. **Credit Cards** None. **Check-In/Out** 3–9 p.m./11 a.m. **Smoking** No. **Pets** No. **Kids** No. **No-Nos** No arrivals after 9 p.m. **Minimum Stay** 2 nights w/ some exceptions. **Open** All year. **Hosts** Prudence & Dan Heston, 1535 New Suffolk Rd., Cutchogue, 11935. **Phone** (631) 734-4180. **E-mail** freddyshouse@aol.com. **Web** wickhamsfruitfarm.com.

J. HARPER POOR COTTAGE, East Hampton

OVERALL ★★★★★ | QUALITY ★★★★½ | VALUE ★★★ | PRICE $225–$595

In July and August, Ferraris and Mercedes move at a snail's pace along East Hampton's main thoroughfares. It will be practically impossible to get a room reservation here at the height of the summer season, anyway—so, why not wait for a quieter time to savor this premier property in the heart of The Hamptons. The location is great—across from the famous town pond and near Guild Hall, which offers cultural programs, lectures, and art exhibits year-round. You can walk to three museums. The innkeeper can bring you up-to-the-minute on which celebrities are in town—or at least where they dined the last time they visited. It's a place where guests feel like part of the in-crowd. The hospitality is extraordinary.

SETTING & FACILITIES

Location On Main St. 0.3 mile from town center, across from Guild Hall. **Near** 0.9 mi. to Atlantic Ocean beaches, 20 mi. west of Montauk, 50 mi. east of MacArthur Airport in Central Islip. **Building** 1910 Arts & Crafts built over 1648 core; Tudor half timbers, multi-paned windows, pointed gables, guardian angel door frame. **Grounds** 0.5 acre semi-walled sunken garden, ivy, boxwood, magnolia, lavender & white wisteria, flower borders, bird bath fountain, 2 patios w/ lawn chairs, antique wood door. **Public Space** Lobby, entry/library, LR, DR, breakfast room, powder room, spa. **Food & Drink** Full breakfast served buffet style plus eggs or griddle item; specialties—smoked salmon on Sundays, lemon cornmeal waffles, blueberry pancakes, vegetable frittata; light eats at 5 p.m.; tea on request; licensed bar on site. **Recreation** Cultural programs, kayaking & canoeing, water sports, fishing, golf nearby. **Amenities & Services** On-site workout equipment including treadmill, stationary flume pool, massage, spa tub, & sauna; extensive video library, laundry on request, fax & e-mail; beach passes, towels; meetings (40), weddings (120).

ACCOMMODATIONS

Units 5 guest rooms. **All Rooms** AC, TV & VCR, phone, safe, ceiling fan, hair dryer, robes, noise machines, double blackout curtains. **Some Rooms** Fireplaces (4), balcony (1). **Bed & Bath** King (1), queen (3), twin (1 set), egg crate foam avail.; all private baths, whirlpool tubs (3), claw-foot tub w/ antique plumbing (2). **Favorites** #11—garden view, spacious bath w/ spa tub. **Comfort & Decor** The inn faces busy Main Street, but the back of the house is quiet. Decor ranges from rustic to upscale. Breakfast is particularly elegant.

RATES, RESERVATIONS, & RESTRICTIONS

Deposit 50%, refund w/ 14-days notice less $10 per night. **Discounts** No. **Credit Cards** AE, V, MC, D. **Check-In/Out** 2 p.m./noon. **Smoking** No. **Pets** No (collie on premises). **Kids** No. **Minimum Stay** 3 nights in summer, 2 nights all other weekends. **Open** All year. **Hosts** Rita & Gary Reiswig, 18 Main St., East Hampton, 11937. **Phone** (631) 324-4081. **Fax** (631) 329-5931. **E-mail** info@jharperpoor.com. **Web** jharperpoor.com.

MILL HOUSE INN, East Hampton

OVERALL ★★★★ | QUALITY ★★★★ | VALUE ★★★ | PRICE $200–$425

This inn offers warmth and character from a past era overlaid with stylish modern amenities. Rooms are small, but some views include the Old Hook Mill. The porch faces a busy main thoroughfare, but you can escape to a quiet backyard. Gary is an accomplished chef whose professional kitchen offers an unusually extensive breakfast menu. Sylvia, who has a hospitality background, oversees the front of the house and makes it look easy. Her decorating style is distinctive—simple but serviceable. Younger couples and young families will feel right at home. Genuine hospitality and good food are the hallmarks of this cozy getaway.

SETTING & FACILITIES

Location Across from working windmill, 2 blocks to town center. **Near** 1.6 mi. to ocean beaches, 4 mi. to bay & harbor beaches, 20 mi. west of Montauk. **Building** 1790 Colonial saltbox, enlarged; 1896 gambrel roof, 6 sets of French doors on front porch. **Grounds** 0.5 acre, lawn, bluestone patio w/ Adirondack chairs, butterfly plants, hydrangeas, day lilies, rose of Sharon, privet hedge. **Public Space** LR, DR, porch, backyard. **Food & Drink** Extensive breakfast menu w/ 7 starters, 10 entrees plus juice, fruit, cereals, salmon platter; specialties—French toast, egg white omelet w/ fine herbs, spinach, asparagus, & mushrooms; 8 cookies & goodie jars avail. anytime; guests can bring dinner from outside & use inn cutlery. **Recreation** Beach activities, antiquing, boating, fishing, cultural programs at Guild Hall, Hampton Classic Horse Show (Aug.). **Amenities & Services** Videos, massage avail., fax & e-mail, games, puzzles, & books avail.; beach pass & towels provided; disabled access (garden room); meetings (16) w/ catering avail.

ACCOMMODATIONS

Units 8 guest rooms. **All Rooms** AC, TV & VCR, CD player, phone w/ private voice mail, hair dryer. **Some Rooms** Gas fireplace (6), ceiling fan (6), robes (2). **Bed & Bath** King (3), queen (5), daybed (1), featherbeds atop all mattresses; all private baths, 4 whirlpools. **Favorites** #7 Hampton Holiday—sky light in bathroom, whirlpool, king bed, fireplace, green & white decor. **Comfort & Decor** The living room has dark leather sofas, Asian antiques, Arts and Crafts–style mica lights and exposed ceiling beams. Dining room furniture is handcrafted American oak & French country pine. Guest rooms are small with quality details; themes include local attractions and personalities.

RATES, RESERVATIONS, & RESTRICTIONS

Deposit 50% or 1st night, refund w/ 30-days notice less 15%. **Discounts** 15% for stays over 7 days, except July & Aug. **Credit Cards** All major. **Check-In/Out** 3 p.m./11 a.m. **Smoking** No. **Pets** No. **Kids** Yes. **Minimum Stay** 3 nights on summer weekends, 2 nights off-season, 3–4 nights for holidays, special events. **Open** All year. **Hosts** Sylvia & Gary Muller, 33 N. Main St., East Hampton, 11937. **Phone** (631) 324-9766. **Fax** (631) 324-9793. **E-mail** innkeeper@millhouseinn. **Web** millhouseinn.com.

QUINTESSENTIALS, East Marion

OVERALL ★★★★ | QUALITY ★★★★ | VALUE ★★★ | PRICE **$100–$190**

This multi-talented, Jamaican-born hostess acquired a fondness for beautiful things while living in Europe and working as financial senior vice president for American Express. She is now a licensed massage therapist and skin care consultant, as well as a color image consultant. And, she loves to cook, using Jamaican vegetables from the garden to create a variety of island-style recipes. When restoring this historic house, she brought craftsmen from the island and from Mexico to help create an appealing series of rooms. Open since 1994, she has fine-tuned her skills to offer a unique B&B experience.

SETTING & FACILITIES

Location North Fork on Rte. 25. **Near** Orient State Wildlife Preserve, 8-mi. bike path, 2 mi. east of Greenport, 7 mi. west of Orient Point. **Building** 1840 Victorian w/ widow's walk, wraparound porch. **Grounds** 1 acre w/ 2-story barn, blacksmith shed, rock, vegetable, & flower gardens. **Public Space** 2 parlors, DR, library, sun deck, massage alcove. **Food & Drink** Elaborate brunch w/ fruit platter, fish & meat dish, homemade baked goods; specialties—crab w/ zucchini, quiche, fried plantains, Mediterranean salad, cornbread w/ jalapeno and cheddar, afternoon tea w/ sweet and savory fare, fruit iced tea in silver service, lace napkins. **Recreation** Golf, biking, boating, beach activities. **Amenities & Services** Videos, fax, e-mail, beach passes; on-site shiatsu, Swedish, & Thai massage, energy balancing, aromatherapy, body wraps, cardiovascular workouts; groups (20), weddings (70).

ACCOMMODATIONS

Units 4 guest rooms. **All Rooms** AC, ceiling fan, robes, alarm clock radio, fresh flowers, phone jack, chocolate, mineral water. **Bed & Bath** King (1), queen (3); 2 private baths, 2 detached baths. **Favorites** Savannah—warm peach tones, Florentine-style walls, Spanish antiques, hand-carved wood accessories, large detached private bath. **Comfort & Decor** Well-placed antiques, original art, two fireplaces and comfy furnishings fill the public rooms, and there's a classic Victorian staircase.

RATES, RESERVATIONS, & RESTRICTIONS

Deposit 50%, refund w/ 14-days notice less $25. **Discounts** Available. **Credit Cards** AE, V, MC. **Check-In/Out** 3 p.m./11 a.m. **Smoking** No. **Pets** No. **Kids** 8 and older preferred. **Minimum Stay** 2 nights on weekends, 3 nights Memorial, July 4, & Labor Day weekends. **Open** All year. **Host** Sylvia Daley, 8985 Main Rd., Box 574, East Marion, 11939. **Phone** (631) 477-9400. **Fax** (631) 477-9471. **E-mail** bandb@quintessentials inc.com. **Web** quintessentialsinc.com.

VICTORIAN ON THE BAY, Eastport

OVERALL ★★★★½ | QUALITY ★★★★½ | VALUE ★★★ | PRICE $150–$350

Feng shui played an important role in the construction from scratch of this B&B. The curved driveway, furniture placement, and accessories were chosen to maximize positive feelings—apparent from the moment you enter. The house is light, airy, and open to great water views. Entertainers Michael Bolton, Renee Taylor, and Jacqueline Smith have been guests. It's a way to get a taste of the best of Hamptons' living. By day, Fred is an estate planner, and Rosemary is Director of Admission for a nearby college. But, they enjoy running the B&B so much, they're planning to build another next door. Their goal is to give guests more than expected, and they do.

SETTING & FACILITIES

Location On Moriches Bay across from marina—0.75 mi. south of Montauk Hwy. **Near** The Hamptons, Atlantic Ocean beaches, theater, Splish Splash waterpark, Tanger Mall, wineries, Eastport antique stores. **Building** 1997 Victorian-style w/ wraparound porch. **Grounds** 2 acres, expansive lawn, flower borders. **Public Space** Piano room, LR, dining area, front & back porch, lower level gym, massage room. **Food & Drink** Full breakfast w/ juice, muffins, beverages; specialties—pancakes w/ melon, 2-inch French toast w/ baked apple, quiche w/ pear. **Recreation** Beach activities, golf, boating, biking, horseback riding, people watching; inn offers Feng Shui classes, golf outings, swing and Latin dance classes, holiday events, plus sweetheart, holistic, murder-mystery, & wine-tasting weekends. **Amenities & Services** Workout room open 24-hours w/ 2-man Universal system, bikes, treadmill, weights; massage avail.; groups (20).

ACCOMMODATIONS

Units 5 guest rooms. **All Rooms** Water view, cable TV & VCR, individual climate control, alarm, hepa filter, central vacuum system, sherry & chocolate. **Some Rooms** Balcony (1). **Bed & Bath** King feather beds (5), canopy (1), four-poster (2); all private bath w/ whirlpool. **Favorites** Master Suite—four-poster bed, balcony, large tile bath, bright (Michael Bolton stayed here). **Comfort & Decor** Big, showy furnishings, including a grand piano, create an eye-popping first impression; bold patterns offset white tile floors. Guest rooms, featuring lots of white on white, are gorgeous as well.

RATES, RESERVATIONS, & RESTRICTIONS

Deposit 50%, balance 2 weeks before arrival; credit for another stay w/ 2 weeks notice. **Discounts** Sundays through Thursdays 25%, depending on season; some Fridays on short notice; packages offered. **Credit Cards** V, MC, D. **Check-In/Out** 3 p.m./11 a.m. **Smoking** No. **Pets** No. **Kids** Age 12 and over. **Minimum Stay** 2 nights on weekends, all July & Aug.; 3 nights on holidays. **Open** All year. **Hosts** Rosemary & Fred Barone, 57 South Bay Ave., Eastport, 11941. **Phone** (888) 449-0620 or (631) 325-1000. **Fax** (631) 325-9659. **E-mail** rbarone@hamptons.com. **Web** victorianonthebay.com.

BARTLETT HOUSE, Greenport

OVERALL ★★★ | QUALITY ★★★ | VALUE ★★ | PRICE $95–$150

Michael, who was born in Ireland, recently moved to the area from Australia, while Patricia is a Long Island native. Both are newcomers to the bed-and-breakfast business. Their large Victorian house was built by John Bartlett, a New York State Assemblyman, and it remained a family residence for 60 years. Then for many years it served as a convent. Rooms on the third floor are unheated, so their water is turned off in winter. But the rest of the house offers guests an opportunity to experience the quiet season on the North Fork. There are lots of activities, including the ferry at Orient Point, which heads for Connecticut's casinos and Native American museums.

SETTING & FACILITIES

Location Residential block area, 2 blocks from downtown. **Near** Wine country, Shelter Island, The Hamptons, 75 mi. east of New York City, 8 mi. to Orient Point. **Building** 1908 manor house w/ Corinthian columns & widow's walk. **Grounds** 0.25 acre. **Public Space** LR, DR, front porch. **Food & Drink** Early coffee; buffet breakfast w/ juice, fruit, yogurt, cereal, baked goods, toast. **Recreation** Golf, hiking, sailing, swimming, biking, sightseeing; concerts, plays, art galleries, antique & nautical shops, ferry service to Connecticut. **Amenities & Services** Maps, brochures avail.

ACCOMMODATIONS

Units 10 guest rooms. **All Rooms** AC, phone, dataport. **Some Rooms** Fireplace (#2), stained glass window. **Bed & Bath** Bed sizes vary, brass headboards; some detached baths, 2 shared. **Favorites** #2 master room—Oriental carpet, fireplace, leaded window, large bath, antique tub, antique manual typewriter. **Comfort & Decor** A Dutch door at entrance and stained glass windows add interest. The extensive wood trim has been painted, and there's a fireplace. Second floor guest rooms are the most spacious, while third floor rooms are smaller (#4 and #5 have makeshift plastic closets).

RATES, RESERVATIONS, & RESTRICTIONS

Deposit 1 night, refund w/ 7-days notice in season & holidays. **Discounts** Mid week, 6-day stay earns 15% off. **Credit Cards** AE, V, MC. **Check-In/Out** 3–6 p.m./11 a.m. **Smoking** No. **Pets** No. **Kids** Over age 12. **Minimum Stay** 2 nights on weekends in season, 3 nights some holiday weekends. **Open** All year. **Hosts** Patricia & Michael O'Donoghue, 503 Front St., Greenport, 11944. **Phone** (631) 477-0371. **E-mail** bartletthouseinn@aol.com. **Web** www.greenport.com/bartlett.

HOME PORT, *Peconic*

OVERALL ★★★★½ | QUALITY ★★★★ | VALUE ★★★★ | PRICE $120–$130

Jack carves primitive bird decoys, specializing in egrets, cranes, and shore birds. He's an outdoorsman with a passion for fly-fishing. One ground-floor room is devoted to his interest in former President Teddy Roosevelt, a noted game hunter and naturalist. This masculine-looking retreat has leather furniture, mounted deer and fish, small-scale boat models, books on fishing and hunting, and antique rods, reels, and tackles. A second parlor offers a more formal ambience. Check out the wallpaper throughout the house—all chosen with taste and an eye for design. It's no surprise to learn that Pat is now a wallpaper and paint consultant at a local store.

SETTING & FACILITIES

Location Country road 0.25 mi. north of Rte. 25. **Near** Peconic Bay, Long Island Sound, wine country, town park. **Building** 1876 Victorian, wraparound porch w/ awnings. **Grounds** 1.25 acres, cultivated but relaxed garden, weeping beech tree over 100 years old, black walnut trees. **Public Space** 2 sitting rooms, DR, porch. **Food & Drink** Cont'l buffet breakfast w/ fresh fruit, juice, muffins, hot beverages. **Recreation** Host conducts 2-day fly-casting school, provides wading salt water fly-fishing guide service, & can arrange excursions to fish for striped bass, albacore, & bluefish; bike rentals delivered, kayaking tours nearby, maritime and folk art festivals, weekly winery events (summer & fall). **Amenities & Services** Seasonal summer beach pass, hair dryer avail.; meetings (12).

ACCOMMODATIONS

Units 3 guest rooms. **All Rooms** AC, robes, bottled water. **Some Rooms** Alarm clock, iron & board. **Bed & Bath** King (1), queen (1), double (1), four-poster (1); 2 shared baths, 1 tub. **Favorites** #3—king bed, lace curtains, foyer w/ book wallpaper, large bath, floral & blue design. **Comfort & Decor** The club-like main parlor has dark wood trim and evokes understated elegance. The Teddy Roosevelt parlor displays fishing and hunting paraphernalia. There's a formal dining room, an appealing porch with wicker furniture, and a hammock. Guest rooms and hallways have handsome wall coverings.

RATES, RESERVATIONS, & RESTRICTIONS

Deposit 50%, refund w/ 7-days notice less 20%. **Discounts** 1-week stay or more. **Credit Cards** No. **Check-In/Out** 2 p.m./11 a.m. **Smoking** No. **Pets** No (3 Jack Russell dogs on premises). **Kids** No. **Minimum Stay** 2 nights on weekends May through Oct., 3 nights on holiday weekends. **Open** All year. **Hosts** Pat & Jack Combs, Peconic Ln., Peconic, 11958. **Phone** (631) 765-1435. **Web** www.northfork.com/homeport.

RAM'S HEAD INN, *Shelter Island*

OVERALL ★★★★½ | QUALITY ★★★★ | VALUE ★★★ | PRICE $80–$290

What could be better than a hilltop inn on a secluded island with a gourmet kitchen, hammocks to laze in, and boats and kayaks to explore nearby creeks and harbors? You can relax under huge oak trees, play tennis on the private court, or enjoy an 800-foot private sand beach. Nearby, you can explore Mashomack Preserve, a mosaic of tidal creeks, woodland, fields, and ten miles of coastline. Come evening, the sunsets are glorious and fine dining on the deck is excellent. A plaque explains that in 1947 physicists Enrico Fermi and Edward Teller and chemist Linus Pauling were part of a meeting held here that led to remarkable developments in physics.

SETTING & FACILITIES

Location Overlooking Coecles Harbor w/ private beach. **Near** Shelter Island North Ferry & South Ferry, Mashomack Nature Preserve. **Building** 1929 Victorian. **Grounds** 5 acres of rolling lawn w/ shade trees, spectacular sunsets. **Public Space** Sun porch, DR, patio, lounge, spa. **Food & Drink** Buffet cont'l breakfast w/ fruit, juice, baked goods, hard boiled eggs; full service restaurant & bar on premises. **Recreation** Water sports, fishing, hiking in nature preserve; 2 sailboats, 1- & 2-man kayaks avail.; exercise room, sauna, Stairmaster, pool table, board games on premises. **Amenities & Services** Mooring for guest boats on first-come basis, videos.

ACCOMMODATIONS

Units 17 guest rooms. **All Rooms** AC, phone, smoke detector, deadbolt lock (TV & VCR avail.). **Some Rooms** Balcony (3). **Bed & Bath** King (8), queen (4), double (5); some private, some shared baths. **Favorites** #1—balcony w/ water view, mint green carpet, white spread, restful. **Comfort & Decor** The sunporch has a brick floor, wood stove and comfortable seating. Lots of windows and sliding glass door reveal multiple views. Guest rooms are quaint and small with pretty wicker, white furniture and floral wallpaper.

RATES, RESERVATIONS, & RESTRICTIONS

Deposit 50%, refund w/ 10-days notice. **Discounts** None. **Credit Cards** AE, V, MC. **Check-In/Out** 3–6 p.m./11 a.m. **Smoking** No. **Pets** No. **Kids** Yes. **Minimum Stay** 2 nights on weekends year round, 3 nights on holiday weekends. **Open** All year. **Hosts** Linda & James Eklund, 108 Ram Island Dr., Shelter Island Heights, 11968. **Phone** (631) 749-0811. **Fax** (631) 749-0059. **Web** shelterislandinns.com.

EVERGREEN ON PINE, Southampton

OVERALL ★★★ | QUALITY ★★★★ | VALUE ★★ | PRICE **$100–$295**

These innkeepers aimed to create a home away from home, so guests can relax. They live in a remodeled barn next door, but maintain a very hands-on presence. She decorates; he paints, gardens, and, on Sundays mornings, prepares French toast. Peter is also a golfer, who has access to tee times at courses in the area. The couple moved here from Stamford, Connecticut in 1996, after selling a residential garbage business. One standout on this property is the garden, where ample seating invites guests to enjoy the flowers and shade trees. One elm tree on the property was planted in the 1800s.

SETTING & FACILITIES

Location Residential area 2 blocks from Main St., 1 mi. south of Rte. 27. **Near** Beaches, museums, vineyards. **Building** 1860 Victorian w/ white siding, green shutters. **Grounds** 0.33 acre w/ evergreen & Japanese cherry trees, Chinese lanterns, birdbath, flower borders, hydrangeas, day lilies. **Public Space** LR/DR, kitchen, patio. **Food & Drink** Cont'l breakfast Mon.–Sat. w/ fruit, juice, coffee, muffins, cereal; on Sunday mornings French toast is added. **Recreation** Beach activities, golf, tennis, boating, antiquing, kayaking. **Amenities & Services** Massage avail., fax & e-mail, groups (25).

ACCOMMODATIONS

Units 5 guest rooms. **All Rooms** AC, phone & answering machine, ceiling fan. **Some Rooms** TV (suite). **Bed & Bath** Queen (4), full (1), four-poster (1); 2 detached baths, 1 tub (#1). **Favorites** Mahogany room—four-poster, Chinese screen, maroon lamps, bowers, wall borders, pine floor, detached private bath. **Comfort & Decor** This property houses traditional furniture, wood floors, quality carpet, reproduction antiques, wallpaper borders, a wood fireplace, patio furniture with umbrellas, and a feel-at-home kitchen. The house faces a busy street, and guest rooms are accessed via steep stairs with railings.

RATES, RESERVATIONS, & RESTRICTIONS

Deposit Prepaid in full June, July, Aug., refund w/ 10-days notice less 15%. **Discounts** AAA. **Credit Cards** AE, V, MC, D. **Check-In/Out** 4 p.m./11 a.m. **Smoking** No. **Pets** No. **Kids** Over age 12. **Minimum Stay** 2 nights on weekends in May, June, Sept., Oct.; 3 nights on weekends in July & Aug. **Open** All year. **Hosts** JoAnn & Peter Rogoski, 89 Pine St., Southampton, 11968. **Phone** (877) 824-6600 or (516) 283-0564. **Fax** (516) 283-0564. **E-mail** Rogoski@hotmail.com. **Web** evergreenonpine.com.

THE IVY SOUTHAMPTON, Southampton

OVERALL ★★★★½ | QUALITY ★★★★½ | VALUE ★★★ | PRICE $135–$325

This dynamic duo met in 1996 at their 30th high school reunion and married two years later. Her background is in fashion with stints at Ann Taylor and Donna Karin. She's a Francophile who relaxes by knitting, cooking, and gardening. A golfer, he can get valuable tee times at public courses and country clubs, even playing with guests on occasion. Together, they've created a stunningly beautiful house with eye-popping decor in public rooms and more conservative tones in the guest rooms. The cool seclusion of the garden patio or the warmth of the fireplace invite guests to enjoy afternoon refreshments or curl up with a good book.

SETTING & FACILITIES

Location Residential street 0.5 mi. north of the village. **Near** 2 blocks to railroad station, 0.25 mi. to Hampton Jitney. **Building** 1860 2-story farmhouse, reconfigured.

Grounds 0.75 acre, lawn, garden, swimming pool. **Public Space** LR, DR, powder room, pool & deck. **Food & Drink** Full breakfast w/ fresh fruit, juice, homemade muffins, gourmet coffee; specialties—4 styles of omelets, French toast w/ fruit and sausage, blueberry pancakes w/ sausage or bacon, eggs any style; afternoon wine & tea. **Recreation** Kayaking, horseback riding on the beach (beach towels provided), golf, tennis, boating, antiquing, wine tasting, biking, numerous festivals include Hampton Classic (late Aug.). **Amenities & Services** Massage avail., fax & e-mail.

ACCOMMODATIONS

Units 5 guest rooms. **All Rooms** AC, TV, individual heat, private phone line & answering machine, hair dryer, robes. **Some Rooms** Ceiling fan. **Bed & Bath** King (1), queen (4), sleigh (1), four-poster (1), feather duvets; all private baths, 3 tubs. **Favorites** #3—queen four-poster, yellow walls, floral fabric, huge armoire, ginger jar lamps, mohair throw, large tile bath w/ easy chair. **Comfort & Decor** Vibrant colors on main floor include barn siding painted butter yellow, a green staircase, and a vibrant pink dining room. Brick flooring, a fireplace, French antiques, and a 1929 baby grand piano add charm. Guest rooms are more subdued, using quality fabrics and some antiques.

RATES, RESERVATIONS, & RESTRICTIONS

Deposit 50%, refund w/ 14-days notice, less $25. **Discounts** 10% Southampton College parents. **Credit Cards** AE, V, MC, DC. **Check-In/Out** 3 p.m/noon. **Smoking** No. **Pets** No. **Kids** Over age 12. **Minimum Stay** 2 nights on weekends May–July, 3 nights on weekends Sept. &. Oct., 4 nights on major holidays. **Open** All year. **Hosts** Melody and Phillip Tierney, 244 N. Main St., Southampton, 11968. **Phone** (631) 283-3233. **Fax** (631) 283-3793. **E-mail** theivy@earthlink.net. **Web** theivy.com.

WILLOW HILL HOUSE, Southold

OVERALL ★★★ | QUALITY ★★★ | VALUE ★★★ | PRICE $90

There aren't many amenities at Willow Hill, but there's lots of warmth. Gayle made creative use of castoff furnishings and quirky spaces to create this friendly bed-and-breakfast. A homemaker and artist, her oil paintings are part of the decor. Her greenhouse burgeons with flowers and plants. After raising five children, empty nest syndrome prompted her to open her home to guests. That and the retirement of her husband, formerly a train engineer. Some guests say a visit feels like they're staying with relatives. Across the street is Willow Hill town cemetery, where tombstones remember locals who served under George Washington at the Battle of Brooklyn.

SETTING & FACILITIES

Location Heart of North Fork wine country. **Near** South shore beaches & The Hamptons, 8 mi. west of Greenport, 17 mi. west of Orient Point. **Building** 1850 country house. **Grounds** 0.5 acres w/ fish pond, barn, hammock. **Public Space** LR, DR, kitchen, powder room, greenhouse, patio. **Food & Drink** Full country breakfast; specialties—eggs any style, sausage or bacon, grits, omelets, pain perdu (French toast); beverages anytime. **Recreation** Beach activities, golf, antiquing, wineries.

ACCOMMODATIONS

Units 3 guest rooms. **All Rooms** Simple. **Some Rooms** Ceiling fan (2), AC (2). **Bed & Bath** Queen sleeper sofa (1), double (2); all rooms have detached shared bath.

Favorites Upstairs rooms. **Comfort & Decor** The dining room is the focal point. Rooms are decorated informally.

RATES, RESERVATIONS, & RESTRICTIONS

Deposit 50%, refund w/ 1-week notice or room rented. **Discounts** No. **Credit Cards** No. **Check-In/Out** 2–8 p.m./11 a.m. **Smoking** Downstairs only. **Pets** No. **Kids** Yes. **Minimum Stay** 2 nights holiday weekends. **Open** All year. **Host** Gayle Birkmier, 48850 Main Rd., Southold, 11971. **Phone** (631) 765-1575. **Web** www.bbonline.com.

INN AT BOX FARM, Water Mill

OVERALL ★★★★ | QUALITY ★★★★ | VALUE ★★★ | PRICE $275–$325

This quirky house provides guests with a taste of authentic East End history and an overlay of Hamptons' chic. You'll find stark white slipcovered chairs and sofas, French country sideboards, and unusual accessories, many purchased on world travels. Fireplaces, original wide-plank floors, Oriental carpets, and custom-made curtains add to the ambience. The house, which is listed as a Historic National Landmark, was decorated on the principal that less is more. The owner has a fine eye for detail. It's a great choice for people who appreciate quality. The expansive grounds, with lounge chairs and hammock, are a plus.

SETTING & FACILITIES

Location Rte. 27A in the center of The Hamptons. **Near** 3.5 mi. east of Southampton, 1 mi. east of Water Mill, 7 mi. west of East Hampton, 0.75 mi. to Atlantic Ocean. **Building** 1690 Colonial w/ clapboard exterior. **Grounds** 2 acres adjacent to wetlands, expansive lawn, 200-year-old trees, lounge chairs, hammock, neighboring lily pond. **Public Space** 2 LR, DR, kitchen, porch, powder room. **Food & Drink** Early coffee, full breakfast w/ fruit, juice, muffins, croissants; specialties—pancakes, waffles, eggs any style; evening wine and cheese; coffee, lemonade, snacks anytime. **Recreation** Beach activities, golf, swimming, biking, deep sea fishing, wine tasting. **Amenities & Services** Beach towels and chairs, beach permits, 6 bikes, barbecue grill, massage, videos, fax & e-mail, numerous special events; meetings (12).

ACCOMMODATIONS

Units 5 guest rooms. **All Rooms** AC, TV, fresh flowers, robes, radio, fax line. **Some Rooms** Fireplace (4), balcony and private entrance (garden room). **Bed & Bath** 5 twin sets/can be joined; 2 private baths, 3 detached private baths, 1 tub. **Favorites** Garden room—large, light-filled, lawn view, king bed, sliding door to balcony, pine floor, eclectic library; Pond room—rustic, pond view, king bed, tub. **Comfort & Decor** Stylish French antiques are blended with simple country furniture and fine art. Guest rooms feature white on white with wood trim, using quality accessories to create a clean, pleasant look.

RATES, RESERVATIONS, & RESTRICTIONS

Deposit 50%, refund w/ 14-days notice less 10%. **Discounts** No. **Credit Cards** AE, V, MC, D. **Check-In/Out** 3 p.m./11:30 a.m. **Smoking** Limited areas. **Pets** Conditional (small, good pets may be allowed). **Kids** Yes. **Minimum Stay** 3 nights July & Aug. weekends, 2 nights all other times. **Open** All year, except Jan. & Feb. **Hosts** Elaine Markolf & Gabrielle Barrett, 78 Mecox Rd., Water Mill, 11976. **Phone** (631) 726-9507. **Fax** (631) 726-3623. **E-mail** inn@boxfarm.com. **Web** boxfarm.com.

1880 HOUSE, Westhampton Beach

OVERALL ★★★★½ | QUALITY ★★★★ | VALUE ★★★★ | PRICE $150–$200

The Collins family moved here in 1972 and Elsie converted her home to a bed-and-breakfast ten years later. Her many personal antiques and family photos add warmth to this 14-room house. It has all the amenities of a perfect Hamptons' address—a pool, tennis court, and fine dining and shopping within easy walking distance. Even more important is the conscious effort to appease all five senses with pleasant-looking surroundings, classical music, a tasty breakfast, and myriad creature comforts.

SETTING & FACILITIES

Location 2 blocks to village center. **Near** Quogue, Southampton. **Building** 1890 farmhouse, remodeled. **Grounds** 1 acre w/ trees, floral borders, swimming pool, tennis court. **Public Space** LR, library, enclosed porch, pool & deck (DR avail. in winter). **Food & Drink** Full breakfast w/ fruit, juice, hot beverage, homemade baked goods; specialties—cheese soufflé, French toast, pancakes; tea, sherry, almond shortbread cookies anytime. **Recreation** Biking, fishing, golf, boating, antiquing, tennis (3 racquets & balls avail.). **Amenities & Services** *New York Times*, free local phone calls, beach parking.

ACCOMMODATIONS

Units 2 guest suites, 1 carriage house. **All Rooms** AC, TV, small fridge, robes, dried flowers, hair dryer, sitting room, heated blanket. **Some Rooms** Microwave, dishes/silverware, ceiling fan, blackout shades (carriage house). **Bed & Bath** Queen (2), antique brass bed (1); all private baths, 3 tubs. **Favorites** Kim suite—delicate floral wallpaper, marble sink; Carriage House—multiple handmade quilts, wood paneling, extra high-riser, old trunk, country knick-knacks, megaphone, colorful rag rugs, angel doll collection. **Comfort & Decor** Eclectic Victorian furnishings include caned rocker, piano, hurricane lamps, antique apothecary chest, Shaker benches, and Chinese and English porcelain. A fireplace and potbelly stove add winter warmth; the porch offers delightful summer dining.

RATES, RESERVATIONS, & RESTRICTIONS

Deposit Credit card, cancellations receive credit for another stay. **Discounts** No. **Credit Cards** AE, V, MC. **Check-In/Out** Noon/11 a.m. **Smoking** No. **Pets** No. **Kids** No. **Minimum Stay** 2 nights. **Open** All year. **Host** Elsie Collins, 2 Seafield Ln., Westhampton Beach, 11978. **Phone** (800) 346-3290 or (631) 288-1559. **Fax** (631) 288-7696. **E-mail** bb1880house@worldnet.att.net. **Web** 1880-house.com.

Part Two

New Jersey

Close your eyes. Imagine you're sitting outside enjoying the feeling of a gentle breeze. In front of you, sheep graze in a mountain-framed pasture. Or, perhaps there's an old-growth forest infused with a sense of enchantment, an isolated marshland beside a narrow horseshoe-crab-covered beach, or a quiet towpath along a historic canal.

Where are you? The British Isles, the French countryside, a remote African coast, the byways of Belgium? Guess again. You're in New Jersey.

This may be our nation's most densely populated state, but a few miles from its wall-to-wall townships, New Jersey offers surprisingly green vistas, pastoral countryside, even wilderness landscapes. The Garden State has 38 state parks, 11 state forests, 57 historic sites, 42 natural areas, and 3 national recreational areas. In the north, mountains, forests, and lakes are commonplace. In the south, pine barrens and beaches dominate.

In keeping with the its reputation as a state of commuters, you can drive straight though New Jersey, north to south, on the 148-mile New Jersey Turnpike or 173-mile Garden State Parkway. Or, you can slow down and explore the other 33,669 miles of roadways. One of the prettiest driving routes is the **Coastal Heritage Trail,** which hugs the shores of the Delaware Bay and the Atlantic Ocean. New Jersey's 127 miles of Atlantic Ocean shoreline is legendary, but there are also over 4,100 freshwater lakes, ponds, rivers, and streams. The wetland areas are a magnet for water fowl, wildlife, and birds that migrate along the Atlantic flyway.

For traveler's seeking wildlife of another kind, **Atlantic City**'s glamorous casinos and six-mile boardwalk beckon. Accommodations at the state's biggest attractions are pretty much the antithesis of a homey bed-and-breakfast. In the lobbies of casino hotels, bells, whistles, and blinking lights create a sound and light show geared to spur visitors to action. But fortunately, vacationers wishing to see Atlantic City don't have to stay there. A short drive and they can see the state's pastoral side at a country inn or enjoy small-town charm at a bed-and-breakfast.

For travellers seeking culturally, rather than financially, enriching entertainment, New Jersey has much to offer, as well. In **Madison,** the **New Jersey Shakespeare Festival** showcases works by the Bard and other world-class playwrights. **Newark** offers two world-class cultural venues, **Newark Museum** and the **New Jersey Performing Arts Center,** as well as the spectacular **Cathedral Basilica of the Sacred Heart.**

New Brunswick makes a major contribution to the arts in New Jersey. The **Jane Voorhees Zimmerli Art Museum** has a renowned collection of Russian and Soviet non-conformist art, Japanoise, and graphics. One block of the city houses both the **State Theatre** and **George Street Playhouse.** Nearby, at **Princeton University,** Orange Key tours show off the 1756 **Nassau Hall** and other architectural gems. The **Princeton University Art Museum** is a repository of classical, European, Chinese, and pre-Columbian art. Twentieth-century outdoor sculptures enliven campus lawns, while public concerts, plays, and lectures are frequent.

One last word about New Jersey's image problem. It's gotten to the point that some residents keep a list handy of native-born celebrities to impress out-of-staters. Among them are Frank Sinatra and Paul Simon, (both from Hoboken); Connie Francis, Whitney Houston, Jerry Lewis, and Eva Marie Saint (all Newark natives); Bruce Springsteen (Freehold); Bette Midler (Paterson); Jon Bon Jovi (Sayreville); Michael Douglas (New Brunswick); Meryl Streep (Summit); John Travolta (Englewood); Danny DeVito and Jack Nicholson (both from Neptune); Tom Cruise (Glen Ridge); and Joe Pesci, Bruce Willis, and Elisabeth and Andrew Shue (all from South Orange).

Their list of heavy hitters is kept in reserve: names like Thomas A. Edison, who invented the incandescent light bulb, movie camera, and phonograph in his West Orange laboratory; Edwin E. "Buzz" Aldrin, Jr., who went from Montclair to the moon; and Grover Cleveland of Caldwell, who became President of the United States—twice. Though you're not likely to see these celebrities and luminaries on your visit, you can count on finding lots of pleasant surprises—and excellent bed-and-breakfasts.

FOR MORE INFORMATION

New Jersey Commerce, Economic, & Growth Commision
20 W. State St. CN826
Trenton, NJ 08625
(609) 292-6963

B&B Innkeepers Association of New Jersey
(732) 449-3535; njinns.com

Zone 5

Northern New Jersey

Most of New Jersey's residents and major attractions are in the northern half of the state. If you're adventurous, you can float down the river through the 37-mile-long **Delaware Water Gap National Recreation Area** or the 70-mile-long **Delaware and Raritan Canal State Park.** Or, you can climb in the Kittatinny Mountains, where a monument in **High Point State Park** marks the state's loftiest point at 1,803 feet.

You can spend a quiet afternoon at the **New Jersey State Botanical Garden** at Ringwood in the Ramapo Mountains. The gardens are part of **Skyland Manor,** a 44-room English Jacobean mansion designed by John Russell Pope, who also designed the Jefferson Memorial.

From there, it is a 1.5 mile drive to **Ringwood Manor,** the nineteenth-century 51-room country estate that was home to a succession of iron masters over 200 years. The Cooper-Hewitt family furnished it with a valuable collection of Americana and paintings by artists of the Hudson River School. Today, it is open for touring.

Sterling Hill Mining Museum in **Ogdensburg** preserves the region's unique geological history, even allowing visitors to tour a mine. For Colonial history, visit the **Morristown National Historic Park,** the site of two encampments organized by George Washington during the Revolutionary War. Solider's huts and elegant mansions are showcased there now.

From April to October, **Stanhope** draws crowds to **Waterloo Village,** where concerts, craft demonstrations, and wagon tours take place against a backdrop of a recreated Lenape Indian village and Colonial dwellings.

The metropolitan center of **Newark** offers a world-class museum and cultural events. From Jersey City, there is ferry access to **Liberty State Park**, the **Statue of Liberty** and **Ellis Island.** And, **Liberty Science Center** is a family-oriented museum with 250 interactive exhibits.

Meadowland Sports Complex in **East Rutherford** is the only stadium in the country to house two NFL teams—the New York Giants and the New York Jets. The complex is also a venue for basketball, hockey, soccer, and horse racing.

Exploring **Hunterdon County,** to the west, feels a little like poking around a treasure-filled attic. Fire-engine red barns, solid stone mills, and white-steepled churches appear as pleasant surprises on the horizon. Sixty horse farms add character to the gently rolling hills and fertile valleys.

In a restored stone mill, the **Hunterdon Art Center** displays the work of local artists and craftsmen. Nearby, the **Hunterdon Hills Playhouse** presents musicals and comedies—often at matinees. Afterwards, it's worth the drive to dine at the **Frenchtown Inn,** home to one of the state's best restaurants. Frenchtown and it's riverfront neighbors are abuzz with boutiques, art galleries, and upscale eateries.

Ironically, the northern half of New Jersey has relatively few bed-and-breakfasts, and most of those thrive due to a healthy midweek corporate business.

FOR MORE INFORMATION

Skylands Tourism Council
(973) 383-7004; njskylands.com

Gateway Regional Tourism Council
(877) 428-3930

Meadowlands Chamber of Commerce
(201) 939-0707

North Jersey Chamber of Commerce
(973) 470-9300

Hunterdon County Chamber of Commerce
(908) 735-5955

Sussex County Chamber of Commerce
(973) 579-1811

Warren County Department of Economic Development and Tourism
(800) 554-8540

Hope Area Chamber of Commerce
(908) 459-5700

Lambertville Area Chamber of Commerce
(609) 397-0055

WOODEN DUCK, *Andover Township*

OVERALL ★★★★½ | QUALITY ★★★★½ | VALUE ★★★★ | PRICE $110–$175

While house hunting for a retirement home, Bob and Barbara fell in love with this beautiful 20-year-old house surrounded by peaceful woodlands. Having never stayed in a bed-and-breakfast themselves, they casually commented that it would make a good bed-and-breakfast. The seller agreed to take it off the market for six months until they got a variance from Andover Township, and the rest is history. After lots of painting and wallpapering, the inn initially opened with three guest rooms. More were gradually added. Some guests like it so much they claim to have "slept around" in each of the seven guests rooms.

SETTING & FACILITIES

Location 1.5 mi. east of Rte. 206; 9 mi. north of Rte. 80 Exit 25. **Near** Adjacent to Kittatinny Valley State Park. **Building** 1978 Colonial, white 2-story. **Grounds** 17 acres of woodlands dominated by dogwood & oak trees, in-ground pool. **Public Space** LR, DR, game room, guest kitchen, pool deck. **Food & Drink** Full breakfast w/ fruit, breads & muffins; specialties—peach French toast, egg bake w/ green chilies, omelet pie; baked goods & beverages avail. **Recreation** Hiking on 50 plus mi. of trails, mountain biking, horseback riding, fishing, birding, antiquing. **Amenities & Services** Videos, fax & modem outlet, trail maps.

ACCOMMODATIONS

Units 7 guest rooms. **All Rooms** AC, hair dryer, TV & VCR, iron & board, phone, desk, extra seating, portable fan. **Some Rooms** Fireplace (2), balcony (2), private entrance (2). **Bed & Bath** Queen (7), four-poster (2), sleigh (1); private baths, two-person soaking tubs (2), quality fixtures. **Favorites** Golden Eye & Harlequin—both have 2-sided gas fireplace, soaking tub, CD player, private porch, skylight, woodland view. **Comfort & Decor** Surrounded by nature, you'll enjoy watching the activity at birdfeeders outside the dining room window. Tasteful, comfortable furnishings fill spacious rooms. No opportunity is missed in carrying out the duck theme—books, pictures, decoys, and plaques all add color. Guest rooms are named mallard, canvas back, ruddy duck, harlequin, pintail, etc.

RATES, RESERVATIONS, & RESTRICTIONS

Deposit 1 night, refund w/ 7-days notice. **Discounts** Corp. **Credit Cards** AE, V, MC, D. **Check-In/Out** 2–8 p.m./11 a.m. **Smoking** No. **Pets** No. **Kids** Over age 8. **Minimum Stay** 2 nights holiday weekends. **Open** All year. **Hosts** Barbara & Bob Hadden, 140 Goodale Rd., Newton, 07860. **Phone** (973) 300-0395. **Fax** (973) 300-0395. **Web** woodenduckinn.com.

MAIN STREET MANOR, Flemington

OVERALL ★★★★ | QUALITY ★★★★ | VALUE ★★★ | PRICE $95–$135

These hosts restored a Queen Anne house before tackling this large Victorian home, once the social hub of Flemington and home to its mayor. They are avid collectors of authentic antiques and continually trade up for more valuable pieces. One prize possession is a handsome reclamier (fainting couch). "I like to do things nicely," says Elinor, who serves breakfast on her grandmother's china, using antique silver and damask napkins. Her family history in New Jersey goes back to the 1700s. She learned inn-keeping skills by osmosis while watching her mom run an informal bed-and-breakfast for relatives on the Jersey shore each summer.

SETTING & FACILITIES

Location 0.5 block from Rtes. 112 & 31. **Near** Outlet shopping, vineyards, New Hope, PA. **Building** 1901 Victorian mansion, restored. **Grounds** 0.75 acre w/ flower garden, roses. **Public Space** Front parlor, side parlor, DR, guest pantry, porch. **Food & Drink** Cont'l breakfast mid-week, full breakfast weekends; fresh fruit, beverages; specialties—Belgian waffles, omelets, baked eggs w/ 3 cheeses, zucchini frittata. **Recreation** Public golf course, wineries, state parks, Northlantz model railroads. **Amenities & Services** VCR, microwave, speaker phone, fax, flip chart, modem-ready outlets; meetings (20).

ACCOMMODATIONS

Units 5 guest rooms. **All Rooms** AC, ceiling fans, alarm clocks, phones, pillow-top mattresses, handmade afghans & quilts. **Some Rooms** 1 balcony, 1 window seat. **Bed & Bath** Queen beds, four-poster (1), sleigh (1); private baths, 1 tub. **Favorites** Thomas Edison—sleigh bed, rosewood furniture, lace curtains, oak armoire, claw-foot tub, peach quilt. **Comfort & Decor** Attention is paid to perfect placement of antiques and quality reproductions, *Gone-With-the-Wind* lamps and chandeliers help achieve a sense of purity. A gas-burning fireplace adds coziness.

RATES, RESERVATIONS, & RESTRICTIONS

Deposit 50% of first night, refund w/ 2-days notice less $15 (7-days notice on holidays). **Discounts** AAA, corp. **Credit Cards** AE, V, MC. **Check-In/Out** 2–8 p.m./11 a.m. **Smoking** No. **Pets** No (2 cats on premises, but not in guest area). **Kids** Over age 12. **Minimum Stay** 2 nights for some holidays. **Open** All year. **Hosts** Dennis & Elinor Lengle, 194 Main St., Flemington, 08822. **Phone** (908) 782-4928. **Fax** (908) 782-7229. **E-mail** innkeeper @mainstreetmanor.com. **Web** mainstreetmanor.com.

CROSSED KEYS, Green Township

OVERALL ★★★ | QUALITY ★★★★ | VALUE ★★★ | PRICE $130–$185

This bed-and-breakfast was reopened in May 1999 by a couple who also run a successful catering business in Cedar Knolls, so you can expect super breakfast menus. Lovely paintings accent attractive eighteenth-century furnishings in a large parlor, comfortable reading room, and hallways. A stone cottage overlooks a formal flower garden often used for wedding parties. Be sure to ask if a private function is scheduled during your stay, or you may find 100 people milling around and the lawn sprouting huge tents. If not, you're apt to be left on your own and have the run of this lovely setting.

SETTING & FACILITIES

Location Facing Rte. 03. **Near** Newton, Kittatinny Valley State Park. **Building** 1730 farm estate w/ additions. **Grounds** 12.5 acres with pond, old stone wall, swing, birdhouses. **Public Space** Large formal LR, library, DR, sunporch, back porch, formal garden. **Food & Drink** Country breakfast; specialties—vegetable frittata, blueberry pancakes, blintz soufflé, French toast; afternoon snacks. **Recreation** Horseshoes, fishing, chess, videos. **Amenities & Services** Meetings (25).

ACCOMMODATIONS

Units 4 guest rooms, 1 cottage. **All Rooms** Perfumes, wit & wisdom books. **Some Rooms** High beds w/ stools, TV. **Bed & Bath** All well-appointed; private baths, cottage has 2-person whirlpool tub. **Favorites** Meadows—large closed porch, four-poster canopy bed, TV. **Comfort & Decor** Lots of good art, a marble-faced fireplace, and nice carpets enhance the property.

RATES, RESERVATIONS, & RESTRICTIONS

Deposit 1 night, refund w/ ample notice. **Discounts** Corp. **Credit Cards** AE, V, MC. **Check-In/Out** 2–9 p.m./11 a.m. **Smoking** No. **Pets** No. **Kids** No. **Minimum Stay** 2 nights on weekends. **Open** All year. **Hosts** Katherine & Celso Rodriguez, 289 Pequest Rd., Andover, 07821. **Phone** (973) 829-9922. **Fax** (973) 829-1636. **Email** info@crossed keys.com. **Web** crossedkeys.com.

INN AT MILLRACE POND, Hope

OVERALL ★★★★ | QUALITY ★★★★ | VALUE ★★★ | PRICE $120–$170

A sense of Moravian and Colonial character permeates this property. The inn is located in a village founded in 1769 by Moravians. (Followers of John Huss began this Protestant sect in Saxony in 1722.) The gristmill supplied flour to George Washington's army when it was camped at Jockey Hollow in Morristown. You'll see the skeleton of a 100-year-old water wheel and a stream flowing through the building in a narrow stone channel. The only thing plastic to interfere with the sense of time travel in your room will be a touch-tone telephone. The hosts, both graduates of Princeton University, set high standards for quality and add their own genial hospitality.

SETTING & FACILITIES

Location Junction of Rtes. 519 & 521, 1 mi. south of Rte. 80, Exit 12. **Near** Land of Make Believe, Delaware Water Gap, Jenny Jump State Park, Waterloo Village. **Building** 1769–70 Colonial stone gristmill; wheelwright's cottage & millrace house dating from the early 19th century, conference center. **Grounds** 24 hilly acres, partially wooded w/ pond. **Public Space** 2 parlors, library, game room, 65-seat restaurant. **Food & Drink** Cont'l breakfast served by the hosts in on-site restaurant w/ juice, hot beverages, fresh fruit, hot & cold cereal, muffins & croissants; afternoon tea on request; special requests met w/ prior notice; fine-dining restaurant serves upscale comfort food by candlelight; tavern on lower level. **Recreation** Hiking, public golf courses, antiquing, tennis court on property w/ rackets, crafts fair, Christmas Fair. **Amenities & Services** Fax & e-mail, walking tour maps, groups (25).

ACCOMMODATIONS

Units 16 guest rooms, 1 suite. **All Rooms** A/C, phone. **Some Rooms** 1 fireplace (#4), 10 TV & VCR. **Bed & Bath** Queen (15), twin (2), canopy (4), four-poster (3), loft (1); private baths, 17 tubs, 5 whirlpools. **Favorites** #5—four-poster bed, chenille spread, dust ruffle, red/white check curtains, crocheted accessories—like visiting your great grandmother. **Comfort & Decor** Parlors are austere but pleasant, capturing the quiet simplicity of Colonial life. Guest rooms have clean, pure lines and quality details. Comfortable beds, wide-plank wood floors, Oriental carpet; tailored curtains dress up white-washed walls; stenciling adds color. Old-fashioned iron door latches look authentically Colonial. Good lighting; but limited closet space.

RATES, RESERVATIONS, & RESTRICTIONS

Deposit 1 night by credit card, refund w/ 7-days notice. **Discounts** Sun.–Thur. **Credit Cards** AE, V, MC, DC, D, CB. **Check-In/Out** 3 p.m. on/noon. **Smoking** No. **Pets** OK w/ prior approval. **Kids** All ages. **No-No's** Open fires. **Minimum Stay** 2 nights on weekends late April–New Years. **Open** All year except Christmas Day **Hosts** Charles & Cordie Puttkammer, Box 359, Hope, 07844. **Phone** (800) 746-6467 or (908) 459-4884. **Fax** (908) 459-5276. **E-mail** millrace@epix.net. **Web** innatmillracepond.com.

CHIMNEY HILL FARM, Lambertville

OVERALL ★★★½ | QUALITY ★★★★ | VALUE ★★★ | PRICE $95–$295

Enjoy songbird sounds and woodland views in this patrician-looking home high above the Delaware River. Make yourself at home in the gracious living room and light-flooded fieldstone sunporch. Tastefully chosen accessories create the feeling that you're house-sitting for a rich relative. Guests in the main house have the sun as their only alarm clock. The absence of phones and TVs is also a plus. However, guest room quality varies; third floor rooms look like servant quarters. Innkeeper Mary Kay Fischer is gracious and friendly, giving guests the run of the house. She knows from experience that most guests want to be left alone. Up-to-date barn suites show a decorator's eye for rustic elegance and provide even more privacy as well as the sense of being close to nature. Look out your window to see squirrels and maybe some deer.

SETTING & FACILITIES

Location Hilltop site in semi-isolated area 0.5 mi. from junction of Rtes. 29, 179, & 518. **Near** The Delaware River separating Lambertville, NJ & New Hope, PA. **Building** 1820 stone-faced country house. **Grounds** 8 acres of woodlands, sunken garden, greenhouse, apple cellar, rebuilt barn, carriage house; apple, tulip, holly trees. **Public Space** Large LR, DR, powder room, fieldstone sunporch, butler's pantry. **Food & Drink** Candlelight cont'l breakfast included; full breakfast additional $15 (skip this and head for town); hot entrees include pancakes w/ fruit, or French toast on weekends; homemade cookies, sodas, tea, sherry, cider, or lemonade avail. **Recreation** Board games, backyard swing, hiking, horseback riding, biking, boating on the Delaware Canal, antiquing, vineyards, theater. **Amenities & Services** Laundry, fax & e-mail, special diets accommodated; meetings (20–100).

ACCOMMODATIONS

Units 8 guest rooms, 4 suites. **All Rooms** AC, fresh flowers, robes. **Some Rooms** Balcony (1), fireplace (8), private entrance (4), TV & VCR (4), hair dryer. (8), separate phone line (4), computer access (4). **Bed & Bath** King (3), queen (9), ceiling canopy (3), four-poster (3); 3 private detached baths, 3 tubs, one 2-person shower w/ stereo; note that some main house fixtures & doors creak, but barn suite plumbing is state-of-the-art. **Favorites** Garden Room #5—fireplace, stenciled walls, pretty floral fabrics; Library #6—full canopy bed (both #5 & #6 are in a separate, quiet wing); suites #3 & #4—loft bedroom, double-sided fireplace, double whirlpool. **Comfort & Decor** The attractive living room with fireplace, grand piano, silver tea service, comfortable seating, wide-plank wood floors, and Persian carpet invites socializing. There's an overall feel of English country elegance. Old-fashioned door latches and family portraits add distinction.

RATES, RESERVATIONS, & RESTRICTIONS

Deposit 1 night or 50% for longer stay. **Discounts** AAA, corp., seniors. **Credit Cards** AE, V, MC. **Check-In/Out** 3 p.m./11 a.m. **Smoking** No. **Pets** No. **Kids** Over age 12. **No-No's** No coolers or candles. **Minimum Stay** 1 night Sun.–Fri., 2 nights if Sat. requested. **Open** All year. **Hosts** Terry & Rick Anderson, owners; Mary Kay & Harry Fischer, innkeepers, 207 Goathill Rd., Lambertville, 08530. **Phone** (609) 397-1516. **Fax** (609) 397-9353. **E-mail** chbb@erols.com. **Web** chimneyhillinn.com.

CHESTNUT HILL ON THE DELAWARE, Milford

OVERALL ★★★★½ | QUALITY ★★★★½ | VALUE ★★★★ | PRICE $90–$150

Linda and Rob collect old photographs, Victorian antiques, vintage clothing, flotsam from the Delaware River and friendships. Most of the 200-plus teddy bears displayed throughout the three-story main house were gifts from contented guests. Many regard this house as a haven from the storms of life. Room diaries are filled with testimonials from guests who feel cared for and safe, even touched and blessed to be here. Linda and her staff put a lot of effort into keeping the house looking fresh for the many repeat guests. If asked, she can go beyond her traditional role, giving good advice on nutrition, lifestyle, and spiritual well-being. After nearly two decades, these innkeepers still find joy in their work and it shows.

SETTING & FACILITIES

Location Facing the Delaware River at the Milford Upper Black Eddy Bridge. **Near** Bucks County, Frenchtown, New Hope. **Building** 1860 main house w/ rounded Neo-Italianate windows, Victorian wrought iron trim w/ acorn details, tall windows, large veranda; 1830 smaller house w/ gingerbread trim. **Grounds** 1 acre includes 40-foot waterside deck w/ benches, private dock located across infrequently used freight railroad tracks (trains run about 5 mph & warnings are sounded, but deaf guests could be in danger); 3 picnic areas; fountain garden w/ caladium, snap dragons, vegetables, parsley border, tiger lilies, roses. **Public Space** Drawing room, parlor, DR, veranda, powder room. **Food & Drink** Full breakfast w/ fresh fruits, homemade baked goods; specialties—German apple pancakes, tomato mushroom pie, omelets w/ goat cheese, corn, & spinach; cookies & beverages avail. mid-day & bedtime. **Recreation** Boating, canoeing, tubing, kayaking, fishing for catfish, bass, shad, & more; some guests swim in the river (floating chairs, rafts, & hammocks avail.); antiquing, Lambertsville's Shad Festival (April). **Amenities & Services** Accommodate special celebrations & dietary needs; massage therapist avail., videos, faxes received; meetings (12).

ACCOMMODATIONS

Units 6 guest rooms, 1 cottage. **All Rooms** AC, fresh flowers, hair dryers. **Some Rooms** TV (4), phone (4), tabletop waterfalls; access to third floor rooms is via steep, narrow stairs w/ ample railings. **Bed & Bath** Bed sizes vary; decor themes include

Pineapple, Peaches & Cream, Bayberry, Rose Garden; 5 private baths, 3 tubs, 1 whirlpool; all baths have rubber duckies & colorful decor. **Favorites** Teddy's Place—a fantasy experience for the young-at-heart w/ more than 60 small bears in outfits, fixtures, children's books & art; Country Cottage—fireplace, whirlpool, private entrance, veranda, TV & VCR, four-poster featherbed, full kitchen stocked for cook-your-own breakfasts, country French furnishings w/ teal, aqua, & peach accents, carousel horses theme. **Comfort & Decor** You'll find extraordinary attention to detail throughout the house. The formal drawing room has an upright piano, a display cabinet of conversation pieces, a family Bible, lace curtains, bowers, and mannequins dressed in vintage Victorian gowns. The smaller parlor has cozy seating by a wood-burning fireplace. Enjoy great river views.

RATES, RESERVATIONS, & RESTRICTIONS

Deposit 1 night. **Discounts** Corp., extended stays. **Credit Cards** No. **Check-In/Out** 3 p.m./11 a.m. **Smoking** No. **Pets** No. **Kids** Over 12. **Minimum Stay** 2 nights on weekends w/ Sat. **Open** All year. **Hosts** Linda & Rob Castagna, 63 Church St., Milford, 08848. **Phone** (908) 995-9761. **Fax** (908) 995-0608. **E-mail** chhillinn@aol.com. **Web** chestnuthillnj.com.

WHISTLING SWAN INN, Stanhope

OVERALL ★★★★ | QUALITY ★★★★ | VALUE ★★★★ | PRICE $95–$150

These are well-organized hosts. Room notebooks contain thorough data on local sporting events, attractions, and eateries. Explanations and labels are everywhere to help you get oriented. If you're too tired to go out, almost-room-service allows you to order pizza with free delivery. Cable TV with 60 channels and 70 movies on video are available. This inn is very much a team effort. Both hosts were project managers for AT&T in Chicago before retiring to their new career 14 years ago. The swan theme is promoted everywhere, including on vases, doorstops, salt and pepper shakers, an umbrella stand, and the wood trim on a reproduction fainting couch. Joe says they chose the theme because swans are territorial, elegant—and they mate for life.

SETTING & FACILITIES

Location Quiet street in rural village, 1 mi. from Rte. 80, exit 27B. **Near** Waterloo Village, Sterling Hill Mine, Morristown Revolutionary War sites, U.S. Equestrian Team, Delaware Water Gap, Lake Hopatcong. **Building** Streamlined 1905 Queen Anne–style neo-classic Victorian, gray & white. **Grounds** 1 acre w/ Victorian garden, fountain, tulips, daffodils, butterfly plants, ferns, tea roses, native New Jersey plants. **Public Space** Entry foyer, front & back parlor, DR, bathroom, three-sided wraparound porch. **Food & Drink** Buffet-style breakfast w/ fruit, yogurt, juice, cereal, homemade breads, hot entrée from inn's recipe book; specialties—oatmeal, waffles, poultry sausage, Italian strata; carry-out breakfast on request. **Recreation** Geraldine Dodge Poetry Festival every other September; antiquing, horseback riding, rafting, swimming, ice skating, ice fishing. **Amenities & Services** Daily newspapers, *New York Times* on weekends; laundry/dry cleaning service, copy machine, message taking, fax; meetings (10).

ACCOMMODATIONS

Units 10 guest rooms. **All Rooms** AC, iron & board, hair dryer, TV & VCR, phone, dataport. **Some Rooms** Sitting room, 2 TVs, fridge. **Bed & Bath** Queen beds, private baths. **Favorites** Third floor rooms are best; Stillwater—large period dresser, gable, peach tones, 1940s items such as handheld mirror, family photos, antique radio; Lenape—pretty blue & yellow patchwork quilt, fringe lamp, claw-foot tub. **Comfort & Decor** Enjoy a log-burning fireplace in the foyer each morning and a gas-burning fireplace in back. Tables are available for fair-weather dining on the porch; there are also a swing, rocking chairs, and 2 hammocks. An apothecary cabinet and stained glass panels give the dining room special flair and family photos add interest, as does handsome woodwork with spindles.

RATES, RESERVATIONS, & RESTRICTIONS

Deposit 1 night, refund w/ 2-days notice, 7-days on holidays. **Discounts** Corp., 15% Sun.–Thur.; 7th night free on full week stay. **Credit Cards** AE, V, MC, D, DC. **Check-In/Out** 1–8 p.m./11 a.m. **Smoking** No. **Pets** No, can arrange kennel off premises. **Kids** 12 and over. **Minimum Stay** 2 nights in Sept. and Oct. & holiday weekends. **Open** All year. **Hosts** Paula Williams & Joe Mulay, 110 Main St., Stanhope, 07874. **Phone** (973) 347-6369. **Fax** (973) 347-3391. **E-mail** wswan@worldnet.att.net. **Web** whistlingswaninn.com.

STEWART INN, Stewartsville

OVERALL ★★★½ | QUALITY ★★★★ | VALUE ★★★★ | PRICE $95–$125

This innkeeper has had multiple careers including town mayor, tax collector, race car competitor, and glider plane pilot. An avid collector of animals, both real and stuffed, her prodigious indoor menagerie includes small hens, cats, pigs, sheep, and every critter you can imagine. There are conversation pieces everywhere, creating a pleasing clutter in the foyer and all public rooms. Even the dining room mantle is filled with tiny animals, birds, and tea sets. While living in luxury, you'll awaken to the crow of a real rooster to eat farm-fresh eggs for breakfast. Outside, giant evergreen trees give the hint of an enchanted forest.

SETTING & FACILITIES

Location 0.2 mi. from Rte. 78, Exit 4 (westbound), 5 mi. to the Delaware River. **Near** Bethlehem, PA, Delaware Water Gap. **Building** 1770 fieldstone-faced Georgian style. **Grounds** 16 acres w/ 2 barns, swimming pool, trout stream; farm animals include llama, pony, goats, sheep, ducks. **Public Space** LR, DR, kitchen, screened porch, patio, pool deck. **Food & Drink** Full breakfast w/ fruit, fresh sausage or bacon, buttermilk pancakes, eggs; cake, cookies, & beverage avail. for snacks. **Recreation** Hiking, canoeing, biking. **Amenities & Services** Disabled access (1), iron & board avail., laundry, fax, modem-ready, meetings (14).

ACCOMMODATIONS

Units 7 guest rooms. **All Rooms** AC, TV, phone, fridge. **Some Rooms** Fireplace (3). **Bed & Bath** King (1), four-poster (6); private baths (some detached), 7 tubs. **Favorites** #4—four-poster, big sitting room, nice wall hanging; #5—fireplace w/ Beatrice Potter tiles, pretty quilt, animal collectibles, sunny. **Comfort & Decor** The house is beautifully furnished with light-hearted collectibles everywhere (some would call it cluttered). There's a delightful pool area. Some guest rooms can be joined to create suites.

RATES, RESERVATIONS, & RESTRICTIONS

Deposit None. **Discounts** Corp.; one person pays just $75. **Credit Cards** AE, V, MC, DC. **Check-In/Out** 3 p.m. on/11 a.m. **Smoking** No. **Pets** No. **Kids** Over age 10. **Minimum Stay** 2 nights on holiday weekends. **Open** All year. **Hosts** Lynn McGarry, Box 6, Stewartsville, 08886. **Phone** (908) 479-6060. **Fax** (908) 479-4211.

WOOLVERTON INN, Stockton

OVERALL ★★★★ | QUALITY ★★★★ | VALUE ★★★ | PRICE $100–$265

This well-worn gentleman's farm is run by three young ex-Chicagoans (two ex-bankers and a former photo archivist) who scoured the East Coast for the perfect inn to manage. Carolyn, Mark, and Matthew bring style, humor, and hands-on attention to their new profession. Mark is a pottery enthusiast and Matthew studied art and photography, so it's no surprise art and pottery enliven the public rooms. You hear no road noise, only the calming sound of twittering songbirds. Pastoral views come complete with two well-fed sheep (Betty and Pate). Yet just minutes away you'll find surprising sophistication. The knowledgeable hosts will steer you to fine dining, world-class wines, theater, and art galleries.

SETTING & FACILITIES

Location Country road 10 mi. from Rte. 29. **Near** Walk to Delaware and Raritan Canal State Park & towpath; drive to New Hope, Flemington, Peddler's Village. **Building** 1792 Colonial-style stone manor house; early-Victorian additions w/ mansard roof, tall windows. **Grounds** 10 acres of rolling woodlands facing PA hills; sheep pen and pasture; spring house, carriage house, dual-entry stone barn; antique yew trees, apple grove, trellised rose garden; herb & cutting gardens; adjacent to 300-acre state-protected farm. **Public Space** Colonial-style parlor w/ log-burning fireplace, DR, long porch, guest pantry. **Food & Drink** Full country breakfast w/ fruit, juice, muffins; specialties—French toast, vegetable frittata, apple-turkey sausage, German-style puff pancakes w/ sautéed apples; afternoon tea w/ homemade baked goods. **Recreation** Biking, tubing, hiking, museums, antiques, wineries, art & craft studio tours by appointment. **Amenities & Services** Health club access, in-room massage avail., fresh flowers, dinner reservations; meetings (15).

ACCOMMODATIONS

Units 8 guest rooms, 1 cottage. **All Rooms** AC, featherbeds, fresh flowers, terry robes, bottled water, chocolates. **Some Rooms** Light-blocking shades (5), fireplace (4). **Bed & Bath** A mix of king & queen beds w/ canopy (3) & four-poster (1); 7 private baths, 2 detached baths, 3 whirlpools, 7 tubs. **Favorites** Dorothy's Alcove—blue accents, Chinese jar, pretty trim; Amelia's Room—canopy bed, fireplace, and sitting room; Cottage—stained glass, exposed beams, private entrance/garden, four-poster canopy bed, 2-person shower, log-burning fireplace. **Comfort & Decor** The inn has an overall look of country elegance. The parlor features a mix of antiques and overstuffed down seating with a grand piano, wood-burning fireplace, and Oriental carpets. Floor-to-ceiling windows have great views Quality framed prints and photos are interesting accessories. Guests rooms are attractive, but sound-proofing is poor and whirlpools create annoying noise.

RATES, RESERVATIONS, & RESTRICTIONS

Deposit 1 night or 50% of stay. **Discounts** Packages avail. **Credit Cards** AE, V, MC. **Check-In/Out** 3 p.m./11 a.m. **Smoking** No. **Pets** No. **Kids** Over 12. **Minimum Stay** 2 nights if Sat. included. **Open** All year. **Hosts** Matthew Lovette, Mark Smith, Carolyn McGavin, 6 Woolverton Rd., Stockton, 08559. **Phone** (888) 264-6648 or (609) 397-0802. **Fax** (609) 397-0897. **E-mail** woolinn@voicenet.com. **Web** woolvertoninn.com.

ALPINE HAUS, Vernon

OVERALL ★★★ | QUALITY ★★★½ | VALUE ★★★ | PRICE **$110–$180**

Location makes this property a success. It's just down the road from a major recreation complex that functions as a ski area in winter and morphs into a water park in summer. Golf courses add to the mix of activities nearby. The innkeepers are keen to provide a friendly atmosphere where guests can get to know each other. The ambience—a Swiss chalet with basic comforts—will appeal to a more active crowd. There are lots of steep steps, so older folks in search of a quiet atmosphere and spacious rooms would be happier elsewhere. But fun-loving younger couples who just need a clean bed and a warm breakfast will appreciate the proximity to activities and the chance to meet other like-minded folks.

SETTING & FACILITIES

Location Adjacent to Mountain Creek Resort on Rte. 94. **Near** Sussex County airport, Wywananda State Park, Appalachian Trail 2 mi. away. **Building** 1887 4-story Federal-style Victorian painted green w/ cream trim. **Grounds** 7 acres of hilly landscape overlooking Vernon Valley, small pond. **Public Space** LR, DR, family room, upper & lower back deck. **Food & Drink** Full breakfast; specialties—French toast, quiche, ham dandy; beverages on request. **Recreation** Waterpark, downhill skiing & snowboarding, birding. **Amenities & Services** Massage, disabled access, sprinkler system, fax & e-mail.

ACCOMMODATIONS

Units 8 guest rooms, 2 suites. **All Rooms** AC, TV, phone, dataport. **Some Rooms** fireplace (2), private entrance (2); coffee pot, fridge, hair dryer in suites only. **Bed & Bath** Queen (7), double (2), twin (1), canopy (1), four-poster (2); private baths, 2 whirlpool tubs. **Favorites** Forget-Me-Not—four-poster bed, blue decor w/ lace curtains (some road noise); Alpine Pink—antique bed, sunny; Buttercup suite—bed and couch, gas fireplace, TV, whirlpool. **Comfort & Decor** Guest rooms are named for wildflowers—Snowberry, Lilly-of-the-Valley, Edelweiss, Alpine Jasmine, etc. Decor is minimal. "Closets" are poles with hangers.

RATES, RESERVATIONS, & RESTRICTIONS

Deposit 1 night; refund w/ 3-days notice or re-rented. **Discounts** None. **Credit Cards** AE, V, MC. **Check-In/Out** 3–9 p.m./11 a.m. **Smoking** No. **Pets** No. **Kids** All ages if well-behaved. **No-No's** Candles. **Minimum Stay** 2 nights on holidays. **Open** All year. **Hosts** Jack & Allison Smith, 217 Rte. 94, Vernon, 07462. **Phone** (973) 209-7080. **Fax** (973) 209-7090. **E-mail** alpinehs@warwick.net. **Web** alpinehausbb.com.

Zone 6

The Jersey Shore

In the 20,000-acre Brigantine division of the **Edwin B. Forsythe National Wildlife Refuge,** you can explore the tidal salt meadow and marsh via an eight-mile dirt road, a former raised railroad bed now called Wildlife Drive. In the foreground, herons, black ibis, terns, red wing black birds, and egrets vie for attention. Butterflies flit among yellow mullen, thistle, and white Queen Anne's lace. Five miles across the bay, the faint outline of Atlantic City's skyline is etched in the horizon.

The **Noyes Museum** near the refuge's entrance is worth a brief stop to see galleries devoted to duck decoys and carvers. Another eco-tourism attraction is the **Marine Mammal Stranding Center** in Brigantine, which responds to calls about stranded whales, dolphins, seals, and sea turtles.

South of Atlantic City is **Leamings Run Gardens and Colonial Farm** where a one-mile, self-guided tour through 30 acres of pine barrens passes 25 themed gardens of annual flowers. Forested spaces between each garden provide a pleasant interlude of shadow and shade. Signs advise visitors to "please look back" and get a different perspective.

The **Wetlands Institute** in Stone Harbor overlooks 6,000 acres of state-protected coastal marsh, upland, and barrier islands. You can explore the area on the boardwalk trail or join a group canoe or kayak safari. And, nearby is **Ocean City**'s 2.5 mile boardwalk, with rides, fun, and food.

For overcast days, inland attractions include **Batsto Village** and the surrounding **Wharton State Forest,** where you can hike, canoe, horseback ride, hunt, and fish. Batsto is the site of a former bog-iron and glassmaking industrial center (1766–1867) which early settlers created because local lands were too sandy for farming. They fashioned bog-iron, made from water, pine needles, and a sandstone composite, into everything from cannon balls to camp kettles. On a walk through the 36-room Italianate mansion at Batsto, you learn about owner Joseph Wharton, and the huge Cohansey aquifer, an underground lake of potable water which still sits under the property he amassed.

From Wharton State Forest, you can explore one of the state's great natural treasures, the **New Jersey Pinelands,** which occupies 22 percent of the state's land area. But, nobody should venture into the remote region without good preparation—including a map, compass, and cell phone.

One of the most unique beaches on the Jersey Shore is at **Ocean Grove,** where both mansions and Main Street have made an impressive comeback. Each spring, original camp meeting tents are still set up in a semicircle around the 1893 Great Auditorium. Religious meetings, concerts, and general entertainment promote family values and old-fashioned fun.

Island Beach State Park, a pristine strip of barrier island, stretches from Seaside Park to Barnegat Inlet and between the Atlantic and Barnegat Bay. At its northernmost tip is "Old Barney," the much-photographed 172-foot-high Barnegat lighthouse and museum. Farther north, **Twin Lights State Historic Site** in Highlands offers a dramatic hilltop view of New York Harbor and a chance to tour two 1862 brownstone lighthouses.

For action, head for **Seaside Heights** where the wall-to-wall amusements include rides at **Casino Pier** and **Water Works Park.** Nearby, **Freehold Raceway** is the oldest and fastest daytime half-mile harness racing track in the country. Or, travel to **Six Flags Great Adventure Theme Park & Wild Safari** in Jackson to see 1,200 animals from six continents without leaving your car. Kids will enjoy the amusement rides and musical performances.

In all, the Jersey Shore region boasts 35 beaches and boardwalks, and many of its towns are in the midst of refurbishing. Bed-and-breakfasts are plentiful and popular—both established standbys and delightful newcomers. But remember, there's more to explore than the beach.

FOR MORE INFORMATION

Shore Region Tourism Council
(732) 544-9300

Atlantic Highlands Chamber of Commerce
(732) 872-8711; atlantichighlands.org

Belmar Chamber of Commerce
(7732) 681-2900; belmar.com

Highlands Chamber of Commerce
(732) 872-8711

Manasquan Chamber of Commerce
(732) 223-8303

Ocean Grove Chamber of Commerce
(800) 388-GROV (732) 774-1391

Spring Lake Chamber of Commerce
(732) 449-0577; springlake.org

ATLANTIC VIEW INN, Avon-by-the-Sea

OVERALL ★★★½ | QUALITY ★★★½ | VALUE ★★★ | PRICE **$90–$265**

These innkeepers raised three children, both come from big families (with a total of ten siblings)—and they still like having people around. So, they opened their inn in 1999. Nita, a former culinary director at Bloomingdales, says she wants to create a place that guests never want to leave. She likes to offer birthday and anniversary surprises—perhaps a heart-shaped chocolate cake with candles at breakfast or an ordered-at-cost gift basket. "Basically, most people are overworked and overstressed and just need a little bit of extra care and special attention. They need to be pampered, and it doesn't take much extra effort," she says. Who could argue with that?

SETTING & FACILITIES

Location Quiet residential street. **Near** 200 feet to the beach, 30 min. to Six Flags Great Adventure. **Building** 1900 3-story frame beach house w/ blue shutters & awnings, wraparound porch. **Grounds** City lot w/ manicured lawn & flower beds. **Public Space** LR, DR, porch. **Food & Drink** Full breakfast w/ juice, fresh fruit, homemade muffins; specialties—pecan French toast, fresh vegetable strata, Belgian waffles w/ warm berry compote; afternoon refreshments include fresh-baked cookies, hot & cold beverages; special requests. **Recreation** Horseback riding & bicycles trails at Allaire State Park; sailing, fishing, golf, Ocean Grove concerts, Belmar seafood festival, volleyball tournaments nearby. **Amenities & Services** Massage therapy (on & off site), fax & e-mail, guest fridge; meetings. (25).

ACCOMMODATIONS

Units 11 guest rooms, 2 suites. **All Rooms** AC, ceiling fan. **Some Rooms** Phone (10), fireplace (2), balcony (1). **Bed & Bath** King (3), queen (4), double (2), twin (2), canopy (4); all rooms have featherbed mattress & down comforter; 10 private baths, 3 detached baths, 2 tubs, 1 whirlpool. **Favorites** Newport—crisp blue & white wall covering and chintz fabric, wicker seating, nice bath w/ tub, white metal four-poster queen bed, lace pillow case; Avon by the Sea—yellow & blue floral decor, fireplace, blue & white tile bath, double whirlpool, small balcony, ocean view. **Comfort & Decor** The house has high ceilings and good bones. The decor, which includes some family heirlooms, is rather sparse. The emphasis is on comfort. Guest rooms have shore themes with pleasant-sounding names like Martha's Vineyard, Savannah, Nantucket, and Key West.

RATES, RESERVATIONS, & RESTRICTIONS

Deposit 50%, refund w/ 10-days notice. **Discounts** Off-season packages w/ entertainment or activities included. **Credit Cards** AE, MC, V, D. **Check-In/Out** 2–8 p.m./11 a.m. **Smoking** No. **Pets** No (yellow lab and cat on premises). **Kids** 2 suites only. **Minimum Stay** 3 nights on July & Aug. weekends, 2 nights midweek July, Aug., & fall weekends. **Open** All year. **Hosts** Nita & Pete Rose, 20 Woodland Ave., Avon-by-the-Sea, 07717. **Phone** (732) 774-8505. **Fax** (732) 869-0187. **E-mail** nita@monmouth.com. **Web** atlanticview.com.

AVON MANOR INN, Avon-by-the-Sea

OVERALL ★★★½ | QUALITY ★★★½ | VALUE ★★★ | PRICE $65–$200

Greg opened this inn in 1998, but he continues to do some consulting work in the fiber optics industry. He was a golf instructor for 15 years, but had to retire from full-time teaching due to a shoulder injury. However, that doesn't stop him from putting his golf expertise to work helping his guests improve their games. Working on a small putting green in the backyard, he enjoys giving complimentary lessons on request. As for the overall experience, he wants to make sure everyone finds their niche—whether it's curling up in a quiet, private corner to relax, or being gregarious and interacting with other guests. It's your choice. He has compiled a thorough description of area activities. You're in good hands with this personable young man.

SETTING & FACILITIES

Location Residential neighborhood, 1 block from beach, 4 blocks from town. **Near** Allaire State Park, Six Flags Great Adventure, Monmouth & Freehold race tracks, wineries. **Building** 1907 Colonial Revival w/ wraparound porch, green & white striped awnings. **Grounds** City lot, small lawn w/ some flowers. **Public Space** LR, DR, veranda, small putting area. **Food & Drink** Full breakfast w/ juices, fruit, hot beverages; specialties—raspberry-chocolate crêpes, Mexican omelet, cashew pancakes, 2 guest fridges, water cooler avail.; picnic lunch baskets avail. at minimal cost. **Recreation** Beach activities, boating, antiquing, theater in Spring Lake & Ocean Grove; 8 bikes (1 tandem) & golf clubs avail., Christmas tours, wine tastings. **Amenities & Services** Massage, fax & e-mail, beach badges, chairs, umbrellas & towels, barbecue, use of cooler and picnic basket; complimentary golf lesson, golf excursions & instruction; meetings (30), weddings. (75).

ACCOMMODATIONS

Units 9 guest rooms, 1 suite. **All Rooms** AC, cable TV, clock radio. **Some Rooms** VCR (3), ceiling fan (2), mini-fridge (3), private entrance (suite). **Bed & Bath** King (1), queen (8), twin (1 set), 1 sleigh; 2 shared baths, 2 tubs, 1 double whirlpool. **Favorites** Bye Bye Birdie—king bed, futon couch, TV, golf art, green decor (guys will love it). **Comfort & Decor** The spacious living room has a gas fireplace and entertainment alcove with a 52" TV and video library. Chestnut oak paneling enhances the dining room. Overall, the house has a lived-in look. You won't be afraid to stretch out and put your feet up. Guest rooms have whimsical names, reflecting the host's sense of humor.

RATES, RESERVATIONS, & RESTRICTIONS

Deposit 50%, refund w/ 14-days notice or re-rented less $20. **Discounts** Midweek, quiet season specials. **Credit Cards** AE, V, MC, D. **Check-In/Out** 2 p.m./11 a.m. **Smoking** No. **Pets** No. **Kids** Limited. **Minimum Stay** 2 nights July & Aug. weekends. **Open** All year. **Hosts** Greg Dietrich, 109 Sylvania Ave., Avon-by-the-Sea, 07717. **Phone** (732) 776-7770. **Fax** (732) 776-7476. **E-mail** gregmav@aol.com. **Web** avonmanor.com.

CASHELMARA, Avon-by-the-Sea

OVERALL ★★★½ | QUALITY ★★★★ | VALUE ★★★ | PRICE $83–$276

Cashelmara is a Gaelic word for house by the sea. Although the sea is just around the corner, the sound of water that you hear is a waterfall placed in the lake by this inn's owner, Marty Mulligan. He lifeguarded locally as a young man, then worked as a Kodak sales representative. These days, he's mostly an absentee innkeeper, spending part of his time at the Corner Stone, another B&B he owns in Landenberg, Pennsylvania. However, he has spared no expense in acquiring unique amenities to please his guests—some of whom have been regulars since the inn opened. Mary Wiernasz does a good job of keeping the place looking ship shape and see worthy.

SETTING & FACILITIES

Location North border of Avon, facing Sylvan Lake, across from ocean beach. **Near** 55 mi. south of New York City, 65 mi. north of Atlantic City, 55 mi. east of Philadelphia, 22 mi. east of Six Flags Great Adventure. **Building** 1901 Greek Revival, gray w/ white pillars, white trim, green shutters, striped awning. **Grounds** Large city lot w/ shrubs, flower beds, hanging baskets, topiaries. **Public Space** Large foyer, 2 parlors, DR, breakfast room, Mulligan's Victorian theater, 2 guest amenity areas, front veranda. **Food & Drink** Full breakfast w/ juice, fruit, hot beverages, freshly baked muffins, meats, selection of 5 entrees including the Cashel McMara sandwich (a toasted English muffin w/ pork, tomato, melted cheese). **Recreation** Boating, charter fishing, golf, horseracing, tennis, swimming, summer music events; beach towels, chairs, umbrellas, windbreakers, & badges provided; movie room has 80-inch screen surround-sound TV. **Amenities & Services** Videos & DVD, massage avail., fax & e-mail, computer access, *New York Times*; meetings (20).

ACCOMMODATIONS

Units 12 rooms, 2 suites. **All Rooms** AC, cable TV. **Some Rooms** Ceiling fan (12), fireplace (7), mini-fridge (7), private entrance (1). **Bed & Bath** King (4), queen (6), double (3), twin set (1), canopy (1), four-poster (1); private baths, 2 whirlpools, 2 tubs. **Favorites** #20—antique four-poster king bed, large armoire, gas fireplace, butternut & blue tones w/ red accents, small bath; #12—suite, four-poster queen canopy bed, double whirlpool, gas log fireplace, elaborate drapes, Victorian antiques, leather sofa, Tiffany-style lamp, fridge, TV & VCR. **Comfort & Decor** The formal arrangement of maroon velvet sofas and chairs, sideboards, bronze statuary, antique clocks, an oversized hall tree, and stained glass windows includes many museum-quality antiques. This is high Victoriana—a bit chichi for a beach setting these days. The theater, also with comfortable velvet seating, is great fun, including the Laurel and Hardy carvings and reproduction wall sconces. Guest rooms are nicely done, but baths are ordinary.

RATES, RESERVATIONS, & RESTRICTIONS

Deposit 50%, refund w/ 10-days notice or re-rented. **Discounts** 5% cash or check, 10% 4 nights or more (except summer & holidays). **Credit Cards** V, MC, D. **Check-In/Out** 2–9 p.m./11 a.m. **Smoking** No. **Pets** No (2 golden retrievers on premises). **Kids** Yes. **No-No's** Sleeping bags. **Minimum Stay** 3 nights summer weekends, 2 nights summer midweeks, off-season weekends, July 4 & Labor Day. **Open** All year. **Hosts**

Martin J. Mulligan, owner; Mary Wiernasz, resident innkeeper, 22 Lakeside Ave., Avon-by-the-Sea, 07717. **Phone** (800) 821-2976 or (732) 776-8727. **Fax** (732) 988-5819. **Web** www.avon-by-the-sea.com/cashelmara.

INN-TO-THE-SEA, Avon-by-the-Sea

OVERALL ★★★★ | QUALITY ★★★★ | VALUE ★★★★ | PRICE $100–$255

John calls Roberta the Martha Stewart of the Jersey Shore because she decorates, oversees the gardening, and prepares gourmet breakfasts, while he does the major hosting, handles the phone calls, and oversees the finances. After he retired as an engineer from Bell Labs and she finished mothering six children, the couple became full-time, hands-on innkeepers. "We thought we had the skills to do a good job," says John, and many guests agree. If you're looking for a picture-perfect living space, enjoy the sounds of classical music, and appreciate good hospitality, you'll enjoy this quiet corner property with easy access to the beach.

SETTING & FACILITIES

Location 400 yards to beach, 5 mi. east of Garden State Parkway Exit 9; 55 mi. south of New York City, 55 mi. east of Philadelphia. **Near** Sandy Hook Lighthouse, Twin Lights of Navesink Museum, Monmouth Park Race Track, PNC Arts Center, historic Allaire Village, Six Flags Great Adventure. **Building** 1890s Queen Anne Victorian w/ turret, arched entry. **Grounds** City lot w/ shrubs, flowers, manicured lawn. **Public Space** Entry hall, LR, DR, powder room, large wraparound porch. **Food & Drink** Full breakfast w/ juices, fresh fruit, hot beverages, baked goods, egg soufflé. **Recreation** Swimming, surfing, fishing, jogging, golf, antiquing, boating, whale watching, concerts, theater, historic sites; bikes, beach badges, & chairs avail.; special events include 5-K race, volleyball tournaments, Italian festival, craft fair, nightly concerts in summer. **Amenities & Services** Videos, outdoor shower (for beach-goers), fax & e-mail; meetings (12), weddings (25).

ACCOMMODATIONS

Units 8 guest rooms. **All Rooms** AC, TV & VCR, clock radio, phone w/ dataport, small fridge, ceiling fan. **Some Rooms** Fireplace (3), ocean view (4). **Bed & Bath** King (3), queen (4), twin (1), four-poster (1), all have featherbed mattress; private baths, 1 double whirlpool, 2 double showers. **Favorites** #2—king bed, ocean view, turret seating area, fireplace, double shower, fridge, TV. **Comfort & Decor** Attractive Victorian-era wall coverings, chestnut staircase, cherry wood and tile fireplaces, antiques, wooden floors with Oriental carpets, and cut glass accessories create distinction. Family photos add warmth.

RATES, RESERVATIONS, & RESTRICTIONS

Deposit 1 night or 50%, refund if rented less $25. **Discounts** 10% 4 nights or more, 15% 7 nights or more. **Credit Cards** AE, V, MC, D. **Check-In/Out** 2–8 p.m./11 a.m. **Smoking** Porch only. **Pets** No. **Kids** No. **Minimum Stay** 2 nights on weekends June–Sept.; 3 nights on major holidays. **Open** All year. **Hosts** Roberta & John Gunn, 101 Sylvania Ave., Avon-by-the-Sea, 07717. **Phone** (732) 775-3992. **Fax** (732) 775-2538. **E-mail** john@inntothesea.com. **Web** inntothesea.com.

INN AT THE SHORE, Belmar

OVERALL ★★★ | QUALITY ★★★½ | VALUE ★★★ | PRICE $105–$135

Couples looking for seclusion are better off coming here in winter. In summer the property is family-oriented, with plenty of games and CDs, plus three drawers of family-type videos to watch. Public rooms are very spacious and furnishings are geared to a casual, relaxed style—even a bit worn in spots. Nice touches include the gas fireplace, large dollhouse, and books featuring the paintings of Norman Rockwell. Like many area residents, Tom is Irish. Before opening their inn in 1993, he worked for J.C. Penny and Rosemary was a secretary. Wedding pictures of their three children are prominently displayed along with family photos. A small aquarium in the dining room is also a focal point.

SETTING & FACILITIES

Location 0.5 block walk to Silver Lake, 2 blocks to ocean beach. **Near** 22 mi. east of Six Flags Great Adventure. **Building** 1880 Country Victorian w/ wraparound porch. **Grounds** City lot w/ brick patio. **Public Space** LR, DR, guest pantry, patio w/ gas grill. **Food & Drink** Full breakfast w/ juice, fruit, baked goods; specialties—crème brûlée French toast, sunrise pancakes w/ vanilla cream syrup & bacon or sausage, homemade granola. **Recreation** Antiquing, fishing, live theater, beach activities, sporting events, seafood festival (June), kite festival (Sept.); 5 bikes avail.; beach badges, chairs, towels, & blankets provided. **Amenities & Services** Videos; massage, fax & e-mail avail.; informal murder mystery weekends held here Oct. & April; meetings & weddings (40).

ACCOMMODATIONS

Units 12 guest rooms. **All Rooms** AC, phone w/ dataport, robes & slippers. **Some Rooms** Cable TV (3), VCR (3). **Bed & Bath** King (4), double (5), twin (3); 3 private baths, 9 shared baths, 1 tub. **Favorites** Maureen Grace—beachy look, shells, stripes, twin beds w/ chenille spreads, multi-patterned chair, beach chair wall border; Emily Dickenson—one wall has wallpaper w/ her poetry, video of "The Belle of Amherst." **Comfort & Decor** The tone is casual and the look is old-fashioned. Many guest rooms are very small and in some cases the furniture is a tight fit. All guest rooms are named for family members and friends. The innkeeper collects dolls.

RATES, RESERVATIONS, & RESTRICTIONS

Deposit 1 night, refund w/ 14-day notice. **Discounts** 10–15% Sept. 15–May 15. **Credit Cards** AE, V, MC. **Check-In/Out** 2 p.m./noon. **Smoking** Porch only. **Pets** No. **Kids** Yes, all ages. **Minimum Stay** 4 nights major holidays, 3 nights June, July, & Aug. weekends; 2 nights all other weekends for rooms w/ private bath. **Open** All year. **Hosts** Rosemary & Tom Volker, 301 4th Ave., Belmar, 07719. **Phone** (732) 681-3762. **Fax** (732) 280-1914. **E-mail** volker@aol.com. **Web** theinnattheshore.com.

MORNING DOVE, Belmar

OVERALL ★★★★ | QUALITY ★★★½ | VALUE ★★★ | PRICE $100–$200

The hostess is a Baltimore native and former system's leader and business analyst for IBM. For ten years, in her spare time, she volunteered at the national crisis hotline, helping people overwhelmed by personal problems. She won awards for this important work. The key, she says, is active listening, helping people identify their real problem, then helping them examine different ways to solve it. Opening this bed-and-breakfast in 1999 was an opportunity to put her other talents to work: gardening, decorating, baking, furniture refinishing, cross stitching, and, of course, good people skills. The location is mesmerizing, as light reflected from the lake changes the mood hour by hour.

SETTING & FACILITIES

Location Faces Silver Lake. **Near** Sandy Hook Lighthouse, Twin Lights of Navesink Museum, Monmouth Park Race Track, PNC Arts Center, historic Allaire Village, Six Flags Great Adventure. **Building** 1895 summer cottage, 3 story, peach stucco w/ teal trim. **Grounds** City lot w/ sculpted hedges, floral borders, hanging flower baskets. **Public Space** LR, DR, solarium, piano alcove, front porch, outdoor shower, guest fridge. **Food & Drink** Early coffee; full breakfast w/ juice, fruit, home-baked goods, cereals; specialties—French toast, eggs Mexicana, cheese blintzes; traditional afternoon refreshment is dove-shaped sugar cookies and beverages; chocolate candy in each room. **Recreation** Dinner cruises, ocean fishing, antiquing, horse racing, living history at Allaire Park, Six Flags Great Adventure, seafood festival, kite festival, concerts, volleyball tournaments; puzzles, books, games, TV & VCR in parlor; beach chairs, bird books & binoculars avail. **Amenities & Services** Massage avail.; meetings (15).

ACCOMMODATIONS

Units 6 guest rooms, 2 suites. **All Rooms** AC, ceiling fan. **Some Rooms** Lake/ocean view (4). **Bed & Bath** King (4), queen (1), double (3), brass (1); private baths, 1 double whirlpool, 2 claw-foot tubs. **Favorites** Goldfinch—pale yellow print, cheery; Swan suite—love seat w/ bay window, nice view, double whirlpool. **Comfort & Decor** Fireplace and comfy furnishings are inviting. Collections include bells and ceramic glass. The breezy front porch is a popular place to congregate and dine. Guest rooms are named for birds that migrate through this area.

RATES, RESERVATIONS, & RESTRICTIONS

Deposit Greater of 50% or one night. **Discounts** Midweek. **Credit Cards** AE, V, MC. **Check-In/Out** 3–7 p.m./11 a.m. **Smoking** No. **Pets** No. **Kids** No. **Minimum Stay** Second floor rooms are 2 nights on weekends, 3 nights on Memorial & Labor Day holidays. **Open** All year. **Host** Carol Lee Tieman, 204 Fifth Ave., Belmar, 07719. **Phone** (732) 556-0777. **E-mail** info@morningdoveinn.com. **Web** morningdoveinn.com.

SEASCAPE MANOR, Highlands

OVERALL ★★★★ | QUALITY ★★★★ | VALUE ★★★★ | PRICE $95–$150

Pay careful attention to the driving directions, because this secluded property is a bit difficult to find. It's well worth the ride, once you're there surrounded by nature. (You may even see deer grazing on the lawn.) Trees and shrubs frame a distant view of the sea and a sliver of beach. At night, you have a front row seat for a bug chorus that includes frisky crickets and a frog or two. The house has an interesting history.

Built by an attorney named Benjamin Trask, it was the site of notable parties during prohibition, because the location allowed easy access to bootleg liquor arriving by boat on nearby beaches. The current owners are two sisters and the husband of one—all with day jobs in the computer field. It's a great find—a place to relax, restore, and recreate.

SETTING & FACILITIES

Location Hilltop 230 ft. above sea level w/ distant view of Sandy Hook Gateway National Recreation Area and the Atlantic Ocean. **Near** 8 mi. east of Red Bank. **Building** Late 1889 Georgian Colonial Revival w/ gray siding, brown shutters, 1928 addition. **Grounds** 2 acres: upper half w/ lawn & stately oak trees, small lily pond w/ fishing, decorative garden, 3 picnic tables, 5 neighborhood deer; lower half overgrown w/ brush & vines. **Public Space** LR, large deck w/ tent. **Food & Drink** Full breakfast w/ fresh fruit, juices, just-baked breads & muffins, hot beverages; specialties—waffles, French toast, soufflés, crêpes. **Recreation** Boating, tennis, golf, whale watching, fishing; Monmouth Race Track, Navesink Lighthouse, ranger-led program at Gateway National Recreation Area, 16 mi. of ocean & bay beaches at Sandy Hook, ferry to Manhattan; use of volleyball net, tree swing, horseshoes, board games. **Amenities & Services** Videos, massage & laundry avail., fax & e-mail; meetings (12).

ACCOMMODATIONS

Units 4 guest rooms. **All Rooms** AC, TV & VCR, robes. **Some Rooms** Ceiling fan (3), balcony (2), private entrance (1). **Bed & Bath** Bed sizes vary; private baths (1 detached), 2 tubs, 1 double soaking tub. **Favorites** Precious Moments—lilac, green, & white decor, ocean view from bed, painted dresser, Aubusson carpet, tile bath, double soaking tub by picture window, Texas star quilt, live plants. **Comfort & Decor** The focal point of the living room is a Mercer tile fireplace, which is joined by wood floors, a grandfather clock, and eclectic antiques. Collections include Precious Moments figurines, ginger jars, cut glass figurines, and books on American Indians, the Civil War, and fitness. Whimsical stuffed animals are perched throughout the house. Hallways are narrow. The breakfast setting is extraordinary, including tiny border lights, individual tables set with candles and begonias, and a dramatic ocean view. It's like a party in the morning.

RATES, RESERVATIONS, & RESTRICTIONS

Deposit 1 night for up to 3-night stays, 25% for longer stays; refund w/ 7-days notice less $25. **Discounts** Corp., longer stays. **Credit Cards** AE, V, MC. **Check-In/Out** 1–9 p.m./11 a.m. **Smoking** No. **Pets** No (3 manor cats: Gatsby, Molly, & Robin Hood). **Kids** Over age 8. **Minimum Stay** 2 nights on holidays. **Open** All year. **Hosts** Robert Adamec, Gloria Miller, & Sherry Ruby, 3 Grand Tour, Highlands, 07732. **Phone** (732) 291-8467. **Fax** (732) 872-7932. **E-mail** sherryruby@worldnet.att.net. **Web** www.bbianj.com/seascape.

NATHANIEL MORRIS INN, Manasquan

OVERALL ★★★ | QUALITY ★★★★ | VALUE ★★★ | PRICE $90–$185

The inn is named for Nathaniel Morris, a local judge and early developer of the Jersey Shore. It was built by William Longstreet, son of Confederate General James Longstreet. The property has a colorful history. In the 1930s it housed the Spruce House Restaurant and Tea Room. During World War

II, it provided lodging for soldiers, sailors, and travelers. It's also been a summer home for a wealthy Philadelphia family, a dress factory, and private residence. The current owners moved here in 1997 because a hurricane destroyed their home in the Virgin Islands. Joe collects antique Kodak cameras, Italian Deruta porcelains, old postcards, bird cages, and CDs. Of the 150 vintage cameras, the oldest dates from 1892. His 700 CDs are available for guests to use. Look, touch, enjoy is the motto here.

SETTING & FACILITIES

Location On Rte. 71. **Near** Next door to Spring Lake, 3 blocks to New Jersey Transit train station, 0.75 mi. to beach, 15 mi. east of Six Flags Great Adventure. **Building** 1882 Carpenter Gothic. **Grounds** City lot w/ shaded lawn, flowering bushes. **Public Space** Front parlor, LR, DR, breakfast room, shade porch, 2nd floor porch. **Food & Drink** Full breakfast served buffet style, separate tables; specialties—crème brûlée French toast, Italian French toast, breakfast burritos. **Recreation** Bikes, beach badges, towels, & chairs provided. **Amenities & Services** Videos, fax & e-mail, internet access; privileges at the Atlantic Club (2 mi. away); pick up at train station.

ACCOMMODATIONS

Units 6 guest rooms. **All Rooms** AC, TV, ceiling fan. **Some Rooms** Balcony (3). **Bed & Bath** Queen (6), four-poster (1), antique brass (2); private baths, 1 tub. **Favorites** #324—high four-poster bed, balcony; #230—gable window, damask spread, 2 wingback chairs, dresser as sink, old postcards of local scenes framed. **Comfort & Decor** The innkeepers call it real furniture, with some family heirlooms. Guest rooms have numbers that refer to significant addresses in their lives.

RATES, RESERVATIONS, & RESTRICTIONS

Deposit 50%, refund w/ 10-days notice less $25. **Discounts** American Legion VFW, corp. **Credit Cards** No (deposit only). **Check-In/Out** 2–7 p.m./11 a.m. **Smoking** No. **Pets** No (cat named Thurmond on premises). **Kids** Over age 12. **Minimum Stay** 2 nights on weekends April 15–Oct. 15; 3 nights on holiday weekends. **Open** All year. **Hosts** Barbara & Joe Jackson, 117 Marcellus Ave., Manasquan, 08736. **Phone** (732) 223-7826. **Fax** (732) 223-7827. **E-mail** joej@monmouth.com. **Web** nathanielmorris.com.

CARRIAGE HOUSE, Ocean Grove

OVERALL ★★★★½ | QUALITY ★★★★½ | VALUE ★★★★ | PRICE $80–$150

To make your stay more pleasant, these hosts redesigned an 18-room house with two bathrooms to create a more spacious eight-room house with eight bathrooms. They added new walls, fireplaces, and a dining room, plus upbeat, elegant furnishings. The result of these interior changes is beautiful. Now they have plans for the exterior. Visitors to this unique community can attend a full schedule of dynamic speakers, classical concerts, and inspiring lecturers. You can stroll on an old-fashioned boardwalk and enjoy a renovated business district. Kathi, a former nurse, and Phil, who continues to work in the corporate world, invite you to leave your hectic lifestyle behind and enjoy this revitalized town—and the fruits of their labors.

SETTING & FACILITIES

Location In the historic district. **Near** 1 block south of Main St., 1 block from the ocean. **Building** 1920 Victorian w/ mansard roof. **Grounds** Large city lot w/ shrubs & floral borders. **Public Space** LR, DR, guest kitchen. **Food & Drink** Full breakfast w/ juice, fruit, hot beverages; specialties—kugel, quiche, bread pudding, sausage strata w/ vegetables; spontaneous treats. **Recreation** Bikes avail. (3), beach towels & chairs provided, beach badges avail. at a reduced price. **Amenities & Services** Videos, massage avail., fax & e-mail; meetings (20), weddings. (25).

ACCOMMODATIONS

Units 8 guest rooms. **All Rooms** AC, TV, phone, alarm clock, candy, bottled water, fresh flowers. **Some Rooms** Fireplace (6), balcony (2). **Bed & Bath** Queen (6), twin (1), full (1); private baths, 1 tub. **Favorites** #1—French art, toile spread, fireplace, partial ocean view from balcony. **Comfort & Decor** The living room has a Southampton look—fresh and crisp with elegant French & English antiques and accessories. Steep steps lead to the renovated basement dining room where guests eat breakfast on Limoge china seated at separate tables. Most guest rooms offer an easy chair in front of a cozy fire plus quality amenities. Ocean views are partial, with other buildings and phone lines in the foreground.

RATES, RESERVATIONS, & RESTRICTIONS

Deposit 50%, refund w/ 14-days notice. **Discounts** Extended stay. **Credit Cards** V, MC. **Check-In/Out** 2–9 p.m./11 a.m. **Smoking** No. **Pets** No. **Kids** No. **Minimum Stay** In summer, 2 nights on weekends, 3 nights on holidays. **Open** All year. **Hosts** Kathleen & Phil Franco, 18 Heck Ave., Ocean Grove, 07756. **Phone** (732) 988-3232. **Fax** (732) 988-9441. **E-mail** carriagehouseog@aol.com. **Web** carriagehousenj.com.

MELROSE, Ocean Grove

OVERALL ★★★★ | QUALITY ★★★★ | VALUE ★★★★ | PRICE **$85–$175**

These hosts are known for their elaborate Christmas decor, which wins them a city award for excellence every year that they're eligible. Guests are welcome to lend a hand with this project, which begins just after Thanksgiving. Other perks to consider are the outdoor cookouts on Memorial Day, July 4, and Labor Day weekends, when guests can indulge in hot dogs, hamburgers, bourbon baked beans, cole slaw, and all the trimmings as part of the regular tariff. And, if you're staying over Thanksgiving weekend, expect an invite to join the family for turkey dinner at no extra charge. No need to inquire about the source of the dense arrangement of antiques and accessories. The hosts own two antique shops in Lambertville, which means everything you see in the house is literally for sale.

SETTING & FACILITIES

Location Residential street in the historic district, 1.5 blocks to ocean. **Near** Asbury Park, Freehold. **Building** 1895 Victorian cottage w/ turret. **Grounds** City lot w/ floral border, fountain. **Public Space** Small sitting alcove, 2 reading nooks, 3rd floor TV room, 3 porches. **Food & Drink** Full breakfast w/ fruit, juice, hot beverages; specialties—homemade cinnamon swirl bread made into almond French toast, eggnog pancakes w/ cranberries in merlot, southwestern egg bake w/ homemade fries & fresh biscuits. **Recreation** Tennis, golf, shuffleboard, fishing, deep sea charters, bike rentals nearby, spring & fall flea markets, Christmas holiday house tour, chocolate lovers weekend (Feb.). **Amenities & Services** Videos, massage avail., fax & e-mail; meetings (15), weddings. (24).

ACCOMMODATIONS

Units 10 guest rooms. **All Rooms** AC, ceiling fan. **Some Rooms** Gas fireplace (3), sauna (1), microwave & fridge (8). **Bed & Bath** King (1), queen (7), full (2); 9 private baths, 1 private detached, 1 tub. **Favorites** English Drawing Room—faux bookshelf wallpaper, tapered dresser, English oak spool headboard, stenciled English settee. **Comfort & Decor** Ground floor sitting alcove and breakfast room have an original tin ceiling, appealing French Provincial & American antiques, plus a handmade grandfather clock & gas fireplace. Spaces are tight. Upstairs halls and alcoves are cleverly used and attractively furnished. Painted wood floors add a beachy look.

RATES, RESERVATIONS, & RESTRICTIONS

Deposit 1 night, refund w/ 7-days notice. **Discounts** 5th consecutive night or more 20%. **Credit Cards** AE, V, MC. **Check-In/Out** 3–8 p.m./11 a.m. **Smoking** No. **Pets** Yes, but call first. **Kids** Yes. **Minimum Stay** 2 nights on weekends May 15–Sept. 15. **Open** All year. **Hosts** Don Margo & Randy Bishop, 34 Seaview Ave., Ocean Grove, 07756. **Phone** (800) 378-9004. **Fax** (732) 774-9004. **E-mail** melroseog@aol.com. **Web** melroseog.com.

OCEAN PLAZA, Ocean Grove

OVERALL ★★★★★ | QUALITY ★★★★ | VALUE ★★★★ | PRICE $75–$190

The porches are key at this bed-and-breakfast. Built on three levels, they offer views of the Atlantic Ocean, a wide, grassy expanse lined with Victorian cottages, and Ocean Grove's 6,000-seat Great Auditorium, home to religious, cultural, and entertainment events. In summer, rocking chair enthusiasts have a nearly front row seat for musical concerts in the town's oceanside bandstand a few doors away. The house was once owned by a founding father of this Methodist community, which was chartered in 1870. The current owners have been officers and trustees of Ocean

Grove's Camp Meeting Association. Not only did Jack save this house from dereliction, but his skills as a building contractor helped renovate a religious retreat and young people's temple nearby. This focus of the entire town is on spiritual renewal.

SETTING & FACILITIES

Location Facing the pathway to the auditorium. **Near** 1 block to the ocean, 45 mi. south of Newark Airport. **Building** 1870 Victorian w/ wraparound porch, 4 stories. **Grounds** Corner city lot. **Public Space** Parlor, breakfast room in winter, 3 porches. **Food & Drink** Cont'l breakfast w/ 2 juices, fruit, yogurt, cereals, homemade breads & muffins, coffee, tea; help yourself to tea, cookies, & chocolates anytime. **Recreation** Beach activities, biking, golf, tennis, concerts, auditorium programs, full schedule of summer events. **Amenities & Services** Videos, massage avail., disabled access, fax & e-mail; meetings (20).

ACCOMMODATIONS

Units 16 guest rooms, 2 suites. **All Rooms** AC, TV, phone, alarm clock, ceiling fan. **Some Rooms** Private porch (2). **Bed & Bath** Queen (15), twin (3); private baths, 6 tubs. **Favorites** #11—wicker seating, floral fabrics, Avenue view; #16—pine chest, antique wicker, wall stenciling, own large porch; Stokes suite—private porch, mini-kitchen, bigger bath. **Comfort & Decor** The elegantly furnished living room includes a baby grand piano, antique love seat, a grandfather's desk, and antique family portraits. There are no particularly Victorian items. High windows are uncurtained to maximize the views and let in more light. The indoor dining area, with wicker seating, is small, but the porches are magnificent. Instead of headboards, all beds have some sort of wall painting above them.

RATES, RESERVATIONS, & RESTRICTIONS

Deposit 30% within 30 days, refund w/ 14-days notice less $25. **Discounts** Off-season. **Credit Cards** AE, V, MC, D. **Check-In/Out** 2–9 p.m./11 a.m. **Smoking** No. **Pets** No. **Kids** Yes. **Minimum Stay** 3 nights on weekends, 2 nights on weekdays May 15–Sept. **Open** All year. **Hosts** Val & Jack Green, 18 Ocean Pathway, Ocean Grove, 07756. **Phone** (888) 891-9442 or (732) 774-6552. **Fax** (732) 869-1186. **E-mail** oplaza@aol.com. **Web** ogplaza.com.

ASHLING COTTAGE, Spring Lake

OVERALL ★★★½ | QUALITY ★★★★ | VALUE ★★★ | PRICE $110–$325

Opened in 2000, this inn is the new kid on the block. The property, which needed work, is getting a gradual facelift. The innkeepers returned to the Jersey Shore from Westport, Connecticut, because Bill's roots are in nearby Avon. After 20 years as a corporate relocater, Joanie was also ready for a change. It took them ten years to find Ashling Cottage. For now, Bill, who once worked for General Electric, continues to do consulting work and hosts only on weekends. Nevertheless, their first season was a success. Already they were named one of the ten great getaways in a spring issue of *Travel & Leisure* magazine. The inn fits right in with the serenity and beauty of Spring Lake.

SETTING & FACILITIES

Location 1 block to ocean & lake. **Near** Sandy Hook Lighthouse, Twin Lights of Navesink Museum, Monmouth Park Race Track, PNC Arts Center, historic Allaire Village, Six Flags Great Adventure. **Building** 1877 Victorian Cottage, cream siding w/ white trim. **Grounds** Large city lot w/ flower border, trellis, hanging baskets. **Public Space** Foyer, LR, DR, glass-enclosed sunporch, front porch. **Food & Drink** Full breakfast w/ fresh fruit, warm breads, beverages; specialties—omelets, Belgian waffles, French toast, blueberry pancakes. **Recreation** Beach activities (badges, umbrellas, & chairs provided), boating, biking (bikes avail.), antiquing, community theater, wine tastings, concerts. **Amenities & Services** Videos, fax & e-mail, hammock on site, guest privileges at Atlantic Club; cottage has disabled access.; meetings (20).

ACCOMMODATIONS

Units 10 guest rooms, 1 cottage. **All Rooms** AC, ceiling fan. **Some Rooms** Private entrance (1). **Bed & Bath** King (1), queen (11), four-poster (1); 9 private baths, 2 shared baths. **Favorites** #3—iron bed, rocker, step-down bathroom w/ claw-foot tub; #8—blue & white quilt, wicker, summery look, quiet, claw-foot tub. **Comfort & Decor** Forget formal Victorian. This downstairs decor is informal, beachy, laid-back—with wood and slate floors, comfortable furniture, and an oversized TV. Third floor rooms are less appealing. The cottage sleeps five, including children of any age.

RATES, RESERVATIONS, & RESTRICTIONS

Deposit 50%, refund w/ 10-days notice less 20%. **Discounts** Corp. **Credit Cards** AE, V, MC. **Check-In/Out** 2–8 p.m./11 a.m. **Smoking** No. **Pets** No. **Kids** Over age 14 (any age in the cottage). **Open** All year. **Hosts** Joanie & Bill Mahon, 106 Sussex Ave., Spring Lake, 07762. **Phone** (888) 274-5464 or (732) 449-3553. **Fax** (732) 449-9067. **E-mail** billmahon@compuserve.com. **Web** ashlingcottage.com.

LA MAISON, Spring Lake

OVERALL ★★★★½ | QUALITY ★★★★ | VALUE ★★★ | PRICE $125–$325

If you can't be in Paris, consider this romantic bed-and-breakfast as a stand-in. The house was built by William V. Reid as a home for traveling peddlers and craftsmen. It gradually evolved into what looks like a private European residence. The decor is warm, elegant, and geared to the elite. The art collection, which fills every wall, is a visual treat. Great music selections uplift the spirit. A platter of muffins on the dining room table beckons. Good books are abundant. Overall, the property has style. Julie managed real estate in New York before turning her talents and enthusiasm towards innkeeping.

SETTING & FACILITIES

Location Quiet residential street. **Near** Town parks, lake, 4 blocks to ocean beach. **Building** 1870 Victorian w/ mansard roof, blue & white awning. **Grounds** City lot w/ holly, daisies, begonias, impatiens. **Public Space** Library, DR, powder room. **Food & Drink** Early coffee; full breakfast w/ freshly squeezed juice & muffins of the day; specialties—goat cheese & herb omelet à la Provence, crème brûlée French toast, tomato & basil frittata, mimosas, cappuccino; afternoon crackers & cheese, tea. **Recreation** Beach activities (badges for pool or ocean & outdoor shower provided), biking (bikes avail.), tennis, gazebo concerts, Christmas B&B tours. **Amenities & Services** Fax & e-mail, guest privileges at Atlantic Club, massage avail., current magazines & books from the *New York Times* best seller list; weddings (40).

ACCOMMODATIONS

Units 5 guest rooms, 2 suites, 1 cottage. **All Rooms** AC, TV, phone, robes, fresh flowers, chocolates. **Some Rooms** Skylights. **Bed & Bath** Queen (8), twin (2), sleigh (5), fluffy white duvets; 7 private, 1 shared bath, 1 double skylit whirlpool, 2 tubs. **Favorites** Louis XVI—iron bed, French linens, wicker armoire, whirlpool; guest cottage—casual comfort, outside barbecue, claw-foot tub, suitable for family of 4. **Comfort & Decor** Public rooms have floor-to-ceiling windows, fresh flower bouquets, a private art collection of great depth and beauty, and leather-bound editions of over 100 great literary works. Antique chairs, chess set, and elegant wall coverings add distinction. There are lots of extras, including festive napkins and home-grown herbs to accent the cuisine.

RATES, RESERVATIONS, & RESTRICTIONS

Deposit 50%, refund w/ 14-days notice less $25. **Discounts** Midweek, corp. **Credit Cards** AE, V, MC, D. **Check-In/Out** 2–10 p.m./11 a.m. **Smoking** No. **Pets** No. **Kids** Over age 16 (any age in cottage). **Minimum Stay** 3 nights July, Aug., & holiday weekends, 2 nights all other times w/ exceptions. **Open** All year. **Hosts** Julianne Corrigan, 404 Jersey Ave., Spring Lake, 07762. **Phone** (800) 276-2088 or (732) 449-0969. **Fax** (732) 449-4860. **E-mail** lamaisonnj@aol.com. **Web** lamaison.com.

NORMANDY INN, Spring Lake

OVERALL ★★★★ | QUALITY ★★★★ | VALUE ★★★ | PRICE $90–$320

Built by the Audenreid family of Philadelphia as a summer home and rental property, this is the only bed-and-breakfast in Spring Lake listed on the National Register of Historic Places. The owners, who come from Staten Island, are new—as recent as January 2001. But little has changed. Jeri and Michael Robertson, who have been managing the inn since 1997, continue at the helm. They still use their computer to ensure their many repeat guests are remembered and well cared for. And, the inn continues to set the standard for all the others in town, says Jeri. The unique building has a life of its own—boasting a unique combination of authentic antiques, a relaxing ambience, and proximity to the beach.

SETTING & FACILITIES

Location 0.5 block from beach & non-commercial boardwalk, walking distance to village and lakes. **Near** Allaire State Park, Six Flags Great Adventure, PNC Arts Center, outlet shopping. **Building** 1888 Italianate villa w/Queen Anne modifications. **Grounds** City lot w/Victorian floral patterns. **Public Space** 2 parlors, large DR, sunporch, front porch w/ wicker chairs & rockers. **Food & Drink** Full breakfast w/ fruit, pastries, beverages; specialties—apple & cheddar omelet, pecan pancakes, raisin French toast; afternoon tea 3–5 p.m., complimentary wine anytime. **Recreation** Beach (guests have use of 10 beach badges, chairs, towels, & umbrellas), golf, antiquing, community theater, house tours. **Amenities & Services** Videos, massage arranged, fax & e-mail, flip charts, overhead projector avail.; meetings (20), weddings (50).

ACCOMMODATIONS

Units 17 guest rooms, 1 suite. **All Rooms** AC, TV, phone, iron & board, clock radio. **Some Rooms** Fireplace (6), balcony (1), VCR. **Bed & Bath** King (1), queen (12), twin (1), canopy (2); 17 private baths, 1 whirlpool, 5 tubs. **Favorites** 201—four-poster tester canopy bed, lace trim, soft pastel florals, wash stand, Victorian lamp; 200—tower, beach view, gasolier, iron headboard, white coverlet (detached bath). **Comfort & Decor** This is a mini-museum of Victorian arts and artifacts framed by reproduction wallpaper. Prized possessions include an antique English tall case clock, a Rococo damask parlor set, and authentic marble sculpture. Guest room headboards are extraordinarily ornate.

RATES, RESERVATIONS, & RESTRICTIONS

Deposit 50%, refund w/ 7-days notice less $20 (modified for longer stays). **Discounts** 10% 4 nights Sun.–Thurs. **Credit Cards** AE, V, MC. **Check-In/Out** 2–10:30 p.m./11 a.m. **Smoking** No. **Pets** No. **Kids** Yes, well-behaved. **No-No's** Large groups on summer weekends. **Minimum Stay** 2 nights on weekends; July & Aug. only—3 nights on weekends, 2 nights midweek; 3 nights all holiday weekends. **Open** All year. **Hosts** Mark Valori & Felix & Lillian Valori (a son and his parents), 21 Tuttle Ave., Spring Lake, 07762. **Phone** (732) 449-7172. **Fax** (732) 449-1070. **E-mail** Normandy@bellatlantic.net. **Web** normandyinn.com.

SEA CREST BY THE SEA, Spring Lake

OVERALL ★★★★½ | QUALITY ★★★★ | VALUE ★★★ | PRICE $155–$275

Close your eyes and imagine you can hear the waves breaking on the beach, smell the salt air, and feel the soft breezes. It's all just a phone call away. Special services at this couples-only retreat include a full moon picnic with champagne, fruit, cheese, and crackers to take to the beach or a romance package with chocolate candy and chilled champagne to enjoy on the porch. These innkeepers are dedicated to making romantic fantasies come true. They say: leave the kids, cell phones, and laptops at home and come here to relax and rejuvenate. In addition to the fantasy, you'll find some of the most comfortable beds in the business. It is a place you'll want to revisit.

SETTING & FACILITIES

Location Residential street, 0.5 block to Atlantic Ocean. **Near Building** 1885 Queen Anne Victorian, restored, w/ wraparound porch, turret. **Grounds** City lot, landscaped lawn. **Public Space** Sitting room, 2 dining rooms, porch. **Food & Drink** Full breakfast: specialties—piña colada French toast, southwestern omelets, Greek frittata; afternoon tea w/ fresh baked goodies. **Recreation** 2 mi. long non-commercial boardwalk, beach (beach passes, towels, umbrellas, & chairs avail.), biking (13 on site), antiquing, outlet mall. **Amenities & Services** Video library, privileges at Atlantic Club in Manasquan (1.5 mi.), tennis privileges.

ACCOMMODATIONS

Units 9 guest rooms, 2 suites. **All Rooms** AC, TV/VCR, fresh flowers, robes, hair dryer, phone, Godiva chocolates. **Some Rooms** Fireplace (8), private porch (1), fridge (3). **Bed & Bath** Queen (11), canopy (1), four-poster (1), sleigh (1), all w/ featherbed mattress covers; private baths, 6 double whirpools. **Favorites** Casablanca—cord entry, Bogart pictures, African wood carvings, movie poster, raincoat (but tiny bath); Papillon—framed butterflies, butterfly stencils, peach tones; Sleigh Ride—brass bed, blue walls, white trim, fainting couch, large bath, whirlpool. **Comfort & Decor** The parlor has cranberry walls, white woodwork, floral drapes, tiled gas fireplace with Empire mantel, two Victorian sofas, chairs, a piano, and a gasolier. The dining rooms capture a sense of gentility and civility. Guest rooms stress comfort.

RATES, RESERVATIONS, & RESTRICTIONS

Deposit Larger of 50% or 2 nights, refund w/ 15-days notice less $25. **Discounts** Special themed packages. **Credit Cards** AE, V, MC. **Check-In/Out** 3–11 p.m./11 a.m. **Smoking** No. **Pets** No. **Kids** No. **Minimum Stay** In season—3 nights weekends, 2 nights midweek; off season—2 night weekends. **Open** All year. **Hosts** Barbara & Fred Vogel, 19 Tuttle Ave., Spring Lake, 07762. **Phone** (800) 803-9031. **Fax** (732) 974-0403. **E-mail** jk@seacrestbythesea.com. **Web** seacrestbythesea.com.

SPRING LAKE INN, Spring Lake

OVERALL ★★★½ | QUALITY ★★★★ | VALUE ★★★ | PRICE $135–$225

Irish is spoken here. The parents of both innkeepers came from Ireland and every two years the couple returns to visit their large extended families in county Clare. Many of today's guests have Irish connections, so they've made it a tradition to have homemade Irish soda bread on the breakfast table each morning. Pat has a good sense of humor and lots of anecdotes to share. Before moving to Spring Lake in 1994, she was a cardiac nurse. Jim continues to work in New York City in the theatrical business. Together, they've renovated the property and created a warm, informal atmosphere. It's a pleasure to sit on the 80-foot front porch and swap stories.

SETTING & FACILITIES

Location Residential area 1 block from the ocean, 6 blocks from downtown. **Near** Allaire airport and state park, Wreck Pond, Spring Lake, 20 min. to PNC Arts Center. **Building** 1888 Victorian w/ turret. **Grounds** City lot, small lawn w/ floral border. **Public Space** Large foyer, parlor, DR, front porch. **Food & Drink** Buffet; cont'l in summer w/ 3 breads, 2 kinds of muffins, juices, 4 fruits, beverages; hot breakfast in winter; specialties—challah bread French toast, blueberry pancakes, frittata; afternoon tea. **Recreation** Beach badges, chairs, towels, 2 bikes avail.; 5K run Memorial Day. **Amenities & Services** Videos, fax & e-mail; meetings (30).

ACCOMMODATIONS

Units 15 guest rooms. **All Rooms** AC, hair dryer. **Some Rooms** Fireplace (2). **Bed & Bath** Queen (14), double (1), twin (1), canopy (1), four-poster (4), sleigh (4); private baths, 1 tub. **Favorites** Sunrise—yellow theme; Americana—spindle four-poster bed, flag pillows, wood floor w/ hook rug. **Comfort & Decor** Look for angel theme wall decor. The dining room has a 12-foot ceiling. You can relax on a great porch amidst the hanging flower baskets, floral sconces, and pots, wicker seats, rockers, lounges, and ice cream tables and chairs.

RATES, RESERVATIONS, & RESTRICTIONS

Deposit 50% by check only, refund w/ 10-days notice less $25. **Discounts** No. **Credit Cards** V, MC. **Check-In/Out** 2 p.m./11 a.m. **Smoking** No. **Pets** No. **Kids** Over age 12. **Minimum Stay** 2 nights May 1–Nov. 1. **Open** All year. **Hosts** Pat & Jim Gatens, 104 Salem Ave., Spring Lake, 07762. **Phone** (732) 449-2010. **Fax** (732) 449-4020. **E-mail** sprnglkinn@aol.com. **Web** springlakeinn.com.

VICTORIA HOUSE, Spring Lake

OVERALL ★★★★ | QUALITY ★★★★ | VALUE ★★★ | PRICE **$130–$335**

These innkeepers have put a lot of thought into giving their guests a unique experience. They've succeeded in creating a place to clear your mind and rekindle your relationship. There's a friendly porch setting for those who want lots of interaction with other guests. And, there are quiet corners to escape and unwind. Louise and Robert moved here from Middletown, where she was a homemaker and mother of three. He worked for AT&T as a strategic planner and then for Lucent, traveling to Europe and Saudi Arabia. In 1997, he retired to join her as a full-time innkeeper.

SETTING & FACILITIES

Location Less traveled residential area, 2.5 blocks from ocean, 0.5 block from Spring Lake. **Near** 6 blocks from New Jersey shoreline train station, 60 mi. south of New York City, 60 mi. northeast of Philadelphia, 46 mi. north of Atlantic City. **Building** 1882 Queen Anne w/ full wraparound porch, 5 types of gothic shingles. **Grounds** City lot, voluminous spring bulbs, perennial garden, colorful side garden w/ bench, giant snow ball trees, lot of birds. **Public Space** LR, foyer, DR, front & side porch, powder room. **Food & Drink** Full breakfast w/ juice, fresh fruit, coffee; specialties—banana crunch cake, oven baked French toast, blueberry bucket cake; guest fridge w/ soda, lemonade, water. **Recreation** Guest privileges at Atlantic Club w/ tennis center, workout machines, beauty salon, massage, fitness trails; beach activities (badges, chairs, towels, & outdoor shower avail.), windsailing, & kayaking on Wreck Pond, surfing (bring your own board), charter boat fishing, horseback riding, biking (10 avail.), living history museums, walking-tour audio tapes about Spring Lake history, St. Patrick's Day Parade, 5K race (Memorial Day weekend). **Amenities & Services** More than 30 videos, massage by Yvonne Perry, fax & e-mail.

ACCOMMODATIONS

Units 6 guest rooms, 2 suites. **All Rooms** AC, hair dryer, live plant, ceiling fan. **Some Rooms** TV, VCR, CD player, surround sound (1), phone jack, fireplace (4). **Bed & Bath** King (3), queen (5), twin (split king); antique iron, brass, mahogany, & refinished heirloom headboards; 6 private baths, 2 detached private baths, 2 double whirlpools, 2 tubs. **Favorites** Manor Suite #102—gas fireplace, CD player, 2 TVs, whirlpool tub w/ candles, liqueurs, fridge, every comfort; #7—wicker, slanted ceiling, pretty blue & white theme. **Comfort & Decor** The parlor has a chess set, fox and geese game, TV & VCR, and old photos. The dining room features a hand-carved walnut sideboard, ten chairs carved with scenes of Venice, an English tea cup collection, and an Eastlake Rocker. Accessories include original Victorian art, stereoscopic pictures, vintage frames. The foyer has four stained glass windows. It all looks formal, but feels comfortable.

RATES, RESERVATIONS, & RESTRICTIONS

Deposit 50%. **Discounts** Added value specials. **Credit Cards** AE, V, MC. **Check-In/Out** 2 p.m./11 a.m. **Smoking** No. **Pets** No. **Kids** Over age 14 w/ own room. **Minimum Stay** 3 nights July and Aug. weekends. **Open** All year. **Hosts** Louise & Robert Goodall, 214 Monmouth Ave., Spring Lake, 07762. **Phone** (888) 249-6252 or (732) 974-1882. **Fax** (732) 974-2132. **E-mail** victoriahousebb@worldnet.att.net. **Web** victoria house.net.

Zone 7

Southern New Jersey/ Cape May

It's a good bet that Cape May has more bed-and-breakfasts than any other American town—about 70 at last count.

In fact, Cape May has so many authentic Victorian-era buildings that in 1976 the entire city was designated a National Historic Landmark. Many of these buildings are architectural gems, with hand-carved façades, porches, turrets, and well-tended gardens.

Only one, the 18-room **Emlen Physick Mansion,** is maintained as a museum to reflect daily life in a turn-of-the-twentieth century household. Built in 1879, architect Frank Furness gave it a medieval look with lots of lacy gothic bric-a-brac, corbelled (upside-down) chimneys, boxy projections, and a dark gray exterior with tomato-soup red trim. During the 45-minute guided tours, visitors explore luxury furnishings upstairs and the working world downstairs.

To capture the flavor of the city's Victorian neighborhoods, climb aboard a carriage pulled by a Belgium draft horse—or take a trolley tour. On **Washington Street Mall,** where guided trolley tours begin, a plaque honors Capt. Cornelius Jacobson Mey, the Dutch explorer who founded Cape May in 1621. (The English later changed Mey to May.)

Afternoon tea is a Cape May tradition. It's typically served in formal parlors or dining rooms. Sipping Earl Gray is incidental to an exchange of pleasantries between fellow guests and eager-to-please hosts.

When you tire of all that lacy, fussy, teddy-bear Victoriana, you can drive to the 1859 newly-restored **Cape May Lighthouse,** which is especially attractive by moonlight. Cape May is one of North America's premier places for birding—at its peak in spring and autumn. There's a hawk observation platform near the lighthouse, and hiking trails fan out through the marshlands.

A full moon in May provides ideal opportunity to explore a 10- to 12-mile stretch of the **Delaware Bay coastline** that attracts one of the world's greatest concentrations of horseshoe crabs—sometimes so thick they form a solid carpet. Millions of birds en route from South America to Arctic tundra breeding territories stop here to gorge on the plump crab eggs, which these blue-blooded arachnids deposit—up to 80,000 per female. When these corn-kernel-sized eggs are uncovered by gently lapping waves they become fuel for sandpipers, plovers, dowagers, skimmers, and terns.

Birders can hire a naturalist to take you into **Dennis Creek Wildlife Management Area** to capture the beauty of these birds on film, as they flit and swoop through the sky and peck intensely at the wet, sandy tideline.

The **Mid-Atlantic Center for the Arts** runs numerous events to attract visitors in the shoulder seasons, including wine tastings and cooking workshops. House tours, lectures, dine-a-rounds, and nineteenth-century dance lessons are part of weeklong events. For Sherlock Holmes mystery weekends in March and November, some participants dress in plumes, bustles, deerstalker caps, and Victorian-era clothing. And, decorations are particularly ornate for Christmas tours and teas.

Come March, **North Wildwood** is one of several New Jersey shore towns that is a magnet for the Irish. It hosts the area's largest St. Patrick's Day parade, a signal that the next beach season is soon to arrive.

But, you'll have to wait for summer to tour **Historic Cold Spring Village,** a living history museum just north of Cape May. Here, characters and craftsmen in period dress portray daily life during the 1800s. And, don't forget to sign up for a sailboat ride on the ***A.J. Meerwald,*** a 115-foot Delaware Bay oyster schooner, departing from the Delaware River coast.

Overall, Cape May's bed-and-breakfast business is thriving, but properties tend to be pricey. Consider a visit in the quiet season, beginning shortly after Labor Day. That's when many bed-and-breakfasts begin to reduce their midweek prices.

FOR MORE INFORMATION

Atlantic City Convention & Visitors Authority
(609) 348-7100

Cape May Chamber of Commerce
(609) 884-5508

Cape May County Chamber of Commerce
(609) 465-7181

Ocean City Chamber of Commerce
(800) BEACHNJ

Southern Shore Region Tourism Council
(609) 463-6415

CAPTAIN MEY'S, Cape May

OVERALL ★★★★ | QUALITY ★★★★ | VALUE ★★★★ | PRICE $85–$225

The name of this house honors Dutch explorer Cornelius J. Mey, who discovered these shores and claimed them for the Dutch West India Co. in

1621, finding the climate similar to Holland's. It was built by Dr. Walter L. Phillips, a homeopathic physician. The Blinns have been fulltime innkeepers here since 1994. (He was an electrician and she worked for a New Jersey newspaper.) At first glance, the large collection of Victorian wardrobe items and underwear in the parlor may be off-putting. But, if you ask questions, you'll get some interesting insights into the Victorian era. "I collect anything that was tortuous to Victorian ladies," says Kathleen.

SETTING & FACILITIES

Location Heart of historic Cape May. **Near** 2 blocks to ocean, 0.5 block to pedestrian mall. **Building** 1890 Colonial Revival, light beige w/ eggplant trim. **Grounds** City lot w/ borders of purple petunias, impatiens, tulips. **Public Space** Foyer, parlor, DR, wraparound veranda, courtyard. **Food & Drink** Full family-style breakfast at set time; specialties—omelet w/ vegetables, flavored French toast, fruit crêpes; hot drinks always avail. **Recreation** Swimming (beach chairs & towels provided), kayaking, birding, carriage rides, trolley tours, theater. **Amenities & Services** Afternoon tea at 4 p.m.; access to fridge, free local calls on hall phone; meetings (10).

ACCOMMODATIONS

Units 7 guests rooms, 1 suite. **All Rooms** AC, ceiling fans, ironing board. **Some Rooms** TV (3), mini-fridge (3), hair dryer (1). **Bed & Bath** All queen beds, 7 are antique; private baths, 2 whirlpools. **Favorites** Capt. Mey's suite—lace canopy; Piet Hein—fainting sofa, pink & green decor. **Comfort & Decor** You'll see Dutch antiques throughout. The parlor's antique coat racks holds Victorian dresses, hats, high-top shoes, 4 corsets, 6 bustles, and hoop cages for crinoline skirts dating from 1860. The ceiling medallion is hand-painted. The dining room has Eastlake chestnut and oak paneling, a gas fireplace with Dutch tile, and an 1870 carved oak sideboard. The leaded glass on foyer panels and dining room bay windows is original. Collections include Victorian butter dishes and Delft Blue China. All guest bedrooms have crocheted ivory coverlets.

RATES, RESERVATIONS, & RESTRICTIONS

Deposit 50%, refund w/ 21-days notice if rented, less $20. **Discounts** No. **Credit Cards** AE, V, MC. **Check-In/Out** 2–8 p.m./11 a.m. **Smoking** No. **Pets** No. **Kids** Over age 8. **Minimum Stay** Varies. **Open** All year, weekends only Jan.–mid-Mar. **Hosts** Kathleen & George Blinn, 202 Ocean St., Cape May, 08204. **Phone** (800) 981-3702 or (609) 884-7793. **Fax** (609) 884-7793 (call to alert). **Web** captainmeys.com.

FAIRTHORNE, Cape May

OVERALL ★★★★ | QUALITY ★★★★ | VALUE ★★★ | PRICE $120–$225

Both of these amiable hosts were born in Cape May County, and both retired from Bell Atlantic before taking up innkeeping. They've created an informal retreat where rooms are compact, immaculately clean, and comfortable. In warm-weather months the parlor is so seldom used it disappears to become an extra bedroom. Guests prefer to sit in rocking chairs on the porch, catching the sea breeze and watching the action on one of Cape May's busiest residential street. Details to spot inside are the two-tiered ship-style mantel, ship-type front door, and leaded window panels in the foyer. After all, a ship captain built this house. We noticed that guys felt very comfortable in this environment—enough so to wear a baseball cap backwards to breakfast.

SETTING & FACILITIES

Location Heart of historic Cape May. **Near** Exit 1 Garden State Parkway, Cape May–Lewes Ferry, 40 mi. south of Atlantic City Airport. **Building** 1892 main building is Colonial Revival, adjacent 1880 Carpenter Gothic cottage w/ red, green, & yellow trim. **Grounds** City lot w/ gazebo, fountains. **Public Space** 2 parlors, DR, wraparound veranda, screened porch. **Food & Drink** Full family-style breakfast w/ 2 seatings, served on porch in warm weather; specialties—eggs Benedict, strata w/ cream cheese & blueberries, stuffed French toast w/ strawberries, fruits of summer soufflé; tea at 4 p.m. **Recreation** Water sports (beach chairs & towels avail.), biking (8 on site), antiquing, numerous festivals. **Amenities & Services** Fax, meetings (14).

ACCOMMODATIONS

Units 10 guest rooms. **All Rooms** AC, TV, hair dryer. **Some Rooms** Fridge (8), gas fireplace (3), Patricia's room has private entrance. **Bed & Bath** All king or queen beds, 2 four-poster, 1 sleigh; 2 detached private baths, 4 tubs, Gabrielle's Room has claw-foot tub. **Favorites** Emma Kate suite—four-poster, cream & rose colors, bay window view. **Comfort & Decor** The parlor has a rococo-style sideboard. Most furnishings are eclectic. The main house guest rooms are named for women owners, while the cottage rooms honor three granddaughters.

RATES, RESERVATIONS, & RESTRICTIONS

Deposit Credit card to hold, full refund w/ 3-weeks notice if rented. **Discounts** Midweek mid-Sept.–mid-June. **Credit Cards** AE, V, MC, D. **Check-In/Out** 2–9 p.m./11 a.m. **Smoking** Veranda only. **Pets** No (1 cat in main building). **Kids** Age 10 & over. **Minimum Stay** 2 nights Sept.–June weekends; 3 nights July, Aug., & holidays. **Open** All year. **Hosts** Diane & Ed Hutchinson, 111 Ocean St., Box 2381, Cape May, 08204. **Phone** (800) 438-8742 or (609) 884-8791. **Fax** (609) 884-1902. **E-mail** wehfair@aol.com. **Web** fairthorne.com.

HUMPHREY HUGHES HOUSE, Cape May

OVERALL ★★★★ | QUALITY ★★★★½ | VALUE ★★★ | PRICE $105–$235

The namesake of this house, Captain Humphrey Hughes, arrived in Cape May in 1692 to become an original landowner. The current house stayed in the hands of Hughes' descendants for 50 years, and it is now one of Cape May's grandest bed-and-breakfasts. Spacious public rooms look authentically Victorian. Beautiful handmade wallpapers, fringed lamps, and leaded glass windows add interest. If furnishings feel a bit museum-like, you can retreat to the sunporch, where white wicker and floral cushions provide creature comforts. Ditto the veranda. Gracious innkeepers take time to help select a good restaurant and give directions. Breakfast is both formal and fun.

SETTING & FACILITIES

Location Heart of historic Cape May. **Near** Cape May Point State Park, 0.5 block from Atlantic Ocean. **Building** 1903 Colonial Revival w/ cedar shake, wraparound veranda, glass-enclosed sunporch. **Grounds** City lot. **Public Space** Large LR, DR, heated sunroom, outside shower. **Food & Drink** Full breakfast at 9 a.m. in DR or on porch in summer; specialties—egg soufflé & emphasis is on healthy fare; tea at 4 p.m. **Recreation** Birding, biking, horseback riding, fishing, tennis, golf, antiquing, house tours, trolley & horse-drawn carriage ridings; music festival (May/June), Dickens Festival (Dec.). **Amenities & Services** Beach chairs & towels.

ACCOMMODATIONS

Units 10 guest rooms. **All Rooms** AC, TV, radio, hair dryer, ceiling fan. **Some Rooms** Doctor's Suite has private entrance. **Bed & Bath** King (2), queen (7), double (1); private baths w/ ceramic tile, 3 tubs. **Favorites** Ocean View—bright, spacious blue satin & lace spread, ruffles, antique armoire, fringe lamp; Rose Room—dramatic, walls white & red rose motif, dark shutters; Doctor's Suite—spacious, white wicker cottage decor (not Victorian), intense floral patterns. **Comfort & Decor** A knockout parlor has polished wood flooring, an Oriental carpet, a rosewood square grand piano, delicate lace curtains, half shutters, bronze statuary and fringed lamps, filigree picture frames, Corinthian pillars, and pocket doors. Both the living and dining rooms have a gas fireplace. Guest rooms feature Victorian beds, comfortable seating, and eclectic accessories.

RATES, RESERVATIONS, & RESTRICTIONS

Deposit 50%, refund w/ 14-days notice less $20. **Discounts** Midweek Oct.–April. **Credit Cards** V, MC. **Check-In/Out** 2–9 p.m./11 a.m. **Smoking** No. **Pets** No. **Kids** No. **Minimum Stay** 3 nights on weekends mid-May–mid-Oct. **Open** All year (weekends only Nov.–Mar. w/ exceptions). **Hosts** Lorraine & Terry Schmidt, 29 Ocean St., Cape May, 08204. **Phone** (800) 582-3634 or (609) 884-4428. **Fax** (609) 898-1845. **Web** humphreyhugheshouse.com.

INN ON OCEAN, Cape May

OVERALL ★★★★ | QUALITY ★★★★ | VALUE ★★★ | PRICE **$129–$279**

Jack Davis honed his hospitality skills in a former career with the Pontiac Division of General Motors. Part of that job was being a professional host—in charge of enlivening groups and getting people to laugh. Part of his innkeeping philosophy he learned from contact with Disney executives: take a calm, reassuring approach to everything and recognize that there are no problems, only opportunities. Jack's wife, Katha, is the detail person at Inn on Ocean. She oversees everything from extensive spring cleaning to on-going domestic chores. Together they strive to orchestrate a seamless B&B experience. If you like playing pool, there's a huge pool table in one of the front parlors. It's a clue to just how relaxed and unpretentious this house can be.

SETTING & FACILITIES

Location Heart of historic district. **Near** 0.5 block from Atlantic Ocean. **Building** 1880 French Second Empire. **Grounds** City lot w/ awning covered porch overlooking flower beds. **Public Space** Foyer, parlor, billiard room, DR. **Food & Drink** Early coffee, formal breakfast at 9 a.m., table set w/ different linens & dishes daily (the inn can go 14 days w/out duplicating a setting); specialties emphasize local produce and include spinach baked eggs, Parmesan eggs w/ potatoes & ham, sherried French toast; tea at 4 p.m. **Recreation** Water sports, antiquing, birding. **Amenities & Services** On-site parking.

ACCOMMODATIONS

Units 4 guest rooms, 1 suite. **All Rooms** AC, cable TV, robes, mini-fridge, hair dryer, fresh flowers. **Some Rooms** VCR w/ movie library, fireplace (2), balcony (2). **Bed & Bath** King (3), queen (2); 2 Victorian soaking tubs, 3 whirlpools. **Favorites** Captain's Quarters Penthouse—entire 3rd floor w/ LR, king bed, strawberry motif, claw-foot tub. **Comfort & Decor** The mood is lighthearted Victorian and accessories are changed seasonally. We noted original painted wood floors with Oriental carpet, a Victorian hat display on the hall tree, an antique lantern collection, and Charles Dana Gibson prints. From the second floor porch you can enjoy great sea views without the sand.

RATES, RESERVATIONS, & RESTRICTIONS

Deposit 50% at booking, refund if rebooked less $25. **Discounts** At discretion of innkeeper. **Credit Cards** All major. **Check-In/Out** 1–10 p.m./11 a.m. **Smoking** No. **Pets** No. **Kids** No. **Minimum Stay** Varies. **Open** March 1–Jan. 1. **Hosts** Katha & Jack Davis, 25 Ocean St., Cape May, 08204. **Phone** (800) 304-4477 or (609) 884-7070. **Fax** (609) 884-1384. **E-mail** innocean@bellatlantic.net. **Web** theinnonocean.com.

JOHN F. CRAIG HOUSE, Cape May

OVERALL ★★★ | QUALITY ★★★½ | VALUE ★★★ | PRICE $85–$185

Named in honor of its turn-of-the-twentieth-century owner, John F. Craig, a wealthy Philadelphia sugar broker, this house is believed to be the oldest on the block. It remained in one family for three generations and was restored to authentic Victorian elegance in the mid-1980s. You'll feel a strong sense of history, thanks to Eastlake and Renaissance Revival antiques, period light fixtures, reproduction wallpapers, and photographs of the current owners' ancestors. A friendly newsletter keeps guests informed about Cape May's astonishingly full events calendar—including the annual Monarch butterfly migration, Jazz festival, World Series of Birding, Craft Show, Food & Wine Festival, Sherlock Holmes Weekends, and more.

SETTING & FACILITIES

Location Heart of historic Cape May. **Near** Walk to beach & pedestrian mall. **Building** 1866 restored Carpenter Gothic. **Grounds** City lot w/ English garden. **Public Space** LR, DR, small library, enclosed porch, sunporch. **Food & Drink** Early coffee, full candlelight breakfast w/ two seatings on weekends; specialties—pancakes, French toast, eggs Florentine; afternoon tea w/ sweet & savory snacks. **Recreation** Water sports, antiquing, bird watching. **Amenities & Services** Beach chairs & towels, newsletter to former guests.

ACCOMMODATIONS

Units 7 guest rooms, 1 suite. **All Rooms** AC, fresh flowers, hair dryer. **Bed & Bath** Bed sizes vary; 7 private baths, 1 detached private bath, 3 tubs. **Favorites** John & Emma Craig—classic Victorian bed, can sleep 3. **Comfort & Decor** Renaissance revival-style antiques dominate. The overall feeling is pleasant and relaxed.

RATES, RESERVATIONS, & RESTRICTIONS

Deposit 1 night or 50%, refund if rented less $15. **Discounts** 10% for 1-week stay, birders. **Credit Cards** V, MC, D. **Check-In/Out** 2–9 p.m./11 a.m. **Smoking** No (open porch only). **Pets** No (2 cats, Heckle & Jeckle, in residence). **Kids** Over age 12. **Minimum Stay** Varies. **Open** All year (except Jan. & Feb.). **Hosts** Connie & Frank Felicetti, 609 Columbia Ave., Cape May, 08204. **Phone** (877) 544-0314 or (609) 884-0100. **Fax** (609) 898-1307. **E-mail** fe6119@belllatlantic.net. **Web** johncraig.com.

MANOR HOUSE INN, Cape May

OVERALL ★★★½ | QUALITY★★★★ | VALUE ★★★ | PRICE **$90–$220**

This property may remind you of your grandmother's house. It's filled with a mixture of antiques, comfortable seating, and homey touches. Eight rocking chairs on a wide porch provide a place to get acquainted with other guests. Nancy is a good cook and a collector of tea pots and mustard jars. She carries on a long tradition of serving homemade sticky buns with mashed potatoes as the secret ingredient. If you've got a sweet tooth, you'll also love the afternoon tea and evening cookie jar that's filled with freshly baked goodies. Tom is a sailboat racing enthusiast and an intermediate-level tennis player who welcomes competition from guests. He can arrange games at the local tennis club.

SETTING & FACILITIES

Location Heart of historic Cape May. **Near** Walk to beach & pedestrian mall. **Building** 1906 Colonial Revival. **Grounds** City lot w/ small garden. **Public Space** Foyer, parlor, fireplace room, DR, porch. **Food & Drink** Four-course breakfast, 2 seatings; specialties—baked egg with bacon, inn-made granola, cheese-egg soufflé, lemon ricotta pancakes, sticky buns; 4 p.m. tea, 7 p.m. cookie jar. **Recreation** Festivals, antiquing, water sports (beach chair and towels provided). **Amenities & Services** Massage.

ACCOMMODATIONS

Units 9 guest rooms, 1 suite. **All Rooms** AC, hair dryer, robe, perfume, hand cream. **Some Rooms** TV (1). **Bed & Bath** King (3), queen (6), full (1); 1 detached bath; 5 tubs, 1 whirlpool. **Favorites** Suite #6 on 3rd floor—green wainscoting, tan wicker, floral cushions, whirlpool, Victorian dresser; Room #9—high bed, floral wallpaper, antique dresser, blue accents, needlepoint pillows, light & airy. **Comfort & Decor** Interesting details include the chestnut and oak lined foyer with pocket doors, Victorian print wallpaper, a player piano, and original stained glass in the staircase window.

RATES, RESERVATIONS, & RESTRICTIONS

Deposit 50%, refund if re-rented less $20. **Discounts** Single occupancy. **Credit Cards** V, MC. **Check-In/Out** 2–9 p.m./11 a.m. **Smoking** No. **Pets** No (2 dogs on premises). **Kids** Over age 12. **No-No's** Candles. **Minimum Stay** 2 nights some weekends; 3 nights July, Aug., & Sept. weekends. **Open** All week April through Dec., weekends only Feb. & Mar. **Hosts** Nancy & Tom McDonald, 612 Hughes St., Cape May, 08204. **Phone** (609) 884-4710. **Fax** (609) 898-0471. **E-mail** innkeepr@bellatlantic.net. **Web** manorhouse.net.

RHYTHM OF THE SEA, Cape May

OVERALL ★★★★ | QUALITY ★★★★ | VALUE ★★★ | PRICE $89–$255

These international innkeepers share a passion for simple, clean lines and a harmony with nature expressed by Arts and Crafts furniture. They've decorated their spacious B&B entirely with L. and J. G. Stickley furniture and Mission-style accessories. Handmade the old-fashioned way, Mission-style goods were popularized at the beginning of the twentieth century as a reaction to overwrought, mass-produced items of the Victorian era. Hues in accessories and trim are faithful to the natural colors of that movement, especially rose, pumpkin, and olive. Original wood floors, interesting art, and ocean views add to the beauty. This is a place to rest and be tranquil. The food is great and the nearly-deserted beach in the front yard is a bonus.

SETTING & FACILITIES

Location Facing the Atlantic Ocean. **Near** 0.5 mi. north of central historic district. **Building** 1915 Swiss chalet in Craftsman style, stucco exterior. **Grounds** 2 lots w/ natural landscaping. **Public Space** Grand salon w/ inglenook fireplace, DR, glass-enclosed porch used in summer. **Food & Drink** Host is a European-trained pastry chef & restaurateur; breakfast specialties—banana split fruit dish, brioche French toast w/ baked custard & seasonal berries, peppered bacon, salmon omelet w/ Dijon crème fraîche & croissant, eggs Oscar, white asparagus; afternoon refreshments. **Recreation** Bikes avail., beach activities (chairs and towels provided), sunset sailboat rides on host's boat. **Amenities & Services** Special occasion dinners, meetings (20).

ACCOMMODATIONS

Units 7 guest rooms, 1 suite. **All Rooms** TV & VCR, AC, ceiling fan. **Some Rooms** Balcony (1), fireplace (2). **Bed & Bath** All queen beds, private baths, 4 tubs. **Favorites** #2—warm tones; #3—nice armoire, gas fireplace, tile bath; #1—sturdy, simple look, tan wicker. **Comfort & Decor** Large living room has six over one windows and furniture that celebrates simple lines, the wood itself, and the construction. The Stickley furniture has Craftsman and Fayetteville finish. Coffeetable books describe the Arts & Crafts movement.

RATES, RESERVATIONS, & RESTRICTIONS

Deposit 50%. **Discounts** Midweek, quiet season. **Credit Cards** Checks preferred. **Check-In/Out** 2–6 p.m./11 a.m. **Smoking** No. **Pets** No (cat and dog on premises). **Kids** Young children would find it tiresome. **Minimum Stay** 2 nights in quiet season; 3 nights July & Aug., 4 nights holiday weekends. **Open** All year. **Hosts** Robyn & Wolfgang Wendt, 1123 Beach Dr., Cape May, 08204. **Phone** (800) 498-6888 or (609) 884-7788. **Fax** (609) 884-7799. **E-mail** rhythm@alogrithms.com. **Web** rhythmofthesea.com.

SUMMER COTTAGE INN, Cape May

OVERALL ★★★½ | QUALITY ★★★★ | VALUE ★★★ | PRICE $85–$275

The theme here is lighthearted. The mood is relaxed and informal. In fact, these innkeepers consider it a compliment when guests kick off their shoes and put their feet up. There's a great view of The Abbey, another bed-and-breakfast with elaborate turrets and towers, from the porch. And, what a pleasure to spend time in the secret flower and herb garden on the side of the house, where you'll find a three-tiered fountain, a bench, a cherry blossom tree, a trellis with climbing clematis, and a pallet of seasonal flowers. Besides gardening and cooking for guests, Linda takes a leadership role in running Cape May's Sherlock Holmes Mystery Weekends in March and November.

SETTING & FACILITIES

Location Heart of historic Cape May. **Near** Emlen Physick Estate, Cape May Lighthouse, 2 blocks to beach. **Building** 1867 Italianate w/ cupola. **Grounds** City lot w/ side Victorian flower & herb garden. **Public Space** Parlor, DR, informal sitting room, porch. **Food & Drink** Full buffet breakfast; specialties—cheese-potato bake, cinnamon stuffed French toast, strawberry croissant w/ almond; 4–5 p.m. tea and treats. **Recreation** Biking, games provided, trolley tours, walking tours. **Amenities & Services** Meetings (18).

ACCOMMODATIONS

Units 9 guest rooms. **All Rooms** AC, ceiling fan. **Some Rooms** 1 private entrance (Wicker Garden), period antiques. **Bed & Bath** All queen beds, private baths, 2 tubs. **Favorites** Café Outlook—wicker furnishings. **Comfort & Decor** Parlor has Eastlake period furnishings, baby grand piano, pocket windows with lace curtains, pressed glass, and a hurricane lamp collection on a white brick fireplace. Pick your own teapot from a display in the dining room. Guest rooms offer Empire, Eastlake, or Renaissance furnishings.

RATES, RESERVATIONS, & RESTRICTIONS

Deposit 50%, refund if rented less $20. **Discounts** No. **Credit Cards** V, MC, D. **Check-In/Out** 2–9 p.m./11 a.m. **Smoking** Veranda area only. **Pets** No. **Kids** 1 room avail. for age 12 & over. **Minimum Stay** 2 nights most weekends, 3 nights July and Aug. weekends. **Open** All year. **Hosts** Linda & Skip Loughlin, 613 Columbia Ave., Cape May, 08204. **Phone** (609) 884-4948. **E-mail** sumcot@bellatlantic.net. **Web** summercottageinn.com.

THE MANSE, Cape May

OVERALL ★★★½ | QUALITY ★★★★ | VALUE ★★★ | PRICE $115–$175

Guests can expect to feel like part of this family and be surrounded by the things of their lives. Karsten, who is Danish, and Anita, who is half-Jewish, half-Italian, have four children and eight grandchildren. Lots of photographs document their family relationships. Anita collects heirloom paperweights, including two she says were carried to this country by ancestors. Original blue wainscoting distinguishes the dining room, where she displays American pressed glass, German china, and silver tea sets. Six sets of china are available. Original stained-glass windows and heart-pine floors are attractions. But most appealing is the warmth of the hostess.

SETTING & FACILITIES

Location Heart of historic Cape May. **Near** 1.5 blocks to beach & center of town. **Building** 1906 American Four-square Hip-roof Colonial Revival. **Grounds** City lot w/ secret garden, herb garden. **Public Space** LR, parlor, DR, large porch, powder room.

Food & Drink Full breakfast at 9 a.m. in DR in winter, porch in summer; specialties—homemade donuts, vegetable frittata w/ corn & tomato salsa, cinnamon buns, crêpes, tortilla stuffed w/ pork, herbs, sour cream, & cheese; 4 p.m. tea. **Recreation** Water sports (beach chairs, bogey boards, & outdoor showers avail.), antiquing, birding, local festivals. **Amenities & Services** Videos, music, books; meetings & weddings (20).

ACCOMMODATIONS

Units 8 guest rooms. **All Rooms** AC, ceiling fan, hair dryer. **Some Rooms** #1 has stained glass bathroom window. **Bed & Bath** King (2), queen (3), double (3), four-poster (3); 4 private baths, 4 shared baths. **Favorites** Room #2—Oriental treasures from living abroad; #3—bay windows, blue tones, nice art; avoid #8—worn furniture, odd opening to deck with EXIT sign lighted all night. **Comfort & Decor** The look is eclectic and multi-patterned, including a player piano, lots of comfortable sofas, two fireplaces, skirted tables, books, and family photos.

RATES, RESERVATIONS, & RESTRICTIONS

Deposit 50%. **Discounts** Single, 7th night. **Credit Cards** No. **Check-In/Out** after 1 p.m./11 a.m. **Smoking** No. **Pets** No. **Kids** Under age 1; age 5 and over. **Minimum Stay** 3 nights Memorial Day–Labor Day. **Open** All year. **Hosts** Anita & Karsten Dierk, 510 Hughes St., Cape May, 08204. **Phone** (609) 884-0116. **E-mail** themanse@bellatlantic.net. **Web** themanse.com.

THE QUEEN VICTORIA, Cape May

OVERALL ★★★★★ | QUALITY ★★★★½ | VALUE ★★★ | PRICE $95–$290

Quality is the hallmark at The Queen Victoria and the adjacent Prince Albert. Everything down to the symbolic wallpaper in these user-friendly houses was carefully hand-picked and positioned in eye-pleasing arrangements. Both innkeepers have a background in preservation and are valued resources for renovation and restoration projects. Originally from Montana, Joan is a former curator of the Molly Brown House in Denver and Executive Director of the Victorian Society of America. After more than 20 years and numerous expansions, they still make time for a high degree of interaction with guests. They've become the deans of innkeeping in Cape May—knowledgeable about their town and fun to talk to.

SETTING & FACILITIES

Location Heart of historic Cape May. **Near** 1 block to beach, 2 blocks to Washington St. pedestrian mall, 1 mi. to Garden State Pkwy., 40 mi. south of Atlantic City International Airport. **Building** 1800/1881 Second Empire w/ fishtail mansard roof, green w/ rust red trim; adjacent modified Stickley-style house, yellow w/ orange & green trim. **Grounds** Two city lots w/ Victorian-style gardens, elephant ears, heather and heath, day lilies, over 2,000 daffodils. **Public Space** 2 parlors, 2 DR, sitting room, library, pantry, 2 powder rooms, sundeck, large porches w/ 50 rocking chairs. **Food & Drink** Early coffee, ample breakfast buffet (breakfast in bed avail.); specialties—bread pudding w/ poached pear, cheese, & potato bake, gourmet pastries; afternoon tea; beverages & popcorn anytime; special requests honored. **Recreation** Biking (bikes avail.), water sports (beach towels & chairs provided), bird watching, lighthouses, horse-drawn carriage rides, antiquing, festivals, 3 theaters. **Amenities & Services** Free local phone calls; can stay all day after checkout w/ luggage storage, bikes & shower use, even afternoon tea.

ACCOMMODATIONS

Units 15 guest rooms, 4 suites, 2 cottages. **All Rooms** AC, hair dryer, fridge, fresh flowers. **Some Rooms** Fireplace (3), balcony (1), private entrance (6), TV (6), phone (2), coffeemaker (2). **Bed & Bath** Stearns & Foster beds, queen (17), double (4), canopy (1), four-poster (7); private baths, 12 whirlpools, 4 tubs (2 claw-foot). **Favorite** Queen Victoria—high ceiling, crown-canopied bed, plush period furnishings. **Comfort & Decor** Small public areas have orchids, Stickley furniture, Mission-style accessories, plus Bradberry, Schumacher, and Waverly wallcoverings and fabrics. Collections include Van Briggle pottery, pithy sayings in frames, and English prints by Cecil Alon.

RATES, RESERVATIONS, & RESTRICTIONS

Deposit Greater of 50% or 2 nights, refund w/ 21-days notice or if re-rented, less $20. **Discounts** Midweek Nov.–Mar., special packages. **Credit Cards** V, MC. **Check-In/Out** 2–10 p.m./11 a.m. **Smoking** No. **Pets** No (cat on premises). **Kids** In certain rooms. **No-No's** Candles. **Minimum Stay** 2 nights winter weekends; 3 nights spring, summer, fall weekends. **Open** All year. **Hosts** Joan & Dane Wells, 102 Ocean St., Cape May, 08204. **Phone** (609) 884-8702. **E-mail** qvinn@bellatlantic.net. **Web** queenvictoria.com.

VELIA'S SEASIDE INN, Cape May

OVERALL ★★★½ | QUALITY ★★★★ | VALUE ★★★ | PRICE $95–$255

This is one of Cape May's newest properties. John and Kathy Mendolia are former pastors of a non-denominational church in Swedesboro, New Jersey. That's where they met Sue Kulman, who is a nurse. Their inn is a favorite with birders interested in seeing the annual arrival of migratory birds, especially in late spring and early summer when horseshoe crabs spawn on local shores. Shorebirds descend by the hundreds of thousands to gorge on their eggs, which fuel the bird's herculean flights to far-flung mating grounds. Sea views from the inn are partial, but the beach is a mere stroll from the pleasant, multi-seat front porch.

SETTING & FACILITIES

Location 75 steps to beach, in the historic district. **Near** Emlen Physick Estate, Cape May Lighthouse. **Building** Newly-renovated Victorian. **Grounds** City lot w/ flower garden. **Public Space** Parlor, porch. **Food & Drink** Buffet-style cont'l breakfast w/ juice, fruit, baked goods, cereals. **Recreation** Water sports (beach chairs, towels, & umbrellas provided), Cape May Zoo, Historic Cold Spring Village, World Series of Birding (May). **Amenities & Services** Complimentary pass to Cape May Bird Observatory.

ACCOMMODATIONS

Units 4 suites. **All Rooms** Individual AC, heat control; phone, cable TV & VCR. **Some Rooms** Microwave, fridge, coffeemaker. **Bed & Bath** King (2), queen (2); private baths. **Favorites** #4 on 3rd floor—sitting room, crisp colors w/ white background, nautical theme, lighthouse stencils, partial ocean view, rocker. **Comfort & Decor** Interiors are refreshingly light and airy. We liked the love seat, sea shells, and wicker porch furniture.

RATES, RESERVATIONS, & RESTRICTIONS

Deposit 50%, refund w/ 21-days notice less $25. **Discounts** Audubon Society, extended stay midweek. **Credit Cards** V, MC. **Check-In/Out** 2–9 p.m./10:30 a.m. **Smoking** No. **Pets** No. **Kids** Age 12 & older. **Minimum Stay** 2 nights on weekends, holidays. **Open** All year. **Hosts** John & Kathy Mendolia, Sue Kulman, 16 Jackson St., Cape May, 08204. **Phone** (609) 884-7004. **Fax** (609) 884-7884. **Web** veliasinn.com.

WHITE DOVE COTTAGE, Cape May

OVERALL ★★★ | QUALITY ★★★★ | VALUE ★★★ | PRICE **$80–$225**

After 28 years as a police detective in Philadelphia, Frank began his career as an innkeeper in 1991, in his words "to be appreciated for what I do." He keeps his hand in the anti-crime business by running Mystery Weekends at his B&B in the quiet season—the last weekends of January through March. Six scripts were written exclusively for him by a playwright and artistic director. Clues are given out, a crime scene is set up, and participants play the part of colorful Cape May characters. Guests need no costumes, just a sense of humor and desire to have fun. Frank takes on the full responsibility of running a clean, friendly place year-round, even cooking for guests. His wife, a retired teachers' aide, says she married Frank, not the inn.

SETTING & FACILITIES

Location Downtown historic district. **Near** 2 blocks to beach. **Building** 1866 Second Empire w/ original slate mansard roof, octagonal tiles w/ daisy motif. **Grounds** City lot w/ seasonal flowers. **Public Space** LR, DR. **Food & Drink** Full breakfast 8:30–10 a.m.; specialties—stuffed French toast, ham & cheese soufflé, skillet cake w/ sautéed apples; 4 p.m. tea. **Recreation** Water sports (beach chair & towels provided), carriage rides, museums, lighthouse tours. **Amenities & Services** Massage avail., fax, winter Murder Mystery weekends.

ACCOMMODATIONS

Units 4 guest rooms, 2 suites. **All Rooms** AC, hair dryer, safe, umbrella. **Some Rooms** Fireplace (2), teddy bears. **Bed & Bath** King (1), queen (4), double (1); private baths, 1 whirlpool. **Favorites** Lady Kathy cottage—privacy, gas fireplace, peaches & cream colors, soft romantic look, own entrance, 2-person whirlpool; Lord Jason—small but sweet with rose-petal pink dormer. **Comfort & Decor** Along with Victorian and country English furnishings, you can enjoy a player piano (with 600 rolls), a beer stein collection, and a cabinet filled with 170 teddy bears. Guest room names identify people in Frank's family.

RATES, RESERVATIONS, & RESTRICTIONS

Deposit 50%. **Discounts** Over age 60, AAA, active duty military. **Credit Cards** No. **Check-In/Out** 2–9 p.m./11 a.m. **Smoking** No. **Pets** No. **Kids** 12 & over. **Minimum Stay** 2 nights weekends in July & Aug.; 3 nights holidays. **Open** All year. **Hosts** Susann & Frank Smith, 619 Hughes St., Cape May, 08204. **Phone** (800) 321-3683 or (609) 884-0613. **Fax** (609) 884-8241. **Web** whitedovecottage.com.

WOODEN RABBIT, Cape May

OVERALL ★★★½ | QUALITY ★★★★½ | VALUE ★★★ | PRICE $100–$265

This house is an exception to the area's dominant Victoriana. It has distinctively Colonial furnishings and an unusual history to match. According to legend, it was a summer retreat for Gen. Robert E. Lee and his wife, who visited former owner Albert Henry Hughes. (After all Cape May lies south of the Mason-Dixon line.) The house may also have been a stop on the underground railroad. The current owners arrived in 1998, leaving the corporate world and a career in education. He's an antique buff who loves sports cars and collects miniature lead British soldiers—and he weaves reproduction Nantucket baskets. She's a good cook and a skilled decorator.

SETTING & FACILITIES

Location Historic district. **Near** 2 blocks to beach, 1 block to mall. **Building** 1838 Federal. **Grounds** City lot w/ perennial garden, small pond. **Public Space** LR, DR, garden room. **Food & Drink** Full homemade breakfast at 8:30 a.m.; specialties—eggs with leeks, prosciutto, & cheese, homemade granola, heart-shaped waffles w/ 3-berry sauce, apricot glazed stuffed French toast—all served on hand-signed Dedham pottery made in Massachusetts; 4 p.m. tea, guest fridge avail. **Recreation** Day spa nearby, water sports; bikes, beach chairs, & towels provided. **Amenities & Services** Videos, on-site parking, faxes received; meetings (8), weddings (15).

ACCOMMODATIONS

Units 2 guest rooms, 2 suites. **All Rooms** AC, TV, fresh flowers. **Some Rooms** VCR (3). **Bed & Bath** King (3), queen (1), four-poster (2); private baths, 1 whirlpool, 1 tub. **Favorites** Sunporch w/ white wicker, floral cushions, porcelain tile, heated floor. **Comfort & Decor** The living room has period American country furnishings, original hardwood floors, gas fireplace, and an assortment of samplers, baskets, salt-glazed stoneware, folk art, duck decoys, and carved birds. The dining room features an Amish farm table, antique chocolate molds of rabbits, and a fireplace.

RATES, RESERVATIONS, & RESTRICTIONS

Deposit 50% or 1 night w/ refund if rented less $20. **Discounts** No. **Credit Cards** V, MC. **Check-In/Out** 2–10 p.m./11 a.m. **Smoking** No. **Pets** No. **Kids** 12 & older. **Minimum Stay** 2 nights on weekends, 3 nights holiday weekends. **Open** All year (except

Jan.). **Hosts** Nancy & Dave McGonigle, 609 Hughes St., Cape May, 08204. **Phone** (609) 884-7293. **E-mail** wrabbit@jerseycape.com. **Web** woodenrabbit.com.

DOCTORS INN, Cape May Courthouse

OVERALL ★★★ | QUALITY ★★★½ | VALUE ★★★½ | PRICE **$140–$175**

The history of Doctors Inn at King's Grant began with a 1690 land grant to reward a Dr. Cox for loyalty to the King of England. Past owners of this prominent house, built by Dr. John Wiley in the mid-nineteenth century, include both MD's and PhD's. Restored and reopened in 1993, the current owner is Dr. Carolyn Crawford, a neonatologist specializing in children's heart surgery. The doctor's hobby is collecting Victorian-era antiques, including oversized armoires, elaborate mantels, and stained glass. Her leaded glass and jewel-toned stained windows add a lighter tone to this high-Victorian assemblage. Some Victorian pieces appear to be museum quality. A capable young housekeeper looks after the guests.

SETTING & FACILITIES

Location Main street of town. **Near** Cape May, Wildwood, Avelon, Mid-Atlantic Performing Arts Center. **Building** 1856 restored Victorian, pink w/ rust-red trim. **Grounds** City lot w/ flowers & shrubs. **Public Space** Parlor, DR, small exercise room. **Food & Drink** Full breakfast served in restaurant on main floor; specialties—French toast, eggs Benedict, quiche, Sunday brunch. **Recreation** Zoo, shore boardwalk, birding. **Amenities & Services** Fax & e-mail.

ACCOMMODATIONS

Units 6 guest rooms. **All Rooms** TV & VCR, fireplace, phone, alarm clock, coffeemaker, iron & board, fridge. **Some Rooms** Balcony (1), sitting room (1). **Bed & Bath** King (1), queen (5), four-poster (1); private baths, 5 whirlpools, 1 steam shower. **Favorites** #1—high Victorian look w/ strong patterns, fringed curtains/bedspread; double mantel w/ mirror, plush seating, overhead lamp. **Comfort & Decor** An ornate parlor features a tufted velvet sofa, ceiling medallion, cornice, bold reds and greens, a gas fireplace, china cabinet, Oriental carpet, bridal doll, and gold picture frames. The lamp newel post in hallway is notable. The dining area has unusual white lotus flower chairs and stained/leaded glass windows. Guest rooms have family names. Avoid room #3 with its slanted eaves if you're claustrophobic.

RATES, RESERVATIONS, & RESTRICTIONS

Deposit 50%, refund w/ 10-days notice less $20. **Discounts** 10% AAA, 15% corp. midweek. **Credit Cards** AE, V, MC. **Check-In/Out** 2–10 p.m./11 a.m. **Smoking** No. **Pets** Yes. **Kids** Yes. **Minimum Stay** 2 nights May 1–Sept. 30. **Open** All year. **Host** Dr. Carolyn Crawford, 2 N. Main St., Cape May, 08210. **Phone** (609) 463-9330. **Fax** (609) 463-9194. **Web** doctorsinn.com.

CANDLELIGHT INN, North Wildwood

OVERALL ★★★½ | QUALITY ★★★★ | VALUE ★★★ | PRICE $110–$200

Organization and efficiency are hallmarks of this compact house in a residential North Wildwood neighborhood. Bill, a retired Navy pilot, works as a computer techie during the week. Nancy, a former college administrator at Georgetown University, runs the inn full time. The cozy Inglenook fireplace in the foyer, which caught their eye during an extensive search for a new home and new careers, is a great place for relaxing. Ditto the wraparound porch. Every nook and cranny of this property is utilized. On weekends, both hosts make and serve breakfast, whip up afternoon baked goods, and look for ways to enhance your B&B experience. Access to a community hot tub and outdoor grill encourages camaraderie among the guests.

SETTING & FACILITIES

Location Quiet residential neighborhood. **Near** 2 blocks to beach/Atlantic Ocean, near restored Hereford Inlet Lighthouse, 4 mi. to. Garden State Parkway. **Building** 1905 Queen Anne Victorian, cream w/ red & blue trim; carriage house. **Grounds** 4 city lots, off-street parking, butterfly garden. **Public Space** Large foyer w/ inglenook wood-burning fireplace, parlor, DR, powder room, sun deck, veranda. **Food & Drink** Early coffee; full 3-course breakfast, 2 seatings, guests pre-select from two entrée choices; afternoon wine, ice tea, lemonade, Italian ice, baked goods. **Recreation** Murder Mystery weekends, fishing, golf, barbecues, hot tub; fireworks visible from the veranda every Friday night July 4–Labor Day, East Coast's largest Irish Festival (3rd weekend in Sept.). **Amenities & Services** Hammocks, porch swing, massage arranged, fax & e-mail.

ACCOMMODATIONS

Units 8 guest rooms, 2 suites. **All Rooms** AC, ceiling fan, fresh flowers, sherry. **Some Rooms** TV, fridge, microwave, fireplace (2), private entrance (4). **Bed & Bath** King (3), queen (6), double (1); private baths, 2 whirlpools, 3 tubs. **Favorites** Satin and Lace—pretty; 2 carriage house suites—more privacy. **Comfort & Decor** Warm-toned mahogany, chestnut, and oak were used in the paneling, trim, pocket doors, and breakfront in the public room. Curved glass, triple columns, and bay windows add distinction. The dining room has a 105-year-old walnut table. Guest rooms are Victorian or contemporary. The innkeepers collect miniature lighthouses.

RATES, RESERVATIONS, & RESTRICTIONS

Deposit 1 night, refund w/ 2-weeks notice or rented less $25. **Discounts** 10% AAA. **Credit Cards** AE, V, MC, D. **Check-In/Out** After 1 p.m./11 a.m. **Smoking** No. **Pets** No. **Kids** 12 & over. **Minimum Stay** 3 nights weekends May 15–Sept. 30 and holiday weekends. **Open** All year. **Hosts** Nancy & Bill Moncrief, 2310 Central Ave., North Wildwood, 08260. **Phone** (609) 522-6200. **Fax** (609) 522-6125. **E-mail** info@candlelight-inn.com. **Web** candlelight-inn.com.

Part Two

Delaware

Small and flat can be beautiful, too.

Delaware, which is 96 miles long and 9 to 35 miles wide, did not bulldoze its historic buildings or obliterate its small towns or ruin most of its landscape with shopping malls. It remains predominantly a state of intact small towns, with an impressive array of B&Bs. But, too often, people don't take the time to slow down and enjoy them.

Typically, most of Delaware's 13 million annual visitors drive right through on the 16-mile section of Interstate 95 in the state's northeast corner. "The bridge was nice, we actually took a picture of it because we thought it was so beautiful," reported one New Yorker en route to Virginia. "That's all we saw of Delaware." That view left a lot unnoticed.

More than half of Delaware's land is devoted to agriculture, and about 90 percent of that grows corn and soybeans for chicken feed. Poultry production is big business; it accounts for nearly half the state's farm income. Consequently, officials made the Blue Hen Chicken the state bird.

The native du Pont family has historically been an economic powerhouse in Delaware. Now, the state has world-class gardens thanks to the du Pont family, which spent a fortune beautifying the state. Their homes, including **Winterthur** and **Nemours,** are spectacular. Both of these houses are open for tours, as are the **Hagley Museum** and nearby **Longwood Gardens.** These properties are located in or near the Brandywine Valley, an idyllic countryside that remains pristine largely because the family took steps to save the land and preserve its history.

Another of the state's famous sons, illustrator Howard Pyle (1853–1911), was born in **Wilmington,** where some 250 of his works are today housed in the **Delaware Art Museum.** It was Pyle who taught Newell Convers Wyeth, the first of a three-generation family of artists that includes Andrew Wyeth and his son Jamie Wyeth. Families on vacation should know that admission to all state museums is free.

Besides fields, charming towns, grand estates, and museums, visitors will find throughout Delaware reminders of the state's rich past.

The Dutch were the first to settle Delaware, establishing **Lewes** in 1631, but their colony was ultimately wiped out by Indians. Today, visitors can see the **Zwaanendael Museum,** dedicated to the area's maritime history. The museum's gabled façade is an adaptation of the City Hall in Hoorn, the Netherlands, and celebrates the city's Dutch roots.

Swedish immigrants did an admirable job of farming the land in the eighteenth century, but their homeland was reluctant to send needed support and reinforcement. So it was left to the English to provide the technology to build and run local grain and textile mills. They brought progress to the area and freed the people from backbreaking labor.

In a **New Castle** park facing the Delaware River, a plaque marks the spot where William Penn first stepped ashore in the New World in 1682. Nearby, the **George Read II House and Gardens** show the lifestyle of a signer of both the Declaration of Independence and U. S. Constitution. It was on the **Dover** village green that, in 1787, delegates to Delaware's Constitutional Convention voted to ratify the U. S. Constitution, making it the first state to do so.

In **Georgetown,** the **Nutter D. Marvel Museum** recalls the state's past with 20 horse-drawn carriages, a school house, a church, and barns full of memorabilia.

In its early days, Delaware had an ethnic and religious mix of citizens that only Pennsylvania could match. As early as 1775, the legislature voted to forbid importing slaves, but the English governor vetoed the bill. It was tried again after ten years and lost by only one vote. Unofficial support of the anti-slavery movement was so strong that Quaker merchant Thomas Garrett (who reportedly helped more than 2,000 fugitive slaves during his lifetime) is thought to be the model for a Quaker farmer in *Uncle Tom's Cabin.*

From Delaware City, it's a short boat ride to **Fort Delaware State Park** on **Pea Patch Island** to see a Civil War–era prison fort, which now houses a museum. **Cape Henlopen State Park,** near Lewes, offers six miles of beaches, nature trails, and a bird sanctuary. The scenery is marred only slightly by remnants of decommissioned Fort Miles, which was part of the World War II coastal defense system and closed in 1959.

Despite centuries of inhabitation, there's still plenty of unspoiled land in the Delaware countryside, including some 15,000 acres of marshland protected at **Bombay Hook National Wildlife Refuge.**

Despite its small appearance on the map, Delaware offers visitors a wealth of things to see and do, and you're sure to add to this list if you make a trip of your own.

Zone 8

Delaware

Flat, flatter, flattest. That pretty much sums up the geography of Delaware's three counties, from north to south.

The state's northwest boundary is unusual because when New Castle was designated its Colonial capital in 1704, somebody thought to use a compass to outline the state's boundary with Pennsylvania. The arc was drawn from the spire of New Castle courthouse. Today, two-thirds of the state's 754,000 residents live in it's northeast corner. Wilmington is a small city by national standards (population 72,000), yet, owing to favorable laws, more than half of the top 500 U.S. companies are incorporated there.

Wilmington has long been home to the world headquarters of the DuPont Company. At **Hagley Museum,** you can retrace the du Pont family's remarkable story, which began with the arrival of French chemist E.I. du Pont in 1800. During the Civil War the du Ponts manufactured black powder, which supplied 50 percent of the ammunition used by the Union Army. After 1921, the family got out of the gunpowder business and bought into other industries. Today, their biggest business is textiles.

Alfred I. du Pont invested his part of the family fortune to build **Nemours,** a 102-room Louis XVI-style chateau on a 300-acre estate that is open for touring. **Winterthur Museum,** built on an even grander scale, displays the world's largest collection of American antiques and decorative arts dating from 1640 to 1860. This was Henry Francis du Pont's house, and now his 89,000-piece collection is displayed here on nine floors and in 175 rooms. Its grounds are spread over almost 1,000 acres.

South of Wilmington, the town of **New Castle** is a model of historic preservation. Brick-paved streets, eighteenth-century Dutch cottages, Federal mansions, and gabled Victorians line its 20-square-block historic area.

Kent County, in central Delaware, offers a change of pace. Here, you can see horse-drawn carriages of Old Order Amish communities. Historic houses lend character to the area's small towns. Even **Dover,** the state capital, has an old-fashioned look with its brick sidewalks and grand Georgian and Victorian homes.

Southernmost **Sussex County** contains all 25 miles of Delaware's oceanfront beaches, which stretch from Cape Henlopen to Fenwick Island. State parklands comprise more than half of that coastline. **Rehoboth Beach,** Delaware's largest resort town, began as a Methodist meeting camp in the 1870s.

Lewes, at the southern terminus of the Cape May–Lewes Ferry, has one of the Mid-Atlantic region's prettiest main streets. The town's historical complex comprises eight restored buildings that were moved here to preserve the state's architectural heritage. The entire town of **Bethel,** a former ship building center, is on the National Register of Historic Places.

Several bed-and-breakfast owners we met in Deleware are retirees or transplants from other states. Others are long-time residents passionate about preservation. You'll find great properties in this often-overlooked state, aptly dubbed a small wonder.

FOR MORE INFORMATION

Delaware Tourism Office
99 Kings Hwy., Box 1401
Dover, DE 19903
(800) 866-7483; visitdelaware.com

Greater Wilmington CVB
(800) 489-6664

Central Delaware Kent County Tourism
(800) 233-5368

Southern Delaware Visitor Information
(800) 357-1818

ADDY SEA, Bethany Beach

OVERALL ★★★★½ | QUALITY ★★★★ | VALUE ★★★ | PRICE $100–$235

This handsome Bethany Beach landmark was built by John M. Addy, a Pittsburgh industrialist and one of the town's original settlers. *Washingtonian* magazine voted it "Best at the Beach" and Delaware architects named it one of the state's top ten architectural structures. Guests have been welcomed since the Depression, when the Addy family rented it for Church of Christ retreats. The current owner first stayed here with his family in 1944, then purchased the house in 1974 for $100,000. The location—right on the dunes—is stunning. It's a view you'll never forget. Even the food is memorable. The late *Washington Post* cartoonist Herb Block lived next door.

SETTINGS & FACILITIES

Location Oceanfront property on Rte. 1 between 3rd & 4th Sts. **Near** Baltimore, Wilmington, Rehoboth Beach. **Building** 1901 Victorian w/ cedar shingles, gingerbread trim. **Grounds** 4 adjoining lots in residential area, lawn, dune grass, wood arbor. **Public Space** LR, DR, wide porch w/ rocking chairs. **Food & Drink** Full breakfast; specialties—eggs of all kinds, bacon, waffles, sausage, French toast, ham, muffins; tea at 3:30 p.m.

Recreation Golf, biking, beach activities, bandstand concerts on Bethany boardwalk. **Amenities & Services** Groups (30).

ACCOMMODATIONS

Units 14 guest rooms. **All Rooms** Ceiling fans, framed art. **Some Rooms** Fireplace (2). **Bed & Bath** King (5), queen (12), double (2); two-person spa (1), 1900 copper tub (1), whirlpool (2); 7 private baths, 2 shared baths, 1 tub. **Favorites** #6—king bed w/ carved headboard, corner beach view & 2 wing chairs to enjoy it; #10—king bed, large tub w/ jets, fan, Victorian lamp, 2 wing chairs facing dramatic ocean view. **Comfort & Decor** Victorian-style decor features crystal chandeliers, period wall covering, original woodwork, classic tin ceilings, double-hung windows with starburst muntins, heavy wood pocket doors, marble mantels and reindeer gaslight fixtures. All this, and a storybook setting.

RATES, RESERVATIONS, & RESTRICTIONS

Deposit 50%. **Discounts** No. **Credit Cards** AE, V, MC, D. **Check-In/Out** 2 p.m./11 a.m. **Smoking** No. **Pets** No. **Kids** Age 7 & older. **Minimum Stay** No. **Open** All year. **Host** Leroy R. Gravatte, III, 99 Ocean View Parkway & N. Atlantic Ave., Bethany Beach, 19930. **Phone** (800) 418-6764. **Fax** (302) 539-7263. **E-mail** addyseabb@aol.com. **Web** addysea.com.

ROSE TOWER, Camden

OVERALL ★★★½ | QUALITY ★★★½ | VALUE ★★★★ | PRICE $89–$120

Rose Tower is locally known as the L.D. Caulk House, named for Dr. Levin Caulk, a dentist who patented numerous dental inventions. The current owners, who converted it to a B&B in 1996, are self-described restoration fanatics. On-going projects are painting and restoring exterior walls and uncovering the original cooking fireplace. Ed works as a test and evaluation engineer; on weekends he enjoys growing roses and acting as chef. A civil service retiree, Jane was the first woman to manage the Air Force's fighter plane acquisition program. The business principals of running a B&B are similar, she says. You must be diligent about managing the financial side in order to enjoy the fun side, like making muffins.

SETTINGS & FACILITIES

Location On busy street at crossroads of Rtes. 13 & 10. **Near** Dover museums, Delaware Wildlife Refuges, Atlantic Ocean beaches. **Building** 1807 Federal stucco-over-brick faux ashlar style, w/ wide hall & wide center staircase. **Grounds** 1 acre, w/ rose garden, birdfeeders, 100-year-old boxwoods, unrestored tower. **Public Space** LR, DR, foyer, TV room, 2 sitting rooms, powder room, porch. **Food & Drink** Full breakfast w/ fresh fruit, homemade breads, beverages; specialties—egg soufflé w/ cream sauce in puff pastry, sausage soufflé w/ potato pancakes; blueberry pancakes & butter pecan syrup, country sausage; classic English tea on request at $15 per person. **Recreation** Harness racing, antiquing, Amish bike tour; access to Old Dover Days, peach, film, & jazz festivals. **Amenities & Services** Videos, laundry facilities, fax & e-mail avail.; groups (10).

ACCOMMODATIONS

Units 3 guest rooms. **All Rooms** AC, phone, fresh flowers. **Some Rooms** Quilts. **Bed & Bath** King (3), sleigh (1); private baths, 1 whirlpool. **Favorites** Blue Rose—Colonial style, French Chinoise wallpaper, white Williamsburg-candlewicking quilt, Queen Anne–style highboy, great bathroom w/ tile, brass fixtures, glass shower (closet is small). **Comfort & Decor** Highlights include a grandfather clock from Germany, lots of art, Lladro figurines, and a tea cup collection. Traditional furniture sits on wood floors with area rugs. Guest room themes are Colonial, American quilts, and Asian fantasy.

RATES, RESERVATIONS, & RESTRICTIONS

Deposit Credit card to hold, refund w/ 24-hours notice. **Discounts** Military, Feb.–March, Oct.–Nov. **Credit Cards** AE, V, MC. **Check-In/Out** 3–6 p.m./noon. **Smoking** No. **Pets** No. **Kids** No. **Minimum Stay** No. **Open** All year. **Hosts** Jane & Ed Folz, 228 E. Camden-Wyoming Ave., Camden, 19934. **Phone** (877) 893-3031 or (302) 698-9033. **Fax** (302) 698-0629. **E-mail** rosetowerb&b@aol.com. **Web** rosetower.com.

DARLEY MANOR INN, Claymont

OVERALL ★★★★ | QUALITY ★★★★ | VALUE ★★★★ | PRICE **$99–$119**

This inn is listed on the National Register of Historic Places. For 30 years, beginning in 1859, it was owned by the artist Felix O. C. Darley, whose skillful drawings illustrated books by Nathaniel Hawthorne, Washington Irving, Edgar Allen Poe, Harriet Beecher Stowe, and Alfred L. Tennyson. He also illustrated 25 of James Fennimore Cooper's 32 books and Henry W. Longfellow's "Evangeline." As the American illustrator for Charles Dickens, he hosted Dickens in this home in March 1867. More recently, the house was a community center and a setting for plays and literary events. Rooms are named for historical and literary figures associated with the house, now decorated with an impressive collection of Darley's work.

SETTINGS & FACILITIES

Location Northern suburb of Wilmington, 1 block from Rte. 495, 1 mi. from I-95 Exit 10. **Near** 8 mi. to Winterthur, 7 mi. to Hagley Museum, 18 mi. to Longwood Gardens. **Building** 1775–1790 Colonial, 3-story pale gray w/ green shutters, scrollwork bargeboards, triple chimney pots. **Grounds** Lot facing Philadelphia Pike, across from 1805 school, next to 1850 Episcopal Church; garden w/ 100 rose bushes. **Public Space** Twin parlors, DR, foyer, small exercise porch. **Food & Drink** Nutrition-oriented kitchen serves full breakfast; specialties—berry or pecan pancakes w/ all-natural ingredients, 3-cheese quiche, homemade biscuits; cookies, snacks & beverages avail. **Recreation** 2 mi. from Bellevue State Park w/ tennis, walking trails, horseback riding stables; 7 mi. to Brandywine State Park w/ annual Civil War reenactment. **Amenities & Services** Business center w/ fax, copier, 2 computers; 5-person Jacuzzi in garden open April–Oct. Large video collection.

ACCOMMODATIONS

Units 2 guest rooms, 4 suites. **All Rooms** AC, cable TV w/ HBO, VCR, hairdryer, robes, recliner chair, computer port, good lighting, desk, phone, ironing board, sound machines to counteract road noise. **Some Rooms** Fireplace (3), small fridge (4), two TVs (4), full canopy beds (2). **Bed & Bath** Bed sizes vary, canopy (2); private baths. **Favorites** Wren's Nest—fireplace, large sitting area, four-poster carved beds w/ finials, lace and tassels, 20 Darley prints; Darley Suite—sitting room fireplace, tapestry headboard, French phone, Victorian lamp, 3 Darley prints. **Comfort & Decor** Antiques and reproductions circa 1850–1900, damask drapes with fringe, Oriental rugs, and Moorish arches endow this property. The North-South suite displays Confederate war tax receipts, a Union discharge paper, and a Civil War–era newspaper.

RATES, RESERVATIONS, & RESTRICTIONS

Deposit 1 night, refund w/ 3 or 7-days notice (depending on the date) less $10. **Discounts** Jan., Feb., corp., multiple nights, short notice. **Credit Cards** AE, V, MC, D, DC. **Check-In/Out** 4 p.m./noon. **Smoking** Outside only. **Pets** No. **Kids** 8 & older. **Minimum Stay** 2 nights some weekends (May, Oct., & all holidays). **Open** All year. **Hosts** Judith & Ray Hester, 3701 Philadelphia Pike, Claymont, 19703. **Phone** (800) 824-4703 or (302) 792-2127. **Fax** (302) 798-6143. **E-mail** Judith@darinn.com. **Web** darinn.com.

MANOR AT COOL SPRING, Cool Spring

OVERALL ★★★ | QUALITY ★★★★ | VALUE ★★★ | PRICE **$130–$160**

Pauline's passion for purple-flowered plants pervades Delaware's only lavender farm. A native of Norfolk, England and daughter of a prominent horticulturist, she earned a degree in English literature from Cambridge, then studied cooking at France's Sorbonne. Joe is from Pennsylvania's coal-mining region. He's a writer specializing in the energy business. Together they oversee two acres of lavender plants, in 50 varieties. The pungent crop does well in Delaware's sandy soil, blooming from May until fall's first frost. The owners make lavender bath and massage oil, soap, candy, jelly, flavored honey, and potpourri. Both hosts say they are living their dream.

SETTINGS & FACILITIES

Location 4.5 mi. west of Rtes. 1 & 9. **Near** 8.5 mi. to Atlantic Ocean, 7 mi. to Cape Henlopen State Park. **Building** 1902 white clapboard Victorian extensively remodeled. **Grounds** 5 acre farm, sweeping lawn, fruit trees, conifers, garden, commercial lavender production. **Public Space** 2 LR, DR, spa room w/ hot tub. **Food & Drink** English breakfast w/ grapefruit, bacon, sausage, rumbled eggs, pancakes, toast; other choices include salmon, stuffed French toast, tomatoes, eggs; afternoon tea, room refreshments. **Recreation** Guided tours of lavender farm, Lavender Fair (first weekend in June), biking, horseback riding, visiting a nearby bison farm, antiquing. **Amenities & Services** Fax, e-mail, turn-down service, massage by appointment, lavender samples.

ACCOMMODATIONS

Units 2 guest rooms. **All Rooms** AC, fresh flowers. **Some Rooms** 1 whirlpool. **Bed & Bath** Queen beds, canopy (1); private baths. **Favorites** Hidcote room—window sitting area, queen four-poster bed w/ bunches of lavender tied at each corner, hand-crocheted canopy, books, whirlpool tub. **Comfort & Decor** The inn has an eclectic mix of comfortable 1930s- and 1940s-style furnishings, a fireplace, and collections of English teapots, cup-and-saucer sets, and antique china.

RATES, RESERVATIONS, & RESTRICTIONS

Deposit 1 night. **Discounts** No. **Credit Cards** V, MC. **Check-In/Out** Noonish. **Smoking** No. **Pets** No (dog & 8 cats on premises). **Kids** No. **Minimum Stay** No. **Open** All year. **Hosts** Pauline Pettitt-Palenik & Joe Palenik, R.D. 2, Box 238, Milton, 19968. **Phone** (302) 684-8325. **Fax** (302) 684-8326. **E-mail** lavender@dmv.com. **Web** www.desu.edu/dhgma/lavender.html.

LITTLE CREEK INN, Dover

OVERALL ★★★★★ | QUALITY ★★★★½ | VALUE ★★★★★ | PRICE $200–$250 (INCLUDES DINNER)

A couple of transplants from Eastern Long Island have brought a touch of The Hamptons style and upscale cuisine to central Delaware. They transformed this former potato farm into a light-filled, tastefully-decorated retreat. The emphasis is on food. Bob is a member of the James Beard Foundation and has appeared on the Food Network. He's known for his seafood dishes. The elaborate gourmet dinners he prepares for B&B guests are served with bone china, silver, and fine linens, yet the ambience is decidedly casual and relaxed. This inn, listed on the National Register of Historic Places, is an ideal place to unwind and recharge.

SETTINGS & FACILITIES

Location On Rte. 8, 2 mi. east of Rte. 13. **Near** Rehoboth Beach, museums, NASCAR & harness racing at Dover Downs. **Building** 1860 Italianate. **Grounds** 8 acres of farmland w/ perennial garden, swimming pool, 2 barns. **Public Space** LR, DR, screened porch, powder room, front porch w/ swing, swimming pool, deck. **Food & Drink** Breakfast is fresh fruit plate, homemade muffins or scones, frittata or eggs cooked to order, meat, coffee/tea; gourmet dinners served w/ fine linens, china, and sterling silver. **Recreation** Swimming, 6 bikes avail., indoor tennis nearby. **Amenities & Services** Massage, laundry facilities, fax & e-mail.

ACCOMMODATIONS

Units 3 guest rooms, 1 suite. **All Rooms** AC, TV, private number phone, fresh flowers, robe, ceiling fan. **Some Rooms** Jacuzzi (2). **Bed & Bath** King (1), queen (3), double (1), four-poster (1), sleigh (1); 1 private bath, 3 rooms have detached bath; 4 tubs. **Favorites** Blue Room—four-poster bed, wood floor, Chinese rug, Queen Anne highboy, Scalamandre fabrics, Jacuzzi and glass shower; King Room—beige toile bed covers, pine floor, Aubusson rug, classic wallpaper, Jacuzzi. **Comfort & Decor** The spacious living room has high ceilings with a ceiling medallion, comfortable seating, reproduction oil paintings, antiques, and a fireplace. Colors are neutral. Guest rooms feature lovely Italian and French linens.

RATES, RESERVATIONS, & RESTRICTIONS

Deposit 1 night, refund w/ 48-hours notice; 50% charge w/ less notice. **Discounts** Midweek corp. rate. **Credit Cards** V, MC. **Check-In/Out** 3 p.m./11 a.m. **Smoking** Porch only. **Pets** Well behaved dogs (two dogs on premises). **Kids** Over age 12. **Minimum Stay** No. **Open** All year. **Hosts** Carol & BobThomas, 2623 N. Little Creek Rd., Dover, 19901. **Phone** (302) 730-1300. **Fax** (302) 730-4070. **Web** littlecreekinn.com.

SPRING GARDEN, Laurel

OVERALL ★★★½ | QUALITY ★★★★ | VALUE ★★★★ | PRICE $85–$115

Like the house that Topsey built, this one is a hodgepodge of architectural styles and accessories. It's one of 800 structures earning Laurel the status of a historic district—plus it's on the National Register of Historic Places. The original 400-acre plantation was run by Capt. Kendell Lewis, whose family was in residence here for more than 100 years. The clan included Warren K. Lewis, said to be the father of American Chemical Engineering. The current innkeeper grew up here, after her parents bought the property in 1954. She returned years later to open one of the first B&Bs in Sussex County. The garden is particularly attractive—an ideal place to relax.

SETTINGS & FACILITIES

Location 0.5 mi. east of town center, 0.2 mi. west of Rte. 13. **Near** Salisbury, MD Airport, Rehob0th & Bethany beaches. **Building** 1760 Colonial white brick Flemish bond w/ Georgian overtones; 1870 Victorian clapboard addition. **Grounds** 2.7 acres w/ stream, large barn, plus herb, flower, tomato, & shade gardens. **Public Space** LR, DR, 2 decks, screened porch. **Food & Drink** Full breakfast w/ seasonal fruit, cereals, beverages; specialties—Scotch eggs w/ Dijon mustard, zucchini nut muffins; Belgian waffles w/ strawberries, sausage; fruit, soda, & coffee anytime. **Recreation** Bike tours, antiquing, bird-watching, canoeing, fresh-water fishing, old-fashioned July 4th celebration, Sussex County Days. **Amenities & Services** Videos, games, croquet, badminton; meetings (12).

ACCOMMODATIONS

Units 4 rooms, 1 suite. **All Rooms** AC, fresh flowers. **Some Rooms** Fireplace (1), TV/VCR (1). **Bed & Bath** Double (4), twin (3), canopy (2); 4 private baths, 1 whirlpool, 1 tub. **Favorites** Naomi's Room—Colonial style w/ high four-poster canopy bed, white walls w/ blue trim, gas fireplace, wing chair, sofa, sleeps 3; one caveat: the detached bath is accessed via a private stairway. **Comfort & Decor** Varied styles include Federal, Colonial, and Victorian antiques.

RATES, RESERVATIONS, & RESTRICTIONS

Deposit 1 night, refund w/ 7-days notice less $10. **Discounts** Travel agents. **Credit Cards** No. **Check-In/Out** 3 p.m./11 a.m. **Smoking** In designated areas. **Pets** No (resident dog is jealous). **Kids** Over age 10. **No-Nos** Boom boxes. **Minimum Stay** 1 night. **Open** All year. **Host** Gwen North, Box 283A, Laurel, 19956. **Phone** (302) 875-7015. **Fax** (302) 875-7132. **E-mail** Gwen@ddmg.net.

BAY MOON, Lewes

OVERALL ★★★★ | QUALITY ★★★★½ | VALUE ★★★★ | PRICE $95–$150

Greek architect John Pigonas traveled from Washington, D.C. on weekends to create this house over a 15-year period. Then he got mad, sold the property, and left town in 1995. He left an eye-pleasing treasure distinguished by handsome wainscoting, bay windows, a two-sided fireplace, and a cozy pub room. The current innkeepers transformed his handiwork into a relaxing environment for vacationers. Pamela owned a custom interior design business for 13 years in Bridgeville, Delaware, before changing careers. During the week, Albert still works as a biologist with the U.S. Fish and Wildlife Service in Annapolis. But on weekends, he enjoys chatting with guests.

SETTINGS & FACILITIES

Location One block from town center. **Near** Rte. 1 and Rte. 404, Cape Henlopen State Park, Delaware Bay, across from a Presbyterian church & cemetery. **Building** 1897 Victorian w/ pillars, shutters, wraparound porch. **Grounds** City lot w/ several small flower gardens, outdoor Jacuzzi. **Public Space** LR, DR, library, bar, brick patio, 2 porches. **Food & Drink** Full breakfast w/ homemade baked goods, breakfast in bed available; complimentary wine, beverages/snacks on request. **Recreation** Canoe and kayak rental, 100 outlet stores; access to British Car Show (May), Garden Show (June), house tours. **Amenities & Services** Video & novel library, barbecue grill, beach gear.

ACCOMMODATIONS

Units 3 guest rooms, 1 suite. **All Rooms** AC, TV, VCR avail., comfortable seating. **Some Rooms** Fresh flowers, balcony (Silver Moon). **Bed & Bath** King (1), queen (3), double (2), twin beds (3), four-poster (3); private baths, 2 tubs. **Favorites** #2—four-poster bed, lace curtains, quilt, wainscoting on one wall (caveats: tiny bath, in-room sink); #5—quiet, light-filled, half-shuttered windows w/ church view, wood trim, rocker, craft accessories, great mattress (one caveat: detached bath). **Comfort & Decor** The peach-toned living room has varied antiques accessorized with a spinning wheel, roll-top desk, and birdhouse clock. The wood-paneled bar room resembles a cozy English pub. Patios have abundant flowers and floral borders.

RATES, RESERVATIONS, & RESTRICTIONS

Deposit 1 night, check or money order. **Discounts** 10% after 3rd day, some mid-week, gov. **Credit Cards** AE, V, MC, D. **Check-In/Out** 3 p.m./11 a.m. **Smoking** No. **Pets** No. **Kids** No. **Minimum Stay** 2 nights on weekends. **Open** All year. **Hosts** Pamela & Albert Rizzo, 128 Kings Hwy., Lewes, 19958. **Phone** (302) 644-1802. **E-mail** baymoon@dmv.com. **Web** baymoonbnb.com.

BLUE HERON INN, Lewes

OVERALL ★★★★½ | QUALITY ★★★★ | VALUE ★★★★ | PRICE **$80–$98**

After enjoying the bustle of noisy boardwalks and beaches, return to the quiet of a country marsh. Weather permitting, you're encouraged to leave windows open and enjoy nature's mellower sounds—throaty frogs, chirping birds, even flopping fish. The wetland views are magical. Guests are ensconced in the top two floors, accessible by a private entrance. Linda tried to think of everything a family would need. She spent a year designing the rooms, then nine months overseeing every detail of construction—all the while working as a hospice nurse and raising two children. Already Blue Heron, opened in 1998, has a huge repeat clientele. Linda says it's the view, but her enthusiasm and warm personality are factors as well.

SETTINGS & FACILITIES

Location 0.5 mi. east of Rte. 1 on Old Mill Creek. **Near** 5 mi. to Lewes Beach, 6 mi. to Cape Henlopen State Park, 8 mi. to Rehoboth. **Building** 1997 cedar-sided three-story gray house, owner-designed. **Grounds** Total 7.25 acres w/ 1,000-ft. creekside, 3-acre wooded meadow, trails, goat pen. **Public Space** 2 sitting areas, DR, kitchen, 2 screened porches. **Food & Drink** Full breakfast w/ juice, fresh fruit; specialties—popovers, eggs Benedict, French toast, bacon, sausage, eggs to order, Belgian waffles, quiche, homemade strawberry jam; coffee & tea anytime. **Recreation** Canoe to Broad Kill River (tide permitting) and on to Delaware Bay; near many area festivals including balloon, kite, chocolate, jazz, film, punkin chunk; NASCAR races in Dover (June & Sept.). **Amenities & Services** TV & VCR on 3rd floor, games, outdoor grill, outdoor shower; groups to 10.

ACCOMMODATIONS

Units 3 guest rooms. **All Rooms** AC, clock radio **Some Rooms** Water view (2). **Bed & Bath** Queen (2), twin (2), canopy (1), sleigh (1); private baths. **Favorites** Sussex—four-poster bed, double window w/ creek view. **Comfort & Decor** The spacious, light-filled family room on the third floor has windows on four sides, comfortable wicker furnishings, TV, and games including chess and checkers. The second floor sitting area has a more limited view and more sedate decor. Guest rooms are pristine and pleasing.

RATES, RESERVATIONS, & RESTRICTIONS

Deposit 1 night. **Discounts** Entire inn, 3 days or more. **Credit Cards** V, MC. **Check-In/Out** 3 p.m./11 a.m. **Smoking** No. **Pets** Outside only. **Kids** Over age 5. **Minimum Stay** 2 nights April 1–Nov. 1; 3 nights major holidays. **Open** All year. **Hosts** Linda & Bob LeKites, 11 Willow Creek Rd., Lewes, 11958. **Phone** (302) 645-9898. **Fax** (302) 645-1998. **E-mail** lekites@bwave.com. **Web** www.beach-net.com/blueheron.

BLUE WATER HOUSE, Lewes

OVERALL ★★★★½ | QUALITY ★★★½ | VALUE ★★★ | PRICE $85–$150

A sign "celebrate life" hangs over the reception desk. Almost every wall, nook and cranny is part of what looks like a combination modern art gallery and child's fantasy house. The owner's overall theme is fun at the beach, and he's achieved nothing less than a tour de force. He did it by combining a palette of pleasing colors, eye-boggling mobiles, and whimsical sculpture. Among them are faux animal trophies, giant masks, oversized paintings, pottery, puppets, statues, and surreal floral arrangements. Even the top floor sitting room, with wraparound windows, is wired with colored lights to create some after-dark fantasy. All this, plus the owner's effervescent personality, will please the young and young at heart.

SETTINGS & FACILITIES

Location Residential area, beach side of Lewes. **Near** 1.5 mi. to Cape Henlopen State Park w/ pristine ocean beach, 2.5 mi. to bay beach. **Building** 1993 w/ cedar siding inspired by Chesapeake Bay lighthouse; white, pink, yellow, & blue trim, 2nd-floor wraparound balcony. **Grounds** City lot adjacent to wetlands on two sides w/ sea grass, reeds, shrubs, eclectic mix of trees; dolphin and mermaid sculpture fountain, benches, wood carvings. **Public Space** 2nd floor breakfast room, wet bar; 3rd floor sitting room/observatory. **Food & Drink** Gourmet cont'l breakfast: fruit tray, granola, cereal, yogurt, pudding, muffins, biscotti, bagels, beverages. **Recreation** Beach chairs, towels, umbrellas, 10 bikes avail. at no charge. **Amenities & Services** Videos, massage, outside grill/shower, laundry, fax & e-mail.

ACCOMMODATIONS

Units 9 guest rooms. **All Rooms** AC, VCR, handmade soap. **Some Rooms** balcony (6). **Bed & Bath** King (1), queen (6), twin (2); 7 private baths, 2 shared baths, 5 tubs. **Favorites** #1—basic furnishings enlivened w/ a rainbow of colors (teal green, pale peach, plus blue & yellow accents), double doors open to porch w/ ice-cream table, chairs; #7—art deco look w/ blue walls, red accessories, black furniture, gold trim; #9—if avail. the spacious owners suite offers fine art, luxury furnishings. **Comfort & Decor** "Awesomely adequate" sums up this color-saturated property. Furnishings are the adequate part of the equation, plus a few luxury touches. The color scheme is bright, bold, and unusual. The soothing sound of running water is a constant—heard in the dining and porch areas. The walls are a bit thin, but hopefully you'll have quiet neighbors.

RATES, RESERVATIONS, & RESTRICTIONS

Deposit 1 night, refund w/ 7-days notice. **Discounts** Age 65 & older, Sept. 6–May 14. **Credit Cards** V, MC. **Check-In/Out** 2 p.m./11 a.m. **Smoking** No. **Pets** No. **Kids** All ages. **Minimum Stay** 2 nights on weekends May 15–Sept. 15. **Open** All year. **Host** Richard M. Quill, 407 E. Market St., Lewes, 19958. **Phone** (800) 493-2080 or (302) 645-7832. **Fax** (302) 644-3704. **E-mail** rick@erols.com. **Web** www.lewes-beach.com.

JOHN PENROSE VIRDEN HOUSE, Lewes

OVERALL ★★★★ | QUALITY ★★★★½ | VALUE ★★★★ | PRICE **$125–$150**

This is one of Lewes' most elegant historic homes. It was built by John Penrose Virden, founder and 21-year president of the Delaware Bay and River Pilots Association. In 1999, a New Jersey couple redecorated the property and opened it as a B&B. Ruth is an artist with the instincts of a perfectionist. Her hobby is to paint folk art on stools, chests, and small objects, which she displays discretely. Formerly an upper-elementary teacher, she met her husband while teaching at the American School in

Germany. For now, Jim continues his career with AT&T. Together they have polished a town jewel in a way that would make the Virdens proud.

SETTINGS & FACILITIES

Location Adjacent to Lewes-Rehobeth Canal Yacht Basin. **Near** Henlopen State Park, Lewes Historical Society, Delaware Bay, Atlantic Ocean. **Building** 1888 Victorian, 3-story green w/ white trim, awning. **Grounds** Large city lot, hedges, garden, brick patio, bird hotel. **Public Space** Parlor, grand ballroom, DR, powder room, porch w/ swing, patio. **Food & Drink** Full breakfast w/ fresh fruit; specialties—baked eggs with Canadian bacon, baked orange French toast w/ apple sausage ring, ham-egg-brie strudel w/ endive tomato salad, steamed asparagus; afternoon wine & cheese, snacks. **Recreation** Museums, water sports, fishing, house & garden tours, parades, art festivals, auctions. **Amenities & Services** Videos, massage, laundry & fax on request; meetings (30).

ACCOMMODATIONS

Units 2 guest rooms, 1 cottage. **All Rooms** AC, TV, radio, fresh flowers, hair dryer, fresh fruit. **Some Rooms** 1 private entrance, 1 small fridge (cottage). **Bed & Bath** Queen beds w/ antique walnut frames; private baths, 1 tub. **Favorites** Cottage—TV, fridge, breakfast table to eat in, crystal glassware, glass shower. **Comfort & Decor** The overall look is elegant. The ballroom has crown molding, cranberry walls, heart-pine floors with Oriental rugs, antique/Victorian furnishings, Gone-with-the-Wind lamps, and a butler's chest. The dining room bar comes from a ship. The second floor bedroom has Eastlake antique bed, bird-and-flower wallpaper, and hand-painted bathroom walls. The mahogany stairway continues to the third floor. Wicker furniture invites relaxation on the porch.

RATES, RESERVATIONS, & RESTRICTIONS

Deposit 1 night. **Discounts** 10% for 5 nights or more. **Credit Cards** No. **Check-In/Out** 3 p.m./11 a.m. **Smoking** No. **Pets** No. **Kids** No. **Minimum Stay** 2 nights. **Open** All year. **Hosts** Ruth & Jim Edwards, 217 Second St., Lewes, 19958. **Phone** (302) 644-0217. **Fax** (302) 644-0217. **E-mail** redwards@virdenhouse.com. **Web** http://virdenhouse.com.

ROYAL RETREAT, Lewes

OVERALL ★★★½ | QUALITY ★★★½ | VALUE ★★★ | PRICE **$60–$145**

According to legend, the house was built by Danish Sea Captain Lars Petersen, the only survivor of a shipwreck on the sands off Cape Henlopen. The Birches moved to Lewes because it has old world charm similar to villages in Cornwall in England. Roy enjoys reminiscing with guests about his career in the British navy. At age 13, he started aboard a training ship, and he retired from the Royal Navy in 1984 after serving as a Commander in the Falklands War. British nautical items—including a sword, original tots used to measure rum, and a bosun's whistle—add to the ambience. Even the friendly dogs are named "Maggie" and "Fergie." Roy now runs the B&B full time, while Joann continues her nursing career.

SETTINGS & FACILITIES

Location 4 blocks from town center, minutes to Atlantic Ocean. **Near** Henlopen State Park, Cape May Ferry, tax-free shopping outlets. **Building** 1890 three-story house w/

mansard roof, white siding. **Grounds** 0.5 acre w/ garden, screened gazebo, hammock, birdhouse, bird bath. **Public Space** Sitting room, DR, upstairs library, TV lounge, guest pantry. **Food & Drink** Early coffee; English breakfast at 9 a.m.; specialties—baked French toast, breakfast pie; daily refreshments—served on Blue Willow China at 5 p.m. —include port or sherry w/ cheese, flavored tea w/ sandwiches, scones w/ Cornish cream, strawberries & champagne. **Recreation** Biking (5 avail.), beach activities (towels & chairs provided), old car show, garden tour, charter fishing boats. **Amenities & Services** Exercise bike; champagne turn-down service.

ACCOMMODATIONS

Units 3 guest rooms. **All Rooms** AC, fresh flowers, hair dryer, robes. **Some Rooms** Private entrance. **Bed & Bath** King (1), queen (2); 1 private bath, 2 shared. **Favorites** Blue Willow—pretty blue & yellow wallpaper, antique dresser, fine china display;. Admiral Lord Nelson Suite—fantasy version of *HMS Victory* quarters, but light and cheerful w/ nautical accents. **Comfort & Decor** The living room has brick-front log fireplace, traditional style homey furnishings, and lots of personal mementos. The upstairs library displays personal documents, photos, and military hats.

RATES, RESERVATIONS, & RESTRICTIONS

Deposit 1 night, refund w/ 7-days notice less $10. **Discounts** No. **Credit Cards** V, MC. **Check-In/Out** 2–7 p.m./11 a.m. **Smoking** No. **Pets** No (2 dogs on site). **Kids** No. **Minimum Stay** 2 nights on weekends in July & Aug., 3 nights on holidays. **Open** All year. **Hosts** Joann & Roy Birch, 425 Kings Hwy., Lewes, 19958. **Phone** (877) 645-9698 or (302) 645-8913. **Fax** (302) 645-8913. **E-mail** Rbirch3232@aol.com. **Web** www.lewestoday.com.

WILD SWAN INN, Lewes

OVERALL ★★★½ | QUALITY ★★★★ | VALUE ★★★ | PRICE **$85–$150**

This house seems to say, "Look at me, how pretty I am." It was built by Captain Arthur Hudson, who gussied it up with three Queen Anne glass windows plus etched ruby glass over the front door. The exterior wood trim is equally fanciful, with bargeboard scrollwork in wagon-wheel design, finials, turnings, and gables. An integral part of the B&B experience here is Michael's after-breakfast mini-lecture on old phonographs and Thomas Edison. He cranks up his authentic antique player and puts on old recordings, including opera singer Enrico Caruso. On Sunday mornings, Mike gives a short concert on his player piano, inviting you to step back 100 years to an era when the piano was a focal point in family life.

SETTINGS & FACILITIES

Location Residential area, east side of Lewes. **Near** Cape Henlopen State Park, Zwaanendael Museum, Maritime Museum, Cape May–Lewes Ferry, Prime Hook Federal Wildlife Preserve, Delaware Bay, 3 mi. to Atlantic Ocean. **Building** 1899 Queen Anne Victorian in the Charles Eastlake style, pinkish beige w/ pale green, burgundy, rose, & white accents. **Grounds** Corner city lot, Victorian-style landscaping, flowering trees, garden. **Public Space** Parlor w/ library, DR, wraparound porch, backyard gazebo, patio, swimming pool.

Food & Drink Full breakfast; specialties—award-winning asparagus pie w/ corn muffins, poached pear almondine, sunshine bread, honey-banana raisin bread w/ porcupine mango, maple-walnut waffles w/ fresh berries, blueberry muffins, boiled grapefruit; bottled water, biscotti, & snacks avail. **Recreation** Swimming, fishing, boating, cycling (6 bikes provided), birding, photography, museums, British Motorcar Show (April–May), Memorial Day parade, 4th of July fireworks & parade, Coast Day, kite festival, garden tours, antiques fairs, crafts shows, art shows, Christmas parade. **Amenities & Services** Games & puzzles.

ACCOMMODATIONS

Units 3 guest rooms. **All Rooms** AC, fresh flowers, hair dryer, reading lamp, upholstered chair. **Some Rooms** Artwork and antiques. **Bed & Bath** Queen beds, private baths, 1 tub. **Favorites** Delaware room—quilt, painted floor, interesting art & area memorabilia including a Wyeth print, a 1926 lighthouse picture, & an old map. **Comfort & Decor** Displays include heirloom antiques, old photos, collections of swans, plates, cameras, and baby feeding dishes. Nan's room has host's grandmother's 1890 wedding certificate and dress. The rose room has rose wallpaper, a ceiling medallion, a hanging quilt, and a wash stand base as its sink.

RATES, RESERVATIONS, & RESTRICTIONS

Deposit 1 night, refund w/ 7-days notice less $10. **Discounts** No. **Credit Cards** No. **Check-In/Out** 2–7 p.m./11 a.m. **Smoking** No. **Pets** No. **Kids** No. **No-Nos** No more than 2 people in a room. **Minimum Stay** 2 nights weekends July through Labor Day, 3 nights on holiday weekends. **Open** All year except Jan. **Hosts** Hope & Michael Tyler, 525 Kings Hwy., Lewes, 19958. **Phone** (302) 645-8550. **Fax** (302) 645-8550. **E-mail** wildswan@udel.edu.

ZWAANENDAEL INN, Lewes

OVERALL ★★★ | QUALITY ★★★★ | VALUE ★★★ | PRICE **$60–$225**

Now on the National Register of Historic Places, this building (until recently known as the New Devon Inn) had a somewhat checkered past. It has housed the town hall, a jail, bus counter, and, some say, a brothel. The turnaround began in 1987, when the interior was gutted to create an upscale inn. The lobby is spacious and interesting. Thoughtful touches in all guest rooms include plants, books, and a silver tray holding crystal drinking glasses. When new owners took over in July 2000, they added all new bedding and linens. Cloth napkins, china, and good stemware are used for the continental breakfast. And, right outside the door, the main street of Lewes awaits—chockablock with gift shops, boutiques, antique stores, and an old-fashioned ice cream parlor.

SETTINGS & FACILITIES

Location Main street of town, near Rte. 1. **Near** 0.75 mi. to Delaware Bay, 1.5 mi. to Atlantic Ocean; Cape Henlopen State Park. **Building** 1926 brick building, renovated. **Grounds** Street front sidewalk. **Public Space** Main lobby, garden room, lower lobby, small elevator. **Food & Drink** Cont'l breakfast as "a start for your day" w/ juice, bagels, muffins, coffee, tea. **Recreation** Cape May–Lewes Ferry, fishing, boating, whale watching, dinner train, garden tour (June), coastal celebration (Oct.), Christmas house tour, art, antique, & craft shows. **Amenities & Services** Evening turndown service w/ candy, handicap accessible, fax, copier; meetings (45), weddings (60).

ACCOMMODATIONS

Units 18 guest rooms, 5 suites. **All Rooms** AC, phone, hardwood floor w/ Oriental rug, books, plants, upholsltered chair, hair dryer, silver tray w/ crystal glasses, silver ice bucket, nice toiletries. **Some Rooms** Bay views. **Bed & Bath** King (5), Queen (12), double (4), twin (2), sleigh (1); private baths, 14 tubs. **Favorites** #106—French headboard, oak dresser, desk & chair, wool carpet, red & rose tones, street view; #108—largest standard room, view to canal & bay, cross-ventilation, high bed w/ dust ruffle, teal floral fabrics w/ gold & wine accents; #208—same corner view, blue & white floral fabrics. **Comfort & Decor** Twin teakwood carved elephant chairs from Thailand are the centerpieces of the lobby.

RATES, RESERVATIONS, & RESTRICTIONS

Deposit Credit card, refund w/ 3-days notice. **Discounts** Corp. rate on weekdays Sept.–May. **Credit Cards** AE,V, MC. **Check-In/Out** 2 p.m./11 a.m. **Smoking** No. **Pets** No. **Kids** Yes ($20 each plus $20 for rollaway). **Minimum Stay** 2 nights on weekends. **Open** All year. **Host** Michael Cryne, 142 Second St., Lewes, 19958. **Phone** (800) 824-8754 or (302) 645-6466. **Fax** (302) 645-7196. **E-mail** zwaanendaelinn@dca.net. **Web** zwaanendaelinn.com.

THE TOWERS, Milford

OVERALL ★★★★½ | QUALITY ★★★★½ | VALUE ★★★★★ | PRICE $95–$135

In spite of being 36 miles upstream, Milford was an early shipbuilding center. It's forests grew sturdy woods and finished products could be transported to sea via the Mispillion River, which runs through town. The Towers, one of 29 houses in Milford listed on the National Register of Historic Places, has been a residence, millinery shop, and general store. In the 1880s, heiress Rhoda Roudebush lavishly remodeled it, hiring local shipbuilders to lower the living room floor, install a coffered ceiling, extensive wood paneling, ornamental mantels, and colored glass windows and doors. On the exterior, they added a corner turret, balconies, porches, shingling, and ornamental woodwork. Recent and current owners have restored all this to mint condition—with stunning results.

SETTINGS & FACILITIES

Location Southern Delaware, Rte. 14, downtown Milford. **Near** Atlantic beaches, Bombay Hook National Wildlife Refuge. **Building** 1783 Victorian w/ 1891 addition; exterior has elaborate interior wood & stained glass to create a Steamboat Gothic look. **Grounds** 0.25 acre w/ enclosed garden, deck, swimming pool, goldfish pool, fountain. **Public Space** Foyer, music room, parlor, dining room, 3rd floor sitting area, guest pantry. **Food & Drink** Full breakfast; specialties—ricotta pancakes, eggs Benedict, quiche Lorraine; sherry and fruit drinks avail. anytime. **Recreation** Beach activities, bird & wildlife viewing. **Amenities & Services** Cable TV & videos in public rooms; groups (30).

ACCOMMODATIONS

Units 2 guest rooms, 2 suites. **All Rooms** AC, ceiling fans. **Some Rooms** Balcony (1). **Bed & Bath** Queen (1), double (3); private baths, 4 tubs. **Favorites** Tower room—pink canopy bed w/ lace, 2 wing chairs, claw-foot tub, tile floor, stained-glass window; Garden room—tailored, light-filled, quieter, garden view, Czarist money displayed (detached bath). **Comfort & Decor** The large music room has an 1899 Knabe grand piano, elaborate carved doorscreens, and sycamore coffered ceiling. Furnishings are primarily French Victorian—formal, yet friendly. Both the dining and music rooms have gas fireplaces. Guest rooms retain historic ties yet offer modern comforts.

RATES, RESERVATIONS, & RESTRICTIONS

Deposit Credit card to hold, refund w/ 7-days notice. **Discounts** Corp., 20% Sun.–Thurs. **Credit Cards** AE, V, MC. **Check-In/Out** 3–6 p.m./11 a.m. **Smoking** No. **Pets** No. **Kids** Over age 12. **Minimum Stay** 2 nights on weekends May–Sept. **Open** All year. **Hosts** Rhonda & Dan Bond, 101 NW Front St., Milford, 19963. **Phone** (302) 422-3814. **Fax** (302) 422-4703. **E-mail** mispillion@ezd.com. **Web** mispillion.com.

INN AT MONTCHANIN VILLAGE, Montchanin

OVERALL ★★★★★ | QUALITY ★★★★★ | VALUE ★★★ | PRICE **$160–$375**

This former working-class compound contains stone walls, carriage lanes, and gardens reminiscent of an English or Irish village. Originally, residents worked at nearby DuPont Company powder mills and factories along the Brandywine River. The compound thrived from 1859 to 1910. But, by 1991 when Missy and Dan inherited the property, it was neglected and in disrepair. These du Pont descendants spared no expense in transforming it into one of Delaware's best inns. The old blacksmith shop is now a fine-dining restaurant and the 1889 railroad station a carry-out gourmet shop. The aptly named Privy Lane is lined with small concrete buildings. It's all part of the charm of this historic property, named for Anne de Montchanin, grandmother of the DuPont Company founder.

SETTINGS & FACILITIES

Location 6 mi. north of Wilmington. **Near** Rte. 95 & Rte. 202, Winterthur, Longwood Gardens, Chaddsford. **Building** Mid- to late-1800s stucco, stone, & wood, 11 separate buildings. **Grounds** 5 acres, sloping terrain w/ carriageways, paths, gardens, stone walls. **Public Space** Lobby/lounge, Krazy Kat's restaurant. **Food & Drink** Full breakfast Mon.–Sat., brunch on Sun. includes fresh-squeezed juice, muffins, cereals, yogurts; specialties—Belgian waffles, eggs Benedict, omelets. **Recreation** Antiquing, visiting museums. **Amenities & Services** Restaurant, groups (55).

ACCOMMODATIONS

Units 13 guest rooms, 14 suites. **All Rooms** AC, TV & VCR, kitchenette w/ microwave, mini-fridge stocked w/ complimentary soda & water, coffeemaker, tableware & glasses, terry robes, heated towel bar, make-up mirror, hair dryer, phone, fresh flowers, linen sheets. **Some Rooms** Gas fireplace (14), porch w/ furniture (14), private entrance. **Bed & Bath** King (8), queen (22), twin (3), four-poster (4); private baths, 1 Jacuzzi, 1 jet tub, 6 oversize soaking tubs. **Favorites** Suites—the ultimate in luxury, no two are alike. **Comfort & Decor** Room sizes and quality vary. Period and antique furnishings are enlivened with animal prints mixed with floral, striped, and plaid fabrics. Comfort is key with plenty of oversized, sink-in sofas, and wingback chairs.

RATES, RESERVATIONS, & RESTRICTIONS

Deposit Credit card to hold, refund w/ 24-hours notice. **Discounts** No. **Credit Cards** AE, V, MC, DC, D. **Check-In/Out** 3–10 p.m./11 a.m. **Smoking** No. **Pets** No. **Kids** Yes, cribs avail. **Minimum Stay** No. **Open** All year. **Hosts** Missy & Dan Lickle, Rte. 100 and Kirk Rd., Montchanin, 19710. **Phone** (800) 269-2473 or (302) 888-2133. **Fax** (302) 888-0389. **Web** montchanin.com.

ARMITAGE INN, New Castle

OVERALL ★★★★ | QUALITY ★★★★ | VALUE ★★★ | PRICE **$110–$185**

The house was named for Ann Armitage, the third wife of patriot Zachariah Van Leuvenigh, who was a town magistrate. The nearby dock was a strategic ferrying point across the Delaware River between Washington, D.C. and New York City. During his residency, from 1765 to 1789, Van Leuvenigh provided hospitality to post riders bringing word of Revolutionary War battles. In an earlier era, the house gained fame for sitting only a few feet away from the spot where William Penn first set foot in the New World. In fact, one wing is believed to have been built in the 1600s. You can still see the original "walk in" cooking fireplace. If you arrive early enough, you can dine in one of the two nearby Colonial-style restaurants (they close early), then take a stroll along the grassy river bank.

SETTINGS & FACILITIES

Location Northern Delaware, at the edge of the historic district, facing the Delaware River & Battery Park. **Near** Philadelphia & Baltimore airports, Longwood Gardens; Winterthur, Brandywine River & Hagley Museums. **Building** 1732 Colonial brick Georgian w/ additions/restorations. **Grounds** Brick patio, walled garden, boxwoods, pond, statuary, Victorian playhouse. **Public Space** Parlor, DR. **Food & Drink** Juice, fresh fruit, Ethiopian coffee, homemade cinnamon-nut & kiwi muffins, yogurt, cereals; specialties—French toast, waffles, silver dollar pancakes, apple crisp, breakfast pudding w/ vanilla cream sauce. **Recreation** Antiquing, 1.25 mi. scenic river walk, public tennis courts accessible, annual Day in Olde New Castle. **Amenities & Services** Fax avail.

ACCOMMODATIONS

Units 4 guest rooms, 1 suite. **All Rooms** A/C, Cable TV, dataport, hair dryer, telephone. **Some Rooms** Water views. **Bed & Bath** King (2), queen (3), canopy (2), four-poster (4); private baths, 3 whirlpool, 3 tubs. **Favorites** Hawthorn—high king four-poster bed w/ drapery, attractive paintings, antique photos, lace curtains, water view, whirlpool; White Rose—high king four-poster canopy bed, bay window to watch river traffic, spacious, bathroom w/ whirlpool tub. **Comfort & Decor** The spacious living room has wood floors, an Oriental carpet, a gas fireplace, and interesting coffee table books. The formal dining room features a gas fireplace, collections of fine china, Armenian pottery, brassware, and a silver service. There are partial water views.

RATES, RESERVATIONS, & RESTRICTIONS

Deposit 1 night. **Discounts** No. **Credit Cards** AE, V, MC, D. **Check-In/Out** 4–7 p.m./11 a.m. **Smoking** No. **Pets** No. **Kids** 12 and older. **Minimum Stay** 2 nights on most weekends. **Open** All year. **Host** Stephen Marks, 2 The Strand, New Castle, 19720. **Phone** (302) 328-6618. **Fax** (302) 324-1163. **E-mail** armitageinn@earthlink.net. **Web** armitageinn.com.

WILLIAM PENN, New Castle

OVERALL ★★★½ | QUALITY ★★★½ | VALUE ★★★★ | PRICE $69–$89

Make yourself at home in one of four cozy guest rooms in this small, but beautifully restored historic home. It's comfortable, warm, and inviting right down to the original wide-plank floors. Outside, cobblestone streets bring to mind a time when life was simpler. New Castle, with its quiet tree-lined streets and historic Colonial-era homes, is definitely a walking town. Townspeople take great pride in renovating and preserving its architectural beauty. These hosts are old-timers. They opened their B&B in 1956, so they know the area and have interesting stories to tell.

SETTINGS & FACILITIES

Location Northern Delaware, heart of New Castle's historic district. **Near** Longwood Gardens, Winterthur, Brandywine River, Hagley Museums, Nemours Mansion, Delaware Art Museum, Old Swedes Church. **Building** 1682 Colonial brick w/ additions. **Grounds** City lot w/ garden, over 50 rose bushes. **Public Space** LR, DR, patio. **Food & Drink** Cont'l breakfast includes juice, fruit, cereal, bagels, hot beverages. **Recreation** River walk, public tennis courts access, annual Day in Olde New Castle. **Amenities & Services** Knowledgable hosts offer concierge-like services.

ACCOMMODATIONS

Units 4 guest rooms. **All Rooms** AC, TV. **Some Rooms** Ceiling fan (2). **Bed & Bath** King (1), double (2), twin beds (2); 1 private, 1 detached, 2 shared baths. **Favorites** 3rd floor #2—twin beds, floral pattern, very small but sweet. **Comfort & Decor** Plaster over brick walls, American and English heirlooms, and comfortable furnishings are notable. The dining room features a storybook teapot collection.

RATES, RESERVATIONS, & RESTRICTIONS

Deposit 1 night w/ credit card, refund w/ 5-days notice. **Discounts** No. **Credit Cards** V, MC. **Check-In/Out** 11 a.m./10:30 p.m. **Smoking** No. **Pets** No. **Kids** Age 10 & over. **Minimum Stay** 2 nights on holidays. **Open** All year (except Feb.). **Hosts** Irma & Dick Burwell, 206 Delaware St., New Castle, 19720. **Phone** (302) 328-7736. **Fax** (302) 328-0403.

DELAWARE INN, Rehoboth Beach

OVERALL ★★★ | QUALITY ★★★½ | VALUE ★★★ | PRICE $95–$190

One of Rehobeth Beach's oldest continuously-operated inns, it was established by a Mrs. Moore, who ran it until she was in her 80s. She rented rooms for $10 a night, primarily to sport fishermen. Today, the inn offers tastefully-decorated, antique-filled rooms along with warm hospitality and a country atmosphere. The hosts are thoughtful and thorough in creating a pleasant retreat. Stained-glass panels created by Tom are displayed throughout the house, and his aromatic plants thrive in garden borders that enhance the yard. Outside, the inn flies a rainbow-hued banner, indicating that it is alternative-lifestyle friendly. In fact, everyone is welcome at this ideally-located inn near the sea.

SETTINGS & FACILITIES

Location 1.5 blocks from Atlantic Ocean. **Near** Cape Henlopen State Park, Outlet Shopping Center. **Building** 1930 beach cottage, enlarged. **Grounds** City lot w/ interesting floral & plant borders. **Public Space** LR, DR, glassed-in, heated porch. **Food & Drink** Buffet-style cont'l breakfast Mon.–Sat. includes homemade muffins & breads; hot breakfast Sun. may include spinach quiche or apple cinnamon French toast; wine & cheese after 5 p.m.; boxed lunches avail. **Recreation** Golf, birding, fishing, biking (6 on site), beach activities (beach chairs & umbrellas provided); inn offers off-season Murder Mystery weekends w/ professional actors. **Amenities & Services** Fax & e-mail, extensive paperback & board game collection, outdoor shower.

ACCOMMODATIONS

Units 7 guest rooms, 2 suites. **All Rooms** AC, ceiling fan. **Some Rooms** TV (4). **Bed & Bath** King (2), queen (6), double (2), twin beds (4); canopy (1), four-poster (1), sleigh (1); 3 private, 2 shared baths, 3 tubs. **Favorites** Magnolia—large room w/ comfortable bed, green tones, stripes, & flowers; Southwestern—metal four-poster bed, Santa Fe pottery, cactus, dream catcher, stained glass art. **Comfort & Decor** The living room has an area rug, tin chandelier, Flow Blue china, hanging baskets, stained glass collection, and antiques. Themed guest rooms include Southwest, Far East, and Victorian.

RATES, RESERVATIONS, & RESTRICTIONS

Deposit 50% in summer, refund w/ 10-days notice less $10 fee. **Discounts** 10% for week or longer stay. **Credit Cards** V, MC, D. **Check-In/Out** 3 p.m./11 a.m. **Smoking** Porch only. **Pets** No (2 dogs on premises are confined). **Kids** Over age 12. **Minimum Stay** 2 nights May 1–Oct. 1. **Open** All year (except Jan.). **Hosts** Ron Baird & Tom Peters, 55 Delaware Ave., Rehoboth Beach, 19971. **Phone** (302) 227-6031. **Fax** (302) 226-1788. **E-mail** innkeeper@delawareinn.com **Web** delawareinn.com.

Part Four

Pennsylvania

Pennsylvanians are avid archivists and preservationists.

Many key chapters of American history took place in the Keystone State, and efforts to preserve that history began at a grassroots level long before sites were codified by state commissions or Congressional decree.

One early site is in **Baumstown,** where the 1734 birthplace of frontiersman Daniel Boone was recreated on a 570-acre site that includes his family's house, barn, blacksmith shop, and sawmill.

The town of **Bethlehem** on the Lehigh River preserves the traditions of Moravians who established a religious community in 1741. Special events are numerous at Christmastime. Because Moravians brought the first serious music to the colonies, Bach concerts are a tradition each May.

No great battle was fought at **Valley Forge,** but it was the site of a great victory of the human spirit. Troops led by George Washington encamped here, endured dire conditions, overcame uncertainty, and forged an efficient fighting force. A local women's group, Daughters of the Revolution, helped to create what became a 3,300-acre memorial to the endurance and determination of the first Americans.

Near **Chadds Ford,** a small park commemorates the 1777 Battle of the Brandywine, and each September reenactment ceremonies feature a Washington look-alike and musket firing. In December, at **Washington's Crossing Historic Park,** you can relive George Washington's daring maneuver to re-cross the ice-choked Delaware River on Christmas Day. The 500-acre park is split between two areas five miles apart and offers 13 historic buildings, a nature preserve, and five picnic pavilions.

One of the state's most unusual archivists, Dr. Henry Chapman Mercer, preserved buildings and objects in **Doylestown.** At the **Mercer Museum of the Bucks County Historical Society,** you can see his encyclopedic collection of 14,000 household items and farm tools from the eighteenth and nineteenth centuries. His home, now **Fonthill Museum,** and his workplace, the still-active **Moravian Pottery and Tile Works,** preserve a slice of Americana.

In **Lancaster County**, an entire culture survives from the mid-1700s, when the first Amish refugees emigrated to America. For Old Order Amish, dress remains medieval, the standard mode of transportation is still by horse-drawn buggy, and religious beliefs are mostly intact from the days when the Amish were transplanted from Europe.

Painters and artists in **Bucks County** continue to preserve the beauty of the region's Cotswolds-like landscapes on canvas. Art galleries and studios throughout the county display eye-popping art that evolved from the Bucks County art colony, begun about 1898.

Philadelphia is a living library of American history. Imbedded in the modern city are attractions that evoke the eighteenth century—an era of knee britches, periwigs, and haversacks. You can stroll down the cobblestone and brick walks on **Elfreth's Alley,** an enclave of houses built for working- and middle-class families from 1728 to 1836 (all the houses are inhabited—one is a museum).

The house where flag-maker **Betsy Ross** lived is one of the city's top ten attractions, as are the **Liberty Bell Pavilion, Independence Hall, Congress Hall,** and **Carpenters' Hall.** A museum and print shop explores the daily life and work of patriot **Benjamin Franklin.**

City Tavern, which first opened its doors in 1773, still serves tasty candlelight meals brought by wenches in Colonial garb. **Independence National Historic Park** helps visitors feel a connection to those bygone days. Philadelphia's **Rosenbach Library** carefully preserves the literature of yesteryear, including prized first editions.

Hiring a private guide for a two-hour drive through **Gettysburg National Battlefield Park** is the best way to make the events of the Civil War come alive. It was at Gettysburg where 51,000 Union and Confederate troops were killed or wounded in the July 1, 2, and 3, 1863, battles and where President Abraham Lincoln delivered his Gettysburg address.

Only in **Pittsburgh,** the state's second largest city, do you see a reluctance to hold onto the past. The city fathers have successfully engineered a stunning transformation from dreary mill town to sophisticated metropolis.

The Mid-Atlantic's second largest state is home to a variety of bed-and-breakfasts. Hospitality is a long-practiced tradition, which will add special value to your experience.

FOR MORE INFORMATION

Pennsylvania Bureau of Travel
453 Forum Building
Harrisburg, PA 17120
(800) VISITPA or (717) 787-5453

Zone 9

Philadelphia Area/ Bucks County

Okay, you've seen the **Liberty Bell, Congress Hall,** and **Benjamin Franklin's print shop**. What more can you do besides steep yourself in eighteenth-century history?

Plenty. America's fifth-largest city offers gleaming skyscrapers and majestic boulevards. It is filled with top-flight cultural attractions, including its symphony at the **Kimmel Center for the Performing Arts,** the world-class **Philadelphia Museum of Art,** and the **Walnut Street Theater.** The 30-gallery **University of Pennsylvania Museum of Archaeology and Anthropology,** one of our great science museums, deserves an unhurried visit.

For children, Philadelphia offers **Franklin Institute Science Museum and Fels Planetarium, Please Touch Museum,** and **The Academy of Natural Science Museum.** History buffs will enjoy the **Civil War Library & Museum** and the **Colonial mansion in Fairmont Park.**

The city is home to many additional museums and attractions, as well as a lively downtown that hosts frequent festivals.

When you tire of the urban scene, you can head for **Bucks County,** where taverns and inns have hosted overland travelers en route to New York for a couple of centuries. Bucks County is a wooded, hilly terrain bordered on the east by the Delaware River. Hints of a bygone era are seen in fieldstone houses, old stone fences, and the 12 covered bridges.

Doylestown is a horticultural center, where springtime garden tours are beyond the ordinary. Downtown, the old Bucks County jail was reborn as the **James A. Michener Arts Center.** Art galleries are numerous. Not far from town, you can visit **Pearl S. Buck's House,** where the Pulitzer and Nobel Prize–winning author wrote novels and ran a small dairy.

New Hope, on the Delaware River, has been a haven for free-thinkers and artists for over a century. You can hop on a steam train. Or, you can ride a nineteenth-century gravel barge pulled by two mules while a costumed host entertains on his dulcimer. Canal paths along the Delaware River invite hiking and biking.

History buffs will enjoy **Pennsbury Manor,** a reconstruction of William Penn's seventeenth-century country manor. Formal and kitchen gardens, craft demonstrations, and hands-on workshops evoke the life of Pennsylvania's founding father. In **Montgomery County,** northwest of Philadelphia, the **Peter Wentz Farmstead** is a restored and furnished mid-eighteenth-century country mansion, which was twice occupied by George Washington during his Pennsylvania campaign. **Longwood Gardens,** southwest of Philadelphia, evolved from the estate of Pierre S. du Pont. Bring walking shoes to explore the 350 acres of gardens.

You'll find so much to see in the Philadelphia area and Bucks County, you'll wonder why you don't visit more often.

FOR MORE INFORMATION

Philadelphia CVB
1515 Market St., Suite 2020
Philadelphia, PA 19120
(800) 537-7676; pcvb.org

Bucks County B&B Association
(215) 862-7145; visitbucks.com

Bucks County Tourist Commission
Box 912
Doylestown, PA 188901
(215) 345-4552

CENTRE BRIDGE INN, Centre Bridge

OVERALL ★★★½ | QUALITY ★★★½ | VALUE ★★★ | PRICE **$135–$200**

Centre Bridge Inn overlooks the water and sits next to a metal bridge that was once part of a major route between New York and Philadelphia. The bridge, which looks a bit like the Eiffel Tower sitting on its side, hums with the rattle of passing traffic—but you get used to it. In the lobby, look for six prints of paintings by Edward Redfield, a prominent local artist and former neighbor. Nearby are three signed prints by local artist Randolph Bye. One owner, Joe Luccaro, worked at Martha's Vineyard, Princeton, and Peddler's Village, before moving to this area, where his wife has roots. He's known for cutting-edge menus in the 200-seat restaurant downstairs.

SETTINGS & FACILITIES

Location On the Delaware River facing Roosevelt State Park towpath & the center bridge to Stockton. **Near** 3 mi. north of New Hope, 2 mi. south of Cutalossa. **Building** 1960 Williamsburg Colonial–style (the original 1705 home burned down). **Grounds** 1 acre w/ brick patio, fountain. **Public Space** Foyer, breakfast room w/ sitting area, powder room, terrace. **Food & Drink** Cont'l plus breakfast w/ fruit, breads & muffins, beverages. **Recreation** Biking, hiking, fishing, canoeing, ice skating, tubing. **Amenities & Services** Meetings (30), weddings (100).

ACCOMMODATIONS

Units 7 guest rooms, 3 suites. **All Rooms** AC, TV. **Some Rooms** Balcony access. **Bed & Bath** King (3), queen (4), double (3), canopy (4); private baths, 9 tubs. **Favorites** #9—

four-poster canopy bed, river view, private terrace, wood paneled bath; #8 two-room suite, queen brass bed, nice bath. **Comfort & Decor** Original beams, stone walls, and a walk-in fireplace with a crane for kettles add distinction to the downstairs area. Pleasant porches are good for relaxing in warmer weather. Guest room quality varies widely.

RATES, RESERVATIONS, & RESTRICTIONS

Deposit 50%, refund w/ 14-days notice less 20%. **Discounts** Corp. **Credit Cards** V, MC, D. **Check-In/Out** 2 p.m./11 a.m. **Smoking** No. **Pets** No. **Kids** In some rooms. **Minimum Stay** 3 nights on holiday weekends. **Open** All year. **Hosts** Joe Luccaro & Jerry Horan, 2998 River Rd., New Hope, 18938. **Phone** (215) 862-2048. **Fax** (215) 862-3244. **E-mail** innkeeper@centrebridgeinn.com. **Web** centrebridgeinn.com.

INN AT FORDHOOK FARM, Doylestown

OVERALL ★★★★★ | QUALITY ★★★★★ | VALUE ★★★ | PRICE **$195–$295**

The Inn at Fordhook Farm reopened in April 1999 after extensive renovations. Not only is it beautifully restored and substantially staffed, but new owner George Ball has installed a personal art collection of high quality. Think English country manor house. Listed on the National Register of Historic Places since 1987, the home was formerly owner by W. Atlee Burpee and his son, David, who did pioneering work on seed cultivation on the adjacent acreage. Fordhook Farm was their family home—and home to Big Boy Tomatos, Fordhook Lima Beans, Black Beauty Eggplants, stringless snowpeas, white marigolds, and more. Ball, now CEO of Burpee Seed, maintains a seed house on the property to store millions of seeds.

SETTINGS & FACILITIES

Location 1.5 mi. south of Doylestown, across from Delaware Valley College. **Near** New Hope, Peddler's Village, Delaware Canal, Washington's Crossing, 28 mi. north of Philadelphia. **Building** 1760s French Colonial fieldstone farmhouse w/ 1903 additions, 1869 carriage house, 1893 seed house, barn. **Grounds** 60 acres w/ gardens, woodland walking paths, benches & chairs. **Public Space** Parlor, DR, study, powder room, butler's pantry, veranda. **Food & Drink** Full breakfast. **Recreation** Biking, hiking, art galleries, museums, historic sites. **Amenities & Services** Access to Doylestown YMCA; weddings & meetings (50).

ACCOMMODATIONS

Units 6 guest rooms. **All Rooms** AC, alarm clock, hair dryer, robes. **Some Rooms** Duraflame fireplace (3), private balcony (2). **Bed & Bath** Queen beds, 2 four-poster; private baths, 1 Jacuzzi, 2 claw-foot tubs. **Favorites** Burpee—private entrance & balcony, 11-ft. ceiling w/ gold chandelier, Mercer tile fireplace, antique armoire w/ mirror, fainting chaise, draped claw-foot tub; Simons—built-in bookshelves, crystal chandelier, half-crown canopy bed w/ gold spread, antique dressing table, tile bath w/ claw tub. **Comfort & Decor** Spacious, elegantly furnished rooms and bucolic views make this a standout. The parlor has a high ceiling, fireplace, and French paintings. The study features a cathedral ceiling, chestnut wainscoting, and palladian windows. A polished antique table, leaded glass windows, beamed ceiling, and Mercer fireplace enhance the dining room. French doors open onto a terrace shaded by a 200-year-old linden tree.

RATES, RESERVATIONS, & RESTRICTIO

Deposit Credit card to hold, refund w/ 7-days no None. **Credit Cards** AE, V, MC. **Check-In/Out** 3–9 p. No. **Kids** Over age 12. **Minimum Stay** 2 nights on week George Ball, 105 New Britain Rd., Doylestown, 18901. **Pho** (215) 345-1791. **E-mail** innatfordhook@aol.com. **Web** fordhoo

PINE TREE FARM, Doylestown

OVERALL ★★★★½ | QUALITY ★★★★½ | VALUE ★★★ | PRICE $175–$20

The owners of this inn are life-long Bucks County residents. Joy's mat nal ancestors came over with William Penn on the *Good Ship Welcome.* After years of nurturing a family, volunteering, and entertaining, she began applying her impeccable taste and her master's degree in nutrition to this bed-and-breakfast. Named for the trees that dot its magnificent lawn, the house has grown over the years with seamless additions. Originally it belonged to Doylestown's first doctor. In spite of the elegant look, the current owners want you to relax, enjoy their collection of good books and magazines, and make yourself at home. Chances are good that you'll come away with a sense of having discovered the best of Bucks County.

SETTINGS & FACILITIES

Location Residential area, next to Delaware Valley College. **Near** 1.5 mi. west of central Doylestown. **Building** 1730 fieldstone farmhouse plus addition, partly covered with white stucco, dark green shutters. **Grounds** 16 acre sloping lawn, gorgeous trees, wishing well, brick patio, 3 ponds, barn, carriage & spring house. **Public Space** LR, library, DR, solarium, upstairs sitting room, guest pantry, powder room, swimming pool. **Food & Drink** Early coffee, full breakfast at separate tables; first course served buffet style w/ bircher muesli, granola, fruit, juice; specialties—Cotswold cheddar & garden herb omelet, home-smoked bacon, lemon or puffed apple pancakes, Pennsylvania maple syrup; fruit, sodas, Perrier, Tollhouse cookies anytime. **Recreation** Hiking, biking, & horseback riding on the towpath, antiquing, art galleries, hot air balloon rides from the front yard, Doylestown farmer's market on Sat. mornings; local festivals & house tours. **Amenities & Services** VIP pass to Doylestown YMCA; meetings (10).

ACCOMMODATIONS

Units 3 guest rooms. **All Rooms** AC, phone, hair dryer, fresh flowers, 3-way bulbs, nice views. **Some Rooms** Antiques. **Bed & Bath** Queen beds, linens w/ eyelet borders; private baths, 1 tub. **Favorites** Yellow room—reading nook, low-poster bed, well-lit. **Comfort & Decor** A 1730s grandfather clock, an antique blanket chest, Windsor chairs, and ecletic antiques are attractively arranged. Collections include antique linens and heirloom baptismal and dressing gowns. The common areas are lovely with expansive views. Guest rooms are smaller.

RATES, RESERVATIONS, & RESTRICTIONS

Deposit 1 night, refund w/ 10-days notice less $10. **Discounts** Corp. (midweek, 1 person). **Credit Cards** AE, V, MC. **Check-In/Out** After 4 p.m./11 a.m. **Smoking** No. **Pets** No (Bernese mountain dog on premises). **Kids** Over age 16. **Minimum Stay** 2

r. **Hosts** Joy & Ron Feigles, 2155 -0632.

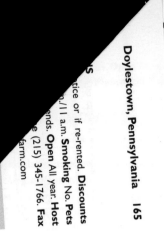

r | PRICE **$95–$195**

pread of 600 acres and sold stine. In 1818 it passed to see at Stone Ridge Farm this property to develop a house (now a two-room shed. Jackie and Bob pur- ive in the farmhouse and on the acreage. The idea for the bed-and-breakfast came nearly 15 years later. The 40-foot ceiling, original ladder to the loft, and most of the barn's other interior features remain intact. Guests will experience an authentic dairy environment with a dash of country chic.

SETTINGS & FACILITIES

Location Adjacent to the Pearl Buck Estate, 1 mi. south of Rte. 313. **Near** Nockamixon State Park, Peace Valley County Park, Peace Valley Winery, 4 mi. east of Doylestown. **Building** 1818 German-style bank barn w/ 2 stone walls, converted. **Grounds** 10 acres w/ silo, pastures, country garden sunflowers, perennials, swimming pool. **Public Space** Open barn divided into LR, DR, loft library; butler's pantry, powder room, deck. **Food & Drink** Full breakfast w/ juice, baked goods; specialties—slab bacon, fried potatoes & eggs, quiche w/ ham or vegetables, blueberry pancakes, croissant French toast w/ bacon; complimentary snacks, sodas, bottled water. **Recreation** Lessons at Haycock Riding Stable ($20/hr.), biking (some avail.), boating, fishing, canoeing, sailing, paddleboating, cross-country skiing, museums; hot tub on premises. **Amenities & Services** Disabled access (#4); meetings (20), weddings (50)

ACCOMMODATIONS

Units 6 guest rooms. **All Rooms** AC, extra bed or sofa. **Some Rooms** Cathedral ceiling w/ fan, private entrance. **Bed & Bath** Queen beds; private baths, 2 whirlpools. **Favorites** #6—watch horses graze in the pasture a few feet from your private porch, whirlpool, microwave. **Comfort & Decor** One huge open space is dominated by the living room area, which has exposed fieldstone walls, hand-hewn beams, plank floors plus Victorian seating and lamps, a Franklin stove, and large screen TV. The dining area features separate tables with checkered tablecloths. A collection of ship models sits in the foyer. Guest rooms furnishings are comfortable.

RATES, RESERVATIONS, & RESTRICTIONS

Deposit 50%, refund w/ 7-days notice less $25. **Discounts** Corp. **Credit Cards** AE, V, MC, D. **Check-In/Out** 3 p.m./11 a.m. **Smoking** No. **Pets** No (6 horses on premises). **Kids** Age 12 & older. **Minimum Stay** 2 nights if Saturday included. **Open** All year. **Hosts** Jackie & Bob Walker, Box 105, Dublin, 18917. **Phone** (215) 249-9186. **Fax** (215) 249-9185. **E-mail** innkeeper@stoneridge-farm.com. **Web** stoneridge-farm.com.

EVERMAY-ON-THE-DELAWARE, Erwinna

OVERALL ★★★★½ | QUALITY ★★★★½ | VALUE ★★★ | PRICE $145–$350

If you're looking for a quiet, old-fashioned getaway with an edge of luxury, consider this riverside home. There's not a television in sight. Instead, you can play croquet, explore woodland walking paths, lie in a hammock contemplating the flowers and cornfields, or rock on the front porch ogling the waterside views. With a chef from the Culinary Institute of America on staff, even afternoon teas are a gastronomical experience. The property earned its place on the National Register of Historic Places because in the late 1800s it was an inn run by the locally-prominent Stover family. Today's hands-on owners arrived in 1995. Both golfers, they retired from the real estate business in the Philadelphia area.

SETTINGS & FACILITIES

Location On Rte. 32 w/ front facing the Delaware River & rear bordering the Delaware Canal. **Near** 13 mi. north of New Hope, 40 mi. north of Philadelphia, 65 mi. southwest of Manhattan. **Building** 1780 stone-filled frame Victorian, enlarged & remodeled in 1871 & 1985. **Grounds** 25 acres of pastures, woodland paths, 2 corn fields, English garden, cutting garden, hammock, benches. **Public Space** Double parlor, formal DR, foyer, garden room, 2 powder rooms, sunporch, 2 brick patios, 1 flagstone patio. **Food & Drink** Cont'l plus breakfast; 4 p.m. tea & 5 p.m. sherry, cordial at turndown; fresh fruit in room; box lunches can be ordered; 6-course dinners served Friday, Saturday, & Sunday evenings plus Thanksgiving, New Year's Eve, & Valentine's Day. **Recreation** 60 mi. Delaware Canal towpath, lawn croquet, antiquing, art galleries, historic sites, parks, canoeing, boating, fishing, golf, tennis, horseback riding, hunting, cross-country & downhill skiing. **Amenities & Services** Copier, fax & e-mail, massage arranged; meetings (22), weddings (60).

ACCOMMODATIONS

Units 16 guest rooms, 2 suites. **All Rooms** AC, phone, computer jack, fresh flowers, hair dryer, iron & board, magnifying mirror, bottled water, ice bucket, combination lock. **Some Rooms** Private entrance (6), ornamental fireplace (2), Vermont castings gas stove (4), robes. **Bed & Bath** King (3), queen (15); private baths, 2 detached; whirlpool (3), tub (2). **Favorites** Pearl S. Buck—3 windows w/ river view, soft floral prints, her photo & books; David Burpee—sunny corner, nice headboard, pale floral Waverly fabrics, plant pictures; James A. Michener—3rd floor hideaway w/ antiques, yellow tones, florals & stripes; Edward Redfield Suite—claw-foot Victorian tub, love seat, great fabrics. **Comfort & Decor** The parlors are dense with plush antiques and vintage collectibles plus Mercer-tile and gas fireplaces. The owner collects antique clocks. Guest rooms provide biographies and art of their namesake local artists.

RATES, RESERVATIONS, & RESTRICTIONS

Deposit 1 night, refund w/ 7-days notice. **Discounts** Travel agent, spring promotion. **Credit Cards** AE, V, MC. **Check-In/Out** 2 p.m./11 a.m. **Smoking** No. **Pets** No. **Kids** Not appropriate for young children. **Minimum Stay** 2 nights if includes a Saturday night, 3 nights Memorial, Labor, Columbus, & President's Day weekends. **Open** All year. **Hosts** Danielle & Bill Moffly, River Rd., Box 60, Erwinna, 18920. **Phone** (610) 294-9100. **Fax** (610) 294-8249. **E-mail** moffly@atevermay.com. **Web** evermay.com

GOLDEN PHEASANT INN, Erwinna

OVERALL ★★★½ | QUALITY ★★★★½ | VALUE ★★★★ | PRICE $95–$125

The inn was built as a stop for bargemen working the Delaware Canal, which extends from Easton to Bristol. The men stopped here to change mules, buy beers, eat salt cakes, and bed down for the night. After the canal was abandoned in 1931, the property fell on hard times until it was rescued in 1967 and named Golden Pheasant Inn. The Faures have run it since 1986—fine tuning the decor and creating outstanding cuisine. Michel, a native of Grenoble, France, is an accomplished chef. He worked previously at Le Bec-Fin in Philadelphia and the Hotel du Pont in Wilmington. To sample his cuisine, you'll have to reserve a table for dinner, since the breakfast menu is limited. Or, stay for midweek cooking classes, which are popular with locals.

SETTINGS & FACILITIES

Location On Rte. 32 adjacent to the Delaware River & Delaware Canal. **Near** Next door to Sand Castle Winery, 12.5 mi. north of New Hope. **Building** 1857 fieldstone inn w/ window boxes. **Grounds** 4.5 acres w/ plants & flower borders, herb garden, hammock, swing, greenhouse. **Public Space** Covered porch, 2nd floor reading room, 3 back terraces, breakfast room, DR. **Food & Drink** Cont'l plus breakfast. **Recreation** Canal boat rides, antiquing, art galleries, museums. **Amenities & Services** Fax; culinary classes Mondays through Wednesdays; dinner served Wednesdays through Sundays, brunch avail. Sunday; special events at Peddler's Village; meetings (125), weddings (150).

ACCOMMODATIONS

Units 4 guest rooms, 1 suite, 1 cottage. **All Rooms** Phone, flowers, hair dryer, CD player/radio/clock. **Some Rooms** Fireplace (3), private entrance (1), fridge & microwave (1), TV & VCR (1), extra beds (3), AC (1). **Bed & Bath** King (1), queen (5), all four-posters w/ canopy; all private baths, 1 Jacuzzi, 3 tubs. **Favorites** #5—stone wall, nice decor; cottage—a super cozy hideaway w/ high pencil-post king bed, 3 ceiling fans, river view, porch on canal, French country furnishings, hand-painted armoire, antique wicker, quilts, floral café curtains, original paintings. **Comfort & Decor** One dining room is a plant-filled greenhouse with a canal view. A large bar dominates the original tavern room, which features a wood-burning fireplace, exposed fieldstone walls, recessed windows, beamed ceilings, and burnished copper pots. Displays in the center room include wicker baskets, Quimper French pottery from Brittany, and tin chandeliers. The hall stenciling is attractive. There's no parlor and not much indoor space to merely hang out. But, guest rooms are lovely, featuring 1850s-style French, English, and American antiques.

RATES, RESERVATIONS, & RESTRICTIONS

Deposit 50%, refund w/ 21-days notice less $25. **Discounts** Long term, midweek, AAA, Mobil. **Credit Cards** AE, V, M, D. **Check-In/Out** 3 p.m./noon. **Smoking** No. **Pets** Cottage. **Kids** Cottage. **No-Nos** Food in rooms. **Minimum Stay** 2 nights on weekends. **Open** All year. **Hosts** Barbara & Michel Faure, 763 River Rd., Erwinna, 18920. **Phone** (800) 830-4474 or (610) 294-9595. **Fax** (610) 294-9882. **E-mail** barbara@goldenpheasant.com. **Web** goldenpheasant.com.

RAVENHEAD, Hartsville

OVERALL ★★★★½ | QUALITY ★★★★★ | VALUE ★★★ | PRICE $175–$190

Even talented decorators and antique dealers can learn from Carol about how to place furniture and mix accessories. She's particularly adept at decorating walls, using the upper half like an artist's palate. She likes to blend periods and styles. Look for everything from a Victorian fainting couch to freeform stenciling. Her collections are prodigious—Victorian knife rests, oil lamps, Flow Blue porcelain, cut glass and crystal, antique hats, clothing, toys, dolls, hat boxes, plates, sewing baskets, and more. Carol transferred her energy from a demanding career in the theater world to making this property a showcase. It's part serious, part whimsical—and all fun.

SETTINGS & FACILITIES

Location 0.5 block west of Rte. 263, 2.5 mi. east of Rte. 611. **Near** 13 mi. south of New Hope, 5 mi. east of Doylestown. **Building** 1849 Greek revival Colonial, 3 story fieldstone sealed w/ stucco, wooden columns. **Grounds** 2 acres w/ gardens, patio, fountain. **Public Space** LR, DR. **Food & Drink** Full breakfast w/ juices, fruit, biscuits or muffins; specialties—eggs any style, corn fritters w/ pineapple & orange glaze, choice of pancakes (apple, strawberry, etc.), egg hash w/ potatoes & ham; turndown treat, brandy & liquor avail.; juice, soda, water, cappuccino anytime; cheese platter w/ fruit on arrival. **Recreation** Art galleries, antiquing, golf, tubing, rafting, kayaking, fishing, scenic boat rides, theater, wineries, cultural attractions—Mercer Museum, Fonthill Museum, Michener Museum, Pearl S. Buck House, Washington Crossing Historic Park. **Amenities & Services** Over 100 videos, massage on special weekends, laundry, e-mail & fax.

ACCOMMODATIONS

Units 4 guest rooms. **All Rooms** AC, TV & VCR, fridge, phone, hair dryer, iron & board, robes, magnifying mirror, cologne, sewing kit, coffee pot, books, games. **Some Rooms** Fireplace (1). **Bed & Bath** King (1), queen (3); high canopy four-poster (2); 3 private baths, 1 detached private bath, 1 tub. **Favorites** Lodge—If you love surprises you'll love this small log-cabin themed room. Accessories include antique women's bathing gear, a fishing pole and basket, horse saddle, duck decoy, old suitcase, and tennis racket—anything to do with the sporting world; Garden room—accessories here include a picket fence headboard, tree branches, picnic basket, swallow's nest, antique rakes & garden tools, frog collectibles, etc. (naturally, the color green dominates); Country room—features over 50 Raggedy Anne dolls. **Comfort & Decor** The parlor and dining room are formal Victorian with high ceilings as well as period antiques and collectibles carefully placed to look rich and right. The guest rooms are wildly creative and dense with furniture, toys, and dolls. There are no blank spaces. The themes even extend into the bathroom decor. Recreational shoppers and collectors will love it.

RATES, RESERVATIONS, & RESTRICTIONS

Deposit 1 night, refund w/ 15-days notice, $15 fee may apply. **Discounts** AAA, over age 65 10%. **Credit Cards** AE, V, MC. **Check-In/Out** 3 p.m./11 a.m. **Smoking** No. **Pets** No (miniature dachshund on premises). **Kids** Over age 16. **Minimum Stay** None. **Open** All year. **Hosts** Carol & Bill Durborow, 1170 Bristol Rd., Hartsville-Warminster, 18974. **Phone** (800) 448-3619 or (610) 687-3565. **Fax** (215) 328-9401. **E-mail** rvnhdinn@aol.com. **Web** ravenheadinn.com.

ASH MILL FARM, Holicong

OVERALL ★★★★ | QUALITY ★★★★ | VALUE ★★★★ | PRICE $100–$160

Both hosts here are originally from West Virginia. W. C. was vice president of human resources at Scott Paper for 28 years and Madonna owned a folk art and reproduction furniture business before they changed careers. He likes to putter and interact with the guests, while she does the cooking. They have a mutual interest in gardening—and it shows. Under their care, the house has undergone a major renovation and upgrade. Old timers from the area will be surprised at just how attractive they have made it. Madonna did all the samplers, hooked rugs, and cross-stitch work herself. A former guest hand painted a hallway mural that interprets Bucks County scenery. Folk art reproduction pieces throughout the house come from a shop in Boston.

SETTINGS & FACILITIES

Location North side of Rte. 202, 1 mi. southwest of Peddler's Village; 5 mi. southwest of New Hope. **Near** Doylestown Airport, Delaware River, Lake Noximixon. **Building** 1790 manor house, plaster over stone, pale mustard w/ moss green shutters. **Grounds** 11 acres w/ gardens, meadows, grazing sheep, lily pond w/ fish & frogs, shade & herb garden, split rail fence, corncrib, 2 barns, mill house. **Public Space** LR, DR, front porch, patio. **Food & Drink** Full country breakfast served in original dining area w/ walk-in fireplace; fruit & juice, breads; specialties—crêpes w/ roasted red pepper & pesto sauce, cinnamon raisin French toast w/ bourbon cream sauce, blackberry & peach cobbler w/ cream; afternoon refreshments on weekends; guest fridge w/ sodas & snacks. **Recreation** Hosts can arrange hot air balloon rides, fly-fishing w/ guide; also enjoy Michener Museum, New Hope Canal boat ride, New Hope & Ivyland Railroad, biking, local wineries. **Amenities & Services** Fax & e-mail avail., massage arranged, bike storage; weddings (150).

ACCOMMODATIONS

Units 3 guest rooms, 2 suites. **All Rooms** AC, down comforter. **Some Rooms** Fireplace (2). **Bed & Bath** Queen (4), double (2), four-poster (2); 3 private baths, 2 detached private, 1 tub. **Favorites** Library—high pencil-post queen bed, wood floor w/ rag rugs, hand stenciling, pristine Colonial look, 1st floor location is good for seniors; Meadow view—2 modified antique rope beds, tin chandeliers, blue & white decor, huge detached bath w/ tub. **Comfort & Decor** The look is Colonial. Details contributing to the early Americana theme include high ceilings, a central stairway, original random flooring, deep set windows, and a Rumford-style fireplace. These hosts collect antique clocks and redware.

RATES, RESERVATIONS, & RESTRICTIONS

Deposit Credit card to hold, refund w/ 7-days notice. **Discounts** Corp., midweek. **Credit Cards** AE, V, MC. **Check-In/Out** 3 p.m./11 a.m. **Smoking** No. **Pets** No (2 dogs on premises). **Kids** Over age 12 on weekends. **No-Nos** Candles in the room. **Minimum Stay** 2 nights on weekends April through Dec. & holidays. **Open** All year. **Hosts** Madonna & W. C. Bird, 5358 York Rd., Box 202, Holicong, 18928. **Phone** (215) 794-5373. **Fax** (215) 794-9578. **E-mail** info@ashmillfarm.com. **Web** ashmillfarm.com.

BARLEY SHEAF, Holicong

OVERALL ★★★½ | QUALITY ★★★★ | VALUE ★★★ | PRICE $105–$215

From 1936–53, Pulitzer Prize–winning playwright George S. Kaufmann owned this property. His guests included the Marx brothers, Lillian Hellman, S. J. Perelman, and neighbor Moss Hart. The Department of Interior designated part of the 200-year-old estate a National Historic Site because an underground river here once supplied water for Delaware Indians before their final westward migration. It's been a B&B for nearly two decades, and continues to offer tranquil farm vistas and warm hospitality. New owners have updated furnishing, spruced up public rooms and added visual appeal throughout. You can kick back and live the lifestyle of a country squire.

SETTINGS & FACILITIES

Location Set back from Rte. 263. **Near** New Hope, Doylestown, 1 mi. to Peddler's Village. **Building** 1740 stone farmhouse, summer house, renovated barn. **Grounds** 30 acres of rambling park-like setting, 2 ponds. **Public Space** Large country parlor, DR, TV room. **Food & Drink** Full country breakfast w/ fruit, yogurt, granola, Swiss breads, homemade jams, farm honey; specialties—stuffed baked apples, scrambled eggs w/ salmon, ham, or sausage. **Recreation** Olympic-size pool. **Amenities & Services** Meetings (50).

ACCOMMODATIONS

Units 8 guest rooms, 4 suites. **All Rooms** Comfy furnishings. **Some Rooms** Fireplace, TV. **Bed & Bath** King (1), some full, mostly queen beds; roll away, safety bed, trundle, extra beds ($20 fee); private baths, Jacuzzi (3), claw-foot tub (1). **Favorites** #1—brass sleigh bed, sitting area faces fireplace, writing desk, French windows w/ garden & pond view; #6—private staircase, Jacuzzi for 2, garden/pool view. **Comfort & Decor** All rooms are cheerful. Colonial-style furnishings are accented with Americana folk art. The brick-floored dining room and sunporch overlook the lawn, pool, and pond. Guest rooms vary in size and decor.

RATES, RESERVATIONS, & RESTRICTIONS

Deposit 1 night or 50%, refund w/ 10-days notice less $20. **Discounts** $15 off for single occupancy. **Credit Cards** AE, V, MC. **Check-In/Out** 2–9 p.m./11 a.m. **Smoking** No. **Pets** No. **Kids** Age 8 and older. **Minimum Stay** 2 nights some weekends; 3 nights holidays. **Open** All year. **Hosts** Veronika & Peter Suess, Box 10, Holicong, 18928. **Phone** (215) 794-5104. **Fax** (215) 794-5332. **E-mail** info@barleysheaf.com. **Web** barleysheaf.com.

WHITEHALL INN, Lahaska

OVERALL ★★★★ | QUALITY ★★★★ | VALUE ★★★ | PRICE **$150–$210**

A four-course candlelit breakfast is the highlight of a stay at this country hideaway. It begins at 9 a.m. with fresh squeezed juice and Whitehall's own blend of coffee plus delicious family-recipe baked goods. Before every course, the host explains the painstaking preparation of each recipe. You might continue with a fruit compote and a seafood quiche, but the meal always ends with something chocolate: a mousse, soup, or cake. After a day of sightseeing or shopping, plan to return for afternoon tea and sit by the wood-burning fireplace in the antiques-filled living room enjoying more of Suella's culinary creations. If prices seem a bit high, it's the food.

SETTINGS & FACILITIES

Location Quiet country road. **Near** 4 mi. to New Hope, 2.5 mi. to Peddler's Village. **Building** 1794 farmhouse. **Grounds** 13 acres of rolling farmland w/ barn, swimming pool, tennis court. **Public Space** Large parlor, DR, sunroom. **Food & Drink** Elaborate four-course breakfast; table set w/ heirloom sterling, European crystal and china, white linen; specialties—chilled banana bisque or hot spiced apple & honey soup, strawberries w/ custard, red pepper Swiss cheese soufflé, wild strawberry–filled French toast; menu file insures no repeats unless requested; afternoon tea w/ cucumber & blue cheese sandwiches, tarts, scones, & silver teapot at 4 p.m. **Recreation** Horseback riding, tennis, swimming. **Amenities & Services** Crabtree & Evelyn toiletries, evening turndown service w/ homemade truffles, bottle of Buckingham Vineyard wine, crystal glasses.

ACCOMMODATIONS

Units 5 guest rooms. **All Rooms** AC, canopy bed. **Some Rooms** Fireplace (2). **Bed & Bath** Bed sizes vary, canopy (5), flannel sheets in winter; 3 private baths, 2 shared baths, homemade bath salts & potpourri. **Favorites** Albert Hibb—handmade furniture, large tile bath. **Comfort & Decor** The living room has a high ceiling, a wide plank floor with an Oriental rug, deep window sills, family portraits, samplers, antique clocks, and a piano. The sunroom offers a bowl of apples, a puzzle-in-progress, and great farmland vistas. Guest rooms are furnished with a mix of late Victorian and American country antiques.

RATES, RESERVATIONS, & RESTRICTIONS

Deposit 1 night. **Discounts** 1 night stay midweek. **Credit Cards** AE, V, MC, D, DC. **Check-In/Out** 3–7 p.m./11 a.m. **Smoking** No. **Pets** No. **Kids** No. **Minimum Stay** 2 nights on weekends, 3 nights on holidays. **Open** All year. **Hosts** Mike & Suella Wass, Box 250, Pineville Rd., New Hope, 18938. **Phone** (215) 598-7945.

MANSION INN, New Hope

OVERALL ★★★★★ | QUALITY ★★★★½ | VALUE ★★★ | PRICE $210–$307

Charles Crook, a prosperous businessman, built this stately house for his wife, who was an ardent admirer of French Victorian architecture. It is said to have had the first running water in Bucks County—pumped by windmill from the river. In the mid-1930s, Dr. Kenneth Leiby, a physician, purchased the house and raised his family here. When he retired, it fell into disrepair and was scheduled for the wrecking ball in 1995. It was saved by Dr. Elio Filippo Bracco and Keith David, who have done a superb job in restoring it to its former glory. During the restoration, a workman's signature was uncovered. It stated: "John—wallpaperer '65—just heard Lincoln shot—Ford's Theatre. Will be all right—Horray for Abe!" This is one case where the walls did talk—and had quite a story to tell.

SETTINGS & FACILITIES

Location Center of downtown New Hope. **Near** Delaware River, walking bridge to Lambertville, Michener Museum, Washington Crossing Historic Park. **Building** 1865 Second Empire Baroque manor house, sunny yellow w/ white trim. **Grounds** Large city lot w/ shaded gardens, gazebo, flagstone terrace, 1867 wrought iron grape cluster fence, herb garden, swimming pool, deck. **Public Space** Foyer, LR, DR, porch, swimming pool. **Food & Drink** Early coffee, full breakfast ordered the previous night from menu, served at individual tables; buffet of freshly baked breads & muffins, seasonal fruit, homemade granola; specialties—French toast croissant w/ raspberry sauce & whipped cream, brie, tomato, & chive omelet, cheese soufflé (egg substitute or egg white on request); afternoon wine & cheese on Saturdays, complimentary wine every afternoon; fruit bowl & candy anytime. **Recreation** Bucks County Playhouse, mule barge rides, scenic railroad tour, antiquing, wineries, Delaware Canal towpath, biking. **Amenities & Services** Turndown service w/ cookies, weather report, bottled water; meetings (10).

ACCOMMODATIONS

Units 5 guest rooms, 3 suites. **All Rooms** AC, phone, clock radio, cable TV & VCR, fresh flowers, hair dryer, antique clock, sherry decanter, daily newspaper delivered to room.

Some Rooms Private entrance, private porch, terry robes (suites), fruit bowl (suites), fireplaces (3). **Bed & Bath** King (3), queen (5), four-poster (3), all featherbed down comforters & down pillows, ironed sheets; private baths, 3 whirlpool, 1 tub. **Favorites** Ashby Suite—dramatic blue & white floral fabrics & wallpaper, king canopy rice bed, whirlpool tub, bay window w/ sitting area, Victorian love seat; Windsor Suite—rose floral fabrics, king canopy rice bed, sitting room w/ fireplace, double. whirlpool tub. **Comfort & Decor** Enjoy the elegance of original etched glass doors, lace curtains on ceiling-to-floor windows, original wood moldings, arched doorways with split brass hinges, Washington red pine floors, a spiral staircase, and quality antiques and art. Collections include antique clocks, Depression-era glass, and first edition books.

RATES, RESERVATIONS, & RESTRICTIONS

Deposit Full payment, refund in the form of a gift certificate only, w/ 21-days notice or room re-rented. **Discounts** AAA, Sunday through Thursday. **Credit Cards** AE, V, MC. **Check-In/Out** 2 p.m./11 a.m. **Smoking** No. **Pets** No. **Kids** Over age 16. **No-Nos** No food in the room. **Minimum Stay** 2 nights on weekends, 3 nights on holiday weekends. **Open** All year (except Christmas Day). **Hosts** Keith David, 9 South St., New Hope, 18938. **Phone** (215) 862-1231. **Fax** (215) 862-0277. **E-mail** mansion@pil.net. **Web** themansioninn.com.

WEDGEWOOD COLLECTION, New Hope

OVERALL ★★★½ | QUALITY ★★★★ | VALUE ★★★ | PRICE $85–$225

Since 1982, Carl Glassman has built a solid reputation in the innkeeping industry. A self-described expert in historic renovation and management, he also teaches classes on the fine points of hospitality. These houses are visually busy, with subtle patterns on every surface including colorful hand-painted walls. The effect is pleasing, but definitely not for the claustrophobic. History buffs will enjoy the tie-in with George Washington's famous crossing of the Delaware to fight the Battle of Trenton. Part of his army bivouacked here. In the dining room, you'll see results of an archeological dig that links the present to an earlier era. The best feature of all is that you can walk to everything.

SETTINGS & FACILITIES

Location New Hope's historic district, 5 mi. southwest of Rtes. 179 and 32. **Near** Walk to town, canal, Cannon Square. **Building** Side-by-side Victorian-era homes built in 1830 (the Umpleby House) & 1870. The latter is painted five shades of blue w/ white and red trim; details include pillars, deep eaves, scrolled brackets, porte cachere. **Grounds** 2 landscaped acres, brick walks, flagstone patio, flower gardens, 2 gazebos. **Public Space** 2 parlors, DR, 2 covered wraparound porches, 2 guest pantries. **Food & Drink** Welcome refreshments; cont'l plus breakfast w/ pastries, fresh juice, fruit salad or fruit crisp, homemade yogurt, granola; specialties—daily quiche served on Wedgewood china; trays avail. for garden dining; will serve breakfast in bed. **Recreation** Badminton & croquet on property, bike rentals delivered, walk to canal towpath w/ mule-drawn canal boat rides, drive to 14 covered bridges, 1890 stream train, Pennsylvania Dutch Surrey. **Amenities & Services** Kosher, salt-free, sugar-free cuisine; disabled access (1), fax. and e-mail access; meetings (30).

ACCOMMODATIONS

Units 12 guest rooms, 6 suites, 1 carriage house. **All Rooms** Smoke detector sprinkler system, phone w/ voice mail, AC, fresh flowers, antiques, extra pillows, original art, hand-stenciled walls, homemade almond cordial. **Some Rooms** Kitchenette (3), 2-person whirlpool (5), TV & VCR (7), private entrance (3), balcony (5), fireplace (8). **Bed & Bath** King (5), twin (1), mostly queen beds, canopy (5), four-poster (3), sleigh (3); private baths, 7 tubs, 5 whirlpools, chrome waterfall faucets. **Favorites** Carriage house—wood stove, kitchenette & 2nd-floor deck, the most privacy; all newly-decorated main house guest rooms are color saturated & highly individual—choose your favorite. **Comfort & Decor** Extensive wall paintings add energy. An attractive parlor is enhanced with lace curtains and gingerbread treats. Guest rooms are comfortable and varied in size. Two ghosts are said to inhabit the Umpleby House.

RATES, RESERVATIONS, & RESTRICTIONS

Deposit 50%. **Discounts** Midweek. **Credit Cards** All. **Check-In/Out** 3 p.m./11 a.m. **Smoking** No. **Pets** Small dogs in some rooms. **Kids** All ages. **No-Nos** Candles, incense. **Minimum Stay** 2 nights if including Sat., 3 nights on holidays. **Open** All year. **Hosts** Nadine and Carl Glassman, 111 W. Bridge St., New Hope, 18938. **Phone** (215) 862-2520. **Fax** (215) 862-2570. **E-mail** stay@new-hope-inn.com. **Web** new-hope-inn.com.

10–11 CLINTON, Philadelphia

OVERALL ★★★½ | QUALITY ★★★½ | VALUE ★★★ | PRICE $135–$200

Location counts here. Like other well-kept, restored row houses on Clinton Street, this one has wrought iron railings, large shutters, and old-fashioned street lamps. It's on one of Philadelphia's toniest streets, and the look is decidedly nineteenth century. Inside, individually decorated suites will appeal to business people, singles, and families. Expect to find privacy and a touch of hominess. After a travel-intensive career, innkeeper and host Judith Cills wanted to create a home-away-from-home environment, and she has. It feels like borrowing a friend's apartment for the weekend. And, she's not done yet. Plans are in the works to renovate a third property around the corner.

SETTINGS & FACILITIES

Location Washington Square West. **Near** Antique Row, Society Hill. **Building** Two attached 3-story brick townhouses built in 1836. **Grounds** Faces quiet tree-lined residential street. **Public Space** Narrow hallway, small courtyard. **Food & Drink** Do-it-yourself breakfast & snack in your suite's private kitchen stocked w/ fruit, juice, cereals, breads, eggs, coffee & tea; attractive crockery & accessories provided. **Recreation** Bike rentals 2 blocks away, antiquing on Pine St., sightseeing. **Amenities & Services** AC, cribs & cots ($10 fee for 3rd person), iron & board, phone w/free local calls, internet access, movies, fireplaces, turndown upon request.

ACCOMMODATIONS

Units 7 suites. **All Rooms** Private entrance, living room/sitting area, full kitchen w/ microwave, coffee pot, toaster; TV & VCR, hair dryer, clock radio. **Some Rooms** High ceiling, gas fireplace, ceiling fan, four-poster bed, deck. **Bed & Bath** Bed sizes vary;

private baths w/ tub & shower. **Favorites** English Suite—lighthearted English country look, chintz-covered sofas by gas fireplace, floral wallpaper, TV console, corner cabinet w/ pretty dishes. **Comfort & Decor** Rooms are made inviting with plates, plants, art, candlesticks, and imaginative accessories.

RATES, RESERVATIONS, & RESTRICTIONS

Deposit Credit card, refund w/ 14-days notice. **Discounts** AAA, monthly or longer. **Credit Cards** AE, V, MC. **Check-In/Out** 3 p.m./11 a.m., call for early arrival. **Smoking** No. **Pets** Quiet dogs. **Kids** Well-behaved children welcome. **Minimum Stay** 2 nights. **Open** All year. **Host** Judith Talbot Cills, 1011 Clinton St., Philadelphia, 19107. **Phone** (215) 923-8144. **E-mail** 1011@concentric.net. **Web** teneleven.com.

SHIPPEN WAY INN, Philadelphia

OVERALL ★★★½ | QUALITY ★★★½ | VALUE ★★★ | PRICE $80–$110

The hosts here are brother and sister who have been innkeeping together for more than ten years. Their parents own three connecting buildings and use one for a private residence. It takes some adjustment to settle in, even for a history buff. But overall, a sense of warmth permeates the buildings. Guests can relax and enjoy a sense of connection with bygone days and experience first hand what it was like to live in Colonial-era Philadelphia. Specifically, you see how working-class citizens lived, including Betsy Ross, whose house on Arch Street is similar in style and construction. Regard this as an authentic cultural experience.

SETTINGS & FACILITIES

Location Eclectic downtown neighborhood w/ tea shops, macrobiotic eateries, tattoo parlors, Americana craft, jewelry, & fetish shops. **Near** South St., Penn's Landing Presbyterian Historical Society, 6 blocks to Independence Hall. **Building** One Colonial frame, one brick building w/ connecting walls. Built in 1750 & restored. **Grounds** 2 city lots, w/ iron gate leading to interior garden & patio w/ table & chairs, roses & rare trees. **Public Space** Colonial-style parlor, sunny breakfast room. **Food & Drink** Cont'l breakfast w/ fruit, granola, cereals, juice, yogurt, features Walnut Acres natural organic products; wine, cheese, cookies, crackers, and beverages anytime. **Recreation** Walk to historic & cultural attractions. **Amenities & Services** Hot/cold spring water; iron, hair dryer available.

ACCOMMODATIONS

Units 9 guest rooms. **All Rooms** AC, phone, books. **Some Rooms** TV (3). **Bed & Bath** Varied sized beds, some four-poster; small bathrooms. **Favorites** Dormer Room—narrow spiral stairs lead to 3rd floor, walls slant so severely the ceiling is only 3-feet wide; spinning wheel, woven carpet, patriotic colors, separate sitting area, stenciled & tiled bath; a phone is your only link to the 21st century. **Comfort & Decor** Two-thirds of the building dates from the eighteenth century, so rooms are small. Many have original flooring and exposed beams. Four guest room were remodeled to look old. All are individually decorated, some with country floral fabrics, stenciling, and quilts. The parlor has a working fireplace with cooking crane, stovepipe wing chairs, writing desk, antique drop-leaf table, settle (bench), hand-loomed carpet, linsey-woolsey curtains, and tin sconces.

RATES, RESERVATIONS, & RESTRICTIONS

Deposit Credit card; refund w/ 3-days notice. **Discounts** 10% off for singles. **Credit Cards** AE, V, MC. **Check-In/Out** 3–7 p.m./11 a.m. **Smoking** Garden only. **Pets** No (2 cats on premises, advise hosts about strong allergies and book the #418 address). **Kids** Age 8 and older. **Minimum Stay** No. **Open** All year. **Hosts** Ann Foringer & Raymond Rhule, 418 Bainbridge St., Philadelphia, 19147. **Phone** (800) 245-4873 or (215) 627-7266. **Fax** (215) 627-7781. **Web** http://shippenwayinn.members.easyspace.com.

THOMAS BOND HOUSE, Philadelphia

OVERALL ★★★★ | QUALITY ★★★★ | VALUE ★★★★ | PRICE $95–$175

Thomas Bond built this townhouse for his son, Thomas, Jr., a physician. Along with Benjamin Franklin and Dr. Benjamin Rush, Bond helped found Pennsylvania Hospital, the first public hospital in the U.S. Today, the National Park Service owns the building and leases it to investors. Electric candles shine from every windowsill. It's a safe neighborhood with numerous good restaurants within a three-block radius. The tone is friendly, as guests gather in the parlor for evening wine tastings and conversation. Guest rooms are individually decorated. In keeping with Federal period customs, second floor rooms are more elaborate, while some third-floor rooms are unusually small.

SETTINGS & FACILITIES

Location In Independence National Park, overlooking Welcome Square, 2 blocks from I-95. **Near** Visitors Center, Penn's Landing, waterfront district, Society Hill. **Building** Important example of classic revival Georgian-style from 1769 w/ 1824 & 1840 additions. **Grounds** City lot facing a paved public square, a memorial to William Penn. **Public Space** Large parlor, center hall, informal and formal DR. **Food & Drink** Cont'l breakfast Mon.–Fri., full breakfast Sat. & Sun. w/ fruit, juice, cereal; specialties—banana French toast w/ sausage, cheese quiche w/ bacon, cranberry/orange muffins; nightly wine & cheese reception; homemade cookies & beverages anytime. **Recreation** Biking, jogging, sightseeing. **Amenities & Services** Access to Sheraton Hotel health club for small fee, dinner & theater reservations.

ACCOMMODATIONS

Units 12 guest rooms. **All Rooms** TV, writing desk, period furnishings, hair dryer, clock radio. **Some Rooms** Gas fireplace (2); 5 3rd-floor rooms are unusually small. **Bed & Bath** Varied bed sizes, 1 canopy, some four-posters; private baths, brass fixtures, 3 whirlpool tubs. **Favorites** #201—suite w/ canopy high-poster, fireplace, whirlpool, Oriental rug, sofa bed, and sitting area; #304—raspberry walls, botanical prints. **Comfort & Decor** The spacious parlor has a Rumford-style fireplace, reproduction Chippendale furniture, antique prints, and a ten-generation family tree. The dining rooms are attractive and well lit. Guest rooms are named for people associated with Thomas Bond, among them: Robert Fulton, William Penn, and Benjamin Franklin.

RATES, RESERVATIONS, & RESTRICTIONS

Deposit 1 night, refund w/ 2-days notice. **Discounts** 10% AAA members. **Credit Cards** AE, V, MC, D, DC. **Check-In/Out** 3–9 p.m./noon. **Smoking** Rooms #305 and

#306 only. **Pets** No. **Kids** Over age 10. **No-Nos** No cots avail. **Minimum Stay** No. **Open** All year. **Hosts** Rita McGuire, 129 South Second St., Philadelphia, 19106. **Phone** (800) 845-2663 or (215) 923-8523. **Fax** (215) 923-8504. **Web** www.winston-salem-inn.com/philadelphia.

TATTERSALL INN, Point Pleasant

OVERALL ★★★★ | QUALITY ★★★★ | VALUE ★★★★ | PRICE $105–$145

For 150 years this was the main homestead and part of a 140-acre tract owned by the ubiquitous Stover family, a clan of 11 siblings who were mill owners in Bucks County. You get a hint of the life of a country squire when entering the wainscoted hall and formal dining room. Instead of televisions and whirlpools, you can enjoy rocking on shaded porches and hear bells chiming from a local church. The current owners, who originally came from Summit, N.J., have lived in this area since 1990—exchanging long commutes for Bucks County serenity. He collects history books, while her library features gardening tomes. Open since 1998, the B&B reflects their mutual interest in preservation.

SETTINGS & FACILITIES

Location Between Rte. 32 & Cafferty Rd., adjacent to Hickon Valley Park. **Near** 8.5 mi. north of New Hope, 7 mi. south of Frenchtown, 1.5 mi. south of Ralph Stover Sate Park. **Building** 1750 plastered fieldstone Colonial w/ 1850 Gothic additions, celery color w/ cream trim. **Grounds** 2.5 acres w/ perennial & butterfly gardens, spring bulbs, reproduction of 1750 dovecote. **Public Space** Common room, DR, library, powder room, 5 porches. **Food & Drink** Full breakfast downstairs or cont'l delivered to your room; specialties—mushroom, broccoli, egg, & cheese casserole, cinnamon apple French toast, eggs Benedict; afternoon biscotti, cider, cheese, and fruit. **Recreation** 100 yards to Bucks County River Country for tubing, kayaking, rafting May to Labor Day plus weekends by appointment; bike rental, swimming, & tennis nearby; newly-paved towpath, 15 min. to Doylestown museums, events at Tinicum county park & Peddler's Village, antiquing. **Amenities & Services** Fax; meetings (15).

ACCOMMODATIONS

Units 6 guest rooms. **All Rooms** AC, fresh flowers, hair dryer. **Some Rooms** Fireplace (2), porch (2). **Bed & Bath** Queens, canopy (1), four-poster (1); private baths, 1 tub. **Favorites** Wintergreen—brass bed, sitting room, wicker, garden view, lace curtains, nice fabric, light-hearted, tub. **Comfort & Decor** It feels like country. The entry mural was painted by Donna's dad. The Colonial-era common room has a homey, welcoming ambience, created by the walk-in fireplace with warming oven, exposed beams, haying tools, quilts, a whiskey jug, bed warmer, and more. There are six working fireplaces throughout. The 18–24 inch walls help to buffer traffic from roads that border two sides of the house. Pleasant guest rooms have access to second floor porches.

RATES, RESERVATIONS, & RESTRICTIONS

Deposit 1 night, refund w/ 10-days notice or re-rented. **Discounts** Over age 55, AAA. **Credit Cards** V, MC. **Check-In/Out** 3 p.m./11 a.m. **Smoking** No. **Pets** No. **Kids** Over age 12. **Minimum Stay** 2 nights w/ a Sat. **Open** All year. **Hosts** Donna & Bob Trevorrow, Cafferty & River Rds., Point Pleasant, 18950. **Phone** (800) 297-4988 or (215) 297-8233. **Fax** (215) 297-5093. **E-mail** tattersallinn@aol.com. **Web** tattersallinn.com.

HOLLYHEDGE ESTATE, Solebury Township

OVERALL ★★★½ | QUALITY ★★★½ | VALUE ★★★ | PRICE **$115–$185**

Step back into Revolutionary times, when this inn was an overnight stop on the main stage route between New York and Philadelphia. Today, it boasts expansive lawns surrounded by leafy woodland and forest, a trickling stream, and a natural pond. It's an ideal backdrop for large wedding parties to celebrate, and often they do. As many as 110 weddings or corporate events take place here each year. In fact, catering is the primary business at the sprawling country estate. So, be sure to ask if there's a wedding scheduled during your stay and request a room that's sheltered from the hubbub. Better yet, plan a visit during the week when you're apt to have the entire estate to yourself. Then, pretend you have a staff to mow all that grass and trim all those hedges.

SETTINGS & FACILITIES

Location On a hillside facing Upper York Rd. (Rte. 263), 0.5 mi. south of Centre Bridge. **Near** 4.5 mi. northwest of New Hope. **Building** 1730 Federal-style stone manor (white stucco & clay red trim) w/ additions, carriage house, summer cottage. **Grounds** 22 acres w/ English country courtyard, stone outbuildings & barn, stream, pond. **Public Space** LR, library, TV room, DR, pool deck. **Food & Drink** Cont'l breakfast Mon.–Fri. w/ fresh fruit, muffins, croissants, pastries, & beverages; full breakfast Sat. & Sun.; specialties—omelet, frittata, French toast, served family style. **Recreation** A place to relax. **Amenities & Services** Fax; meetings & weddings (180).

ACCOMMODATIONS

Units 15 guest rooms. **All Rooms** AC, phone, dataport. **Some Rooms** Fireplace (3), private entrance (4), ceiling fan (5), kitchenette (2), TV. **Bed & Bath** King (8), queen (4), full (3), canopy (1), four-poster (1), sleigh (1); private baths, 14 tubs. **Favorites** #9—spacious, fireplace & sitting area, king bed; #15—carriage house w/ stone walls & efficiency kitchen. **Comfort & Decor** The living room is a vision in pale sea green with wood trim, deep set windows, chair rails, and modern to Victorian country furnishings. Guest rooms are scattered through several buildings; some can be combined to create suites.

RATES, RESERVATIONS, & RESTRICTIONS

Deposit 50%, refund w/ 14-days notice less 20%. **Discounts** No. **Credit Cards** V, MC, D. **Check-In/Out** 2 p.m./11 a.m. **Smoking** No. **Pets** No. **Kids** Yes. **Minimum Stay** 3 nights on holiday weekends. **Open** All year. **Hosts** Amy & Joseph Luccaro, 6987 Upper York Rd., New Hope, 18938. **Phone** (800) 378-4496 or (215) 862-3136. **Fax** (215) 862-0960. **E-mail** hlyhdge@voicenet.com. **Web** hollyhedge.com.

Zone 10

Eastern Pennsylvania/ The Poconos

If you're expecting to have your senses bombarded by jarring billboards, glitzy trailer park–like accommodations, and all-you-can-gorge buffets, think again. This wooded plateau in Northeastern Pennsylvania has changed a lot since the 1950s.

Today, you'll find family-oriented accommodations and quiet retreats where the focus is on nature and nurturing the soul.

Technically, the Pocanos aren't mountains at all but an uplifted land mass that was scoured by glaciers into hundreds of rolling hills. The tallest peak, Mt. Ararat, rises a modest 2,654 feet. The four-county region is mostly about trees—nearly 2,400 square miles of maple, oak, birch, hemlock, and beech. And, about streams and lakes—thousands of trout streams tumble through forests filled with mountain laurel, blueberry, and rhododendron.

There's an impressive list of attractions: 9 state parks, 150 lakes, 10 miles of rivers (the Delaware, Lehigh, and Lackawaxen), 25 miles of the Appalachian Trail, 20 museums, 35 golf courses, 12 whitewater rafting facilities, and 14 waterfalls.

The **Lackawaxen River** is particularly lovely. Novelist and ardent fisherman Zane Grey described it as "a little river hidden away…dashing white sheeted over ferny cliffs, wine-brown where the whirling pools suck the stain from the hemlock roots." Grey's home at the edge of the river is now a museum. One section of the Lackawaxen runs through the nineteenth-century town of **Hawley**. Nearby, the nine-square-mile **Lake Wallenpaupack** is a prime bass fishing area, and **Dorflinger Glass Museum** appeals to collectors.

Along the Delaware River, a canyon through the **Kittatinny Mountains** rises nearly a quarter-mile high. The National Park Service administers an area of unspoiled land where you can canoe, boat, hunt, and fish. Nearby, **Dingmans Falls** and **Silver Thread Falls** are the highest waterfalls in the Poconos.

In **Easton,** the **National Canal Museum** captures the flavor of life on the water. In **Scranton,** you can don a hard hat and ride a coal mining car 300 feet underground into dark, damp, slippery terrain. **Colony Village** near **Canadensis** has a mineral museum and mine replica as well as demonstrations of musket operation, tool making, and farm activities year round, and admission is free.

Stroudsburg offers **Stroud Mansion** built by the town's founding father. At nearby **Quiet Valley Living Historical Farm,** costumed guides demonstrate seasonal farm activities and show off a 1765 log house.

Skiing is available at **Alpine Mountain, Jack Frost, Big Boulder, Blue Mountain, Elk Mountain, Shawnee Mountain,** and **Camelback Ski Areas**. Poconos golf courses are also good.

There aren't many bed-and-breakfasts in the region, but those we've identified are faithful to the Poconos tradition of genuine hospitality.

FOR MORE INFORMATION

Pocono Mountains Vacation Bureau
1004 Main St.
Stroudsburg, PA 18360
(800) POCONOS
800poconos.com

BLUEBERRY MOUNTAIN INN, *Blakeslee*

OVERALL ★★★★ | QUALITY ★★★★ | VALUE ★★★★★ | PRICE $81–$135

This innkeeper claims that most guests rebook before they leave. To insure that they have a wonderfully relaxing and peaceful stay, Grace bought up 68 acres of adjacent property from a local hunt club. In addition she granted a conservation easement on several hundred acres to the Nature Conservancy. A key segment of the Thomas Darling Nature Preserve along Two Mile Run, this is an area where guests can explore a diverse set of plant communities, including peat bogs, shrub swamp, spruce-tamarack balsam swamp, beech-maple forest, and one of the largest native undisturbed spruce forests in Pennsylvania. Grace bought the property in 1988 and opened her bed-and-breakfast in 1995. Before that, she owned a school bus company and auto repair garage in Spotswood, New Jersey.

SETTINGS & FACILITIES

Location On a Pocono plateau. **Near** Hickory Run State Park. **Building** 1994 Southwest stucco, peach. **Grounds** 440 acres, lawn, conifer forest, protected glacial woodlands, 4-acre lake, blueberry bushes, 2 mi.of maintained trails. **Public Space** 2 great rooms, sunroom, billiard room, upstairs TV room/library, 9-foot-deep indoor pool w/ exercise equipment, powder room. **Food & Drink** Full breakfast w/ 2 juices, fresh fruit, breadbasket served family style; specialties—semolina French toast w/ bacon, 2 kinds of quiche, potato pancakes, cornbread w/ blueberries, oatmeal, crêpes stuffed with cottage cheese served w/ hot strawberry sauce, Sunday buffet; afternoon tea avail. **Recreation** Horseback riding, whitewater rafting, fishing, skiing, golf; 2 canoes & a row boat provided. **Amenities & Services** Massage avail., disabled access (1), laundry equip., fax & e-mail; 4-day yoga seminars include chef-prepared vegan food, in-house masseuse; meetings (20).

ACCOMMODATIONS

Units 5 guest rooms, 1 suite. **All Rooms** AC, TV, hair dryer, robes, clock, ceiling fan. **Some Rooms** Balcony (3). **Bed & Bath** King (3), queen (6), four-poster (1); private baths, 5 tubs. **Favorites** Violet—hydrangea & violet floral decor, large & airy; Blueberry—suite w/ sitting area, full kitchen, balcony. **Comfort & Decor** The house was built on a grand scale—spacious enough to show off large family heirlooms handed down by Grace's Syrian ancestors and collectibles from her travels. She is passionate about Japanese and Chinese culture and displays Oriental sculpture, murals, figurines, and paintings on velvet. One great room, where a carved Oriental breakfront is a focal point, has a cathedral ceiling, gas fireplace, and access to the cedar-paneled indoor swimming pool room. Guest rooms are comfortable, but more modest in scale and decor.

RATES, RESERVATIONS, & RESTRICTIONS

Deposit $50, refund w/ 30-days notices less $10 (or can reschedule). **Discounts** No. **Credit Cards** AE, V, MC, D. **Check-In/Out** Noon/11 a.m. **Smoking** No. **Pets** 1 room (5 cats, 1 dog on premises). **Kids** Yes. **Minimum Stay** 2 nights on weekends. **Open** All year. **Host** Grace Hydrusko, Box 1102, Blakeslee, 18610. **Phone** (570) 646-7144. **Fax** (570) 646-6269. **Web** blueberrymountaininn.com.

CHESTNUT HILL, Brodheadsville

OVERALL ★★★★ | QUALITY ★★★★ | VALUE ★★★ | PRICE $89–$158

The innkeeper's art work, including oil paintings and watercolors, add a delightful dimension to this cozy country home. Her other hobby is growing herbs, which she keeps in a small pink shed on the property. The house faces a babbling stream, but the rights to this waterway are owned by a local fishing club and no one else, including guests here, can legally use it. The house is rather isolated and it's a bit of a drive to the area's numerous activities—everything from golf, tennis, and rafting to skiing, hiking, and horseback riding. However, you may just want to bring an easel and some paints, stay put, and be inspired by the beauty of the locale.

SETTINGS & FACILITIES

Location On Rte. 715 3 mi. north of Brodheadsville. **Near** Tannersville; Camelback, Alpine, & Blue Mountain ski villages. **Building** 1860 German-crafted country home. **Grounds** 4 acres w/ gardens, woodlands, 3 ponds, trails. **Public Space** LR, DR, TV room. **Food & Drink** Full breakfast w/ juice, fruit plate, muffins; specialties—crab strata, blueberry waffles, decadent French toast. **Recreation** Skiing, hiking, antiquing. **Amenities & Services** Videos, fax & e-mail; meetings (12), weddings (60).

ACCOMMODATIONS

Units 2 guest rooms, 2 suites. **All Rooms** Ceiling fan, clock, fresh flowers. **Some Rooms** AC (3), private entrance (1), phone (1), TV (1), kitchen (1). **Bed & Bath** King (1), queen (4), canopy (1), all have feather mattresses; private baths, 2 tubs. **Favorites** Port Charleston—a mini suite, blue walls, red bathroom, tub. **Comfort & Decor** Imaginative use of color brightens this cozy country home. Standouts include the grandfather clock, egg collection, and framed watercolors.

RATES, RESERVATIONS, & RESTRICTIONS

Deposit 1 night. **Discounts** No. **Credit Cards** V, MC. **Check-In/Out** 3 p.m./11 a.m. **Smoking** No. **Pets** No (2 dogs in residence). **Kids** Yes. **Minimum Stay** No. **Open** All year. **Host** Sally Nolan, Box 1330, Brodheadsville, 18322. **Phone** (800) 992-1860.

MERRY INN, Canadensis

OVERALL ★★★ | QUALITY ★★★½ | VALUE ★★★★ | PRICE $80–$95

After just one bed-and-breakfast experience in New Hampshire, this Long Island couple decided to uproot themselves and start hosting guests. After a search, they chose this perky, bright blue property in the Poconos. Meredyth forfeited a career in counseling in the Oyster Bay area. Chris traded his construction job in Levittown, New York but he continues to make a daily commute from Canadensis to New York City. For guests, there's plenty to do in the area, including the use of facilities at large resorts nearby—plus regional events throughout the year. Or, you can just plan to relax on their deck and soak in the hot tub surrounded by woodlands.

SETTINGS & FACILITIES

Location Rte. 390, just outside the village. **Near** Stroudsburg, Delaware Water Gap. **Building** 1940 Cape Cod. **Grounds** 1.5 acres w/ lawn, garden, outdoor hot tub on deck adjacent to woodlands. **Public Space** LR, DR. **Food & Drink** Full breakfast w/ juice, muffins; specialties—eggs any style, stuffed French toast w/ sausage or bacon. **Recreation** Hiking, fishing, antiquing, golf, boating, swimming, whitewater rafting, tennis, horseback riding, NASCAR (June/July), Logging Festival, Chili Festival, Irish Festival. **Amenities & Services** Videos, discount at Bushkill Golf Course, massage avail., fax; meetings (25).

ACCOMMODATIONS

Units 6 guest rooms. **All Rooms** TV, clock, fan. **Some Rooms** Antiques. **Bed & Bath** King (3), queen (2), double (1); private baths. **Favorites** #6 King room—burgundy walls, floral spread, settee, antique sewing machine, detached private bath is nice. **Comfort & Decor** The decor is simple. The innkeepers collect cobalt blue glassware, salt and pepper shakers, and antique typewriters.

RATES, RESERVATIONS, & RESTRICTIONS

Deposit $50, refund w/ 2-weeks notice, 4-weeks on holidays. **Discounts** No. **Credit Cards** V, MC. **Check-In/Out** 2 p.m./noon. **Smoking** LR, upstairs hall only. **Pets** 1 room. **Kids** Yes. **Minimum Stay** 2 nights on holidays & NASCAR weekends. **Open** All year. **Hosts** Meredyth & Chris Huggard, Box 757, Canadensis, 18325. **Phone** (800) 858-4182. **E-mail** merryinn@ezaccess.net. **Web** www.pbcomputerconsulting.com/themerryinn.

SHEPARD HOUSE, Delaware Water Gap

OVERALL ★★★★ | QUALITY ★★★★ | VALUE ★★★ | PRICE $99–$120

Staying at this B&B feels like visiting family. In fact, the basement and third floor are occupied by long-term tenants, and the MacWilliams actually live just up the street. However, they are very accommodating hosts, and when our car battery died, Ruth pitched in to provide transportation. When the problem was solved, she sent us on our way with a bag of freshly-made cookies. A native of Delaware Water Gap, she's a great concierge. We were grateful for the tip about Aerole, an extraordinary restaurant a few blocks away. And we were glad to be steered to the Antoine Dutot School and Museum, which relives this town's glorious past as a resort mecca for East Coast families. A short film captures the flavor of the big hotels that once thrived here. Delaware Water Gap is still a very nice, if quieter, place.

SETTINGS & FACILITIES

Location Residential area, 2 mi. up the hill from town. **Near** 1 block to Appalachian Trail, 3 mi. southeast of Shawnee ski area, 3 mi. east of Stroudsburg. **Building** 1910 country Victorian. **Grounds** City lot w/ floral borders. **Public Space** LR, DR, wraparound porch, guest fridge. **Food & Drink** Full breakfast w/ juice, fruit, homemade muffins; specialties—baked pancakes w/ fruit, baked egg casserole, bananas foster French toast; welcome cheese tray, cookie jar. **Recreation** Hiking, fishing, canoeing, antiquing; canoe rental nearby, Jazz Festival (Sept.), Balloon Festival (Oct.). **Amenities & Services** Videos, massage avail.

ACCOMMODATIONS

Units 4 guest rooms. **All Rooms** AC, fresh flowers, hair dryer, clock, bottled water, sherry. **Some Rooms** CD player (1). **Bed & Bath** Queen (3), double (1), canopy (1), four-poster (2); all private baths, 2 detached. **Favorites** Forsythia—detached sitting room w/ bath, CD player; Hibiscus—black & white patterned wallpaper, four-poster bed, sturdy oak furnishings, fringed Victorian lampshades (like visiting a great aunt).**Comfort & Decor** This unpretentious home is filled with sturdy oak sideboards, desks, and bureaus, plus comfy sofas and chairs. The look is softened by lace curtains, pretty Victorian lamps, and heirloom photos. A small rock fountain adds audio appeal. Guest rooms look old-fashioned but deliver up-to-date amenities.

RATES, RESERVATIONS, & RESTRICTIONS

Deposit 1 night or 50% for longer stays, refund w/ 14-days notice. **Discounts** Longer stays. **Credit Cards** V, MC. **Check-In/Out** 3 p.m./11 a.m. **Smoking** No. **Pets** No. **Kids** Over age 12. **Minimum Stay** 2 nights holiday weekends. **Open** All year. **Hosts** Ruth & Wayne MacWilliams, 108 Shepard Ave., Delaware Water Gap, 18327. **Phone** (570) 424-9779. **E-mail** shepardhouse@enter.net. **Web** shepardhouse.com.

LAFAYETTE INN, Easton

OVERALL ★★★★ | QUALITY ★★★★ | VALUE ★★★ | PRICE $105–$160

It's a big bonus that this inn welcomes children, because there are lots of great family attractions in town. The Crayola Factory is at the top of the list because it's fun, colorful, and engaging. Right next to the "factory" you'll find hands-on exhibits about the heyday of barge canals that thrived in this area—and nearby you can ride on a mule-drawn canal boat. Also in town is the Weller Health Center, with exhibits that entertain and inform. And, it's not far to amusements parks with both old-fashioned and state-of-the-art rides. These innkeepers provide excellent concierge services to ensure a pleasant, rewarding stay. They deserve extra kudos for rescuing and restoring this impressive-looking property and creating the area's premier inn.

SETTINGS & FACILITIES

Location On a hilltop, 2 blocks to Lafayette College. **Near** Delaware River, Lehigh Valley, 60 mi. north of Philadelphia, 70 mi. west of Manhattan. **Building** 1895 Georgian mansion, brick w/ 100-foot-long wraparound porch. **Grounds** 1 acre w/ gardens, waterfall, fountain. **Public Space** Lounge/dining area, sunroom/DR walk-through kitchen w/ wood-burning fireplace. **Food & Drink** Full breakfast w/ 3 juices, fresh fruit, home-baked goods; specialties—Belgian waffles w/ sautéed apples, Irish soda bread, French toast, quiche egg casserole; hot beverages, fruit, pastries, soda always avail. **Recreation** Canoeing, kayaking, & tubing on the Delaware River; hot air ballooning, mule-drawn canal rides, Crayola Factory, Dorney Park, Bushkill Park, Weller Health Center, Nazareth Speedway; Music Fest (Aug.), Shad Fishing Tournament (April), 8th of July Heritage Festival. **Amenities & Services** Videos, massage avail., access to fitness center, disabled access (1), fax & e-mail, *New York Times* & *Wall Street Journal* avail.

ACCOMMODATIONS

Units 14 guest rooms, 2 suites. **All Rooms** AC, TV & VCR, phone w/ dataport, hair dryer, bottled water. **Some Rooms** Fireplace (3), balcony (2), robes (3), CD player (2). **Bed & Bath** King (1), queen (13), double (2), canopy (1), four-poster (1), sleigh (2); private baths, 3 whirlpools, 10 tubs. **Favorites** #21—suite w/ gas fireplace, whirlpool, balcony, CD player; #27—half canopy bed, striped wallpaper, tub. **Comfort & Decor** The first and second floors have ten-foot ceilings. The foyer's marble mirror with ionic columns is impressive. Guest rooms are okay.

RATES, RESERVATIONS, & RESTRICTIONS

Deposit Credit card, refund w/ 2-days notice. **Discounts** No. **Credit Cards** AE, V, MC, DC, D. **Check-In/Out** 3 p.m./11 a.m. **Smoking** No. **Pets** No (1 dog, Arthur, on premises). **Kids** Yes. **No-Nos** Candles. **Minimum Stay** No. **Open** All year. **Hosts** Marilyn & Scott Bushnell, 525 W. Monroe St., Easton, 18042. **Phone** (610) 253-4500. **Fax** (610) 253-4635. **E-mail** lafayinn@fast.net. **Web** lafayetteinn.com.

MORNING GLORIES, Hawley

OVERALL ★★★½ | QUALITY ★★★½ | VALUE ★★★★★ | PRICE $55–$75

A sharp turn and a steep dirt road leads you up to this unexpected find on a hillside overlooking Hawley. The interior makes a delightful impression, thanks to one light-filled area that has two-story glass walls, a goldfish pond, and an assembly of greenery. It's all meant to foster relaxation and good health. Roberta shares the inn-keeping chores with her niece, Natalie. She moved here from upstate, New York in 1992 and bought several houses on this hillside. The location is especially good for antique enthusiasts. But everyone has access to shopping, summer theater, and fine restaurants.

SETTINGS & FACILITIES

Location Hillside overlooking Rte. 6, across from Hawley Antique Exchange. **Near** Lake Wallenpaupack. **Building** 1885 Victorian. **Grounds** 1 acre w/ Japanese rock garden in back. **Public Space** LR, kitchen, 2-story conservatory w/ plants & goldfish pond, exercise room, balcony. **Food & Drink** Full breakfast w/ juice, fresh fruit, muffins & pastries, hot beverages; specialties—waffles, pancakes, omelets, quiche w/ meats. **Recreation** fishing, boating, hiking, museum visits, antiquing. **Amenities & Services** Videos, massage avail.

ACCOMMODATIONS

Units 3 guest rooms. **All Rooms** Fresh flowers, robe, clock. **Some Rooms** TV (1), ceiling fan (2). **Bed & Bath** Queens; 1 private bath, 2 shared baths, 1 tub. **Favorites** Master bedroom—sitting room, private bath. **Comfort & Decor** Unusual features include a solarium overlooking a homemade rock garden, an attractive loft area outfitted with wicker sofas, chairs, and a porch swing as well as an adjoining exercise room. Guest rooms are modestly furnished.

RATES, RESERVATIONS, & RESTRICTIONS

Deposit 1 night, refund w/ 2-days notice. **Discounts** Returning guests & longer stays. **Credit Cards** V, MC, D. **Check-In/Out** 4 p.m./11 a.m. **Smoking** No. **Pets** No. **Kids** Age 9 & older. **Minimum Stay** No. **Open** All year. **Host** Roberta Holcomb, 204 Bellemonte Ave., Hawley, 18428. **Phone** (570) 226-0644.

SETTLER'S INN, Hawley

OVERALL ★★★★★ | QUALITY ★★★★ | VALUE ★★★★ | PRICE $95–$160

If it's ripe and ready to pick, you'll find it in this renowned dining room. Grant, the self-taught owner-chef, specializes in fresh fish, pheasant, and venison, and does interesting things with vegetables. Most produce comes from local farmers. An Amish cheese maker provides the cheese. Trout comes from a local hatchery, and Grant smokes all his own fish and game on site. The bakery produces slow-rise artisan breads each day—and the birdseed bread is famous. To walk off the calories, Jeanne provides a map route of a two-mile nature trail through town, past Victorian houses and along the Lackawaxen River. Or, a walking path on the Delaware and Hudson Canal. On the job for 20 years, these experienced innkeepers produce lots of interesting special events year-round, naturally built around food.

SETTINGS & FACILITIES

Location North edge of town across from Bingham Park. **Near** Lake Wallenpaupack, Delaware River, Promised Land State Park, Zane Grey Museum. **Building** 1927 Tudor mansion, English Arts & Crafts. **Grounds** 6 acres w/ herb & flower gardens. **Public Space** Chestnut Tavern, restaurant, powder room, potting shed (gift shop). **Food & Drink** Full breakfast w/ fruit, yogurt, & breads, buffet & daily menu; specialties—omelet, eggs Florentine. **Recreation** Tennis (rackets avail.) golf, canoeing, fishing, antiquing, hiking, biking, boating, cross-country & downhill skiing, Glass Museum. **Amenities & Services** Privileges at Paupack Hills Country Club (health club, pool), massage avail., laundry, fax & e-mail; full calendar of events on site; meetings (20–40), weddings (200).

ACCOMMODATIONS

Units 20 guest rooms. **All Rooms** AC, TV, phone, hair dryer. **Some Rooms** Sitting area. **Bed & Bath** Queen (14), double (4), full (4); private baths, whirlpool (6), tubs (10). **Favorites** #14—large, canopy-style four-poster, antiques, double whirlpool, floral & wicker, rose tones; #9—wicker sitting area, big windows face park, bright cabbage roses dominate. **Comfort & Decor** A great look is achieved with chestnut-wood walls, fulper tiles, and mission lighting. Relax in comfortable antiques by a large hearth. Hand-screened artisan wallpaper enhances the dining room. Guest rooms are rather small, but the decor is nice—white wicker with pretty flowered walls and white spreads.

RATES, RESERVATIONS, & RESTRICTIONS

Deposit Credit card to hold, refund w/ 3-days notice. **Discounts** AAA & AARP 10%. **Credit Cards** AE, V, MC, D. **Check-In/Out** 2 p.m./noon. **Smoking** No. **Pets** No, in-house Labrador retriever. **Kids** Yes, any age. **Minimum Stay** 2 nights on weekends. **Open** All year. **Hosts** Jeanne & Grant Genzlinger, 4 Main Ave., Hawley, 18428. **Phone** (800) 833-8527. **Fax** (570) 226-1874. **E-mail** settler@ptd.net. **Web** thesettlersinn.com.

ROEBLING INN ON THE DELAWARE, Lackawaxen

OVERALL ★★★★ | QUALITY ★★★½ | VALUE ★★★★ | PRICE $65–$130

This decidedly un-touristy area will appeal to couples who want to enjoy quiet woodland hikes, river-watching, fishing, relaxing by the fire, and a good meal. "It's a place for stressed-out people who want to be pampered a little," says JoAnn. The property, listed on the National Register of Historic Places, was formerly the home of Judge Thomas J. Ridgeway, a superintendent and tallyman for the Delaware and Hudson Canal Company, which financed the nearby Roebling Bridge in 1848. It is our country's oldest suspension bridge and a forerunner of the Brooklyn Bridge. Having lived here since 1985, JoAnn and D. J., a former country club manager, can direct you to hidden waterfalls and fill you in on local history.

SETTINGS & FACILITIES

Location Northern Pocono Mountains, on a bend in the Delaware River. **Near** Across from Roebling Bridge, same block as the Zane Grey Museum, next door to the winter field office of The Eagle Institute. **Building** 1870 Greek Revival, white clapboard w/ green shutters. **Grounds** 1 acre w/ grassy area, Adirondack chairs riverside, hammock, maple trees, window boxes, campfire site. **Public Space** Sitting room, breakfast room, buffet room, front porch. **Food & Drink** Full breakfast w/ fruit, baked goods; specialties—eggs any style w/ bacon, pancakes, omelets, oatmeal; beverages & cookies avail. anytime. **Recreation** Excellent fishing for bass, shad, & trout; ski at Masthope (5 mi.) & Tanglewood (15 mi.); local museums, eagle watching, hiking to waterfalls, drift boat river rides, summer theater; Jazz Fest, St. Patrick's Day Parade, Shad Festival (Memorial Day weekend), Wildflower Concerts (summer), October Fest. **Amenities & Services** Fax.

ACCOMMODATIONS

Units 5 guest rooms. **All Rooms** AC, TV, clock. **Some Rooms** Fireplace (3), private entrance (1), ceiling fan (4). **Bed & Bath** Queen (4), double (3), twin (1); private baths, 2 tubs. **Favorites** #2—river view, gas fireplace, yellow & blue quilt, white iron bed, carved Eastlake dresser; cottage—fireplace, tub, extra sofa bed, big kitchen. **Comfort & Decor** Simple, unpretentious furnishings are comfy and welcoming. (Note that #1 has its bathtub in a closet—literally.) Antique garment stretchers are displayed. There's a cemetery next door.

RATES, RESERVATIONS, & RESTRICTIONS

Deposit 1 night, refund w/ 7-days notice. **Discounts** No. **Credit Cards** AE, V, MC, D. **Check-In/Out** 2:30 p.m./11:30 a.m. **Smoking** Cottage only. **Pets** No. **Kids** No. **Minimum Stay** 2 nights on weekends May–Oct., 3 nights most holidays. **Open** Yes. **Hosts** JoAnn & Donald Jahn, Scenic Drive, Lackawaxen, 18435. **Phone** (570) 685-7900. **E-mail** roebling@itis.net. **Web** roeblinginn.com.

BLACK WALNUT, Milford

OVERALL ★★★½ | QUALITY ★★★ | VALUE ★★ | PRICE **$60–$175**

The owner's only daughter has just taken over the responsibilities for running this inn—with great enthusiasm. We wish her well in the daunting task of returning this venerable old property to its former glory. The setting is magnificent, complete with ponds, farm animals, and natural vistas. "The inn needs a bit of love, care, and attention," says Robin, who's jumped in with both feet to see that it gets it. The location is a bit isolated, but all the better to enjoy such country experiences as picking fresh berries, catch-and-release fishing, hiking, horseback riding, and bird watching. The public rooms are the most inviting, and there are facilities for a full-service restaurant. Brides-to-be take note.

SETTINGS & FACILITIES

Location On a lake surrounded by woodlands. **Near** 3 mi. west of Milford. **Building** 1897 Tudor farmhouse w/ stone exterior. **Grounds** 162 acres w/ tree-lined drive, pine & walnut trees, 3-acre lake, ponds, lawn. **Public Space** LR, 2 DR, bar, game room, outdoor hot tub, petting zoo. **Food & Drink** Full breakfast w/ fruit salad & assorted breads; specialties—eggs any style, French toast, lox & cream cheese; evening treat w/ coffee. **Recreation** Catch & release fishing (license required), floating dock for swimmers; 4 paddleboats, 1 row boat, fishing poles, horseshoes, volleyballs, croquet avail. **Amenities & Services** Meetings (100), weddings (200).

ACCOMMODATIONS

Units 12 guest rooms. **All Rooms** Basic furnishings. **Some Rooms** AC (4), TV (2), private entrance (1), kitchen (1). **Bed & Bath** Queen (4), double (6), twin (2), four-poster (1); 4 private baths, 4 shared baths, 2 tubs, 4 rooms have half baths. **Favorites** Living room. **Comfort & Decor** The house's best feature is its attractive living room where a gorgeous marble fireplace is flanked by three floral sofas and a big-screen TV. The glass-enclosed dining room has windows on two sides with nice lake view. Guest rooms are small, even cramped, and several have hall baths, but they are being upgraded.

RATES, RESERVATIONS, & RESTRICTIONS

Deposit Credit card to hold, refund w/ 3-days notice, 14-days on holidays. **Discounts** AAA, groups over 10. **Credit Cards** AE, V, MC, D. **Check-In/Out** 2 p.m./11 a.m. **Smoking** No. **Pets** No (2 dogs on premises). **Kids** Yes. **No-Nos** Drinking or eating in guest rooms. **Minimum Stay** 2 nights on weekends, 3 nights on holidays. **Open** All year. **Hosts** Robin Schneider & William Jura, 179 Fire Tower Rd., Milford, 18337. **Phone** (570) 296-6322. **Fax** (570) 296-7696. **E-mail** tourguide@poconovacation.com. **Web** theblackwalnutinn.com.

CLIFF PARK INN & GOLF COURSE, Milford

OVERALL ★★★½ | QUALITY ★★★½ | VALUE ★★ | PRICE $110–$170 (MAP $160–$220)

Golf is spoken here. First and foremost, this is a golfer's inn. Its links-style, nine-hole course has wide, long fairways (2 holes are over 500 yards), which makes it attractive to high handicap players. Greens are said to play fast. The course is quite hilly and a cart is suggested. Overall, it's said to be challenging. In fine, summer weather the views are especially grand, as you sit on the long porch or patio and watch players tee off just steps away from the front door. The property has been in the Buchanan family for five generations. In fact, their ancestors received the original land grant directly from King George. Much of the land remains in pristine condition.

SETTINGS & FACILITIES

Location Facing a 9-hole golf course. **Near** 1.5 mi. south of Milford, 2 mi. west of Delaware River, 75 mi. north of George Washington Bridge. **Building** 1820 farmhouse, remodeled, white clapboard w/ green trim, clubhouse. **Grounds** 500 acres w/ 65-acre golf course, apple trees, & 7 mi. marked, ungroomed trail for hiking, biking, & cross-country skiing. **Public Space** 2 LR, 2 DR, front porch, golf pro area. **Food & Drink** Full breakfast w/ juice, home baked goods; specialities include homemade baked goods, chocolate chip pancakes, three-egg omelet with home fries, French toast. **Recreation** Golf, hiking, cross-country skiing; golf club and ski rentals. **Amenities & Services** MAP guests pay twilight greens fee of $15 weekends, $7.50 midweek, no discount for B&B guests, individual and group lessons avail.; 6 rooms have disabled access, fax & e-mail; meetings (24), weddings (200).

ACCOMMODATIONS

Units 18 guest rooms. **All Rooms** AC, phone, clock. **Some Rooms** Fireplace (2), balcony (3), private entrance, (6) TV & VCR (4). **Bed & Bath** King (6), queen (3), twin (9), canopy (1); all private baths, 16 tubs. **Favorites** #8 3rd floor—blue/butternut theme, king bed, full bath, 1950s look; #4 2nd floor—magnolia wallpaper, king bed, porch overlooks golf course. **Comfort & Decor** This venerable, well-worn property could use some sprucing up. The large living room has a hearth and collection of family heirlooms. But some of the inn's rugs are especially dreary and many need replacing. However, many visitors love the easy access to golf.

RATES, RESERVATIONS, & RESTRICTIONS

Deposit Credit card or $50, refund w/ 5-days notice. **Discounts** AAA, AARP (room only). **Credit Cards** AE, V, MC, DC, D. **Check-In/Out** 2 p.m./noon. **Smoking** Yes, some rooms. **Pets** 2 rooms. **Kids** Yes. **Minimum Stay** 1 night on weekends Memorial Day–Oct. 31. **Open** All year. **Hosts** Barbara C. & Harry W. Buchanan III, 155 Cliff Park Rd., Milford, 18337. **Phone** (800) 225-6535 or (717) 296-6491. **Fax** (717) 296-3982. **E-mail** cpi@warwick.com. **Web** cliffparkinn.com.

MOUNTAINTOP LODGE, Pocono Pines

OVERALL ★★★★½ | QUALITY ★★★★ | VALUE ★★★ | PRICE $95–$205

Merrily is part of the fifth generation of a family that has pioneered in developing this area of the Poconos with a focus on conservation, recreation, and upscale housing. The family's membership in two country club facilities within one mile of this property extends to guests of this lodge—making it a real find. Both hosts are friendly and accommodating. Colin, an avid golfer, can steer guests to the best local courses and other sporting venues. Merrily, who earned a degree in interior design and art, has created an attractive setting for a relaxing getaway. She has set aside one room in the lodge to display antique ice harvesting equipment, old photos, and town memorabilia owned by the Historical Association of Tobyanna Township. Her mom is the curator.

SETTINGS & FACILITIES

Location On Rte. 940. **Near** 18 mi. northwest of Stroudsburg. **Building** 1928 Colonial boarding house, remodeled. **Grounds** 3.5 acres w/ woodlands, flower gardens, tall pines, trail to Lake Naomi. **Public Space** Great room/dining area, foyer w/ espresso bar, 100-foot-long porch. **Food & Drink** Early coffee, full breakfast w/ fruit, juice, homemade baked goods, gourmet coffee, cereal, yogurts; specialties—eggs Benedict, cinnamon raisin French toast, strata w/ fruit & cream cheese, side meats; beverages avail. anytime. **Recreation** Mountain biking, hiking, whitewater rafting, river floats, boating, kayaking, canoeing, swimming, fishing, tennis, golf, downhill & cross-country skiing, snow tubing, hunting, paintball, doing absolutely nothing; NASCAR, Jazz weekend (spring), Blues weekend (Aug.), Biker Rally (fall); beach chairs, towels provided. **Amenities & Services** Club privileges at Lake Naomi Club & Pinecrest Lake Golf & Country Club for tennis, fitness, golf, boating, swimming; massage avail., disabled access (room C-1), fax & e-mail; meetings (50), weddings (85).

ACCOMMODATIONS

Units 10 guest rooms, 2 suites. **All Rooms** AC, hair dryer, clock, iron & board, ceiling fan. **Some Rooms** Fireplace, private entrance, TV, phone w/ dataport (4). **Bed & Bath** King (3), queen (9), double (3), canopy (1), four-poster (3), all have down comforters & pillow top mattresses; private baths, whirlpools (4), tubs (4). **Favorites** Cottage suite #1—king canopy bed, gas fireplace, whirlpool, TV & VCR. **Comfort & Decor** In the living room area, three pairs of wing chairs and sofas are arranged compactly on pine floors with area rugs. Lots of ceiling fans circulate the air, warmed by a gas fireplace. Books, framed heirloom clothing, and photos add interest. In the foyer, you'll see backgammon and chess tables, antique sports equipment, and country collectibles. The halls have hand stenciling. Guest rooms are lined up dormitory style, but decor is individualized with attractive fabrics, great attention to detail, and thoughtful amenities. The cottage suites are a bit more deluxe and private.

RATES, RESERVATIONS, & RESTRICTIONS

Deposit 50%, refund w/ 14-days notice. **Discounts** Corp. **Credit Cards** AE, V, MC. **Check-In/Out** 3 p.m./11 a.m. **Smoking** No. **Pets** No. **Kids** 12 & older (well-behaved). **Minimum Stay** 2 nights on weekends, 3 nights holiday weekends. **Open** All year. **Hosts** Merrily Baxter-Mackay & Colin Mackay, Box 1097, Rte. 940, Pocono Pines, 18350. **Phone** (570) 646-6636. **Fax** (570) 643-0904. **E-mail** mtnlodge@epix.net. **Web** mountaintoplodge.com.

THE FRENCH MANOR, South Sterling

OVERALL ★★★★★ | QUALITY ★★★★½ | VALUE ★★★ | PRICE $135–$275

Titanium czar Joseph Hirshhorn built The French Manor to look like his chateau in the South of France, which was destroyed in World War I. He also used his wealth to amass fine art and sculpture, creating one of our country's premier collections. (Look for it at the Hirshhorn Museum in Washington, D.C.) Subsequent owners of this property have included department store magnate Samuel Kress and Bucknell University. In 1990, the Logans bought it to complement their more homespun Sterling

Inn, a short drive away. They make annual improvements, with a big investment in 1999 to create six new suites with upscale furnishings and amenities. It's a bit isolated, but dinner is available six nights a week in summer, and Thursday through Sunday in winter. The menu is ambitious, so hopefully they won't run out of ingredients mid-meal.

SETTINGS & FACILITIES

Location On Huckleberry Mountain off Rte. 191. **Near** 5 mi. south of Lake Wallenpaupack, 14 mi. north of Mt. Pocono, 25 mi. south of Hawley. **Building** 1932 French chateau, stone exterior, w/ detached addition. **Grounds** 45 acres w/ garden, groomed trails, forest, valley view. **Public Space** Common room, DR, terrace, powder room. **Food & Drink** Full breakfast w/ juices, homemade baked goods, fresh fruit; specialties—custard French toast stuffed w/ fresh fruit, fruit pancakes, eggs Benedict; sherry, cheese, & fruit in your room; afternoon tea; dinner Tues.–Sun. in summer, Thurs.–Sun. off peak; breakfast in bed is $10 extra. **Recreation** Cross-country skiing, sledding, snowshoeing & hiking on site; ice skates, sleds, snow tubes avail.; access to Sterling Inn (a sister property 1.5 mi. away) w/ lake, paddleboats, indoor pool, whirlpool, tennis courts, self-guided nature trail & guided walks, ice skating; drive 7 mi. to golf, horseback riding, & sleigh rides; races at Pocono Raceway (June, July), Balloon Fest (Oct.). **Amenities & Services** Videos, massage avail., guided nature treks, disabled access, laundry, fax & e-mail; meetings (30), weddings (200).

ACCOMMODATIONS

Units 6 guest rooms, 9 suites. **All Rooms** AC, phone w/ dataport, voice mail, hair dryer, robes, cable TV, clock, fresh flowers. **Some Rooms** Balcony (6), gas fireplace (8), private entrance (7), iron (11), ceiling fan (6), wet bar (7), coffeemaker & fridge (8), VCR (8). **Bed & Bath** King (7), queen (8), four-poster (7), canopy (2); private baths, whirlpools (8), tubs (9). **Favorites** Turret suite (original)—view, split-level, king bed; Chambord suite (new)—spacious, balcony, view, fireplace, VCR, large tile bath. **Comfort & Decor** Wood details give the original mansion a rustic feel. Six new fireplace & Jacuzzi suites in La Maisonneuve are upscale and contemporary. Public space is limited. Carriage house rooms are named for French castles, European cities, and two of the owners' daughters. The property has been upgraded to a new level of luxury.

RATES, RESERVATIONS, & RESTRICTIONS

Deposit $100, refund w/ 14-days notice less $15 (letter of credit given w/ 3-days notice). **Discounts** Midweek packages include meals. **Credit Cards** AE, V, MC, D. **Check-In/Out** 3 p.m./11 a.m. **Smoking** No. **Pets** No. **Kids** No. **Minimum Stay** 2 nights if Saturday included, 3 nights some holidays. **Open** All year. **Hosts** Mary Kay & Ron Logan, Box 39 Huckleberry Rd., South Sterling, 18460. **Phone** (800) 523-8200 or (570) 676-3244. **Fax** (570) 676-9786. **E-mail** thesterlinginn@ezaccess.net. **Web** thesterlinginn.com.

Zone 11

Central Pennsylvania/ Amish Country

You can observe the slower, more peaceful lifestyle of the Old Order Amish on the back roads of **Lancaster County.** Amish families clip-clop past in buggies pulled by fine trotting horses grown too slow to race in nearby tracks. In spring planting season, barefoot youths and bearded patriarchs in black britches, vests, and broad-brimmed black hats work their tobacco, alfalfa, and corn fields with ploughs drawn by horse and mule teams. You'll see prosperous triple-tiered farmhouses where wholesome looking women in dark purple pinafores, aprons, and organdy prayer caps hoe vegetable gardens, hang out laundry, and tend roadside stands piled with freshly baked bread and relishes.

Lancaster County is one of the few places where bed-and-breakfasts encourage you to bring young children. Several properties are on farms, where families can interact with the animals.

At the **People's Place,** an interpretive center in **Bird-in-Hand,** kids can try on Amish clothes and learn about their beliefs. Exhibits at **Hands On House** teach kids ages two to ten about growing food, having a job, shopping, and creating art—then they can climb into a realistic-looking space capsule and pretend to blast off. Next door, **Landis Valley Museum** is a restored village with 20 buildings and costumed crafters.

Visitors can twist a soft pretzel by hand at the 1784 **Sturgis Pretzel Factory** in **Lititz,** and learn historic lore about chocolate at **Wilbur Candy Museum.** A steam train ride and a railroad museum filled with real train engines, parlor cars, and cabooses draws crowds to **Strasburg.**

Older children may be interested in touring the **Amish Village,** where guides explain how Jacob Amman broke from the Swiss Mennonites and founded the sect that adopted his name in 1693. You'll learn that the average Old Order Amish family has seven children, schooling ends with grade eight, men grow beards after marriage, and women fasten their clothes with straight pins, never buttons.

To taste local produce, head for **Central Market** in **Lancaster.** The 1889 building is no longer dominated by Amish vendors, but you can still buy whoopee pies, scrapple, and German bratwurst. Family-style dining is inexpensive throughout the area, and, if it's Friday, you're likely to sit near a large Amish or Mennonite family—that's their night on the town. It's increasingly common for local Amish women to cook and serve dinners for travelers in their homes. No cameras, smoking, or pre-arrival alcohol consumption are allowed. Your bed-and-breakfast host can put you in touch.

Northeast of Lancaster, it's worth a detour to see **Ephrata Cloister,** until 1934 home to a community of recluses who dressed in white habits.

In westernmost Lancaster County, a history-rich necklace of towns borders the Susquehanna River. Before prohibition, this area was a magnet for "gun-toting Irish and whiskey-drinking German" according to locals. Today, unusual museums, farm tours, and craft shops await. In **Columbia,** you can tour the 1738 **Wright's Gerry Mansion,** an old-fashioned bank museum and world-class collection of time pieces. **Marietta** is awash with Victorian homes, and **Mount Joy** is home to **Bube's Brewery,** the only American brewery surviving intact from the 1800s.

Overall, the region has an eclectic mix of bed-and-breakfasts, ranging from homespun properties to historic restorations to modern estates.

FOR MORE INFORMATION

Pennsylvania Dutch CVB
501 Greenfield Rd.
Lancaster, PA 17601
(800) PA DUTCH
padutchcountry.com

WEST RIDGE GUEST HOUSE, Elizabethtown

OVERALL ★★★ | QUALITY ★★★★ | VALUE ★★★★★ | PRICE $60–$120

Tucked away in a quiet corner of rural Pennsylvania, this peaceful retreat has attracted a loyal following since opening in 1987. Running the guest house for 13 years was Alice Heisey, a self-described idea person who began by restoring the main building then adding an annex. After taking a short course, she did her own decorating. Husband Wayne, a builder, is developing 18 homes on land they own across the road, which will give the area a more residential feeling. Alice decided to retire in 2000 and chose long-time employee Susan Miller to take the reins. The house is still kind of out in the boonies, but the value is there so people find it.

SETTINGS & FACILITIES

Location On Rte. 743, 2.5 mi. west of Elizabethtown, 4 mi. northwest of the Rheems/ Elizabethtown Exit on Rte. 283. **Near** 15 min. from Harrisburg International Airport, close to Amish country, outlet malls, Hershey Park. **Building** European manor-style main house w/ 2-story annex. **Grounds** 23 acres includes gazebo, 2 fishing ponds, tennis court. **Public Space** LR, family room w/ dining area. **Food & Drink** Full country breakfast served in guest house at separate tables; specialties—waffles, quiche, French toast. **Recreation** Exercise room w/ hot tub, 2 bikes w/ helmets, 2 golf courses w/in 5 mi. **Amenities & Services** Video library, make dinner reservations, fax, copier; meetings (25).

ACCOMMODATIONS

Units 7 guest rooms, 2 suites. **All Rooms** TV & VCR, phone. **Some Rooms** Deck (4), fridge, fireplace (4), ceiling fan (6), coffeemaker (4). **Bed & Bath** King (2), queen (7), canopy (1), four-poster (2); quality private baths, 3 whirlpools, 8 tubs. **Favorites** Executive suite—glowing peach tones, king bed plus sofa bed, fireplace, 2 TVs, fridge, whirlpool, seperate shower; Loft suite—dramatic entrance faces double forest green whirlpool, 2-story layout, good amenities, sitting area w/ fireplace & sofa bed. **Comfort & Decor** The main house's formal living room is traditional, but looks a bit plastic. The adjacent building's family room has an attractive double tower buffet, cane chairs, and a beanie doll collection Guest rooms reflect styles of various decades. Swimming pool is not zoned for guests.

RATES, RESERVATIONS, & RESTRICTIONS

Deposit 1 night. **Discounts** Extended stays, corp. **Credit Cards** AE, V, MC, D. **Check-In/Out** 1 p.m/10:30 a.m. **Smoking** No. **Pets** No. **Kids** Yes. **Minimum Stay** 2 nights holiday weekends. **Open** All year. **Hosts** Susan & Wayne Miller, 1285 West Ridge Rd., Elizabethtown, 17022. **Phone** (877) 367-7783 or (717) 367-7783. **Fax** (717) 361-9755. **E-mail** wridgeroad@.aol.com. **Web** westridgebandb.com.

TWIN PINE MANOR, Ephrata

OVERALL ★★★★½ | QUALITY ★★★★★ | VALUE ★★★★ | PRICE $95–$189

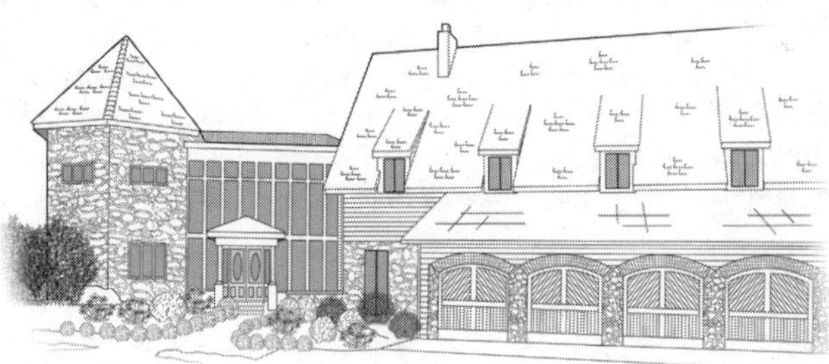

Owner Norman Kurtz collects designer furniture and classic sports cars, including Jaguars and Lamborghinis. You, too, can live like a king for a day in the manor house that showcases his spare-no-expense lifestyle. Strongly-themed furniture collections are deftly accessorized and cleverly placed in spacious rooms. The details are overwhelming. A player grand piano entertains in the A-frame living room filled with plants, art, and super-comfortable seating. A pool table is dwarfed in the recreation room, which adjoins a mini-spa and patio overlooking green pastures. Every guest room is a tour-de-force. What's next? Perhaps a lap pool next to the alfalfa fields.

SETTINGS & FACILITIES

Location Rte. 322, 3 mi. west of Ephrata, 30 mi. southeast of Hershey, 30 mi. northeast of Lancaster. **Near** Landis Valley Farm, Ephrata Cloisters, Adamstown, Horst Auction House. **Building** Manor house superimposed on Swiss chalet–style A-frame. **Grounds** 15 acres, 2 ponds, 2 gazebos; front faces busy commercial road, back adjoins farmland with unobstructed view of 20 farms, silos. **Public Space** Great room, DR, library, powder room, recreation room, spa, 2nd-floor sitting area, outdoor hot tub, patio, rooftop deck. **Food & Drink** Buffet-style breakfast; specialties—casseroles, quiche, wet-bottom shoo-fly pie, apple French toast, pastries, muffins, homemade granola, elaborate fruit plate; beverages always avail. **Recreation** Sauna, steam room, tanning booth, weights, treadmill, bike equipment, outdoor hot tub, antiquing nearby. **Amenities & Services** Portable TV, free local calls.

ACCOMMODATIONS

Units 7 guest rooms, 1 suite. **All Rooms** AC, phone, cable connect, robes. **Some Rooms** Dataport, fireplace. **Bed & Bath** King & queen beds, elaborate bedspreads & window treatments; private marble baths, 3 Jacuzzis, 2 tubs, luxury fixtures, double sinks, thick towels. **Favorites** Windsor—castle-like feel; shades of mustard, black, & gold, dental molding, stone fireplace, brocade spread w/ fringe, chandelier, antique chest; Fox Hunt—hunt scene wall mural, boots & dog sculpture; Valentine—lighthearted Victorian look, canopy bed w/ lace from India, chandelier, floral wallpaper, faux dogwood tree, balcony, glass shower, & Jacuzzi. **Comfort & Decor** This 21-room mansion with 7 stone-faced gas fireplaces comprises more than 9,000 square feet. The look is contemporary, with granite and hardwood floors plus open airy spaces. Strongly-themed guest rooms with quality wall-coverings, fixtures, and accessories.

RATES, RESERVATIONS, & RESTRICTIONS

Deposit Credit card ($50), refund w/ 2-days notice. **Discounts** Entire house. **Credit Cards** V, MC. **Check-In/Out** 4 p.m./11 a.m. **Smoking** No. **Pets** No. **Kids** 10 & over. **Minimum Stay** $30 surcharge for one night stay on weekends Memorial Day to Labor Day. **Open** All year (except Jan. & Feb.). **Host** Norman Kurtz, 1934 W. Main St., Ephrata, 17522. **Phone** (888) 266-0099 or (717) 733-8400. **Fax** (717) 733-8300. **E-mail** twinpinemanor@desupernet.net. **Web** twinpinemanor.com.

INTERCOURSE VILLAGE SUITES, Intercourse

OVERALL ★★★ | QUALITY ★★★★ | VALUE ★★★ | PRICE $99–$239

If you've always wanted to stay in the village with the funny name, here's your chance. The main house was opened for guests in 1998 by a father and son team, who also own the town's Best Western. Past tenants were a local hardware store, country doctor, and two dentists—then it became Intercourse's first bed-and-breakfast. It features antique tables, sofas, sideboard, and bureaus but new beds. Particularly fetching are the loveseat, old Victrola, sewing machine, and antique lighting fixtures in the parlor and sitting room. Wicker furniture on the front porch invites guests to relax and get acquainted. Suites in the annex buildings are comfortable, but look more like an upscale motel.

SETTINGS & FACILITIES

Location On busy Rte. 340, the main thoroughfare through Intercourse. **Near** Antique malls, farmers market, quilt shops, Sight & Sound theaters, Hershey Park. **Building** 1909 Victorian w/ 3 modern buildings added in back. **Grounds** Shrubs, perennials, seasonal window boxes. **Public Space** Sitting room, parlor, DR, porch. **Food & Drink** 3-course candlelight breakfast served on fine china, snacks avail. **Recreation** Amish attractions, buggy rides, farm visits, crafts & antique shows, quilt festivals. **Amenities & Services** Videos, cable TV & VCR.

ACCOMMODATIONS

Units 3 guest rooms, 9 suites. **All Rooms** Working gas fireplace, AC, hair dryer. **Some Rooms** Private entrance (8), wet bar with microwave, fridge, coffeemaker (9). **Bed & Bath** King (3), queen (6), four-poster (3), sleigh (1); private baths, 3 double whirlpools, 4 tubs. **Favorites** Johnson room—four-poster bed w/ white canopy, floral wallpaper, pretty Victorian accessories; Summer House suite—heart-shaped whirlpool, four-poster bed & great wallpaper, fully accessorized for cook-in convenience. **Comfort & Decor** In the main house, guest rooms feature Victorian furnishings, original woodwork, pocket doors, wood floors, and Oriental carpets. In the annex buildings, rooms are themed in a crisp country style.

RATES, RESERVATIONS, & RESTRICTIONS

Deposit Credit card to hold, refund w/ 2-days notice or re-rental. **Discounts** Clergy, winter coupons. **Credit Cards** V, MC, AE. **Check-In/Out** 4–7 p.m./noon. **Smoking** No. **Pets** No. **Kids** No. **Minimum Stay** 2 nights on autumn weekends & all holidays. **Open** All year. **Host** Elmer Thomas, Main St., Rte 340, Intercourse, 17534. **Phone** (800) 664-0940 or (717) 768-2626. **E-mail** ivbbs@aol.com. **Web** amishcountryinns.com.

COUNTRY VIEW, Kinzer

OVERALL ★★★ | QUALITY ★★★½ | VALUE ★★★★ | PRICE **$49–$79**

This property was rescued and restored by a Mennonite plumber who raises chickens on an adjacent farm. The outside looks spic and span, with new aluminum siding. Interior rooms have been gradually renovated to create a plain, but comfortable place for families to vacation without having to worry about the children breaking somebody's antique chandelier. Eli Smucker is handy with tools and is always looking for ways to improve his property. Now that he's finished converting the chicken coop into a family and TV room for guests, he's eyeing other out buildings to spiff up. If asked, he sometimes invites visitors to his farm to see the animals—goats, sheep, ducks, and, of course, chickens.

SETTINGS & FACILITIES

Location Junction of Rte. 340 and Rte. 897 N, 6 miles east of Intercourse. **Near** Quilt shops, farmers markets, outlet malls, Sight & Sounds theatres. **Building** 1903 2-story farmhouse. **Grounds** 30-acre active farm growing corn & alfalfa. **Public Space** Dining area, front porch, back deck, detached sitting room. **Food & Drink** Cont'l breakfast served 7–10 a.m. w/ homemade baked goods, fresh fruit, cereal, beverages. **Recreation** Buggy rides, antiquing. **Amenities & Services** Fridge, microwave, toaster.

ACCOMMODATIONS

Units 3 guest rooms, 1 suite. **All Rooms** AC, ceiling fan, clock. **Some Rooms** Whirlpool (1), Amish quilt. **Bed & Bath** Adequate; one detached bath. **Favorites** Suite. **Comfort & Decor** Lace window curtains, floral wallpaper, rocking chairs, and quilts add a bit of hominess to guest rooms, but avoid room #3 which has a detached bath and lace curtain to create a makeshift closet

RATES, RESERVATIONS, & RESTRICTIONS

Deposit $20 returned w/ 24-hours notice. **Discounts** After 3 nights deduct $10 per night. **Credit Cards** No. **Check-In/Out** Noon–5 p.m./11 a.m. **Smoking** No. **Pets** No. **Kids** Yes. **Minimum Stay** None. **Open** All year. **Hosts** Barbara & Eli Smucker, 5463 Old Philadelphia Pike, Kinzer, 17535. **Phone** (717) 768-0936. **Fax** (717) 768-8520. **Web** countryviewpa.com.

KING'S COTTAGE, Lancaster

OVERALL ★★★ | QUALITY ★★★★ | VALUE ★★★ | PRICE **$105–$200**

This B&B faces the former King's Highway, renamed Lancaster Turnpike in 1794 when it became the nation's first paved roadway. It's listed as Totten House on the National Register of Historic Places, for dentist Frank Totten who owned it from 1913 to 1916. A subsequent owner earned the title Great Gatsby of Lancaster. The Spanish Revival style is unique in Lancaster County. The interior look is definitely upscale. Spacious public rooms contain a pleasant mix of Chippendale reproductions, a smattering of antiques, cozy fireplaces, and an airy enclosed porch. Jim, a consulting engineer, and Karen no longer live on the premises. They've moved a few blocks away, leaving details to a capable young staff.

SETTINGS & FACILITIES

Location On Rte. 462. **Near** 1.5 miles east of downtown Lancaster; Amish country. **Building** 1913 Spanish Revival, cream w/ red tile roof. **Grounds** City lot w/ small lily pond, herb garden. **Public Space** LR, DR, Florida room/foyer, library, panty, terrace. **Food & Drink** Full breakfast; specialties—quiche Lorraine, orange stuffed French toast, apple pancake, meat, fruit and juice; afternoon tea, cordials, evening snack. **Recreation** Weekly list posted for area events, Lancaster central market, private tour of Amish country, dinner w/ Amish family, antiquing, buggy ride. **Amenities & Services** Disabled access (1), fax, VCR and videos; written directions to restaurants; special events: Hershey Auto Show, Quilt Festival, Renaissance Faire, arts & crafts shows.

ACCOMMODATIONS

Units 8 guest rooms, 1 carriage house. **All Rooms** AC, hair dryer, iron, telephone jack, TV if requested. **Some Rooms** Fireplace (1), 2-person Jacuzzi (1), private entrance (2). **Bed & Bath** King (3), queen (6) canopy (3), four-poster (3); 8 tubs, several very large bathrooms with quality decor; 3 baths are detached but private. **Favorites** Princess room—private balcony (w/ view of garage), chandelier, floral/powder blue color scheme, light floods in through 9 windows, large bath w/ claw-foot tub, tiny closet. **Comfort & Decor** Enjoy a spacious, light-filled parlor with art deco brick fireplace. Also, a marble fireplace in the library, a grand staircase, original stained glass windows, antiques, and interesting coffeetable books. Guest rooms have antique wardrobes and marble-topped sinks. Street noise is a factor, so bring ear plugs.

RATES, RESERVATIONS, & RESTRICTIONS

Deposit 50%. **Discounts** AAA, corp., extended stays. **Credit Cards** V, MC, D. **Check-In/Out** 4–7 p.m./11 a.m. **Smoking** No. **Pets** No. **Kids** 12 and over. **No-Nos** Breakfast & afternoon tea for guests only. **Minimum Stay** 2 nights weekends, 3 nights holidays & special events. **Open** All year. **Hosts** Karen & Jim Owens, 1049 East King St., Lancaster, 17602. **Phone** (800) 747-8717 or (717) 397-1017. **Fax** (717) 397-3447. **E-mail** kingscottage@earthlink.net. **Web** www.innbook.com/inns/kings/.

O'FLAHERTY'S DINGELDEIN HOUSE, Lancaster

OVERALL ★★★½ | QUALITY ★★★★ | VALUE ★★★★ | PRICE $95–$150

The Leath family, who founded the Strasburg Railroad, were past owners here. For the Whittles, who moved here in 1999, one stay at a B&B in Rockport, Massachusetts was all it took for them to give up successful careers in Kentucky to become innkeepers. (He was a city planner, she a social worker and nursing home administrator.) Born in Tennessee and trained in the art of southern hospitality, both seem right for the job. They enjoy chatting with guests and their guesthouse looks and feels like a real home. On Saturday mornings, they celebrate their southern heritage by serving imported Tennessee country ham and Nancy's scratch biscuits topped with white gravy from a cookbook used by Danny's mother.

SETTINGS & FACILITIES

Location Rte. 462, 1.5 mi. east of downtown Lancaster. **Near** Amish countryside, outlet malls. **Building** 1910 Dutch Colonial home w/ additions. **Grounds** City lot w/ flower garden, 1,000 spring bulbs, small pond w/ Japanese fish. **Public Space** LR, DR, library, porch. **Food & Drink** Full country breakfast served 8–9 a.m.; specialties—omelets, French toast, egg & meat casserole, plus homemade muffins, special blend coffee. **Recreation** 3 theaters nearby, museums, Amish attractions, Strasburg railroad. **Amenities & Services** Book & video library about Amish/Pennsylvania culture, area itineraries/maps.

ACCOMMODATIONS

Units 3 guests rooms, 1 suite, 1 cottage. **All Rooms** AC. **Some Rooms** Soundproofed (1). **Bed & Bath** Queen (7), twin (2); 3 private baths, 2 detached baths, 6 tubs. **Favorites** Master suite has appliquéd comforter, chintz wallpaper, full drapes, elegant bathroom w/ 2-person shower & tub, antique pedestal sink. **Comfort & Decor** Enjoy sharing two fireplaces, traditional furnishings, and lots of personal photographs and family heirlooms.

RATES, RESERVATIONS, & RESTRICTIONS

Deposit 1 night, refund w/ 7-days notice. **Discounts** Seniors, winter season (Jan–March). **Credit Cards** V, MC, DC, D. **Check-In/Out** 2 p.m./11 a.m. **Smoking** No. **Pets** No (kennel 0.5 mi. away). **Kids** Yes. **Minimum Stay** 2 nights weekends, 3 nights holiday weeks. **Open** All year. **Hosts** Nancy & Danny Whittle, 1105 E. King St., Lancaster, 17602. **Phone** (800) 779-7765 or (717) 293-1723. **Fax** (717) 293-1947. **E-mail** rooms@dingledeinhouse.com. **Web** dingledeinhouse.com.

MT. GRETNA INN, Mount Gretna

OVERALL ★★★★½ | QUALITY ★★★★ | VALUE ★★★ | PRICE **$95–$145**

The Pennsylvania Chautauqua Society founded Mt. Gretna in the 1890s. In summer, the tradition of education and culture continues with daily offerings of first-rate music, theater, and cultural events. Bring your easel, sketch pad, and/or musical instrument to participate in classes and mingle with folks who share your interests. Miles of hiking and mountain biking trails range in level of challenge from family-suitable to expert. In autumn, the heavily wooded area displays some of the Northeast's most stunning fall foliage. In winter, cross-country skiers can enjoy picturesque trails. Staying at Mt. Gretna Inn gives you entrée into a unique community.

SETTINGS & FACILITIES

Location Appalachian foothills, walk to village. **Near** 0.5 mi. east of Conewago Lake, 12 mi. east of Hershey, 25 mi. east of Harrisburg, 18 mi. northwest of Lancaster. **Building** 1921 Arts & Crafts. **Grounds** 1.25 acres w/ forested canopy of hardwood & pine trees, gardens. **Public Space** Parlor, 2 DR, small library, porch, guest pantry, powder room. **Food & Drink** Full breakfast served by candlelight w/ heirloom silver including juice, fresh fruit, baked goods; specialties—egg puff, various stuffed French toast, soufflés, quiches. **Recreation** Hiking, canoeing, miniature golf, roller rink, carriage rides, mountain biking, skiing; summer theater, chamber music, & art workshops. **Amenities & Services** Massage, meetings (25), weddings (75).

ACCOMMODATIONS

Units 7 guest rooms. **All Rooms** AC, clock radio, ceiling fan, robes, flowers in summer. **Some Rooms** Fireplace (6). **Bed & Bath** King (1), queen (6), canopy (4); private baths, whirlpool (1). **Favorites** Black Walnut—bay window, gas fireplace, porch, massage steam shower; Wild Cherry—wing chair near the fireplace, marble top dresser & washstand, flapper costume display. **Comfort & Decor** White walls with dark trim, crushed velvet sofas, the glow of polished wood, and flamboyant Victorian antiques set a classic tone. A wood fireplace and four-foot grand piano, beveled lead glass, and lace curtains add old-fashioned style. Clean, simple architectural lines and comfy furnishings invite relaxation. Accessories include antique clothing and wall stenciling.

RATES, RESERVATIONS, & RESTRICTIONS

Deposit 50%, refund w/ 14-days notice less $10. **Discounts** Packages avail. **Credit Cards** AE, V, MC, D. **Check-In/Out** 3–7 p.m./11 a.m. **Smoking** No. **Pets** No. **Kids** Over age 12. **Minimum Stay** None. **Open** All year. **Hosts** Robin & Keith Volker, 16 W. Kauffman Ave., Mt. Gretna, 17064. **Phone** (800) 277-6602 or (717) 964-3234. **Fax** (717) 964-3234. **E-mail** kvolker@mtgretna.com. **Web** mtgretna.com.

COUNTRY GARDENS, Mount Joy

OVERALL ★★★★ | QUALITY ★★★½ | VALUE ★★★★★ | PRICE **$65–$85**

These Mennonite hosts spent most of their lives working their farm and now delight in sharing it with guests. With 7 children and 20 grandchildren, they understand and welcome kids. The family begins meals with a short prayer, and don't be surprised to find vegetables from the garden on the table. Bring old clothes, because after breakfast you don't just stand on the sidelines. Guests are urged to explore a big barn, gather eggs from the hen house, pick off corn to fill the animals' feeding trough, even swing on a rope and drop in a straw pit. The hosts like to join in the fun and are apt to be right behind you.

SETTINGS & FACILITIES

Location 5 mi. north of Rte. 30, 5 mi. south of Rte. 283, 20 mi. west of Lancaster. **Near** Amish country, Hershey Park, Gettysburg, Marietta. **Building** 1860s brick Georgian-style Colonial. **Grounds** 103-acre farm w/ colorful flowers, vegetable garden. **Public Space** LR, DR, family room, kitchen, porch. **Food & Drink** Hearty farm breakfast served at set hour; specialty—filled French toast with homemade raspberry jam. **Recreation** Swings, kittens, feeding chickens, cows, & sheep. **Amenities & Services** Hayrides, bonfire to roast marshmallows, arrange dinner w/ Amish family; a piano is avail., Dotty plays the marimba; groups (8).

ACCOMMODATIONS

Units 3 guest rooms, 1 suite. **All Rooms** AC, clock. **Some Rooms** Balcony (1). **Bed & Bath** Queen (3), double (2); 2 private baths, 2 shared baths, 1 tub. **Favorites** Lilac room—spacious, sweet wallpaper, lace curtains, Dotty's own painting of lilacs (separate bath). **Comfort & Decor** Enjoy handmade crafts, original oil paintings, and family heirlooms.

RATES, RESERVATIONS, & RESTRICTIONS

Deposit 1 night. **Discounts** No. **Credit Cards** V, MC. **Check-In/Out** 4–7 p.m./11 a.m. **Smoking** No. **Pets** No. **Kids** Yes ($10 extra per child). **Minimum Stay** 2 nights on weekends April–Oct. **Open** All year. **Hosts** Dotty & Andy Hess, 686 Rock Point Rd., Mount Joy, 17552. **Phone** (717) 426-3316. **Web** www.metrocast.com/countrygardens.

COUNTRY LOG HOUSE FARM, *Mount Joy*

OVERALL ★★★★★ | QUALITY ★★★★ | VALUE ★★★★★ | PRICE $75–$85

This Mennonite farm is a great place for families with young children. A short scripture reading and prayer precedes a hearty breakfast. Then, host Jim Brubaker, who resembles Paul Newman, takes guests on an hour-long farm tour. Everyone gets to pet, feed, and milk the goats. You ride a tractor-drawn wagon filled with hay to an adjoining farm to see calves and learn how cows are milked. Our group sang a few lines of "Old McDonald Had A Farm" as we rolled along. For a finale, everyone gets a basket to gather "hot" eggs from a little red hen house. Checkout time is flexible: guests are invited to linger and enjoy the bucolic ambience.

SETTINGS & FACILITIES

Location 4 mi. west of Rte. 283. **Near** Groff's golf complex, Amish country, Hershey Park, Gettysburg. **Building** Renovated 1800 farmhouse, two additions. **Grounds** 48-acre dairy farm milking 90 cows, fields planted w/ rye and corn. **Public Space** DR, family room w/ original logs exposed, brick patio. **Food & Drink** 8 a.m. farmer's breakfast w/ eggs, meats, waffles, pancakes, baked oatmeal, beverages. **Recreation** Basketball hoop, double swing, country road for hiking, jogging, biking; feed sheep, goats, kittens; gather eggs, milk goat, hayride to dairy farm. **Amenities & Services** Farm tour, groups to 8.

ACCOMMODATIONS

Units 4 guest rooms, 1 suite. **All Rooms** AC. **Some Rooms** Amish quilt, fridge & microwave (Loft), TV (2). **Bed & Bath** Varied bed sizes; 2 private baths, 3 shared. **Favorites** Loft room—handmade crafts depict farm critters, tiny bath. **Comfort & Decor** This is country chic superimposed on an original log building. A modern, open kitchen adjoins a sky-lit living room with a gas fireplace. French doors open to a patio, and ceiling beams are hung with baskets of dried flowers. Teddy bears are everywhere. Guest rooms are cozy but not all are well-designed. One bathroom is on a lower floor.

RATES, RESERVATIONS, & RESTRICTIONS

Deposit 1 night by check. **Discounts** No. **Credit Cards** No, cash or check only. **Check-In/Out** 4–7 p.m./10:30 a.m. **Smoking** No. **Pets** No. **Kids** Yes ($10 per child). **Minimum Stay** 2 nights on weekends Memorial to Labor Day. **Open** All year. **Hosts** Joanne & Jim Brubaker, 1175 Flory Rd., Mount Joy, 17552. **Phone** (717) 653-4477. **Web** www.pamall.net/CLHF.

GREEN ACRES FARM, Mount Joy

OVERALL ★★★ | QUALITY ★★★ | VALUE ★★★★ | PRICE $75–95

This property has been a bed-and-breakfast for 39 years and looks it. The brick-floored country kitchen and the public rooms are awash with collectibles and pleasant clutter. A living room trampoline and elaborate outdoor playhouse set the tone for welcoming families. But avoid weekends, when scout troops move in. The setting is magnificent—a hilltop surrounded by green pastureland and bucolic splendor. Formerly Mennonite, the innkeepers are pleasant and well-connected in the community. They provide a detailed written itinerary for exploring backcountry roads that lead to places like the Hands-On and Landis Farm Museums, pretzel and candy factories in Lititz, and Amish attractions.

SETTINGS & FACILITIES

Location 7 mi. west of Lancaster, 2 mi. south of Mount Joy. **Near** Amish country, Landis Farm Museum, Lititz. **Building** 1850 farmhouse. **Grounds** 150 acres of corn & soybeans, nut grove, pasture for sheep, goats, & donkeys. **Public Space** LR, 2 DR, porch, playhouse and play barn. **Food & Drink** Early coffee, family-style farmer's breakfast at 8 a.m. w/ fruit, juice, hot beverages; specialties—pancakes, waffles or French toast, quiche, eggs, meat, casseroles. **Recreation** Pet goats, sheep, & kittens; swing, outdoor trampoline, hayrides to dairy farm, donkey rides, volleyball net, biking, nearby golf & miniature golf, bowling, water slide, farmers market Tues., Fri., & Sat. **Amenities & Services** A collection of Amish clothes for children to try on.

ACCOMMODATIONS

Units 7 guest rooms. **All Rooms** AC. **Some Rooms** Fireplace (1), balcony (4), private entrance (4), rocking chair, TV if requested. **Bed & Bath** Some canopy, several bunk beds, 1 detached bath. **Favorites** The kitchen. **Comfort & Decor** The living room has a fireplace, baby grand piano, doll collection, dried flowers, family photos, and antique music box. The warm, friendly kitchen displays candle molds and country implements. Bedrooms have antique furnishings and vary in quality.

RATES, RESERVATIONS, & RESTRICTIONS

Deposit 1 night or $100 for groups, credit cards accepted for reservation only. **Discounts** No. **Credit Cards** No. **Check-In/Out** As you please/11 a.m. then invited to spend the day. **Smoking** No. **Pets** Yes. **Kids** Yes, add $5 per child. **Minimum Stay** 2 nights weekends June–Oct. **Open** All year. **Hosts** Yvonne & Wayne Miller, 1382 Pinkerton Rd., Mount Joy, 17552. **Phone** (717) 653-4028. **Fax** (717) 653-2840. **Web** thegreen acresfarm.com.

CREEKSIDE INN, Paradise

OVERALL ★★★★ | QUALITY ★★★★ | VALUE ★★★★ | PRICE $75–$105

These innkeepers have nurtured friendships with their Amish neighbors. They can introduce you to a gazebo maker who loves to talk about history, a quilt maker with an impresive private collection, and an Amish housewife who welcomes diners in her home. If asked, they can also direct you to secret places in Lancaster County to make your visit memorable. These hosts invite guests to sit and talk in the parlor, and there's no shortage of conversation pieces. Cabinets contain over 50 hand-blown pre–World War I communion sets made in Czechoslovakia. Predominantly coral, red, and blue, they look like large Easter eggs. Cathy collects pottery made in Torquay, England—each painted with a saying.

SETTINGS & FACILITIES

Location Heart of Amish country. **Near** 0.25 mi. north Rte. 30, 8 mi. east of downtown Lancaster. **Building** 1781 Georgian-style limestone w/ original fireplaces, woodwork, doors, hardware. **Grounds** 2 acres next to Pequea Creek, part of an original William Penn land grant. **Public Space** Foyer, LR, 2 DR, porch w/ rockers. **Food & Drink** Early coffee, full country breakfast at 8:30 a.m. w/ home-baked treats, farm eggs & milk, Lancaster county meats; evening snack. **Recreation** Amish community & farm tours, theater, Strasburg Railroad, golf; shop for crafts, furniture, antiques, local foods, & art. **Amenities & Services** Amish culture & Pennsylvania history books; use of fridge.

ACCOMMODATIONS

Units 4 guest rooms, 1 suite. **All Rooms** AC, ceiling fan. **Some Rooms** Stone fireplace (2). **Bed & Bath** Queen beds, 3 four-poster; private baths, 3 tubs. **Favorites** Pequea—crisp, pure tone, nice quilt, Amish hats, good view; Witmer—1 stone wall, four-poster bed, antique dresser & desk, wood floor, big closet, 1781 portraits, creek view; Creekside—fireplace, four-poster bed, antique dresser & desk, blue wall-to-wall carpet, blue & white plaid curtains, nice lamp, stenciling in bathroom. **Comfort & Decor** Antiques and locally-made Amish quilts are featured.

RATES, RESERVATIONS, & RESTRICTIONS

Deposit One night or 50%, refund w/ 5-days notice less $20. **Discounts** 7th night free. **Credit Cards** AE, V, MC, D. **Check-In/Out** 3 p.m./11 a.m. **Smoking** No. **Pets** No. **Kids** No. **Minimum Stay** 2 nights most weekends. **Open** All year. **Hosts** Cathy & Dennis Zimmermann, Box 435, 44 Leacock Rd., Paradise, 17562. **Phone** (717) 687-0333. **Fax** (717) 687-8200. **E-mail** cathy@thecreeksideinn.com. **Web** thecreeksideinn.com.

Zone 12

Harrisburg/ Western Pennsylvania

Harrisburg, Pennsylvania's capital city, is a far different place than it was two decades ago. Mayor Stephen Reed was the catalyst for transforming this community on the Susquehanna River from almost derelict in 1982 to a dynamic urban center. Today, visitors can see the restored **State Capitol, State Museum, Governor's Mansion, John Harris/Simon Cameron museum,** a vibrant market, and **City Island,** a mid-river recreation hub.

Heading west, you may sense a hint of untamed energy and frontier spirit in downtown **Carlisle.** Once the last bastion of English speaking civilization, many a Conestoga wagon left from Carlisle towards the setting sun and an uncertain fate. You can visit a museum focusing on **The Indian Industrial School** (1879–1918), which tried to transform buffalo hunters, warriors, and Indian girls into skilled craftsmen and laborers. Olympic athlete Jim Thorpe was once a student.

To the south, **Gettysburg National Military Park,** one of the state's most visited sites, has a powerful story to tell. An electric map at the Visitor Center shows troop movements during the three-day battle. Consider hiring a private guide to show you the land where 168,000 men fought and explain some of the 1,300 granite or bronze monuments, markers, and tablets plus 375 cannons.

Your itinerary should include **East Cemetery Hill,** the **Gettysburg National Cemetery, Little Round Top, Devil's Den,** the **Wheatfield and Peach Orchard, Seminary Ridge,** the **Eternal Light Peace Memorial,** and the **Memorial to State Units.** Often these sites are viewed in hushed silence. The battlefield area is very different from the town of Gettysburg, which has run amuck with commercial outlets attempting to capitalize on its fame.

Adjoining the battlefield is the **Eisenhower National Historic Site,** where visitors can tour the only house owned by President Dwight D. Eisenhower and his wife, Mamie.

The **Allegheny National Forest,** in the state's northwest corner, extends through Warren, Frost, Elk, and McKean Counties. Resources include 500 miles of fishing streams, 226 miles of hiking and cross-country ski trails and 297 miles of snowmobile trails, 106-miles of bike routes, and several boat launches. In a word, it is huge.

In the southwest corner of the state, you'll find **Fort Necessity National Battlefield,** where the French and Indian War began on July 3, 1754. The fort and earthworks ordered to be built by George Washington have been reconstructed. An audio-visual program tells about the Washington-led campaign.

Rivers, bridges, and roadways bisect a maze of hills and ravines in **Pittsburgh,** a city that has transformed itself from a sooty industrial town into an admired metropolis offering impressive cultural attractions.

This large area has a number of distinctive bed-and-breakfasts, many offering unique experiences.

FOR MORE INFORMATION

Gettysburg CVB
35 Carlisle St.
Gettysburg, PA 17325

PA Capital Regions Vacation Bureau
1255A Harrisburg Pike
Carlisle, PA 17013
(800) 995-0969; pacapitalregions.com

JACOB'S RESTING PLACE, Carlisle

OVERALL ★★★★ | QUALITY ★★★½ | VALUE ★★★★ | PRICE $75–$95

From 1801 to 1835, this property was a colonial inn called The Sign of the Green Tree. It also served as a toll station along the Harrisburg-Chambersburg Pike. Today, it sits at the edge of a busy highway, but you can relax in the backyard, which offers a hot tub and small swimming pool. And, at the far end of the lawn, you can fish in the famed Letort Trout Stream—catch-and-release, of course. Visitors with an interest in the Civil War will enjoy seeing Terry's collection of items—from belt buckles to buckshot. The house is made cozy by its seven fireplaces.

SETTINGS & FACILITIES

Location 1.5 mi. east of the center of Carlisle, adjacent to Letort Trout Stream, Carlisle Barracks, & U.S. Army War College. **Near** 18 mi. west of Harrisburg, 28 mi. north of Gettysburg. **Building** 1790 five-bay Georgian w/ Flemish bond brick, 1986 addition. **Grounds** 3 acres w/ stream access, formal Colonial garden w/ indigenous plants or those imported before 1790, cottage garden w/ herbs, medicinal plants & flowers, mature pine & walnut trees. **Public Space** Original keeping room, sitting room, herringbone brick patio, pavilion, swimming pool. **Food & Drink** Full breakfast w/ seasonal fresh fruit plate, homemade breads, hot beverages served on porcelain w/ crystal & linen; specialties—stuffed crêpes, Dutch babypuff, stuffed French toast w/

berry sauce; snacks anytime, guest fridge & microwave. **Recreation** Catch-&-release fly-fishing year-round (trout season runs mid-April–Oct.); hiking the Appalachian Trail, antiquing, visiting the Military History Institute & Carlisle Barracks; numerous street fairs & festivals. **Amenities & Services** Hot tub, exercise equipment, videos (Colonial, Civil War, & contemporary), golf privileges at Carlisle Barracks Golf Course, beach towels avail., fax & e-mail; meetings (22).

ACCOMMODATIONS

Units 4 guest rooms. **All Rooms** AC, ceiling fan, phone, TV, clock radio, fresh flowers, robes, hair dryer. **Some Rooms** Fireplace (3). **Bed & Bath** King (1), queen (2), single (3), double (3); 1 private bath, 3 rooms share a bath (attractive w/ English tile), tubs. **Favorites** Victorian—a more feminine room w/ fireplace, king bed, marble top tables & 1870s Austrian bedroom suite; Blue & Grey—Civil War art, adjoining room can be added. **Comfort & Decor** A case in the sitting room contains museum-quality Civil War memorabilia. You'll find antiques and early-American furnishings throughout. The keeping room has a beamed ceiling, fireplace, Welsh grandfather's clock, and Scandinavian dough box. Collections include earthen jugs and yellow ware.

RATES, RESERVATIONS, & RESTRICTIONS

Deposit Credit card to hold or $20, refund w/ 10-days notice less $20; policy differs on special event weekends. **Discounts** Military. **Credit Cards** AE, V, MC, D. **Check-In/Out** 2 p.m./11 a.m. **Smoking** No. **Pets** No. **Kids** Over age 12. **Minimum Stay** 2 or 3 nights for special event weekends. **Open** All year. **Hosts** Marie & Terry Hegglin, 1007 Harrisburg Pike, Carlisle, 17013. **Phone** (888) 731-1790. **Fax** (717) 241-5010. **E-mail** jacobsrest@pa.net. **Web** www.jacobsrest.cvbednbreakfasts.com.

PHEASANT FIELD, Carlisle

OVERALL ★★★★ | QUALITY ★★★★ | VALUE ★★★★ | PRICE **$85–$100**

"Come home to the country" is the motto of this pleasant rural retreat, where Denise and Chuck enjoy sharing local history and steering guests towards the area's best attractions. Denise always goes the extra mile. While traveling extensively in a previous career, she learned first-hand that travelers need to be comfortable and relaxed. Chuck works in the computer field, but takes an active role in the B&B on weekends. Ask him to show you the false floor in the family room, which leads to an underground hideaway for runaway slaves. The hospitality at Pheasant Field is genuine. Once a guest, you'll be on the Christmas letter list for updates on new projects, shared recipes, and family happenings.

SETTINGS & FACILITIES

Location Rural setting, 3 mi. east of Carlisle. **Near** U.S. Army War College, Dickinson College; 32 mi. north of Gettysburg, 35 mi. west of Hershey, 14 mi. west of Harrisburg Airport. **Building** 1800–1810 Federal, red brick. **Grounds** 10 acres, horse pasture, pond w/ island & pergola, perennial garden w/ rhododendron, mountain laurel, day lilies. **Public Space** Family room, LR, DR, front porch, patio. **Food & Drink** Full country breakfast w/ fruit, juice, homemade baked goods; specialties—oatmeal pancakes, baked French toast, quiches; guest fridge stocked w/ soft drinks, fruit. **Recreation** 0.25 mi. to

Appalachian Trail, 1 tennis court w/ balls & racquets provided, fly-fishing at Yellow Breeches & Letort Spring Run, antiquing; Classic Car show April–Oct. at Carlisle Fairgrounds. **Amenities & Services** Videos, fax & e-mail, overnight boarding for horses (no trail rides provided); meetings (12), weddings (200).

ACCOMMODATIONS

Units 4 guest rooms, 1 cottage. **All Rooms** AC, phone w/ answering machine, TV, clock radio. **Some Rooms** Cottage has private entrance & kitchenette. **Bed & Bath** King (2), queen (3), four-poster (1), sleigh (1); private baths, 2 tubs. **Favorites** General Miller's Retreat—king bed, sitting area, blue tones. **Comfort & Decor** Comfy rooms have attractive furnishings, including a piano. Bedrooms were named by guests in a contest.

RATES, RESERVATIONS, & RESTRICTIONS

Deposit 1 night, refund w/ 3-days notice. **Discounts** Corp., gov. **Credit Cards** AE, V, MC. **Check-In/Out** 4–7 p.m./11 a.m. **Smoking** No. **Pets** Barn for horses, other pets welcome in cottage only (1 dog in residence). **Kids** Age 8 & older (all ages in cottage). **Minimum Stay** 2 nights for special car show & college weekends. **Open** All year. **Hosts** Denise Fegan and Chuck DeMarco, 150 Hickorytown Rd., Carlisle, 17013. **Phone** (877) 258-0717 or (717) 258-0717. **E-mail** pheasant@pa.net. **Web** pheasantfield.com.

CASHTOWN INN, Cashtown

OVERALL ★★★½ | QUALITY ★★★★ | VALUE ★★★ | PRICE $95–$145

Most of the Confederate army marched past this inn's front door en route to the battle at Gettysburg in July 1863. For two nights, Confederate General A. P. Hill headquartered here. In the foyer, a dozen photos show actors and scenes filmed here in 1992 for the movie *Gettysburg*, including Sam Elliot, who stayed here while portraying General Buford. Artist Dale Gallon's print *Serious Work Ahead* shows Hill meeting with General Robert E. Lee at the inn on July 1, 1863. Artist Mort Kunstler's dramatic painting *Distant Thunder* is also displayed. A dining room mural shows the red brick inn in a more pastoral nineteenth-century setting—very similar to the way the building appears today. Civil War buffs will appreciate this historic treasure.

SETTINGS & FACILITIES

Location On Rte. 30 facing an apple orchard. **Near** 7 mi. west of Gettysburg National Military Park. **Building** 1797 Federal. **Grounds** 2.5 acres w/ herb garden, flower gardens, koi pond. **Public Space** Mini-parlor, 2 DR. **Food & Drink** Full breakfast w/ juice, fruit, baked goods; specialties—egg & cheese strata, Belgian waffles w/ bacon, stuffed French toast; full-service restaurant on premises. **Recreation** Historic and Civil War battlefield–related tours & attractions. **Amenities & Services** Videos, fax; wine dinners, murder mystery & psychic weekends; meetings & weddings (55).

ACCOMMODATIONS

Units 7 guest rooms. **All Rooms** AC, fresh flowers, hair dryer, robes, clock. **Some Rooms** Porch (2), private entrance (2), ceiling fan (2). **Bed & Bath** King (1), queen (5), double (1), canopy (1), four-poster (4); private baths, 2 tubs. **Favorites** Gen. Robert E. Lee Suite—king bed w/ pillowtop mattress, TV & VCR, slant roof; #3—four-poster canopy bed, possibly the room where A. P. Hill stayed. **Comfort & Decor** Eclectic furnishings feature reproduction antiques. The sitting area is part of the foyer. Teddy bears are everywhere. Civil War art is shown on consignment.

RATES, RESERVATIONS, & RESTRICTIONS

Deposit 1 night, return w/ 14-days notice less $100. **Discounts** Extended stay. **Credit Cards** AE, V, MC, D. **Check-In/Out** 3–6 p.m./11 a.m. **Smoking** Tavern only. **Pets** No. **Kids** In suites only. **Minimum Stay** 2 nights most weekends. **Open** All year. **Hosts** Eileen & Dennis Hoover, son Jason, 1325 Old Rte. 30, Box 103, Cashtown, 17310. **Phone** (800) 367-1797. **Fax** (717) 334-1442. **E-mail** cashtowninn@cvn.net. **Web** cashtowninn.com.

BECHTEL MANSION INN, East Berlin

OVERALL ★★★½ | QUALITY ★★★★ | VALUE ★★★ | PRICE $85–$150

East Berlin's artists and craftsmen display their wares in quaint village shops along Main Street. The town is awash in Colonial structures, earning it a place in the National Register of Historic Places. In May, 1764, it was laid out in 85 lots, with one main street, four cross streets, and five alleys—and hasn't gotten much bigger. Restored buildings include the 1769 school house, 1794 stone mill, and a 1790 house, now a museum. The Holtzschwamm Church was rebuilt in the mid-nineteenth century, but tombstones in the cemetery are older. Founder John Frankenberger named the town after his native German city, and the post office added "East" because there was another Berlin in the state. This property is low-key—a no-pressure zone with plenty of hospitality.

SETTINGS & FACILITIES

Location Center of historic district on Rte. 234. **Near** 18 mi. northeast of Gettysburg, 10 mi. north of Hanover, 52 mi. northwest of Baltimore. **Building** 1897 Queen Anne Victorian w/ turret & wraparound porch, exterior is red brick w/ white trim. **Grounds** City lot, bulb garden. **Public Space** Guest parlor, DR, 3rd floor sitting room. **Food & Drink** Full breakfast w/ juice, fresh fruit, homemade baked goods; specialties—orange French toast, apple cinnamon pancakes, bacon & cheese casserole; afternoon tea w/ cookies. **Recreation** Antiquing, historic Gettysburg, factory tours, biking tours; antique show (May), Colonial Days—juried arts & crafts show w/ period costumes (early Sept.). **Amenities & Services** Videos, bike storage; meetings (12), weddings (20).

ACCOMMODATIONS

Units 7 guest rooms, 2 suites. **All Rooms** AC. **Some Rooms** Fireplace (1), balcony (3), TV (2). **Bed & Bath** King (1), queen (6), double (2), canopy (1); private baths, 3 tubs. **Favorites** Balcony suite—queen bed w/ ornate walnut headboard, small sitting room w/ TV, claw-foot tub, balcony overlooking Victorian gardens. **Comfort & Decor** Tasteful Victorian charm and antique furniture are the highlights here.

RATES, RESERVATIONS, & RESTRICTIONS

Deposit Credit card to hold, refund w/ 10-days notice; during Gettysburg reenactments 1 night by check w/ no refund. **Discounts** More than 4 nights. **Credit Cards** AE, V, MC, D. **Check-In/Out** 1–4 p.m./11 a.m. **Smoking** No. **Pets** No. **Kids** Over age 12. **Minimum Stay** 2 nights on special event weekend; 3 nights for Gettysburg reenactments. **Open** All year. **Hosts** Carol & Richard Carlson, 400 W. King St., East Berlin, 17316. **Phone** (800) 331-1108 or (717) 259-7760. **Web** www.bbonline.com/pa/bechtel/rooms.html

BALADERRY INN, Gettysburg

OVERALL ★★★½ | QUALITY ★★★½ | VALUE ★★★ | PRICE **$115–$145**

If it's Civil War authenticity you're looking for, this inn is a good choice. Located just outside the main Gettysburg battlefield, the property was part of a Union field hospital during what locals call The War Between the States. Guests dine in the main house, which is the more historic building. Rooms in the carriage house are newer and have pastoral views and a sense of privacy. Our bed was not very comfortable, but who can complain when, in an earlier era, soldiers slept on the ground. You can relive the war via a collection of videos in the TV room. "My main mission is to help people enjoy the real Gettysburg. I don't want people to go away thinking this is a honky-tonk, T-shirt town," says host Caryl.

SETTINGS & FACILITIES

Location Adjacent to Gettysburg battlefield, 2 mi. south of downtown Gettysburg. **Near** Little Round Top, National Park Visitor Center, Eisenhower farm. **Building** 1812 Federal brick, restored. **Grounds** 3.7 acres w/ brick terrace, giant spruce trees, flower gardens, gazebo, tennis court. **Public Space** Great room, DR, sitting room, powder room, guest fridge. **Food & Drink** Early coffee, full country breakfast w/ juice, fresh fruit, cereal; specialties—eggs Baladerry, French toast, waffles with bacon or sausage. **Recreation** Bike tour of Gettysburg battlefield, horseback riding, golf, skiing, antiquing, tennis (rackets & balls avail.); Civil War reenactments. **Amenities & Services** Videos, fax & e-mail; meetings (40).

ACCOMMODATIONS

Units 8 guest rooms (4 in cottage). **All Rooms** AC, phone, clock radio. **Some Rooms** Private patio (2), gas fireplace (2). **Bed & Bath** Queen beds; private baths. **Favorites** Cottage's Yellow Room—gas fireplace, pullout sofa, access to TV room with Civil War videos & patio. **Comfort & Decor** A massive brick fireplace dominates the two-story great room, which doubles as a dining and gathering area. Guest rooms in the cottage are plain; two upstairs rooms have a fireplace, while downstairs rooms offer patios.

RATES, RESERVATIONS, & RESTRICTIONS

Deposit $25 per night, refund w/ 7-days notice. **Discounts** None. **Credit Cards** AE, V, MC, D, DC, CB. **Check-In/Out** 2 p.m./11 a.m. **Smoking** No. **Pets** No. **Kids** Over age 12 welcome. **Minimum Stay** 2 nights on weekends, holidays, & special events. **Open** All year. **Hosts** Caryl O'Gara, 40 Hospital Rd., Gettysburg, 17325. **Phone** (717) 337-1342. **Fax** Call first. **E-mail** baladerry@mail.wideopen.net. **Web** baladerryinn.com.

BATTLEFIELD INN, Gettysburg

OVERALL ★★★★★ | QUALITY ★★★½ | VALUE ★★★ | PRICE **$145–$193**

Every Gettysburg visitor should meet Charlie, a Civil War reenactor with a degree in and a life-long passion for military history. Dressed in battle uniform, he communicates his knowledge of Civil War lore to inn guests each morning in a lively hour-long presentation about some facet of the three-day battle in 1863. His presentations sparkle with humor, insights, and colorful descriptions. Weather permitting, horse-drawn carriage rides are part of a stay. The inn's simple farmhouse decor and a family-style breakfast invite guests to get acquainted. The shadow of a Civil War soldier is painted on one wall and Civil War flags, weapons, books, and videos are plentiful. The house sits four miles north of the Mason-Dixon line, facing a pond with a stone wall and open spaces. It's an ideal place for families.

SETTINGS & FACILITIES

Location Bordering Gettysburg National Military Park. **Near** Big Round Top. **Building** 1809 stone & wood farmhouse. **Grounds** 46 acres w/ field, woods, pond & streams. **Public Space** Parlor, DR, Lincoln sitting room. **Food & Drink** Full breakfast served by costumed staff; first course specialties—orange section in cream sauce w/ cream cheese pecan pastry, apple cobbler w/ whipped cream topping, poached pears & raisin rum muffins; main course specialties—heart-shaped pancakes w/ bacon, fried eggs, and farm potatoes, apricot French toast w/ kielbasa slices & potatoes, fritatta w/ Italian sausage, raspberry cream crêpes w/ ham & potatoes. **Recreation** A rotation of 15 hands-on history demonstrations presented at 8 a.m. daily; learn to fire a musket & crew a cannon, watch cavalry train for battle, try on uniforms; ranger tours focus on the Peach Orchard, Pickett's Charge, & Little Round Top; carriage rides Apr.–Nov., weather permitting; Friday night ghost stories; golf, biking, horseback riding. **Amenities & Services** Civil War & children's videos, central phone, TV, carrots to feed horses; meetings (30), weddings (100).

ACCOMMODATIONS

Units 6 guest rooms, 2 suites. **All Rooms** AC, quilts, Civil War art. **Some Rooms** Gas fireplace (2). **Bed & Bath** Queen (7), pair of doubles (2), canopy (1); private baths w/ tubs. **Favorites** 7th Georgia—view of pond, nice fabrics; Harts—romantic; Reilly's—good for families. **Comfort & Decor** History permeates the inn, with guest rooms named for military units. Low water pressure can be a problem during morning showers.

RATES, RESERVATIONS, & RESTRICTIONS

Deposit Credit card, refund w/ 7-days notice. **Discounts** None. **Credit Cards** AE, V, MC, DC, D. **Check-In/Out** 2:30–8 p.m./11:30 a.m. **Smoking** No. **Pets** No. **Kids** Yes, w/ guidelines. **Minimum Stay** 2 nights when a Saturday is included (exceptions possible). **Open** All year. **Hosts** Florence & Charlie Tarbox, 2264 Emmitsburg Rd., Gettysburg, 17325. **Phone** (888) 766-3897 or (717) 334-8804. **Fax** (717) 334-7330. **E-mail** battlefieldinn@hotmail.com. **Web** gettysburgbattlefield.com.

DOUBLEDAY INN, Gettysburg

OVERALL ★★★★½ | QUALITY ★★★★ | VALUE ★★★ | PRICE $95–$130

This is one of Gettysburg's most prestigious addresses—right in the middle of the battlefield. Rooms are small but cheery. The atmosphere is low-key, and the decor is a visual treat, with eye-catching collectibles in every nook and cranny and a wood-burning fireplace to add warmth. The friendly innkeepers, who moved here from Illinois in 1994, did a total make-over on the property—with complete success. Breakfast is served by candlelight. Evening programs on Civil War history on Wednesday and Saturday nights by a licensed battlefield guide are a bonus. The inn's namesake, West Point graduate Abner Doubleday, had a distinguished military career. But, you'll learn, he didn't really invent baseball as many claim—although he probably refined the sport and modified some of the basic rules.

SETTINGS & FACILITIES

Location On Oak Ridge, the center of the first day's battle. **Near** 1 mi. north of downtown Gettysburg, 15 mi. east of the Appalachian Trail, 70 mi. northwest of Baltimore, 90 mi. north of Washington, D.C. **Building** 1929 Colonial w/ 1940s addition. **Grounds** 1 acre w/ flower gardens, surrounded by 6,300 acres of Gettysburg National Military Park. **Public Space** LR, DR, covered porch, 2 patios, 2nd floor deck. **Food & Drink** Full breakfast w/ juice & fresh fruit; specialties—alternate between a baked eggs dish w/ muffins and variations of baked French toast w/ sausage; afternoon tea & lemonade w/ cookies. **Recreation** Immediate access to the battlefield, mountain biking, fishing, skiing, golf, fitness center, reenactments, living history demonstrations; Remembrance Day (Nov.), Apple Blossom & Harvest Festivals. **Amenities & Services** Massage avail., bike storage; meetings (12), weddings (25).

ACCOMMODATIONS

Units 9 guest rooms. **All Rooms** AC, clock, named for senior officers who fought nearby. **Some Rooms** Library area (1). **Bed & Bath** Double (8), twin (3), four-poster (1); 7 private baths, 2 shared baths, 7 tubs. **Favorites** Ramsure—a small but nifty room w/ horse border wallpaper; O'Neal—blue plaid, roman numeral wall border, tiny bath. **Comfort & Decor** Colorful, classic decor features lots of interesting accessories. The wood-burning fireplace adds to the coziness. Every window has a battlefield view.

RATES, RESERVATIONS, & RESTRICTIONS

Deposit 50%, refund w/ 10-days notice less $10. **Discounts** Friends of Nat'l Parks at Gettysburg. **Credit Cards** V, MC, D. **Check-In/Out** 2–6 p.m./11 a.m. **Smoking** No. **Pets** No. **Kids** Age 8 & up. **Minimum Stay** None. **Open** All year (except Thanksgiving, Dec. 24–25, some midweek days in Jan. & Feb.). **Hosts** Ruth Anne & Charles Wilcox, 104 Doubleday Ave., Gettysburg Battlefield, 17325. **Phone** (717) 334-9119. **Fax** (717) 334-7907. **E-mail** doubledayinn@blazenet.net. **Web** doubledayinn.com.

GASLIGHT INN, Gettysburg

OVERALL ★★★★ | QUALITY ★★★★ | VALUE ★★★ | PRICE $100–$175

Six old-fashioned gaslights surround this house, evoking the ambience of an earlier era. The house, built by a prosperous carriage maker, grew in stages. Pocket doors, wood trim, and frosted and beveled glass panels are original and ceiling medallions were added. Art from local galleries perks up the hallways. The hosts excel at helpful concierge services, steering guests to the best private guides, attractions, and restaurants. Follow their advice, then share your experiences at the breakfast table, where one recent menu included strawberries with lemon curd sauce, a choice of six juices, toffee scones, cheese omelets, and homemade veal and turkey sausage.

SETTINGS & FACILITIES

Location Center of town. **Near** 7 blocks to Gettysburg Visitors Center. **Building** 1872 peaked roof farmhouse w/ Italianate front, Eastlake carvings. **Grounds** Double city lot w/ annual gardens. **Public Space** 2 parlors, DR, 2nd floor TV room, 2 powder rooms. **Food & Drink** Full breakfast w/ juice, fresh fruit, homemade baked goods; specialties—lemon spice waffles, apple French toast, omelets; cookies & beverages avail. anytime. **Recreation** Civil War attractions & reenactments (July), golf, tennis horseback rides on the battlefield, wineries, antiquing; Apple Blossom Festival (May), Apple Harvest Festival (Oct.). **Amenities & Services** Videos, club privileges at YMCA, massage avail., disabled access (1 room); meetings (14), weddings (60).

ACCOMMODATIONS

Units 9 guest rooms. **All Rooms** AC, TV, phone, clock. **Some Rooms** Fireplace (6), private entrance (4), balcony (3), ceiling fan (6), VCR (2). **Bed & Bath** King (1), queen (8); private baths, 2 whirlpools, 4 steam showers. **Favorites** Violet—pretty colors, cheerful; Heather—floral fabrics, gas fireplace, steam shower, front view (some traffic noise). **Comfort & Decor** Public rooms feature quality reproductions and family antiques with a look that is consciously un-Victorian. Accessories include a Taiwan screen, Chinese funeral urn, Iranian bass bowl, and pre-Czarist samovar.

RATES, RESERVATIONS, & RESTRICTIONS

Deposit 50%, refund w/ 7-days notice less $10. **Discounts** No. **Credit Cards** AE, V, MC, D. **Check-In/Out** 3 p.m./11 a.m. **Smoking** No. **Pets** No (1 chocolate lab in residence). **Kids** Over age 12. **Minimum Stay** 2 nights on weekends April 1–Nov. 30, 3 nights for special events. **Open** All year (except Dec. 24–25). **Hosts** Roberta & Denis Sullivan, 33 E. Middle St., Gettysburg, 17325. **Phone** (717) 337-9100. **Fax** (717) 337-1100. **E-mail** info@thegaslightinn.com. **Web** www.virtualcities.com/ons/pa/g/page97702.htm.

SHEPPARD MANSION, Hanover

OVERALL ★★★★★ | QUALITY ★★★★★ | VALUE ★★★★ | PRICE $140–$220

The remarkably well-preserved Sheppard Mansion is one of the most opulent properties in the Mid-Atlantic. It's the kind of place you usually gawk at from behind velvet ropes on historic home tours but never can touch—much less lounge on its fine brocade and silk upholstery. Kathryn has lovingly restored it to the way it looked when her great grandparents, H. D. Sheppard and his wife, were in residence. You'll be astonished at the size of the rooms, the quality of the workmanship of the decor and furnishings, and the details that remain from an earlier era. Kathy, a recent college graduate, is a hands-on owner and delightful hostess. Tim Bobb adds his expertise as a host and chef extraordinaire. Some folks may feel intimidated by so much grandeur, but these hosts want you to feel right at home.

SETTINGS & FACILITIES

Location 1 block from city center at intersection of Rte. 194 & Rte. 116. **Near** 15 mi. east of Gettysburg, 15 mi. west of York, 34 mi. northwest of Baltimore. **Building** 1913 Neo-classic Greek Revival, red brick w/ 4 marble columns. **Grounds** 1.5 acres w/ English gardens, boxwoods, stone benches. **Public Space** Gentlemen's parlor, ladies parlor, DR, den, powder room, breakfast room, 2 libraries, terrace. **Food & Drink** Full breakfast w/ juices, fresh fruit, baked goods, coffees; specialties—stuffed French toast w/ cream cheese, apricots, & walnuts; mushroom, red pepper, broccoli, & smoked gouda frittata; banana & blueberry strata; help yourself to beverages in guest fridge anytime. **Recreation** Factory tours of local snack food companies, fitness facility on premises; meetings (16), weddings (125). **Amenities & Services** Spa treatments avail., laundry, fax.

ACCOMMODATIONS

Units 5 guest rooms, some w/ adjoining bedrooms. **All Rooms** AC, TV, phone, dataport, robes, fresh flowers, alarm clock, luggage rack, Oriental rug, iron & board, water candles. **Some Rooms** VCR, fireplace (1), hand-painted ceiling (2), noise machine avail. **Bed & Bath** Queen (7), double (4), canopy (1); private baths, cast-iron soaking tubs (4). **Favorites** Ayres room—fireplace, hand-painted ceiling, sitting area w/ antiques, 2-person shower, claw-foot tub, elegant furnishings, very spacious; Lee room—rose, gold, blue, & green accents, canopy bed, Oriental rug, hand-painted ceiling, marbled-floor bath w/ soaking tub. **Comfort & Decor** Silk wall panels, velvet room dividers, crystal wall sconces, marble lamps and sculptures, and carved sofas with rich fabrics create a knock-your-socks-off impression. The property is in pristine condition, including a grand staircase which splits at the landing and beveled glass windows that add rainbow hues to everyday light.

RATES, RESERVATIONS, & RESTRICTIONS

Deposit Credit card to hold, refund w/ 14-days notice. **Discounts** Corp., 7th night free. **Credit Cards** AE, V, MC, DC, D. **Check-In/Out** 2–8 p.m./11 a.m. **Smoking** No. **Pets** No. **Kids** Over age 12. **Minimum Stay** 2 nights on weekends May to Oct. **Open** All year. **Hosts** Kathryn Sheppard, owner & Timothy Bobb, innkeeper, 117 Frederick St., Hanover, 17331. **Phone** (877) 762-6746 or (717) 633-8075. **Fax** (717) 633-8074. **E-mail** katsheppard@hotmail.com. **Web** sheppardmansion.com.

DOUBLEDAY COUNTRY INN & FARM, Landisburg

OVERALL ★★★★★ | QUALITY ★★★½ | VALUE ★★★ | PRICE $65–$75

The focus here is on baseball and, in summer, guests can play more of it than most people do in a lifetime. Guests have the use of vintage uniforms and all the necessary equipment. As many as four games take place daily on a beautifully groomed, well-lighted field where you can field, hit, and pitch in games with former baseball professionals. Among them are Hall of Famers, All-Stars, World Series champs, Most Valuable Players, and Rookies of the Year. (The roster in recent seasons included Harmon Killebrew, Tug McGraw, and Gaylord Perry.) Or, you can pull up a lawn chair and just watch. The unique concept was the brainchild of Brad Shover, a former team-owner and college coach. He also provides horses for trail rides through gorgeous meadows and on ridges overlooking the farm.

SETTINGS & FACILITIES

Location Rural farmland w/ views of meadow, woods, & hills. **Near** 10 min. south of Little Buffalo State Park, 20 mi. north of Carlisle. **Building** 19th century farmhouse. **Grounds** 90 acres w/ 50 acres planted with corn, soybeans, & hay, a 5-acre regulation baseball field, 5 horses, llamas, 3 goats, 2 pot-bellied pigs. **Public Space** Sitting room, TV room, 2nd floor DR, upstairs sunporch & balcony, powder room. **Food & Drink** Full breakfast w/ juice, fresh fruit, baked goods; specialties—egg casserole, pancakes & sausage, eggs any style. **Recreation** Horseback riding lessons ($25 per hour), trail rides ($20 per hour); fantasy baseball. **Amenities & Services** Meetings (12), weddings (150).

ACCOMMODATIONS

Units 7 guest rooms. **All Rooms** AC. **Some Rooms** Phone (1), TV (2), fireplace (1), private entrance (1), ceiling fan (3). **Bed & Bath** Queen (5), twin (2); 3 private baths, 4 shared baths, 1 tub. **Favorites** Ground floor #2—quiet, wicker rocker; 2nd floor green room—pleasant decor. **Comfort & Decor** The public areas have jazzy wallpaper, simple furnishings, wood floors, and lots of baseball books and art. Guest rooms are small and simply decorated—comfortable, but no frills. Each window has a pastoral view, and baseball games are visible from the upstairs porch.

RATES, RESERVATIONS, & RESTRICTIONS

Deposit $20, refund w/ 7-days notice. **Discounts** No. **Credit Cards** AE, V, MC. **Check-In/Out** 2 p.m./noon. **Smoking** No. **Pets** Yes, stay in the barn (3 labs on premises). **Kids** Yes. **Minimum Stay** No. **Open** All year. **Hosts** Ann & Brad Shover, Box 617, Landisburg, 17040. **Phone** (717) 789-2456. **Fax** (717) 789-2456. **E-mail** d2dayfarm@aol.com. **Web** doubledayfarm.com.

FARM FORTUNE, New Cumberland

OVERALL ★★★★ | QUALITY ★★★★ | VALUE ★★★ | PRICE $95–$185

Phyllis has lived in this house since 1976, and she turned it into a bed-and-breakfast in 1986 after her three children had left home. She added five bathrooms in the house and one in the cottage, which was formerly her antique shop. She collects blue and white spongeware, decorated crocks, tin, redware, and ironstone plus a cache of antiques, including kitchen utinsels. Unfortunately, the front of the property overlooks a nondescript off-putting commercial park. But you soon forget that once you're inside the carefully maintained Georgian-style home, in remarkably good condition after so many centuries.

SETTINGS & FACILITIES

Location Hilltop overlooking Yellow Breeches Creek, 1 mi. south of New Cumberland. **Near** 2 mi. west of Harrisburg; Hershey, Amish country, Gettysburg, York. **Building** 1784 Georgian-style limestone w/ 1734 cottage. **Grounds** 2.5 acres w/ gardens, fishing area. **Public Space** Keeping room, formal parlor, DR. **Food & Drink** Full breakfast w/ juice, fresh fruit, homemade breads & muffins; specialties—orange oatmeal pie, French toast w/ pecan topping, apple puff. **Recreation** fly-fishing (license needed), antiquing, factory tours, minor-league baseball games; Apple Festival (fall), York Fairgrounds, hot rod shows, model train shows, Dapona River Festival in Harrisburg. **Amenities & Services** Videos, books, fax & e-mail; meetings (15), weddings (50).

ACCOMMODATIONS

Units 4 guest rooms, 1 cottage. **All Rooms** AC, TV, phone, fresh flowers, hair dryer, robes, clock radio. **Some Rooms** Balcony (1). **Bed & Bath** King (1), queen (3), canopy (2), four-poster (1); private baths, 2 tubs. **Favorites** Cottage—2-story hideaway, rustic, wood fireplace, TV & VCR, microwave, fridge; King—four-poster canopy bed. **Comfort & Decor** Formal early American furnishings and Williamsburg powder blue trim throughout lend a classic look. Two-foot thick horsehair and plaster walls cushion the outside noise. The two-story cottage is rustic with some modern amenities.

RATES, RESERVATIONS, & RESTRICTIONS

Deposit One night, refund w/ 7-days notice. **Discounts** Corp. **Credit Cards** AE, V, MC, DC. **Check-In/Out** 3–9 p.m./11 a.m. **Smoking** No. **Pets** No. **Kids** Over age 10. **Minimum Stay** None. **Open** All year. **Host** Phyllis Combs, 204 Limekiln Rd., New Cumberland, 17070. **Phone** (717) 774-2683. **Fax** (717) 774-5089. **E-mail** frmfortune@aol.com. **Web** http://members.aol.com/frmfortune/.

KANAGA HOUSE, New Kingstown

OVERALL ★★★★ | QUALITY ★★★★ | VALUE ★★★ | PRICE $75–$110

A mother and son team run this bed-and-breakfast, which was originally built by Joseph Junkin, son of one of Cumberland County's earliest settlers. The setting is ideal for weddings, and lots of brides book the property. It's well located to explore the surrounding region, including car shows and antique shows at the fairgrounds. You can golf at local courses and fish in the best limestone troutstreams in the East. You can hike the Appalachian Trail for nine miles, then have lunch at a historic tavern (phone Kanaga and you have a ride back.) In winter, Roundtop ski area has a night chairlift. From April to November, Allenberry Playhouse offers entertaining fare.

SETTINGS & FACILITIES

Location On Rte. 11, 6 mi. east of Carlisle. **Near** PA turnpike, I-81, Dickinson College, 9 mi. west of Harrisburg. **Building** 1775 limestone manor house. **Grounds** 3 acres w/ bulb garden, 1880s gazebo, lawn, mature trees. **Public Space** LR, DR, family room, sunroom, powder room, eat-in kitchen, tavern room, upstairs sitting area, guest pantry. **Food & Drink** Full breakfast w/ juice, fresh fruit; specialties—omelets, frittatas, egg casserole, stuffed French toast. **Recreation** Car shows, antique shows, trout fishing, hiking the Appalachian Trail, golf, skiing, cooking classes, Allenberry Playhouse (April–Nov.). **Amenities & Services** Meetings (15), weddings (225).

ACCOMMODATIONS

Units 6 guest rooms. **All Rooms** AC, hair dryer, robes, clock radio. **Some Rooms** TV (2), phone (5), ceiling fan (2), fireplace (1), private entrance (1). **Bed & Bath** Queen (5), double (1), canopy (4); 4 private baths, 2 shared baths. **Favorites** Dr. George Junkin—four-poster canopy bed, Oriental screen, homemade draperies & spread, TV. **Comfort & Decor** The house is filled with antiques, many from a family-owned antique business. The rule growing up, says Dave, was "never get too attached to anything." Rooms are a bit staid and dimly lit. The family room has a wood-faced brick fireplace, leather sofa, and chair, plus wingback chairs. Guest rooms are named for family members.

RATES, RESERVATIONS, & RESTRICTIONS

Deposit 1 night, refund w/ 4-days notice less $10. **Discounts** Corp., gov. **Credit Cards** AE, V, MC, D. **Check-In/Out** 3 p.m./11 a.m. **Smoking** No. **Pets** No. **Kids** Over age 10. **Minimum Stay** 1 night. **Open** All year. **Hosts** Mary Jane & Dave Kretzing, 6940 Carlisle Pike, New Kingstown, 17072. **Phone** (717) 697-2714. **Fax** (717) 766-8654. **E-mail** kanaga@ezonline.com. **Web** kanagahouse.com.

FIELD & PINE, Shippensburg

OVERALL ★★★★ | QUALITY ★★★★ | VALUE ★★★★ | PRICE **$50–$80**

This home's spacious interior is beautifully decorated. Guests enjoy a hearty breakfast in the formal dining room or, on cold winter mornings, by the kitchen's walk-in fireplace. Besides being a good cook, Mary Ellen has a green thumb. Pretty flowers fill her terraced gardens, where you'll find two small fish ponds and can see sheep grazing in the meadow. Nearby, you can fish in Big Spring trout stream. Or, stroll through Shippensburg's town center, which has several eighteenth- and nineteenth-century buildings, earning it a listing on the National Register of Historic Places. The inn has its own pedigree—first as a tavern called Sign of the Indian King, then as John Stough Tavern. For a time, it even served as a weigh station for wagons and a whiskey bonding station for bootleggers.

SETTINGS & FACILITIES

Location Cumberland Valley. **Near** 14 mi. south of Carlisle. **Building** 1790 stagecoach stop & tavern, limestone. **Grounds** 80 acres w/ pasture, meadow, grazing sheep, pine trees, hiking trails, two fish ponds, gardens w/ boxwood hedges, ivy, terraced flowers, barn. **Public Space** Foyer, formal parlor, keeping room, family room, DR, alcove w/ fireplace, powder room. **Food & Drink** Full breakfast w/ juice, fresh fruit, homemade breads; specialties—peaches & cream French toast, asparagus puff, veggie frittata w/ ingredients from the garden in season, home-cured ham, bacon, or fresh sausage from a Mennonite butcher; cookies & beverages avail. **Recreation** 1 mi. to trout fishing at Big Spring. **Amenities & Services** Weddings (50).

ACCOMMODATIONS

Units 2 guest rooms, 1 suite. **All Rooms** AC, TV, radio, robes. **Some Rooms** Working fireplace (1). **Bed & Bath** King (1), queen (1), double (1); 2 shared baths. **Favorites** Blue Room—queen canopy bed, fireplace, antiques. **Comfort & Decor** Colonial-style furnishings with a homey feeling. The family has lived here since 1970 and filled every room with attractive antiques and collectibles. There are seven working fireplaces.

RATES, RESERVATIONS, & RESTRICTIONS

Deposit 1 night, refund w/ 5-days notice less $10. **Discounts** Gov't. **Credit Cards** V, MC. **Check-in/Out** 2 p.m./11 a.m. **Smoking** No. **Pets** No (golden retriever on premises). **Kids** Over age 12. **Minimum Stay** 2 nights on car show & local college graduation weekends. **Open** All year. **Hosts** Mary Ellen & Allan Williams, 2155 Ritner Hwy., Shippensburg, 17257. **Phone** (717) 776-7179. **Fax** (717) 776-0076. **E-mail** fieldpine @cvbednbreakfasts.com. **Web** www.fieldpine.cvbednbreakfasts.com.

WARRINGTON FARM, Wellsville

OVERALL ★★★★ | QUALITY ★★★★ | VALUE ★★★★ | PRICE $64–$90

While honeymooning in the mid-1980s, Megan and Brad discovered bed-and-breakfasts in New England. "We decided it would be neat to have one of our own someday," says Megan. Eleven years later, they found this property and took a year off to remodel and enlarge it. The results, opened in 1996, are two side-by-side houses (one that they live in) separated by a large one-story dining room. Now, Megan is home to raise her two children while still involved in the business. And, Brad has taken on other building projects. Guests who lead stressed, harried lifestyles will especially enjoy the home's simplicity plus the chance to sit on the back porch and look out at the old barn, wooded area, and open fields. It's definitely is a calming environment—and a great place to relax.

SETTINGS & FACILITIES

Location On Rte. 74. **Near** 12 mi. north of York, 5 mi. from Ski Roundtop, 1 mi. from Gifford Pinchot State Park. **Building** 1860 Shaker-style gentleman's farm. **Grounds** 3.75 acres w/ flower borders. **Public Space** LR, DR, summer kitchen, porch. **Food & Drink** Full breakfast w/ seasonal fruit, baked goods; specialties—waffles, strata, French toast; guest fridge. **Recreation** Fishing, hiking, boating & swimming in the state park; hunting, snow skiing, golf; car show (April), hot rod show (June); train collector's show (April), folk art show in York (April). **Amenities & Services** Videos, ski packages, fax & e-mail; meetings (36), weddings (150).

ACCOMMODATIONS

Units 5 guest rooms. **All Rooms** AC, flowers, clock radio. **Some Rooms** Pull-out bed (1). **Bed & Bath** Queen beds; private baths. **Favorites** Elk Lake—regatta prizes, fishing & sailing items, quality quilts are accessories; Snowed-in room—skis, long johns, mittens, & ice skates add personality. **Comfort & Decor** The house is done completely in Shaker-style furnishings, with pencil-post beds, narrow-legged furniture, lots of Shaker pegs, and straight, clean-cut lines. Colorful accessories add beauty and whimsy. Guests can watch TV in the sitting room or relax by the kitchen fireplace or on the porch.

RATES, RESERVATIONS, & RESTRICTIONS

Deposit 1 night, refund w/ 10-days notice. **Discounts** Extended stays. **Credit Cards** V, MC, D. **Check-In/Out** 3–9 p.m./11 a.m. (10 a.m. Sunday mornings). **Smoking** No. **Pets** No (white Bichon Frise on the premises). **Kids** Over age 9. **Minimum Stay** 1 night. **Open** All year. **Hosts** Megan & Brad Hakes, 7680 Carlisle Rd., Wellsville, 17365. **Phone** (717) 432-9053. **Fax** (717) 432-4537. **E-mail** wfarm@conewago.com. **Web** conewago.com.

Part Five

Maryland

Maryland isn't likely to be the first place where you'd plan to vacation—unless you're a Civil War buff, a convention-goer headed to Baltimore, or a sportsman exploring the Chesapeake Bay.

Big mistake.

Maryland's attractions and treasures are not as heavily promoted as those of its neighboring states, but the reasons to visit are legion.

There's variety— everything from history and nature to cityscapes and culture. The calendar is littered with festivals and special events. And, it's a place to learn about national as well as state history. It was Lord Baltimore's brother, Leonard Calvert, who knelt on St. Clements Island and named the state's first town in honor of Henrietta Maria, wife of Charles I, King of England. A commitment to the concept of religious freedom by his band of religious refugees survived to influence the writers of our Declaration of Independence—and shape the character of our nation.

Nevertheless, Maryland's Colonial history is often overshadowed by its role in the Civil War, as a state bordering the Mason-Dixon line. How do you define a border state, which even after the war retained characteristics of both North and South? You could point out that for many decades, its economy was sustained by profits from growing tobacco. It evolved as modern factories, ironworks, and mills grew up around Baltimore. Shipping ports, railroads, and canal traffic brought more commercial success, and the state remained a crossroads. Nevertheless, much of the state's agrarian ambiance and country charm remains.

One thing is sure: Marylanders know how to enjoy themselves. The state is known for its race tracks, including **Pimlico** and **Laurel.** Hunting is a favorite pastime on the **Eastern Shore,** where you can shop for gear at top-notch outfitters. The boating community is vast, with hundreds of marinas along the state's 3,190 miles of shoreline on the **Chesapeake Bay** and its tributaries. Maryland also offers 31 miles of **Atlantic beaches.**

In the west, the state's largest lake, **Deep Creek,** was manmade to generate electric power, then adapted for recreational use. Ski slopes and a golf course have been added, and now you can find every activity from snowshoeing and fly-fishing to rock climbing and spelunking. You can reach the lake from the east via a major highway that passes through the state's slimmest point near **Hanover,** where Maryland's northern and southern borders are constricted to within a mere two-and-a-half miles apart. The pinched-waist effect is created by the crazily meadering Potomac River, which defines the western half of the state's southern border.

In another tight squeeze, the **Eastern Shore,** part of the 200-mile-long DelMarVa peninsula shared with Delaware and Virginia, is linked to the rest of Maryland by the 4.35-mile-long **Chesapeake Bay Bridge.** It seems people leave their stress behind when crossing the bridge, as the lifestyle on the Eastern Shore is more laid back than in most of the state.

Southern Maryland, as defined here, is the peninsula that begins south of Washington, D.C. and is bounded by the Potomac River and Chesapeake Bay. The area's pièce de resistance is **Annapolis,** a more than 350-year-old city with a brick-lined Main Street and market, eighteenth-century-style street lamps, and parking garages hidden behind red brick façades.

The best way to see Annapolis is on foot. On walking tours, guides in colonial garb pepper their speeches with eighteenth century words and carry covered baskets filled with items that evoke the spirit of Colonial life (a tussie mussie to offset body odor, face wax to hide pox holes, and ground beetles for cheek color). The **U.S. Naval Academy** is a centerpiece of Annapolis today. Walking tours of the academy begin with a film about life as a midshipman and include a visit to the **Sports Hall of Fame.** You also see **Bancroft Hall,** the only dormitory, which houses all 4,000 midshipmen and has 1,800 rooms, five miles of corridors, even its own zip code.

Even with pedestrian-friendly cities, Maryland's back roads and quiet byways offer some of the best places to visit in the state. And, many of the bed-and-breakfasts found here are so unique and special that they themselves have become destinations worth taking extra time to savor and enjoy. Best of all, Maryland's enviable inventory of bed-and-breakfasts tends to be more affordable than many on the eastern seaboard.

FOR MORE INFORMATION

Maryland Department of Business
and Economic Development
Office of Tourism Development
217 East Redwood St.
Baltimore, MD 21202
(410) 767-3400 or (410) 767-6299

Zone 13

Western Maryland

Western Maryland is accessible via Interstate 70, which begins in Baltimore and continues 99 miles before veering north into Pennsylvania near Hancock, Maryland.

Frederick, now a hub of biotech firms and a bedroom community for Washington, D.C., is the first pleasant surprise. A strong sense of history permeates Maryland's second largest city, where patriot Barbara Fritche and poet Francis Scott Key once lived. Particularly distinctive are the clustered spires of four downtown churches, described in a John Greenleaf Whittier poem. A first-rate Civil War medical museum interprets an era when doctors used primitive tools and were efficient at moving great numbers of people through the medical system. Nearby are the less-well known battle sites of South Mountain (1862) and Monocacy (1864).

In **Sharpsburg,** one feels compelled to whisper. This subdued town includes hallowed ground where Union and Confederate troops fought the Battle of Antietam. Some visitors are emotionally overcome trying to comprehend the day that left nearly 25,000 Americans dead or wounded.

By contrast, **Hagerstown** is a busier city, home to the **Maryland Symphony,** trendy upscale restaurants, and lively theater productions. Then, everything changes, as you head further west, climbing gently into the more rugged landscape of the **Allegheny Mountains.**

Until Interstate 68 was finished in 1991, traveling beyond this area was limited to the slower National Pike, which follows a trail George Washington took during the French and Indian War more than 200 years ago.

The role of transportation is key to understanding the history of western Maryland. In **Cumberland,** exhibits at the **Western Maryland Railroad Station Museum** preserve the story of a race between two modes of transportation: canals and railroads.

At the **C&O Canal National Historical Park Visitors Center,** you get a vivid sense of the bawdy, raucous life of families who lived like water gypsies, tending the boats and mules that ferried coal, grain, and wood from the inland mines and farms to cities on the eastern seaboard. It may be called the Chesapeake & Ohio, but the canal stopped at Cumberland, because by the time the canal arrived there, the railroads had proved they could provide cheaper and faster delivery of people and products.

Farther west, the forests, waterfalls, and wildlife of **Garrett County** have attracted well-to-do visitors since the late nineteenth century, when cottages and large hotels were built. Old photographs show Thomas Edison, Henry Ford, and Harvey Firestone dressed to the nines, holding court near the state's highest waterfall. Properties they owned or frequented, such as the old Deer Park Inn, were eventually destroyed by fire or financial reversal.

The creation of a 12-mile-long lake in this area set the stage for rediscovery. **Deep Creek Lake,** Maryland's largest, was made in 1925 to provide hydroelectric power to regional urban areas. Recreational development was gradual. **Wisp Ski and Golf Resort,** across from Lake Pointe Inn, opened in 1956 with a rope tow, and it now has 23 ski slopes on 80 acres of skiable terrain. An 18-hole golf course opened in 1980.

Outfitters are available for everything from deer hunting and fishing to spelunking and rock climbing. In winter, you can cross-country ski, go sledding or snowshoeing, or hunt for wild turkey, grouse, and deer. During warmer months, you can mountain bike, hunt for fossils, go rafting, kayaking, and fishing.

Western Maryland is a visual paradise thanks to greenery, heights, and wildlife—a huge contrast to the skyscrapers of Baltimore.

FOR MORE INFORMATION

Allegany Country CVB
13 Canal St., Suite 406
Western Maryland Railway Station
Cumberland, MD 21502
(800) 425-2067 or (301) 777-5132

Tourism Council of Frederick
19 E. Church St.
Frederick, MD 21701
(800) 999-3613 or (301) 663-8687

Garrett County Chamber of Commerce
15 Visitors Center Dr.
McHenry, MD 21541
(301) 387-6171

Washington County CVB
16 Public Square
Hagerstown, MD 21740
(301) 791-3246

INN AT BUCKEYSTOWN, Buckeystown

OVERALL ★★★★ | QUALITY ★★★★ | VALUE ★★★ | PRICE $125–$190 ($190–$260 MAP)

The focus here is on regional sports and activities. Innkeeper Melinda Hensley is a true concierge who's done extensive homework. If you want to be active and explore the area, she'll put you in touch with numerous seasonal pursuits. Much of the pre-planning is done over the phone before you arrive, so that you can maximize your time. The number of choices are amazing—everything from Frederick Keys baseball games and beer tastings at Frederick Brewing Company to the Koi Festival at Lily Ponds Water Gardens, the East Coast's largest water gardening facility. Owner Janet Wells is also a professional wedding coordinator who can help with everything from shopping for a dress (she owns a bridal boutique nearby) to catering. The MAP price above includes a five-course dinner for two.

SETTINGS & FACILITIES

Location Rte. 85, 4 mi. south of Rte. 270, Rte. 70, & Rte. 40 intersection. **Near** Gettysburg, Antietam, 5 mi. south of downtown Frederick. **Building** 1897–99 Victorian w/ wraparound porch. **Grounds** 2.5 acres, Victorian garden w/ herbs, vegetables, wildflowers, roses, pine grove. **Public Space** Ladies parlor, music room, DR, tearoom, 3rd floor chess area, downstairs tavern. **Food & Drink** Full breakfast; specialties—omelets, eggs Benedict, pancakes; hot beverages available anytime; wine and cheese; prix fixe lunch & dinner by reservation; high tea served on alternate Sundays 2–5 p.m. for $15 per person. **Recreation** Lawn croquet, ping pong, bocce, horseshoes, badminton, dartboard, hot air ballooning, spelunking, whitewater rafting, horseback riding, day spa, area festivals. **Amenities & Services** Welcome food platter, golf packages, special occasion celebrations.

ACCOMMODATIONS

Units 7 guest rooms. **All Rooms** Fresh flowers, candles, room journals. **Some Rooms** Fireplace (1), TV & VCR (1) fridge (2), bay window (2), daybed (2), dataport (2), private porch (1). **Bed & Bath** Queen (1), double (6), down comforters, egg crates; 5 private baths, 2 shared baths, private label amenities. **Favorites** Déjà View—sleigh bed, fireplace, blue walls w/ maroon trim, large bathroom; Love Garden—bright, floral theme, garden view. **Comfort & Decor** Elegant chandeliers and three working fireplaces add romance and style. Porch sitting is popular. Special occasions and holidays are celebrated with festive foods and decorations.

RATES, RESERVATIONS, & RESTRICTIONS

Deposit 50%, refund w/ 2-days notice. **Discounts** 10% for ages 55 and over; corporate rate $90 Sun.–Thur. **Credit Cards** AE, V, M, D. **Check-In/Out** 4–7 p.m./11 a.m., call to arrange late check-in. **Smoking** No. **Pets** No. **Kids** Discouraged, house is not child-proofed. **No-Nos** Kinky behavior. **Minimum Stay** No. **Open** All year, except Dec. 24–25. **Hosts** Janet Wells, owner, Melinda Hinsley, innkeeper, Box 546, Buckeystown, 21717. **Phone** (800) 272-1190 or (301) 874-5755. **Fax** (301) 831-1355. **E-mail** innlove@gte-mail.net. **Web** innatbuckeystown.com.

INN AT WALNUT BOTTOM, Cumberland

OVERALL ★★★½ | QUALITY ★★★½ | VALUE ★★★ | PRICE $87–$131

The Dent House was the birthplace of the father of Julia Dent, who became First Lady, as the wife of Ulysses S. Grant. Public areas are family-oriented, with toys and books for kids of all ages. Families can use two suites, extra day beds in some guest rooms, and a portable crib if needed. Danish-born Kirsten is an expert at Afspaending, a muscular therapy that combines massage, gentle stretching, and relaxation exercises. An hour of "unbuckling" (as the Danes call it) costs $50 and is worth the investment. Breakfasts are good, and the host is knowledgeable about local attractions. The drawback at this urban inn is its proximity to a major highway. It's no longer in a walnut grove. Light sleepers should bring ear plugs.

SETTINGS & FACILITIES

Location Heart of historic Cumberland, on busy road near major highway. **Near** Two blocks to C&O Canal towpath & Western Maryland Scenic Railroad; 65 mi. west of Hagerstown, 65 mi. east of Morgantown, WV. **Building** 1820 Federal (Cowden House) & 1890 Queen Anne (Dent House). **Grounds** Large city lot. **Public Space** Parlor, DR, powder room. **Food & Drink** Full breakfast w/ fresh fruit, homemade muffins, & coffee bread; specialties—herbed ham & cheese frittata, English muffin w/ ham, poached egg, chive lemon sauce; buckwheat blueberry or lemon ricotta pancakes. **Recreation** Hiking, canoeing, whitewater rafting, cross-country skiing; biking the C&O canal towpath (bikes avail.); visit Frank Lloyd Wright's Fallingwater; steam train rides to Frostburg (May–mid-Dec.), leaf peeping; Rail Fest (Oct.), Heritage Festival (June). **Amenities & Services** Massage, fax & e-mail; meetings (20).

ACCOMMODATIONS

Units 12 guest rooms. **All Rooms** AC, TV w/ expanded cable, phone, alarm clock/radio. **Some Rooms** Hair dryer, ceiling fan, adjoining rooms. **Bed & Bath** Bed sizes vary; 5 in-room private baths, 3 locked private hall baths, 4 rooms share 2 detached baths. **Favorites** Dent #2—blue wallpaper, rose spread, small, but quieter; Cowden #6—king bed, private bath. **Comfort & Decor** The large, informal parlor has ample seating, books to browse, a stack of local menus, and snacks anytime. Meals are served in the basement, where white brick walls and separate tables are spic-n-span. Guest rooms are attractive and there are stylish fixtures, but the age of the house shows.

RATES, RESERVATIONS, & RESTRICTIONS

Deposit Credit card to hold, refund w/ 10-days notice. **Discounts** AAA & AARP 10%; corp. rate is $81 Sun.–Thur. **Credit Cards** AE, V, MC, D. **Check-In/Out** 3 p.m./11 a.m. **Smoking** No. **Pets** No. **Kids** All ages welcome. **Minimum Stay** 2 nights on weekends. **Open** All year. **Hosts** Kirsten Hansen & Grant Irvin, 120 Greene St., Cumberland, 21502. **Phone** (800) 286-9718 or (301) 777-0003. **Fax** (301) 777-8288. **E-mail** iwb@iwbinfo.com. **Web** www.iwbinfo.com.

CAMEL COVE INN, Deep Creek Lake

OVERALL ★★★★ | QUALITY ★★★★ | VALUE ★★★ | PRICE $100–$160

Be aware that you do not get a view of Deep Creek Lake from this inn. But the lake is easily accessible via a five-minute walk on a leafy path through the woods. And, once there, you can swim, fish, and navigate a canoe or paddleboat. The inn, built as a monastery for a group of Discalced Carmelite Fathers, retains a bit of a churchy look. (Discalced means barefoot or wearing strapped sandals.) A cross still decorates a wall where an altar once stood. That area also now contains a pool table, and, nearby, guests can relax in comfy sofas and chairs. Large picture windows in the dining room let in forest views, and you can expect to see wild turkey and deer during your visit. The host provides plenty of equipment to explore the area's natural beauty, so take advantage of it and enjoy.

SETTINGS & FACILITIES

Location Secluded vacation community 200 yards from Deep Creek Lake, 2 mi. west of Rte. 219, 4 mi. south of McHenry. **Near** 6 state parks, Wisp Ski Area; 90 mi. south of Pittsburgh, 180 mi. northwest of Baltimore. **Building** Renovated 1945 monastery w/ clock tower, blue shingles, painted cinderblock. **Grounds** 2 acres w/ forest trails, downhill path to Deep Creek Lake, dock. **Public Space** Common room, DR, deck, hot tub. **Food & Drink** Full breakfast served at separate tables, room service avail.; specialties—Belgian waffles w/ fresh strawberries, cheesy sausage mushroom quiche, pancakes w/ Maryland maple syrup, southern bourbon French toast w/ Amish sausage. **Recreation** Pool table & tennis on premises; swimming, fishing, hiking, snowmobiling, downhill & cross-country skiing, hunting, boating; free use of tandem & mountain bikes, tennis rackets, canoeing, paddleboating, snowshoes, fishing gear, cross-country skis. **Amenities & Services** Videos & cable TV in the common room, hot tub outside; meetings (50), weddings (50).

ACCOMMODATIONS

Units 10 guest rooms. **All Rooms** AC, phone, robes. **Some Rooms** Fireplace (2), private deck (4). **Bed & Bath** Queen (9), full (1), sleigh (1); private baths, whirlpools (3), tubs (2). **Favorites** #2—Laura Ashley fabrics, balcony w/ forest view, in-room breakfast; #7—stacked stone wood-burning fireplace, whirlpool, black & gold decor, in-room breakfast (but no view); #9—small but charming w/ high antique headboard, pretty sheets, Stickley bench. **Comfort & Decor** The long common room was formerly a chapel. Eclectic furnishings are arranged to create conversation, reading, and movie-viewing areas. A Vermont castings stove adds warmth, but cinderblock walls detract. Guest rooms are pleasant, but small; they vary in amenities.

RATES, RESERVATIONS, & RESTRICTIONS

Deposit 50%, refund w/ 5-days notice. **Discounts** AAA, extended stay. **Credit Cards** V, MC. **Check-In/Out** 4–9 p.m./11 a.m. **Smoking** No. **Pets** No. **Kids** Over age 12 (2 person max. per room). **Minimum Stay** 2 nights on weekends (except winter). **Open** All year. **Host** Mary Bender, Box 644, Oakland, 21550. **Phone** (301) 387-0067. **Fax** (301) 387-2394. **E-mail** carmelcove@aol.com. **Web** carmelcoveinn.com.

LAKE POINTE INN, Deep Creek Lake

OVERALL ★★★★½ | QUALITY ★★★★ | VALUE ★★★ | PRICE **$118–$189**

The state's tallest waterfall roars nearby. Backbone Mountain, the tallest point in Maryland, looms to the south. This is wilderness country—a far cry from the skyscrapers of Baltimore. Lake Pointe Inn is right in the heart of this newly developed—and haphazardly planned—vacation community. You'll eat well. Then, choose to rock on the porch and enjoy water views. You can also enjoy the water in the hot tub or fish from a dock on site. There is a huge array of sports and activities to take part in.

SETTINGS & FACILITIES

Location Edge of Deep Creek Lake w/ view of Marsh Run Cove, across from trailer park. **Near** Across from Wisp Ski and Golf Resort, 11.25 mi. northeast of Swallow Falls

State Park, 14 mi. northeast of Harrington Manor, 50 mi. to Fallingwater & Kentuck Knob. **Building** 1890 farmhouse w/ wood siding, green tin roof & green trim, porch w/ stone pillars, restored. **Grounds** 1 acre w/ fir trees, swimming dock, lakeside seating. **Public Space** Great room, powder room, wraparound porch w/ rocking chairs, back deck. **Food & Drink** Full breakfast w/ fruit, juice; specialties—scrambled eggs w/ leeks, puff pastry & mushroom tarragon sauce, French toast w/ rum butter & sautéed apples, rolled omelet w/ corn, basil red pepper couli; complimentary soda, wine, beer, fruit bowl, popcorn, homemade cookies, & banana nut bread anytime; hot cider on arrival. **Recreation** Outdoor hot tub, swimming, boating, fishing from own dock; complimentary bikes (6), canoes (2), and kayak (1); tennis court, walk to downhill & cross-country skiing; near antiquing, whitewater rafting, ice & rock climbing, horseback riding, skydiving; Autumn Glory festival (Oct.). **Amenities & Services** 130 videos, written directions to attractions; meetings (20).

ACCOMMODATIONS

Units 8 guest rooms. **All Rooms** AC, TV & VCR, phone w/ private line, hair dryer, robes, ice bucket, fresh flowers, book light, ceiling fan, radio/sound machine. **Some Rooms** Private entrance (2). **Bed & Bath** Queen beds w/ down comforters & down pillows; 6 private baths, 2 detached private baths, 5 tubs, 1 whirlpool. **Favorites** Browning—lake view, small bath; Garrett—large room w/ private entrance, tiny bath is detached. **Comfort & Decor** Guests gather around a nine-foot stacked stone fireplace and Arts & Crafts sofas and chairs accessorized with handcrafted ironwork and pottery, mica and glass lamps, William Morris fabrics, and wall coverings. Brown and burgundy colors and wormy chestnut paneling create a hearty, masculine look.

RATES, RESERVATIONS, & RESTRICTIONS

Deposit Credit card to hold, refund w/ 7-days notice less $25. **Discounts** None. **Credit Cards** V, MC, D. **Check-In/Out** 4–6 p.m./11 a.m. **Smoking** No. **Pets** No. **Kids** Over age 16. **Minimum Stay** 2 nights on weekends. **Open** All year, except Christmas. **Hosts** Caroline McNiece, innkeeper; Linda & George Pettie, owners, 174 Lake Pointe Dr., Deep Creek Lake, 21541. **Phone** (800) 523-LAKE or (301) 387-0190. **Fax** (301) 387-0190. **E-mail** info@deepcreekinns.com. **Web** deepcreekinns.com.

SAVAGE RIVER LODGE, Deep Creek Lake

OVERALL ★★★★★ | QUALITY ★★★★½ | VALUE ★★★★★ | PRICE $180

A one-and-a-half-mile gravel road crosses the headwaters of the Savage River and winds through a state forest to the gate of this extraordinary retreat. The focus here is on what lies outside your log cabin door—acres of hardwood and evergreen forest, fields, streams, and the wildlife of Maryland's Allegheny Mountains. To coax you to fully enjoy the surroundings, the hosts maintain miles of forest trails. In the future, they plan workshops in wildlife photography, stream ecology, fly-fishing, wildflower identification, and gourmet cooking. Of course, you could just relax and breathe deeply of the deliciously fresh air.

SETTINGS & FACILITIES

Location Hilltop in pristine Allegheny Mountains forest. **Near** 3.7 mi. off I-68, 10 mi. west of Frostburg. **Building** Hand-hewn log lodge w/ wide chinking; 18 luxury log cabins. **Grounds** 43 acres surrounded by 700-acre Savage River State Forest, extensive trails. **Public Space** Great room, library, bar, DR, wraparound porch, upstairs meeting room. **Food & Drink** Early juice & muffins delivered to your cabin; full breakfast from menu; specialties—omelet, breakfast pizza, eggs any style w/ bacon or sausage. **Recreation** Hiking, mountain biking, cross-country skiing, snowshoeing, picnicking, fossil hunting, bird watching, fly-fishing, hunting for turkey, grouse, & deer; outfitters avail. for rafting, caving, rock climbing; 5-K run (Labor Day), wine tastings, themed weekends. **Amenities & Services** Massage avail., fax; meetings (35), weddings (70), personal guide service; therapeutic massage by reservation, 1 disabled access.

ACCOMMODATIONS

Units 18 guest cabins. **All Rooms** Ceiling fan, gas fireplace, fridge, hair dryer, coffee pot, dataport, flashlight. **Some Rooms** Disabled access. **Bed & Bath** Queen beds w/ down comforters; private baths w/ oversized soaking tub. **Favorites** #11—end cabin w/ porch overlooking forest, atrium LR, soaking tub, muted colors & earth tones **Comfort & Decor** The great room has a double-sided stone fireplace, rough-hewn wood walls, forest views, and comfy furnishing in earth tones. Accessories include old saws and farm tools, antique license plates, a stuffed turkey (Mike is a champion turkey caller), and vintage sporting equipment. The mood is casual and the look is western. (You'll wonder if you aren't really in Wyoming or Colorado.) Guest cabins are basically alike.

RATES, RESERVATIONS, & RESTRICTIONS

Deposit 1 night, refund w/ 14-days notice less 10%. **Discounts** No. **Credit Cards** AE, V, MC, D. **Check-In/Out** 3 p.m./noon. **Smoking** No. **Pets** Well-behaved by advance arrangement, $20 per night per pet plus $100 deposit (yellow lab on premises). **Kids** Yes. **Minimum Stay** 2 nights on weekends w/ exceptions. **Open** All year. **Hosts** Jan Russell & Mike Dreisbach, Box 655, Grantsville, 21536. **Phone** (301) 689-3200. **Fax** (301) 689-2746. **E-mail** savageriverlodge@mindspring.com. **Web** savageriverlodge.com.

DEER PARK INN, Deer Park

OVERALL ★★★★½ | QUALITY ★★★★½ | VALUE ★★★★ | PRICE $98–$135

Josiah Pennington, a Baltimore architect and lawyer for the B & O Railroad, built a cottage across the street from a fancy 208-room hotel that closed in 1929 and was eventually torn town for war material. The cottage survived to be listed on the National Register of Historic Places and is now the Deer Park Inn. It does look a bit worn and unappealing from the outside, but don't let that fool you. Open the door and step into an exquisite foyer and elegantly furnished public and guest rooms. Pascal, the French chef, retired as Executive Chef with Westin Hotels in Washington, D.C. to live here and spend more time with his family. (He's known for his confit of duck.) Guest rooms have no phone or TV. They offer a real change from city life, so bring a good book, kick back, and relax.

SETTINGS & FACILITIES

Location Western edge of Deer Park Village, rural Allegheny Mountains, across from Deer Park Water Bottling Company. **Near** 1 mi. southeast of Deep Creek Lake, 6 mi. southeast of Wisp Ski Resort, 20 minutes to the Savage & Youghiogheny Rivers. **Building** 1889 Victorian cottage. **Grounds** 9.5 acres on the grounds of the former Deer Park Hotel, surrounded by fields & forest. **Public Space** Parlor, DR, wraparound porch. **Food & Drink** Full breakfast w/ juice, fruit; specialties—apple & blueberry pancakes, vegetable fritatta, eggs w/ bacon & potatoes; afternoon refreshments; full service restaurant, candlelight dining. **Recreation** Antiquing, outdoor sports, horseback riding, ski & lake sports, golf, whitewater rafting, rock climbing; masseuse & hot tub on site, 2 bikes avail.; Autumn Glory festival (Oct.). **Amenities & Services** Fax & e-mail; meetings (25), weddings (60).

ACCOMMODATIONS

Units 3 guest rooms. **All Rooms** Hairdryer, iron. **Some Rooms** Non-working fireplace (2). **Bed & Bath** Queen (1), full (2); private baths w/ tubs, 1 detached. **Favorites** Rose—4 tall windows w/ lace curtains emit radiant light, maple tiger wood bed & dresser, ceramic fireplace, soft floral & beige wallpaper; Blue—old furniture from Sears

& Roebuck mail order, original chandelier, huge bath w/ wood paneling, antique pull toilet. **Comfort & Decor** Large rooms with 13-foot ceilings are decorated with Victorian antiques, many original to the cottage. Chandeliers and a Victorian brothel chair are unusual details. Six fireplaces, wood wainscoting, and a grand staircase add character.

RATES, RESERVATIONS, & RESTRICTIONS

Deposit Credit card to hold, refund w/ 7-days notice. **Discounts** No. **Credit Cards** AE, V, MC, D. **Check-In/Out** 4–10 p.m./11 a.m. **Smoking** No. **Pets** No (dog & cat on site). **Kids** Yes. **Minimum Stay** 2 nights weekends (during daylight savings). **Open** All year. **Hosts** Sandy & Pascal Fontaine, 65 Hotel Rd., Deer Park, 21550. **Phone** (301) 334-2308. **Fax** (301) 334-2308. **E-mail** deer_park_inn@hotmail.com. **Web** deerparkinn.com.

MCCLEERY'S FLAT, Frederick

OVERALL ★★★★ | QUALITY ★★★★ | VALUE ★★★★ | PRICE $100–$135

The people skills of these friendly hosts make a difference. A stewardess who retired from United Airlines after 26 years, Jutta says "running a bed-and-breakfast is very much the same—minus the turbulence. I'm still in the galley cooking—but this is a dream come true for me." George retired from the Army and works as a consultant. You'll be right in the heart of a dynamic small town—where you can walk to art and antique galleries, museums, and 32 restaurants. There's plenty to see, including lovely European-style church spires and several museums—one honoring Barbara Fritchie, another Francis Scott Key. And, don't forget to check out the angel paintings on the buildings and the three-dimensional painting on the bridge.

SETTINGS & FACILITIES

Location Downtown. **Near** Civil War Medical Museum, Weinberg Theater, Cultural Arts Center. **Building** 1876 French Empire brick townhouse, detached. **Grounds** City lot, garden w/ fountain & courtyard. **Public Space** Double parlor, DR. **Food & Drink** Full breakfast; specialties—frittatas, pancakes, waffles, eggs w/ fresh vegetables; dessert on Sunday; complimentary Irish whiskey; parlor tea $20 by reservation. **Recreation** Civil War sites, antiquing. **Amenities & Services** Free local phone calls, reimbursement for public lot parking; TV, VCR, & large movie selection avail.

ACCOMMODATIONS

Units 5 guest rooms. **All Rooms** AC, phone & computer jacks, radio alarm clock. **Some Rooms** Radiator & baseboard heat (can be noisy). **Bed & Bath** Bed sizes vary, high thread-count sheets; private baths, 4 tubs. **Favorites** Ben Franklin—1 brick wall, four-poster, wall-size bookshelf, highboy, spire view. **Comfort & Decor** A townhouse with high ceilings, wood trim, working gas fireplace, pocket shutters, a collection of birdcages, wall stenciling, and appealing antiques. Some guest rooms are strongly themed.

RATES, RESERVATIONS, & RESTRICTIONS

Deposit Credit card to hold, refund w/ 5-days notice less 20%. **Discounts** Corp. 10%. **Credit Cards** AE, V, MC, D. **Check-In/Out** 3–5 p.m./11 a.m. **Smoking** No. **Pets** No, cat on premises. **Kids** Age 15 and older. **Minimum Stay** None. **Open** All year. **Hosts** Jutta & George Terrell, 1212 E. Patrick St., Frederick, 21701. **Phone** (800) 774-7926 or (301) 620-2433. **Web** www.fwp.net/mccleerysflat.

TYLER SPITE HOUSE, Frederick

OVERALL ★★★★ | QUALITY ★★★★ | VALUE ★★ | PRICE $200–$300

If you're interested in Frederick's who's who past and present, this is the place to learn. Your host, Bill Myer, has been around seemingly forever and knows every facet of local history. The Nelson House down the block (#112) is his second B&B, with five rooms in a less formal atmosphere. We prefer the grandiose style of Tyler Spite, which captures the era of Victorian excess—lots of fringe, velvet, and dramatic detail. Breakfast is a highlight, with an oh-so-formal table set with tall candlesticks, colorful plateware, and lots of silver. A butler in tails is there to serve you.

SETTINGS & FACILITIES

Location Courthouse Square in central historic district. **Near** Francis Scott Key law office. **Building** 1814 Federal building, cream stucco w/ green shutters. **Grounds** Restored historic garden, swimming pool. **Public Space** Parlor, library, TV room, library, music room, DR, sunporch. **Food & Drink** Full breakfast; specialties—Belgian waffles, egg soufflé, hot apples, fruit muffins; public teas Fri. and Sat. by reservation; 24-hours hospitality bar w/ wine, cider, sodas, fruit, nuts. **Recreation** Golf, tennis, biking, antiquing, museums, theater, C&O Canal, Potomac River. **Amenities & Services** Arrange a horse-drawn carriage ride; garden weddings (150).

ACCOMMODATIONS

Units 5 guest rooms. **All Rooms** Spring water, hair dryer. **Some Rooms** Fireplace. **Bed & Bath** Bed sizes vary; 4 shared baths. **Favorites** John Hanson—four-poster, fireplace, chest w/ secret drawers; Mosby Suite—sitting room, private bath w/ Swedish shower. **Comfort & Decor** Over-the-top elegance in all public rooms, but a bit dated. Enjoy marble fireplaces, Oriental carpets, comfortable antique furnishings, and paintings.

RATES, RESERVATIONS, & RESTRICTIONS

Deposit 1 night, refund w/ 7-days notice less 30%. **Discounts** Corp. $90–$125 Mon.–Thurs. **Credit Cards** V, MC. **Check-In/Out** 3–7 p.m./11 a.m. **Smoking** No. **Pets** No. **Kids** No. **No-Nos** Check-in after 9 p.m. **Minimum Stay** Major holidays 2 days. **Open** All year (closed New Year's Day to last weekend in Jan.). **Hosts** Andrea & Bill Myer, 112 W. Church St., Frederick, 21701. **Phone** (301) 831-4455. **Fax** (301) 662-4185.

BEAVER CREEK HOUSE, Hagerstown

OVERALL ★★★★ | QUALITY ★★★½ | VALUE ★★★★ | PRICE $75–$95

Beaver Creek dates from the 1700s when three German brothers named Newcomer bought land near the creek. It has remained a quiet, rural area conducive to rest and relaxation. The hosts were both born and raised in the Hagerstown area. Don headed the Maryland Bed & Breakfast Association for years. Like many innkeepers, he and Shirley got the idea for their new career while staying in bed-and-breakfasts in Britain. They said to themselves, I can do this. They bought this house in 1988 and continue to "enjoy it immensely, especially meeting so many interesting people."

SETTINGS & FACILITIES

Location West of historic village w/ South Mountain view. **Near** 4 mi. east of Hagerstown, 0.5 mi. to antique & auction mecca. **Building** 1905 Victorian w/ wraparound porch. **Grounds** 2 acres w/ red barn, country garden, pond, brick patio w/ fountain. **Public Space** Parlor, DR, screened porch, courtyard w/ fountain. **Food & Drink** Full breakfast; specialties—buttermilk pecan pancakes, baked apple, bananas Edgar (the host's middle name); snacks avail. **Recreation** Golf, hiking the Appalachian Trail, biking, skiing, horseback riding, ice skating, canoeing, outlet shopping; National Historical Parks of Antietam, Harpers Ferry; C&O Canal; Blues Fest (June), German Festival (Aug.), Boonsboro Days (Sept.). **Amenities & Services** Fax; Antietam audio tape for drive-through visit, lots of Civil War books.

ACCOMMODATIONS

Units 5 guest rooms. **All Rooms** AC, hair dryer, robes, ceiling fan. **Some Rooms** private entrance (1). **Bed & Bath** Double (4), twin (1); private baths, 1 detached, 2 tubs. **Comfort & Decor** Family heirloom antiques and memorabilia include Hummel figurines, antique glassware and toys, and 11 striking clocks. Wedgewood china, Waterford crystal, and sterling silver are used routinely for breakfast.

RATES, RESERVATIONS, & RESTRICTIONS

Deposit One night, refund w/ 3-days notice. **Discounts** Mon.–Thur. **Credit Cards** AE, V, MC (cash or check preferred). **Check-In/Out** 1 p.m./11 a.m. **Smoking** No. **Pets** No. **Kids** Age 10 & older. **Minimum Stay** 2 nights most weekends & holidays. **Open** All year. **Hosts** Shirley & Don Day, 20432 Beaver Creek Rd., Hagerstown, 21740. **Phone** (888) 942-9966 or (301) 797-4764. **Fax** (301) 797-4978.

WINGROVE MANOR, Hagerstown

OVERALL ★★★½ | QUALITY ★★★★½ | VALUE ★★★★★ | PRICE $95–$140

The breakfast was skimpy but the conversation sparkled. Much of it revolved around Winnie's interesting career as a professional basketball player and a mover and shaker in the hospitality industry. Her resumé includes a stint as regional director for 47 hotels and as food and beverage manager of Governor's House in Bethesda. She has managed three country clubs, opened several hotels, and owned six other bed-and-breakfasts. "Hotels were fun, but this is hard work, because I'm also the maid," she says, adding, "but it's keeping me young."

SETTINGS & FACILITIES

Location On a hill 0.5 mi. north of town center. **Near** 11 mi. north of Antietam National Battlefield, 71 mi. northwest of Baltimore; 18 mi. east of Whitetail Ski Resort, Gettysburg. **Building** 1905 Victorian w/ Greek Revival details, porch has 20 fluted white columns. **Grounds** City lot w/ shrubs, trees, terraces. **Public Space** LR, DR, foyer, porch. **Food & Drink** Cont'l plus breakfast w/ homemade muffins & breads, fruit & hot beverage. **Recreation** Antiquing, hiking, jogging, biking, swimming, skiing, golf, tennis, fishing, horseback riding, museums, art galleries, symphony. **Amenities & Services** Fax, day spa nearby; meetings (12).

ACCOMMODATIONS

Units 4 guest rooms. **All Rooms** AC, TV & VCR, phone jack. **Some Rooms** Ceiling fan (1), electric fireplace (1), private entrance (1). **Bed & Bath** King (1), queen (3), canopy (3), four-poster (1); private baths, 2 whirlpool, 2 tubs. **Favorites** Rose room—four-poster bed, white w/ pink accents, double shuttered bay windows, spacious. **Comfort & Decor** At Christmas season the house is a vision of beribboned trees, garlands, tiny white lights, candles, and antique Santas. White striped satin wallpaper, an impressive spiral staircase, white sofas and chairs, a fireplace, Oriental screen, polished mahogany dining room table, and lots of cut glass create an elegant look.

RATES, RESERVATIONS, & RESTRICTIONS

Deposit Credit card, refund w/ 4-days notice. **Discounts** Corp. rate $54. **Credit Cards** AE, V, MC, D. **Check-In/Out** 1 p.m./11 a.m. **Smoking** No. **Pets** No. **Kids** Yes (no special equipment provided). **Minimum Stay** None. **Open** All year. **Host** Winnie Price, 635 Oak Hill Ave., Hagerstown, 21740. **Phone** (301) 733-6328 or (301) 797-7769. **Fax** (301) 797-8659. **E-mail** dmgrove@msn.com. **Web** wingrovemanor.com.

ANTIETAM OVERLOOK FARM, Keedysville

OVERALL ★★★★ | QUALITY ★★★★★ | VALUE ★★★★★ | PRICE $115–$165

The house, the location, the views. They're all so spectacular, one wonders why the hosts are willing to share their hilltop hideaway. (Perhaps it gets lonely at the top.) In any case, this is one of the most successful B&Bs in the area. Barbara's prior career was running a carryout deli business in Towson. John continues to work as a building contractor and is now chief building officer for Howard County. They moved here in 1990 and built the bed-and-breakfast portion of the building from scratch, with John supervising the entire project. You'll enjoy the sense of exclusivity.

SETTINGS & FACILITIES

Location Mountaintop overlooking Antietam National Battlefield & Burnside Bridge. **Near** 2 mi. from Rte. 34. **Building** 1990 farmhouse, gated w/ electronic dial-in, standing seam metal roof w/ snowbirds, wood cupola. **Grounds** 95 acres w/ stunning vistas of 4 states, walking trails. **Public Space** Country room, foyer, guest pantry, porch. **Food & Drink** Early coffee, full country breakfast w/ fruit, juice, baked goods; specialties—creamed pears, southwest French toast; wine & beer avail. **Recreation** Civil War sites at Gettysburg, Bull Run, & Harpers Ferry, golf, antiquing; Heritage Festival (mid-Sept.), Luminaries (1st Sat. in Dec.).

ACCOMMODATIONS

Units 5 guest rooms. **All Rooms** AC, gas fireplace, ceiling fan, curling iron, bath brush, hair dryer, live plants, Civil War art. **Some Rooms** Antiques vary. **Bed & Bath** Queens; private baths, 5 Kohler steeping tubs. **Favorites** #3—rustic beams, old chest, gas fireplace, screened porch, whirlpool; Overlook room—for peace, quiet, & privacy. **Comfort & Decor** The living room looks like a centerfold for *Architectural Digest*. The home's casual elegance is accessorized with duck decoys, stained glass, lots of books, and a cozy wood-burning limestone fireplace. Bathrooms are spacious and full of extra amenities.

RATES, RESERVATIONS, & RESTRICTIONS

Deposit 1 night, refund w/ 1-day notice. **Discounts** No. **Credit Cards** AE, V, MC. **Check-In/Out** 3–4 p.m./11 a.m. **Smoking** No. **Pets** No (Cocker Spaniel, Max, in residence). **Kids** Over age 12. **Minimum Stay** 2 nights on weekends. **Open** All year. **Hosts** Barbara & John Dreisch, Box 30, Keedysville, 21756. **Phone** (800) 878-4241 or (301) 432-4200. **Fax** (301) 432-5230. **E-mail** antietamoverlookfarm@erols.com. **Web** www.innbook.com/inns/antietam/index.html.

STONE MANOR, Middletown

OVERALL ★★★★★ | QUALITY ★★★★ | VALUE ★★ | PRICE $150–$275

The host's family has lived in this valley for five generations, making their home a social and cultural gathering place for the community. The restaurant of chef Charles Zeran, an attorney who "changed to a profession where people are happy," is exceptionally good. It bothers us, at these prices, that indoor public areas are limited and some guest rooms are so small that the bathtub is in the dining and/or living room area. However, the location is ideal. Sunsets are magnificent. Ditto the night sky. And, it's quiet enough to hear songbirds. For a true rest, a first-rate kitchen, and a wine list that earned *Wine Spectator* awards of excellence, Stone Manor is worth a detour.

SETTINGS & FACILITIES

Location Dairy farmland in Middletown Valley at the foot of the Catoctin Mountains. **Near** 11 mi. west of Frederick, 35 mi. southwest of Gettysburg, PA. **Building** 1760s fieldstone farmhouse w/ restorations and additions. **Grounds** 114-acre working farm w/ formal garden, cutting garden, bank barn, corn cribs, smokehouse. **Public Space** LR w/ dining area, upstairs library. **Food & Drink** Cont'l plus breakfast w/ fruit from local orchards & strata, pancakes, or eggs, no meats; welcome plate of fruit & cheese; full service restaurant in dry county w/ no liquor license. **Recreation** White Tail Ski Resort; hike, bike, & raft on the C&O Canal; visit local artist studios, antique shops, Civil War sites; Keep The Cup tea party (Feb.) artist studios tour (April). **Amenities & Services** Movies avail.; meetings (60), weddings (100).

ACCOMMODATIONS

Units 6 guest rooms. **All Rooms** AC, TV & VCR. **Some Rooms** Covered porch (2), sitting room (5), fireplace (3), private entrance (3). **Bed & Bath** Queens; private baths, 5 whirlpools. **Favorites** Gardenia—carved rice bed, 2 fireplaces, antique English armoire (1860s), double whirlpool, garden view; Laurel—sunken living room w/ fireplace, queen mahogany canopy bed, double whirlpool w/ underwater lighting, pond view. **Comfort & Decor** The overall look is upscale traditional, with ten fireplaces to add a cozy touch.

RATES, RESERVATIONS, & RESTRICTIONS

Deposit 1 night, refund w/ 2-days notice less $25. **Discounts** Dinner packages. **Credit Cards** AE, V, MC, D. **Check-In/Out** 2 p.m./11 a.m. **Smoking** No. **Pets** No. **Kids** Not recommended (no special rooms or dining facilities for young children). **No-Nos** Cell phones discouraged in dining room. **Minimum Stay** None. **Open** All year except Christmas & New Year's Day. **Host** Judith Harne, 5820 Carroll Boyer Rd., Middletown, 21769. **Phone** (301) 473-5454. **Fax** (301) 371-5622. **E-mail** themanor@stonemanor.com. **Web** stonemanor.com.

INN AT ANTIETAM, Sharpsburg

OVERALL ★★★★★ | QUALITY ★★★★½ | VALUE ★★★★ | PRICE $110–$175

The hosts' personalities are key here. For years, they were partners in running the Rochester Music Theater, presenting nine musicals in nine weeks each summer. Then, for five months each winter, they sang on cruise ships for companies like Norwegian American and Carnival. Both enjoy chatting with guests late into the night as they did on world cruises, and they both like to cook. They've collected lots of show business friends and theater memorabilia over the years. Much of it is displayed in the narrow, light-filled upstairs hallway. The house is filled with positive energy in spite of being surrounded by the hallowed ground of Antietam National Battlefield.

SETTINGS & FACILITIES

Location Adjacent to Antietam National Cemetery, 2 blocks to town center. **Near** 2.5 mi. north of C&O Canal towpath & Shepherdstown, WV, 12 mi. southeast of Hagerstown, 17 mi. northwest of Harper's Ferry National Park. **Building** 1908 Victorian w/ wraparound porch. **Grounds** 8 acres w/ gardens, holly pine, magnolia, dogwood, & English walnut trees, plus 14 boxwoods lining main walkway. **Public Space** Solarium, parlor, library, brick patio. **Food & Drink** Full breakfast w/ juice, fruit, hot beverages; specialties—egg casserole, baked Swiss eggs, quiche w/ Swiss cheese & spinach, Belgian waffles; tea sodas & cookies avail. **Recreation** Bike & hike the C&O Canal towpath; golf & swim at Greenbrier State Park; hike the Appalachian Trail; fish, canoe, raft, & kayak on the Potomac & Shenandoah Rivers; performances by American Contemporary Theatre, Millbrook Orchestra, Maryland Symphony; Heritage Festival (mid-Sept.), Luminaries at Antietam (1st Sat. in Dec.). **Amenities & Services** 400 videos, privileges at Crest Creek Golf Club, massage avail., fax & e-mail, laundry.

ACCOMMODATIONS

Units 5 suites. **All Rooms** AC, fresh flowers, robes. **Some Rooms** TV & VCR (2), fireplace (1). **Bed & Bath** Queen (4), double (1); four-poster (2), hand-embroidered pillow cases; private baths w/ tubs. **Favorites** Garden suite—cozy, pencil-post bed, floral wall border, quilt chair, cemetery view. **Comfort & Decor** The living room is Victorian with a noteworthy Civil War chess set. General Burnside's smokehouse is dark and rustic, with a low-ceilinged loft and one brick wall. The penthouse has skylights and a contemporary look. The upstairs hall is a mini-shrine to the owners' stage careers.

RATES, RESERVATIONS, & RESTRICTIONS

Deposit Credit card to hold, refund w/ 3-days notice. **Discounts** None. **Credit Cards** AE, V, MC. **Check-In/Out** 3 p.m./11 a.m. **Smoking** No. **Pets** No (dog on premises). **Kids** Age 6 & over. **Minimum Stay** 2 nights on holidays & special events. **Open** All year (except January). **Hosts** Charles Van Metre & Bob Leblanc, 220 E. Main St., Box 119, Sharpsburg, 21782. **Phone** (877) 835-6011 or (301) 432-6601. **Fax** (301) 432-5981. **E-mail** innatantietam@juno.com. **Web** innatantietam.com.

JACOB RORHBACH HOUSE, Sharpsburg

OVERALL ★★★★ | QUALITY ★★★½ | VALUE ★★★★ | PRICE $85–$105

Antietam National Battlefield, site of the bloodiest day in American history, casts a wide shadow over this town. Residents call it hallowed ground, and you soon understand why. It's well worth taking a private tour with knowledgeable local historians. You'll learn that the three arch stone bridge, now named Burnside's Bridge, was called Rohrbach Bridge prior to the battle. The Rohrbachs, who had farmed in this area since the eighteenth century, had their nearby farmhouse occupied by Burnside during the 1862 battle. This bed-and-breakfast was the Rohrbach's more formal town house, which remained in the family for five generations. One of the area's finest, these innkeepers have done a diligent job in restoring its former beauty.

SETTINGS & FACILITIES

Location Residential street in historic district w/ battlefield on 3 sides. **Near** 1 mi. to Antietam Battlefield Visitors Center, 2 mi. to C&O Canal towpath, near Harper's Ferry. **Building** 1830s Federal house w/ stone base & brick walls, fanlights, 6 chimneys, original iron fencing & trim. **Grounds** 1 acre w/ flower beds, herb garden. **Public Space** Foyer, LR, DR, kitchen, 4 porches, summer kitchen (converted to sitting area), hot tub. **Food & Drink** Full breakfast w/ fruit, juices, breads; specialties—apple crisp, Belgian waffles w/ bacon, eggs Benedict, mushroom omelets; hot beverages, sodas, cookies avail. in afternoon. **Recreation** Steeping yourself in Civil War lore; biking, antiquing, golf; Heritage Festival (mid-Sept.), Luminaries (1st Sat. in Dec.). **Amenities & Services** Video series on Antietam National Battlefield, laundry, fax & e-mail; lectures.

ACCOMMODATIONS

Units 4 guest rooms. **All Rooms** AC, fresh flowers, robes, hair dryer, access to mobile phone. **Some Rooms** Porch (2), private entrance (2). **Bed & Bath** Queen (2), full (2), twin (1), four-poster (4); 2 private baths, 2 shared baths, 1 tub. **Favorites** Stonewall Jackson Room—old glass panes, non-working fireplace w/ faux marbling, tiny porch. **Comfort & Decor** This is a good example of a Federal period home, with fan light door and windows and irreplaceable iron works at the entrance. Interior details include painted stair backs and faux marbling. The simple yet comfortable decor emphasizes history.

RATES, RESERVATIONS, & RESTRICTIONS

Deposit Credit card to hold, refund w/ 2-days notice for weekdays, 7-days for weekends. **Discounts** Senior, military (10%). **Credit Cards** AE, V, MC. **Check-In/Out** 3–8 p.m./11 a.m. **Smoking** No. **Pets** No (dog on premises). **Kids** Over age 10. **Minimum Stay** 2 nights for holidays & special events. **Open** All year (except Dec. 20–Jan. 10). **Hosts** JoAnne & Paul Breitenbach, 138 W. Main St., Sharpsburg, 21782. **Phone** (877) 839-4242 or (301) 432-5079. **Fax** (301) 473-1797. **E-mail** jbreiten@gschclone.com. **Web** jacob-rohrbach-inn.com.

PIPER HOUSE, Sharpsburg

OVERALL ★★★★★ | QUALITY ★★★★ | VALUE ★★★★★ | PRICE $85–$95

These innkeepers—a former cop and nurse—are resident curators of this mini-museum on Civil War lore. The house, which is actually on Antietam National Battlefield, is owned by the National Park Service and leased to their bed-and-breakfast. It opened in 1994. The hosts welcome world travelers and enjoy engaging them in that lost art—good conversation. They share their extensive collection of diaries, letters, photos, books, and memorabilia about Antietam. The house, spotless, well-ordered, and pristine, feels peaceful and isolated, like a bastion of sanity in a world that is now the battlefield. Some visitors are emotionally affected by the surroundings. The hosts try to lighten things a little, but are very respectful.

SETTINGS & FACILITIES

Location Geological center of the Confederate Line of Antietam National Battlefield, just south of Bloody Lane. **Near** 0.5 mi. north of Sharpsburg, 4 mi. east of Shepherdstown, WV, 12 mi. south of Hagerstown. **Building** 1840 log & stone farmhouse, coffee siding w/ blue & red trim; 6 out buildings include 1740 slave quarters, 1830 barn & root cellar, plus smokehouse, corn crib, & blacksmith's shop. **Grounds** 187 acres w/ cattle (including one huge bull), cornfields, hay, winter wheat, & other crops indigenous to the Civil War era. **Public Space** 2 parlors, kitchen, front porch, upstairs parlor w/ library, screened porch. **Food & Drink** Cont'l plus farm breakfast w/ juice, fruit, fresh baked goods; may include pancakes, eggs or oatmeal; tea & cookies anytime. **Recreation** Ranger-led battlefield tour, free use of auto tour tape, lectures by historians, medical & artillery demonstrations; C&O canal towpath; Heritage Festival (mid-Sept.), Luminaries at Antietam (1st Sat. in Dec.). **Amenities & Services** Extensive Civil War book and video library.

ACCOMMODATIONS

Units 3 guest rooms. **All Rooms** AC, private entrance. **Some Rooms** One once slept General Longstreet. **Bed & Bath** Full (2), twin (2), four-poster (1), painted (1); private baths w/ tubs. **Favorites** D. H. Hill room—pretty painted bed, period rope trim, private entrance to porch. **Comfort & Decor** Plain but quality furnishings place a heavy emphasis on history, including dramatic framed prints of Antietam events. The kitchen is the hub, where you can see videos and talk Civil War.

RATES, RESERVATIONS, & RESTRICTIONS

Deposit Credit card to hold, refund w/ 7-days notice. **Discounts** No. **Credit Cards** V, MC. **Check-In/Out** 4–6 p.m./11 a.m. **Smoking** No. **Pets** No. **Kids** Behaved & over age 10. **Minimum Stay** 2 days on holidays. **Open** All year. **Hosts** Regina & Louis Clark, Box 100, Sharpsburg, 21782. **Phone** (301) 797-1862. **Web** www.nps.gov/anti.

TURNING POINT INN, Urbana

OVERALL ★★★★ | QUALITY ★★★★½ | VALUE ★★★★ | PRICE **$80–$150**

For decades this house enjoyed a solitary view of the pastoral countryside and the Blue Ridge and Sugarloaf Mountains. But in recent years, the land across the road was transformed into a sea of houses, which somewhat detracts from the country ambience. Emphasis at the inn is on the restaurant, open to the public for dinner and Sunday brunch. Chef William Erlenback specializes in contemporary American cuisine that blends Mediterranean, Southern, and Asian flavors. The wine list offers more than 300 selections. The Club Room offers lighter fare in a more casual setting.

SETTINGS & FACILITIES

Location Junction of Rte. 80 & Rte. 355 overlooking a rolling landscape. **Near** 5 mi. south of Frederick, 40 mi. north of Washington, D.C. **Building** 1910 Georgian-style white w/ black shutters. **Grounds** 6 acres w/ pine & maple trees, gardens, fountain. **Public Space** LR, DR, clubroom. **Food & Drink** Full breakfast; specialties—banana stuffed French toast w/ bourbon pecan syrup, house-cured pancetta, brie & spinach omelet, oatmeal w/ dried cranberries & apples; full service dining w/ touring wine cellar (pick your bottle). **Recreation** 3 golf courses within 15 min., antiquing, Monocacy Battlefield, Lily Ponds Bird Sanctuary, Civil War Medical Museum. **Amenities & Services** Meetings (10).

ACCOMMODATIONS

Units 5 guest rooms, 2 cottages. **All Rooms** Cable TV, phone (free local calls), dataport. **Some Rooms** Fireplace, small fridge/wet bar (cottage). **Bed & Bath** King (3), queen (2), double (2); private baths. **Favorites** Carriage house—2 story, large bedroom; Dairy house—country antiques, king bed, reclining chairs. **Comfort & Decor** The inn has the look of luxury with a mix of original and reproduction antiques.

RATES, RESERVATIONS, & RESTRICTIONS

Deposit Credit card to hold, refund w/ 2-days notice. **Discounts** Corp. $70 Mon.–Fri. **Credit Cards** AE, V, MC, D. **Check-In/Out** 3 p.m./11 a.m. **Smoking** No. **Pets** No. **Kids** Yes, any age. **Minimum Stay** No. **Open** All year except Christmas and New Year's Day. **Host** Charlie Seymour, 3406 Urbana Pike, Frederick, 21701. **Phone** (301) 831-8232. **Fax** (301) 831-8092. **Web** theturningpoint.com.

Zone 14

Baltimore & Central Maryland

America's 15th largest city is a tour de force in urban redevelopment. Its visually-stunning **Inner Harbor** is layered with unique architecture and its first-rate attractions are accessible by water taxi.

Maryland Science Center and the **National Aquarium** are well suited for younger travelers. Historic ships at the **Baltimore Maritime Museum,** include the Coast Guard cutter *Taney,* the World War II submarine *Torsk,* and the lightship *Chesapeake.* You can shop in block-long glass pavilions, a four-story atrium mall, and a two-story bookstore with chairs placed to give you a harbor view. **Oriole Park at Camden Yards** baseball stadium is one of the nation's most attractive downtown sports venues.

Beyond Baltimore's bustling Inner Harbor, adventurous visitors can find nifty older neighborhoods, offbeat museums, and character-filled bed-and-breakfasts. You can get a new perspective on Baltimore's role in the Civil War, dental history, and the phenomenon of sideshows. Particularly interesting is the hands-on **Museum of Industry,** which highlights Baltimore's pivotal role in America's food canning, bottling, and labeling industries in the nineteenth century.

Harbor City Tours buses take you to Italian, Greek, Polish, and Russian communities, as well as Canton, Fell's Point, Mt. Vernon, and Federal Hill. It's worth extra time to see the first-rate **Walters Art Gallery**, which sits opposite **Peabody Institute,** a renowned music academy and library. And, the **Baltimore Museum of Art** has a dynamite fine art collection.

Hampden, a working class neighborhood in northwest Baltimore, is a mini-version of Greenwich Village, with its funky art galleries, retro clothing stores, and hole-in-the-wall eateries. And don't miss **Café Hon,** the down-home eatery that launched an annual big hair contest each June.

At **Cross Street Market** you can rub shoulders with working-class Baltimoreans who jockey for a spot at the "raw bar," where fleet-fingered oyster shuckers fill lunch platters with succulent shellfish.

Other areas to explore in Central Maryland? Consider **Ellicott City,** a hilly community with a railroad museum dedicated to the oldest railroad in America. And, consider **Havre de Grace,** a modest waterfront town with a maritime tradition. It offers three museums, carved waterfowl collections, and one of East Coast's oldest operating lighthouses at Concord Point.

A pleasant surprise, one of the Mid-Atlantic's most elegant bed-and-breakfasts is in tiny, rural **Taneytown.**

FOR MORE INFORMATION

Baltimore Area Convention and Visitors Association
100 Light St., 12th Floor
Baltimore, MD 21202
(800) 343-3468

Baltimore County CVB
Hunt Valley Mall, 2nd Level
118 Shawan Rd.
Hunt Valley, MD 21030
(877) STAYNDO

Discover Harford County Tourism Council
121 N. Union Ave., Suite B
Havre de Grace, MD 21078
(800) 597-2649

Howard County Tourism Council
Box 9
Ellicott City, MD 21043
(800) 288-8747

ABERCROMBIE BADGER, Baltimore

OVERALL ★★★★ | QUALITY ★★★★ | VALUE ★★★★ | PRICE $85–$150

This elegant townhouse is ideally located for music and art patrons. The innkeeper, a former antique dealer, specializes in collecting small boxes and ecclesiastical antiques. He furnished this townhouse with vivid pieces that create an eye-popping impression the minute you enter. The mix includes an antique sofa and sideboard, as well as patterned fabrics with matching window swags, drapes, and pillows. A gold rug with white fringe, wall sconces, porcelain, and a fresh flower bouquet add distinction. The breakfast room is also unique—with faux watermelons and lively pink and green wall covering.

SETTINGS & FACILITIES

Location Mount Vernon/Belvedere section of downtown Baltimore, busy city intersection. **Near** Across from Meyerhoff Symphony Hall, 2 blocks from Lyric Opera House, 1 mi. to Baltimore Harbor. **Building** 1880s American baronial townhouse. **Grounds** City lot w/ adjacent parking. **Public Space** Parlor, breakfast room. **Food & Drink** Large cont'l breakfast w/ help-yourself gourmet homemade breads, meat, cheese, juice, fruit, beverages; a small Italian restaurant on the lower floor is open for dinner. **Recreation** Walk 6 blocks to Walter Art Gallery, sightseeing. **Amenities & Services** *New York Times,* voice mail, personal phone number.

ACCOMMODATIONS

Units 12 guest rooms. **All Rooms** AC w/ individual controls, private phone w/ voice mail, TV, clock radio. **Some Rooms** Antiques vary. **Bed & Bath** Queen (9), twin (3), canopy

(2), four-poster (1); private baths, 7 tubs. **Favorites** Rose room #201—four-poster bed, quality accessories. **Comfort & Decor** Lavish hall and living room decor is chic Middle Eastern–style with a chandelier, antique sofa, drapes with matching side chairs, a Moroccan chest, and an antique mirror. Guest rooms are attractive but some are small. Light sleepers should bring ear plugs to ignore a noisy heating system and road noise.

RATES, RESERVATIONS, & RESTRICTIONS

Deposit 1 night, $15 charge for any cancellation. **Discounts** Musicians. **Credit Cards** V, MC, D, DC. **Check-In/Out** 4–6 p.m./11 a.m. **Smoking** No. **Pets** No. **Kids** Well-mannered, over age 10. **No-Nos** Late arrivals w/out notification. **Minimum Stay** 2 nights on weekends. **Open** All year. **Host** Paul Bragaw, 58 W. Biddle St., Baltimore, 21201. **Phone** (888) 922-3437. **Fax** (410) 244-8415. **E-mail** Abadger722@aol.com.

CELIE'S WATERFRONT, Baltimore

OVERALL ★★★½ | QUALITY ★★★★ | VALUE ★★★★ | PRICE **$120–$220**

Location is everything at this stylish urban hideaway. Recently built from scratch in a former parking lot, it fits right into the eclectic eighteenth and nineteenth century-era neighborhood surrounding Baltimore's first deep water port. You enter through a narrow brick alleyway past an iron gate and register in a cozy back room with a fireplace and garden view. Once settled in, you can explore a vibrant community lined with pubs, boutiques, antique shops, and eateries. It's a short walk to a water taxi to Baltimore's Inner Harbor. However, finding a car taxi to downtown can be difficult. If not too busy, the innkeeper will rescue guests by providing a ride. On weekday mornings, business people can reserve this car service.

SETTINGS & FACILITIES

Location Fells Point historic area. **Near** Inner Harbor, city museums, Johns Hopkins University. **Building** 3-story building built in 1991. **Grounds** Sidewalk entrance, courtyard w/ garden. **Public Space** LR, DR, roof deck. **Food & Drink** Cont'l breakfast w/ juice, 6 kinds of homemade bread, jams, granola, fruit, house-blend coffee. **Recreation** Boating from Brown's Wharf Marina, sightseeing. **Amenities & Services** Car service to downtown Baltimore on weekdays, free local calls, local newspapers, ice, fax.

ACCOMMODATIONS

Units 7 guest rooms. **All Rooms** Small TV & VCR, answering machine, fresh flowers, robe, night light, iron & board, hair dryer, dataport. **Some Rooms** Fireplace, balcony, book nook, whirlpool (4). **Bed & Bath** King (3), queen (4), rough-textured flannel sheets, down comforters; private baths, shower gel dispenser, bathsheet-size towels, clothesline, magnifying makeup mirror. **Favorites** Harborfront 1—3 windows & window seats facing harbor, wicker seating by wood-burning fireplace, soft pastels, whirlpool; Harborfront 2—same window treatment, canopy king bed, wicker chaise, fireplace, whirlpool. **Comfort & Decor** Eclectic furnishings reflect this historic working-class neighborhood, including small dressers, subdued lighting, quality art, and a noisy heater.

RATES, RESERVATIONS, & RESTRICTIONS

Deposit 50% or 1 night, refund with 10-days notice (21-days for holidays), 24-hours corp. **Discounts** Corporate. **Credit Cards** AE, V, MC, D. **Check-In/Out** 3–6 p.m./11 a.m. **Smoking** Garden, courtyard, roof deck, or private balcony only. **Pets** No. **Kids** Age 10 and older. **Minimum Stay** 2 or 3 nights for weekends for whirlpool rooms (1, 2, 5, & 6); all rooms holidays and event weekends. **Open** All year. **Host** Celie Ives, 1714 Thames St., Baltimore, 21231. **Phone** (800) 432-0184 or (410) 522-2323. **Fax** (410) 522-2324. **E-mail** celies@aol.com. **Web** celieswaterfront.com.

MR. MOLE, Baltimore

OVERALL ★★★★½ | QUALITY ★★★★★ | VALUE ★★★★★ | PRICE **$115–$175**

Expectations should be high, since this B&B has won four stars from *Mobil Travel Guide* continuously since 1995. The parlors showcase a mania for collecting fine antiques from around the world—all pleasingly displayed. What surprises is the creativity and originality in the guest rooms. One pays homage to characters from *Wind in the Willow,* a story by Beatrix Potter, another is dense with artifacts and equipment related to the sporting world—skis, golf clubs, and safari gear. A third goes over the top with a garden theme; another recalls a Victorian gentlemen's boudoir. It's an experience—but not for everybody. By the way, former neighbors were F. Scott and Zelda Fitzgerald, who lived around the corner.

SETTINGS & FACILITIES

Location Bolton Hill, a quiet residential neighborhood. **Near** 6 blocks to Meyerhoff Symphony Hall & Lyric Opera House; Baltimore's Antique Row, Walters Art Gallery, Amtrak's Pennsylvania Station, Johns Hopkins University. **Building** 1860s row house, brick & stone. **Grounds** Narrow city lot. **Public Space** LR, drawing room, breakfast room. **Food & Drink** Dutch-style breakfast w/ tea, coffee, & juice; specialities—poached pear w/ raspberry sauce, honey & oat bread, 3 Amish meats & cheeses, non-fat sour cream mousse cake. **Recreation** Concerts, art galleries, museums, antiquing. **Amenities & Services** Private covered parking garage w/ automatic door opener.

ACCOMMODATIONS

Units 3 guest rooms, 2 suites. **All Rooms** AC, private phone number w/ voice mail, clock radio, dataport, robes, hair dryer. **Some Rooms** Coal-style fireplace (non-working). **Bed & Bath** Queen (5), double (2); private baths w/ tubs, Caswell Massey amenities. **Favorites** Garden Suite—wicker, bird cages, basket of fake vegetables, framed seed envelops, bordered wallpaper, very colorful. **Comfort & Decor** The ground floor rooms are dense with Chinese and English porcelain and Irish crystal, along with eighteenth- and nineteenth-century antiques. Portraits and beautiful fabrics compete for attention at all eye levels. Ceilings soar to 14-feet and thumb-painted hanging vines decorate the walls.

RATES, RESERVATIONS, & RESTRICTIONS

Deposit 1 night, refund w/ 10-days notice less $15. **Discounts** No. **Credit Cards** AE, V, MC, D. **Check-In/Out** 4–6 p.m./11 a.m. **Smoking** No. **Pets** No. **Kids** Age 10 & over if very well mannered. **No-Nos** Late check-in unless prearranged. **Minimum Stay** 2 nights on weekends, special events, & holidays. **Open** All year. **Host** Collin Clarke, 1601 Bolton St., Baltimore, 21217. **Phone** (410) 728-1179. **Fax** (410) 728-3379. **E-mail** MrMoleBB@aol.com. **Web** mrmolebb.com.

WAYSIDE INN, Ellicott City

OVERALL ★★★★ | QUALITY ★★★★ | VALUE ★★★★ | PRICE $95–$135

Following an old English custom, electric window lights here are extinguished at a set hour to signal there's no room at the inn. Apparently, this doesn't faze the resident ghost, a 45-year-old cleaning woman named Jennie, who lived here in the early 1800s—and continues to clean. Whoever's responsible, the inn is spotless. But that's not the only virtue. The current innkeepers are a perfect match for the bed-and-breakfast industry—eager to provide good food and comfortable surroundings. David, a former executive with a food service company, oversees the inn full time, while Susan, a certified public accountant, continues her career with the Justice Department. They like innkeeping enough to plan a major expansion.

SETTINGS & FACILITIES

Location Residential area, 2.5 mi. south of historic Ellicott City. **Near** 14 mi. west of Baltimore, 40 mi. north of Washington, D.C. **Building** 1780 Federal farmhouse w/ 20-inch granite walls. **Grounds** 2 acres w/ pond, gardens, mature trees (one dated to 1776). **Public Space** LR, DR, library, hallways, sunroom. **Food & Drink** Full breakfast w/ fruit & fresh baked goods; specialties—French toast w/ Grand Marnier & orange rum sauce, caramel apple French toast, fritatta w/ ham, apples, & sage; afternoon refreshments. **Recreation** Antiquing, B & O Railroad Museum, Howard County African American Culture Museum, & African Art Museum of Maryland; Maryland Sheep & Wool Festival (May), Wine Festival (May), Columbia Arts Festival (June). **Amenities & Services** Videos, e-mail, disabled access; meetings (20), weddings (30).

ACCOMMODATIONS

Units 4 guest rooms (4 more open soon). **All Rooms** AC, cable TV & VCR, phone, dataport, fresh flowers, hair dryer, robes, bottled water, sound machine, turn-down service. **Some Rooms** Fireplace (2). **Bed & Bath** Queen beds, four-poster (1), sleigh (2); 2 private baths, 2 shared, 4 tubs (no showers), 1 claw-foot tub. **Favorites** Betty's suite—sitting room has a sleeper sofa for kids, doors for privacy, the bath is separate but private; Banneker suite—bright w/ antique rice bed, wood-burning fireplace, custom quilt, pond view (a shared bath means a lower price). **Comfort & Decor** The house has lots of character. Period Williamsburg paints, heart pine floors, an Oriental carpet, and pre-1800 antiques enhance the living room. Dining room decor features a handmade farm table, dry sink, wash rack, Windsor chairs, and antique whisky jug. Books in the library focus on Maryland history. The house is close to the road, but thick walls reduce traffic noise.

RATES, RESERVATIONS, & RESTRICTIONS

Deposit 1 night, refund w/ 1-day notice (3-days on holidays). **Discounts** Gov't, long-term. **Credit Cards** AE, V, MC. **Check-In/Out** 4 p.m./11 a.m. **Smoking** No. **Pets** No (cat in residence). **Kids** Yes, any age. **Minimum Stay** None. **Open** All year. **Hosts** Susan & David Balderson, 4344 Columbia Rd., Ellicott City, 21042. **Phone** (410) 461-4636. **E-mail** bnbboy@aol.com. **Web** waysideinn.com.

CURRIER HOUSE, Havre de Grace

OVERALL ★★★★ | QUALITY ★★★★ | VALUE ★★★★ | PRICE $95–$115

Jane inherited this house from her father in 1991, but left it untouched for years before opening the bed-and-breakfast in 1996. Most of the furnishings were found stored in the basement, including enough photographs of past residents to cover an entire dining room wall. Collections are displayed everywhere—antique string instruments, World War I memorabilia, vintage toys, old documents, carving tools, guns, a saddle and riding paraphernalia, you name it. One relative aided the underground railroad, another was a master duck decoy carver, so there are lots of stories to tell. It's the strong flavor of Maryland history that sets this property apart. Staying here is a chance to get acquainted with one of the old-time families of Havre de Grace, a heavy-duty boating town.

SETTINGS & FACILITIES

Location Residential area w/ view of Chesapeake Bay. **Near** Concord Point Lighthouse, Decoy Museum, Maritime Museum, city yacht basin, Tidings Park. **Building** 1790 house w/ 1900 additions, cedar shake covered w/ vinyl siding. **Grounds** 1 acre w/ garden restored to 1800s-era style. **Public Space** 2 parlors, DR, wraparound porch, 2 patios. **Food & Drink** Full breakfast, specialties—Denver omelet, cinnamon toast casserole, sautéed oysters; evening tea. **Recreation** Cruise on the skipjack *Martha Lewis,* paddleboat dinner cruise, duck decoy museum, antiquing. **Amenities & Services** Videos, outdoor hot tub.

ACCOMMODATIONS

Units 4 guest rooms. **All Rooms** AC, TV & VCR, hair dryer. **Some Rooms** Balcony (2), robes (1). **Bed & Bath** Queen beds, four-poster (1); 3 private baths, 1 private detached, tubs (3). **Favorites** Crawford—iron bed, Currier & Ives lithographs, acrylic paintings by the host, wood-lined bath w/ tile floor, private porch, water view. **Comfort & Decor** The rooms are small and crowded with artifacts, but folks interested in Maryland history should find this fascinating.

RATES, RESERVATIONS, & RESTRICTIONS

Deposit Credit card to hold, refund w/ 10-days notice less 20%. **Discounts** None. **Credit Cards** AE, V, MC, D. **Check-In/Out** 3–6 p.m./11 a.m. **Smoking** No. **Pets** No (2 dogs in residence). **Kids** No. **Minimum Stay** 1 night. **Open** All year. **Hosts** Jane & Paul Belbot, 800 S. Market St., Havre de Grace, 21078. **Phone** (800) 827-2889 or (410) 939-7886. **Fax** (410) 939-6145. **E-mail** janec@currier-bb.com. **Web** currier-bb.com.

SPENCER-SILVER MANSION, Havre de Grace

OVERALL ★★★½ | QUALITY ★★★★ | VALUE ★★★★ | PRICE $70–$140

Carol moved from a career in international banking to innkeeping. The house, which she bought in 1987, was built by John Spencer to show off the fortune he made in the canning, fish packing, and pipe fitting businesses. It was the grandest of three side-by-side houses he owned on this block. Mr. Silver, another canning magnate, was a subsequent owner, followed by Edward Simon, a local doctor. Carol says she's been collecting antiques since she was 14. This is the second house she's restored and filled with her treasures. Being an innkeeper allows her to combine all the things she loves to do—including cooking a good breakfast.

SETTINGS & FACILITIES

Location Residential street, 2 blocks from the Chesapeake Bay. **Near** Concord Point Lighthouse, Havre de Grace Decoy Museum, Susquehanna Tidewater Lockhouse Canal Museum. **Building** 1896 Queen Anne w/ turret, made of Port Deposit granite, burgandy & cream trim, painted wreath detailing. **Grounds** 1 acre w/ flower gardens. **Public Space** Parlor, family room, DR, powder room, upstairs sitting room, guest fridge. **Food & Drink** Full breakfast w/ fresh fruit, juices, hot beverages, cereals, homemade muffins & breads, one hot entrée; specialties—quiche, apple French toast, eggs Benedict. **Recreation** Antique book dealers, tennis golf, boat & kayak rentals, summer concerts, art shows, theater; art & antique shows, seafood, music, maritime & Scottish festivals, Christmas candlelight tour. **Amenities & Services** Massage avail., fax & e-mail, videos; meetings (20); weddings (100).

ACCOMMODATIONS

Units 4 guest rooms, 1 carriage house. **All Rooms** AC. **Some Rooms** TV (3), fireplace (1), kitchen area (1). **Bed & Bath** King (1), queen (2), full (3); 3 private baths, 2 shared baths, 2 whirlpools, 2 tubs. **Favorites** Irish Room—stained glass doors, antique marble sink, double whirlpool tub; Carriage House—a stone cottage w/ spiral staircase, oak antiques, wood floors, gas fireplace, 3-person whirlpool, TV & VCR. **Comfort & Decor** Authentic pre-Victorian, Victorian, and Eastlake antiques are set amidst warm wood trim, moldings, pocket doors, and a grand staircase. You'll see lots of marble-topped tables and unusual lamps, including gasoliers with original fixtures. Parquet inlaid floors and original stained glass windows add authenticity. High ceilings feature decorative plasterwork and wide wallpaper borders. Seating in public areas is limited.

RATES, RESERVATIONS, & RESTRICTIONS

Deposit 1 night, refund w/ 10-days notice. **Discounts** $10 less Mon.–Thur. **Credit Cards** AE, V, MC. **Check-In/Out** 2 p.m./11 a.m. **Smoking** No. **Pets** Limited (3 cats on premises). **Kids** Yes, all ages. **Minimum Stay** None. **Open** All year. **Host** Carol Nemeth, 200 South Union Ave., Havre de Grace, 21078. **Phone** (800) 780-1485 or (410) 939-1097. **Fax** (410) 939-9340. **E-mail** spencersilver@erols.com. **Web** spencer silvermansion.com.

PATERNAL GIFT FARM, Highland

OVERALL ★★★★½ | QUALITY ★★★★½ | VALUE ★★★★★ | PRICE $95–$125

This inn was part of a 510-acre tract purchased in 1803 by Dr. Charles Alexander Warfield, an activist in Maryland history. When giving the land to his son Gustavaus, he patented it under the name "Paternal Gift." The original, asymmetrical section of the house has one large chimney serving two fireplaces, which sets it apart from local houses of that era. The walnut flooring in the dining room and cherry floor in the den were made from trees grown on the property. But the real beauty here is the setting—pastoral views of rolling hills and dales and a front-row seat for magnificent sunsets. That, plus a swimming pool and tennis court, makes it well worth the trip.

SETTINGS & FACILITIES

Location Rural hilltop facing 75 acres of open pastureland. **Near** Rte. 108 & Rte. 29, 15 mi. south of Ellicott City, 22.5 mi. southwest of Baltimore, 22.5 mi. northwest of Washington, D.C. **Building** 1850 farmhouse, asymmetrical w/ 1937–47 additions, renovated. **Grounds** 3.75 acres w/ giant boxwoods, holly, hardwood, & evergreen trees, barn, gazebo, clay tennis court, swimming pool, access to trails. **Public Space** LR, DR, enclosed porch, powder room, patio. **Food & Drink** Cont'l plus w/ juice, fruit, bread, or muffins, granola, yogurt; specialties—egg casserole w/ broiled tomatoes. **Recreation** Swim & tennis on premises, rackets avail; riding ring & 50 miles of riding trails in adjacent county park; biking on C&O Canal towpath; Maryland Sheep & Wool Festival. **Amenities & Services** Fax, massage, phone line; meetings (10), weddings (25).

ACCOMMODATIONS

Units 3 guest rooms. **All Rooms** AC, fresh flowers. **Some Rooms** Art & antiques vary. **Bed & Bath** Queen (2), double (1), four-poster (2); 2 private baths, 1 detached, tub (1). **Favorites** Victorian—hand-painted four-poster, faux finish walls, mirrored Scottish armoire from 1870s, grandfather's chair, light from 3 windows, yellow & gold decor. **Comfort & Decor** The house is a mini–art gallery, with a stunning array of oil paintings, photographs, water colors, and prints. They accompany an eclectic collection of antiques. A 1790 Hepplewhite table, 1820-era sideboard, and 1789 grandfather clock are standouts. A large floral painting dominates the white-on-white sunroom.

RATES, RESERVATIONS, & RESTRICTIONS

Deposit Credit card, refund w/ 7-days notice. **Discounts** 10 days or more. **Credit Cards** AE, V, MC. **Check-In/Out** 4–6 p.m./11 a.m. **Smoking** No. **Pets** No (dog & cat in residence; horses welcome by special arrangement). **Kids** Not encouraged. **Minimum Stay** None. **Open** All year (except Thanksgiving & Christmas Day). **Hosts** Barbara & Bob Allen, 13555 Rte. 108, Highland, 20777. **Phone** (301) 854-3353. **Fax** (301) 854-3353. **E-mail** ballen1036@aol.com. **Web** bbonline.com/md/paternal.

ANTRIM 1844, Taneytown

OVERALL ★★★★★ | QUALITY ★★★★★ | VALUE ★★★ | PRICE $150–$375

The property is named for Antrim County, Ireland. Guest rooms are divided among the main house, adjacent cottages, and a renovated barn. The smokehouse was converted to an award-winning restaurant, overseen by chef Lynn Kennedy-Tilyou, a Culinary Institute of America graduate and James Beard Foundation chef. The public rooms are gorgeous, with lots of space, high ceilings, elegant furnishings, and huge bouquets of fresh flowers. Service is extraordinary, including extra touches like a morning tray with coffee, a muffin, and a newspaper delivered to your room, so you can wake up slowly. Then, there's a full, seated breakfast between 9 and 10 a.m. in the dining room overlooking the gardens. The multi-course dinners alone are worth the trip. The wine list, with bottles from $18 to $1,800, earned the restaurant Best of *Wine Spectator* Awards in both 1999 and 2000.

SETTINGS & FACILITIES

Location Foothills of the Catoctin Mountains, 12 mi. south of Gettysburg, PA. **Near** Frederick, Baltimore. **Building** 1844 3-story brick plantation house w/ several dependencies. **Grounds** 23 acres w/ formal garden, swimming pool, tennis court, croquet lawn, golf chipping green, barn, carriage house, ice house, cottage. **Public Space** Drawing rooms (2), library, pub, powder room, veranda in main mansion; common areas in several out buildings. **Food & Drink** Early coffee; full breakfast w/ fresh fruit, juices, homemade baked goods; specialties—eggs Benedict, Belgian waffles, spicy country sausage, Grand Marnier French toast; afternoon tea by request; evening butler's tray w/ chocolates & cordials; dinner served by reservation nightly. **Recreation** Tennis, swimming, horseshoes, croquet, golf at the Links at Gettysburg, skiing; tennis rackets & balls, croquet equip., practice golf clubs provided. **Amenities & Services** Videos, massage avail., disabled access, fax & e-mail; wine dinners, cooking classes, decorating seminars; a glass enclosed pavilion for meetings (300), weddings (300).

ACCOMMODATIONS

Units 11 guest rooms, 9 suites. **All Rooms** AC, hair dryer, robes, fresh flowers. **Some Rooms** Fireplace (16), sauna (2), TV (2), balcony (10), private entrance (6). **Bed & Bath** King (6), queen (16), four-poster (13), canopy (4), sleigh (1), all featherbeds; private baths, double Jacuzzis (14), tubs (6). **Favorites** Ice House—in formal garden, 2-room English-style cottage w/ period antiques; Taney suite—balcony overlooking garden, 3-rooms, steam shower, Jacuzzi next to wood-burning fireplace, cable TV & VCR, CD & tape player; Robert E. Lee suite—queen four-poster featherbed, 2-person Jacuzzi, separate shower, gas fireplace, private courtyard, sitting room w/ pull-out sofa, tape player. **Comfort & Decor** Enter to a grand three-story staircase in the wide entrance hall. Oriental rugs, wide-plank floor, elegant fabrics, and textiles are enhanced by warm jewel tones. The tavern has a walk-in fireplace and fabric-covered walls. Brick floors add a romantic touch to the original summer kitchen, now a restaurant.

RATES, RESERVATIONS, & RESTRICTIONS

Deposit $100 to reserve, non-refundable; applied to another stay w/ 7-days notice. **Discounts** Corp. **Credit Cards** AE, V, MC, D. **Check-In/Out** 3 p.m./11 a.m. **Smoking** No, except in pub. **Pets** No. **Kids** Over age 12. **Minimum Stay** 2 nights if Saturday included. **Open** All year (except Christmas Eve & Day). **Hosts** Dort & Richard Mollett, 30 Trevanian Rd., Taneytown, 21787. **Phone** (800) 858-1844 or (410) 756-6812. **Fax** (410) 756-2744. **E-mail** antrim1844@erols.com. **Web** antrim1844.com.

Zone 15

Eastern Shore Maryland

Most bed-and-breakfasts in Maryland's Eastern Shore are tied in some way to the water. No surprise there.

What is surprising is just how elegant some of these properties are. You may think you need special connections to approach these grand dames of architecture, many built in the eighteenth and nineteenth centuries by the tycoons of their time. Not so. On the back roads of this tidewater landscape, you'll find venerable properties that welcome overnight visitors. Nearby are quaint fishing villages, historic small towns, and wetlands that attract migrating waterfowl.

The premier property, **Inn at Perry Cabin** in **St. Michaels,** has 41 rooms, which falls outside the perimeters of this book. But we found wonderful bed-and-breakfasts—some on huge plantations—that offer a smaller number of rooms and come with a wide choice of ambience and activities.

Chesapeake City sits at the western end of the Chesapeake and Delaware Canal, a waterway that connects the ports of Baltimore and Philadelphia. Specialty stores, antique shops, and boutiques line the old-fashioned streets. The bed-and-breakfasts are quaint and eclectic.

Chestertown on the Chester River was the Eastern Shore's chief port for shipping in Colonial times. Elegant brick townhouses built by merchants and planters made wealthy by trading tobacco and wheat now dominate the handsome historic district.

On the Miles River, St. Michaels is one of the best-known yachting centers on the East Coast. An important shipbuilding center in the seventeenth century, it has evolved into a picturesque town with Federal brick and frame houses, four historic churches and a first-rate maritime museum.

Oxford thrived as a Colonial seaport hub for wealthy tobacco plantations and British importers. Now a waterman's town, it is enjoying new prosperity based on leisure activities. The Oxford-Bellevue Ferry is still running and is one of the nation's oldest.

Easton is a more sophisticated town. Each fall it hosts the popular **Waterfowl Festival,** which features dog trials, decoy carving, and duck-calling contests. At nearby **Blackwater National Wildlife Refuge,** visitors can take a five-mile "wildlife drive" through a 21,000-acre tidal marsh and woodland sanctuary that protects birds, fish, and other critters. Expect to see great blue herons and bald eagles. Winter visitors include thousands of Canadian geese and migratory ducks.

Salisbury is home to the **Ward Museum of Wildfowl Art,** the world's most comprehensive collection of wildfowl carvings. You can see a re-created workshop of Len and Steve Ward, brothers who were barbers in Cresfield, Maryland, and decoy carving hobbyists. They were discovered in 1948 after entering a carving contest and credited with elevating decoy carving to an art form. At the museum, you can see examples of their real-looking decoys, a retrospective of 100 years of regional decoy-making, winners of Best in World competitions, plus boats and equipment used in duck hunting. It's a slice of Maryland heritage you won't want to miss.

Everywhere you go in Maryland, you're apt to find crab cakes on restaurant menus. But, the best-tasting crab cakes, in our experience, are served up right here—on Maryland's Eastern Shore.

FOR MORE INFORMATION

Kent Office of Tourism
400 High St.
Chestertown, MD 21620
(410) 778-0416

Queen Anne County Department of Business & Tourism
425 Piney Narrows Rd.
Chester, MD 21619
(888) 440-7787

Talbot County Office of Tourism
Courthouse
11 N. Washington St.
Easton MD 21601
(888) BAYSTAY

ATLANTIC HOTEL, Berlin

OVERALL ★★★★ | QUALITY ★★★★ | VALUE ★★★ | PRICE **$65–$175**

It seems that things will never be the same here again after scenes from the movie *Runaway Bride,* starring Julia Roberts and Richard Gere, were filmed in and around the Atlantic Hotel. Then, in the spring of 2001, the Disney folks made it the backdrop of a family-oriented film titled *Tuck Everlasting.* Placed on the National Register of Historic Places in 1980, the hotel underwent an extensive restoration in 1988 to restore its elegance and grandeur. In the early years, it catered to traveling salesmen known as "drummers" who ended each day with a fine dinner of local delicacies. The dining room is still a major attraction.

SETTINGS & FACILITIES

Location Town center. **Near** 7 mi. west of Ocean City, 7 mi. west of Assateague Island National Seashore. **Building** 1895 red brick Victorian. **Grounds** Large city lot w/ lawn, floral borders. **Public Space** Ladies parlor, upstairs hall, front porch, 2 levels of back porches, patio. **Food & Drink** Full breakfast buffet w/ juices, fruit, baked goods, 1 hot item; specialties—egg casserole, French toast, corned beef; lunch & dinner avail. **Recreation** Canoeing, kayaking, fishing, birding, antiquing, 2 beaches 13 golf courses. **Amenities & Services** Elevator, massage avail, disabled access (3), fax; meetings (75), weddings (200).

ACCOMMODATIONS

Units 16 guest rooms. **All Rooms** AC, TV, phone. **Some Rooms** Brass beds. **Bed & Bath** Queen (6), double (7), pair of doubles (3); private baths. **Favorites** #6 & #10—similar corner rooms w/ Victorian-style furnishings in rich burgundy tones. **Comfort & Decor** Expect lots of velvet, tassels, and period elegance plus warm wood trim. Rich green, delicate rose, aqua, and deep mahogany colors plus etched glass, brass beds, and brass light fixtures help to transport you to a gentler, quieter time.

RATES, RESERVATIONS, & RESTRICTIONS

Deposit 1 night, refund w/ 2-days notice less $10. **Discounts** Corp. **Credit Cards** AE, V, M, D. **Check-In/Out** 3 p.m./11 a.m. **Smoking** No (bar only). **Pets** No. **Kids** Yes, no charge to stay in the same room under age 12. **Minimum Stay** 2 nights if staying Sat. between Memorial Day & Labor Day; 3 nights for 4th of July, Memorial Day, & Labor Day weekends. **Open** All year. **Host** Gary Weber, innkeeper, 2 North Main St., Berlin, 21811. **Phone** (800) 814-7672 or (410) 641-3589. **Fax** (410) 641-4928. **E-mail** inquire @atlantichotel.com. **Web** atlantichotel.com.

CAMBRIDGE HOUSE, Cambridge

OVERALL ★★★★½ | QUALITY ★★★★ | VALUE ★★★★ | PRICE $95–$120

This is another example of an historic property that fell on hard times and was rescued by an influx of capital and TLC. The hero, in this case, was a former restaurateur from Manhattan, who formerly worked for NBC and Paramount. Stuart takes pride in his former sea captain's house, as you can see from many details in its large rooms. "From the beginning it felt like a happy place. If it's haunted it would be by happy ghosts," he says. The house is furnished with items he found at flea markets and auctions, and he made all his own curtains and drapes. A people-person, Stuart keeps conversations lively and knows the area well. An enthusiastic cook, he prepares five-course dinners for guests on weekend getaway packages.

SETTINGS & FACILITIES

Location Residential street in historic district. **Near** 1 block to the Choptank River, 10 mi. northwest of Blackwater National Wildlife Refuge. **Building** 1847 Queen Anne style. **Grounds** City lot w/ Victorian gardens, English boxwood trees, pond. **Public Space** Foyer, LR, DR, deck, 3 porches. **Food & Drink** Full breakfast served on china & linen w/ fruit, juice, homemade muffins & breads, hot beverages; specialties—eggs any style, omelet of the day, banana pecan griddle cakes w/ praline syrup; 5-course dinner avail. w/ weekend package. **Recreation** Water sports, motorboat tours, skipjack sailing vessel excursions, antiquing, golf. **Amenities & Services** Hot tub; meetings (20) w/ overnight stay.

ACCOMMODATIONS

Units 6 guest rooms. **All Rooms** AC, phone/modem, TV & VCR. **Some Rooms** Fireplace (4), balcony (2), private entrance (2). **Bed & Bath** King (1), queen (5), four-poster (3), canopy (1); private baths. **Favorites** Queen Anne—four-poster bed, needlepoint Edwardian armchair, antiques, fireplace; Hunt room—four-poster, tea roses theme, map wallpaper in bathroom, spacious. **Comfort & Decor** High ceilings, hardwood floors with area rugs, and an eclectic mix of antiques create a pleasant, homey feel. The innkeeper collects wooden carved boxes and heirloom clocks. Guest rooms look lived-in.

RATES, RESERVATIONS, & RESTRICTIONS

Deposit Credit card to hold, refund w/ 3-days notice. **Discounts** Corp., weekly. **Credit Cards** AE, V, MC. **Check-In/Out** 2–6 p.m./11 a.m. **Smoking** No. **Pets** No (cat on premises). **Kids** Age 8 & older. **Minimum Stay** 2 night on weekends April–Nov. **Open** All year. **Host** Stuart D. Schefers, 112 High St., Cambridge, 21613. **Phone** (410) 221-7700. **Fax** (410) 221-7736. **E-mail** camhausb-b@shorenet.net. **Web** cambridge housebandb.com.

GLASGOW INN, Cambridge

OVERALL ★★★★ | QUALITY ★★★★ | VALUE ★★★ | PRICE $90–$150

Religious tolerance wasn't always the norm in Maryland. In the early 1700s, factions in power confiscated property owned by the Catholic Church. As a counter measure, clergy designated private homes as Mass Houses so the devout could continue to gather and worship. This was such a house. Guest room #4 served as a chapel for a time, and a small closet was the neighborhood confessional. The original owner of the house, William Vans Murray, was appointed by George Washington as Ambassador to The

Hague in 1782. President John Adams sent him abroad again to help negotiate the Treaty of Paris. Once surrounded by an 800-acre plantation, the house now thrives under the tutelage of two former school teachers.

SETTINGS & FACILITIES

Location Residential street in historic district. **Near** Across from the Choptank River, blue heron rookery next door, 44 mi. southeast of Annapolis. **Building** 1760 Georgian w/ 6 chimneys. **Grounds** 3.5 acres w/ centuries old trees, roses, hydrangeas, ponds, cultivated gardens, mini-playground in rear. **Public Space** LR, DR, porch. **Food & Drink** Full country breakfast w/ juice, biscuits & homemade jam; specialties—French toast a la Choptank, veggies omelet, fruit tarts in season, sausage, egg, & cheese casserole. **Recreation** Fishing, kayaking, canoeing, swimming, tennis, boating, antiquing. **Amenities & Services** Videos, club privileges at 2 golf courses, massage avail., laundry facility, fax & e-mail; meetings (30), weddings (40).

ACCOMMODATIONS

Units 7 guest rooms. **All Rooms** AC, robes. **Some Rooms** Phone (4), TV (4), fireplace (3), private entrance (1), ceiling fan. **Bed & Bath** King (1), queen (6), four-poster (2); 3 private baths, 4 rooms share 2 baths; 7 tubs w/ shower. **Favorites** #3—a spacious room w/ park-like view, French furnishings, 2 wing chairs, painted floor, a book alcove, king bed. **Comfort & Decor** The philosophy here is less is more, but you'll find good lights for reading and comfortable corners to relax in. The innkeepers collect angels and crèche scenes, which are displayed discreetly in most rooms.

RATES, RESERVATIONS, & RESTRICTIONS

Deposit Credit card to hold, refund w/ 2-days notice. **Discounts** No. **Credit Cards** No. **Check-In/Out** 4–7 p.m./11 a.m. **Smoking** No. **Pets** No. **Kids** Conditionally. **Minimum Stay** 2 nights on weekends April–mid-Nov. **Open** All year. **Hosts** Louiselee Roche & Martha Ann Roche, 1500 Hambrooks Blvd., Cambridge, 21613. **Phone** (800) 373-7890 or (410) 228-0575. **Fax** (410) 221-0297. **E-mail** glasgow@dmv.com.

BLUE MAX INN, Chesapeake City

OVERALL ★★★★★ | QUALITY ★★★★½ | VALUE ★★★★ | PRICE $95–$215

This house was once occupied by author Jack Hunter who wrote *The Blue Max,* a novel about a German aviator in World War I. (It was made into a movie starring George Peppard and Ursula Anders.) Among the parlor conversation pieces are Max, a large stuffed dog, and a player grand piano. The porch faces the high bridge and there's public boat anchorage within walking distance. After raising six children, Wendy opened the B&B in 1998. Wayne did renovating on weekends and in 2000 he retired as an electrical engineer from Dupont. Their property is one of many delightful facets of Chesapeake City, which began as a workingman's town during construction on the Chesapeake and Delaware Canal.

SETTINGS & FACILITIES

Location Historic area, 3 blocks from the canal. **Near** 6 mi. south of Elkton. **Building** 1854 Federal-style. **Grounds** City lot, rock garden w/ waterfall, gazebo, koi pond, floral borders. **Public Space** LR, DR, breakfast porch, 2 outside porches. **Food & Drink** Full breakfast w/ juice, fresh fruit, fresh breads; specialties—country skillet omelet, caramel pecan French toast, apple crisp pancakes; afternoon refreshments. **Recreation** Fishing, boating, carriage rides, summer concerts, water tours, golf, Elk Neck State Park, horseback riding, boating, birding. **Amenities & Services** Disabled access (1), meetings (16).

ACCOMMODATIONS

Units 8 guest rooms. **All Rooms** AC, phone, cable TV, modem jacks, alarm clock, robes. **Some Rooms** Ceiling fan (6). **Bed & Bath** King (5), queen (3), four-poster (2), canopy (1); private baths, 2 detached, whirlpools (2). **Favorites** Suite—queen four-poster, whirlpool, private balcony, fridge, TV & VCR, teal & raspberry motif. **Comfort & Decor** These innkeepers love color and use it effectively throughout the house. The formal living room has a grand player piano, gas fireplace, tall windows, comfy seating, and lots of silk flowers. The cheerful guest rooms have quality details.

RATES, RESERVATIONS, & RESTRICTIONS

Deposit Credit card, refund w/ 10-days notice. **Discounts** Corp. **Credit Cards** AE, V, MC, DC, D. **Check-In/Out** 2–6 p.m./11 a.m. **Smoking** No. **Pets** No. **Kids** Over age 10. **Minimum Stay** 2 nights May–Oct. **Open** All year. **Hosts** Wendy & Wayne Mercer, Box 30, Chesapeake City, 21915. **Phone** (410) 885-2781. **Fax** (410) 885-2809. **E-mail** innkeeper@bluemaxinn.com. **Web** bluemaxinn.com.

INN AT THE CANAL, Chesapeake City

OVERALL ★★★★★ | QUALITY ★★★★½ | VALUE ★★★★★ | PRICE $85–$130

Known locally as the Brady-Rees house, this home was originally owned by a successful family of tugboat owners. One original touch of elegance is the hand-painted ceiling on the first floor. In the living room the motif is Egyptian, with a sphinx, lotus blossom, and papyrus. Griffins watch over the dining room. Family heirlooms include a cabinet filled with fine china that was saved, piece by piece, as a troupe of jugglers tossed them from a burning house. The innkeepers own an antique shop in the back of the house and take pride in helping restore this unique town. Very hands-on with their guests, they both changed careers to become innkeepers (she was an occupational therapist and he worked for the Department of Energy).

SETTINGS & FACILITIES

Location Heart of the historic district, adjacent to Back Creek Basin of the Chesapeake & Delaware Canal. **Near** Elk Neck State Park, Fair Hill Natural Resources Mangement Area, C & D Canal Museum, Philadelphia, Wilmington & Baltimore-Washington airports. **Building** 1870 Victorian. **Grounds** 0.5 acres w/ gardens, floral borders, peonies. **Public Space** Parlor, DR, waterside porches, courtyard. **Food & Drink** Full breakfast w/ juice, fruit, hot beverages; specialties—Southwestern egg bake, blueberry French toast w/ blueberry sauce, & lemon poppy seed muffins & bacon, apricot bread pudding w/ sausage patties & banana muffins; afternoon refreshments. **Recreation** Boating, fishing, swimming, biking, sightseeing; Scottish Game (May), Canal Day (June), Apple Butter Festival (Oct.), Fair Hill International "Festival in the Country" (Oct.), Equestrian Championship, Christmas Candlelight House Tour. **Amenities & Services** Fax.

ACCOMMODATIONS

Units 6 guest rooms, 1 suite. **All Rooms** AC, TV, phone w/ modem hookup, room darkening shades. **Some Rooms** Hair dryer, iron. **Bed & Bath** King (1), queen (4), double (2), four-poster (3), canopy (2); private baths, 4 European soaking tubs. **Favorites** #11—maroon tones, dresser sink, canal view; #6—cozy, nice colors, ceiling glows w/ stars at night, pillowtop mattress. **Comfort & Decor** The house has 12-foot ceilings, original hand-painted details and stenciling, floor-to-ceiling windows, a winding open staircase, and period lighting fixtures. Furnishings and accessories are antiques and reproductions, yet the feeling is less formal. The innkeepers collect antique quilts, doorstops, Victorian lamps, blue touch crocks, blue sponge ware, rolling pins, and cast iron bake ware.

RATES, RESERVATIONS, & RESTRICTIONS

Deposit 1 night on credit card, refund w/ 10-days notice less $15. **Discounts** AAA, corp. **Credit Cards** AE, V, MC, DC, D. **Check-In/Out** 2–6 p.m./11 a.m. **Smoking** No. **Pets** No (cat on premises). **Kids** Over age 10. **Minimum Stay** 2 nights on weekends April–Oct., special event weekends, & holidays. **Open** All year. **Hosts** Mary & Al Ioppolo, Box 187 (104 Bohemia Ave.), Chesapeake City, 21915. **Phone** (410) 885-5995. **Fax** (410) 885-3585. **E-mail** innkeeper@innatthecanal.com. **Web** innatthecanal.com.

SHIP WATCH INN, Chesapeake City

OVERALL ★★★★ | QUALITY ★★★★ | VALUE ★★★ | PRICE $95–$140

Most Chesapeake City homes are family-occupied, creating a real neighborhood—not the tourist trap you might expect. The homes are not grand, but they are beautifully maintained, giving visitors an authentic glimpse of an earlier era. This inn was formerly a carriage house for the larger property next door, now a nice waterfront restaurant. It has stayed in Tom's family for six generations, and he's a direct descendant of original owner Captain Firman Layman. When guests ask Linda what there is to do here, she replies "not much, that's why you're here." The house is perfectly situated for the town's best show—sitting on the porch watching the boats go by.

SETTINGS & FACILITIES

Location Facing the Chesapeake & Delaware Canal. **Near** Philadelphia & Baltimore-Washington airports. **Building** 1930s Arts & Crafts w/ 3-story porch, renovated in 1996. **Grounds** City lot w/ gardens featuring bulbs, natural grasses, window boxes. **Public Space** Foyer/LR, DR, 3 decks. **Food & Drink** Full breakfast w/ juice, fruit; specialties—waffles w/ bacon, Mennonite baked oatmeal, eggs Benedict w/ lump crabmeat on Sundays; complimentary soft drinks & snacks. **Recreation** Fishing, golf, trail riding, boating, sightseeing; horseshoes & bikes avail.; Fair Hill Races, Canal Day, Christmas Tour. **Amenities & Services** Hot tub, disabled access (#2), if-you-forget-it closet; meetings (15).

ACCOMMODATIONS

Units 8 guest rooms. **All Rooms** AC, phone, cable TV, clock radio, binoculars, waterfront balcony. **Some Rooms** Private entrance (1). **Bed & Bath** Kings (3), queen (3), double (2), four-poster (1), canopy (2); private baths, whirlpools (4). **Favorites** #5—crown canopy bed, French lady's chest, antique desk, period safe, pale green decor, whirlpool. **Comfort & Decor** The living room/foyer has William Morris wallpaper, Eastlake chairs, and an English oak sideboard reflecting the 1920s era. Collections include birdhouses, nautical prints by local artists, and duck decoy art by Paul Shertz and other major carvers. Small guest rooms have period antiques and all feature great water views.

RATES, RESERVATIONS, & RESTRICTIONS

Deposit Credit card to hold, refund w/ 10-days notice less $25. **Discounts** Corp. **Credit Cards** AE, V, MC. **Check-In/Out** 2–6 p.m./11 a.m. **Smoking** Private deck only. **Pets** No. **Kids** Limited. **Minimum Stay** None. **Open** All year. **Hosts** Linda & Thomas Vaughan, Box 153 (401 First St)., Chesapeake City, 21915. **Phone** (410) 885-5300. **Fax** (410) 885-5300. **Web** chesapeakecity.com.

BRAMPTON INN, Chestertown

OVERALL ★★★★★ | QUALITY ★★★★½ | VALUE ★★★ | PRICE $125–$215

This house, listed on the National Register of Historic Places, was once home to Henry Ward Carville, the area's most prominent peach grower and slave owner. Tradition holds that he was a pioneer in crop rotation in this area. Danielle, a native of Switzerland, and Michael were involved in all aspects of the restoration of the house, creating a mood of antebellum elegance. They live in a separate property on the grounds with their two daughters. Chestertown, population 3,500, is located on the banks of the Chester River in Maryland's smallest county. It was a thriving Colonial port and shipbuilding center and is now home to Washington College, one of the country's oldest liberal arts schools. It has unusually fine restaurants for a town of this size.

SETTINGS & FACILITIES

Location 0.9 mi. west of town. **Near** 1 hour east of Annapolis. **Building** 1860 Greek Revival plantation house. **Grounds** 35 acres w/ old buildings, paulownia trees, an organic farm, woods. **Public Space** Parlor, DR, study, front porch. **Food & Drink** Early coffee, full breakfast at seperate tables; juice, fruit, homemade baked goods; specialties—French toast, eggs any style w/ Amish sausage; afternoon tea. **Recreation** Antiquing, biking, birding, boating, crabbing, fishing, horseback riding; horseshoes avail. **Amenities & Services** Videos, disabled access (1), bike storage, board games & books (some in French & German); meetings (20), wedding (180).

ACCOMMODATIONS

Units 10 guest rooms (3 in a cottage). **All Rooms** AC, hair dryer. **Some Rooms** Ready-to-light fireplaces avail. Oct.–April (1 gas & 8 wood), TV (3), private entrance (4). **Bed & Bath** King (3), queen (7), four-poster (1), canopies (4), down pillows & comforters; private baths, whirlpools (5), tub (1). **Favorites** Yellow room—barrel canopy bed, fireplace, whirlpool, double sink; Garden cottage—floral walls, plush Victorian sofa, wood-burning fireplace, private patio, double whirlpool, spacious, quiet. **Comfort & Decor** The eye-catching central staircase is made of walnut and ash. The parlor has a Sheraton sofa with eight side chairs, a handmade cabinet, and inlaid secretary, plus an Oriental carpet and antique tables. Tall walnut windows and doors, some original bubble glass, original heart pine floors, and plaster ceiling medallions add elegance. A TV and VCR with videos are available in the pine-paneled study.

RATES, RESERVATIONS, & RESTRICTIONS

Deposit 1 night, refund w/ 7-days notice less $15. **Discounts** None. **Credit Cards** AE, V, MC, D. **Check-In/Out** 3–9 p.m./11 a.m. **Smoking** No. **Pets** No. **Kids** Limited in some rooms. **Minimum Stay** 2 nights w/ a Sat., 3 nights Memorial Day weekend. **Open** All year, except Christmas Day. **Hosts** Danielle & Michael Hanscom, 25227 Chestertown Rd., Chestertown, 21620. **Phone** (410) 778-1860. **E-mail** innkeeper@bramptoninn.com. **Web** bramptoninn.com.

GREAT OAK MANOR, Chestertown

OVERALL ★★★★★ | QUALITY ★★★★½ | VALUE ★★★★ | PRICE $124–$235

This is a destination property that will encourage you to stay put and enjoy the surroundings. As their brochure says, the only honking you'll hear comes from the geese, and the only traffic you see from your room are the boaters sailing the crystal waters a few dozen yards away. The house was built with bricks used as ballast on W. R. Grace sailing ships in an era when grandeur was more important than cost. Formerly a 1,700-acre estate, it served as a hunters' retreat in the 1950s and, rumor has it, a haven for illegal gambling. Guests have now traded their guns for binoculars. And, the house is part of a small community with its own golf and tennis facilities. The current gracious owners began restoring the property in 1992. Diane is a stained glass artist, and Don a retired marketing professional.

SETTINGS & FACILITIES

Location Overlooking the Chesapeake Bay. **Near** 8 mi. west of Chestertown, 70 mi. southwest of Philadelphia & east of Baltimore. **Building** Built in 1938 to mimic a 1700s Georgian manor. **Grounds** 12 acres w/ extensive lawns, mature trees, gazebo, 1,000-foot waterfront w/ private beach, rockers for sunset watching, hammocks, croquet, badminton, volleyball. **Public Space** Library, music room, game room, DR, sunporch, awning-covered patio. **Food & Drink** Full breakfast w/ fruit, cereal, yogurts, oatmeal, juices, coffee & tea; specialties—eggies (strata), quiche, oyster fritters, French toast; afternoon refreshments. **Recreation** Bird watching, lawn games, charter sailboats, fishing; 9-hole executive golf course, swimming pool, & 2 tennis courts next door; golf clubs & tennis rackets avail., 6 10-speed rental bikes avail. **Amenities & Services** Extensive equipment for business meetings (26), weddings (250).

ACCOMMODATIONS

Units 11 guest rooms. **All Rooms** AC, phone, safe, iron & board, hair dryer, binoculars, Perrier, live plant. **Some Rooms** TV (5), duraflame fireplace (5). **Bed & Bath** Kings, four-poster (1), canopies (4); 10 private baths, 1 detached private bath, tub/shower combinations (9). **Favorites** Marmaduke—overlooks the bay, king bed, fireplace, large bath. **Comfort & Decor** Imagine a 25-room manor house with a grand spiral staircase and spacious, tastefully decorated rooms. One favorite room is the library, done in teal blue tones, with a fireplace and wood flooring covered with an Oriental carpet. There are many more—each one a beauty. The house is listed on the Maryland Historic Register.

RATES, RESERVATIONS, & RESTRICTIONS

Deposit 1 night, refund w/ 7-days notice. **Discounts** AARP 10%. **Credit Cards** V, MC. **Check-In/Out** 3–9 p.m./noon. **Smoking** No. **Pets** No (yellow Lab in residence). **Kids** No. **Minimum Stay** 2 days on 3-day weekends & special events. **Open** All year (except last 3 weeks of Dec. & mid-Feb. to mid-March). **Hosts** Dianne & Don Cantor, 10568 Cliff Rd., Chestertown, 21620. **Phone** (800) 504-3098 or (410) 778-5943. **Fax** (410) 778-5943. **E-mail** inndeeper@greatoak.com. **Web** greatoak.com.

INN AT MITCHELL HOUSE, Chestertown

OVERALL ★★★★½ | QUALITY ★★★★ | VALUE ★★★★ | PRICE $95–$120

You'll find lots to talk about with this interesting couple. Tracy uses her intimate knowledge of the area to help guests design custom bike routes through the countryside. Previously she worked as an analyst in the White House correspondence department. Jim continues to teach environment and outdoor studies. Opening a bed-and-breakfast here in 1986 allowed them to raise a family and have one parent stay home. Their collections include hunting caps, duck decoys, and ship art. One portrait is of Sir Peter Parker, a British soldier brought to this house for aid after being wounded in the War of 1812. According to legend, after he died here his body was sent back to England preserved in a barrel of rum. The off-the-beaten path house is especially appealing for birders and bikers.

SETTINGS & FACILITIES

Location Overlooking Stoneybrook Pond on an isolated country road. **Near** 0.5 mi. east of the Chesapeake Bay, 10 mi. west of Chestertown. **Building** Circa 1743 Colonial

& 1825 Federal, red brick w/ hunter green shutters. **Grounds** 10 acres w/ rolling lawns, woods, pond, formal herb garden, access to private beach. **Public Space** 2 parlors, DR, porch. **Food & Drink** Full country breakfast w/ juice, fruit, hot beverages; specialties—crustless quiche, blueberry vanilla French toast, featherbed eggs; guest fridge w/ soda & juice. **Recreation** Tennis, biking, boat & fishing charters, horseback riding, kayaking, hunting, skeet shooting, bird watching, golf, bocce. **Amenities & Services** Use of private beach & tennis court; meetings (16), weddings (150).

ACCOMMODATIONS

Units 6 guest rooms. **All Rooms** AC. **Some Rooms** Fireplace (4). **Bed & Bath** King (1), queen (4), double (1), four-poster (2), canopy (2); 5 private baths, 1 shared, tubs (3). **Favorites** Joseph T. Mitchell—spacious, sitting area w/ fireplace, queen canopy bed plus sleeper sofa, a 2nd bedroom adjoins if needed **Comfort & Decor** The look is relaxed-Colonial with a polished wide-board floor, several fireplaces, and a mix of period antiques and reproductions. Stuffed wildfowl suspended in flight decorate the entry, providing a stunning first impression. Stenciling in some bedrooms adds to the country look.

RATES, RESERVATIONS, & RESTRICTIONS

Deposit 1 night. **Discounts** No. **Credit Cards** V, MC. **Check-In/Out** 3 p.m./noon. **Smoking** No. **Pets** No (1 cat on premises). **Kids** Yes. **Minimum Stay** 2 nights on weekends. **Open** All year. **Hosts** Tracy & Jim Stone, 8796 Maryland Pkwy., Chestertown, 21620. **Phone** (410) 778-6500. **Fax** (410) 778-6500. **E-mail** innatmitch@friendly.net. **Web** www.chestertown.com/mitchell/.

WHITE SWAN TAVERN, Chestertown

OVERALL ★★★★ | QUALITY ★★★★ | VALUE ★★★ | PRICE **$120–$200**

If you treasure quiet mornings, the sound of birdsongs, and small town ambience, you'll find it here. Restoration of the tavern began in 1978 with an archeological dig. It appears that the tenant prior to 1733 was a tanner named John Lovegrove. After changing hands numerous times, the building served as a tavern from 1803 to 1853. Today, it has been restored to its 1793 appearance, with artifacts found at the site displayed in a museum case. Two rooms were furnished with historic inventories as guides. For the rest of the building, the focus is on Colonial simplicity and modern comforts. Antique items add to the feeling of authenticity.

SETTINGS & FACILITIES

Location Heart of the historic district, 0.5 block from the Chester River. **Near** Wilmer Park, Bay beaches. **Building** Meticulously restored 1733 tavern & adjacent townhouse. **Grounds** City lots w/ original terrace, exotic trees, herb, rose, & winter gardens. **Public Space** Lounge, sitting room, formal parlor, breakfast/tea room, museum. **Food & Drink** Cont'l breakfast w/ fruit basket, fresh-squeezed juice, scones, biscuits, muffins, cereal; afternoon tea, beverage set ups, complimentary wine. **Recreation** Sightseeing, water sports, antiquing; Christmas tour, Jazz, Teaparty, & Wildlife Festivals. **Amenities & Services** Massage avail, disabled access, laundry facilities, fax & e-mail.

ACCOMMODATIONS

Units 4 guest rooms, 2 suites. **All Rooms** AC, fresh flowers, hair dryer. **Some Rooms** Non-working fireplace (4), private entrance (1). **Bed & Bath** King (1), queen (1), double (4), twin (5), four-poster (4), canopy (4); private baths, 6 tubs. **Favorites** John Lovegrove Kitchen—oldest room in the inn, brick floor, open-beam ceiling, fireplace; Sterling Suite—queen canopy bed, sitting room. **Comfort & Decor** The public areas have three working fireplaces that contribute to the cheery, welcoming ambience. Five guest rooms have Colonial-style furnishings and one is Victorian.

RATES, RESERVATIONS, & RESTRICTIONS

Deposit 1 night, refund w/ 7-days notice. **Discounts** No. **Credit Cards** V, MC. **Check-In/Out** 3–10 p.m./noon. **Smoking** No. **Pets** No. **Kids** Yes. **Minimum Stay** 2 nights for some weekends & weddings. **Open** All year. **Hosts** Mary Susan Maisel & Wayne McGuire, 231 High St., Chestertown, 21620. **Phone** (410) 778-2300. **Fax** (410) 778-4543. **E-mail** whiteswan@vtechworld.com. **Web** www.chestertown.com/whiteswan/.

BISHOP'S HOUSE, Easton

OVERALL ★★★ | QUALITY ★★★★ | VALUE ★★★ | PRICE $110–$120

This house was built for former Governor Philip Francis Thomas and his wife, Clintonia. In the 1890s, it was sold to the Episcopal Church as a residence for the Bishop of the Diocese of Easton. Ever since it's been known as the Bishop's House. The ambience is decidedly Victorian, complemented by the innkeepers extensive hat collection—with more than 100 pieces of headgear decorating everything from the hat tree to hallways. Extensive plasterwork was done on the first floor, including the restoration of ceiling medallions. The location is convenient to Easton's many fine shops and restaurants.

SETTINGS & FACILITIES

Location Historic district, 3 blocks from Talbot County Courthouse. **Near** 7 mi. south of Pickering Creek, 10 mi. northeast of St. Michaels, 22 mi. north of Blackwater National Wildlife Refuge, 40 mi. to Annapolis, 75 mi. to Baltimore or Washington, D.C. **Building** 1880 Victorian w/ gabled roof. **Grounds** Almost 1-acre lawn w/ flower beds. **Public Space** 2 parlors, DR, wraparound porch. **Food & Drink** Full family-style breakfast w/ 6 juices, fruit, fresh muffins/breads/scones; specialties—blueberry pancakes, banana flavored Belgian waffles, French toast, specialty egg dishes. **Recreation** Antiquing, biking, boating, fishing, tennis, bird watching. **Amenities & Services** Cycling tour maps of Talbot County avail., 6 bikes to rent on site, secure overnight storage for bikes; meetings (10).

ACCOMMODATIONS

Units 5 guest rooms. **All Rooms** AC, cable TV, modem hookup, robes, hair dryer, iron & board. **Some Rooms** Fireplace (3), CD player, ceiling fan. **Bed & Bath** King (2), queen (3); private baths, 1 detached on a different floor, 2 whirlpools, 1 claw-foot tub. **Favorites** #1—the largest room features an antique bedstead & armoire, sterno fireplace, lace accents, CD player, & whirlpool. **Comfort & Decor** First floor rooms have 14-foot ceilings and Victorian-style antiques. Second floor guest rooms offer 12-foot ceilings and working fireplaces. Antique tubs add interest.

RATES, RESERVATIONS, & RESTRICTIONS

Deposit 50% of entire stay, refund w/ 2-days notice less $10. **Discounts** No. **Credit Cards** No. **Check-In/Out** 4–5 p.m./11 a.m. **Smoking** No. **Pets** No (dog on premises). **Kids** Age 12 & older. **Minimum Stay** 2 nights for all stays, 3 nights on holiday weekends. **Open** All year. **Hosts** Diane M. Laird-Ippolito & John B. Ippolito, 214 Goldsborough St., Easton, 21601. **Phone** (800) 223-7290 or (410) 820-7290. **Fax** (410) 820-7290. **E-mail** bishopshouse@skipjack.bluecrab.org. **Web** bishopshouse.com.

INN ON THE OCEAN, Ocean City

OVERALL ★★★★½ | QUALITY ★★★★½ | VALUE ★★★ | PRICE $125–$290

This bed-and-breakfast is one of a kind in Ocean City, where most oceanfront homes were torn down and replaced with high rises. The gracious hosts have distinct talents for decorating and cooking. Guests enjoy luxury beachfront living with immediate views of the sand and sea. Two framed posters in the living room—one dressed up and one dressed down—speak volumes. "We want our guests to be comfortable, anything goes," says Vicki. The couple changed careers to be near Vicki's mom, naming their onsite tearoom in her honor because she always talked about owning a tearoom. Before returning to her roots on Maryland's Eastern Shore, Vicki was director of education at the Wang Center Theater in Boston and Charlie was in business management.

SETTINGS & FACILITIES

Location Adjacent to the boardwalk facing the ocean. **Near** Assateague Island National Seashore & Assateague State Park. **Building** 1938 Victorian cottage. **Grounds** Corner city lot w/ beach plantings. **Public Space** LR, DR, veranda, guest pantry, powder room. **Food & Drink** Full breakfast w/ juice, fruit; specialties—crème brûlée French toast, breakfast burrito, ham & cheese French toast w/ bourbon apples, cheese soufflé. **Recreation** Golf, deepwater fishing, water sports, harness horse racing, antiquing, biking, ocean swimming, boardwalk activities; beach chairs & umbrellas avail., outdoor shower; 12 bikes

(1 tandem & 1 fringed surrey) to use. **Amenities & Services** Videos, health club privileges, fax, concierge service, murder mystery weekends; meetings (12), weddings (60).

ACCOMMODATIONS

Units 6 guest rooms. **All Rooms** AC, TV & VCR, ceiling fan, hair dryer, robes, room-darkening shades. **Some Rooms** Balcony (2). **Bed & Bath** King (3), queen (3), twin (1); private baths, whirlpools (4), tubs (4). **Favorites** Oceana room—king bed, private porch to watch sunrise, mural-style bathroom wallpaper w/ water lily theme, whirlpool. **Comfort & Decor** Lovely family heirlooms accent a collection of antiques. Wicker pieces lighten the look for summer. The living room has a grand piano, fireplace, and interesting art. Attention to detail is key. Guest room themes include canopy, tapestry, veranda, hunt, and Victorian. The cleaning staff is fastidious.

RATES, RESERVATIONS, & RESTRICTIONS

Deposit 1 night or 50%, refund w/ 3-weeks notice less $50. **Discounts** No. **Credit Cards** AE, V, MC, D. **Check-In/Out** 1 p.m./11 a.m. **Smoking** No. **Pets** No. **Kids** No. **Minimum Stay** 2 nights on weekends, 3 nights for Memorial Day & Labor Day weekends & Sunfest. **Open** All year. **Host** Vicki & Charlie Barrett, 1001 Atlantic Ave., Ocean City, 21842. **Phone** (888) 226-6223 or (410) 289-8894. **Fax** (410) 289-8215. **E-mail** innontheocean@aol.com. **Web** innontheocean.com.

COMBSBERRY 1730, Oxford

OVERALL ★★★★★ | QUALITY ★★★★★ | VALUE ★★★ | PRICE $250–$395

This is one of Talbot County's premier historic homes. Notable architectural features include an unusual stair tower, glazed headers, a hidden cellar, and arched fireplaces. The ambience is conducive to relaxing and staying put to enjoy the property. You can fish for crabs and rockfish from the pier, or stroll amidst the daffodils, magnolias, and weeping willows. From the cove shore, you can watch swans, heron, and geese or the tawny glow of the sunset reflected on the water. The current owners, a cardiologist and his wife, opened Combsberry as a bed-and-breakfast in 1996. It's run by full-time innkeeper Cathy Magrogan, who formerly hosted at The Ashby, now closed. Her goal is to make guests feel like they're part of the family. "While you're here, this is your house," she says.

SETTINGS & FACILITIES

Location Facing Brigham's Cove off Island Creek. **Near** Easton airport 10 min. away. **Building** 1730 English-style country estate w/ carriage house, cottages. **Grounds** 9.7 acres w/ extensive lawns, mature magnolia & willow trees, boxwood, brick walkways, walled garden, fountain, hammock. **Public Space** LR, DR, library, kitchen, patio. **Food & Drink** Full breakfast w/ fresh fruit, homemade breads; specialties—strata, baked French toast, crab omelet. **Recreation** Antiquing, skipjack races, wildfowl & deer hunting, golf, tennis, biking; Blackwater National Wildlife Refuge; paddleboats & canoes avail; Art & Crafts Festivals (spring), Seafood Festival, House & Garden tours, Waterfowl Festival (Nov.). **Amenities & Services** Fax, disabled access (1), laundry facilities, small elevator; 6-foot dock for boats; meetings (20), weddings (30).

ACCOMMODATIONS

Units 6 guest rooms, 1 suite. **All Rooms** AC, hair dryer. **Some Rooms** Balcony (1), fireplace (4), private entrance (2). **Bed & Bath** King (3), queen (4), four-poster (2), canopy (2); private baths, whirlpools (4). **Favorites** Magnolia suite—four-poster, floral fabrics, huge balcony w/ water view, spacious bathroom w/ whirlpool, beautiful in every aspect. **Comfort & Decor** Elegance is the key. The living room is a vision in chintz, with sofas flanked by an oversized fireplace and offsetting polished wood floors. In the spacious library a leather sofa and tapestry rocker invite reading and conversation by the fire. A huge kitchen has unusual floral patterns and one wall of glass doors. You won't find telephones or televisions in the bedrooms—the views are enough. A cottage provides extra privacy.

RATES, RESERVATIONS, & RESTRICTIONS

Deposit 50%, refund w/ 7-days notice. **Discounts** No. **Credit Cards** AE, V, MC. **Check-In/Out** 3 p.m./11 a.m. **Smoking** No. **Pets** Yes (cottage only). **Kids** Over age 12. **Minimum Stay** None. **Open** All year (except Christmas & Easter). **Hosts** Cathy Magrogan, 4837 Evergreen Rd., Oxford, 21654. **Phone** (410) 226-5353. **Fax** (410) 228-1453. **Web** combsberry.com.

WATERLOO COUNTRY INN, Princess Anne

OVERALL ★★★★½ | QUALITY ★★★★½ | VALUE ★★★ | PRICE **$105–$245**

In pre-Revolutionary times this mansion was one of the focal points of Eastern Shore social life. Built by prominent Somerset country landowner Henry Waggaman, it is now listed in the National Register of Historic Places. The current owners, who are from Switzerland, have done a fine job renovating the house. Although the tone of the decor is a bit formal, the details are relaxed. Elegant chandeliers and antique clocks are interspersed with their collections of irons and coffee mills plus a gramophone, Victorian doll on a bike, and wash stand. Guest books indicate they host lots of international guests, with many comments in German or French. To welcome both children and pets is rare for an historic manor of this quality.

SETTINGS & FACILITIES

Location On Rte. 363 adjacent to Monie Creek, 5 mi. west of Princess Anne. **Near** 13 mi. south of Salisbury. **Building** 1750 Georgian plantation house, 3-story Flemish bond brick, w/ glazed header checkerboard patterns & distinctive quoins on 3 principal corners. **Grounds** 317 acres w/ forest, cultivated fields, 20 acres of gardens, lawn, rare trees, tidal pond, walking trails, swimming pool. **Public Space** Lounge, DR, library. **Food & Drink** Full breakfast w/ juice, fresh fruits, homemade breads, hot beverages, jams, cereals, yogurt; specialties—eggs any style w/ bacon or sausage; welcome drink and afternoon tea avail. **Recreation** Golf, tennis, fishing, sailing, hunting, swimming, antiquing, Teackle Mansions tour, Olde Princess Anne Days, Assateague State Park, Assateague Island National Seashore, Smith & Tangier Island Cruises, Blackwater National Wildlife Refuge, Ward Museum, canoe on Monie Creek, ferry ride across the Wicomico River; canoes (4) w/ life jackets & bicycles (6) on site, books & games avail. **Amenities & Services** Videos, disabled access (w/ ramp to the Manokin room), fax & e-mail; meetings (40), weddings (200).

ACCOMMODATIONS

Units 3 guest rooms & 2 suites in main building, 1 cottage. **All Rooms** AC, TV, phone, clock radio, hair dryer, fresh flowers. **Some Rooms** Fireplace, VCR, coffee maker (2). **Bed & Bath** King (4), queen (2), twin (1), canopy (1); private baths, whirlpools (2), tubs (4). **Favorites** Somerset suite—sitting area w/ gas fireplace, loveseat & wing chairs, antique armoire, desk, TV & VCR, coffeemaker & radio, queen bed, whirlpool tub, durable fabrics in browns w/ mauve accents; Tangier room—privacy, pet-friendly. **Comfort & Decor** A collection of art by Swiss artist Rudolf Mirer (each with a price tag), heirloom antiques, and Swiss country collectibles (such as a butter churn, laundry tub, and super-sized cow bell) add character to the public areas. Bedrooms are heavy on amenities. Overall, it's the setting that propels this property to stardom.

RATES, RESERVATIONS, & RESTRICTIONS

Deposit 1 night by credit card, refund w/ 7-days notice. **Discounts** No. **Credit Cards** AE, V, MC, D. **Check-In/Out** 3–7 p.m./11 a.m. **Smoking** No. **Pets** Yes, 1 room only. **Kids** Welcome. **Minimum Stay** 2 nights may be required on weekends & holidays. **Open** All year (except Jan. & Feb.). **Hosts** Theresa & Erwin Kraemer, 28822 Mount Vernon Rd., Princess Anne, 21853. **Phone** (410) 651-0883. **Fax** (410) 651-5592. **E-mail** innkeeper@waterloocountryinn.com. **Web** waterloocountryinn.com.

DR. DODSON HOUSE, St. Michaels

OVERALL ★★★★★ | QUALITY ★★★★★ | VALUE ★★★★ | PRICE $170–$180

These innkeepers provide lots of amenities and attention. Each evening they prepare gourmet delicacies and join their guests for conversation at happy hour (except for Wednesday evenings when they race their sail boat, weather permitting). Their elaborate breakfasts are a visual and gastronomic treat. Every nook and cranny of their house works. "For us, this house is like a great big toy," says Janet. It has a colorful history, first as a tavern, then the first town post office, and finally the office where Dr. Dodson practiced medicine in what is now the dining room. After carefully charting their course, Janet gave up her practice as a civil litigator and Gary retired from IBM to move from California with their 30-foot sailboat, *Penniless.*

SETTINGS & FACILITIES

Location Corner of Cherry St. & Locust St. in historic district. **Near** 0.5 blocks to harbor & Miles River, 1 block to Chesapeake Bay Maritime Museum, 2 blocks to St. Mary's Square Museum, 12 mi. to Easton airport. **Building** 1799 Federal 3-story brick w/ 1872 Victorian addition, 2-story porch w/ gingerbread trim. **Grounds** City lot w/ circular brick courtyard, fountain, gardens, white picket fencing & arbors. **Public Space** Parlor, DR, guest pantry. **Food & Drink** Full breakfast w/ juice, fruit, assorted muffins, hot beverages; specialties—eggs Benedict, banana pecan waffles, French toast w/ rum & spices, blueberry pancakes; evening hors d'oeuvres in the parlor; morning room service trays w/ *Baltimore Sun* or *Washington Post* avail. **Recreation** Sailing, fishing, river tour boat rides, skipjack rides, kayaking, canoeing, horse-drawn carriage rides, horseback riding, golf, biplane flights, biking, sightseeing, house tours, concerts in the park; bikes, coolers, & folding chairs avail.; Maritime Arts Festival (May), Boat Festival (June), Crab Days (Aug.), Small Craft Festival (Oct.), OysterFest & Waterfowl Festival (Nov.). **Amenities & Services** Videos & games, fax & e-mail, cordless phone avail.; meetings (6).

ACCOMMODATIONS

Units 2. **All Rooms** AC, TV, clock radio w/ CD player, wood-burning fireplace, hair dryer, robes, heated mattress pad, chocolate truffles. **Some Rooms** VCR. **Bed & Bath** Queen (2), canopy (2); private baths. **Favorites** Dodson room—blue, yellow, & white decor, lace canopy iron bed, antique quilt, in-room marble sink, white shutters, silk flowers, lots of charm. **Comfort & Decor** Although the rooms are smallish, every detail is attended to. The living and dining rooms' walls are deep raspberry with white trim. Rich green fabrics and plenty of healthy, live plants provide dramatic counterpoint. A Victorian fainting couch, 1800s rocker and desk, and heirloom antiques add interest.

RATES, RESERVATIONS, & RESTRICTIONS

Deposit 1 nights or 50% of longer stays, refund w/ 14-days notice less $20. **Discounts** 4 nights or longer. **Credit Cards** No. **Check-In/Out** 4–6 p.m./11 a.m. **Smoking** No. **Pets** No. **Kids** Not suitable for young children or infants. **Minimum Stay** 2 nights most weekends, 3 nights for Memorial & Labor Day weekends. **Open** All year. **Hosts** Janet Buck & Gary Nylander, 200 Cherry St., St. Michaels, 21663. **Phone** (410) 745-3691. **E-mail** jbuck@bluecrab.org. **Web** drdodsonhouse.com.

FIVE GABLES INN & SPA, St. Michaels

OVERALL ★★★½ | QUALITY ★★★★½ | VALUE ★★ | PRICE $140–$325

Guests claim that even a brief stay here recharges sagging spirits and replaces fatigue and stress with renewed energy. The secret is indulging in some of the treatments in the on-site spa, including herbal baths, holistic massage, reflexology, and facials. The pristine accommodations you see today are the results of a painstaking renovation during the 1990s, bringing formerly derelict properties up to the standards of a charming neighborhood of boutiques and restaurants. The walls in the main building are a bit thin, so noise from other rooms, including the sound of whirlpools, can be bothersome. However, you'll find a gracious and savvy hostess who can direct you to area eateries and fun activities.

SETTINGS & FACILITIES

Location Heart of historic waterfront village. **Near** 50 mi. southeast of Annapolis. **Building** 2 circa 1860 buildings, Colonial & traditional brick. **Grounds** About 1 acre. **Public Space** Breakfast room, swimming pool, sun deck, garden. **Food & Drink** Expanded cont'l breakfast w/ juice, fruit, assorted baked goods, fat-free breads, hot beverages; afternoon snacks. **Recreation** Tennis, golf, sailing, hunting, fishing, biking (bikes avail.). **Amenities & Services** Aveda Concept spa w/ hydrotherapy, therapeutic body & facial massage, scrubs, indoor heated pool, sauna, steam room; disabled access; meetings (20).

ACCOMMODATIONS

Units 15 guest rooms, 2 suites. **All Rooms** AC, TV, CD player, gas fireplace, hair dryer, robes, direct phone line. **Some Rooms** Private porch. **Bed & Bath** King (5), queen (10), twin (2); private baths w/ whirlpool & Aveda amenities. **Favorites** All rooms are similar, with attractive, functional furnishings. Some have larger whirlpools and a small, narrow balcony. Suites offer additional amenities. **Comfort & Decor** There's not much public space. Flick-of-the-switch gas fireplaces are standard in all rooms in the main building, as are whirlpool tubs. Beds are comfortable. Spa services are being expanded.

RATES, RESERVATIONS, & RESTRICTIONS

Deposit 1 night, refund w/ 14-days notice; spa appointments are also held w/ a credit card, refund w/ 24-hours notice. **Discounts** No. **Credit Cards** AE, V, MC. **Check-In/Out** 3–7 p.m./noon. **Smoking** No. **Pets** Yes, w/ notice, rules & restrictions apply. **Kids** Not suitable. **Minimum Stay** 2 nights for all Sat. night stays. **Open** All year. **Hosts** Bonnie & John Booth, owners; Lynsey Rochon, innkeeper, 209 N. Talbot St., St. Michaels, 21663. **Phone** (877) 466-0100 or (410) 745-0100. **Fax** (410) 745-2903. **E-mail** fivegables@crosslink.net. **Web** fivegables.com.

OLD BRICK INN, St. Michaels

OVERALL ★★★ | QUALITY ★★★★ | VALUE ★★★ | PRICE $95–$250

Sunday through Thursday rates are good values here, but weekend prices are high. There's a great deal of individuality in the decor, but overall, the tone is somewhat impersonal. The property will appeal to couples who like privacy and anonymity. Hopefully, the pervasive green carpet will quickly wear out and have to be changed. The original home, built by shipwright Wrightson Jones, morphed into a restaurant, pharmacy, Masonic lodge, bank, real estate office, and antique gallery over the years. Martha Strickland bought it in 1997 and oversaw a major renovation. The annex was added in 1985 by previous owners on the site of the original carriage house. The location is excellent.

SETTINGS & FACILITIES

Location Heart of town, facing the main street. **Near** One block from marina if arriving by boat; 50 minutes drive to Annapolis. **Building** 1816 Federal-style inn & 1985 brick carriage house. **Grounds** Large city lot w/ brick New Orleans–style courtyard, swimming pool. **Public Space** LR, DR. **Food & Drink** Cont'l plus breakfast, w/ juice, bagels, muffins, cereal, fresh fruit, hot beverages. **Recreation** Chesapeake Bay Maritime Museum; biking &

boating (rentals avail. nearby); Waterfowl Festival (Nov.), boat show, oyster & crab festivals. **Amenities & Services** Disabled access (12), fax; meetings (14).

ACCOMMODATIONS

Units 12 guest rooms. **All Rooms** AC, cable TV. **Some Rooms** Non-working fireplace (5), porch (2), ceiling fan (7). **Bed & Bath** Queens, four-posters (3), canopies (2); private baths, 1 whirlpool, 10 tub/showers. **Favorites** Honeymoon suite—a huge room sometimes used for conferences, sleigh bed, Victorian chandelier, painted sink, whirlpool (overlook the green carpet); Sailor room—white four-poster, themed accessories include a ship's wheel, lighthouse, ship model, & art. **Comfort & Decor** The parlor is basic. Individuality reigns in the guests rooms, with accessories carrying out such themes as Annie Oakley and Scarlett O'Hara. A full-sized reproduction suit of armor stands in one corner of the Guinevere room. The Out of Africa room interprets a safari.

RATES, RESERVATIONS, & RESTRICTIONS

Deposit 1 night, refund w/ 7-days notice. **Discounts** No. **Credit Cards** AE, V, MC, DC. **Check-In/Out** 3–7 p.m./11 a.m. **Smoking** No. **Pets** No. **Kids** Over age 12. **No-Nos** Skinny dipping. **Minimum Stay** 2 nights on weekends mid-April–mid-Nov. **Open** All year (except Jan. 2 through Feb. 13). **Host** Martha Strickland, Box 985 (401 S. Talbot St.), St. Michaels, 21663. **Phone** (410) 745-3323. **Fax** (410) 745-3320. **E-mail** mstrickland @expresshost.com. **Web** oldbrickinn.com.

CHANCEFORD HALL, Snow Hill

OVERALL ★★★★★ | QUALITY ★★★★½ | VALUE ★★★★ | PRICE **$130–$150**

You can enjoy the upscale lifestyle of a mid-eighteenth century British family as a guest in this remarkably intact house built by the family of Robert Morris, a financier of the Revolutionary War. With over 6,000 square feet of finished space, it has sturdy 18-inch thick brick walls with trim of virgin forest timber, including elaborate crown moldings, chair rails, fireplace mantels, paneled doors with original hardware, and wide plank wood floors. There's even some original flow glass in the windows.

You won't find televisions in the guests rooms, but the availability of good, current books is remarkable. Alice is southeast sales director for Random House publishing. Randy, an architect, now works from home. Both fascinating conversationalists, the energetic couple takes pride in sharing their architectural and historic treasure.

SETTINGS & FACILITIES

Location Residential area. **Near** 10 mi. west of Assateague Island. **Building** Brick 1759 Greek Revival w/ Georgian & Federal details. **Grounds** 1 acre, mature trees, boxwood, magnolia & holly, narrow lap pool, koi pond, hammock. **Public Space** Salon, DR, solarium, kitchen area. **Food & Drink** Full breakfast w/ smoothie, fresh fruit, fruit pie; specialties—strata, omelets, pancakes, French toast; afternoon cookies, pie, beverages. **Recreation** Golf, kayaking, canoeing, motorized paddle boating, bass fishing, biking; croquet & 4 bikes avail.; Canoe Jousting Tournament (July), Blessing of the Combines (Aug.), Century Bike Tour (Oct.). **Amenities & Services** Meetings (20), weddings (150).

ACCOMMODATIONS

Units 4 guest rooms. **All Rooms** AC, antique quilt, robes. **Some Rooms** Fireplace (3). **Bed & Bath** Queens, four-poster (2), canopy (2); private baths, 2 tubs. **Favorites** Chanceford—1850s ceiling medallion & molding, fireplace, wing chairs, ship & plant art, nice bathroom. **Comfort & Decor** This majestic manor house has appropriate, eye-pleasing antiques and simple, uncluttered surfaces. A unique wood fireplace graces the dining room. The kitchen, once a ballroom, is lined with dark wood cabinets.

RATES, RESERVATIONS, & RESTRICTIONS

Deposit 1 night, refund w/ 7-days notice. **Discounts** No. **Credit Cards** V, MC. **Check-In/Out** 3–7 p.m./11 a.m. **Smoking** No. **Pets** No (2 akita dogs in residence). **Kids** Yes, on occasion. **Minimum Stay** 2 nights June 1–Oct. 31. **Open** All year. **Hosts** Alice Kesterson & Randy Ifft, 209 W. Federal St., Snow Hill, 21863. **Phone** (888) 494-8817 or (410) 632-2900. **Fax** (410) 632-2479. **E-mail** chbnb@aol.com. **Web** chancefordhall.com.

RIVER HOUSE INN, Snow Hill

OVERALL ★★★½ | QUALITY ★★★★ | VALUE ★★★ | PRICE $140–$210

The best feature of this well-worn property is the sloping back lawn, which ends at the edge of the pristine Pocomoke River. It invites you to relax in lawn chairs by the shore or arrange a boat or canoe excursion down stream. The house, listed on the National Register of Historic Places, has four fireplaces on the main floor. The parlor is nicely decorated with brick red walls, floral sofas, balloon curtains, and parquet floors, and you'll find lots of books and current magazines. The TV room is also a popular gathering place. The innkeepers collect oyster plates and teacups, which decorate dining room shelves and walls.

SETTINGS & FACILITIES

Location In the historic district adjacent to the Pocomoke River. **Near** 18 mi. southeast of Salisbury. **Building** 1860 Gothic Revival w/ 1890 carriage barn. **Grounds** Large riverside lawn, 2 ponds, gardens, benches, hammocks. **Public Space** Sitting room, TV room, DR, breakfast room, powder room, 2 porches. **Food & Drink** Full breakfast w/ juice, fruit, cereals, breads, meats; specialties—French toast, pancakes, eggs any style; afternoon wine & cheese. **Recreation** Biking, canoeing, kayaking, birding, pontoon boat river tours, antiquing; Canoe Jousting (July), Blessing of the Combines (Aug.), Century Bike Tour (Oct.). **Amenities & Services** Videos, fax, golf & swimming privileges at Nassawango Country Club, disabled access (#12); meetings (20), weddings (200).

ACCOMMODATIONS

Units 5 guest rooms, 4 suites. **All Rooms** AC, hair dryer, ceiling fan. **Some Rooms** TV (7), gas fireplace (6). **Bed & Bath** King (3), queen (6), four-poster (1), canopy (1); private baths, 3 whirlpools, 5 tub/showers. **Favorites** Lilac suite—sitting room w/ TV & VCR, kitchen. **Comfort & Decor** The public areas look relaxed and informal. Rooms tend to be plain and some have mix-and-match furniture, but necessary items are provided.

RATES, RESERVATIONS, & RESTRICTIONS

Deposit Credit card to hold, refund w/ 7-days notice less $10. **Discounts** 10% AAA, AARP, active duty military. **Credit Cards** AE, V, MC, D. **Check-In/Out** 3–7 p.m./noon. **Smoking** No. **Pets** Welcome (3 standard poodles on premises). **Kids** Welcome if well behaved. **Minimum Stay** 2 nights on weekends April–Oct. & holidays. **Open** All year. **Hosts** Susanne & Larry Knudsen, 201 E. Market St., Snow Hill, 21863. **Phone** (410) 632-2722. **Fax** (410) 632-2866. **E-mail** innkeeper@riverhouseinn.com. **Web** riverhouseinn.com.

CHESAPEAKE WOOD DUCK INN, Tilghman Island

OVERALL ★★★½ | QUALITY ★★★★ | VALUE ★★ | PRICE $149–$219

You cross a drawbridge to reach three-square-mile Tilghman Island, a waterman's village still home to working skipjack captains. You enter this house via a well-worn screened porch and farm-style parlor furnished with heirlooms and antiques. The kitchen is more modern—with clean, bright cabinets and a sophisticated work island. That's the first hint that you're in for some good eats. Jeff is passionate about food and whips up gourmet breakfasts. Collections on display include golf art, old door knobs, and original works by local painter Maureen Bannon. Kim was formerly a district manager of Washington, D.C.–area Disney stores and Jeff a Continental Airlines pilot. They've worked hard to upgrade their property and are enthusiastic about their new roles as innkeepers.

SETTINGS & FACILITIES

Location Overlooking Dogwood Harbor. **Near** St. Michaels, Chesapeake Bay Maritime Museum, Oxford, Blackwater National Wildlife Refuge, Easton, Sandy Point State Park. **Building** 1890 Victorian boarding house w/ cottage. **Grounds** 1.5 acres w/ lawn. **Public Space** LR, DR, sunroom, 3 porches, kitchen. **Food & Drink** Full breakfast w/ fruit, assorted baked goods, juice; specialties—omelet puff w/ asparagus & spiced apples, jumbo lump crab, orange & beet spaghetti, smoked salmon hash w/ poached eggs & tomato/yellow pepper sauce; dinners are avail. w/ advance notice. **Recreation** Biking, golf, tennis, swimming, kayaking, fishing, bird watching, horseback riding, carriage rides, skipjack excursions, antiquing, sunset sails; Tilghman Island Days, Seafood Festival, Waterfowl Festival, sailboat and power boat show, sailboat races. **Amenities & Services** Meetings (10).

ACCOMMODATIONS

Units 6 guest rooms, 1 suite. **All Rooms** AC, fresh flowers. **Some Rooms** Private entrance (1), deck, TV, stereo. **Bed & Bath** Queen (3), double (4); private baths, 5 tubs. **Favorites** Magnolia—nice armoire, etching; cottage—maroon & floral fabrics, four-poster, TV & CD player, small back deck. **Comfort & Decor** Smallish rooms are decorated with antiques and family heirlooms. The living room has a gas fireplace, upright piano, wash stand, and working Victrola. Jeff's mom is an artist, so you'll see lots of her paintings. Stairs to second and third floor rooms are steep and narrow. The cottage has the most amenities.

RATES, RESERVATIONS, & RESTRICTIONS

Deposit Credit card to hold, refund w/ 7-days notice. **Discounts** AAA. **Credit Cards** V, MC. **Check-In/Out** 4–7 p.m./11 a.m. **Smoking** No. **Pets** No. **Kids** Over age 14. **Minimum Stay** 3 nights on weekends May–Oct., 2 nights for other weekends. **Open** All year. **Hosts** Kimberly & Jeffrey Bushey, P.O. Box 202 (21490 Dogwood Harbor Rd.), Tilghman Island, 21671. **Phone** (800) 956-2070 or (410) 886-2070. **Fax** (410) 886-2263. **E-mail** woodduck@bluecrab.org. **Web** woodduckinn.com.

LAZYJACK INN, Tilghman Island

OVERALL ★★★★★ | QUALITY ★★★★★ | VALUE ★★★ | PRICE $130–$230

Tilghman Island is home to the last working sailing fleet in the country. "This is not a pristine harbor. Things happen here… the skipjacks leave at 4:30 a.m. and come back with their catch and unload at the end of the dock between 11 and 2," says Mike, himself the captain of a 16-passenter sailing yacht. As the story goes, Carol and Mike had just set sail from nearby Reston, Virginia and were headed for a two-year sailing venture in the Florida Keys and the Bahamas, when they tied up at a dock here in 1991.

They liked what they saw so much that they never really left—spending the next decade turning this modest-looking house into a treasure. It is a delight to sit in the harbor room watching the tall masts of skipjacks moored at the edge of their property and enjoying sparkling conversation.

SETTINGS & FACILITIES

Location Facing Dogwood Harbor. **Near** 11 mi. west of St. Michaels, 23 mi. west of Easton. **Building** 1855 Colonial, a traditional waterman's house. **Grounds** 1 acre w/ rose-lined driveway, flower & herb gardens, fountains. **Public Space** Library, harbor room, front porch, back deck, guest fridge **Food & Drink** Early coffee, full breakfast w/ fruit, juice, hot beverages; specialties—grilled portabello mushrooms w/ herbed eggs & sweet biscuits, silver dollar pancakes w/ fried apples & baked country sausage, seafood crêpes, vegetable cakes w/ parsley, sour cream, & fresh salsa. **Recreation** Fishing charters, biking, golf, tennis, sailing aboard the innkeeper's 16-passenger boat, *Lady Patty;* Chesapeake Bay Maritime Museum, Oxford Bellvue Ferry; Tilghman Island Seafood Festival (June), Tilghman Island Day (Oct.). **Amenities & Services** Meetings (8).

ACCOMMODATIONS

Units 4 guest rooms. **All Rooms** AC, fresh flowers, sherry, antique quilt, reading lamp. **Some Rooms** Fireplace (2). **Bed & Bath** King (1), queen (3); private baths, 2 whirlpools, 2 tubs. **Favorites** Nellie Byrd suite—brass bed, sofa, chair and 4 windows face river and harbor view; Garden suite—spacious 1st floor room w/ fireplace, whirlpool, private porch overlooking cottage garden. **Comfort & Decor** Family antiques, comfortable furnishings, and nautical-themed art and accessories provide a strong sense of place. Conversation pieces include the maritime library and collections of sea glass, old bottles, duck decoys, and paintings and photography by local artists. Turn-down service, chocolates and Perrier, and a change of towels are part of the luxury treatment.

RATES, RESERVATIONS, & RESTRICTIONS

Deposit 1 night due within 10 days, refund w/ 7-days notice less $20. **Discounts** Ask. **Credit Cards** AE, V, MC. **Check-In/Out** 4–7 p.m./11 a.m. **Smoking** No. **Pets** No (3 cats on premises). **Kids** Age 12 & older. **Minimum Stay** 2 nights on weekends. **Open** All year. **Hosts** Carol & Capt. Mike Richards, Box 248 (5907 Tilghman Island Rd.), Tilghman Island, 21671. **Phone** (800) 690-5080 or (410) 886-2215. **Fax** (410) 886-2635. **E-mail** stay@lazyjackinn.com. **Web** lazyjackinn.com.

INN OF SILENT MUSIC, Tylerton, Smith Island

OVERALL ★★★★½ | QUALITY ★★★★ | VALUE ★★★★ | PRICE $75–$95

Do not expect daily newspapers, a nearby mall, bars with live music, or alcohol for sale (bring your own). Tylerton (three-eighths of a mile long) is a remote waterman's village (population 70) where most people earn a living harvesting the Chesapeake Bay. It's one of three villages on Smith Island, which was settled by English colonists about 1665. Tylerton's landscape is a labyrinth of channels, passages, and creeks that invite canoeing, kayaking, and birding. Or, if you like, sit on the porch and watch the boats come and go. Smith Island's history is one of courage, faith, and tenacity.

Present challenges include sea-level rise, erosion, and assimilation into mainland culture. Many guests find the historical, cultural, and social aspects of this community its most remarkable assets.

SETTINGS & FACILITIES

Location 10 mi. from the mainland, on a small Chesapeake Bay island accessible via ferryboat from Crisfield dock, southwest of Salisbury; ferry service is $20 round trip; the island has no roads or cars, parking is avail. in Crisfield. **Near** Blackwater National Wildlife Refuge, Ward Museum of Wildfowl Art, Ocean City beaches, Tangier Island. **Building** 1916 Maryland-style cottage, remodeled. **Grounds** 1.4 acres w/ salt marsh, loblolly pines, cedars, & mowed yard, surrounded on 3 sides by water. **Public Space** LR, kitchen, screened porch, dock, guest fridge & microwave. **Food & Drink** Early coffee; full breakfast w/ juice, fresh fruit, homemade baked goods, hot beverages; specialties—German apple puffed pancakes, artichoke heart frittata, rolled basil omelet; seafood dinners are avail. for $15 per guest (poultry & vegetarian meals also avail.). **Recreation** Biking, birding, kayaking, boat charter, visit local villages of Ewell & Rhodes Point, local Women's Crab Picking Co-op, Smith Island Cultural Museum; bikes & canoes provided w/ stay; Blessing of the Fleet (spring), Memorial Day & July 4th celebrations on the green. **Amenities & Services** Meetings (10).

ACCOMMODATIONS

Units 4 guest rooms. **All Rooms** AC, books, water views. **Some Rooms** Rocking chairs. **Bed & Bath** Queen (3), double (1), twin (1), four-poster (1); 1 private bath, 3 shared baths, tub (3). **Favorites** Black Walnut Point—queen & twin bed, rocking chair, bright, perky floral accessories. **Comfort & Decor** The public areas have a fresh mix of antiques and flea market finds plus collection of books on Smithiana. Guest room furnishings are English cottage wicker with floral motifs on windows and beds. Quilts add hominess. You can retreat to the balconied greenhouse to read, meditate, bird watch, and enjoy the solitude.

RATES, RESERVATIONS, & RESTRICTIONS

Deposit Personal check for 1 night, refund w/ 21-days notice less 15%. **Discounts** None. **Credit Cards** No. **Check-In/Out** Ferryboats arrive at 1:15 & 5:45 p.m./11 a.m. **Smoking** No. **Pets** No. **Kids** Age 6 & older. **Minimum Stay** 2 nights on weekends. **Open** All year (except Dec., Jan., & Feb.). **Hosts** Sharryl Lindberg & LeRoy Friesen, 2955 Tylerton Rd., Tylerton, 21866. **Phone** (410) 425-3541. **E-mail** silentmu@shore.intercom.net. **Web** innofsilentmusic.com.

Zone 16

Annapolis & Southern Maryland

Southern Maryland was the scene of pivotal moments in American history. Today, **St. Mary's City,** an 800-acre living history site at Maryland's southernmost tip, commemorates the 1634 arrival of 140 settlers who pressed to make religious freedom a cornerstone of local government. Costumed guides interpret seventeenth-century life in the re-created community tavern, tobacco plantation, and Native American hamlet. The largest building is a reconstruction of Maryland's first state house, a Jacobean-style brick building which served as capitol until 1695, when Maryland's government relocated to Annapolis. A modern visitors center emphasizes Maryland's role in establishing religious freedom in the Colonies.

This historic area has a strong sense of authenticity. However, urban sprawl has taken over the outskirts and highways north of the city, where the Patuxent River Naval Air Station helps to fuel the local economy. **Patuxent River Naval Air Museum,** the Navy's official museum, displays 17 naval aircraft, including the F-14 and F-18, a great model collection, and exhibits on G-forces, ejection seats, and propulsion.

Solomons, at the southern end of Calvert County offers fishing and boating, plus the first-rate **Calvert Maritime Museum.** Miocene fossils on display comprise the second largest collection outside the Smithsonian Museum. Even better, you can hunt for whales' teeth and bone bits from the Miocene area on your own at nearby **Calvert Cliffs State Park.**

Chesapeake Beach, a community of modest homes, offers gorgeous water views, a railway museum, and a water park, plus lots of fresh seafood.

In scenic **Annapolis,** traffic moves at a slow pace, because streets fan out from two-lane circles around St. Anne's Episcopal Church and the State House where George Washington resigned his Army commission. Homes of three former residents, all signers of the Declaration of Independence, are open for tours. Most impressive of all is the **Hammond-Harmond House,** a classic example of Georgian architecture.

Local **St. John's College,** the nation's third-oldest college, bases its curriculum on reading literary classics known as "The Great Books." A few blocks away is the **U. S. Naval Academy,** known as the Yard. Here, visitors can see the Rogers Ship Models Collection, the Chapel with Tiffany stained-glass windows, and the marble crypt of naval hero John Paul Jones.

Annapolis is a sailing town. But if skies are cloudy and the wind is still, consider a visit to the archaeological dig at **LondonTown,** in a 23-acre county park on the South River. Only one house survives in what was once a bustling tobacco port of 300 residents. Now a museum, it is adjacent to a trash dump packed with Colonial artifacts including pieces of plates, ale-tankard handles, pipe stems—real evidence of a once-lively community.

Annapolis and southern Maryland are home to numerous well-run bed-and-breakfasts. Prices tend to be higher in Annapolis, but there's much to do throughout the area—and this description only scratches the surface.

FOR MORE INFORMATION

Annapolis & Anne Arundel County
26 West St.
Annapolis, MD 21401
(410) 280-0445

Calvert County Dept. of Economic Development & Tourism
176 Main St., Suite 101
Prince Frederick, MD 20678
(800) 331-9771

St. Mary's County Dept. of Economic and Community Development
23115 Leonard Hall Dr.
Leonardtown, MD 20650
(800) 327-9023

55 EAST, Annapolis

OVERALL ★★★★ | QUALITY ★★★★ | VALUE ★★★ | PRICE $140–$150

An art historian, Mat specialized in nineteenth- and twentieth-century French and American art and taught art history at Ohio State. Tricia earned her doctorate in English and worked as a professional fund raiser and community volunteer in Columbus. Together, they share enthusiasm for art, cooking, and travel, as well as broad knowledge of the area. Their house is full of books and art, including American graphics and folk art from Mexico, Peru, Puerto Rico, and the Galapagos. One parlor displays Tricia's mother's collection of Japanese items, including a kimono, embroidered fabric, and wood block prints. But there's no need to tiptoe around all these treasures. You're invited to take off your shoes, put your feet up, and relax.

SETTINGS & FACILITIES

Location Historic district. **Near** Naval Academy, state capitol, harbor. **Building** 1864 Federal w/ bracketed wood cornice & lintels. **Grounds** City lot w/ New Orleans–style inner courtyard, garden, & fountain. **Public Space** 2 LR, DR, kitchen, powder room, guest pantry. **Food & Drink** Full breakfast w/ juice, fruit, homemade breads; specialties—toasted pecan corn waffles w/ Creole chicken, Napoleon cornbread w/ smoked turkey, scrambled eggs & cream cheese sauce, apricot-raisin bread pudding w/ sausage & sautéed zucchini; evening cookies, M&Ms anytime. **Recreation** Boating & fishing on Spa Creek, the Severn River, and Chesapeake Bay, sightseeing, antiquing. **Amenities & Services** Classic videos, fax & e-mail; meetings (8).

ACCOMMODATIONS

Units 3 guest rooms. **All Rooms** AC, phone jack, computer port, fresh flowers, monogrammed robes, hair dryer, sitting area. **Some Rooms** Porch access (2), gas fireplace (2). **Bed & Bath** King (1), queen (2); private baths w/ tubs. **Favorites** Russell—great fabric & rug, host's art (his medium is crayon), small balcony; Mary S. Johnson—Vermont castings stove, tiny deck, antique chest & sink. **Comfort & Decor** The house blossoms with antiques, family heirlooms, great fabrics, and original art. One parlor features a gas fireplace with cypress mantel, one-and-a-half walls of book shelves with tomes on art, travel, and literature. The Japanese embroidery and Arts & Crafts desk is notable. The upstairs hall displays pre-twentieth-century American Indian pottery. Breakfast is served on fine china with crystal and linens—in the courtyard when weather permits.

RATES, RESERVATIONS, & RESTRICTIONS

Deposit Credit card, refund /w 10-days notice less $25. **Discounts** Extended stay. **Credit Cards** AE, V, MC. **Check-In/Out** By arrangement/11 a.m. **Smoking** No. **Pets** No (terrier in residence). **Kids** Age 12 & over. **Minimum Stay** 2 nights on weekends. **Open** All year (except part of Jan. & Feb.). **Hosts** Tricia & Mat Herban, 55 East St., Annapolis, 21401. **Phone** (410) 295-0202. **Fax** (410) 295-0203. **E-mail** triciah @erols.com. **Web** www.annearundelcounty.com/hotel/55east.html.

ANNAPOLIS INN, Annapolis

OVERALL ★★★★★ | QUALITY ★★★★★ | VALUE ★★★ | PRICE $250–$375

History has touched this house. According to legend, six signers of the Declaration of Independence were guests here, as were numerous slaves, who were smuggled through a brick-lined tunnel which runs through the cellar. It once belonged to Dr. James Murray, who was Thomas Jefferson's doctor when he lived in Annapolis. The current owners arrived in 1998. Joe, a native of New York City, retired from AT&T and Alexander retired from the foreign language department of a Manhattan high school after 25 years. As new innkeepers, they target upscale clients with over the top decor. Their goal is to take your mind off of everything except having fun—and according to some guest diaries, they do.

SETTINGS & FACILITIES

Location Residential street in the historic district. **Near** City Dock, U. S. Naval Academy, state capitol, St. John's College. **Building** 1770 Georgian & Greek Revival row house, 3 stories, stucco w/ 1884 entrance. **Grounds** City lot w/ enclosed yard, shade trees, garden, brick patio, koi pond. **Public Space** Foyer, LR, DR, powder room, 2nd floor deck. **Food & Drink** Full breakfast w/ baked goods, fruit, & beverages; specialties—

Dutch baked apple pancakes, French toast stuffed w/ brie & raspberries, scrambled eggs w/ Italian herbs & tomato in puffed pastry w/ sausage; will cater to dietary restrictions; afternoon tea on request. **Recreation** Sailing, tours of gardens, historic houses, & museums, Naval Academy, antiquing, art galleries, theater, opera, symphony; Jazz Festival (June), boat show (Oct.), renaissance festival (mid-Aug.–mid Oct.). **Amenities & Services** Fax, cable TV, phone & modem access, concierge & laundry service, can arrange massage, Spanish & Italian spoken; meetings (8), receptions (25).

ACCOMMODATIONS

Units 3 suites. **All Rooms** AC, phone jack, hair dryer, fresh flowers, TV avail. **Some Rooms** Balcony (1), wood burning fireplace (2). **Bed & Bath** Kings, can convert to twins, extra beds; private baths, 2 whirlpools. **Favorites** Murray suite—sophisticated & elegant, pocket doors w/ etched glass, marble fireplace, silk damask, French-style cabinet, marble bath w/ hand-painted ceramic sink, bidet, whirlpool; Rutland suite—wooden & plaster angels add a romantic touch, egg & dart wall art, original 1770 floor, hand-carved bed from Portugal, cedar-lined closet, marble bathroom w/ bidet, private 3rd floor location, exclusive use of outside deck. **Comfort & Decor** The foyer has rare alternating dark walnut and pine-planked floors. The living and dining rooms are stately salons with ornate gilded rosette moldings, huge Austrian crystal chandeliers, marble fireplaces, oil paintings, marble and bronze sculptures, antique furnishings, Oriental rugs, and Belgian, French, and English tapestries. Live like an aristocrat for a day.

RATES, RESERVATIONS, & RESTRICTIONS

Deposit 50%, refund w/ 10-days notice less $25, holidays and special weekends vary. **Discounts** Some extended stays. **Credit Cards** AE, V, MC. **Check-In/Out** 3–6 p.m./11 a.m. **Smoking** No. **Pets** No. **Kids** Over age 18. **No-Nos** Quiet hours between 11 p.m. and 8 a.m. **Minimum Stay** 2 nights on weekends, 3 nights on major holidays. **Open** All year. **Hosts** Joe Lespier & Alexander DeVivo, 144 Prince George St., Annapolis, 21401. **Phone** (877) 295-5200 or (410) 295-5200. **Fax** (410) 295-5201. **E-mail** info@annapolisinn.com. **Web** annapolisinn.com.

CHEZ AMIS, Annapolis

OVERALL ★★★★½ | QUALITY ★★★★ | VALUE ★★★★ | PRICE $115–$140

The property is unusual because it was originally three buildings, which were joined together to serve as a grocery store from 1920 to the late 1970s. You still see shelving and details from that configuration. Breakfast is served on pewter and custom-made Annapolis pottery. Guests sit at a homemade picnic-style wooden table called a stammtisch table, a German expression for a table set aside for family and friends. It is a reminder that these hosts spent 6 of Don's 25 years as a U. S. Army lawyer living in Germany. In all they lived in 17 different locations worldwide. Mickie is a retired Washington, D.C. tour guide. They arrived in Annapolis in 1994 and have built up a good business with lots of repeat customers. You'll feel welcome.

SETTINGS & FACILITIES

Location Historic district, 1 block to capitol, Naval Academy, and harbor. **Near** 33 mi. east of Washington, D.C., 25 mi. south of Baltimore. **Building** 1920 corner grocery store, restored (original section 1850). **Grounds** 3 small city lots. **Public Space** LR w/ breakfast area. **Food & Drink** Full breakfast w/ juice, fruit, hot beverages home-baked goods; specialties—eggs Rico, pflannkuchen pancakes, baked blueberry French toast; complimentary sodas, beer, & wine, M & Ms & peanuts anytime. **Recreation** Sailing, golf, sightseeing, Naval Academy football games; boat shows (Oct.), Parade of Lights (Dec.). **Amenities & Services** Videos, fax & e-mail.

ACCOMMODATIONS

Units 4 guest rooms. **All Rooms** AC, cable TV, robes, coffeemaker. **Some Rooms** Capital view (1). **Bed & Bath** King (2), queen (2), down-filled comforters; 3 private baths, 1 detached private bath w/ skylight, tubs (2). **Favorites** Capitol room—king brass bed w/ flag spread, handmade quilts, antique school desk, church pew, dresser & sewing machine, pedestal porcelain sink w/ antique mirror, autographed photos of famous politicians, books on Washington, D. C., history, & the Civil War; Judges Chamber—grandma's quilts, law books, judge art, law journals, gavel bookends, autographed photo of Sandra Day O'Connor with the hosts. **Comfort & Decor** The living room emphasizes the grocery store look with its original tin ceiling, Georgia pine floors (formerly shelving for canned goods), and barrels of flour, sugar, and sweets. Bins in the original oak counter contain nuts, candies, and other foods. Antique quilts, teapots, and eclectic family heirlooms add charm. Cozy anytime, the home is especially joyful when decorated for Christmas.

RATES, RESERVATIONS, & RESTRICTIONS

Deposit Credit card to hold, refund w/ 3-days notice less $15. **Discounts** No. **Credit Cards** V, MC. **Check-In/Out** Flexible/11 a.m. **Smoking** No. **Pets** No. **Kids** Over age 10. **Minimum Stay** 2 nights on weekends. **Open** All year. **Hosts** Mickie & Don Deline, 85 East St., Annapolis, 21401. **Phone** (888) 224-6455 or (410) 263-6631. **Fax** (410) 295-7889. **E-mail** stay@chezamis.com. **Web** chezamis.com.

FLAG HOUSE, Annapolis

OVERALL ★★★★½ | QUALITY ★★★★ | VALUE ★★ | PRICE $140–$200

What's unique about this bed-and-breakfast is that the hosts fly the state and national flags of their guests during their stay. They have about 100 in their repertoire. The location is great—within four blocks of 15 historic sites, numerous art galleries, antique shops and restaurants, two live theaters, plus the Naval Academy, St. Johns College, and the harbor. You can keep very busy, or kick back in a front porch swing. Lighting is good for enjoying a book. Bill, a political science teacher specializing in Russian politics and international relations, now teaches part time at the Naval Academy. Charlotte is a former director of student health. As parents of a USNA graduate, they can help academy visitors understand life on that campus.

SETTINGS & FACILITIES

Location Residential street in the heart of the historic district. **Near** 0.5 block to both the U. S. Naval Academy & waterfront. **Building** 1870 Victorian, originally 2 townhouses, mansard roof on 3 sides. **Grounds** City lot w/ floral border in front, parking (rare in Annapolis). **Public Space** LR, DR, front porch. **Food & Drink** Full breakfast w/ fruit, cereals, baked goods, hot beverages; specialties—egg casserole, French toast, waffles. **Recreation** Visit historic homes, kayaking, boating, waterfront activities, summer theater, water taxis, symphony, ballet, St. John's College; Baltimore–Annapolis Bike Trail, water park, swim at Sandy Ridge State Park; Power & Sail Boat Shows (Oct.), First Night, 4th of July Festival. **Amenities & Services** Fax; meetings (10).

ACCOMMODATIONS

Units 4 guest rooms, 1 suite. **All Rooms** AC, cable TV, ceiling fan, hair dryer. **Some Rooms** Couches; disappointingly small. **Bed & Bath** King (4), twin (1), four-poster (1); private baths. **Favorites** Suite—sitting room w/ 2 couches, blue & white decor, plain, unadorned, quality; B—striped & botanical wallpaper, Chinese chest, twin beds. **Comfort & Decor** The cozy living room/library is enlivened by nautical art and books plus a Chinese wedding chest and objects that emphasize trade with China. The dining room's Russian samovar prompts conversation and prints of Naval history, flags, swords, and sailing mementos add character.

RATES, RESERVATIONS, & RESTRICTIONS

Deposit 1 night, refund w/ 10-days notice less $25. **Discounts** Extended stay. **Credit Cards** V, MC. **Check-In/Out** 4–6 p.m./11 a.m. **Smoking** No. **Pets** No (dog in residence). **Kids** Age 10 and over. **No-Nos** Candles in the rooms. **Minimum Stay** 2 nights on weekends. **Open** All year (except Thanksgiving & Christmas). **Hosts** Charlotte & Bill Schmickle, 24 Randall St., Annapolis, 21401. **Phone** (800) 437-4825 or (410) 280-2721. **Fax** (410) 280-0133. **E-mail** info@flaghouseinn.com. **Web** flaghouseinn.com.

GEORGIAN HOUSE, Annapolis

OVERALL ★★★ | QUALITY ★★★★ | VALUE ★★★ | PRICE $115–$175

An Annapolis historic landmark, the house was the clubhouse of the Forensic Club in pre-Revolutionary times. Members met two Mondays each month for five hours. Along with dinner, they enjoyed a convivial exchange of speeches, discussions, and debates on some political, historical, or ethical question. At the close, members voted on such questions as: is it morally lawful to keep slaves (as early as 1765) and is it justifiable to take up arms against a tyrant or even dethrone a king? Results were kept secret. Club members included William Paca, Samuel Case, and Thomas Stone—all of whom were to sign the Declaration of Independence—and Charles Willson Peale, who painted more portraits of George Washington than any other artist.

SETTINGS & FACILITIES

Location Residential street in the historic district. **Near** Naval Academy, state capitol, museums, art galleries. **Building** 1747 Georgian townhouse, brick w/ black shutters. **Grounds** City lot w/ gardens. **Public Space** Foyer, LR, sitting room, DR, 2nd floor gathering room, brick patio. **Food & Drink** Full breakfast w/ juice, fruit, homemade baked goods, hot beverages; specialties—caramel apple French toast, vegetable frittata, breakfast pizza w/ ham, tomato, & cheese. **Recreation** Waterfront activities, historic tours, boat rides. **Amenities & Services** Videos, laundry facilities; meetings (8).

ACCOMMODATIONS

Units 3 guest rooms, 1 suite. **All Rooms** AC, phone connection, candy. **Some Rooms** TV & VCR (2), ceiling fan (3). **Bed & Bath** Queen beds, four-poster (1), sleigh (1); private baths, tub (1). **Favorites** Thomas Stone suite—queen rice bed, gas log fireplace, wing-backed recliner, sleeper sofa, Oriental rug, wide plank floor, large bath, very traditional. **Comfort & Decor** The house has two staircases and multiple levels. It features original pine floors, six fireplaces, Norman Rockwell prints, period window treatments, and nice floral bouquets. Except for the suite, guest rooms are small. The top floor, with its sloping ceilings and exposed beams, is rustic.

RATES, RESERVATIONS, & RESTRICTIONS

Deposit Credit card to hold, refund w/ 7-days notice less $15. **Discounts** Winter, midweek, extended stay. **Credit Cards** AE, V, MC. **Check-In/Out** 3 p.m./noon. **Smoking** No. **Pets** No. **Kids** No. **Minimum Stay** 2 nights on weekends. **Open** All year. **Hosts** Michele & Dan Brown, 170 Duke of Gloucester St., Annapolis, 21401. **Phone** (800) 557-2068 or (410) 263-5618. **Fax** (410) 263-5618. **E-mail** georgian@erols.com. **Web** georgianhouse.com.

WILLIAM PAGE INN, Annapolis

OVERALL ★★★½ | QUALITY ★★★★ | VALUE ★★★ | PRICE $115–$195

This building was the meeting place for the Democratic Club for more than 50 years before being converted to a bed-and-breakfast. The current owner, a former theatrical lighting designer, arrived in 1987, making him the most seasoned full-time innkeeper in Annapolis. He still enjoys meeting people, but takes lengthy and unusual winter vacations to recharge his own batteries. Amsterdam, Romania, Tibet, and China were recent choices. The house is very traditional, save that four guest rooms are named for characters from the childrens' book *Charlotte's Web*. Breakfasts are not served at the table, but in the common room at informally grouped seating. If you want to relax in the corner with the sports page, you can.

SETTINGS & FACILITIES

Location Heart of historic district. **Near** Waterfront, Naval Academy. **Building** 1908 cedar shake single-family detached home, renovated in 1987, newly reshingled. **Grounds**

Corner city lot. **Public Space** Common room. **Food & Drink** Full breakfast w/ juice, fruit, homemade pastries & breads; specialties—oven egg Florentine, Colonial egg casserole, oven baked French toast w/ brown sugar & pecans. **Recreation** Historic home & garden tours, antiquing, waterfront activities, Naval Academy tour, regional & state parks. **Amenities & Services** Health club access, massage avail, fax & e-mail.

ACCOMMODATIONS

Units 4 guest rooms, 1 suite. **All Rooms** AC, phone jack, fresh flowers in season, hair dryer. **Some Rooms** Cable TV (suite). **Bed & Bath** Queen beds, four-posters (2); sleigh (1); 3 private baths, 2 shared baths, robes provided, whirlpools (2), tub (1). **Favorites** Marilyn suite—spacious, private, dormer windows & window seats, sofa, cable TV, queen sleigh bed, large bath w/ whirlpool tub; Fern room—ground floor w/ private porch. **Comfort & Decor** The pleasant common room has a brick-faced fireplace, wet bar, and formal seating. The style throughout is traditional with lots of antiques and family heirlooms. Two bathrooms have stained glass panels.

RATES, RESERVATIONS, & RESTRICTIONS

Deposit Credit card to hold, refund w/ 10-days notice less $25. **Discounts** Seniors, AAA. **Credit Cards** V, MC. **Check-In/Out** 4–6 p.m./ noon. **Smoking** No. **Pets** No. **Kids** Over age 12. **Minimum Stay** 2 nights on weekends. **Open** All year (except January). **Host** Robert Zuchelli, 8 Martin St., Annapolis, 21401. **Phone** (800) 364-4160 or (410) 626-1506. **Fax** (410) 263-4841. **E-mail** wmpageinn@aol.com. **Web** williampageinn.com.

BACK CREEK INN, Solomons

OVERALL ★★★★½ | QUALITY ★★★★ | VALUE ★★★★ | PRICE $95–$145

These hosts met at a Bible study when their husbands were stationed at the nearby Patuxent River Naval Air Station. Carol is an accomplished artist who works in oils and watercolors. She taught art in Hershey, Pensylvania, and exhibited as far away as Florida. Her paintings adorn numerous walls and most are for sale. Lin expresses her creative talents in the kitchen. Both women are avid gardeners. They've created a peaceful haven where travelers can sit facing the water and experience a quieter, calmer frame of mind. Some guests say that even the birds—among them a pair of swans and a resident blue heron—seem friendlier. This place surrounds you with peaceful pleasures, and there are several good restaurants nearby.

SETTINGS & FACILITIES

Location On the tree-lined banks of Back Creek. **Near** Chesapeake Bay & Pautuxent River, 75 mi. south of Washington, D.C. **Building** 1880 waterman's house, blue w/ white trim. **Grounds** 1 acre w/ 0.5 acre garden of bulbs, azaleas, dogwood, small pond, private deep water dock (you can arrive by boat), outdoor hot tub. **Public Space** Common room, breakfast room, guest fridge. **Food & Drink** Full or cont'l breakfast; specialties—Chesapeake crab quiche, back creek tea scones, baked French toast; beverages & cookies anytime. **Recreation** Boating, fishing, crabbing, biking, museums, antiquing, Cypress Swamp, Calvert Cliffs State Park, Ann Marie Gardens; 2 bikes avail. **Amenities & Services** Fax, picnic baskets avail. w/ 48-hr. notice, pool privileges at Zahniser's; meetings (14).

ACCOMMODATIONS

Units 6 guest rooms, 1 cottage. **All Rooms** AC, cable TV, phone, hair dryer, alarm clock, robes. **Some Rooms** Ceiling fan (4), coffeemaker (3), private entrance (3), fireplace (2), fresh flowers. **Bed & Bath** King (2), queen (5); private baths, tubs (4). **Favorites** Lavender—cottage w/ screened porch, king bed, French doors, fireplace; Chamomile—original master bedroom, large, 6 windows w/ creek view, blue decor, lots of Dorothy ruffles; Thyme—paisley walls, gas fireplace, stenciling, king bed, tub. **Comfort & Decor** The common room is made cozy by tan rattan couches, a Vermont Castings stove, green plants, ceiling fan, and Windsor chairs. Seven windows and two glass doors open to water and garden views. A TV hides in an armoire. Guest rooms vary greatly in size and style, some are cozy while others are upscale.

RATES, RESERVATIONS, & RESTRICTIONS

Deposit Credit card to hold, refund w/ 3-days notice less $5. **Discounts** Corp., gov't. at $66 per diem, 10% off for 3 or more nights. **Credit Cards** V, MC. **Check-In/Out** 1–8 p.m./11 a.m. **Smoking** No. **Pets** No. **Kids** Over age 12. **Minimum Stay** 2 nights on weekends. **Open** All year (except Dec. 20–Jan. 2). **Hosts** Carol Pennock & Lin Cochran, 210 Alexander St., Box 520, Solomons, 20688. **Phone** (410) 326-2022. **Fax** (410) 326-2946. **Web** www.bbonline.com/md/backcreek.

SOLOMONS VICTORIAN INN, Solomons

OVERALL ★★★★ | QUALITY ★★★½ | VALUE ★★★ | PRICE $90–$175

The inn was originally the family home of Clarence Davis, the renowned builder of early-twentieth-century sailing yachts. It sits in the center of a 128-year-old fishing village, on a flat fishhook-shaped bit of land at the confluence of the Pautuxent River and the Chesapeake Bay. Across the street is a deep, protected harbor rimmed with marinas. You can stroll down quiet streets bordered by small houses of weathered wood. Bait and tackle shops, restaurants, gift shops, and ice cream stores beckon. At the Calvert Marine Museum, river otters named Bubble and Squeak perform in a 9,000-gallon tank. Nearby, there are two lighthouses to explore, a marshwalk to meander, and a sculpture garden to enjoy. And, you can dig for fossils in local sandstone cliffs. This inn's appeal lies in its simplicity—a chance to experience the sights and sounds of an earlier, quieter era.

SETTINGS & FACILITIES

Location Facing a working Chesapeake Bay marina. **Near** 75 mi. south of Washington, D. C., 8 mi. northeast of Patuxent River Naval Air Station. **Building** 1906 Queen Anne w/ newly built carriage house, yellow w/ blue trim. **Grounds** Corner city lot w/ lawn, flowering shrubs, trees, fountain, gardens. **Public Space** LR, sitting room, glassed-in breakfast porch, front porch. **Food & Drink** Full breakfast w/ juice, fruit, muffins; specialties—stuffed French toast w/ peach preserves & cream cheese, brie en croissant, shrimp puff; beverages & cookies anytime. **Recreation** Sailing, fishing, strolling the non-commercial Riverwalk, Calvert Marine Museum, Drum Point & Cove Point Lighthouses, fossil hunting, antiquing, charter & party boat fishing; Christmas Walk, 4th of July, Appreciation Day. **Amenities & Services** Fax, disabled access (1); meetings (16).

ACCOMMODATIONS

Units 8 guest rooms. **All Rooms** AC, cable TV, phone, full length mirror, clock radio. **Some Rooms** Private entrance (2), fridge & microwave (2), ceiling fan (2), balcony (1). **Bed & Bath** King (2), queen (6); private baths, whirlpools (3). **Favorites** Harbor Sunset—private entrance, bright, king four-poster, brass chandelier, lace curtains, marble framed double whirlpool, balcony w/ harbor view; Solomon's Sunset—3rd floor privacy, pine walls, dormer roof lines, slant windows, iron & wicker sleigh bed, blue double whirlpool, seating overlooks partial water view & working marina. **Comfort & Decor** Furnishings are eclectic. Guest rooms range from ordinary to elegant, so choose carefully.

RATES, RESERVATIONS, & RESTRICTIONS

Deposit 1 night, refund w/ 2-days notice. **Discounts** Winter, corp., gov't. **Credit Cards** AE, V, MC. **Check-In/Out** 3–8 p.m./11 a.m. **Smoking** No. **Pets** No. **Kids** Over age 13. **Minimum Stay** 2 nights April 1–Nov. 15, 3 nights on some holiday & event weekends. **Open** All year. **Hosts** Helen & Richard Bauer, 125 Charles St., Solomons, 20688. **Phone** (410) 326-4811. **E-mail** solvictinn@chesapeake.net. **Web** www.chesapeake.net/solomonsvictorianinn.

BROME-HOWARD INN, St. Mary's City

OVERALL ★★★★½ | QUALITY ★★★★½ | VALUE ★★★★ | PRICE $80–$160

The main house, which was moved to this location in 1994, sits back from St. Mary's River, with a panoramic view of the area where settlers arrived in 1634 seeking religious freedom. The Kelleys, a young couple from Washington, D.C., spent three years restoring the state-owned house, which was neglected after 130 years in the Brome and Howard families. Michael is a chef and Lisa is a designer. Together they specialize in running a fine-dining restaurant Thursday through Sunday, and catering large weddings and corporate events. The guest rooms, all with water views, are lovely. Especially attractive is the third floor suite, for which journalist Sally Quinn, a neighbor and friend, gifted them with French toile wallpaper.

SETTINGS & FACILITIES

Location On St. Mary's River, adjacent to Historic St. Mary's City museum. **Near** Godiah Spray Tobacco Plantation, Point Lookout State Park, St. Mary's College. **Building** 1840 Greek Revival farmhouse, w/ 4 chimneys, white w/ pale blue shutters. **Grounds** 30 acres of formal British gardens, access to 5 mi. of well-marked hiking trails, slave quarters, carriage, smoke, & dairy houses. **Public Space** Foyer, parlor, 2 DR, 2 porches, patio. **Food & Drink** Full breakfast w/ fruit, fresh baked bread or scones; specialties—blueberry muffins, French toast, smoked duck w/ red pepper & blue saga cheese, dietary requests honored; tea on request. **Recreation** Hiking, biking, charter fishing, kayaking, golf, horseback riding, antiquing, Naval Air Museum, Historic St.Mary's City museum; 4 adult's & 2 child's bikes avail. **Amenities & Services** Videos, massage avail., laundry, fax, phone; meetings (75), weddings (500).

ACCOMMODATIONS

Units 3 guest rooms, 1 suite. **All Rooms** AC, phone, fresh flowers, coffeemaker. **Some Rooms** Fireplace (3). **Bed & Bath** King (1), queen (3), pencil post (1), featherbeds; private baths, tubs (4). **Favorites** McKenney—queen bed w/ partial canopy, fireplace, river view, rattan seating, crimson walls w/ white trim, romantic; Quinn-Bradlee suite—powder blue & white toile wallpaper, slanted walls, antique rugs, a light-filled space. **Comfort & Decor** The parlor has pale green walls, a fireplace, television, games, and a piano. The library features histories and contemporary books. The pink-walled dining room has an Oriental carpet and family heirlooms. Guests sit on Windsor chairs at small tables. The area doubles as a busy restaurant.

RATES, RESERVATIONS, & RESTRICTIONS

Deposit Credit card to hold, refund w/ 14-days notice. **Discounts** Corp., military. **Credit Cards** AE, V, MC. **Check-In/Out** 3 p.m./noon. **Smoking** No. **Pets** No (dog in residence). **Kids** Sometimes. **Minimum Stay** No. **Open** All year (except Christmas Day). **Hosts** Lisa & Michael Kelley, 11821 Rosecroft Rd., Box 476, St. Mary's City, 20686. **Phone** (301) 866-0656. **Fax** (301) 866-9660. **E-mail** kelleyms@tqci.net. **Web** bromehowardinn.com.

Part Six

Virginia

Almost everywhere you go in Virginia, you'll be reminded of or touched by the roles the state's sons and daughters played in American history.

It was Virginia-born Thomas Jefferson's life-long fascination with language history that led him to combine key words from Old English and Latin and translate heartfelt ideals about freedom into the language of politics. The Declaration of Independence, which he drafted, has a profound influence on the lives of Americans. It was Virginia-born George Manson who helped to draft Virginia's Declaration of Rights, which became the model for our federal Bill of Rights. And it was a Virginian, James Madison, who helped to frame our Bill of Rights.

The state's 100 historic sites include the homes of these patriots, along with the homes of George Washington at Mount Vernon and Woodrow Wilson in Staunton—two of the eight former Presidents of the United States who hailed from Virginia.

Land played a prominent role in the state's history, as well. The word plantation conjures up the genteel lifestyle of Virginia's early aristocracy, in a timeless era before wristwatches when people read the classics, bred horses to chase foxes, and swapped sparkling repartee at a seemingly endless series of house parties. Never mind that less than three percent of the population could afford to live on such a grand scale.

Privileged families who owned riverfront plantations would probably be pleased to know that twenty-first-century travelers can still access their homes and appreciate them as architectural masterpieces. They are mostly Georgian or Queen Anne in style, with solid, balanced, and symmetrical exteriors. Interior detailing is exquisite. Period antiques and family heirlooms fill high-ceilinged rooms. Separate dependencies housed the kitchen, meat house, icehouse, laundry, tutor's house, and servants' quarters, while stables and coach houses sat well away to protect the owners from odors and summer flies. Some of these plantations are open for tours. A few are now bed-and-breakfasts where you can experience a bit of Virginia's old-time lifestyle firsthand.

Virginia honors its earliest European settlers at **Staunton's Frontier Culture Museum,** where costumed staff re-enact primitive farming and blacksmithing techniques. In **Williamsburg,** visitors can experience the culture of eighteenth-century Virginia. In **Bristol,** a museum archives major events in the history of country and bluegrass music. At **Big Stone Gap,** a museum depicts the history of Southwest Virginia during the 1890s. A new museum in **Winchester** will honor the history of the Shenandoah Valley.

Civil War battlefields now draw visitors to **Manassas, Fredericksburg, Chancellorsville, The Wilderness, Spotsylvania, Petersburg,** and a ring of military positions around **Richmond.** And the war itself is examined at **Pamplin Historical Park.**

Arlington National Cemetery commemorates all the nation's wars. Among the 200,000 interred remains are three unknown soldiers and two presidents: William Howard Taft and John F. Kennedy. Nearby, the Iwo Jima Statue honors the Marine Corps.

Sightseers based in northern Virginia could spend weeks discovering **Washington, D.C.,** where many attractions are free. The city takes on a dramatically different aspect after dark, when spotlights illuminate the White House, Capitol, Senate and House office buildings, Supreme Court, Library of Congress, Jefferson, Lincoln and Korean War Memorials, and the Washington Monument. If the slightest breeze ripples the water at the Reflecting Pool, the reflection doesn't work. But you may be lucky.

Virginia isn't all about history. There are theme parks, beaches, fishing holes, horseback riding rings, hiking and biking trails, golf courses, and festivals. Clean, pastel-colored, family-friendly **Virginia Beach** is the state's largest city. Shops are set back a block from an oceanfront walkway and parallel a three-mile-long bicycle and skating path. Sculptures add wit and whimsy to the open spaces. Across the state, **Shenandoah National Park** offers fabulous vistas and a host of outdoor recreation. It's famed **Skyline Drive** parallels 94 miles of the Appalachian Trail and extends another 460 miles on the Blue Ridge Parkway through North Carolina.

Most of the bed-and-breakfasts in Virginia are in the state's central area. Many throughout the state are both gracious and gorgeous.

FOR MORE INFORMATION

Virginia Tourism Corp.
1629 K St. NW
Washington, D.C. 20006
(800) 934-9184

Zone 17

Capital Suburbs/ Northern Virginia

Northern Virginia offers both history and high tech. Within hours, you can drive from city pleasures to scenic byways, from high-toned horse country society to humbling Civil War battlefields.

Alexandria's Old Town is a National Historic Landmark, still looking very much as it did when it was George Washington's hometown. This city's finest eighteenth-century building is the restored house of John Carlyle, who hosted a meeting where attendees expressed the ideas that eventually led to the Revolutionary War.

On walking tours through Alexandria guides dressed in waistcoat, breeches, three-cornered hat, and haversack point out Gadsby's Tavern, the Apothecary Shop, Washington's townhouse, and his family pew at Christ Church. Alexandria has a fun side, as well. Pleasure boats line its harbor on the Potomac. Scores of artists produce an astonishing variety of art in studios converted from a former torpedo factory. Trendy boutiques, collectible shops, and upscale coffee bars line the city's main thoroughfares. On weekends, King Street attracts a vibrant cast of street performers, mimes, musicians, and magicians. The atmosphere is so festive, Alexandria now calls itself the "fun side of the Potomac."

Nearby, **Fort Ward** is one of 68 hastily-dug Union forts built in a ring around Washington, D.C. during the Civil War. The fifth largest and best-preserved of that defense system, its elongated, star-shaped design became a prototype. An on-site museum houses Civil War memorabilia, including maps, uniforms, letters, photographs, and camp items.

It's a nine-mile drive from Alexandria to **Mount Vernon.** Down the road is the mansion Washington bought for his niece. Frank Lloyd Wright's **Pope-Leighey House** was moved to the grounds of this estate and it is also open to visitors.

If you head west into **Loudoun County,** horseback riding and gourmet picnicking at historic estates are pleasures to savor in an area dotted with mansions, horse farms, and history-rich towns. At **Oatlands,** built in 1803 by George Carter, imposing white pillars on the three-story front porch may remind you of Tara from *Gone With the Wind.* The mansion escaped the torches of Union soldiers, but the plantation could not survive without slave labor.

Morven Park, home to two former governors, overlooks 1,200 acres of private trust land. Inside, six wall tapestries from Brussels depict the Second Punic Wars. In the north wing, the six-room **Museum of Hounds and Hunting** displays memorabilia from local hunt clubs. A barn protects the antique vehicles of the Winmill Carriage Collection—about 70 in all.

Downtown **Leesburg,** settled about 1758, is a national historic landmark. Wall-to-wall antique, tea, and souvenir shops line its brick sidewalks. Exhibits at **Loudoun Museum** remind you that most major battles of the Civil War's eastern theater took place within 60 miles of the town. The closest was at Ball's Bluff, a small battle that cast a long shadow.

Strip malls, gas stations, and fast food chains line the roads into **Manassas.** But, all of a sudden you cross an invisible line and enter the nineteenth century. **Manassas National Battlefield Park** spreads out before you across lush, green, forested, and totally natural countryside. Silence prevails. The entire 5,500-acre park has just nine plaques and monuments.

Heading west from Washington, you encounter the land of hunting cavalcades, one of rural America's most beautiful sights. Few communities are more focused on equestrian sports than **Upperville** and **Middleburg,** where residents devote fortunes to every phase of horsemanship from fox hunting to point-to-point racing, steeplechasing, polo, and thoroughbred breeding.

Arlington County is the urban center of northern Virginia. **Arlington House** is a national memorial to Robert E. Lee, and a portion of Lee's estate forms **Arlington National Cemetery.** The litany of monuments in nearby Washington, D.C. is well known. The city also offers artistic and cultural attractions as well as dining and nightlife.

Northern Virginia is dominated by cookie-cutter hotels. However, you can also find a variety of bed-and-breakfasts where in-the-know owners will help you maximize your valuable vacation time.

FOR MORE INFORMATION

Alexandria Visitors Center
221 King St.
Alexandria, VA 22314
(800) 388-9119; funside.com

Arlington County Visitors Center
735 18th St. S.
Arlington, VA 22202
(800) 677-6267; stayarlington.com

Fairfax County CVB
8300 Boone Blvd. Ste. 450
Vienna, VA 22182
(703) 790-3329; visitfairfax.org

Loudoun Tourism Council
108-D South St., SE
Leesburg, VA 22075
(800) 752-6118; visitloudoun.org

Prince William County/Manassas Visitor Information Center
200 Mill St.
Occoquan, VA 22125
(703) 491-4045; visitpwc.com

Warrenton-Fauquier County Visitor Center
183-A Keith St.
Warrenton, VA 20188
(800) 820-1021 or (540) 347-4414

Winchester-Frederick County Visitors Center
1360 S. Pleasant Valley Rd.
Winchester, VA 22601
(800) 662-1360;
www.shentel.net/wfcedc

LITTLE RIVER INN, Aldie

OVERALL ★★★★ | QUALITY ★★★½ | VALUE ★★★ | PRICE $105–$225

Aldie, named for founder Charles Fenton Mercer's ancestral home in Scotland, is a convenient stopping place for those planning to explore pricey Middleburg just down the road. The ebullient personality of host Tucker Withers makes a visit to this combination Colonial and rustic property memorable. Guests routinely find a note on the counter with instructions to check themselves in, enjoy a snack of juice, sodas, cheese, and crackers in the fridge and make themselves at home. Tucker can be reached at his antique store a few doors away. In the morning he's on hand to cook breakfast and entertain guests with fact-filled, humor-laden repartee. His Dutch apple baby recipe is a cherished memory of our visit.

SETTINGS & FACILITIES

Location On John S. Mosby Hwy. (Rte. 50). **Near** 5 mi. east of Middleburg, 17 mi. east of the Blue Ridge Mountains, 18 mi. west of Dulles Airport, 12 mi. northwest of Manassas National Battlefield Park. **Building** 1865 Federal w/ 1790s cottage, log cabin. **Grounds** 2.8 acres w/ garden, patios, stone fountain. **Public Space** Sitting room, breakfast room, kitchen. **Food & Drink** Full breakfast w/ juice, fruit; specialties—Dutch apple baby, baked French toast, egg & cheddar cheese casserole; snacks avail. **Recreation** Picnics, swimming, golf, tennis, canoeing; Steeple Chase Racing (spring & fall), Aldie Harvest Festival (Oct.). **Amenities & Services** Laundry, fax, access to Narrowgate for swimming; meetings (20) & receptions (100).

ACCOMMODATIONS

Units 5 guest rooms, 2 suites. **All Rooms** AC, phone. **Some Rooms** Fireplace (3), private entrance (2). **Bed & Bath** Double (6), twin (5); 4 private baths, 3 shared baths. **Favorites** Log cabin—log walls, fireplace, sitting room, 2nd floor bedroom. **Comfort & Decor** Rooms in the main house are small and have prim, tidy furnishings, including antiques, oil paintings, and Colonial details. Two detached buildings offer comfort and privacy. The buildings sit close to Route 50 and share a small backyard used for al fresco breakfasts in good weather.

RATES, RESERVATIONS, & RESTRICTIONS

Deposit Credit card, refund w/ 7-days notice. **Discounts** 2 consecutive nights. **Credit Cards** AE, V, MC, D, DC. **Check-In/Out** 3 p.m./noon. **Smoking** No. **Pets** No. **Kids** Cottages only. **Minimum Stay** 1 night. **Open** All year. **Hosts** Mary Ann & Tucker Withers, Box 117, Aldie, 20105. **Phone** (703) 327-6742. **Fax** (703) 327-6645. **Web** aldie.com.

BERRYVILLE, Berryville

OVERALL ★★★★ | QUALITY ★★★★ | VALUE ★★★★ | PRICE **$95–$145**

Both of these innkeepers enjoy meeting people, so opening a bed-and-breakfast was natural. Jan, who grew up in Mississippi, taught high school English, while Don, who is Canadian, directed a school athletic program. Currently, she finds time to read and cook, while he pursues his love for golf and Civil War history. Together, they enjoy working in the yard. After visiting numerous bed-and-breakfasts in Europe and New England, they opened this property in 1993, and, so far, they seem delighted with their career moves. "We've never had a bad experience. Bed-and-breakfast guests must be the nicest people in the world," says Jan.

SETTINGS & FACILITIES

Location On Rte. 34 in residential area. **Near** 10 mi. east of Winchester, 40 mi. west of Dulles Airport, 70 mi. northwest of Washington, D.C. **Building** 1915 English country manor, white stucco w/ green trim. **Grounds** 1 acre w/ mature trees, grape arbor, boxwoods, flower garden, rockery. **Public Space** LR, sitting room, DR, back porch. **Food & Drink** Full breakfast w/ fruit, juice; specialties—French toast, omelets, crêpes; beverages avail. anytime. **Recreation** Horseback rides, the Appalachian Trail, Harpers Ferry, Civil War sites, Skyline Drive; boating, tubing, kayaking, fishing & swimming in the Shenandoah River. **Amenities & Services** Videos, fax & e-mail; meetings (12).

ACCOMMODATIONS

Units 2 guest rooms, 1 suite. **All Rooms** AC, TV & VCR, phone, fresh flowers, hair dryer, robes. **Some Rooms** Fireplace (1). **Bed & Bath** Queen (2), double (2); private baths, 1 whirlpool, 2 tubs. **Favorites** Victorian—massive antique bed, English wallpaper, Persian rug, wood fireplace, sofa bed. **Comfort & Decor** Traditional upholstered and stuffed furnishings were chosen for comfort. A fireplace and lots of books and magazines invite relaxation.

RATES, RESERVATIONS, & RESTRICTIONS

Deposit Credit card to hold, refund w/ 7-days notice. **Discounts** Corp. **Credit Cards** AE, V, MC, D. **Check-In/Out** 3 p.m./11 a.m. **Smoking** No. **Pets** No. **Kids** Prior notice requested. **Minimum Stay** 2 nights on weekends May, June, Oct., & Nov. **Open** All year. **Hosts** Jan & Don Riviere, 100 Taylor St., Berryville, 22611. **Phone** (800) 826-7520 or (540) 955-2200. **Fax** (540) 955-0922. **E-mail** bvillebb@shentel.net. **Web** berryvillebb.com.

BAILIWICK INN, Fairfax

OVERALL ★★★★★ | QUALITY ★★★★½ | VALUE ★★★ | PRICE $145–$330

Staying here is a virtual history lesson; excellent books and pictures put you in touch with the accomplishments of Virginia luminaries, including Thomas Jefferson, Lord Fairfax, James Monroe, John Mosby, Robert King Carter, Robert E. Lee, Patrick Henry, George Mason, Nelly Custis, and Confederate spy Antonia Ford. During the Civil War, the attic was used as a hospital. In fact, the first Confederate officer death in action took place on the lawn across the street. Don't miss tea in the formal parlor, where ladies don frilly, wide-brimmed hats to partake in old-fashioned style. Consider staying for dinner, prepared in chef Jeff Prather's award-winning restaurant.

SETTINGS & FACILITIES

Location Heart of downtown. **Near** George Mason University, Vienna Metro stop, Wolf Trap Performing Arts Park, 15 mi. southeast of Dulles Airport, 16 mi. southwest of Washington, D.C., 20 mi. east of Manassas. **Building** 1809 Federal townhouse w/ 1830 addition & 1985 restoration, red brick w/ green shutters, white trim. **Grounds** City lot w/ brick patio, flowerpots, hanging baskets, flower borders. **Public Space** 2 parlors, DR, powder room, 2nd floor balcony. **Food & Drink** Full breakfast w/ juice, fruit plate, fresh muffins; specialties—omelet w/ boursin cheese & shrimp, open face fritatta w/ smoked duck & asparagus, maple-smoked sausage & French toast stuffed w/ cream cheese & raspberries, pancakes w/ banana & pineapple; regular afternoon tea 4–5 p.m. w/ scones, 2 jams, Devonshire cream, fruit and cheese tray; high tea 2 days a week includes 5 sweets and 5 savories. **Recreation** Visit historic homes & Civil War battlefields. **Amenities & Services** Privileges at Gold's Gym, murder mystery weekends, monthly winemaster dinners, disabled access (1); meetings (18), outdoor functions (85).

ACCOMMODATIONS

Units 13 guest rooms, 1 suite. **All Rooms** AC, cable TV, dataport, phone, robes, minibar, alarm clock, CD player, American history memorabilia. **Some Rooms** Fireplace (4), oriental rug. **Bed & Bath** King (1), queen (12), twin (1), canopy (3), four-poster (2), sleigh (1); 13 private baths, detached (1), whirlpools (2), tub (1). **Favorites** George Washington—four-poster, dark forest green w/ burgundy & cream trim, log fireplace flanked by bookshelves, part of original house w/ a rustic, early-American look; John Marshall—high bed w/ steps, elaborate leaf molding, chandelier, feels like a library. **Comfort & Decor** Public rooms have 12-foot ceilings, pocket doors, elaborate molding, and chair rails. Furnishings include Early American and Queen Anne pieces, formal drapery, cabinets displaying china, books, and oil portraits. Guest rooms are named for famous Virginia people, including two women. Each one is accessorized with appropriate portrait, biography, newspaper clippings, and clothing items.

RATES, RESERVATIONS, & RESTRICTIONS

Deposit 1 night, refund w/ 14-days notice less $15. **Discounts** Gov't., negotiated corp., shoulder & low season. **Credit Cards** AE, V, MC. **Check-In/Out** 2 p.m./11 a.m. **Smoking** No. **Pets** No. **Kids** Discouraged. **Minimum Stay** None. **Open** All year. **Hosts** Ann & Christopher Sheldon, 4023 Chain Bridge Rd., Fairfax, 22030. **Phone** (703) 691-2266. **Fax** (703) 934-2112. **E-mail** theinn@bailiwick.com. **Web** bailiwickinn.com.

BUCKSKIN MANOR, Hillsboro

OVERALL ★★★½ | QUALITY ★★★★½ | VALUE ★★★ | PRICE **$115–$185**

A lot of time and planning went into choosing and restoring this remote property at the end of a one-third-mile driveway. It attracts students at the Equissage School in nearby Round Hill, which teaches equestrians massage. And, it's next door to the country estate of former Secretary of State Madelaine Albright, where she often entertained foreign dignitaries. The innkeepers moved here after a seven-year assignment with the U.S. NATO mission in Belgium. Gail gave up a career as a clinical psychologist to cook and garden, while Jeff continues to commute to work in Washington, D.C. City folks will find this an unusually restorative environment, but it's a long way to a good restaurant so consider making dinner arrangements.

SETTINGS & FACILITIES

Location Rolling countryside set back from Rte. 671. **Near** 4 mi. west of Hillsboro, 8 mi. east of Harpers Ferry, 30 mi. west of Dulles Airport, 50 mi. west of Washington, D.C. **Building** 1750 log & mortar tavern, American chestnut logs w/ white chinking, restored, plus additions. **Grounds** 65 acres w/ fish pond, floating dock, 2 terrace gardens, paths, swimming pool, horse barn, original spring & smoke houses. **Public Space** 2 LR, library, DR, 2 porches, powder room. **Food & Drink** Full breakfast w/ juice, fruit; specialties—eggs Benedict & Neptune (w/ smoked salmon), ham & cheese crêpes, quiche, French toast; complimentary sherry; dinner can be arranged. **Recreation** Horseback rides, golf, Civil War battlefields (Antietam, Balls Bluff, Gettysburg), vineyards & wine tastings, water sports (fishing poles, kayaks, pedalboats, & row boats provided); Strawberry Festival (spring), Waterford Arts Fair (Oct.). **Amenities & Services** Videos, laundry, e-mail.

ACCOMMODATIONS

Units 3 guest rooms, 1 cottage. **All Rooms** AC, ceiling fan. **Some Rooms** Fireplace (1), private entrance (1), robes. **Bed & Bath** Queen (2), double (2), twin (1); private baths, 1 detached, double whirlpools (2), tubs (2). **Favorites** Squires—exposed log wall, low ceiling, whirlpool. **Comfort & Decor** One living room has eclectic contemporary furnishings with bay windows, a circa 1730 clock, and fireplace. The other is more rustic—a reminder that the original building was a one-room tavern. The decor balances collections of contemporary art and antique Belgian lace.

RATES, RESERVATIONS, & RESTRICTIONS

Deposit Credit card to hold, refund w/ 3-days notice. **Discounts** 3 nights or more 10%, multiple rooms Jan.–Mar. **Credit Cards** V, MC. **Check-In/Out** 3 p.m./11 a.m. **Smoking** No. **Pets** No. **Kids** $40 per child. **Minimum Stay** 2 night minimum May–June, Sept.–Oct. **Open** All year (except Jan.). **Hosts** Gail & Jeff Bogert, 13452 Harpers Ferry Rd., Purcellville, 20132. **Phone** (888) 668-7056 or (540) 688-6864. **E-mail** inndeeper@buckskinmanor.com. **Web** buckskinmanor.com.

GOODSTONE INN & ESTATE, Middleburg

OVERALL ★★★★★ | QUALITY ★★★★★ | VALUE ★★★ | PRICE **$195–$495**

Loudoun County's premier accommodation opened in 1998 for visitors to the quaint town of Middleburg, known for foxhunting and equestrian events as well as vineyards. The swimming pool sits by the ivy-covered remains of the original mansion, built in 1743 by a member of the Leith family. It now neighbors some of the area's finest private estates, including those of the late Paul Mellon and the late Pamela Harriman. Middleburg, population 600, dates back to 1787, and its narrow streets are lined with art galleries, boutiques, and specialty shops. The countryside is dotted with pastureland and thoroughbreds. Taking an elaborately packed picnic hamper to watch horse races from a hilltop is a much-loved tradition.

SETTINGS & FACILITIES

Location In the Blue Ridge Mountain foothills surrounded by private estates & horse farms. **Near** 2.5 mi. northwest of Middleburg. **Building** Carriage house w/ converted horse stalls, French farm cottage, spring house, Dutch cottage. **Grounds** 265-acre estate w/ rolling lawns, 0.5 mi. walking trail. **Public Space** Great room, heated pool.

Food & Drink Full breakfast w/ juice, fresh fruit compote, baked goods; specialties—corned beef hash, Belgian waffles, eggs Aberdeen or Florentine; open bar 24-hours, modest afternoon tea on weekdays, full tea on weekends, Sunday brunch, picnic hampers. **Recreation** Golf, canoeing, mountain biking, bird watching, horseback riding; canoes & mountain bikes avail.; Middleburg Spring Race Meet, Virginia Gold Cup (May), Stable Tour (May), Upperville Horse Show (June), International Gold Cup Race (Oct.), Friday Night Polo (June–Sept.). **Amenities & Services** Outdoor sauna, stereo system, fresh flowers, on-site massage, golf privileges at Stoneleigh Country Club, fax & e-mail; meetings (35), weddings (150).

ACCOMMODATIONS

Units 9 guest rooms, 4 suites. **All Rooms** AC, phone, fresh flowers, hair dryer, seasonal robes, CD player/clock radio, iron & board, ceiling fan. **Some Rooms** Balcony (2), TV (3), private entrance (2). **Bed & Bath** Queens, canopy (4), four-poster (7), sleighs (2); private baths, 11 whirlpools, 2 claw-foot tubs. **Favorites** Warburg suite—queen four-poster, sitting parlor, green & rose country fabrics, whirlpool soaking tub, French doors lead to front porch w/ rockers; Harvest room—ceiling beams, carved armoire, whirlpool bath & steam shower, good views. **Comfort & Decor** The great room features a stone fireplace, heart-of-pine floors, and furniture upholstered with English and French country-style fabrics. Guest rooms have luxury toile and tartan fabrics and wallcoverings. Believe it or not, the carriage house guest rooms are remodeled horse stalls. The three other buildings, located some distance away, range from rustic to country chic. Each has its own common areas—ideal for social networking.

RATES, RESERVATIONS, & RESTRICTIONS

Deposit 1 night, refund w/ 14-days notice. **Discounts** None. **Credit Cards** AE, V, MC. **Check-In/Out** 3–6 p.m./11:30 a.m. **Smoking** No. **Pets** No. **Kids** No. **Minimum Stay** 2 nights on public holidays. **Open** All year. **Host** Keith Halford, Mgr., 36205 Snake Hill Rd., Middleburg, 20117. **Phone** (540) 687-4645. **Fax** (540) 687-6115. **E-mail** goodstone@erols.com. **Web** www.johansens.com/goodstoneinn.

ASHBY INN, Paris

OVERALL ★★★★★ | QUALITY ★★★★½ | VALUE ★★★ | PRICE $145–$300

Fascinated by the rolling hills, winding roads, and estates of Virginia hunt country, these hosts exited Washington, D.C. to open this inn in 1984. The heart of Ashby Inn is its kitchen, run by chef Hilton Hunter. Menus change weekly, producing what some consider one of north Virginia's finest restaurants. Passionate about food, the innkeepers grow their own vegetables and herbs and buy local produce like goat cheese, blueberries, and heirloom apples. Well-connected with the local equestrian set, they help guests explore the area. The bucolic setting is magnificent—a village (population 60) whose name was changed from Punkinville in 1820 to honor the Marquis de Lafayette when he visited local landowner Peter Glascock.

SETTINGS & FACILITIES

Location On a hilltop in the heart of hunt country. **Near** 62 mi. west of Washington, D.C. **Building** 1829 Colonial & converted 1-room schoolhouse. **Grounds** 4 acres, manicured lawns, perennial flower beds, vegetable & cutting gardens. **Public Space** Sitting room, library, restaurant, taproom, porch, patio. **Food & Drink** Full breakfast w/ juice, cereal, baked goods; specialties—pancakes, omelets, frittata, w/ sides of sautéed apples, bacon, roast potatoes, fresh asparagus; dinner Wed.–Sat., Sun. brunch. **Recreation** The Appalachian Trail, the Shenandoah River, point-to-point racing & horse shows, vineyards, antiquing, golf, tennis, Civil War sites, Sky Meadows State Park, Blandy Experimental Farm (Virginia's arboretum); stable tour (May), Upperville Horse Show (June), Daffodil Tour (spring). **Amenities & Services** Club privileges for golf & tennis w/ prior notice, massage avail., fax & e-mail; meetings (20), wedding (150).

ACCOMMODATIONS

Units 10 guest rooms. **All Rooms** Clock, fresh flowers, hair dryer. **Some Rooms** Fireplace (5), balcony (5), coffeemaker (4), TV (4), phone (4), private entrance (1). **Bed & Bath** Queen (9), double (2); private baths, 1 detached, 9 tubs. **Favorites** Glascock & Lafayette—window seats w/ mountain view, pencil-post canopy beds, two easy chairs facing wood burning fireplaces, private decks; Fireplace—main building, painted floor, rustic w/ vaulted ceiling, eggplant walls. **Comfort & Decor** Public space is dominated by three restaurants and a tavern, where accessories include hunt-themed posters and drawings, political cartoons, and horse brasses. The best, most spacious guest rooms are in the restored schoolhouse. Details in the smaller main building guest rooms include handmade quilts, hand-painted wardrobes, and blanket chests.

RATES, RESERVATIONS, & RESTRICTIONS

Deposit Credit card, refund w/ 7-days notice. **Discounts** 15% Sun.–Thur. **Credit Cards** V, MC. **Check-In/Out** 3 p.m./noon. **Smoking** No. **Pets** No. **Kids** Over age 12. **Minimum Stay** None. **Open** All year (except Jan. 1). **Hosts** Roma & John Sherman, 692 Federal St., Paris, 20130. **Phone** (540) 592-3900. Fax (540) 592-3781. **E-mail** celebrate @ashbyinn.com. **Web** ashbyinn.com.

INN AT VAUCLUSE SPRING, Stephens City

OVERALL ★★★★ | QUALITY ★★★★ | VALUE ★★★ | PRICE **$126–$265**

Guests here can choose from a variety of accommodations—from the elegant main house to more casual and family-friendly out buildings. The Mill House cottage, which faces an idyllic pond fed by Vaucluse Spring, was moved here by the late John Chumley, an artist who used it as his studio. Chumley's paintings, some on loan from his widow, are displayed throughout the property. It's hard to believe, but Neil says "this was a scary-looking place" when they came in 1995. But Barry, a builder of custom buildings, had the know-how to transform them all in the next two years. The hosts are gracious and steer guests to the area's best attractions. One drawback is that to get to here you must drive past a junkyard and electric power station. Don't get discouraged, the trip is worthwhile.

SETTINGS & FACILITIES

Location Rural setting 2.5 mi. south of Stephens City, 9 mi. south of Winchester, 10 mi. northwest of Front Royal. **Near** Belle Grove Plantation, Shenandoah National Park, Shenandoah River, Civil War battlefields. **Building** 1780 Federal-style manor house, plus

4 1800s buildings moved here and reconstructed. **Grounds** 100 acres in rolling orchard, strolling gardens, herb garden, swimming pool. **Public Space** Foyer, sitting room, 2 DR, winter kitchen (lower floor), porch. **Food & Drink** 3-course breakfast w/ fresh fruit, juice, home-baked goods; specialties—fresh asparagus quiche, Challah bread French toast w/ crème fraîche, banana-stuffed French toast, eggs Benedict; afternoon cookies, wine & beer avail.; 4-course dinner for guests on Sat. w/ reservation. **Recreation** Golf, horseback riding, wineries, caverns, antiquing, historic homes, hot air ballooning; Apple Blossom Festival (May), Mushroom Festival (June). **Amenities & Services** Disabled access (Stephen's room), fax & e-mail, massage avail.; meetings (15), weddings (100).

ACCOMMODATIONS

Units 9 guest rooms, 1 suite, 2 cottages. **All Rooms** AC, hair dryer, fireplace, clock radio. **Some Rooms** Private entrance (4), ceiling fan (1). **Bed & Bath** King (3), queen (9); private baths, 9 whirlpools, 2 double whirlpools. **Favorites** Jones—main house, upscale traditional w/ slanty floors, 2 remote-control gas fireplaces (1 facing the whirlpool), mountain view; Mill House cottage—on a pond w/ waterfall, double whirlpool, sink, fridge, coffeemaker, private patio. **Comfort & Decor** The manor house features high ceilings, spacious rooms, elegant furnishings, and a wide porch with rocking chairs and a sweeping meadow view. The Chumley Homeplace keeping room has a stone fireplace, beamed ceiling, and log walls; guest rooms have modern touches like plush comforters. The more traditional Gallery Guest House, which faces the swimming pool, is ideal for families.

RATES, RESERVATIONS, & RESTRICTIONS

Deposit 50%, refund w/ 7-days notice less $25. **Discounts** Corp. **Credit Cards** V, MC. **Check-In/Out** 3–5 p.m./11 a.m. **Smoking** No. **Pets** No. **Kids** Over age 10. **Minimum Stay** 2 nights all weekends. **Open** All year. **Hosts** Neil & Barry Myers, 231 Vaucluse Spring Lane, Stephens City, 22655. **Phone** (800) 869-0525 or (540) 869-0200. Fax (540) 869-9546. **E-mail** mail@vauclusespring.com. **Web** vauclusespring.com.

BLACK HORSE INN, Warrenton

OVERALL ★★★½ | QUALITY ★★★★ | VALUE ★★★ | PRICE $125–$295

This house was used as a Confederate hospital during the Civil War. It was named for the Black Horse Cavalry, a group of Confederate lawyers who gathered in 1858 and later led a successful charge at the First Battle of Manassas. Subsequently, they served as bodyguards, escorts, and scouts for Generals Stonewall Jackson and Joseph E. Johnston. Local legend says the house was also used as a courthouse after Union troops burned the town of Warrenton. The current owner is a mining engineer who moved from Connecticut in 1991 to work for the government. An avid equestrian, she enjoys fox hunting and point-to-point racing. Watching her two horses graze in the meadow enhances the picturesque setting.

SETTINGS & FACILITIES

Location Rolling hills & woodlands 1.5 mi. east of Warrenton. **Near** Shenandoah National Park, Fredericksburg & Spotsylvania National Military Parks, Manassas National Battlefield. **Building** 1850 Georgian-style. **Grounds** 20 acres w/ small horse pasture, barn, flagstone terrace. **Public Space** Reception hall, great room, DR, library, 3 enclosed porches. **Food & Drink** Early coffee, full breakfast w/ fresh fruit, baked goods; specialties—French toast, tomato-basil strata, blueberry blintzs, all w/ sausage or bacon; afternoon tea & sherry. **Recreation** Golf, tennis, hot-air ballooning, hiking, fox hunting, horse shows, horseback riding, wineries, antiquing, water sports on the Shenandoah & Rappahanock Rivers;Virginia Gold Cup Race (May & Sept.), Friday polo matches (May-Oct.). **Amenities & Services** Classic videos; meetings & weddings (200).

ACCOMMODATIONS

Units 7 guest rooms, 1 suite. **All Rooms** AC, phone line w/ dataport, hair dryer, clock, turn-down service. **Some Rooms** TV & VCR (1), clock radio (1), private entrance (1), fireplace (4), ceiling fan (5), robes (2). **Bed & Bath** Queen (6), double (1), canopy (5) four-poster (3); private baths, 4 whirlpools, 3 claw-foot tubs. **Favorites** Great Expectations—fireplace, porch w/ sunset views, marble bathroom w/ whirlpool; Fox & Grape—stone walls, hand-hewn beams, kitchenette, whirlpool, fox-hunting motif, cozy; Garden Room—floral fabrics & borders, canopy bed, claw-foot tub. **Comfort & Decor** Spacious rooms have traditional furniture, wood floors, Oriental carpets, antiques, and reproductions. An antique writing desk, formal dining room, book-lined den, and side porch with riding photos and accessories add interest.

RATES, RESERVATIONS, & RESTRICTIONS

Deposit One night, refund w/ 14-days notice. **Discounts** None. **Credit Cards** AE,V, MC. **Check-In/Out** 4–8 p.m./11 a.m. **Smoking** No. **Pets** Yes, horses only. **Kids** Over age 12. **Minimum Stay** 2 nights on weekends May–Oct. **Open** All year. **Host** Lynn Pirozzoli, 8393 Meetze Rd., Warrenton, 20187. **Phone** (540) 349-4020. Fax (540) 349-4242. **E-mail** relax@blackhorseinn.com. **Web** blackhorseinn.com.

INN AT LITTLE WASHINGTON, Washington

OVERALL ★★★★★ | QUALITY ★★★★★ | VALUE ★★★ | PRICE $340–$865 (SURCHARGES MAY APPLY)

Save your money. Because you'll need a bundle to stay and dine in this highly-acclaimed country inn, located in a tiny unspoiled town (now a National Historic District) in the Blue Ridge Mountains. Sitting on property that George Washington surveyed in 1749, it opened as an inn in 1978. Extraordinary attention to detail and an obsession with perfection has placed the Inn at Little Washington atop numerous lists of the best places to stay and dine—in the world. The 15,000-bottle wine cellar has won the *Wine Spectator* Grand Award repeatedly since 1995 and chef Patrick O'Connell was James Beard Chef of the Year in 2001. Besides the ornate decor, unique touches include dinner plates displayed in the elevator and pistachio-flavored mock dog biscuits along with a note from Rose the Dalmation wishing you sweet dreams as part of the turn-down service.

SETTINGS & FACILITIES

Location Center of town surrounded by farmland & Blue Ridge Mountains. **Near** 67 mi. west of Washington, D.C. **Building** Unassuming white building festooned w/ flags.

Grounds Several adjacent town lots w/ courtyard garden, koi pond, small fountain. **Public Space** Lobby, LR, monkey lounge, restaurant, loggia, terrace, powder room. **Food & Drink** Cont'l breakfast is brought to your room or served on a terrace w/ garden view; afternoon tea; 4-course dinners are served nightly in season in an 80-seat restaurant (the prix fixe range is $98–138 per person plus beverages); room service 24-hours, picnic lunches avail., special diets honored. **Recreation** Fly-fishing for mountain trout, horseback riding, golf, wineries, hot-air ballooning, touring Shenandoah Valley; July 4th Parade, Hunt Cup & Gold Cup races. **Amenities & Services** Massage, fax, laundry, disabled access; weddings (24).

ACCOMMODATIONS

Units 9 guest rooms, 5 suites. **All Rooms** Orchids, fresh flowers, safe, lighted magnifying mirror, hair dryer, fireplace, robe, turn-down service. **Some Rooms** Clock radio (2), balcony (9), wet bar (2). **Bed & Bath** King (9), queen (5), half-draped canopy (9), 4-inch featherbeds; private baths, 4 whirlpools, 9 tubs. **Favorites** #3—French toile fabrics, upholstered ceiling w/ moiré & gold stars, Portuguese hutch, king bed with canopy, mirror, & tassels, bath has hand-painted Portuguese tile; #12—blue & gold decor, Chinese antiques & accessories, built-in sofa, ceramic pears, loft bedroom, elaborate bath w/ large tiles, 2 walls of mirrors (it's the most expensive). **Comfort & Decor** A cocoon of luxury and a sense of theater envelops the inn. All decor and guest rooms were created by a London stage and set designer. Layering of expensive fabrics and whimsical touches are everywhere. The dining room has hanging rose silk lampshades with fringe. Even the powder room is gorgeous. Guest room sizes vary and some are shockingly small. Overall, it's a place for the wealthy to be tranquil and connect with nature and for special celebrations when you want all to be perfect. There's a staff of 90 to see to your every need.

RATES, RESERVATIONS, & RESTRICTIONS

Deposit One night, refund w/ 14-days notice. **Discounts** None. **Credit Cards** V, MC. **Check-In/Out** 3 p.m./noon. **Smoking** Monkey lounge only. **Pets** No (2 Dalmatians on premises). **Kids** Yes (babysitter avail., room service provided). **Minimum Stay** No. **Open** All year, except Tuesdays (open 7-days mid-April–May & mid-Sept.–Oct.). **Hosts** Reinhardt Lynch, owner, Patrick O'Connell, chef, Box 300, Washington, 22747. **Phone** (540) 675-3800. **Fax** (540) 675-3100. **Web** "We're very low tech."

L'AUBERGE PROVENCALE, White Post

OVERALL ★★★½ | QUALITY ★★★★ | VALUE ★★ | PRICE $145–$250

These innkeepers sold two restaurants in Key West and set out to find their dream project on an air search of the East Coast, with Alain at the controls of their small plane. It took six months to locate Mount Airy, which they bought in 1980 and renamed L'Auberge Provencale. For the interiors, they achieved the distinctive look they wanted with French country fabrics and walls faux-painted in warm, interesting colors. You can expect good things from the kitchen—breakfasts are a tour de force. Sitting close to the road was an asset when the property served as a stagecoach stop, but nowadays the noise from passing cars drowns out the birdsongs. For seclusion, ask about their Villa La Campagnette, located three miles north. That 18-acre property has only two suites and a guest room, but offers a swimming pool, hot tub, and whirlpool.

SETTINGS & FACILITIES

Location Rural setting in hunt country facing the Blue Ridge Mountains. **Near** On Rte. 340, 1 mi. south of Rte. 50, 9 mi. southeast of Winchester, 12 mi. north of Skyline Drive entrance. **Building** 1753 Federal-style farmhouse w/ blue fieldstone front, gray siding, white pillars, several additions. **Grounds** 9.5-acre farm w/ pond, fruit orchards, herb, perennial, & vegetable gardens. **Public Space** Sitting room, powder room, porch, full-service restaurant. **Food & Drink** Full multi-course breakfast, menu changes daily; specialties—banana crêpes, wild mushroom fritatta w/ smoked bacon, duck breast & potatoes; orange blossom waffles w/ raspberries, poached egg in potato nest w/ spinach & roast quail; poached pear stuffed w/ walnuts, cream cheese egg roll w/ asparagus, mushrooms, & chutney; dinners avail. **Recreation** Horseback riding, golf, vineyard tours, canoeing, ballooning, Sky Meadows State Park, Long Branch Plantation, Glen Burnie Gardens; Apple Blossom Festival (early May), Bastille Day celebration (July 14), Balloon Festival (mid Oct.). **Amenities & Services** Massage avail. club privileges at Dominion Health & Fitness Center in Front Royal (9 mi.); meetings (20), weddings (150).

ACCOMMODATIONS

Units 9 guest rooms, 2 suites. **All Rooms** AC, fresh flowers, hair dryer, coffeemaker. **Some Rooms** Fireplace (6), balcony (3), private entrance (5), dataport (3). **Bed & Bath** King (2), queen (7), double (3), canopy (2), four-poster (5), sleigh (1); private baths, 1 whirlpool, 9 tubs. **Favorites** Suite Romantique—hand-carved king alcove bed, fireplace, French country fabrics, pine antiques, cushy chairs, double whirlpool, Italian tiles, private entrance by herb & flower garden; #9—French country look, four-poster canopy bed, wood fireplace, hand-painted Spanish tile. **Comfort & Decor** Walls have been sponge-painted in warm colors to ressemble leather and accessorized with melon and mustard-colored chairs and couches. A smattering of antiques from Alain's grandfather, who ran a hotel in Avignon, France, includes copper pots, wine racks, and wrought iron utensils. Attractive birds made from reeds by a family of Spanish artisans are for sale. Guest rooms vary from upscale in the main house to a more contemporary, artsy-crafty look in a newly-built wing.

RATES, RESERVATIONS, & RESTRICTIONS

Deposit 1 night, refund w/ 7-days notice. **Discounts** AAA, seniors 10%. **Credit Cards** AE, V, MC, D. **Check-In/Out** 3 p.m./11 a.m. **Smoking** No. **Pets** No (1 cat on premises). **Kids** Over age 10. **No-Nos** Noise after 10 p.m. **Minimum Stay** None. **Open** All year (except Jan. 1–23). **Hosts** Celeste & Alain Borel, Box 190, White Post, 22663. **Phone** (800) 638-1702 or (540) 837-1375. Fax (540) 837-2004. **E-mail** cborel@shentel.net. **Web** laubergeprovencale.com.

Zone 18

Tidewater Virginia

At some point each year, the salt content of Virginia's coastal waterways spikes as river and ocean water mix. But, no matter how salty it gets, there are opportunities for visitors to enjoy water sports and more in this land of patriots, plantations, and beaches.

Virginia Beach is the state's largest city. Its most popular attraction, besides the beach, is the **Virginia Marine Science Museum,** which is dedicated to the state's indigenous life forms. Exhibits simulate coastal river, salt marsh, and Chesapeake Bay habitats.

In **Norfolk,** the annual **Waterfront International Arts Festival** offers a mixture of cultural events. Other key attractions are **Nauticus: The National Maritime Center, Chrysler Art Museum, Norfolk Botanical Gardens,** and a tribute to U.S. Army General Douglas MacArthur.

At **Norfolk Naval Base,** aircraft carriers, submarines, and battleships are lined up like giant toys. At **Newport News,** the **Mariners' Museum** recognizes 3,000 years of nautical history and the **Virginia Living Museum** focuses on natural science. The world-class **Virginia Air & Space Museum** in **Hampton** resembles a glass butterfly with huge steel wings. It's as well endowed as its national counterpart in Washington, but far less crowded.

Fort Monroe at **Old Point Comfort** is the largest enclosed stone fortification ever built in the United States. This "Gibraltar of the Chesapeake" was Union-held throughout the Civil War. Exhibits at the **Casemate Museum** include personal items owned by President Jefferson Davis, who was imprisoned here for five months.

Yorktown's shining hour came in 1781 when the French fleet outmaneuvered British ships and brought the American Revolution to a close. Monuments, historic houses, and sight-and-sound exhibits at **Yorktown Victory Center** capture the moment.

You can learn about the harsh realities of life in Britain's first permanent settlement circa 1607 at **Jamestown Settlement** and **Jamestown**

Colonial National Historical Park. Attractions include reproductions of James Fort, a Powhatan Indian village, and three ships that brought colonists to Virginia.

Williamsburg was Virginia's political, social, and cultural capital for 81 years, until 1780. John D. Rockefeller, Jr. and Dr. W.A.R. Goodwin rescued the town from obscurity in 1926 by initiating a movement to reshape it into a living history monument. Visitors can now see 88 restored buildings, homes, shops, gardens, outbuildings, grazing meadows, and split-rail fencing that evoke the Colonial era. Crafters and interpreters in period garb energize the village, reenact past events, and star in quality programs.

Nearby **Carter's Grove** shows early agricultural practices and life in slave quarters. An archaeological museum interprets a seventeenth-century settlement at this site. Three miles away, **Busch Gardens** offers an array of amusement rides and shows and **Water Country USA** has 30 water rides.

Along a 50-mile stretch of the James River, you have access to restored plantations including **Sherwood Forest, Evelynton,** and **Berkeley.**

For a crowd-free, leisurely pace, the best time to visit the popular historic areas of tidewater Virginia is November through March. The number of high-quality bed-and-breakfasts is limited, but hospitality is tops.

FOR MORE INFORMATION

Chincoteague Chamber of Commerce Visitor Center
6733 Maddox Blvd.
Chincoteague, VA 23336
(757) 336-6161

Hampton Visitors Center
710 Settlers Landing Rd.
Hampton, VA 23669
(800) 800-2202;
www.hampton.va.us/tourism

Newport News Tourist Information Center
13560 Jefferson Ave.
Newport News, VA 23603
(888) 493-7386; newport-news.org

Norfolk Visitors Information Center
4th View St.
Norfolk, VA 23503
(800) 368-3097; www.norfolk.va.us

Virginia Beach Visitors Information Center
2100 Parks Ave.
Virginia Beach, VA 23451
(800) 446-8038; vabeach.com

Williamsburg Area CVB
201 Penniman Rd.
Williamsburg, VA 23187
(800) 368-6511; visitwilliamsburg.com

EDGEWOOD PLANTATION, Charles City

OVERALL ★★★½ | QUALITY ★★★★ | VALUE ★★★ | PRICE $130–$198

Lovers of fanciful, even serious collectibles will appreciate this over-the-top country house. The hosts, who rescued it from dereliction, have filled their mini-museum with antiques bought from estate auctions plus everything from finger purses to a traveling bidet, vintage hats, and toy bunnys enjoying a tea party. In places it looks like a decorator's dream gone bonkers. The house, notable for its exquisite winding staircase, has had multiple lives, as a church, post office, telephone exchange, restaurant, nursing home, and host to Civil War General Jeb Stuart. It has its own legend—the haunting story of "Lizzie," who etched her name on a bedroom window before dying of a broken heart after her lover failed to return from the war. Charm, eccentricity, Southern hospitality—you'll find it here.

SETTINGS & FACILITIES

Location Across from Berkeley Plantation entrance. **Near** 20 mi. west of Richmond, 28 mi. east of Williamsburg. **Building** 1849 Carpenter Gothic Revival, white clapboard w/ green shutters, 5 chimneys. **Grounds** 7 acres w/ 1725 grist mill, slave quarters, swimming pool, English gardens, 2 gazebos. **Public Space** Parlor, 2 DR, kitchen, porch, patio, basement. **Food & Drink** Full breakfast w/ juice, fruit plate, beverages; specialties—almond French toast, scrambled eggs w/ ham biscuits, sausage roll w/ herbed eggs; complimentary beer, tea, & sodas. **Recreation** Fish at Benjamin Harrison Lake hatchery, golf at nearby Jordan Point Country Club; Thanksgiving festival at Berkeley, special Halloween & Christmas tours. **Amenities & Services** Fax; meetings (30), weddings (125).

ACCOMMODATIONS

Units 6 guest rooms, 1 suite, 1 cottage. **All Rooms** AC, TV & VCR w/ tapes, hair dryer. **Some Rooms** Fireplace (4), private entrance (2), kitchenette (1). **Bed & Bath** Queen (7), king (1); 7 private baths, 1 shared bath, 1 whirlpool, 4 tubs. **Favorites** Victoria—a plethora of pillows on the 1850s bed, marble-top dresser, salesmen samplers of hats & clothing, wall display of bustles, hoops, & more; Lizzie—behind layers of vintage clothing, pillows, & borders are a comfortable king bed, a large bathroom w/ blue claw-foot tub & double shower, even a fireplace. **Comfort & Decor** Every available space is filled with a unique, densely-displayed collection of Victoriana, period clothing, bowers of ribbons and faux flowers, dolls, vintage toys, and pillows (up to a dozen per bed). The kitchen looks like a 200-year-old country store—where nothing has sold. One dining room is dark and cluttered with silver, glass, and accessories; the other has shelves lined with tea cups, china, you-name-it. It takes a dedicated staff to dust and polish so much stuff.

RATES, RESERVATIONS, & RESTRICTIONS

Deposit 1 night, refund w/ 15-days notice less $25. **Discounts** AAA. **Credit Cards** V, MC. **Check-In/Out** 3 p.m./11 a.m. **Smoking** Kitchen. **Pets** No. **Kids** Over age 12. **Minimum Stay** 2 nights on holidays. **Open** All year. **Hosts** Dot & Julian Boulware, 4800 John Tyler Memorial Hwy., Charles City, 23030. **Phone** (804) 829-2962 or (804) 829-6908. Fax (804) 829-2962. **Web** edgewoodplantation.com.

NORTH BEND PLANTATION, Charles City

OVERALL ★★★★½ | QUALITY ★★★★ | VALUE ★★★ | PRICE $125–$135

Kinship is everything in this part of Virginia. George Copland has special bragging rights because he's a great grandson of Edmund Ruffin, a prominent pre–Civil War southern politician. (Although a civilian, Ruffin was given the honor of firing the first shot in that war.) The Coplands opened their bed-and-breakfast to help finance restoration. Ridgely, who has a day job in nursing, is there evenings to relate tidbits of history, including the time General Sheridan used the house as his headquarters. George, now retired, is an amiable host during breakfast. "We're comfortable people, and we want you to feel a part of all this," says Ridgely.

SETTINGS & FACILITIES

Location Rural lane off Rte. 619. **Near** 1.5 miles south of historic Rte. 5. **Building** 1819 Greek Revival w/ wide center hall, original wood trim, faux marble, pocket doors. **Grounds** 850 acres w/ farmland, fields, pond, nature trails, Civil War trenches, swimming pool. **Public Space** Foyer, LR, DR, billiard room, upstairs hall, 3 porches. **Food & Drink** Full breakfast w/ juice, fruit, beverages; specialties—omelet & biscuits, waffles w/ bacon, country ham, eggs & biscuits; specialty jelly & syrup; tea avail. **Recreation** Volleyball, croquet, horseshoes, badminton, swimming; numerous James River plantation events. **Amenities & Services** Videos, fax, TV, hair dryer, iron & board; meetings (20), weddings (200).

ACCOMMODATIONS

Units 4 guest rooms, 1 suite. **All Rooms** AC, TV, robes, iron & board. **Some Rooms** Fireplace (2). **Bed & Bath** Queen (4), double (1), four-poster (3); private baths, tub (1). **Favorites** Rose—four-poster bed, chaise, sunny, uncluttered. **Comfort & Decor** The screen door sticks and the floors are worn, but the rooms are attractive and comfortable. Enjoy the authenticity. It's a rare opportunity to stay in a James River plantation, since most are open only for touring. All common rooms are large with high ceilings and heirloom antiques are part of daily life—including mismatched pedigree silverware.

RATES, RESERVATIONS, & RESTRICTIONS

Deposit 1 night. **Discounts** Seniors, AAA. **Credit Cards** V, MC. **Check-In/Out** 3 p.m./11 a.m. **Smoking** Some areas. **Pets** No. **Kids** Over age 6. **No-Nos** Bed wetters. **Minimum Stay** None. **Open** All year. **Hosts** Ridgely & George Copland, 12200 Weyanoke Rd., Charles City, 23030. **Phone** (804) 829-5176. **Fax** (804) 829-6828. **Web** northbendplantation.com.

INN AT WARNER HALL, Gloucester

OVERALL ★★★★★ | QUALITY ★★★★½ | VALUE ★★★★★ | PRICE $130–$195

You may suspect that you've taken a wrong turn at the dramatic entrance of Warner Hall plantation. The driveway, with triple-tiered white fencing, is unusually long, but once you arrive you'll be glad you came. A columned portico and brick dependencies give the manor house a *Gone With the Wind* look. Warner Hall is listed on the National Register of Historic Places because it's where George Washington's great, great grandfather and relatives of explorer Meriwether Lewis once lived. Today's hosts, Troy and Theresa, hired skilled artisans and craftsmen to restore the 17,000-square-foot property. After a genuine welcome and introduction to area attractions, they step back and let you enjoy the spacious public rooms. Breakfast is served on fine china and flavored with good conversation.

SETTINGS & FACILITIES

Location Rural lane 3 mi. east of Rte. 17, overlooking the northwest branch of the Severn River. **Near** 15 mi. northeast of Williamsburg, 7 mi. north of Yorktown Battlefield & Victory Center, 5 mi. south of downtown Gloucester; also near Jamestown, Busch Gardens & Water Country USA, Air & Space Museum. **Building** Colonial Revival plantation rebuilt on 1895 foundation, 2 brick dependencies dating from 1698 & 1730. **Grounds** 38 acres of lawns, gardens, & horse pasture; 250-year-old pecan orchard, American boxwoods, Ohio buckeye trees; water views. **Public Space** Wide center hall, drawing room, parlor, DR, enclosed porch, 2 powder rooms, 2nd floor sitting room w/ library & porch, boathouse. **Food & Drink** Early coffee, full breakfast w/ cereal, juice, baked goods, fresh fruit; specialties—omelets, pancakes, Belgian waffles, Mobjack Bay eggs Benedict (w/ crab & potatoes); guest fridge w/ soft drinks, juice, & cookies; bar on site; reasonably priced 5-course dinners on weekends. **Recreation** Volleyball, badminton, croquet, horseshoe pits, 4 kayaks, 1 canoe, 6 bikes, & fishing equipment provided; biking, hiking, golf, horseback riding; Daffodil Festival (early April), Guinea Jubilee (Sept.), Battle of the Hook reenactment (Oct. 3), Oyster Festival (Nov.), Blessing of the Hounds (Nov.). **Amenities & Services** Video library, massage avail., fax & e-mail, 1 disabled access; meetings (50), weddings (200).

ACCOMMODATIONS

Units 11 guest rooms. **All Rooms** AC, phone, hair dryer, robe, CD player/clock radio, iron & board, VCRs avail., bottled water, chocolates. **Some Rooms** Gas fireplace (6), private entrance (1). **Bed & Bath** King (2), queen (8), twin (1), canopy (2), four-poster (2); down comforters (non-allergienic bedding on request); private baths, 2 steam showers, 2 double Jacuzzis, most have ceramic tile and molded marble. **Favorites** Washington suite—spacious w/ private porch & entrance, antique brass king bed, water view, fireplace, heart of pine floor, Jacuzzi; Mildred Warner—old-fashioned elegance, antique walnut bed, heart of pine floor, corner fireplace, water view; Austin's Desire—exposed brick wall, mahogany sleigh bed, soaking tub, sitting area, best views. **Comfort & Decor** Period antiques and eclectic furnishings are formally arranged but comfortable. Ten-foot ceilings, moldings, art, Schumacher fabrics, and wall coverings add elegance. Guest rooms sizes vary and some are oddly configured.

RATES, RESERVATIONS, & RESTRICTIONS

Deposit 50%, refund w/ 10-days notice. **Discounts** No. **Credit Cards** AE, V, MC, D. **Check-In/Out** 3 p.m./11 a.m. **Smoking** No. **Pets** No. **Kids** Over age 8. **No-Nos** Spiked heels. **Minimum Stay** 2 nights on weekends. **Open** All year. **Hosts** Theresa & Troy Stavens, 4750 Warner Hall Rd., Gloucester, 23061. **Phone** (800) 331-2720 or (804) 695-9565. Fax (804) 695-9566. **E-mail** whall@inna.net. **Web** warnerhall.com.

APPLEWOOD COLONIAL, Williamsburg

OVERALL ★★★★ | QUALITY ★★★★½ | VALUE ★★★ | PRICE $110–$175

These owners grew up in a small Indiana town named for William Tell, hence their 25-year collection of apple-related items . . . 500 strong and still growing. In short, if it looks, smells, or tastes like an apple, it's probably here—everything from sugar bowls, pillows and art to a checkerboard with apple-shaped pieces. Look out the dining room window to see seven apple-shaped birdhouses. The house itself is noteworthy because it was built by Elton Holland, manager of the craftsmen who restored Colonial Williamsburg. It echoes details used in the more formal Governor's House nearby. But, best of all is the apple pie that awaits guests whenever temptation calls.

SETTINGS & FACILITIES

Location Across from College of William & Mary, walk to Colonial Williamsburg. **Near** Richmond, Norfolk. **Building** 1929 Georgian Colonial built by restoration craftsmen. **Grounds** City lot w/ colorful flowers. **Public Space** Parlor, DR. **Food & Drink** Full breakfast w/ apple theme; specialties—scalloped apples, hash brown potatoes, vegetable pie, muffins; peach French toast, glazed bacon; baked apple dumplings, baked tomato & bacon cups, Finnish pancakes; apple pie always avail., plus chocolate chip cookies, sodas, & Virginia peanuts. **Recreation** Williamsburg attractions, pottery factory, candle factory, winery, outlets. **Amenities & Services** Fax & e-mail, videos.

ACCOMMODATIONS

Units 2 guest rooms, 2 suites. **All Rooms** AC, TV, phone, hair dryer, ironing board. **Some Rooms** Fireplace (2), private entrance (1), CD stereo, fridge, ceiling fan. **Bed & Bath** Queen (4), twin (2), canopy (4); private baths. **Favorites** Colonel Vaughn suite—green paneled walls, pencil-post bed, fireplace, tub, sunny private breakfast room, lots of thoughtful details. **Comfort & Decor** Colonial-style furnishings include distinctive dentil molding, which frames the ceilings. The parlor has hand-forged hinges and botanical prints. Walnut paneling on the fireplace was salvaged from a local hospital. The television is concealed in a handsome dollhouse cabinet. Apple theme adds whimsy without overwhelming.

RATES, RESERVATIONS, & RESTRICTIONS

Deposit 1 night, refund w/ 14-days notice (30 days holiday weekends & in Dec.). **Discounts** 4 nights or more. **Credit Cards** V, MC. **Check-In/Out** 4–6 p.m./11 a.m. **Smoking** No. **Pets** No. **Kids** Yes, 1 suite only. **Minimum Stay** 2 nights. **Open** All year. **Hosts** Marty Jones, owner; Donna Pompillio, innkeeper, 605 Richmond Rd., Williamsburg, 23185. **Phone** (800) 899-2753. Fax (757) 229-9405. **E-mail** applewood@tni.net. **Web** www.williamsburgbandb.com.

CEDARS, Williamsburg

OVERALL ★★★ | QUALITY ★★★½ | VALUE ★★ | PRICE $95–$180

From the outside, this property looks unusually appealing. Over the years, the brick has aquired a lovely patina. It was taken from the original Wren building on the William & Mary campus when it became the first reconstruction project at Colonial Williamsburg. Inside, Williamsburg's oldest and largest B&B looked a bit scruffy when we visited. The innkeepers, a husband and wife team plus his sister, live off site. The advantage of staying here is that you can walk to Williamsburg for a daily program of fascinating special events. Read the local newspaper to learn which historic date is being reenacted during your visit. And, plan to attend evening programs that delve into cultural and social life in Thomas Jefferson's era.

SETTINGS & FACILITIES

Location Residential area, flanked by Lutheran & Christian Science churches. **Near** Norfolk, Newport News, Jamestown, Yorktown, Busch Gardens & Water Country USA. **Building** 1933 Georgian. **Grounds** 0.75 acre w/ ancient American elms, flower boxes, front garden. **Public Space** LR, tavern, porch. **Food & Drink** Elaborate breakfast w/ fresh fruit, homemade muffins, juice & beverages; specialties—smoked salmon flan, oatmeal pudding, mushroom egg puff, noodle kuegel, apples & sausage; afternoon drinks, cookies & snacks; Michelob Golf Tournament, Scottish Festival, Shakespeare Theater. **Recreation** Golf, biking. **Amenities & Services** Fax & e-mail; meetings (12).

ACCOMMODATIONS

Units 6 guest rooms, 2 suites, 1 cottage. **All Rooms** AC. **Some Rooms** Fireplace (2), private entrance (2). **Bed & Bath** King (2), queen (7), twin (2), four-poster (7), canopy (3); private baths. **Favorites** Christopher Wren—red walls, king bed, red & white checked sofa, Waverly drapes, American primitive prints, windows on three sides including dormer with seat, large bath; George Washington suite—tailored canopy bed, rose walls, white trim, mirrored armoire, small tiled bath. **Comfort & Decor** The living room has an eighteenth-century desk, reproduction wing chairs, a gas fireplace, and a camelback sofa. Framed original newspapers announce Abe Lincoln's assassination and Grover Cleveland's inauguration. The tone is casual. On the porch are cards, games, and individual tables for buffet-style breakfast.

RATES, RESERVATIONS, & RESTRICTIONS

Deposit 1 night, refund w/ 14-days notice. **Discounts** AAA, travel agents in off-peak season. **Credit Cards** V, MC. **Check-In/Out** 2–10 p.m./11 a.m. **Smoking** No. **Pets** No. **Kids** Welcome. **Minimum Stay** 2 nights most weekends & holidays. **Open** All year. **Hosts** Brona & Jim Melecha; Carol Melecha, 616 Jamestown Rd., Williamsburg, 23185. **Phone** (800) 296-3591 or (757) 229-3591. Fax (757) 229-3591. **E-mail** cedars @widomaker.com. **Web** cedarsofwilliamsburg.com.

COLONIAL CAPITAL, Williamsburg

OVERALL ★★★★ | QUALITY ★★★★ | VALUE ★★★ | PRICE $110–$160

Judging from the basket of thank you notes from their loyal guests, these hosts have found the formula for success. Their collection of pineapples, which appear in the form of candle holders, wall sconces, door plaques, and more, is symbolic of their desire to make your stay memorable. It recalls an era when serving this once-hard-to-get fruit showed guests were held in high esteem. Here, genuine hospitality is dished up with a sense of humor. Canned possum is just one of several conversation pieces that is likely to spark some lively repartee—or can-you-top-this comebacks. Expect to have a happy, light-hearted experience.

SETTINGS & FACILITIES

Location Across from College of William & Mary, 3 blocks from Merchant Square. **Near** Busch Gardens & Water Country USA, 20 mi. to Newport News & Williamsburg Airport. **Building** 1926 Colonial Revival, portico w/ 8 white columns, mint green siding. **Grounds** 0.5 acre corner lot w/ magnolia, white pine, oak, crepe myrtle, yew trees, shrubs, flowering plants, birdfeeders. **Public Space** Parlor, DR, breakfast solarium, screened porch, patio, back deck. **Food & Drink** Full breakfast w/ fresh fruit, juices, beverages; specialties—soufflé, casseroles, pancakes, Virginia pork; afternoon tea & wine. **Recreation** Bike trails, tennis, golf, boating, horseback riding, beaches nearby; 5 bikes avail. (2 tandem); Scottish Festival (Sept.), special events at Williamsburg, Jamestown, & Yorktown. **Amenities & Services** Videos, fax & e-mail; meetings (12).

ACCOMMODATIONS

Units 4 guest rooms, 1 suite. **All Rooms** AC, TV & VCR, radio, phone, hair dryer, remote control ceiling fan. **Some Rooms** Fireplace (1), balcony (1). **Bed & Bath** King (2), queen (3), twin (2), all canopies; 5 private baths, 3 tubs. **Favorites** York—blue floral fabrics, maple four-poster, claw-foot tub w/ shower, pedestal sink; Potomac—pencil four-poster, nice fabrics, small tub. **Comfort & Decor** The traditional parlor has mint green trim, Oriental rugs, velvet wingback chairs, a fireplace. Guest rooms have nice beds and seating.

RATES, RESERVATIONS, & RESTRICTIONS

Deposit Credit card, refund w/ 14-days notice. **Discounts** AAA, returning guests. **Credit Cards** AE, V, MC, D. **Check-In/Out** 3–6 p.m./11 a.m. **Smoking** No. **Pets** No (golden retriever on premises). **Kids** Over age 8. **Minimum Stay** 2 nights on weekends; 3 nights some holidays. **Open** All year. **Hosts** Barbara & Phil Craig, 501 Richmond Rd., Williamsburg, 23185. **Phone** (757) 229-0233. Fax (757) 253-7667. **E-mail** ccbb@widomaker.com. **Web** ccbb.com.

COLONIAL GARDENS, Williamsburg

OVERALL ★★★★½ | QUALITY ★★★★½ | VALUE ★★★★ | PRICE $125–$165

This is an attractive house, but what really draws the eye are Wil's framed watercolors of European landmarks and pencil drawings of local architecture. A major talent, his work has been shown at galleries in Atlanta, Hilton Head, and Manhattan. Here, it is displayed throughout the house. Also beautiful are the woodland views from a multi-windowed sunporch—especially the azaleas and rhododendron in spring and foliage in fall. Bird life is abundant. The hosts retired to this quiet, secluded place in 1995, ten years after they began vacationing regularly in Williamsburg. They're eager to share their enthusiasm for the area.

SETTINGS & FACILITIES

Location Residential area, 1.25 mi. to Colonial Williamsburg. **Near** Jamestown, Yorktown, Busch Gardens & Water Country USA, James River plantations. **Building** 1965 Colonial-style, exterior bricks recycled from 1800s courthouse. **Grounds** About 3 acres, front lawns w/ poplars, oaks, mountain laurels, floral borders; wildlife, often visit extensive rear gardens. **Public Space** Parlor, formal DR, front porch, sunporch, refreshment area. **Food & Drink** Early coffee; full breakfast w/ juices, fruit, beverages; specialties—herb-baked egg on ham w/ muffins, baked croissant French toast w/ sautéed apples & sausage; country casserole w/ buttermilk biscuits; light afternoon snacks & soft drinks; dietary requests met. **Recreation** Historic sites. **Amenities & Services** Videos, nightly turndown w/ gourmet pillow treats; rose bouquet for birthdays & anniversaries.

ACCOMMODATIONS

Units 2 guest rooms, 2 suites. **All Rooms** AC, TV & VCR, phone, ceiling fan, robes, clock radio, hair dryer, fresh flowers, bottled water, wine glasses & corkscrew, ice bucket, 6-item amenity basket. **Some Rooms** Daybed (1). **Bed & Bath** King (2), queen (2), canopy (1), four-poster (1); private baths. **Favorites** Library—iron four-poster bed, 2 walls of bookshelves filled w/ 100 leather-bound books; Azalea—a 2-room suite w/ four-poster bed, light teal w/ pink accents, antiques. **Comfort & Decor** The look is sophisticated with English and American antiques, marble statuary, and Oriental sculpture. Notable pieces include an 1840s slave-made corner cabinet and a 1780s silverware holder. Heirloom quilts and an elaborate four-story dollhouse add personality.

RATES, RESERVATIONS, & RESTRICTIONS

Deposit 1 night, balance due 14 days prior, $10 cancellation fee. **Discounts** None. **Credit Cards** AE, V, MC, D. **Check-In/Out** 4–6 p.m./11 a.m. **Smoking** No. **Pets** No. **Kids** No. **No-Nos** Coolers in rooms. **Minimum Stay** 2 nights on weekends, 3 nights holidays. **Open** All year. **Hosts** Scottie & Wil Phillips, 1109 Jamestown Rd., Williamsburg, 23185. **Phone** (800) 886-9715. Fax (757) 253-1495. **E-mail** colgdns@widomaker.com. **Web** colonial-gardens.com.

LEGACY OF WILLIAMSBURG, Williamsburg

OVERALL ★★★★ | QUALITY ★★★★ | VALUE ★★★ | PRICE $125–$180

A newcomer as a B&B host, Marshall stepped into the role in January 2000, after 13 years working at luxury hotels. He invites guests to escape to an eighteenth-century mindset. Hence, no TVs or dataports in the guest rooms. Furnishings are pristine and Colonial, with pleasing authentic colors and geometric-patterned fabrics. Collecting cookbooks is Marshall's "obsession," as he described it. He enjoys preparing great breakfasts—

sometimes waking at 3 a.m. to research new recipes. Another plus is a full set of official videos from local historic sites, many within walking distance.

SETTINGS & FACILITIES

Location Residential area. **Near** Across from College of William & Mary, 4.5 blocks to Colonial Williamsburg, 45 min. to Richmond airport. **Building** 1976 Colonial clapboard. **Grounds** City lot w/ white picket fence, floral borders. **Public Space** Billiards room, keeping room, library, news room, back porch, gazebo. **Food & Drink** Full breakfast w/ fresh fruit, homemade baked goods; specialties—French toast w/ honey cinnamon syrup, oatmeal soufflé w/ orange cream sauce, puff pastry w/ scrambled egg, mushroom, & cheese sauce; vegetarian requests honored. **Recreation** Explore Colonial Williamsburg, Busch Gardens. **Amenities & Services** Complete video library of sites & attractions at Williamsburg, Jamestown, & Yorktown.

ACCOMMODATIONS

Units 1 guest room, 3 suites. **All Rooms** AC, phone, robes, hair dryer, iron & board. **Some Rooms** Fireplace (3), balcony (3). **Bed & Bath** Queen (3), double (1), all canopies; private baths, 2 tubs. **Favorites** Nicholson suite—green trim, red & white checked fabrics, shirted four-poster, fireplace; Legacy of Williamsburg suite—spacious, maroon canopied four-poster, tall windows, fireplace. **Comfort & Decor** The library features a Shaker bench, Colonial reproductions, and a tri-cornered hat. Patterned after Colonial Williamsburg's Raleigh Tavern, the tavern room has a fireplace and billiards table, plus darts and checkers. Guests dine by a fireplace in the basement-level keeping room. The outside deck is bridged to a gazebo set among bamboo, white dogwoods, and holly.

RATES, RESERVATIONS, & RESTRICTIONS

Deposit Credit card, refund w/ 14-days notice. **Discounts** None. **Credit Cards** V, MC. **Check-In/Out** Noon/10:30 a.m. **Smoking** No. **Pets** No. **Kids** No. **Minimum Stay** 2 nights on weekends. **Open** All year. **Hosts** Marshall Wile, owner; Joan Paul, hostess, 930 Jamestown Rd., Williamsburg, 23185. **Phone** (757) 220-0524 or (800) 962-4722. **Fax** (757) 220-2211. **E-mail** legacy@tni.net. **Web** legacyofwilliamsburgbb.com.

LIBERTY ROSE, Williamsburg

OVERALL ★★★★★ | QUALITY ★★★★★ | VALUE ★★★★ | PRICE **$155–$215**

An interior decorator and wedding planner from California, Sandi excels in providing the best of both b's in bed-and-breakfast. You'll enjoy the finest mattresses, high-thread-count linens, plus down pillows and duvets. You'll also savor fabulous breakfasts and afternoon tea. Fine antiques throughout the house evidence the hosts' sense of beauty, whimsy, and creative flair. You'll see lots of red, because husband Brad buys Sandi something red every Valentine's Day. Most unusual is the hooded red Victorian concierge chair in the parlor. Space is tight in some rooms, but you're sure to find at least one decorating idea you can use. Think of your experience here as tantamount to reading a good decorating book, and feel free to adapt an idea or two at home.

SETTINGS & FACILITIES

Location 1 mi. west of historic district. **Near** Jamestown, Yorktown, Busch Gardens & Water Country USA, College of William & Mary. **Building** 1922 Colonial Revival, white clapboard & brick w/ slate roof. **Grounds** 1 acre wooded hilltop in town, partially walled & shaded stone patio w/ fence, fountain, statuary, flower pots, roses, impatiens, begonias, iron table & chairs, swing. **Public Space** Parlor, breakfast porch. **Food & Drink** Full breakfast served from 8–9 a.m. at tables for 2; specialities—stuffed French toast, fritter hot cakes w/ ham & cheese croissants plus eggs, bacon, or sausage; afternoon tea, lemonade, & homemade cookies; soft drinks always avail.; menus set out each evening, request for changes honored. **Recreation** Local historical sites, tennis, river sports, numerous special events nearby. **Amenities & Services** TV & VCR w/ at least 30 videos, guest fridge.

ACCOMMODATIONS

Units 1 guest room, 3 suites. **All Rooms** AC, TV, private phone line, hair dryer, robes, chocolates, alarm clock. **Some Rooms** Fireplace (3). **Bed & Bath** Four-poster queen beds, canopy (3); private baths, tubs (3). **Favorites** Suite Williamsburg—carved ball-&-claw bed, silk & jacquard fabrics, 6 windows, French sofa, working fireplace, sitting area, Habershams doll mansion hiding a TV, black Italian tile shower, claw-foot tub, porcelain candelabras; Rose Victoria—French canopy bed w/ fringed & tassled bed curtains, red damask wall covering, ivory woodwork, tin ceiling, antique armoire, heart of pine floor, oversize antique tub, red marble shower. **Comfort & Decor** Comfortable turn-of-the-century antiques are complemented by exquisite fabrics and wall coverings, historic reproductions, and a Grand piano. Victorian antique clothing is displayed in halls and on walls.

RATES, RESERVATIONS, & RESTRICTIONS

Deposit Full pre-payment, refund w/ 18-days notice. **Discounts** None. **Credit Cards** AE, V, MC. **Check-In/Out** 3 p.m./11 a.m. **Smoking** No. **Pets** No. **Kids** No. **Minimum Stay** Usually 2 nights, 3 in some seasons. **Open** All year. **Hosts** Sandi & Brad Hirz, 1022 Jamestown Rd., Williamsburg, 23185. **Phone** (800) 545-1825. Fax (757) 253-8529. **Web** libertyrose.com.

Zone 19

Central Virginia/ President's Country/ The Piedmont

George Washington spent his boyhood in **Fredericksburg,** now located 50 miles south of Washington, D.C. Today it is home to a well-preserved 40-block National Historic District. Virginia's hilly Piedmont and President's Country stretch southward from the town.

Residents of Fredericksburg are eager to make history come alive for visitors. You can visit the house and gravesite of Washington's mother, Mary. Guides in period costume give excellent tours of **Rising Sun Tavern,** once home to the first president's brother, Charles. Elegant **Kenmore** plantation was the home of Washington's sister Betty and his brother-in-law Fielding Lewis, who played a major role in the Revolution by providing arms from his gunnery, sometimes without pay. The Washingtons no doubt shopped at **Hugh Mercer's Apothecary Shop,** where docents give vivid descriptions of Colonial health regimes. The **James Monroe Museum** is also in town.

During the Civil War, Fredericksburg was frequently attacked and changed hands seven times. More than 100,000 casualties were suffered in the area. Nearby battlefields are vast and monuments are poignant. Allow time to explore three key battlefields within 15 miles of the city—at **Chancellorsville, The Wilderness,** and **Spotsylvania Court House.**

Memories of the Civil War also color Virginia's capital. One glance at mansion-lined **Monument Avenue,** where Olympian-sized statues of Robert E. Lee, J. E. B. Stuart, Stonewall Jackson, and others perch atop improbably high pedestals, tells you that **Richmond** is no ordinary city. It has inspired so many heroes and seen so many momentous, emotionally-charged events that its history reads like an epic tale from grand opera.

You wouldn't know it from a casual look at today's glittering modern skyline, but, during the Civil War, Richmond was the military, political, industrial, and social center of another nation. It accrued such distinction largely because of money made from worldwide sales of tobacco and the existence of a single factory—the **Tredegar Iron Works,** which made cannon and train rails without which there could have been no war.

The list of attractions in modern Richmond is long: **Valentine Riverside, Richmond National Battlefield Park,** the **Confederate White House, Hollywood Cemetery, Virginia Historical Society, Battle Abbey, Valentine Museum, St. John's Church,** and **Belle Isle,** to name just a few.

Continuing southward, **Petersburg** was the object of a heartbreaking nine-months, three-weeks siege by Union troops, which began June 9, 1864. The war's longest campaign resulted in 70,000 casualties—and when it ended the Confederate capital at Richmond fell the next day.

Petersburg has never fully recovered. To this day, on downtown streets, stark brick walls remain from Civil War–era buildings. Lots were left vacant and one gutted factory now houses musical events. At the **Siege Museum,** an 18-minute film, *The Echo Still Remains,* precedes exhibits that show how a lavish lifestyle gave way to a bitter struggle for survival. At **Blanford Church,** the cemetery has rows of marked graves and a mound dedicated to unknown soldiers. It was here that the practice of decorating graves eventually led to our national holiday—Memorial Day.

At **Petersburg National Battlefield,** a four-mile one-way road passes well-preserved earthworks built to defend the city. At **Pamplin Historical Park,** you'll see more earthworks plus hiking trails, Tudor Hall plantation, and Battlefield Center. The newest addition is the **National Museum of the Civil War Soldier,** which greets visitors with a bronze sculpture of two nondescript soldiers, bearing no insignias.

Heading west, you reach **Appomattox Court House National Historic Park.** At the pristine village of Appomattox, now restored and reconstructed, park rangers and guides in period costume recall events leading up to and including April 9, 1865, when the Civil War finally ended here.

Thomas Jefferson's home has been **Charlottesville's** most popular tourist attraction for more than 100 years. In recent years, up to a half-million people waited in line more than two hours to tour the architectural treasure. Meanwhile, the rest of Charlottesville and surrounding Albemarle County remain largely undiscovered.

The heart of downtown Charlottesville is a revitalized eight-block-long pedestrian mall, which offers theaters, boutiques, even an ice-skating rink. The best way to view the **Academia,** the stunning architectural gem Jefferson designed as the heart of the University of Virginia, is to walk the length of the courtyard. Vest-pocket gardens behind serpentine brick walls add an element of surprise. At **Michie's Tavern,** you can taste punch made from an eighteenth-century recipe, and in the rolling hills around the city more than a dozen vineyards are open for tastings.

Perched on a hilltop southeast of the Charlottesville is **Ash Lawn-Highland,** a 535-acre estate owned by President James Monroe from 1799 to 1823. Guides give a witty and animated 45-minute tour of the house. To the north at **Montpelier** in **Orange** you can visit the home of President James Madison and his wife, Dolly.

A number of grand and historic bed-and-breakfasts and country inns add distinction to this region, including an estate once owned by Thomas Jefferson's daughter. They range widely in quality and ambience.

FOR MORE INFORMATION

Appomattox Visitor Information Center
5 Main St.
Appomattox, VA 24522
(804) 352-2621; appomattox.com

Charlottesville/Albemarle County CVB
Rte. 20 S.
Charlottesville, VA 22902
(804) 977-1783;
charlottesvilletourism.org

Fredericksburg Visitors Center
706 Caroline St.
Fredericksburg, VA 22401
(800) 678-4748; fredericksburgva.com

Petersburg Visitors Center
425 Cockade Aly
Petersburg, VA 23804
(800) 368-3595 or (804) 733-2400;
petersburg-va.org

Richmond CVB
550 E. Marshall St.
Richmond, VA 23219
(800) 370-9004 or (804) 782-2777;
richmondva.org

HENRY CLAY INN, Ashland

OVERALL ★★★½ | QUALITY ★★★½ | VALUE ★★★ | PRICE $90–$165

This inn's exterior is a replica of two predecessors. The first was built in 1858 for Richmonders who came by train to enjoy the country. Then it became a boarding house for Randolph Macon College, but burned down in 1905. Rebuilt in 1906, it took the name of Henry Clay, a prominent local orator, statesman, and three-time presidential candidate. It burned again in 1946. The present innkeeping team started from scratch on the land. They are a mother, her two daughters, and a friend who serves as head cook. Pooling their talents, they've captured the feel of bygone days. The ground-floor gift shop features train items, Virginia products, crafts, and works by local artists. It's a pleasant stopover, but there's little incentive to linger.

SETTINGS & FACILITIES

Location Town center across from State Visitors Center & Randolph Macon College. **Near** 18 mi. north of Richmond. **Building** 1992 Georgian Revival. **Grounds** City lot facing railroad tracks. **Public Space** Lobby, multi-purpose/drawing room, upstairs parlor, 2 porches w/ rockers. **Food & Drink** Cont'l breakfast w/ cereals, fruit, muffins or breads, juices, coffee; brunch avail. Sat. & Sun., dinner avail. Fri. & Sat. **Recreation** Rocking chair reverie & watching trains rumble by; Strawberry Faire (June). **Amenities & Services** Disabled access (#101), computer access, fax & e-mail avail; meetings (33).

ACCOMMODATIONS

Units 14 guest rooms, 2 suites. **All Rooms** AC, cable TV, phone, dataport, sparkling cider. **Some Rooms** Private entrance (3), ceiling fan. **Bed & Bath** King (2), queen (10), double (3), twin (1); sleigh, pencil post, canopy, acorn post, & cannonball bed styles; private baths, w/ tub & shower, whirlpools (3). **Favorites** Suite #100—king canopy bed, whirlpool, ceiling fan, LR w/ wet bar, nice art; #212—pale peach canopy bed, bright, view of railroad station. **Comfort & Decor** The spacious lobby captures small town ambience. An extensive upstairs parlor has a porch for relaxing. There are interesting antique wood fireplaces with mantels and mirrors plus reproduction and period furnishings.

RATES, RESERVATIONS, & RESTRICTIONS

Deposit Credit card, refund w/ 7-days notice or rented. **Discounts** AAA, AARP, 10% gov't, corp. varies. **Credit Cards** AE, V, MC. **Check-In/Out** After 2 p.m./11 a.m. **Smoking** No. **Pets** No. **Kids** Yes. **Minimum Stay** College event weekends. **Open** All year. **Hosts** Carol Martin, Ann-Carol Houston, Susan Sams, & Judy Ashcraft, 114 N. Railroad Ave., Ashland, 23005. **Phone** (800) 343-4565 or (804) 798-3100. Fax (804) 752-7555. **E-mail** information@henryclayinn.com. **Web** henryclayinn.com.

EIGHTEEN SEVENTEEN, Charlottesville

OVERALL ★★★ | QUALITY ★★★½ | VALUE ★★★ | PRICE $89- $199

Thomas Jefferson's master craftsman, James Dinsmore, had a hand in designing this ideally-located house. Dinsmore, an Irishman who came to America in 1789, also worked on three of the area's most famous houses: Monticello, Montpelier, and Poplar Forest. The innkeeper owns an antique shop and displays many of her wares here. Look carefully and you'll see a price tag on just about everything. Consequently, the decor is in a state of flux and may look different each time you visit. Serious antiquers take note: guests receive a 30 percent discount on any purchase they make.

SETTINGS & FACILITIES

Location Downtown. **Near** 2 blocks from Univ. of Virginia, 1 mi. to pedestrian mall. **Building** 1817 Federal-style townhouse. **Grounds** City lot next to Marriott Courtyard. **Public Space** Parlor, DR, porch. **Food & Drink** Cont'l breakfast; afternoon tea & refreshments. **Recreation** Ice skating, historic attractions. **Amenities & Services** Antiques for sale, fax.

ACCOMMODATIONS

Units 4 guest rooms, 1 suite. **All Rooms** A/C. **Some Rooms** Private entrance (1). **Bed & Bath** King (2), queen (2), double (2), four-poster (3); private baths, 1 detached. **Favorites** Suite. **Comfort & Decor** The attractive parlor features a rotating array of antiques. Guest room furnishings are nice, but some walls need repair.

RATES, RESERVATIONS, & RESTRICTIONS

Deposit 1 night or 50%, refund w/ 7-days notice. **Discounts** AARP, AAA Sun–Thur. 10%. **Credit Cards** AE, V, MC. **Check-In/Out** 2–5 p.m./11 a.m. **Smoking** No. **Pets** No. **Kids** Yes. **Minimum Stay** 2 nights some weekends. **Open** All year. **Host** Candace DeLoach, 1211 W. Main St., Charlottesville, 22903. **Phone** (800) 730-7443 or (804) 979-7353. **Fax** (804) 979-7209. **E-mail** the1817inn@aol.com. **Web** http://inngetaways.net/va/1817.html.

INN AT MONTICELLO, Charlottesville

OVERALL ★★★½ | QUALITY ★★★★ | VALUE ★★★★ | PRICE $125–$135

This is the closest inn to Jefferson's Monticello, Monroe's Ash Lawn Pavilion, and historic Michie Tavern, where visitors can dance to an eighteenth-century tune and write their name with a quill pen. While relaxing in a rocking chair on the front porch, you have a full view of Monticello Mountain, which rises just across busy Route 20. The spacious lawn is ideal for playing croquet or bocce. Innkeeper Becky Lindway says she was destined to live near Jefferson's home. Tradition among her ancestors called for naming males after Thomas Jefferson. Among them were engineers and shipbuilders who built vessels and churches in Monmouth, New Jersey before heading west to Cleveland and the Ohio River region.

SETTINGS & FACILITIES

Location Rte. 20 1 mi. south of I-64. **Near** Monticello, Ash Lawn-Highland, Univ. of Virginia, Blue Ridge Mountains, Skyline Drive. **Building** 1856 manor house. **Grounds** 5 acres of rolling lawns, trees, flower borders, brook, hammock. **Public Space** LR, dining area, reading nook, porch. **Food & Drink** Full breakfast w/ juice, fresh fruit, 2 meats, home-baked goods; specialties—crème brûlée French toast, cinnamon raisin French toast, eggs a la Jefferson, mushroom egg bake; 4 p.m. refreshments w/ wine. **Recreation** Access to Willow Lake & hiking trail to Monticello, 0.75 mi. drive to historic Michie Tavern. **Amenities & Services** Complimentary featured Virginia wines.

ACCOMMODATIONS

Units 5 guest rooms. **All Rooms** A/C, fresh flowers, 2 chairs. **Some Rooms** Fireplace (2), private entrance (1), ceiling fan. **Bed & Bath** King (1), queen (4), twin (2), private baths w/ tubs. **Favorites** Lilac room—high four-poster w/ white ruffled canopy, Wedgewood bluewalls, cupboard with family mementos, privacy, side porch w/ birdsounds. **Comfort & Decor** Enjoy elegant antiques and period pieces in the living room and throughout. However, road noise could be disturbing.

RATES, RESERVATIONS, & RESTRICTIONS

Deposit 1 night. **Discounts** Winter specials. **Credit Cards** AE, V, MC. **Check-In/Out** 3 p.m./11 a.m. **Smoking** No. **Pets** No. **Kids** Age 14 & over. **Minimum Stay** 2 nights on weekends. **Open** All year. **Hosts** Becky & Norm Lindway, 1188 Scottsville Rd., Charlottesville, 22902. **Phone** (804) 979-3593. Fax (804) 296-1344. **E-mail** stay@innatmonticello.com. **Web** innatmonticello.com.

SILVER THATCH INN, Charlottesville

OVERALL ★★★★ | QUALITY ★★★★½ | VALUE ★★★ | PRICE $125–$170

A lot of history has happened on this spot since the establishment of the first Native American settlement. It's the site of one of Central Virginia's oldest buildings—a two-story log cabin built by Hessian soldiers who were captured at Saratoga, New York, during the Revolutionary War and marched south to Charlottesville. One part, built in 1812, was used as a boys' school. The property became a tobacco plantation, and, after the Civil War, a melon farm. From 1937 to 1967 it was residence for the Dean of the University of Virginia. Then, in 1998, Jim turned in his lawyer's hat and Terri retired from the healthcare field and they became full time innkeepers and restaurateurs.

SETTINGS & FACILITIES

Location Residential area 6 mi. north of downtown. **Near** Monticello, Montpelier, Ash Lawn-Highland, Skyline Drive, Blue Ridge Mountains. **Building** 1780 white Colonial clapboard w/ additions. **Grounds** 1.25 acres w/ flowers, English-style herb garden, brick patio. **Public Space** LR, 3 DR, powder room, pub. **Food & Drink** Full breakfast w/ fresh vegetables & herbs, breads, muffins; specialties—French toast, eggs & vegetables in a pastry shell, frittata; dinner avail. in fine-dining restaurant w/ a *Wine Spectator* Award of Excellence winning wine list. **Recreation** Horseback riding, golf, fishing, hiking, biking, antiquing, vineyards. **Amenities & Services** Access to Hollymeade community swimming pool next door.

ACCOMMODATIONS

Units 7 guest rooms in two buildings. **All Rooms** AC, robes. **Some Rooms** Fireplace (4). **Bed & Bath** King (1), queen (5), double (1), four-poster (4), canopy (3), sleigh (1); private baths, tubs (3). **Favorites** John Tyler—scrubbed pine canopied bed, fireplace, decor in muted shades of burgundy. **Comfort & Decor** The restaurant ambience is rustic and the cozy pub is warmed by a brick fireplace. The garden adds charm to the property. Several of the consistently attractive guest rooms have sitting areas with wing chairs.

RATES, RESERVATIONS, & RESTRICTIONS

Deposit 1 night, refund w/ 7-days notice. **Discounts** AAA. **Credit Cards** AE, V, MC, DC. **Check-In/Out** 3–9 p.m./11 a.m. Tue.–Sat., 3–6 p.m./11 a.m. Sun. & Mon. **Smoking** No. **Pets** No. **Kids** Over age 8. **Minimum Stay** 2 nights on Fri. & Sat. April–Dec. **Open** All year (except 5 days around Christmas). **Hosts** Terri & Jim Petrovits, 3001 Hollymead Dr., Charlottesville, 22911. **Phone** (800) 261-0720 or (804) 978-4686. Fax (804) 973-6156. **E-mail** info@silverthatch.com. **Web** silverthatch.com.

200 SOUTH STREET, Charlottesville

OVERALL ★★★ | QUALITY ★★★★ | VALUE ★★ | PRICE $135–$220

Location is the key here—guest rooms offer old-world elegance in the midst of a lively downtown. The inn comprises two restored houses. The larger house was built in 1856 for Thomas Jefferson Wertenbaker, son of a close friend of Thomas Jefferson. It was a private residence for years, before operating as a girls' finishing school, then a brothel, then a boarding house. The transformation to an inn was completed in 1986. There's not much public space, just the front porch, rear patio, and a small library that double as the breakfast room. But when you leave your room, it's a quick walk to antique shops, the colorful pedestrian mall, and excellent restaurants.

SETTINGS & FACILITIES

Location Downtown Charlottesville. **Near** 1 mi. from Univ. of Virginia, 4 mi. to Monticello. **Building** Restored 1856 house & smaller 1890 cottage. **Grounds** City lot w/

floral borders. **Public Space** Small library/dining area, veranda, garden patio. **Food & Drink** Cont'l breakfast w/ home-baked breads & coffee cakes; afternoon wine & cheese. **Recreation** Indoor ice-skating; downtown Charlottesville. **Amenities & Services** Disabled access (1).

ACCOMMODATIONS

Units 20 guest rooms. **All Rooms** TV, dataport. **Some Rooms** Fireplace (8), pullout couch (2). **Bed & Bath** Bed sizes vary, canopy (6); private baths, whirlpool (6). **Favorites** #5—teal hues, four-poster, whirlpool; #8—red tones, four-poster, floral fabrics; #24—green tones, four-poster, fireplace. **Comfort & Decor** English and Belgian antiques fill the guest rooms. The main hallway has a solid walnut two-story serpentine banister. Wicker chairs in the neoclassic veranda are inviting.

RATES, RESERVATIONS, & RESTRICTIONS

Deposit No. **Discounts** AAA, local business. **Credit Cards** AE, V, MC. **Check-In/Out** 2–8:30 p.m./11 a.m. **Smoking** No. **Pets** No. **Kids** Yes. **Minimum Stay** 2 nights Fri.–Sat. **Open** All year. **Host** Brendan Clancy, 200 South St., Charlottesville, 22902. **Phone** (800) 964-7008 or (804) 979-0200. Fax (804) 979-4403. **E-mail** clanccyb@cfw.com. **Web** southstreetinn.com.

BELLMONT MANOR, Chesterfield

OVERALL ★★★½ | QUALITY ★★★★ | VALUE ★★★ | PRICE $75–$125

An antiques business is now run out of this house, which is a virtual rabbit warren of rooms added in various eras. Each one is filled with whimsical touches and serious collections. Among them are trivets, china, men's jewelry, porcelain dogs, silver boxes, and roosters. The hospitality is old-fashioned, and guests quickly become a part of the household. Uly Gooch, a retired Episcopalian minister, is a gracious host with well-honed people skills. He loves to cook. And still pinch hits for the ministry, performing what he calls hatching, matching, and dispatching services. Partner Worth Kenyon is a social worker for the Veterans Administration hospital.

SETTINGS & FACILITIES

Location 1.5 mi. south of Rte. 150 (Chippenham Pkwy., Belmont Rd. south exit), 5 mi. west of I-95. **Near** 12 mi. south of Richmond, 15 mi. north of Petersburg. **Building** 1726 farmhouse w/ 1830, 1980, & 1989 additions; lemon yellow shingles w/ rust red accents. **Grounds** 5 acres, w/ gardens, lawn, hammocks, fruit trees, barn, greenhouse, pumphouse, carriage house, chicken house, cow pasture. **Public Space** Joining room, big DR, little DR, old kitchen, library, sunroom, new kitchen & den, "what-the-hell room" (used when there is nowhere else to put something). **Food & Drink** Full breakfast w/ juice, fruit, fried apples, grits, sausage, eggs, muffins, breads; specialties—cheese soufflé, waffles, eggs to order; soda, tea, & juice anytime. **Recreation** Historic sites in Richmond, Petersburg, Williamsburg, Yorktown, Charlottesville, plus James River plantations; croquet. **Amenities & Services** Massage arranged, laundry facilities, fax & e-mail avail.; meetings (25).

ACCOMMODATIONS

Units 3 guest rooms. **All Rooms** AC, TV, fresh flowers, hair dryer, books, sherry, candy, bottled water, flashlight. **Some Rooms** Phones by request, . **Bed & Bath** Queen (2), double (1), sleigh (1); 2 private detached baths, 1 shared bath, 2 tubs. **Favorites** Victoria's room—sleigh bed, desk, portraits. **Comfort & Decor** Cozy, with seven fireplaces, this home is all the more comfortable for being cluttered—there are antiques and collectibles everywhere. Guest rooms, however, are neat and orderly.

RATES, RESERVATIONS, & RESTRICTIONS

Deposit Credit card to hold, refund w/ 14-days notice. **Discounts** Corp. **Credit Cards** AE, V, MC, D. **Check-In/Out** 3–6 p.m./11 a.m. **Smoking** No. **Pets** No (2 dogs in residence). **Kids** No. **Minimum Stay** 2 nights on weekends. **Open** All year. **Hosts** Uly Gooch & Worth Kenyon, 6600 Belmont Rd., Chesterfield, 23832. **Phone** (800) 809-9041 (code 69) or (804) 745-0106. Fax (804) 745-0740. **E-mail** innkeeper@bellmont manor.com. **Web** bellmontmanor.com.

VIRGINIA CLIFFE INN, Glen Allen

OVERALL ★★★★ | QUALITY ★★★★ | VALUE ★★★★★ | PRICE $90–$135

The Cliftons turned their dream house into a bed-and-breakfast after their four children had grown—and Henrico County built its Cultural Arts Center next door. Business has been so successful some kids and grandkids have returned to help out. Besides overnight guests, they host numerous weddings. James designed and built the house to look like an eighteenth-century plantation home, specifically the Morris Jumel house in Manhattan, where George Washington once headquartered. He salvaged some historic elements from an older house on this property. Margaret is an ambitious cook, who says "we work 18-hour days to avoid having a 9 to 5 job." They are gracious hosts offering Southern cuisine, comfort, and culture.

SETTINGS & FACILITIES

Location Historic Mountain Rd., 0.5 mi. west of Rte. 295, 2 mi. west of I-95. **Near** 12 mi. north of Richmond, 1 mi. east of Meadow Farm County Park, a living history museum. **Building** 1973 Georgian w/ stately columns. **Grounds** 6 acres w/ 80 trees, including sycamore, pin oak, poplar, wild cherry, casaba, & pecan; gazebo, rose garden, pond w/ swans, fountain, flower gardens. **Public Space** LR, DR, dinette, family room, 2 powder rooms, Florida room, deck. **Food & Drink** Light breakfast for early risers; full country breakfast served family style w/ fresh fruit, juice, homemade baked goods; specialties—strawberry cheese blintz, quiche, waffles, bacon, ham, cheese grits, biscuits, peach cobbler, spiced apples; soda, juice, bottled water, & snacks anytime. **Recreation** Bikes, fishing poles, jukebox, player piano, pool table, jogging trails; visit Civil War sites; Glen Allen's Cultural Arts Center w/ theater & restaurant is next door. **Amenities & Services** Videos, laundry facilities, fax & e-mail; Meadow Farm Harvest Festival; meetings (100), weddings (300).

ACCOMMODATIONS

Units 4 guest rooms, 1 cottage. **All Rooms** AC, plants. **Some Rooms** Balcony (1), private entrance (1), VCR (2). **Bed & Bath** King (1), queen (2), twin (2), four-poster (4); private baths in main house, shared in cottage. **Favorites** Margaret Aurelia suite—queen canopy bed, balcony, 2nd room w/ sleeper sofa; Virginia Page—queen four-poster bed, quilt, love seat, large bath, peach tones. **Comfort & Decor** The formal living room has a high ceiling with dentil molding, wainscoting, Williamsburg green walls, a fireplace, and a baby grand piano. The foyer, with a crystal chandelier and pine staircase, leads to a formal dining room. You can relax with TV and games in the family room or a separate recreation building. Out back is Cliff House with a sky-lit living room, oak cabinets, hardwood floors, and a tiled kitchen—ideal for families.

RATES, RESERVATIONS, & RESTRICTIONS

Deposit Credit card, refund w/ 7-days notice (rain check avail.). **Discounts** Single, corp., 3 nights or more. **Credit Cards** AE, V, MC, D. **Check-In/Out** 4–8 p.m./11 a.m. **Smoking** No. **Pets** No (kennel 0.5 mi.). **Kids** Yes, w/ supervision by prior arrangement. **Minimum Stay** None. **Open** All year. **Hosts** Margaret & James Clifton, 2900 Mountain Rd., Glen Allen, 23060. **Phone** (877) 254-3346 or (804) 266-7344. Fax (804) 266-2946. **E-mail** vacliffe@aol.com. **Web** bbonline.com/va/cliffeinn.

LITTLEPAGE INN, Mineral

OVERALL ★★★ | QUALITY ★★★★. | VALUE ★★★ | PRICE $99–$215

This is one southern plantation you don't have to admire from behind velvet ropes. Unlike Monticello, Ash Lawn-Highland, and so many others, you can actually sit on the furniture, sip tea in the parlor, and sleep in the beds. The main house, built in 1811, remains as it was after a member of the Holladay family walked back from Civil War battlefields to restore the family farm. Of course, it's been enhanced with a modern kitchen, baths, and climate control. But, you approach down the same lane lined with cypress trees, enter the same vaulted hallway and classic interior. It's well off the beaten track, but if you're a history buff, you'll appreciate the chance to not only see history displayed, but to intimately live it.

SETTINGS & FACILITIES

Location Rural countryside just north of Lake Anna. **Near** 10 mi. north of Mineral, 30 mi. southwest of Fredericksburg, 38 mi. northeast of Charlottesville. **Building** 1811 Federal plantation complex w/ large white-frame main house & 7 dependencies. **Grounds** 200 acres w/ barn, well, ice house, granary, leased farmland. **Public Space** Parlor, sitting room, DR, north porch. **Food & Drink** Full breakfast w/ juice, homemade granola, baked goods; specialties—5-grain pancakes, fresh vegetable omelets, waffles, flaky southern biscuits, ham. **Recreation** Chancelorsville, Wilderness, & Spotslvania battlefields; Lake Anna State Park has boat rentals, swimming, hiking, & fishing; beach towels, croquet, volleyball avail.; Bluegrass festivals. **Amenities & Services** Hot tub in 150-year-old log icehouse, videos, golf privileges at Fawn Lake Country Club, laundry facilities, fax & e-mail; disabled access (1); meetings (25), weddings (175).

ACCOMMODATIONS

Units 7 guest rooms, 1 suite, 1 cottage. **All Rooms** AC, fresh flowers. **Some Rooms** Gas fireplace (6), balcony (3), private entrance (4). **Bed & Bath** King (1), queen (8), some twin; private & shared baths. **Favorites** Cottage—rustic, field view, queen bed, double shower, gas fireplace, washer & dryer; Garden room—pristine look, four-poster bed, claw-foot tub, porch, view of lily pond. **Comfort & Decor** The main house has high ceilings, untreated heart of pine floors, wainscot paneling, and family heirloom furnishings. Accessories include a grandfather clock, family portraits, antique sewing machine, bird cage, and wood carvings. A sense of simplicity and history pervades. The back porch overlooks fertile fields and rooms over bucolic views.

RATES, RESERVATIONS, & RESTRICTIONS

Deposit Credit card, refund w/ 14-days notice. **Discounts** Yes. **Credit Cards** AE, V, MC. **Check-In/Out** 3–7 p.m./11 a.m. **Smoking** No. **Pets** No. **Kids** Yes. **Minimum Stay** No. **Open** All year. **Hosts** The Holladay Family; Holly Currier, innkeeper, 15701 Monrovia Rd., Mineral, 23117. **Phone** (800) 248-1803. Fax (540) 854-7998. **E-mail** little page@earthlink.net. **Web** www.littlepage.com.

INN AT THE CROSSROADS, North Garden

OVERALL ★★★ | QUALITY ★★★½ | VALUE ★★★ | PRICE **$80–$125**

Guests step back two centuries at this inn. Originally built as a tavern and inn, this house is listed on the National Register of Historic Places and as a Virginia historic landmark. The bricks were fired on site, the insulation is clay mixed with horsehair, and the heart of pine floors are original. The kitchen has pine ceiling beams and a brick floor, and breakfast is served on a farm table by a stone fireplace. The scenery remains idyllic: rolling pastureland and the distant Blue Ridge Mountains. John is the full time innkeeper while Maureen continues a career in international banking. The couple formerly owned an inn in Maine. They now reside nearby in the former St. Anne's Parish Anglican Church, which dates to 1785.

SETTINGS & FACILITIES

Location Junction of Rtes. 29 & 692, 10 mi. south of Charlottesville. **Near** Blue Ridge Mountains, Ivy Creek Nature Preserve, Willow Creek. **Building** 1820 red brick Colonial w/ green tin roof, summer kitchen. **Grounds** 4 acres of open lawn, garden, well; adjacent to cattle pasture. **Public Space** LR, keeping room, kitchen, wraparound porch, pergola & deck. **Food & Drink** Full breakfast w/ juice, fruit, hot beverages, specialties—lemon ricotta pancakes, French toast, herbed eggs, vegetable omelet, baked goods; cookies & beverages anytime. **Recreation** Hiking, picnics, golf (7 mi,); swimming, canoeing, tubing & rafting on the James River & Walnut Creek; dogwood festival, garden & vineyard tours near Charlottesville. **Amenities & Services** Vintage sports cars avail. for country touring, picnic supplies at general store.

ACCOMMODATIONS

Units 4 guest rooms, 1 suite, 1 cottage. **All Rooms** A/C, fresh flowers, ceiling fan. **Some Rooms** Fireplace (cottage). **Bed & Bath** King (1), queen (3), double (2); private baths, tubs (3). **Favorites** Cardinal Suite—sitting area, rocking chair, mountain view; Old Summer Kitchen—exposed brick walls, chestnut wood ceiling beams, extensive woodwork, four-poster bed, fireplace, deck. **Comfort & Decor** Authentic Colonial atmosphere includes Federal- and Colonial-style furniture and creaky wide heart of pine wood floors.

RATES, RESERVATIONS, & RESTRICTIONS

Deposit 1 night, refund w/ 2-days notice. **Discounts** Midweek. **Credit Cards** AE, V, MC. **Check-In/Out** 2 p.m. on/11:30 a.m. **Smoking** No. **Pets** No (1 dog & cat on premises, kept outside). **Kids** Yes. **Minimum Stay** 2 nights weekends in April & May. **Open** All year. **Hosts** John & Maureen Deis, 5010 Plank Rd., North Garden, 22959. **Phone** (804) 979-6452. **Web** crossroadsinn.com

MAYHURST PLANTATION, Orange

OVERALL ★★★★ | QUALITY ★★★★½ | VALUE ★★★★ | PRICE $115–$200

This out-of-the-way gem was built by Colonel John Willis, grand nephew of President James Madison. Listed on the National Register of Historic Places, the house has been restored to its former grandeur. Imagine it in 1859 as a bustling 1,700-acre plantation. On August 6, 1862, Stonewall Jackson was a guest. Now a painting depicting his bravery at the Battle of Cedar Mountain hangs over the mantel. During the 1863–64 winter, the Army of Northern Virginia III Corps headquartered here, and General A. P. Hill commanded 18,000 men from a front-yard tent. While living in the mansion, Hill's wife gave birth to Lucy Lee Hill. General Robert E. Lee held her at her christening here on May 1, 1864—four days before he led troops at the Battle of the Wilderness. If only these walls could talk.

SETTINGS & FACILITIES

Location Rte. 15, 0.75 mi. south of Orange. **Near** Montpelier, 30 mi. northeast of Charlottesville, 35 mi. west of Frederick. **Building** 1859 4-story white Italianate w/ rooftop cupola, floor-to-ceiling arched windows, Victorian curlicues. **Grounds** 37 acres of wooded land, rolling hills, pond. **Public Space** 2 large halls, library, DR, 2 porches, upstairs reading area, tower w/ telescope. **Food & Drink** Full breakfast at 3 tables in downstairs dining room, specialties—plantation casserole, Italian scrambled eggs, stuffed French toast w/ apples. **Recreation** Shakespeare plays at Barboursville Ruins, fall steeplechase races, wine festivals. **Amenities & Services** Discount at Fawn Lake golf course; groups (150).

ACCOMMODATIONS

Units 5 guest rooms, 2 suites. **All Rooms** AC, phone jacks. **Some Rooms** Fireplace (5), balcony (1), private entrance (1). **Bed & Bath** King (1), queen (4); private baths, 2 whirlpools, 1 claw-foot tub, 1 regular tub. **Favorites** Southern Charm—double whirlpool tub, king bed, log fireplace, 3 windows, Victorian lamps, Virginia wine. **Comfort & Decor** The house has special architectural merit. Details include the grand parlor and entry hall, high ceiling, and a spiral staircase that ascends four floors.

RATES, RESERVATIONS, & RESTRICTIONS

Deposit 1 night or 50%; refund w/ 14-days notice. **Discounts** No. **Credit Cards** V, MC, AE. **Check-In/Out** 3–7 p.m./noon. **Smoking** No. **Pets** No. **Kids** Yes. **Minimum Stay** 2 nights in May & Oct. **Open** All year. **Hosts** Peg & Bob Harmon, 12460 Mayhurst Ln., Orange, 22960. **Phone** (888) 672-5597. Fax (540) 672-7447. **E-mail** bharmon 527@aol.com. **Web** mayhurstinn.com.

WILLOW GROVE INN, Orange

OVERALL ★★★½ | QUALITY ★★★★ | VALUE ★★ | PRICE $225–$330 (WITH DINNER)

Are you a history buff? Except for bathrooms added in the 1930s, this house has stayed virtually as it was when completed in 1820. One portion was built even earlier by Joseph Clark in 1778. Generals Wayne and Muhlenberg camped here during the Revolutionary War. The house was under siege

during the Civil War, and trenches
nonball was recently removed from
the life of rural Virginia gentry. Old-
this inn a success. That and authentici
ter of Historic Places and it has Virgini

SETTINGS & FACILITIES

Location On Rte. 15, 2 mi. north of downt
Mountains. **Building** 1778 Federal manor hous
additions. **Grounds** 37 acres, sloping lawn, herb
bulbs & English boxwood, lily pond, benches, swin ... , pasture.
Public Space 2 sitting rooms, 2 DR, 1 bar, large br ... porches. **Food & Drink** Full breakfast; specialties—orange cinnamon French toast, open-faced garden omelet, spicy sausage gravy w/ corn muffins; 3-course dinners feature regional cuisine (MAP guests only). **Recreation** Hiking, fishing, cycling, canoeing, badminton, boccie, croquet, vineyard tours; Christmas Tour, Chestnut Festival, Southern Cooking Extravaganza. **Amenities & Services** Fax & e-mail; groups (80 inside, more outside)

ACCOMMODATIONS

Units 7 guest rooms, 3 suites. **All Rooms** AC, fresh flowers. **Some Rooms** Fireplace (3), balcony (1), private entrance (5). **Bed & Bath** King (3), queen (1), double (7), twin (1), canopy (1), four-poster (5), sleigh (1); private bath, 5 whirlpools, 4 tubs. **Favorites** Washington—corner room w/ 6 windows, 1700s furniture, double cherry poster bed, sitting area, fireplace; Cook's Quarters—antebellum cottage, nineteenth-century pine furnishings, double brass and iron bed, sitting room, brass daybed, whirlpool. **Comfort & Decor** The house is handicapped by old walls, but good fabrics, antiques, and gilded picture frames add a touch of elegance. The restaurant uses antique silver, crystal, and china.

RATES, RESERVATIONS, & RESTRICTIONS

Deposit 50%, refund w/ 15-days notice. **Discounts** Weekdays. **Credit Cards** AE, V, MC, D, DC. **Check-In/Out** Flexible. **Smoking** No. **Pets** Yes, in outbuildings. **Kids** Yes. **Minimum Stay** No. **Open** All year. **Host** Angela Mulloy, 14079 Plantation Way, Orange, 22960. **Phone** (800) 949-1778. Fax (540) 672-3674. **E-mail** wginn@ns.gemlink.com. **Web** willowgroveinn.com.

MAYFIELD INN, Petersburg

OVERALL ★★★★½ | QUALITY ★★★★½ | VALUE ★★★★★ | PRICE **$69–$95**

This Georgian-style gem was saved from demolition in 1969. Owners Jamie and Dot Caudle achieved an exquisite restoration, including the Flemish bond brickwork, bay windows, and clipped gable roof. Seven fireplaces add charm to high-ceilinged rooms. "I want travelers to see how we used to live in the South," says Caudle, whose house is now on the National Register of Historic Places. An important part of this aristocratic experience is a sumptuous country breakfast prepared by English-born innkeeper Cherry Turner and served in the formal dining room. The Caudles also own King's Barbecue, a down-home eatery.

ES

I-95, I mi. east of I-85. **Near** Petersburg National Battlefield, Pam- r Museum, Siege Museum, Blandford Church & cemetery, Centre Hill mond airport. **Building** 1750 Colonial. **Grounds** 4 acres w/ award-winning den, shade garden, brick walkways, gazebo, 40-ft. outdoor swimming pool. **Public ce** 2 parlors, DR, pool deck. **Food & Drink** Full breakfast w/ fresh fruit, beverages, home-baked goods; specialties—egg, cheese, & herb casserole, blueberry pancakes, creamy scrambled eggs w/ chives, bacon, sausage, fried apples; afternoon tea w/ home-made cookies & cakes. **Recreation** Horse-drawn carriage rides, historic sites. **Amenities & Services** Videos, laundry facilities, fax; meetings (25), weddings (150).

ACCOMMODATIONS

Units 2 guest rooms, 2 suites. **All Rooms** A/C, phone, fresh flowers, hair dryer. **Some Rooms** Dormer windows. **Bed & Bath** Queen (4), canopy (1); private baths, 1 detached, 2 tubs. **Favorites** Blue room—spacious, canopied bed, antique dressing table. **Comfort & Decor** This authentically restored house showcases antiques and period reproductions. Colonial-themed guest rooms have very comfortable mattresses.

RATES, RESERVATIONS, & RESTRICTIONS

Deposit 1 night, refund w/ 3-days notice. **Discounts** AAA, AARP, National Trust 10%. **Credit Cards** AE, V, MC. **Check-In/Out** 1 p.m. on/11 a.m. **Smoking** No. **Pets** No. **Kids** Yes. **Minimum Stay** No. **Open** All year. **Hosts** Jamie Caudle & Cherry Turner, Box 2265, Petersburg, 23804. **Phone** (800) 538-2381 or (804) 733-0866. Fax (804) 863-1971. **E-mail** mayfieldinn@rcn.com. **Web** mayfieldinn.com.

EMMANUEL HUTZLER HOUSE, Richmond

OVERALL ★★★★ | QUALITY ★★★★ | VALUE ★★★★ | PRICE **$105–$155**

One of Richmond's finest addresses, guests here can walk to major museums and fine restaurants. Built by the youngest son of a prosperous dry goods merchant from Bavaria, the inside is huge and elegantly appointed. It does have a checkered past, serving for a time as a men's social club, then a run-down rooming house. But, current owners have thoroughly renovated it. Lyn was formerly a social worker and an employee in the Governor's office. She collects salesmen's samples of miniature furniture, including an 1860s English washstand, a bed with quilt, and a Dutch corner cabinet. John left the real estate business after finding himself suited for the role of innkeeper.

SETTINGS & FACILITIES

Location Center of 1.3-mi. tree-lined Monument Ave. between statues of Robert E. Lee & Jefferson Davis. **Near** White House of the Confederacy, Virginia Museum of Fine Arts, Science Museum, Agecroft Hall, Maymont, state capitol, Valentine Museum, Louis Ginter Botanical Gardens, Riverwalk, Poe Museum, St. John's Church. **Building** 1914 Italian renaissance, 3-story pale yellow brick w/ 4 columns, granite steps, iron railing, bay windows. **Grounds** City lot. **Public Space** Foyer, LR, DR, kitchen, porch. **Food & Drink** Full breakfast w/ juice, seasonal fruit, natural cereals, homemade breads; specialties—eggs any style, French toast, quiche. **Recreation** Sightseeing, jogging, kayaking the James River, touring Richmond; Easter Parade, Holiday House Tour, Garden Tour, Arts in the Park. **Amenities & Services** Lighted off-street parking, fax & e-mail avail.

ACCOMMODATIONS

Units 4 guest rooms. **All Rooms** AC, phone, cable TV. **Some Rooms** Fireplace (1), desk. **Bed & Bath** King (1), queen (3), four-poster (2), interesting headboards; private baths, 1 whirlpool, 4 tubs. **Favorites** Robinette's suite—largest, bright, Monument Ave. view, decor is pink & peach tones w/ cream molding, chandelier, antique sofa, marble fireplace, four-poster bed, huge bathroom w/ whirlpool; Marion's room—queen bed, iron headboard, sitting area, antique desk, loveseat, nice fabrics, tiled bath. **Comfort & Decor** Spacious public rooms have a classic look. Wood wainscoting with raised paneling, coffered 12-foot ceilings with dropped beams, and leaded glass windows enhance all first floor rooms. The living room has an Italian marble fireplace and mahogany bookcases.

RATES, RESERVATIONS, & RESTRICTIONS

Deposit Credit card to hold, refund w/ 10-days notice (5-days corp., 30-days holidays and special events). **Discounts** Midweek corp., single. **Credit Cards** AE, V, MC, DC, D. **Check-In/Out** 4–6 p.m./11 a.m. **Smoking** No. **Pets** No (T.C. the cat in residence, boarding nearby). **Kids** Over age 12. **No-Nos** Candles. **Minimum Stay** 2 nights on weekends. **Open** All year (except Dec. 30–Jan. 7). **Hosts** Lyn & John Benson, 2036 Monument Ave., Richmond, 23220. **Phone** (804) 355-4885. **E-mail** be.our.guest@bensonhouse.com. **Web** bensonhouse.com.

CHESTER, Scottsville

OVERALL ★★★½ | QUALITY ★★★★½ | VALUE ★★★ | PRICE $165

Chester played a role in the Civil War during General Sheridan's occupation of nearby Scottsville in March, 1865. When the wounded Major James Hill, a local Confederate Army Commander, occupied this house, Sheridan and his aide, Colonel George Custer, visited him here. But, they decided not to arrest what they thought was a dying man. Unexpectedly, Hill survived and went on to become editor of the *Scottsville Courier* newspaper. The house was built by Joseph C. Wright, a retired landscape architect from Chester, England. He transformed the setting to offer both beauty and privacy. The grounds are remarkable for their stands of English boxwoods, and the largest holly tree in Albemarle County.

SETTINGS & FACILITIES

Location 2 blocks from Rte. 205, 18 mi. south of Charlottesville. **Near** Monticello, Michie Tavern, Univ., of Virginia, Ash Lawn-Highland, Charlottesville Airport, James River, Blue Ridge Parkway. **Building** 1847 Greek Revival. **Grounds** 7 acres w/ 2 lily ponds, patio, gardens, boxwoods, trees. **Public Space** LR, DR, library, 2 porches. **Food & Drink** Full breakfast w/ juice, fresh fruit, homemade bread & muffins; specialties—breakfast soufflés, cinnamon orange French toast w/ Canadian bacon; wine & beverages avail.; 5-course candlelight dinner option for 6 or more. **Recreation** Touring Richmond, canoeing on James River. **Amenities & Services** Massage avail., meetings (20), weddings (100).

ACCOMMODATIONS

Units 5 guests rooms. **All Rooms** AC, fireplace, fresh flowers, large chairs. **Some Rooms** Private entrance (1). **Bed & Bath** Queen, four-poster (4), duvets; private baths, tubs (4). **Favorites** #4—large, wood-trimmed bathroom, baby cradle. **Comfort & Decor** Upscale living room furnishings include a baby grand piano, chandeliers, plus sofa, Oriental rugs, and wood-burning fireplace. A cozy library and porches with rocking chairs and swing are inviting.

RATES, RESERVATIONS, & RESTRICTIONS

Deposit Credit card, refund w/ 10-days notice. **Discounts** No. **Credit Cards** V, MC. **Check-In/Out** 4 p.m./11 a.m. **Smoking** No. **Pets** No. **Kids** Over age 8. **Minimum Stay** 2 nights in Oct. & some weekends. **Open** All year. **Hosts** Jean & Craig Stratton, 243 James River Rd., Scottsville, 24590. **Phone** (804) 286-3960. **E-mail** info@chesterbed.com. **Web** chesterbed.com.

HIGH MEADOWS VINEYARD, Scottsville

OVERALL ★★★★ | QUALITY ★★★★ | VALUE ★★★★ | PRICE $99–$265

A lot of heart and hard work were poured into restoring this unique double house and the surrounding grounds, which now produce quality Pinot Noir grapes. Peter was a Navy captain who specialized in submarines and served on Margaret Thatcher's staff. His wife, Jae, had a career with the Securities and Exchange Commission. Together they began restoring the house in 1984, devoting weekends to hands-on projects that ultimately made their dream come true. The result is a mecca for warm hospitality, comfortable lodging, and creative loafing. Their award-winning restaurant is a bonus. Evening wine tastings are fun and spark social interaction among guests. Note that a Saturday stay includes dinner in the on-site restaurant.

SETTINGS & FACILITIES

Location On Rte. 20, 0.5 mi. north of Scottsville. **Near** 15 mi. south of Monticello, 18 mi. south of Charlottesville. **Building** 1832 Federal joined to 1882 Victorian farmhouse. **Grounds** 23 acres of hilltop pasture surrounded by woodlands, fruit tree orchard, antique rose garden, gazebo, pond, 1.4-acre vineyard, walking trail. **Public Space** Parlor, 2 DR, 4 porches. **Food & Drink** Full country breakfast w/ fresh fruit, juice, homemade muffins; specialties—cranberry apple French toast, eggs, bacon, sausage, pancakes, omelets; multi-course dinners begin w/ wine tastings in grand hall or vineyard-side terrace. **Recreation** Tubing, canoeing, & fishing on the James River. **Amenities & Services** Champagne welcome; on-site restaurant.

ACCOMMODATIONS

Units 7 guest rooms, 3 cottages. **All Rooms** AC. **Some Rooms** Fireplace (9). **Bed & Bath** King (1), queen (8), round (1), four-poster (2), canopy (2); private baths, tubs (7), Jacuzzi (1), whirlpool (1), hot tub (2). **Favorites** High View—four-poster bed, fireplace, deck; Vineyards View—exposed beams, naval theme; Music Room—bay windows, hand-carved walnut bed, red/wood/cream tones; Fairview—toile draped bed, claw-foot tub facing fireplace, bay windows filled with dogwood blossoms. **Comfort & Decor** High ceilings, antiques, and gilded mirrors are distinctive elements of the lavish decor.

RATES, RESERVATIONS, & RESTRICTIONS

Deposit 1 night, refund w/ 10-days notice less $25. **Discounts** Midweek. **Credit Cards** V, MC, DC, D. **Check-In/Out** 4–8 p.m./11 a.m. **Smoking** No. **Pets** 3 rooms only. **Kids** Yes. **Minimum Stay** 2 nights some weekends & holidays. **Open** All year except Christmas. **Hosts** Peter & Jae Sushka, 55 High Meadows Ln., Scottsville, 24590. **Phone** (800) 232-1832. **Fax** (804) 286-2124. **E-mail** peterhmi@aol.com. **Web** highmeadows.com.

CLIFTON—THE COUNTRY INN, Shadwell

OVERALL ★★★★★ | QUALITY ★★★★½ | VALUE ★★★ | PRICE $175–$475

Clifton was built by Thomas Mann Randolph, the husband of Thomas Jefferson's beloved daughter, Martha. Randolph served as governor of Virginia and a U.S. Congressman, using this house as a trading center. During another colorful era, Clifton sheltered the wife and children of Confederate Colonel John Singleton Mosby. "The Grey Ghost" left them provisions at a hiding place nearby to elude Union troops. Today, guest rooms in the main house are swathed in elegant English fabrics and wall coverings. More rustic outbuildings provide privacy and charm. Throughout this historic property, the attention to detail is remarkable. The restaurant has earned national recognition for its cuisine and wine list.

SETTINGS & FACILITIES

Location Rte. 729 off Rte. 250, 8 mi. east of Charlottesville. **Near** Univ. of Virginia, Charlottesville Airport. **Building** 1799 Federal & Colonial Revival w/ double level 5-bay porch, box columns; 3 original dependencies (law office, carriage house, livery stable). **Grounds** 40 acres w/ flower & herb gardens, 2 stone walls, 20-acre lake, spring-fed pool w/ waterfall, gazebo, 0.25-mi. hiking trail. **Public Space** Drawing room, library, tea room, 2 DR, powder room, veranda. **Food & Drink** Full breakfast; specialties—frittatas of smoked salmon & scallions, smoked bacon, stone ground herbed grits, buckwheat pancakes w/ strawberry rhubarb compote; afternoon tea; picnic lunches avail. **Recreation** Clay tennis court, hot tub, croquet, horseshoes, fishing, picnicking; rackets, balls, fishing poles, & backpacks provided. **Amenities & Services** TV & VCRs, massage, health club privileges nearby, disabled access (1), fax; groups (25).

ACCOMMODATIONS

Units 7 guest rooms, 7 suites, 3 cottages. **All Rooms** AC, phone, CD player w/ CDs, dataport, cotton robes & slippers, fresh fruit, feather pillows, down comforter. **Some**

Rooms Fireplace (13), private entrance (9), stone courtyard & garden, decanters of port & sherry, Sanderson fabrics & wallcoverings. **Bed & Bath** King (1), queen (12), double (1), canopy (3), sleigh (2), loft (1); private baths, 1 whirlpool, 12 tubs. **Favorites** Thomas Mann Randolph—yellow & white checkered bed canopy; Monticello Suite—canopied valance, sofa facing fireplace, tufted chaise lounge, hand-painted coral & white striped walls, claw-foot tub. **Comfort & Decor** An elegant parlor and small library offer comfortable seating. One dining room overlooks the garden. Guest rooms have Federal-style reproduction antiques and quality amenities. Gourmet 5-course and 6-course dinners are $60 and $70, respectively, and get pricier with wine. Noteworthy are the formal cocktail hour with menu presentation and pianist on Fridays and Saturdays.

RATES, RESERVATIONS, & RESTRICTIONS

Deposit 1 night. **Discounts** AARP 10%. **Credit Cards** AE, V, MC, DC. **Check-In/Out** 3–5 p.m./11 a.m. **Smoking** No. **Pets** No. **Kids** Over age 10. **Minimum Stay** 2 nights on weekends. **Open** All year, except Christmas Eve & Day. **Host** Michael Hebony, 1296 Clifton Inn Dr., Charlottesville, 22911. **Phone** (804) 971-1800. Fax (804) 971-7098. **E-mail** kpurcell@cliftoninn.com. **Web** cliftoninn.com.

PROSPECT HILL PLANTATION, Trevilians

OVERALL ★★★★★ | QUALITY ★★★★★ | VALUE ★★★★ | PRICE $200–$285

These innkeepers say they derive their inspiration from former neighbor Thomas Jefferson, a man who insisted on striving for perfection in all his endeavors. Their overriding goal is to make guests feel at home. And, somehow, in this fairly remote corner of Virginia, they achieve that Herculean task—running a full-service country retreat patterned after a small European hotel while maintaining a cool, gracious demeanor. The setting, property, and cuisine are spectacular. Budget $80 per couple to add dinner to your stay. Being a guest at this historic property in the heart of a gently civilized countryside promotes a sense of peace, tranquility, and well-being.

SETTINGS & FACILITIES

Location Green Springs Historic District, 14 mi. east of Charlottesville, 3 mi. off Rte. 250. **Near** Monticello, Ash Lawn-Highland, Univ. of Virginia, 45 min. to Blue Ridge Mountains. **Building** A complete plantation complex w/ 1732 Colonial main house & 7 dependencies—slave quarters, log cabin, overseer's house, summer kitchen, smokehouse, carriage house, groom's quarters. **Grounds** 50 acres w/ vast park-like lawn, statuary, macadam paths, cutting garden, hammock, benches, swings, rockers, gazebo, pond, swimming pool, boxwoods, hedgerows, rare magnolias, tulip poplars, & giant beeches. **Public Space** Parlor, 3 DR, library, conservatory, parquet room, wine cellar, veranda. **Food & Drink** Cookies in room at check-in; breakfast tray in bed is standard or a 2-course breakfast in DR is avail. w/ fruit, juice, home-baked goods; specialties—omelets, quiche, French toast; afternoon tea; picnic lunches avail.; 5-course gourmet dinner served nightly. **Recreation** Swimming, hiking, golf, hot-air balloon rides, carriage rides, antiquing. **Amenities & Services** Massage, laundry facilities, fax; meetings (20).

ACCOMMODATIONS

Units 10 guest rooms, 3 suites. **All Rooms** A/C, fireplace, fresh flowers, fresh fruit, baked goods, red wine. **Some Rooms** Balcony (1), fridge w/ soft drinks (10). **Bed & Bath** King (1), queen (7), double (5), beehive (1), several canopies & four-posters; private baths, 7 double whirlpools, 1 whirlpool, 3 tubs. **Favorites** Terrill room—comfy bed, fireplace, whirlpool; Carriage House—largest suite, queen bed, deck; Miss Marcie's room—romantic four-poster canopy bed, large sit-in window; Overseer's cottage—cheerful, sun-filled sitting room, small deck overlooking pool, double whirlpool; Summer kitchen—large hearth fireplace, four-poster cannonball bed, double whirlpool, best pastoral views. **Comfort & Decor** The manor house has antique furnishings and quilts plus elegant accessories. Restored outbuildings have beamed ceilings, squeaking floors, and working fireplaces.

RATES, RESERVATIONS, & RESTRICTIONS

Deposit $200 per room. **Discounts** 10% Sun.–Thurs. except April, May, Oct., & holidays. **Credit Cards** AE, V, MC, DC, D. **Check-In/Out** 3 p.m./11 a.m. **Smoking** Bedrooms only. **Pets** No. **Kids** Welcome in some cottages. **Minimum Stay** 2 nights on weekends, 3 nights on some holidays. **Open** All year (except Christmas Eve & Day). **Hosts** The Sheehan Family—Laura & Michael, 2887 Poindexter Rds, Trevilians, 23093. **Phone** (800) 277-0844 or (540) 967-2574. Fax (540) 967-0102. **Web** prospecthill.com.

INN AT SUGAR HOLLOW, White Hall

OVERALL ★★★★ | QUALITY ★★★★½ | VALUE ★★★★ | PRICE $95–$160

Guests here have a front row seat for some of Albemarle County's best scenery. Sunshine streams through bay and palladium windows that overlook Buck's Elbow Mountain, Pasture Fence Mountain, and the rippling crests of Skyline Drive. The name dates back to the early 1900s when local distilleries brought in wagonloads of sugar which often spilled onto bumpy roads. Dick, a former hospital management consultant, is full of good humor, local history, and good advice about day trips. Hayden, a former French and Spanish teacher, helps with the cooking and keeps the place looking cheerful. A stay at this inn offers peace and serenity—plus the soothing sound of a real babbling brook.

SETTINGS & FACILITIES

Location 13 mi. northwest of Charlottesville. **Near** Shenandoah National Park, the Appalachian Trail. **Building** 1995 modern Virginia farmhouse w/ gray cedar siding. **Grounds** 70 acres in a wooded area bordering Moorman's River, herb,vegetable, & flower gardens. **Public Space** Sunroom, study, family room, powder room, guest pantry, reading nook, bluestone terrace, upstairs deck. **Food & Drink** Full country breakfast served buffet style; specialties—vegetable frittata, pumpkin pancakes, zucchini cakes; beverages & cookies anytime; dinners served on Sat. **Recreation** Horseback riding on woodland trails, winery tours, hiking, catch-and-release trout fishing below 80-foot dam, bird watching (binoculars avail.), good biking roads (bring your own bike). **Amenities & Services** Massage, access to laundry facilities, fax & e-mail.

ACCOMMODATIONS

Units 5 guest rooms. **All Rooms** AC, phone jack, hair dryer & phone on request. **Some Rooms** Fireplace (4). **Bed & Bath** King (2), queen (2), twin (1), four-poster (2), sleigh (1); private baths, 2 whirlpools, 2 tubs. **Favorites** Wildflower—master bedroom has pencil-post king draped w/ white organdy, fireplace, bright floral fabrics & pillows, wood floors, double Jacuzzi, bay windows w/ mountain view. **Comfort & Decor** Spacious public areas offer stylish furnishings, a massive stone fireplace, and lots of windows to enjoy woodland views. Quilts and stuffed animals add a touch of whimsy throughout.

RATES, RESERVATIONS, & RESTRICTIONS

Deposit 1 night, refund w/ 7-days notice. **Discounts** 3 nights or more, midweek. **Credit Cards** AE, V, MC, D. **Check-In/Out** 4–7 p.m./11 a.m. **Smoking** No. **Pets** No. **Kids** Over age 12, except some weekends. **Minimum Stay** 2 nights on weekends. **Open** All year (except Christmas). **Hosts** Hayden & Richard Cabell, 6051 Hollow Rd., White Hall, 22932. **Phone** (804) 823-7086. **E-mail** theinn@sugarhollow.com. **Web** sugarhollow.com.

Zone 20

Shenandoah Valley/ Blue Ridge Highlands

The richly-endowed Shenandoah Valley is steeped in both history and natural splendor. Mountains and rivers bound a region that boasts Civil War sites, orchards, caverns, hot springs, and a spectacular valley floor.

Beginning in **Front Royal,** the 105-mile long **Skyline Drive** extends the length of the Shenandoah Valley to just outside of **Staunton.** With a 35-mph speed limit and 75 scenic overlooks, you'll need plenty of time to enjoy the eagle's-eye views of the valley and its picturesque orchards, pastures, and plow-patterned vistas 4,000 feet below. In summer, leafy trees somewhat limit valley views from the roadway, but you can park and explore local flora and fauna on well-marked walking trails. Avoid peak holiday times when traffic is heavy and inclement weather possible.

At **Thornton Gap,** you can leave Skyline Drive to visit **Luray Caverns,** created by underground streams that penetrated the valley's porous limestone base. Sixty steps lead down a paved path that threads through enchanted spaces filled with stalactites and stalagmites. Expert lighting casts an eerie glow on a forest of water-etched columns, fluted stone cascades, and clear pools vaulted by natural ceilings up to 168-feet high.

The Shenandoah Valley was the breadbasket of the Confederacy. Near **New Market,** at the **Hall of Valor,** a 20-foot stained glass window honors ten cadets who died in the Battle of New Market, and circular exhibits survey the entire Civil War. **New Market Battlefield Military Museum** displays a private collection of artifacts dating from 1776 to present, including uniforms, weapons, and letters.

Staunton, set in the fertile valley between the Blue Ridge and Allegheny Mountains, is home to **Woodrow Wilson Birthplace and Presidential Museum.** At the **Museum of American Frontier Culture,** a three-quarter-mile lane connects farmsteads brought from England, Germany, and Northern Ireland, plus an indigenous American farm.

Costumed interpreters demonstrate the daily life of farmers in the eighteenth and nineteenth centuries.

Near **Lexington, Natural Bridge** is a 215-foot-high limestone arch over a deep gorge. George Washington surveyed it, Thomas Jefferson once owned it, and numerous artists have painted it. Today, self-guided tours and a sound and light show require a hefty admission charge.

Roanoke, set in a bowl between the Blue Ridge and Allegheny Mountains, is the cultural, commercial, and industrial center of western Virginia. The **Roanoke Museum of Fine Arts,** the **Science Museum of Western Virginia, Roanoke Valley History Museum,** and **Mill Mountain Theatre** are part of a downtown arts facility called **Center in the Square.**

The southwestern region of the Blue Ridge Highlands offers acres of forest, powerful waterfalls, and quiet lakes and streams—a true change of pace from modern life.

Our bed-and-breakfast choices include a horse farm, rock quarry, and a small town with access to first-rate theater. This is an ideal area to kick back, relax, and enjoy the scenery.

FOR MORE INFORMATION

Shenandoah Valley Visitors Center
Box 1040
New Market, VA 22844(540) 740-3132;
shenandoah.org

Front Royal-Warren County Visitors Center
414 East Main St.
Front Royal, VA 22630
(800) 338-2576; frontroyalchamber.com

Roanoke Valley Visitors Information Center
114 Market St.
Roanoke, VA 24011
(800) 635-5535; visitroanokeva.com

Staunton-Augusta County Travel Information Center
1250 Richmond Ave.
Staunton, VA 24401
(800) 332-5219; www.staunton.va.us

ABINGDON BOARDING HOUSE, Abingdon

OVERALL ★★★★ | QUALITY ★★★★ | VALUE ★★★★ | PRICE $85–$115

Eleanor Roosevelt's father, Elliott, stayed here when he came to town on lumber business years ago. And, it's believed that Eleanor accompanied him on several occasions. The innkeepers moved to this area in 1994, where she has family ties, and just recently opened the bed-and-breakfast. They're off to a good start. Lawrence retired from personnel work and now sells real estate, while Juanita continues her career with a local bank. Theater lovers will be particularly happy here because it's within walking distance of the excellent Barter Theater, which presents quality plays year-round. In earlier times you could exchange a chicken, some milk, or a few eggs for tickets, but a credit card is preferable nowadays.

SETTINGS & FACILITIES

Location Historic district. **Near** Barter Theatre, Holston Lake, Virginia Creeper Trail, Appalachian Trail, Mount Rogers; 130 mi. north of Knoxville, TN, 130 mi. south of Roanoke. **Building** 1840 Colonial. **Grounds** 1 acre w/ flower & vegetable gardens, native trees & shrubs, white picket fencing. **Public Space** LR, parlor, sunroom, DR, breakfast room, porch. **Food & Drink** Full breakfast served on Portmeirion china w/ fresh fruit, homemade baked goods; specialties—waffles, pancakes, eggs any style; coffee & tea w/ snack avail. anytime. **Recreation** Hiking, biking, theater; NASCAR in Bristol (March & Aug.), Virginia Highlands Festival (Aug.). **Amenities & Services** Videos, fax & e-mail (fiber optic connection); groups (10), weddings (30).

ACCOMMODATIONS

Units 3 guest rooms. **All Rooms** Phone, TV, ceiling fan, fresh flowers, clock, fireplace. **Some Rooms** Sizes vary. **Bed & Bath** King (1), queen (1), full (1); private baths, 1 tub. **Favorites** Elliott Roosevelt—four-poster bed, lace curtains. **Comfort & Decor** High ceilings, hardwood floors, Oriental rugs, and antique furnishings suggest the gracious lifestyle of an earlier era. The house was recently renovated.

RATES, RESERVATIONS, & RESTRICTIONS

Deposit 1 night. **Discounts** Long term. **Credit Cards** No. **Check-In/Out** 4 p.m./11 a.m. **Smoking** No. **Pets** No. **Kids** Yes. **Minimum Stay** 2 nights during race weekends, festivals, holidays, special events. **Open** All year. **Hosts** Juanita & Lawrence Campany, 116 E. Main St., Abingdon, 24210. **Phone** (276) 628-9344. **E-mail** campany123@aol.com.

CHESTER HOUSE, Front Royal

OVERALL ★★★★ | QUALITY ★★★½ | VALUE ★★★ | PRICE **$95–$210**

This location is ideal, with Balthus House, the Confederate Museum, and several good restaurants within walking distance and the entrance to Skyline Drive nearby. International lawyer Charles Samuels, who worked on the Treaty of Versaille, built this architectural gem, starting with an older house where his mother grew up. Sparing no expense, he added nine fireplaces, chandeliers from Europe, elegant woodwork, and dentil moldings. The house needed only cosmetic repairs when these enthusiastic innkeepers moved in during 2001—after restoring four other houses. A stay includes candlelight breakfasts served on fine china and good crystal, and old-fashioned southern hospitality.

SETTINGS & FACILITIES

Location Residential street in historic district. **Near** 1 mi. north of Shenandoah National Park/Skyline Drive, 19 mi. south of Winchester, 50 mi. west of Dulles Airport, 70 mi. west of Washington, D. C. **Building** 1905 Italian Renaissance, beige stucco w/ green shutters. **Grounds** 2 acres w/ English herb garden, 1-acre formal walk-through boxwood garden, European statuary, fish pond, fountain, wisteria arbor, double hammock, rope swing. **Public Space** Foyer, 2 front parlors, LR, DR, porch. **Food & Drink** Full breakfast w/ juice, fruit, fresh breads; specialties—waffles w/ blackberries, popovers, pancakes, eggs any style; complimentary beer, wine, sherry, cookies anytime.

Recreation Shenandoah River, Civil War battlefields, wineries, horseback riding, antiquing, caverns, Skyline Drive, Luray Caverns; Wine & Mushroom Festival (May), Fall Leaf Festival (Oct.). **Amenities & Services** Fax & e-mail.

ACCOMMODATIONS

Units 5 guest rooms, 1 cottage. **All Rooms** AC, robes, CD clock, fan, electric blanket. **Some Rooms** Fireplace (3), private entrance (1), TV (1), phones (1), kitchen (1). **Bed & Bath** King (2), queen (3), four-poster (2); private baths, 1 detached, whirlpool, 4 tubs. **Favorites** Carriage House—corner fieldstone fireplace, spiral stairs to loft w/ king bed, stained glass, double whirlpool, full kitchen; Royal Oak—fireplace, best garden view, peach & blue decor. **Comfort & Decor** Spacious public rooms have traditional and eclectic furnishings with antiques, family heirlooms, crystal chandeliers, Oriental rugs, oil landscape paintings, and accessories from worldwide travels. An Austrian sideboard, carved marble fireplace, and elegant table inlaid with three kinds of wood enhance the dining room. Both parlors have a television and fireplace for relaxing.

RATES, RESERVATIONS, & RESTRICTIONS

Deposit 1 night, refund w/ 30-days notice. **Discounts** Corp. 20% Sun.–Thurs. **Credit Cards** AE, V, MC. **Check-In/Out** 3–9 p.m./noon. **Smoking** No. **Pets** Indoor-outdoor dog run avail., call first (1 resident dog). **Kids** Over age 12. **Minimum Stay** 2 nights on weekends April–Nov. **Open** All year except Dec. & Jan. **Hosts** Phillip Inge & Barbara & Allen Hamblin, 43 Chester St., Front Royal, 22630. **Phone** (800) 621-0441 or (540) 635-3937. **Fax** (540) 636-8695. **E-mail** mail@chesterhouse.com. **Web** chesterhouse.com.

KILLAHEVLIN, Front Royal

OVERALL ★★★★ | QUALITY ★★★★ | VALUE ★★★ | PRICE **$135–$235**

Every day is St. Patrick's Day at this comfy hilltop home run by an innkeeper of Irish descent. (Her dad was born in Limerick.) After leaving the corporate world as a personnel consultant for Xerox, she created a bit of the old country in northern Virginia. The decision to create an informal Irish pub in a corner of the main floor has fostered tremendous camaraderie among her guests. "Many of my guests meet at the pub and end up going out to dinner together. Some keep in touch and a few even return together as a group," Susan reports. The sprawling house has lots of public areas. If you want privacy, the dining room has separate tables, the guest house is quieter, and the grounds are large.

SETTINGS & FACILITIES

Location 1.5 mi. north of town center, atop a high hill. **Near** Blue Ridge Mountains, George Washington National Forest, Skyline Drive, Shenandoah National Park. **Building** 1905 modified brick Queen Anne, 4-story guesthouse w/ tower. **Grounds** 10 acres w/ lawn, 2 gazebos, mature trees, pond w/ koi, frogs, goldfish, water lilies, water hyacinth. **Public Space** Parlor, DR, pub, 2 porches, powder room. **Food & Drink** Full breakfast w/ Kona coffee, juice, fresh fruit, gourmet cereals, homemade baked goods; specialties—Belgian waffles w/ country sausage, French toast, eggs Benedict; cookies, free Irish beer, wine, champagne, snacks served in the pub. **Recreation** Antiquing, theater, wineries, Civil War sites, canoeing, golf, hiking, horseback rides, hot-air balloons, caverns; Wine &

Mushroom Festival (May), Octoberfest (Sept.). **Amenities & Services** Private health club privileges, massage avail., disabled access (1); meetings (12), weddings (100).

ACCOMMODATIONS

Units 4 guest rooms, 2 suites. **All Rooms** AC, phone, hair dryer, clock radio, ceiling fan, fireplace, sherry & cookies. **Some Rooms** TV/VCR (2), balcony (4), private entrance (2). **Bed & Bath** Queens, four-poster (3); private baths, 5 whirlpools, 1 claw-foot tub. **Favorites** Jade Tree suite—best fabrics & walls, green double whirpool. **Comfort & Decor** The main house has high ceilings, wood paneling, French doors, and seven fireplaces, including three in the public rooms. Furnishings are eclectic. The pub is a gathering place to meet other guests and kick back and relax. The first to arrive gets to be bartender, dispensing complimentary beer and popcorn to all.

RATES, RESERVATIONS, & RESTRICTIONS

Deposit Credit card, refund w/ 3-days notice. **Discounts** Corp. Sun.–Thurs. **Credit Cards** AE, V, MC, D. **Check-In/Out** 3–9 p.m./11 a.m. **Smoking** No. **Pets** No (1 cat on premises named Oscar Wilde). **Kids** Over age 12. **Minimum Stay** 2 nights on weekends & holidays. **Open** All year. **Host** Susan O'Kelly, 1401 N. Royal Ave., Front Royal, 22630. **Phone** (800) 847-6132 or (540) 636-7335. **Fax** (540) 636-8694. **E-mail** kllhvln @shentel.net. **Web** vairish.com.

JOSHUA WALTON HOUSE INN, Harrisonburg

OVERALL ★★★ | QUALITY ★★★★ | VALUE ★★★ | PRICE $110–$150

The inn is staff-run, and the owners are "not here very much." But everything seems to be running smoothly in this oasis of quiet charm in an urban setting. The tone is somewhat formal and the emphasis is on fine dining. You can relax in the bar area, then have dinner in one of several dining rooms on the first floor. Otherwise, there's not much space set aside for a common area for houseguests to use. Chef Mark Newsome prepares interesting fare using produce from small local farms, and his menu changes seasonally. You can order from an award-winning wine list, and, in warmer months, dine on an attractive outdoor patio. If you're visiting someone at James Madison University, perfect—it's just up the street.

SETTINGS & FACILITIES

Location Urban setting. **Near** 3 blocks to James Madison University, 1 block to Quilt Museum, 26 mi. north of Staunton. **Building** 1888 Victorian. **Grounds** Large city lot w/ herb garden, flower borders. **Public Space** Lounge, 5 DR, brick patio. **Food & Drink** Full breakfast w/ juice, fruit, yogurt, cereal, homemade coffee cake; specialties—blueberry pancakes, poached eggs over Portobello mushroom w/ Dijon mustard sauce, country ham & asparagus omelet; dinner served Tue.–Sat., 100 plus wines, microbrews. **Recreation** Hiking, biking, golf, fishing, snow skiing, antiquing. **Amenities & Services** Club privileges at Wellness Center, fax & e-mail; meetings (25), weddings (130).

ACCOMMODATIONS

Units 5 guest rooms. **All Rooms** AC, phone, hair dryer, robes, clock, plant, ceiling fan. **Some Rooms** Fireplace (1). **Bed & Bath** Queen, canopy (1), feather-top mattresses; private baths, tubs (2). **Favorites** #4—cream w/ soft floral patterns, four-poster w/

canopy, 3 bay windows w/ 2 upholstered chairs, desk, armoire, small bath. **Comfort & Decor** The house has many well-preserved details. Nice features include a leaded-glass front door, high ceilings, parquet floors, a grand staircase with newel post, and painted faux marble fireplaces. Guest rooms have a formal look.

RATES, RESERVATIONS, & RESTRICTIONS

Deposit Credit card, refund w/ 7-days notice. **Discounts** Corp. **Credit Cards** AE, V, MC, DC. **Check-In/Out** 2 p.m./noon. **Smoking** No. **Pets** No. **Kids** Over age 8. **Minimum Stay** 2 nights on homecoming, graduation, & New Year's. **Open** All year (except Christmas Eve & Day). **Hosts** Roberta & Craig Moore, 412 S. Main St., Harrisonburg, 22801. **Phone** (540) 434-4464. **Fax** (540) 432-9525. **E-mail** jwhouse@rica.net. **Web** www.rica.net/jwhouse.

BEDROCK INN, Pounding Mill

OVERALL ★★★★ | QUALITY ★★★★ | VALUE ★★★ | PRICE **$75–$100**

The word unique hardly captures this house, built by Charles Morris Hunter, who went to France during the Civil War to raise money for the Confederacy. After the war, he acquired five quarries, which still produce materials for road building in this relatively remote area of Virginia. The inn, now restored by the fourth generation of Hunters, is set behind a screen of trees that shields it from the sight and noise of heavy machinery—and it all works surprisingly well. Southern belle Sloane Hunter offers a special brand of hospitality. Guests can immerse themselves in the area's wild and wonderful countryside. For example: biking in pristine farmland called Burkes Garden, canoeing on the Clinch River to see dinner-plate sized mussels, and hiking in the Pinnacle Natural Area Preserve to see endangered plants and mollusks.

SETTINGS & FACILITIES

Location Off Rtes. 19 & 460. **Near** 20 mi. west of Tazewell, 30 mi. west of Bluefield. **Building** 1913 country farmhouse. **Grounds** 4 woodland acres w/ flower gardens, 2 ponds, gazebo, treehouse lighted tennis court, swing set, barbecue grill. **Public Space** Great room, DR, sitting room, sunporch, deck. **Food & Drink** Full breakfast w/ fresh fruit, pastries: specialties—stuffed French toast, eggs a la Jefferson, egg & ham soufflé; evening mint juleps. **Recreation** Canoeing, hiking, biking, golf, mussel sighting, fishing, bird watching, whitewater rafting, tennis, spa treatments; Living Pioneer Museum, Burke's Garden, The Cove, Pinnacle Natural Area Preserve. **Amenities & Services** Privileges at 2 country clubs, massage, disabled access, laundry equip., fax & e-mail; meetings (30), weddings (150).

ACCOMMODATIONS

Units 3 guest rooms, 2 suites. **All Rooms** AC, phone, fresh flowers, CD clock. **Some Rooms** TV (4), fireplace (2), private entrance (1), ceiling fan (1). **Bed & Bath** King (1), queen (1), double (3), canopy (1); private baths, 1 whirlpool, 3 tubs. **Favorites** Master bedroom—king four-poster w/ crocheted canopy, fireplace, traditional furnishings, spacious. **Comfort & Decor** This sprawling living space is filled with personal photographs and mementos of a busy family life. Nature art and hunting trophies add to the mix. The emphasis is on comfort.

RATES, RESERVATIONS, & RESTRICTIONS

Deposit 50% on credit card, refund w/ 7-days notice. **Discounts** Corp. **Credit Cards** AE, V, MC. **Check-In/Out** 4 p.m./noon. **Smoking** Yes. **Pets** Yes (outdoor kennel). **Kids** Yes. **Minimum Stay** None. **Open** All year. **Hosts** Sloane & Mike Hunter, Box 105, Pounding Mill, 24637. **Phone** (276) 963-9412. **E-mail** bedrock@netscope.net.

JORDAN HOLLOW FARM INN, Stanley

OVERALL ★★★★ | QUALITY ★★★★ | VALUE ★★★ | PRICE $133–$195

It can't be easy to run a quality bed-and-breakfast in the boonies. But, all you have to do to enjoy this peaceful hideaway in a lush Virginia hollow (read valley) is show up. Horseback riding is available only if you bring your own horse (and many people do). But you can walk the marked trails—about five miles in all. Peacefulness is the main attraction. That, and a good meal at the on-site fine dining restaurant. Oh, and if you enjoy cats, there are a baker's dozen roaming the property, each with a distinct personality. You're invited to adopt one during your stay, even take it your room. The innkeepers have researched several excellent day trip itineraries with detailed instructions—and they will prepare picnics.

SETTINGS & FACILITIES

Location Page Valley section of the Shenandoah Valley at the base off the Blue Ridge Mountains. **Near** Shenandoah National Park, George Washington National Forest, Shenandoah River, Skyline Drive, Massanutten, 40 mi. south of Front Royal, 100 mi. southwest of Washington, D.C. **Building** Restored 1800s farmhouse, 1900s carriage house, wisteria-covered Arbor View Lodge, hewn-log Mare Meadow guesthouse. **Grounds** 150 acres w/ walking trails, barn. **Public Space** Great room, porch, deck, restaurant. **Food & Drink** Full breakfast w/ juice, fruit, baked goods: specialties—omelets, quiche, frittatas, pancakes w/ strawberry & blueberry syrup; picnic lunches avail.; full restaurant features regional cuisine, Virginia wines. **Recreation** Hiking, biking, canoeing, golf, fishing, birding; access to swimming at Hawksbill Recreation Center, wineries, skiing, Civil War sites, caves; Strawberry Festival (May). **Amenities & Services** Massage, fax & e-mail, disabled access (1); meetings (30), weddings (150).

ACCOMMODATIONS

Units 9 guest rooms, 7 suites. **All Rooms** AC, phone, TV, private entrance. **Some Rooms** Fireplace (11). **Bed & Bath** King (6), queen (9); private baths, 7 double thermo-massage spas. **Favorites** Upper level suites—equine theme, access to porch w/ rocking chairs, fireplaces & whirlpools; Mare Meadow Lodge rooms—more rustic, private, view of llama pasture. **Comfort & Decor** The great room has a few games, but the ambience is a bit sterile. In the lodge, pairs of small rooms were joined to create suites. Bathroom amenities are skimpy (two thin bars of soap, period).

RATES, RESERVATIONS, & RESTRICTIONS

Deposit $100 by credit card, refund w/ 2-days notice. **Discounts** Corp. **Credit Cards** V, MC, DC, D. **Check-In/Out** 3 p.m./noon. **Smoking** No. **Pets** Yes, horses can be boarded (llamas, 2 dogs, & myriad cats on premises). **Kids** Yes, well-behaved. **No-Nos** Don't feed the horses in the pasture. **Minimum Stay** 2 nights on holiday weekends.

Open All year. **Hosts** Gail Kyle & Betsy Maitland, 326 Hawksbill Park Rd., Stanley, 22851. **Phone** (888) 418-7000 or (540) 778-2285. **Fax** (540) 778-1759. **E-mail** jhf@jordanhollow.com. **Web** jordanhollow.com.

SAMPSON EAGON INN, Staunton

OVERALL ★★★★ | QUALITY ★★★★ | VALUE ★★★★ | PRICE $98–$125

Forget your toothbrush? Have a headache? Need a taste of chocolate? These eager-to-please hosts provide a range of extra amenities to give you a sense of being in a home away from home. The antiques that raise the level of visual appeal in the spacious, high-ceilinged public rooms recall Laura's former life as an antiques dealer specializing in eighteenth century and American country pieces. The location is ideal: across the street from the Woodrow Wilson Museum, with the Wilson House just a few doors away. Within ten minutes you can be at the American Museum of Frontier Culture, another must-see attraction. In your room you'll find a three-inch thick notebook describing in detail all you can do in the area, an indication of how hard these innkeepers work to make sure you have a good time.

SETTINGS & FACILITIES

Location On Gospel Hill in historic district. **Near** Shenandoah Valley Regional Airport, Skyline Drive, Shenandoah National Park, Blue Ridge Parkway, Museum of American Frontier Culture, across the street from the Woodrow Wilson Birthplace & Museum, 1 block from Black Friars. **Building** 1790 Greek Revival w/ 1840 additions, Italianate elements. **Grounds** Urban lot w/ small cutting garden, 200-year-old boxwoods, iron fence. **Public Space** Parlor, DR, porch, stocked guest fridge. **Food & Drink** Full breakfast w/ juice, fruit, baked goods, specialties—Belgian waffles, soufflé, stuffed French toast, asparagus omelet; complimentary beverages, snacks, & fruit. **Recreation** Fly-fishing, canoeing, biking, horseback riding, the Appalachian Trail, Civil War sites, wineries, antiquing. **Amenities & Services** Videos, laundry access, amenities basket; country club golf privileges.

ACCOMMODATIONS

Units 3 guest rooms, 2 suites. **All Rooms** AC, two-line phone, clock radio, TV & VCR, fresh flowers, flashlight, desk, computer port, Perrier. **Some Rooms** Cassette player (suites). **Bed & Bath** Queen (5), twin (2), canopy (5), four-poster (3); private baths, 4 tubs. **Favorites** Holt—Colonial Revival period, toile fabric, leaded-glass window; David Kayser—American Empire style, 1810 Salem Massachusetts four-poster canopy bed, chandelier, semi–disabled access. **Comfort & Decor** Period antiques and reproduction are in the American Empire, Colonial Revival, and Cottage Victorian styles. Accessories include eighteenth- and nineteenth- century paintings, Japanese Imari porcelain, and antique Persian rugs.

RATES, RESERVATIONS, & RESTRICTIONS

Deposit Credit card. **Discounts** Corp. midweek. **Credit Cards** AE, V, MC. **Check-In/Out** 4 p.m./11 a.m. **Smoking** No. **Pets** No. **Kids** Over age 12. **Minimum Stay** 2 nights on weekends & holidays April–Nov. **Open** All year. **Hosts** Laura & Frank Mattingly, 238 E. Beverley St., Staunton, 24401. **Phone** (800) 597-9722 or (540) 886-8200. **Fax** (540) 886-8200. **E-mail** eagoninn@rica.net. **Web** eagoninn.com.

INN AT NARROW PASSAGE, Woodstock

OVERALL ★★★★ | QUALITY: ★★★★ | VALUE: ★★★ | PRICE **$95–$145**

This Colonial-era inn is one of many that was built as a wagon stop along major trails and toll roads. In a time when traveling was dangerous, sturdy log walls made it a safe haven against Indian attacks at the "narrow passage"—where the roadbed was only one wagon wide. Stonewall Jackson headquartered here in 1862 during the Valley Campaign, and it was here that he commanded his aide Jedediah Hotchkiss to "Make me a map of the Valley." Being so close to the road may be a problem for some guests. But the Shenandoah River is also just a short walk. You can fish, feed the ducks, and cross the river on a rope bridge. The ambience combines rustic and upscale features. Hospitality has been a tradition here for more than 260 years.

SETTINGS & FACILITIES

Location On the Shenandoah River, 2 mi. south of Woodstock (I-81, Exit 283). **Near** 90 mi. southwest of Dulles Airport. **Building** 1740s log & chink structure w/ additions. **Grounds** 5 acres slope to the river, trails, gardens, view of Massanutten Mountains. **Public Space** Common room, DR, conference room, 4 porches. **Food & Drink** Full breakfast; specialties—French toast, bacon & eggs, buffet on weekends; afternoon hot cider & Colonial tea. **Recreation** Hiking, horseback rides, fly-fishing for small-mouthed bass, wine tastings, Civil War sites & museums; Shenandoah Valley Music festival (July, Aug.), Old Times in Edinburgh (Sept.). **Amenities & Services** Fax & e-mail; meetings (25).

ACCOMMODATIONS

Units 12 guest rooms. **All Rooms** AC. **Some Rooms** Fireplace (8), balcony (8), phone (8), private entrance (10). **Bed & Bath** Queen, canopy (8), four-poster (8); private baths, 2 detached, tubs (3). **Favorites** S-4—queen canopy bed, fireplace, river & mountain view. **Comfort & Decor** The dining room has a massive limestone fireplace, beamed ceiling, and Shaker-style tables and chairs. Older guest rooms feature pine floors, stenciling, and the atmosphere of Colonial times. Newer rooms are similar, adding porches with river and mountain views. Among the Colonial antiques and reproductions is a 1700s linen press.

RATES, RESERVATIONS, & RESTRICTIONS

Deposit 1 night, refund w/ 3-days notice. **Discounts** Travel agents 10%. **Credit Cards** V, MC, D. **Check-In/Out** 2:30–9:30p.m. / 11 a.m. **Smoking** No. **Pets** No. **Kids** Yes. **Minimum Stay** 2 nights holidays & some weekends. **Open** All year. **Hosts** Ellen & Ed Markel, Box 608, Woodstock, 22664. **Phone** (800) 459-8002. **E-mail** innkeeper @innatnarrowpassage.com. **Web** innatnarrowpassage.com.

Part Seven

West Virginia

West Virginia is every bit as wild and wonderful as its advertising slogans and auto license plates promise. As a result, tourism now rivals the Mountain State economic mainstays of coal, lumber, and railroads.

The state's sporting opportunities are extraordinary. You can choose from 37 state parks, 9 state forests, and several wildlife management areas that offer 800 miles of hiking trails and 350 miles of mountain bike trails. In summer, you can rock climb, fish, golf, ride horses, and go hot-air ballooning. In winter, alpine and nordic ski areas thrive. When the snow melts, the state is the East Coast's undisputed whitewater capital.

West Virginia's rugged, mountainous terrain is conducive to slowing down to savor life's simpler pleasures. You can hike in wildflower filled glades, see rainbow-hued fish in remote mountain streams, listen to frogs chirp, watch fireflies at twilight, and see brilliant stars in rural night skies. Nearly 80 percent of the state's land is forested, and West Virginia's mountains have the highest total altitudes of any state east of the Mississippi River. Many of them measure over 4,800 feet, with Spruce Knob soaring to a full 4,861 feet high. The loftiest ridges run northeast to southwest in the Allegheny Highlands.

Water is plentiful, too. The state has hundreds of waterfalls and an estimated 2,000 miles of streams and rivers. Indians discovered the medicinal qualities of spring waters at **Berkeley Springs** in the Northern Panhandle. By 1730, infirm travelers from Europe arrived to mingle with local vacationers at makeshift camps. George Washington visited when he was a surveyor for Lord Fairfax and returned frequently—twice as president. **White Sulphur Springs,** where the waters have a more medicinal taste, has been a fashionable destination since the eighteenth century, as well.

For nearly 150 years, the New River Gorge was the source of some of the highest-quality coal in the country. Once 17 towns thrived here. Most are now ghost towns, and some are accessible only by railroad or raft.

Some sections of the river, known collectively as the **Upper New,** are particularly well suited for families (children as young as six), older folks, and anyone looking for a mild introduction to whitewater rafting. Rafting on the **Lower New** is typically more thrilling. Most challenging of all is the **Gauley River** (Upper, Middle, and Lower) which has a 24-mile section of technical whitewater with over 100 rapids.

Underground, the state is peppered with caves. The largest is **Seneca Caverns** in Monongahela National Forest. **Lost World** and **Organ Cave** are two of the more than 100 named caverns in Greenbrier County. The state has more than 1,500 unnamed caverns.

To celebrate the state's culture and heritage, West Virginia holds 200 annual fairs, festivals, races, tournaments, and special events. Bluegrass twang and gospel harmonies radiate from small town bandstands each summer, and foot stompin' square dances are popular year round. Apple butter, strawberries, and quilts are just some of the products highlighted at street fairs and community shindigs.

Some West Virginia towns retain a flavor of the frontier. And, there's plenty of history to absorb, especially in **Harpers Ferry, Charles Town, Charleston, Wheeling, Shepherdstown, Lewisburg,** and **Bramwell.** Fifteen historical sites are part of the **National Civil War Discovery Trail.**

Tamarack: The Best of West Virginia showcases local crafts, arts, and agricultural products at a huge roadside facility in Beckley near Interstates 64 and 77. The 50,000-square-foot building is crammed with juried handcrafts, pottery, furniture, glassware, fiber crafts, jewelry, woodcrafts, painting, sculpture, music, and books by West Virginia authors. Chefs from the legendary Greenbrier Resort prepare all the food for the cafeteria, making it arguably America's best highway-stop eatery.

Traveling to West Virginia's attractions has gotten easier. There are now nine airports and six Interstates. Although the older, windier, steeper back roads still lead to some of the more scenic terrain.

West Virginia's population is relatively small (about 1.8 million). Staying at a bed-and-breakfast is a good way to meet local people—including many transplants who have taken up innkeeping and now call this state home. The number of bed-and-breakfasts is growing and, like everywhere else, the quality is improving. You'll find sophisticated properties with whirlpool tubs, high tech music systems, and remote control fireplaces—and historic buildings that have been lovingly restored.

FOR MORE INFORMATION

West Virginia Division of Tourism & Parks
2101 Washington St. E.
Charleston, WV 25305
(304) 558-2766 or (800) 225-5982

Zone 21

Northern West Virginia

On a map, West Virginia bears an uncanny resemblance to a frog lying on its back with legs extended. The (larger) right foot corresponds to the Eastern Panhandle, an area of rolling countryside and picturesque towns, such as Harpers Ferry, Charles Town, Shepherdstown, Martinsburg, and Berkeley Springs.

Harpers Ferry was the site of abolitionist John Brown's 1850 raid on a U. S. Arsenal, which set off a chain of events that precipitated the Civil War. The state's most visited attraction is **Harpers Ferry National Historical Park,** where you can see historic buildings, museums, interpretive programs, and reenactments.

To the south, sedate **Charles Town** is noted for its Victorian-style houses. It was named for George Washington's youngest brother, who, in turn, named many of the streets for his relatives. History buffs will be interested to know that John Brown was tried and hanged here in 1859. On a lighter note, horse racing is popular at the **Charles Town Raceway.**

To the north, **Shepherdstown** is said to be the state's oldest continuously settled town. The local **Shepherd College** hosts a month-long season of first-rate theater each summer. **Martinsburg** sits in an apple and peach producing area near the entrance of **Shenandoah Valley.** Several Civil War battles were fought here, it was home to Confederate spy Belle Boyd, and numerous eighteenth- and nineteenth- century houses and industrial buildings survive.

Heading west, **Berkeley Springs** is one of America's oldest spas. By the 1830s, it was a summer getaway, especially for families with marriageable-age daughters. After a long decline, the area is once again thriving. A wintertime festival touts the local water, but year-round visitors fill jugs with the high-calcium water from free spigots in a nine-acre downtown state park.

The water, naturally filtered through Oriskany sandstone below the Cacapon Mountains, tastes sweet. Folks not only drink the water, they heat it to 102 degrees and soak in it in the adjacent **Berkeley Spring State Park Bath House.** Massage therapists offer every technique from shiatsu to deep muscle work. Locals say the town has more masseuses than lawyers.

The highest town in West Virginia is **Davis,** which has a frontier style and few pretensions. Nearby, **Blackwater Falls State Park** has a 63-foot waterfall of brown and amber water which flows through a deep river gorge. Naturalists lead interpretative hikes. In season, you can downhill and cross-country ski or go whitewater rafting in the area.

Nearer the center of the state, **Buckhannon** is home to **West Virginia State Wildlife Center,** featuring birds and animals native to the state. It holds a Strawberry Festival in May. At Graceland bed-and-breakfast in Elkins you can actually sleep in the bed of Stephen B. Elkins, who was the town's namesake, a U. S. Senator, and Secretary of War under President Benjamin Harrison. Students from Davis & Elkins College help run Graceland as part of coursework on hospitality and hotel management.

At the 900,000-acre **Monongahela National Forest,** you'll find West Virginia's highest mountains, which spawn the headwaters of the Ohio and Potomac Rivers. Trails range from a half-mile to eight miles. Rock climbers can tackle the more challenging Seneca Rocks, where sandstone juts straight up 900 feet. At **Seneca Caves,** the largest in the state, visitors can descend 165 feet below the surface. Farther north, you can see more weirdly-shaped formations in the **Smoke Hole Caverns.**

Larger cities in the northern half of West Virginia include **Wheeling, Morgantown,** and **Parkersburg.** In the latter, exhibits at the **Blennerhasett Museum** explore the city's past and riverboat cruises on the Ohio River provide present pleasures.

Good bed-and-breakfasts are scattered throughout the northern half of the state, with many of the region's premier properties concentrated in the northeast.

FOR MORE INFORMATION

Buckhannon Chamber of Commerce
(888) 707-1722

Davis Chamber of Commerce
(304) 259-5315

Elkins-Randolph County Chamber of Commerce
(304) 636-2717

Jefferson County Chamber of Commerce
(800) 624-0577

Jefferson County CVB
(800) 848-8687; jeffersoncountycvb.com

Travel Berkeley Springs
(800) 447-8797; berkeleysprings.com

Tucker County CVB
(800) 782-2775; canaanvalley.org

HIGHLAWN INN, Berkeley Springs

OVERALL ★★★★ | QUALITY ★★★★ | VALUE ★★★ | PRICE $85–$185

Algernon R. Unger, a former state legislator and creator of the once-prominent Washington Hotel, built this house for his bride, Chaffie Ziler. When she was widowed, Chaffie opened it as a boarding house. You'll find Berkeley Springs to be a delightful town, and it's one of the few to have a state park downtown, even if it only covers nine acres. From the free public spigots flows high-calcium spring water. Folks not only drink it, they heat it up and soak in it in the adjacent Berkeley Springs State Park Bath House. Local waters have been famous since Indians came to rest and soak in natural pools of the seemingly magical stuff. George Washington first came at age 29 to cure his rheumatic fever. In the nineteenth century, the town was a social mecca of sorts, with families bringing marriageable daughters to meet socially prominent mates. Things are more informal these days.

SETTINGS & FACILITIES

Location On a steep hillside overlooking town. **Near** 9 mi. north of Cacapon State Park, 7 mi. south of Hancock, Maryland. **Building** 1897 Victorian house plus Aunt Pearl's guest house, bath keepers quarters, & carriage house. **Grounds** 4 small city lots w/ flower & herb gardens, pebble path, benches. **Public Space** LR, DR, wraparound veranda, plus Bath Keepers Parlor. **Food & Drink** Full breakfast w/ juice, fruit, baked goods; specialties—fruit oatmeal, confetti-herb squash, light scrambled eggs, crisp bacon, dilled potatoes, homemade croissants; snacks & springwater-based beverages always avail.; prix fixe dinner Sat. nights May–Oct. & on holiday weekends. **Recreation** Golf, tennis, swimming, hiking, horseback riding, mineral spring bathing & spa services, antiquing, Museum of Berkeley Springs; Apple Butter Festival (Oct.), Winter Festival of the Waters (Feb.). **Amenities & Services** Meetings (12), weddings (20).

ACCOMMODATIONS

Units 12 guest rooms. **All Rooms** AC, TV. **Some Rooms** Whirlpool (4), gas fireplace (3), private entrance (4). **Bed & Bath** King (2), queen (9), double (1); private baths. **Favorites** Algernon, the Master's Room—spacious, sitting area, queen bed w/ high carved walnut headboard, double whirlpool; Victorian suite—private sitting porch w/ garden view, hand-painted Victorian furniture, queen bed w/ carved headboard, claw-foot tub. **Comfort & Decor** The sitting/dining room features authentic Victorian antiques and a wood-burning fireplace. The porch is a delight, with nice views overlooking the town. The town has a high density of excellent massage therapists.

RATES, RESERVATIONS, & RESTRICTIONS

Deposit Credit card, refund w/ 5-days notice. **Discounts** Extended stay. **Credit Cards** V, MC. **Check-In/Out** 2 p.m./noon. **Smoking** No. **Pets** No (3 cats in residence). **Kids** Over age 14. **Minimum Stay** 2 nights holidays & most weekends. **Open** All year. **Hosts** Sandra M. Kauffman & Tim Miller, 304 Market St., Berkeley Springs, 25411. **Phone** (888) 290-4163 or (304) 258-5700. **E-mail** highlawn@intrepid.net. **Web** highlawninn.com.

DEERPARK COUNTRY INN, *Buckhannon*

OVERALL ★★★★½ | QUALITY ★★★★½ | VALUE ★★★ | PRICE $80–$185

This inn (with two suites, one bedroom, and a restaurant) combines a nineteenth-century log cabin and turn-of-the-century farmhouse. The latter sits about 400 feet from the lodge, which was reconstructed in 1993 and offers wide verandas and an oversized fireplace. The grounds, open meadows, and woodlands, provide the luxury of seclusion for folks who really want to get away from it all. You can fish in misty ponds where resident geese keep watch, stroll in English Gardens frequented by hummingbirds, watch fireflies at dusk, and hear frogs chirp under clear star-lighted skies. Dining is another highlight of the day. Chef Dale Hawkins features seasonal produce and is known for his Jack Daniels Chocolate Cake.

SETTINGS & FACILITIES

Location Foothills of the Appalachian Mountains. **Near** West Virginia Wesleyan College, 7 mi. east of Buckhannon. **Building** Main Inn & 19th-century log lodge reconstructed in 1993. **Grounds** 100 acres w/ trails, 2 spring-fed ponds, raised gardens, wildflower beds, tree house, hammock. **Public Space** 2 common areas, 4 DR, powder room. **Food & Drink** Full breakfast w/ fresh fruit, sorbet, beverages; specialties—filled omelet, bread pudding French toast, apple cinnamon pancakes; fine dining restaurant open nightly by reservation. **Recreation** Hiking, mountain biking, fishing in private lakes, antiquing, hot-air ballooning, whitewater rafting, skiing, historic sites; fleet of rental bikes & croquet avail., murder mystery dinner, board games; Strawberry Festival (May). **Amenities & Services** Videos, fax & e-mail; meetings (50), weddings (500).

ACCOMMODATIONS

Units 4 guest rooms, 2 suites. **All Rooms** AC, TV, phone, hair dryer, clock. **Some Rooms** Fireplace (1), balcony (2), private entrance (1). **Bed & Bath** King (1), queen (2), double (2); private baths. **Favorites** Randolph suite—9-foot ceiling, antique bed, marble-topped tables, sitting room w/ chandelier, writing desk, porch with wicker furniture & meadow view; Greenbrier—queen sleigh bed, antique wardrobe, writing desk, French doors, veranda. **Comfort & Decor** The mood is rustic elegance with lots of deep wing chairs and nooks and crannies to relax in. Books are tucked everywhere, inviting guests to browse. Cozy fireplaces beckon and Mother Nature is just outside your door.

RATES, RESERVATIONS, & RESTRICTIONS

Deposit Credit card, refund w/ 10-days notice. **Discounts** Corp. **Credit Cards** AE, V, MC, DC, D. **Check-In/Out** 3–8 p.m./noon. **Smoking** No. **Pets** No. **Kids** Yes. **Minimum Stay** No. **Open** All year. **Hosts** Liz & Patrick Haynes, Box 817, Buckhannon, 26201. **Phone** (800) 296-8430 or (304) 472-8400. **Fax** (304) 472-5363. **E-mail** deerpark @deerparkcountryinn.com. **Web** deerparkcountryinn.com.

GOVERNOR'S INN, Buckhannon

OVERALL ★★★½ | QUALITY ★★★½ | VALUE ★★★ | PRICE $69–$115

This century-old brick mansion was built by the second governor of West Virginia, D.D.T. Farnsworth, who lived here with his wife and 15 children. He spared no expense. A unique hand-painted ceiling depicts local history, beginning with Indian mounds, hunting tribes, and the first white man's cabin and continuing with early town buildings, the railroad reaching West Virginia, the arrival of Civil War troops, and the current emphasis on nature and recreation. The ebullient innkeeper is involved in numerous projects and another business out-of-state. But somehow she makes it all work. "If my husband's wallet and my back hold out, we'll get it finished some day," Jerry says of the inn, which she began restoring in 1995.

SETTINGS & FACILITIES

Location Downtown, 1.5 mi. from Rte. 33, 11 mi. east of I-79 (Main St. exit). **Near** Clarksburg Benedum, Bel Meadow Golf Course, Stonewall Jackson Lake, Holly River State Park, Audra State Park, West Virginia Wildlife Center. **Building** 1898 Queen Anne Victorian, 3-story brick w/ turret & gingerbread trim. **Grounds** 2 acres w/ courtyard, gardens, statuary, climbing rose bushes, fruit trees. **Public Space** Reception area, 2 parlors, DR, powder room, 2 upstairs sitting areas. **Food & Drink** Candlelight breakfast w/ juice, fruit, baked goods; specialties—caramel French toast, bread pudding w/ amaretto sauce, egg, cheese, & herb casserole; treasure hunt lunches avail. **Recreation** Biking, fishing, hiking, hunting, antiquing, arts & crafts studios, picnics (tandem bike avail.); Strawberry Festival (May), Italian Heritage Festival (Sept.), Forest Festival (Oct.), Stonewall Jackson Jubilee. **Amenities & Services** VCR w/ videos, massage by appointment, fax; groups (20) weddings (75).

ACCOMMODATIONS

Units 6 guest rooms, 1 suite. **All Rooms** AC, TV, phones, fresh flowers, hair dryer, robes, featherbeds. **Some Rooms** Fireplace (1), balcony (1), private entrance (1). **Bed & Bath** King (3), double (4), twin (1); 4 private baths, 1 shared bath, 1 whirlpool, 1 double tub w/ mood lighting. **Favorites** The Celebrating Suite—2nd floor room w/ gold decor, balloons, queen chair, double whirlpool w/ rose petals, dining area. **Comfort & Decor** Beautiful fireplaces, hand-carved staircase, plus Victorian antiques and period pieces were chosen for comfort. Deep jewel colors create a dramatic look, but accessories add whimsy. The foyer ceiling has hand-painted cherubs. The quality of 3 rooms in Grandma's Attic does not match the standards of the governor's, wife's, and nanny's rooms.

RATES, RESERVATIONS, & RESTRICTIONS

Deposit Credit card, refund w/ 3-days notice. **Discounts** AARP, AAA. **Credit Cards** AE, V, MC, D. **Check-In/Out** after 2 p.m./11 a.m. **Smoking** No. **Pets** By prior arrangement (kennel nearby). **Kids** Yes. **Minimum Stay** 2 nights during college graduation & homecoming, strawberry festival, & square dancers convention. **Open** All year. **Host** Jerry Bruce Henderson, 76 East Main St., Buckhannon, 26201. **Phone** (304) 472-2516. **Fax** (304) 472-1613. **E-mail** henderso@msys.net. **Web** www.bbonline.com/wv/governors.

CARRIAGE INN, Charles Town

OVERALL ★★★★ | QUALITY★★★½ | VALUE ★★★ | PRICE $75–$135

In 1786, George Washington's younger brother, Charles, gave 80 acres to establish the town that now bears his name. Several of his family members owned homes here and have streets named for them. The Carriage Inn is one of the town's grandest properties. In 1864, Generals Ulysses S. Grant and Philip Sheridan met in the East Parlor (now the dining room) to discuss Civil War strategy in the Shenandoah Valley—qualifying it for the Register of National Historic Places. Cuisine is a big attraction at the inn, earning it the 1999 Jones Dairy Farm culinary award. Civil War buffs will appreciate the many mementos on display, and the George Washington Heritage Trail (a National Scenic Byway) passes by the front door. You can walk to restaurants, antique shops, the Charles Town Museum, the Old Opera House, and Charles Town Races.

SETTINGS & FACILITIES

Location On Rte. 51 in historic district. **Near** 5 mi. west of Harpers Ferry, 65 mi. west of Washington, D.C. **Building** 1836 Federal gray brick w/ large porch, swing, rockers & settee. **Grounds** 1 acre tree-shaded lot w/ terraced flower gardens, 2 copper benches. **Public Space** Parlor, DR, 2nd floor landing, powder room, guest fridge. **Food & Drink** Full breakfast w/ juice, fresh fruit, hot beverages; specialties—cheese blintz soufflé with apricot garnish, Canadian bacon, lemon-poppyseed bread; cheese soufflé, sausage patties, baking powder biscuits w/ apricot & honey; southern pecan French toast w/ maple syrup, double chocolate banana muffins; tea, coffee, sodas avail. anytime; special diets accommodated. **Recreation** Rafting, tubing, kayaking, canoeing, golf, tennis, hiking, biking, theater, antiquing, fruit picking in season; umbrellas & bike storage avail. **Amenities & Services** Access to Gold's Gym & Charles Town Athletic Club w/ Olympic-sized pool, weight circuit, racquetball courts; limited disabled access, fax; meetings (10).

ACCOMMODATIONS

Units 4 guest rooms, 2 suites. **All Rooms** AC, fresh flowers, clock radio. **Some Rooms** Fireplace (3), stove (2), ceiling fan (1), private entrance (1), TV (2). **Bed & Bath** Queen (7), twin (1), canopy (3), four-poster (5); private baths w/ tubs. **Favorites** Green room—11-foot ceiling & tall windows w/ lace curtains, four-poster, fireplace, green wallpaper. **Comfort & Decor** High ceilings, period antiques, reproductions, family heirlooms, Oriental rugs, crystal chandeliers, and Civil War books, photos, art, and artifacts found at this site add a sense of authenticity.

RATES, RESERVATIONS, & RESTRICTIONS

Deposit Credit card to hold, refund w/ 3-days notice less $25. **Discounts** Corp. Sun.–Thur., 40% after 4th day. **Credit Cards** AE, V, MC, DC. **Check-In/Out** 3–7 p.m./11 a.m. **Smoking** No. **Pets** No. **Kids** Over age 10 in main house, younger children in Carriage House suite. **No-No's** Inconsiderate behavior. **Minimum Stay** 2 nights in Oct. & on holiday weekends. **Open** All year. **Hosts** Kay & Al Standish, 417 E. Washington St., Charles Town, 25414. **Phone** (304) 728-8003. **Fax** (304) 728-2976. **E-mail** carriage@intrepid.net. **Web** carriageinn.com.

HILLBROOK, Charles Town

OVERALL ★★★★½ | QUALITY ★★★★½ | VALUE ★★★ | PRICE **$200–$325**

This property is a visual stunner. In spring it's framed by a profusion of purple and yellow irises and swans swim in the pond. One-room-wide and one-room-high, the main structure cascades down a limestone ridge. Sloping roofs, mullioned windows, and half-timbered surfaces suggest a European cottage. Inside, the patina of old wood, the gleam of polished brass, jewel-toned Oriental carpets, and elegant, eclectic furnishings delight the eye. The innkeeper collected the Flemish oils, African masks, and unusual sculptures over a lifetime of travel as a diplomat's daughter, a diplomat's wife, then in a professional role developing study abroad programs for Georgetown University. The inn is poetic, the do-it-yourself quality of how it developed is inspiring, and the food is good. It's a find to savor in any season.

SETTINGS & FACILITIES

Location Set back from Rte. 13 amidst rolling lawns & woodlands. **Near** 5 mi. southwest of Charles Town, 60 mi. northwest of Washington, D.C. **Building** 1928 European-style country house superimposed on a late 1700s log structure w/ cottage & gatehouse. **Grounds** 17 acres w/ stream, bridge, 2 duck ponds, boxwood grove, hammock, flowers. **Public Space** DR. **Food & Drink** Full breakfast w/ juice, fruit, baked goods; specialties—frittata, quiche, cranberry French toast, vegetable & mushroom omelets; 7-course candlelight dinner required once during stay, $75 per person w/ unlimited wine. **Recreation**

Hiking, biking, rafting, tubing, kayaking, canoeing, golf, tennis, theater, antiquing; West Virginia Wine & Arts Festival (May), Heritage Arts & Crafts Festival (June & Sept.). **Amenities & Services** Videos, privileges at Cress Creek Golf & Country Club, fax & e-mail, meetings (24), weddings (140).

ACCOMMODATIONS

Units 11 guest rooms (4 in a cottage, 1 in a gatehouse). **All Rooms** AC, phone, clock. **Some Rooms** TV (4), balcony (2), fireplace (6), private porch (5), coffeemaker (4), ceiling fan. **Bed & Bath** King (3), queen (8); private baths, 5 whirlpools, 1 claw-foot tub, 3 reg. tubs. **Favorites** Winter cottage—country chic, rich plum color w/ handpainted walls, over-sized tile floor, antique Persian rug, king bed, tapestry-style curtains, double whirlpool, gas fireplace, TV & VCR, fridge. **Comfort & Decor** Carriage house and gatehouse rooms are spacious and luxurious, but some main house guestrooms are small and some doors are narrow. Overall, it combines sophistication and a beautiful setting—without pretense.

RATES, RESERVATIONS, & RESTRICTIONS

Deposit Credit card to hold, refund w/ 7-days notice. **Discounts** Procrastinator's rate made after noon for that evening is $129. **Credit Cards** AE, V, MC, D, DC. **Check-In/Out** 3 p.m./noon. **Smoking** No. **Pets** No. **Kids** No. **Minimum Stay** None. **Open** All year. **Host** Gretchen Carroll, Rte. 2, Box 150, Charles Town, 25414. **Phone** (800) 304-4223 or (304) 725-4223. **Fax** (304) 725-4455. **E-mail** reservations@hillbrookinn.com. **Web** hillbrookinn.com.

WASHINGTON HOUSE INN, Charles Town

OVERALL ★★★½ | QUALITY ★★★★ | VALUE ★★★ | PRICE $99–$150

Relatives of George Washington built seven homes in Charles Town. This one was erected by descendants of George's brothers Samuel and John Augustine. Members of their families lived here until 1938. In subsequent decades it had various uses until new owners made it a bed-and-breakfast in 1989. Guests can walk to the original Charles Town Courthouse, the site of John Brown's trial. Brochures provide insights and directions for self-guided walking and driving tours past architectural treasures in this unassuming town, which is liveliest during special events like the Mountain Heritage Arts & Crafts Festival, held each June and September.

SETTINGS & FACILITIES

Location One block from town's central square. **Near** Jefferson County Courthouse, Jefferson County Museum, Charles Town thoroughbred race track, Old Opera House, 7 mi. to Harpers Ferry National Historic Park. **Building** 1899 Queen Anne, red brick w/ white mini-pillars, green shutters, wraparound porch. **Grounds** City lot w/ flower borders, gazebo. **Public Space** Foyer, LR, DR, powder room. **Food & Drink** Early coffee, full breakfast w/ fresh baked goods, juices; specialties—caramelized apple French toast, cinnamon toast. **Recreation** Biking on C&O canal towpath, hiking & horseback riding nearby, whitewater rafting & tubing on the Potomac & Shenandoah Rivers, area museums. **Amenities & Services** Massage avail., fax & e-mail; meetings (15).

ACCOMMODATIONS

Units 7 guest rooms. **All Rooms** AC, TV, phone, robes, hair dryer, clock radio. **Some Rooms** Ceiling fan. **Bed & Bath** Queens, 1 sleigh; private baths. **Favorites** Rose—

queen & extra twin beds, pink colors. **Comfort & Decor** The attractive main floor has antiques, carved oak mantles, a carved oak staircase with a newel post statue, and framed portraits of Abraham Lincoln, Robert E. Lee, and George Washington. However, guest room quality varies without appropriate adjustment in price.

RATES, RESERVATIONS, & RESTRICTIONS

Deposit 1 night, refunded w/ 3-days notice or re-rented. **Discounts** Corp., AAA. **Credit Cards** AE, V, MC, D. **Check-In/Out** 3 p.m./11 a.m. **Smoking** No. **Pets** No. **Kids** Over age 10. **Minimum Stay** 2 nights Oct. weekends & holidays. **Open** All year. **Hosts** Nina & Mel Vogel, 216 S. George St., Charles Town, 25414. **Phone** (800) 297-6957 or (304) 725-7923. **Fax** (304) 728-5150. **E-mail** mnvogel@intrepid.net. **Web** washingtonhouseinnwv.com.

BRIGHT MORNING INN, Davis

OVERALL ★★★½ | QUALITY ★★★½ | VALUE ★★★ | PRICE **$75**

Surrounded by over 800,000 acres of Monongahela National Forest, this is a great location for outdoor enthusiasts. The woodlands and canyons of Blackwater Falls State Park, Timberline Four Season Resort, White Grass Nordic Ski Center, Canaan Valley Wildlife Refuge, and Cannan Valley State Park are all a short drive away. When you're done tackling nearby trails, slopes, lakes, rivers, wetlands, and wilderness areas, the hosts provide warm hospitality and a place to put your feet up and relax. Tidy but unpretentious, the inn is a good place for families and anyone who needs a homey retreat after a hard day on the trail.

SETTINGS & FACILITIES

Location Main street of the highest incorporated town in West Virginia. **Near** 2 mi. from Blackwater Falls State Park, 9 mi. from Canaan Valley & Timberline Ski Resorts, 30 mi. northeast of Elkins. **Building** 1890 western frontier-style wood frame w/ cedar siding. **Grounds** 2 city lots w/ flower & herb garden, picnic tables. **Public Space** Sitting room, DR. **Food & Drink** Full breakfast featuring generous helpings of regional cuisine; specialties—wild blueberry pancakes, biscuits & gravy, breakfast burrito. **Recreation** Whitewater rafting, canoeing, hiking, mountain biking, cross-country skiing, hunting, fishing, rock climbing; nearby festivals. **Amenities & Services** Videos & games avail.

ACCOMMODATIONS

Units 7 guest rooms, 1 suite. **All Rooms** Clock, ceiling fan. **Some Rooms** Some singles, some doubles. **Bed & Bath** Bed sizes vary; private baths. **Favorites** #2—larger, nice fabrics. **Comfort & Decor** The sitting area has wood-framed sofas and chairs plus books about West Virginia sites and heritage. Simple, uncluttered guest rooms with Amish-made rugs, hand-crafted quilts, and country antiques create a welcoming feeling.

RATES, RESERVATIONS, & RESTRICTIONS

Deposit Credit card to hold, refund w/ 3-days notice. **Discounts** No. **Credit Cards** No. **Check-In/Out** 11 a.m./3 p.m. **Smoking** No. **Pets** Well-behaved. **Kids** Welcome. **Minimum Stay** None. **Open** All year. **Host** Susan Moore, Box 576, Davis, 26260. **Phone** (304) 259-5119. **E-mail** brightmorninginn@yahoo.com. **Web** brightmorning inn.com.

GRACELAND, Elkins

OVERALL ★★★★★ | QUALITY ★★★★½ | VALUE ★★★★★ | PRICE $65–$130

Rumor has it that fraternity tenants pretty much trashed this grand old building before David & Elkins College designated $4 million to restore it in 1996. Aside for some stains on the floor and the absence of some original antiques, the results are impressive, and operating the inn is now part of the college's degree program in Hospitality and Tourism Management. Built with railroad and coal money by U.S. Senator Henry Gassaway Davis, it is named for his favorite daughter, Grace. A walk through the building reveals several superlatives. From the rooftop turret, you have a 20-mile view of Tygart Valley and Elkins. A conference center adjacent to the mansion offers meeting space and less opulent guest rooms.

SETTINGS & FACILITIES

Location Hilltop site on the campus of Davis & Elkins College. **Near** 0.5 mi. from downtown Elkins, 50 mi. north of Snowshoe Resort, 110 mi. northeast of Charleston. **Building** 1893 Queen Anne Victorian w/ turret, native sandstone, slate roof. **Grounds** 1 acre w/ seasonal gardens. **Public Space** Foyer, library, DR, upstairs sitting area & billiard room, porch. **Food & Drink** Cont'l breakfast w/ juice, fresh fruit, homemade breads, hot beverages; afternoon tea on request. **Recreation** Hiking, mountain biking, canoeing, kayaking, fishing, caving, Blackwater Falls; Augusta Heritage Festival (summer), Mountain State Forest Festival (Oct.). **Amenities & Services** Disabled access (1), fax & e-mail, use of college's outdoor rec. center, gym, & indoor pool; meetings (35), weddings (75).

ACCOMMODATIONS

Units 8 guest rooms, 3 suites. **All Rooms** AC, TV, phone, dataport, clock. **Some Rooms** Views vary. **Bed & Bath** Queen (9), double (1), twin (2), canopy (2); private baths, 3 tubs. **Favorites** Senator's suite—600 sq. ft., high ceilings, elaborately carved bed & dresser, Oriental lamps & accessories, fit for a mogel; Susan Randall Lee—queen bed, antique armoire; Grace's suite—canopy bed, panoramic view. **Comfort & Decor** Original stained glass windows and an original oil painting over a 15-foot-wide mantel enhance the Great Hall. Elaborate woodcarvings adorn the oak-paneled billiard room, the cherry library, and the bird's eye maple parlor. Red oak lines the dining room. A glass conservatory and huge south porch offers additional seating.

RATES, RESERVATIONS, & RESTRICTIONS

Deposit Credit card, refund w/ 3-days notice. **Discounts** AARP, corp. **Credit Cards** AE, V, MC, DC, D. **Check-In/Out** 3 p.m./11 a.m.. **Smoking** No. **Pets** No. **Kids** Yes. **Minimum Stay** None. **Open** Yes. **Host** Frank DeMarco, Executive Director of Graceland Inn & Conference Center, c/o Davis & Elkins College, 100 Campus Dr., Elkins, 26241. **Phone** (800) 624-3157 or (304) 637 1600. **Fax** (304) 637-1496. **E-mail** demarcf@dne.edu. **Web** gracelandinn.com.

THOMAS SHEPHERD INN, Shepherdstown

OVERALL ★★★½ | QUALITY ★★★★ | VALUE ★★★ | PRICE $85–$135

Until 1935, this house was the Lutheran parsonage, then, rooms were added and it was a medical office until 1984. With her children grown, Lori decided to move here from Baltimore in 1999 and take over the inn, leaving a career in sales and marketing in the high tech field. "This is my bliss," says Lori, "I love decorating, cooking, gardening, and people, and now I have time for them all." The small town is remarkably cosmopolitan, with a wealth of cultural activities thanks to the proximity of Shepherd College. Particularly impressive is the annual Contemporary American Theater Festival, when four plays are staged at two venues during July.

SETTINGS & FACILITIES

Location Downtown area. **Near** 4 mi. south of Antietam, Maryland, 8 mi. east of Harpers Ferry. **Building** 1868 Federal. **Grounds** Corner city lot w/ back yard, perennial garden. **Public Space** LR, 2 DR, upstairs library, powder room. **Food & Drink** Full breakfast w/ juice, fresh fruit, baked goods; specialties—eggs on a cloud, blueberry stuffed French toast, eggs w/ artichoke & pesto; beverages anytime. **Recreation** C&O Canal towpath, Antietam Battlefield, Harpers Ferry, Charles Town Races; Back Alley Garden Tour (April), Contemporary American Theater Festival (July), Mountain Heritage Arts & Crafts Festival (June & Sept.). **Amenities & Services** Videos, massage avail., fax & e-mail; meetings (12).

ACCOMMODATIONS

Units 6 guest rooms. **All Rooms** AC, fresh flowers. **Some Rooms** Fireplace (1). **Bed & Bath** Queen (3), double (3), twin (1), canopy (2), sleigh (1); private baths w/ tubs, 1 detached. **Favorites** #6—largest room, canopy queen bed, sofa, claw-foot tub, yard view. **Comfort & Decor** Furnishings are appropriate to an 1867 Federal property. Collections include heirloom photos, architectural drawings, pen and ink sketches, and watercolors—many displayed throughout the house.

RATES, RESERVATIONS, & RESTRICTIONS

Deposit Credit card, refund w/ 7-days notice. **Discounts** AARP. **Credit Cards** AE, V, MC, D. **Check-In/Out** 3–7 p.m./11 a.m. **Smoking** No. **Pets** No. **Kids** Over age 8. **Minimum Stay** 2 nights on weekends & holidays. **Open** All year. **Host** Lori Capettini, Box 3634, Shepherdstown, 25443. **Phone** (304) 876-3715. **Fax** (304) 876-3313. **E-mail** info@thomasshepherdinn.com. **Web** thomasshepherdinn.com.

Zone 22

Southern West Virginia

Some folks may think of West Virginia as basically a fishing rods and hunting rifles kind of place. But, the Mountain State offers much more—indoors and out.

Greenbrier and **Pocohantas Counties** at the southern end of the Monongahela National Forest offer relatively flat terrain, ideal for hiking and biking. The 76-mile **Greenbrier River Trail** begins at the logging town of Cass and keeps the river in sight most of the time. One detour is the **Pearl Buck Museum** in Hillsboro, the birthplace of the Pulitzer and Nobel Prize–winning novelist, now restored to its 1892 appearance.

The trail passes through **White Sulphur Springs,** where you can tour the **Greenbrier Resort** to see where American presidents vacationed and where German and Japanese diplomats were interned during World War II. It ends in **Lewistown,** which offers a historic district with more than 60 notable eighteenth- and nineteenth-century buildings, a collegiate hall donated by Andrew Carnegie, and an upbeat and upscale Main Street.

Bramwell, just north of Bluefield near the Virginia border, is a smaller, quieter backwater town. But its beautiful Victorian houses earned it a listing on the National Register of Historic Places.

At **Beckley Exhibition Coal Mine,** you can take a short ride into a former coal mining tunnel and hear explained in a thick West Virginia drawl what it was like to spend a workday digging for coal. Beckley is also a gateway to **New River Gorge National River,** which flows northwest through 53 miles of some of West Virginia's most ruggedly beautiful scenery.

Sixteen outfitting companies run whitewater raft trips down the New River. Fishing is exceptional, especially for smallmouth bass. In the fall, when dam water is released into it, the Gauley River becomes one of America's premier whitewater runs.

Elk River Cross Country Bike & Ski Center near Slatyford offers rentals and local guides for on-land expeditions. The bed-and-breakfast on site is pretty basic, but guests stay for the restaurant and the access to nature. **Snowshoe Silver Creek Ski Resort** is nearby, and so is the **National Radio Astronomy Observatory** at Green Bank where you can tour the world's largest steerable radio telescope.

When you're ready for civilization again, **Charleston** is a good choice. Architect Cass Gilbert designed the city's capitol building, with its impressive 293-foot-high gold leaf dome. Statues depict state heroes, such as Stonewall Jackson, Booker T. Washington, and Abraham Lincoln. As president, Lincoln declared West Virginia a state on December 31, 1862.

As values shift and people look for less glitzy, more genuine places to vacation, they might consider West Virginia—for adventure and solitude. The scenery is exceptional, as are many of the bed-and-breakfasts we visited.

FOR MORE INFORMATION

Charleston CVB
(304) 344-5075

Charleston Chamber of Commerce
(304) 345-0770

Elkins-Randolph County Chamber of Commerce
(800) 422-3304

Fayetteville CVB
(888) 574-1500; fayettevillecvb.com

Greater Greenbrier Chamber of Commerce
(800) 833-2068

Mercer County CVB
(800) 221-3206; mccvb.com

New River CVB
(800) 927-0263; newrivercvb.com

Pocahontas County CVB
(800) 336-7009; .
pocahontascountywv.com

Princeton-Mercer County Chamber of Commerce
(304) 487-1502

West Virginia Mountain Highlands
(304) 636-8400;
mountainhighlands.com

PERRY HOUSE, Bramwell

OVERALL ★★★½ | QUALITY ★★★½ | VALUE ★★★★ | PRICE $65

This house is next door to the Bank of Bramwell, which is said to have been the richest in the United States for its size at one time. (Funds from here reportedly financed numerous outside projects including the Burning Tree Country Club of Washington, D.C.) The Bank of Bramwell built this house for one of its first cashiers, J. B. Perry, whose family lived in it from 1902 to 1982. Millionaire coal barons, 14 in all, chose to build mansions in Bramwell, because it is one of the few level spots in the area. It sits on a peninsula of the Bluestone River surrounded by mountain peaks. The coal miners towns of Pocahontas and Coopers are close by. In 1992, the Library of Congress and Parks Service photographed local homes, including The Perry House, to preserve the town's history for future generations.

SETTINGS & FACILITIES

Location Main street of small town. **Near** 8 mi. north of Bluefield. **Building** 1902 Revival Tudor, brick w/ cream trim, large porch. **Grounds** 1 acre w/ flower garden, pond, iron fence. **Public Space** LR, DR, music room, porch. **Food & Drink** Full breakfast w/ juice, fresh fruit, baked goods; specialties—egg & cheese strata w/ spinach & tomatoes, sausage casserole w/ roasted red potatoes, baked apple pancakes w/ Canadian bacon & scrambled eggs. **Recreation** Hike to Pinnacle Rock State Park, Coal Mining Museum; 5K road race, House Tours (May & Dec.) Bramwell Theater (July), Octoberfest, Wine Festival. **Amenities & Services** Massage & laundry avail.

ACCOMMODATIONS

Units 4 guest rooms. **All Rooms** AC, robe, clock. **Some Rooms** Antiques vary. **Bed & Bath** Queen (2), double (1), twin (2), canopy (1); 3 privates baths, 1 tub. **Favorites** Macon—four-poster bed, only private bath but still a bargain. **Comfort & Decor** Antiques, reproductions, family heirlooms, and old photographs underscore the Victorian-style interiors. Handsome woodwork, hardwood floors, and a classic Victorian staircase with vivid stained glass windows on the landing add to the period look. Books, magazine, board games, and cards are available, along with television in the parlor, where seating is comfortable.

RATES, RESERVATIONS, & RESTRICTIONS

Deposit No. **Discounts** No. **Credit Cards** No. **Check-In/Out** 3 p.m./11 a.m. **Smoking** No. **Pets** No. **Kids** No. **Minimum Stay** None. **Open** All year. **Hosts** Joyce & Jim Bishop, Box 188, Bramwell, 24715. **Phone** (304) 248-8145. **E-mail** perry house@netlinkcorp.com.

OLD STONE MANSE, *Caldwell*

OVERALL ★★★★½ | QUALITY ★★★★ | VALUE ★★★★ | PRICE $99

This seems a long way from Waverly, Ohio, where these innkeepers noticed a small ad in the local newspaper for a stone house for sale in West Virginia. But fate being what it is, they left the Buckeye State to move here and undertake a major renovation of this property. They are do-it-yourselves innkeepers. Judie is particularly interested in early grain-painting techniques and you can see the results of her hobby throughout the house. Particularly impressive is the elaborate landscape painting that encompasses the entire hallway and stairway. Judie once owned an antique shop and collects antique dolls. You'll see lots of good, practical decorating ideas, and if you ask they make it sound as easy as a quick trip to Home Depot. The results here are stunning.

SETTINGS & FACILITIES

Location Rural setting at milepost 3 of the Greenbrier River Trail. **Near** 4.4 mi. east of Lewisburg, 6 mi. west of White Sulphur Springs. **Building** 1796 Federal w/ 1833 addition, local river stone & sand mortar. **Grounds** 1.4 acres w/ gardens of herbs, flowers, & vegetables. **Public Space** Foyer, LR, DR, 2 porches, summer kitchen. **Food & Drink** Early coffee & tea tray to your room; 9 a.m. candlelight breakfast at fireside; juice, fruit, homemade muffins; specialties—stuffed French toast, pancakes, egg roll w/ ham, sausage avail; menu adjusted for diet or allergies; beverages & cookies avail. anytime. **Recreation** Biking, hiking, fishing, whitewater rafting, hunting; State Fair (Aug.), Taste of Our Town (Oct.). **Amenities & Services** TV avail., massage avail.

ACCOMMODATIONS

Units 2 guest rooms. **All Rooms** AC, clock, ceiling fan. **Some Rooms** Robes (1). **Bed & Bath** Queens, canopy (1), four-poster (1); 1 private bath, 1 detached private bath, 2 tubs. **Favorites** Primitive—exposed beams, pencil four-poster bed, quilt, stenciled walls, vinegar graining on cupboard, antique washstand, wood floors w/ rag rugs, immigrant's chest, 1860s dresses. **Comfort & Decor** The living room has a gas fireplace, Colonial-style furnishings, a painted chair rail, and original marbleized paint on the baseboard. The dining room has a stone-faced gas fireplace, wood mantel, canvas floor covering, and wall stenciling that looks like wallpaper.

RATES, RESERVATIONS, & RESTRICTIONS

Deposit One night, refund w/ 14-days notice. **Discounts** No. **Credit Cards** No. **Check-In/Out** 4 p.m./11 a.m. **Smoking** No. **Pets** No (1 cat in residence). **Kids** No. **Minimum Stay** 2 nights some weekends. **Open** All year. **Hosts** Judie & Dick Lewis, HC 30, Box 13AA, Caldwell, 24925. **Phone** (304) 645-2749. **E-mail** stonemanse @inetone.net. **Web** oldstonemanse.com.

BRASS PINEAPPLE, Charlestown

OVERALL ★★★★ | QUALITY ★★★★ | VALUE ★★★★ | PRICE $79–$129

Lisa first did accounting work for the previous owner, began helping out on weekends with hosting chores, and ended up owning the place in July 2000. Together with her husband, she is now a specialist in financial and business consulting for the printing industry, helping mom-and-pop companies get a sound financial footing and plan for their future. This career puts her on the road approximately every other week, and that's when an assistant innkeeper takes over. The house was built by one of the city's original founders, E. C. Baur, and the quality of its workmanship earned it a listing on the National Register of Historic Places. "I still can't believe I own this beautiful place," Lisa says.

SETTINGS & FACILITIES

Location Residential street in historic district. **Near** 400 yards from state capitol, 200 feet from the Kanawha River, 1.25 mi. east of downtown business district, 3 mi. south of Coonskin Park. **Building** 1907 Arts & Crafts w/ original woodwork, stained glass windows, beveled & leaded glass. **Grounds** City lot w/ mature oak trees, roses, hanging flower baskets. **Public Space** Foyer, LR, DR, porch, patio. **Food & Drink** Full breakfast w/ juice, fruit, baked goods; specialties—blueberry pancakes w/ maple syrup, sausage & egg casserole, cinnamon pecan waffles w/ apple syrup, all w/ side dishes; evening snack basket; beverage & microwave popcorn anytime. **Recreation** Golf, tennis, biking, horseback riding, boating, theater, state museum, symphony, 5-mi. riverside walking track. **Amenities & Services** Videos, fax, copier, laundry facilities, limited airport transport can be arranged; meetings (10), weddings (12).

ACCOMMODATIONS

Units 5 guest rooms, 1 suite. **All Rooms** AC, hair dryer, TV & VCR, phone w/ voice mail & fax modem, robes. **Some Rooms** Decorative fireplace (3). **Bed & Bath** King (1), queen (4), twin (1), high-back canopy (3), four-poster (1); private baths, 2 detached, 3 tubs. **Favorites** Charleston Manor—2 stained-glass windows, mauve w/ solid & patterned walls, Oriental plates, sunken tub. **Comfort & Decor** Sixteen stained glass windows add beauty to the public areas. The dining room has a tiled fireplace, pocket doors, inlaid and patterned hardwood floors, oak woodwork, and high wainscoting. The entry area has beveled and leaded glass.

RATES, RESERVATIONS, & RESTRICTIONS

Deposit Credit card, refund w/ 2-days notice. **Discounts** AAA 10%, over age 65, frequent stays (based on availability). **Credit Cards** AE, V, MC, DC, D. **Check-In/Out** 4–6 p.m./11 a.m. **Smoking** No. **Pets** Dogs under 20 lbs. (with carrier) in 1 room w/ $25 deposit. **Kids** Yes. **No-Nos** Loud noise after 11 p.m. **Minimum Stay** No. **Open** All year, except Christmas, some holidays. **Host** Lisa Elefritz, 1611 Virginia St. E., Charleston, 25311. **Phone** (304) 344-0748. **Fax** (304) 344-0748. **E-mail** pineapp104 @aol.com. **Web** brasspineapple.com.

WHITE HORSE, Fayetteville

OVERALL ★★★½ | QUALITY ★★★½ | VALUE ★★★ | PRICE $100–$125

According to legend, laborers from the local prison helped to build this house for Fayette County Sheriff E. B. Hawkins. It comprises 12,000 square feet, big enough to have its own ballroom—and in fact, it once did. It took two years (1988–90) to restore the house to its former splendor (minus the ballroom) and the house is now listed on the National Register of Historic Landmarks. To carry out the theme of its name, a full-sized carousel horse was placed in one corner of the foyer. In addition to all the spacious interior rooms, the front porch is especially inviting with two swings and several rockers to relax in. The house is located only minutes from the New River Gorge Bridge and access to the excitement of whitewater rafting on the New and Gauley Rivers.

SETTINGS & FACILITIES

Location Residential area. **Near** 17 mi. north of Beckley, 50 mi. southeast of Charlestown. **Building** 1906 Greek Revival w/ cottage, carriage house, & barn. **Grounds** 5 acres w/ lawn, gardens. **Public Space** 2 foyers, parlor, library, sunroom, DR, upstairs sitting room, powder room. **Food & Drink** Full country breakfast w/ juice, breads, specialties—eggs any style, pancakes, waffles; beverages avail. anytime. **Recreation** Biking, rock climbing, fishing, hiking, whitewater rafting, horseback riding; Heritage Festival (July). **Amenities & Services** Disabled access (1); meetings (25), weddings (100).

ACCOMMODATIONS

Units 5 guest rooms, 1 suite, 1 cottage (avail. summer only). **All Rooms** Hair dryer, clock, ceiling fan. **Some Rooms** Private entrance (1). **Bed & Bath** King (1), queen (2), double (2), twin (3), canopy (2); 3 private baths, 4 shared baths, 3 tubs. **Favorites** New River—antique dresser, rocker, lace, bath adjacent but shared; Kanawaha—floral quilt, large tub. **Comfort & Decor** We counted 51 windows on the high-ceilinged ground floor. The living room has a gas fireplace, the music room has an 1850 grand piano, and the foyer boasts a baby grand. The dining room has shoulder-high oak paneling and a hand-painted mural from Paris. Guest room quality varies.

RATES, RESERVATIONS, & RESTRICTIONS

Deposit 50%, refund of 10% w/ 14-days notice. **Discounts** AAA, seniors. **Credit Cards** No. **Check-In/Out** 4 p.m./11 a.m. **Smoking** No. **Pets** Small. **Kids** Yes. **Minimum Stay** No. **Open** All year. **Hosts** Nancy & Dan Porter, 120 Fayette Ave., Fayetteville, 25840. **Phone** (304) 574-1400. **Fax** (304) 574-0070. **Web** historicwhitehorsebandb.com.

CURRENT, Hillsboro

OVERALL ★★★★ | QUALITY ★★★½ | VALUE ★★★★ | PRICE $65–90

The unique thing about this property is the New England–style Beard Chapel church, built in 1922, which the innkeeper owns and has beautifully restored. You can arrange to sleep in it and/or get married in it. The white-steepled, steep-roofed church, which sits just 100 yards across the field in full view of the bed-and-breakfast, is very picturesque. Opened in 1985, the Current is one of West Virginia's oldest bed-and-breakfasts. Leslee, who earned her masters degree in social work, is now a community organizer and currently serves as President of the River Trail Association. Her group monitors the 78-mile biking and hiking trail along the Greenbrier River, and she knows every mile of its terrain. Many of her guests are bikers who complete all or part of that scenic route.

SETTINGS & FACILITIES

Location Pastoral setting at the center of Greenbrier River Valley, mid-point of the Greenbrier River Trail. **Near** 5 mi. southeast of Hillsboro, 12 mi. north of Beartown State Park. **Building** 1904 Victorian-era farmhouse. **Grounds** 42 acres w/ fruit trees, vegetable gardens, pond. **Public Space** LR, DR, kitchen, deck, screened porch, outdoor hot tub. **Food & Drink** Full breakfast w/ juice, fruit, baked goods; specialties—blueberry buckwheat pancakes, vegetable quiche, French toast w/ strawberries & maple syrup; afternoon tea, complimentary wine; dinners avail. by reservation. **Recreation** Mountain biking on 78-mile rail-trail, fishing for catfish, bass & blue gills; kayaking & canoeing, horseback riding, birding, guided nature tours; bikes avail.; Great Greenbrier River Race. **Amenities & Services** Fax & e-mail; meetings (20), weddings (75).

ACCOMMODATIONS

Units 5 guest rooms, 1 suite. **All Rooms** Quilts. **Some Rooms** Fireplace (1), phone (1), ceiling fan (4), private entrance (1), videos (1). **Bed & Bath** Queen (1), double (4), twin (4), four-poster (1); 1 private bath, 2 shared baths, 1 tub. **Favorites** Suite—four-poster, gas fireplace w/ remote, TV, 9 windows, sitting room, small bath; Oak bedroom—stenciled chest, nice quilts. **Comfort & Decor** An eclectic mix of simple country furnishings, include some antiques. Dolls fill a display case in the foyer, a Vermont Castings stove and old ice box are seen in the dining room. Collections include duck decoys, baskets, antique toys, old farm implements, and quilts—creating a cluttered but interesting look.

RATES, RESERVATIONS, & RESTRICTIONS

Deposit Credit card, refund w/ 14-days notice. **Discounts** 2 nights or more. **Credit Cards** V MC. **Check-In/Out** 2–5 p.m./noon. **Smoking** No. **Pets** Yes, on approval (3 dogs, 3 cats on premises). **Kids** Yes. **Minimum Stay** On holiday weekends. **Open** All year. **Host** Leslee McCarthy, HC 64, Box 135, Hillsboro, 24946. **Phone** (866) 537-5336 or (304) 653-4722. **Fax** (304) 653-4744. **E-mail** current@inetone.net. **Web** currentbnb.com.

HUTTON HOUSE, Huttonsville

OVERALL ★★★★ | QUALITY ★★★★ | VALUE ★★★★ | PRICE $75–$85

"They don't build 'em like this anymore," is what visitors say about this distinctive, character-filled house. It was originally built by E. E. Hutton, the third generation of one of the founding families of this town. Hutton's ancestors also established Huttonsville Academy, a local school that was destroyed in the Civil War. The current innkeepers moved here from Swathmore, Pennsylvania in 1991. Loretta retired early after 20 years as a physical education teacher in order to run the bed-and-breakfast. She collects Depression-era glass and an interesting assortment of old toasters. Dean, who formerly owned a house renovation business, now does for himself what he used to do for others—keeps his property in good repair.

SETTINGS & FACILITIES

Location Hilltop overlooking Rtes. 250/219. **Near** 17 mi. south of Elkins. **Building** 1898 Queen Anne Victorian, yellow w/ mustard trim, wraparound porch. **Grounds** 3 acres w/ pond, woodlands, gardens. **Public Space** Foyer, parlor, DR, family room, kitchen, front porch, back deck. **Food & Drink** Full breakfast w/ fruit course; specialties—stuffed French toast, zucchini frittata w/ Italian sausage & carrot stir fry, blintz soufflé w/ blueberry sauce; snacks, cookies, spiced cider, & other beverages anytime; dinner avail. by reservation. **Recreation** Inn-to-inn biking, downhill & cross-country skiing, horseback riding, guided fishing; pool table, music, & games on premises; Ramp Festival (April), Mountain Bike Race (June), International Chili Cookoff (July), Augusta Heritage Festival (summer). **Amenities & Services** Videos, fax & e-mail, TV with videos about West Virginia in common room.

ACCOMMODATIONS

Units 6 guest rooms. **All Rooms** AC. **Some Rooms** Robes, ceiling fan. **Bed & Bath** Queen (2), double (4), twin (4); private baths, 2 detached, 1 whirlpool, 1 tub. **Favorites** E. E.'s room—nice woodwork, 5 windows, tiled fireplace, maroon decor; Sis's room—has tower with rocker, wicker chair, bird cage. **Comfort & Decor** Etched glass, fretwork on the door, a converted gasolier, oak stairs, and lace curtains distinguish the hallway. The parlor has pocket doors and a mix of antiques, reproductions, and collectibles. Lots of books are available. Bathrooms are shoe-horned into corners of the guest rooms.

RATES, RESERVATIONS, & RESTRICTIONS

Deposit Credit card, refund w/ 14-days notice. **Discounts** Seniors. **Credit Cards** V, MC. **Check-In/Out** 2 p.m./noon. **Smoking** No. **Pets** No (3 cats on premises). **Kids** Yes. **Minimum Stay** 2 nights on holidays. **Open** All year. **Hosts** Loretta Murray & Dean Ahren, Box 88, Huttonville, 26273. **Phone** (800) 234-6701 or (304) 335-6701. **Fax** (304) 636-5556. **E-mail** hutton@citynet.net. **Web** wvbandb.com.

LEE STREET, Lewisburg

OVERALL ★★★ | QUALITY ★★★½ | VALUE ★★★★ | PRICE $70–$110

The house once belonged to Brian's mother, who owns an art gallery in town along with his stepfather, a photographer. Brian served in the Air Force for six years, where he developed a specialty as an Arabic linguist and helped to monitor communications in the Middle East. He lived in Florida for a dozen years before buying this property from his mother to open it as a bed-and-breakfast. His projects include building the backyard pond and expanding with more bedrooms. His business partner, Jeff, hails from Michigan. Another member of the household is an African gray parrot who is said to have a several-hundred-word vocabulary, but we found it to be shy in front of strangers.

SETTINGS & FACILITIES

Location Downtown in the historic district. **Near** 8 mi. west of White Sulphur Springs, 50 mi. east of Beckley. **Building** 1876 Victorian w/ additions. **Grounds** 1 acre w/ water, herb, & flower gardens. **Public Space** LR, TV room, upstairs sitting area, 3 porches. **Food & Drink** Cont'l breakfast w/ juice, bagels, bakery items, hot beverages. **Recreation** Hiking, biking, rafting, caving; hot tub on enclosed porch; State Fair (Aug.). **Amenities & Services** Videos, fax.

ACCOMMODATIONS

Units 2 guest rooms, 1 suite. **All Rooms** AC, clock, satellite TV w/ 100-plus channels, DVDs & laser disc movies. **Some Rooms** Ceiling fan (2), balcony (1), private entrance (1). **Bed & Bath** King (1), queen (3), four-poster (1); 1 private bath, 2 shared baths.

Favorites Green room—canopy-style bed, nice quilt, heirloom clock. **Comfort & Decor** Eclectic furnishings were chosen for comfort. Collections include sharks teeth and clocks that chime (which the innkeeper calls music in motion).

RATES, RESERVATIONS, & RESTRICTIONS

Deposit Credit card, refund w/ 10-days notice. **Discounts** No. **Credit Cards** AE, V, MC. **Check-In/Out** 3 p.m./11 a.m. **Smoking** No. **Pets** By prior arrangement, in carriage house only. **Kids** Age 12 & older. **Minimum Stay** No. **Open** All year. **Hosts** Brian Fields & Jeff Guffey, 200 N. Lee St., Lewisburg, 24901. **Phone** (888) 228-7000 or (304) 647-5599. **Fax** (304) 645-1661. **E-mail** innkeeper@leestreetinn.com. **Web** leestreetinn.com.

ELK RIVER TOURING CENTER, Slatyfork

OVERALL ★★★★ | QUALITY ★★½ | VALUE ★★★ | PRICE $50–$100

"We're a hodgepodge of lodging—rustic but not uncomfortable," says innkeeper Mary Willis. But, picture yourself fishing in a thriving native trout habitat—such as the nearby Elk, Slatyfork, Cranberry, and Williams Rivers. The innkeepers can provide water level, hatch information, local guides, and rental equipment. Or, picture yourself with the wind in your hair as you bike past a dense hardwood forest and mountain scenery. The innkeepers can arrange good mountain bike tours on moderate to challenging single-track terrain, with equipment provided. They are experts on hiking, biking, skiing, fishing, and hunting in this section of the Monongahela National Forest. The food is good and the hospitality is warm. The appeal is to active, adventurous vacationers.

SETTINGS & FACILITIES

Location On Rte. 219 in a heavily forested mountain terrain. **Near** 5 mi. from Snowshoe Resort, 17 mi. north of Marlington. **Building** 1988 wood frame inn w/ 2 cabins, deck w/ metal sports sculptures. **Grounds** 148 acres w/ flower & herb gardens, trails to hike, bike, and cross country ski. **Public Space** Sitting room, TV room, restaurant, pub, outdoor hot tub, bike/ski shop. **Food & Drink** Full breakfast w/ juice, fruit & yogurt, home-baked goods; specialties—eggs, bacon, grits, pancakes, sausage gravy & biscuits, pancakes, French toast; a full-service restaurant serves dinner & caters to health-conscious vacationers. **Recreation** Mountain biking, fishing, hiking, canoeing, horseback riding, cross-country skiing (on private trails), downhill skiing, snowboarding, caving; mountain bikes, skis, snowshoes, & snowboards avail; 24 Hours of Snowshoe (June), The Wild 100 (Aug.). **Amenities & Services** Fax, laundry facilities, massage avail.; meetings (15), weddings (125).

ACCOMMODATIONS

Units 14 guest rooms. **All Rooms** Basic. **Some Rooms** Views vary. **Bed & Bath** Queen (3), double (17), twin (10); 5 private baths, 5 shared baths. **Favorites** #10—the best of the lot. **Comfort & Decor** The basics are here and not much else. It's for active people who want to explore the forest. Guest rooms in the main house are best. There's a gas fireplace, television, and phone in the sitting room.

RATES, RESERVATIONS, & RESTRICTIONS

Deposit 2 nights, refund w/ 14-days notice less $25 fee. **Discounts** None. **Credit Cards** V, MC. **Check-In/Out** 4 p.m./11 a.m. **Smoking** No. **Pets** Yes, in the cabins. **Kids** Very kid friendly. **Minimum Stay** 2 nights most weekends. **Open** All year. **Hosts** Mary & Gil Willis, HC 69, Box 7, Slatyfork, 26291. **Phone** (304) 572-3771. **Fax** (304) 572-3741. **E-mail** ertc@ertc.com. **Web** ertc.com.

JAMES WYLIE HOUSE, White Sulphur Springs

OVERALL ★★★★ | QUALITY ★★★★ | VALUE ★★★ | PRICE $75–$140

This is White Sulphur Springs' only registered historic house. The original owner was Richard Dickson, a pioneer of Greenbrier County. Then, the Scotch-Irish James Wylie lived here while farming over 1,300 acres around Howard Creek. The current owner moved from Baltimore, where she managed a hardware store, and took over the bed-and-breakfast in 1999. She collects miniature thimbles, grandparent wedding photos, and old tools, proudly displaying a pitchfork, scissors, ice tongs, and antique screwdrivers. Since rates at the nearby Greenbrier Resort currently range from $422 to $790 per night (including afternoon tea and dinner, plus access to a swimming pool and a theater), this property has become popular with folks attending conventions there.

SETTINGS & FACILITIES

Location In the village. **Near** Greenbrier Resort, Lewisburg, Greenbrier River Trail, Lake Sherwood, Historic Oakhurst Links. **Building** 1819 Georgian Colonial, red brick; 1794 cabin. **Grounds** 1.2 acres w/ flower & vegetable gardens, swing, picnic bench. **Public Space** Parlor, DR, TV room, front, side, & back porches. **Food & Drink** Full breakfast w/ juice, fresh fruit, baked goods; specialties—waffles, sweet corn & bacon quiche, peaches 'n' cream French toast; beverages avail. anytime. **Recreation** Hiking, biking, fishing, canoeing, golf, antiquing; Dandelion Festival (May), State Fair (Aug.), Taste of Our Town Festival (Oct.). **Amenities & Services** Videos, fax & e-mail; meetings (25).

ACCOMMODATIONS

Units 4 guest rooms, 1 suite, 1 log cabin. **All Rooms** AC, cable TV, clock, phone jack. **Some Rooms** Fireplace (1). **Bed & Bath** Queen (5), double (2), twin (3); 5 private baths, 1 detached. **Favorites** Drewery—Williamsburg-blue trim, non-working fireplace, books; Hannah suite—beamed ceiling, quilt bed, built-in dresser, painted wood floors w/ rug, wicker in small sitting area, game basket, sleeps 6, a bargain. **Comfort & Decor** A mix of new and old (mostly old) furnishings in the public and guest rooms.The living room has the innkeeper's great grandmother's travel trunk from Poland.

RATES, RESERVATIONS, & RESTRICTIONS

Deposit Credit card, refund w/ 10-days notice. **Discounts** If renting entire house. **Credit Cards** AE, V, MC. **Check-In/Out** Noon/11 a.m. **Smoking** No. **Pets** No (1 cat on premises). **Kids** Yes. **Minimum Stay** No. **Open** All year. **Hosts** Monica Foos, 208 E. Main St., White Sulphur Springs, 24986. **Phone** (800) 870-1613 or (304) 536-9444. **Fax** (304) 536-2345. **E-mail** mlfoos@access.mountain.net. **Web** www.travelguides.com/bb/james_wylie.

WHITE OAKS, White Sulphur Springs

OVERALL ★★★★ | QUALITY ★★★★ | VALUE ★★★ | PRICE $120–$150

City people will love it here—if they're not too particular about having to share a bathroom. At night you hear crickets and frogs, and at daylight birdsongs are audible. You'll especially enjoy the beauty of seasonal flora and fauna from April to October. From the backyard, you can see the steam rise from hot springs that surface in the nearby wetlands. This has been Mimi's home since 1991. She opened it as a bed-and-breakfast in 1996. As a single mom, she has created one room (the TV room) with lots of kids activities. She goes the extra mile for her guests, being available to pick them up at either the Greenbrier train station or the Lewisburg airport (with advance notice).

SETTINGS & FACILITIES

Location In a forest clearing overlooking wetlands area w/ springs. **Near** 2 mi. east of The Greenbrier Resort, 1.5 mi. east of town, 5 mi. east of Greenbrier River Trail; Oak Hurst Links. **Building** 1949 white clapboard w/ yellow shutters, cottage. **Grounds** 7.5 acres w/ floral borders, wetlands, trail to Howard's Creek. **Public Space** LR, DR, screened porch, brick patio. **Food & Drink** Full breakfast w/ juice, fruit, baked goods; specialties—eggs Benedict, Italian stratta, frittatas, waffles, pancakes; welcome glass of wine, beverages avail. anytime. **Recreation** Biking, hiking, golf, fishing, swimming, picnicking, birding; golf tournaments. **Amenities & Services** Laundry, fax & e-mail; meetings (8).

ACCOMMODATIONS

Units 4 guest rooms, 1 cottage. **All Rooms** AC, coffeemaker, hair dryer. **Some Rooms** Private entrance (1), phone (1), fridge (1). **Bed & Bath** King (1), queen (2), twin (2); 1 private bath, 4 shared baths. **Favorites** The Acorn (cottage)—white decor, bright & clean; Room A—Greenbrier-style cabbage rose wallpaper. **Comfort & Decor** Furnishings in the public rooms look comfy and luxurious, with antique mirrors, Oriental rugs, and a Chippendale couch to add cachet. The large enclosed porch is especially inviting. Guest rooms in the main house are small. (The cottage is fine but it's only open April to October). Your value comes from the peaceful, serene environment and warm hospitality.

RATES, RESERVATIONS, & RESTRICTIONS

Deposit Credit card, refund w/ 3-days notice. **Discounts** No. **Credit Cards** AE, V, MC. **Check-In/Out** 3 p.m./11 a.m. **Smoking** No. **Pets** No (2 black labs on premises). **Kids** Yes, preferably in their own room (1 rollaway avail.). **Minimum Stay** No. **Open** All year. **Host** Mimi Vass, HC 69, Box 974, White Sulphur Springs, 24986. **Phone** (800) 536-3402 or (304) 536-3404. **E-mail** mimi@whiteoaksbb.com. **Web** whiteoaksbb.com.

Appendix

Additional Bed-and-Breakfasts and Small Inns

While our 300 profiles give you a fine range of bed-and-breakfasts and country inns, some may be fully booked when you want to visit, or you may want to stay in areas where we have not included a property. So we have included an annotated listing of 300 additional bed-and-breakfasts and small inns, spread throughout the Mid-Atlantic. All properties meet our basic criteria for this guide: They have about 3–25 guestrooms, a distinct personality and individually decorated guestrooms, are open regularly, and include breakfast in the price (with a few exceptions). Prices are a range from low to high season. Most are highly recommended, but we have not visited all of these properties so we cannot recommend them across the board. We suggest you get a brochure, look on the Internet, or call and ask to find out more. While some of these supplementals are famed and excellent, others may not be up to the level of the profiled properties.

New York

ZONE 1:Northern New York/The Adirondacks

Canton
Ostrander's, $65–$85
(877) 707-2126; ostranders.com

Hague
Ruah, $90–$170
(800) 224-7549; ruahbb.com

Indian Lake
1870 Bed and Breakfast, $54–$75
(518) 648-5377; bandb.bizland.com/

Jay
Book & Blanket, $60–$80
(518) 946-8323; www.adirondackinns.com/bookandblanket

Keene Valley
Trail's End Inn, $59–$175
(800) 281-9860; trailsendinn.com

Little Falls
Overlook Mansion, $100–$120
(315) 823-4222; overlookmansion.com

Plattsburgh
Point au Roche Lodge, $82–$137
(518) 563-8714

Saratoga Springs
Saratoga, $135–$225
(518) 584-0920
Union Gables, $240–$300
(518) 584-1550

Westchester House, $95–$295
(800) 579-8368 or (518) 587-7613; westchesterhousebandb.com

Schroon Lake

Schroon Lake, $90–$175
(800) 523-6755; schroonbb.com

Westport

Victorian Lady, $110 –$125
(877) 829-7128; victorianladybb.com

Zone 2: Western New York/Finger Lakes

Canandaigua

Filigree Inn, $140–$160
(716) 229-5460; filigreeinn.com

Habersham Country Inn, $85–$185
(800) 240-0644 or (716) 393-1510; habershaminn.com

Sutherland House, $85–$185
(800) 396-0375 or (716) 396-0375; sutherlandhouse.com

Candor

Edge of Thyme, $75–$135
(800) 722-7365; edgeofthyme.com

Clarence

Asa Ransom House, $95–$145
(716) 759-2315

Clinton

Artful Lodger, $89–$125
(315) 853-3672

Cooperstown

Angelholm, $150
(607) 547-2483; angelholmbb.com

Landmark Inn, $95–$135
(607) 547-7225; landmarkinnbnb.com

White House, $85–$225
(607) 547-5054; www.cooperstown-chamber.org/stay/

East Aurora

Shepherd Hill Farm, $51–$75
(716) 655-0171

Fredonia

White Inn, $104–$174
(716) 672-2103

Glenora

South Glenora Tree Farm, $85–$125
(607) 243-7414

Gorham

Victoriana, $140–$199
(800) 381-9167 or (716) 526-4531; www.fingerlakesbandb.com

Hammondsport

Elm Croft Manor , $125–$150
(607) 569-3071

Ithaca

Columbia, $95–$250
(607) 272-0204; columbia ithacany.com

Hound & Hare, $85–$150
(800) 652-2821; houndandhare.com

Lansing

Breathe The Dream, A Lakefront Inn, $102
(607) 533-4804

Federal House, $68–$175
(800) 533-7362

Niagara Falls

Rainbow House, $65–$135
(800) 724-3536; rainbowbb.com

Oneida Castle

Governor's House, $94
(315) 363-5643

Rochester

428 Mount Vernon, $125
(800) 836-3159 or (716) 271-0792

Seneca Falls

Guion House, $75–$90
(315) 568-8129

Skaneateles

Sherwood Inn, $75–$170
(800) 374-3796 or (315) 685-3405; thesherwoodinn.com

Syracuse

Beard Morgan House, $79–$99
(800) 775-4234 or (315) 637-4234; www.cnyloding.com

Watkins Glen

Longhouse Manor, $110–$175
(607) 353-2565

Seneca Lake Watch, $85–$105
(607) 535-4490

Westfield

William Seward Inn, $90–$190
(716) 326-4151

Trumansburg

Gothic Eves, $61–$101
(800) 387-7712 or (607) 387-6033

ZONE 3: Central New York/Hudson Valley/New York City

Athens
Stewart House, $70–$90
(518) 945-1357

Averill Park
Gregory House Country Inn, $90–$100
(518) 674-3774

Brooklyn
Bed & Breakfast In The Park, $135–$275
(718) 499-6115

Dover Plains
Old Drovers Inn, $210–$395
(914) 832-9311

Hyde Park
Journey Inn, $95–$155
(845) 229-8972; journeyinn.com
Inn at Rose Hill Farm , $150–$400
(845) 677-5611; rosehillfarmbandb.com

Livingston Manor
Guest House, $153–$225
(845) 439-4000; theguesthouse.com

Montgomery
Mead Tooker House, $85–$225
(845) 457-5770; meadtooker.com

Pine Island
Glenwood House, $90–$250
(845) 258-5066; glenwoodhouse.com

Pine Plains
The Pines, $99–$165
(518) 398-7677

Poughkeepsie
Copper Penny Inn, $90–$150
(845) 452-3045

Red Hook
Grand Dutchess, $95–$155
(845) 758-5818;
www.enjoyhv.com/granddutchess
Red Hook Inn, $75–$125
(845) 758-8445

Rhinebeck
Beckrick House on Chumley's Pond, $99–$175
(845) 876-6416; beckrickhouse.com
Bitter Sweet, $95–$165
(845) 876-7777; www.enjoyhv.com/bittersweet
Hideaway, $159–$275
(845) 266-5673; hideawaysuites bandb.com
Sleeping Beauty, $85–$125
(845) 876-8986
Veranda House, $110–$150
(877) 985-6800 or (845) 876-4133; verandahouse.com

Salisbury Mills
Caldwell House, $135–$245
(845) 496-2954; caldwellhouse.com

Staatsburg
Half Moon, $100–$225
(845) 266-5296; www.enjoyhv.com/halfmoon

Stephentown
Mill House Inn, $90–$140
(518) 733-5606

Stone Ridge
Bakers, $98–$128
(914) 687-9795
Sparrow Hawk, $110–$150
(914) 687-4492

Tannersville
Eggery Inn, $120–$140
(518) 589-5363

Warwick
Warwick Valley, $100–$135
(845) 987-7255; www.bedand breakfast.com

ZONE 4: Long Island/The Hamptons

Centerport
Centerport Harbor, $179–$199
(631) 754-1730

East Quogue
Carole's, $75–$160
(631) 653-5152;
www.bbonline.com/ny/caroles
Grace House, $100–$185
(631) 653-8482

East Hampton
Centennial House , $245–$625
(631) 324-9414; centhouse.com
Pink House , $135–$325
(631) 324-3400

Greenport
Morning Glory, $145–$175
(631) 477-3324; themorningglory.com

Port Jefferson
Golden Pineapple, $110–$125
(631) 331-0706 ; www.portjeff.com/gp

Sag Harbor
Half Moon Hideaway , $150–$400
(631) 725-0992; halfmoon hideaway.com
Southampton
1708 House , $135–$475
(631) 287-1708; 1708house.com
Mainstay, $135–$395
(631) 283-4375;
www.hamptons.com/mainstay
Westhampton Beach
Inn on Main, $75–$250
Westhampton Country Manor, $165–$245
(631) 288-9000; www.hamptonbb.com

New Jersey

ZONE 5: Northern New Jersey

Bernardsville
Bernards Inn, $145–$215
(908) 766-0002
Chatham
Parrot Mill Inn, $125–$235
(973) 635-7722; parrotmillinn.com
Chester
Publick House Inn, $69–$101
(908) 879-6878
Edgewater
Whitebriar, $50–$155
(609) 871-3859
Frenchtown
Hunterdon House, $85–$145
(908) 996-3632
Widow McCrea House, $95–$145
(609) 996-4999; widowmccrea.com
Lambertville
Bridge Street House, $75–$140
(800) 897-2503 or (609) 397-4993;
bridgestreethouse.com
York Street House, $100–$175
(888) 398-3199 or (609) 397-3007;
yorkstreethouse.com
Pittstown
Seven Spring Farm, $85–$175
(908) 735-7675; sevensprings.com
Plainfield
The Pillars of Plainfield, $114–$190
(908) 753-0922; pillars2.com
Wantage
High Point Country Inn, $74–$85
(973) 702-1860
West Milford
Simplicity Inn, $115–$135
(973) 697-0494; siminn.com

ZONE 6: The Jersey Shore

Avon-By-The-Sea
Candlewick Inn, $85–$165
(732) 774-2998; candlewickbnb.com
Bayhead
Bayhead Gables, $100–$195
(732) 892-9844
Bay Head Harbor Inn$75–$175
(732) 899-0767; www.bayhead.org/ harborinn
Conovers, $140–$225
(800) 956-9099 or (732) 892 4664;
conovers.com
Beach Haven
Amber Street Inn, $95–$165
(609) 492-1611
Belmar
Down the Shore, $95–$100
(732) 681-9023
Seaflower, $90–$165
(732) 681-6006;
www.bbianj.com/seaflower
Manahawkin
Goose'N Berry Inn, $75–$155
(609) 597-6350
Ocean Grove
Carol Inn, $45–$100
(732) 502-0303; www.bbianj.com
Chelsea Morning Inn, $40–$135
(732) 775-8847; chelseamorning inn.com
Main Avenue House, $75–$225
(732) 897-9200
Pine Tree Inn, $45–$110
(732) 775-3264; pinetreeinn.com
Spring Lake
Evergreen Inn, $119–$239
(732) 449-9019; evergreeninn.net

Spring Lake *(continued)*
Hamilton House, $145–$225
(732) 449-8282
Sandpiper Inn, $129–$259
(800) U-B-Happy or (732) 449-6060; sandpiper.com
White Lilac Inn, $115–$220
(732) 449-0211; whitelilac.com

Tuckerton
JD Thompson Inn, $75–$155
(609) 294-1331; jdtompsoninn.com

ZONE 7: Cape May

Absecon
Dr. Jonathan Pitney House, $99–$209
(888) 774-8639 or (609) 569-1799 ; pitneyhouse.com

Cape May
Abbey, $100–$275
(609) 884-4506; abbeybedand breakfast.com
Henry Sawyer Inn, $85–$210
(800) 449-5667 or (609) 884-5667; henrysawyerinn.com
Linda Lee, $90–$115
(609) 884-1240 ; thelindalee.com
Mainstay, $100 – $295
(609) 884-8690; mainstayinn.com
Mission Inn, $135–$235
(800) 800-8380 or (609) 884-8380; mission-inn-nj.com

Mays Landing
Abbott House, $89–$99
(609) 625-4400

Ocean City
Barnagate , $70–$160
(609) 391-9366; barnagate.com
Castle by the Sea, $119–$299
(800) 398-3555 or (609) 398 3555; castlebythesea.com
New Brighton Inn, $105–$175
(609) 399-2829; newbrighton.com
Norwood Inn, $120–$185
(609) 399-6071
Serendipity, $78–$139
(609) 399-1554

Ventnor
Carisbrooke Inn, $89–$230
(609) 822-6392; carisbrookeinn.com

Delaware

ZONE 8: Delaware

Dover
Tudor House, $55–$75
(888) 859-5942 or (302) 736-1763

Lewes
Inn at Canal Square, $45–$185
(888) 644-1991; www.beach-net.com /canalsquare

Milford
Marshall House, $95
(800) 366-3814 or (302) 422-5708

New Castle
Fox Lodge at Leslie Manor, $105–$135
(302) 328-0768; foxlodge.com

Rehoboth Beach
Chesapeake Landing, $125–$275
(302) 227-2973; chesapeake landing.com
Mallard Guest House, $55–$265
(888) 872-0744 or (302) 226-3448; themallard.com

Pennsylvania

ZONE 9: Philadelphia Area/Bucks County

Bethlehem
Wydnor Hall, $110–$140
(610) 867-6851

Birdsboro
Brooke Mansion, $110–$145
(800) 544 1094 or (610) 582-9775; brookemansion.com

Fairville
Fairville Inn, $140–$195
(610) 388-5900

Fogelsville
Glasbern, $100–$305
(610) 285-4723; glasbern.com

Kennett Square
Scarlett House, $95–$135
(610) 444-9592

Kintnersville
Bucksville House, $100–$130
(610) 847-8948
Light Farm, $120–$150
(610) 847-3276

Linfield
Shearer Elegance, 475–$140
(800) 861-0308; shearerelegance.com

Malverne
General Warren Inne, $120–$170
(610) 296-3637; generalwarren.com

New Hope
Fox & Hound, $80–$170
(800) 862-5082 or (215) 862-5082
Hotel du Village, $90–$110
(215) 862-9911; hotelduvillage.com

Plumsteadville
Plumsteaville Inn, $85–$165
(215) 766-7500

ZONE 10: Eastern Pennsylvania and the Poconos

Blakeslee
Blueberry Mountain Inn, $90–$120
(570) 646-7144

Canadensis
Pine Knob Inn, $100–$215
(800) 426-1460; pineknobinn.com

Carbondale
Heritage House on the Park, $55–$105
(570) 282-7477

Clarks Summit
Red Barn Village, $79–$249
(800) 531-2567; redbarnvillage.com

Dallas
Ponda-Rowland Inn, $80–$115
(888) 855-9966; pondarowland.com

Eagles Mere
Crestmont Inn, $99–$158
(570) 525-3519
Eagles Mere Inn, $139–$225
(800) 426-3273; eaglesmereinn.com

Hawley
Academy Street, $65–$85
(570) 226-3430; academybb.com

Honesdale
Double W Ranch, $210 - $240
(877) 540-7262 or (570) 226-3118; doublewranchbnb.com

Milford
Inn at Starlight, $165–$255
(570) 798-2519; innatstarlightlake.com

New Milford
Lynn-Lee House, $80–$90
(570) 465-3505; lynn-lee.com

Tunkhannock
Weeping Willow Inn, $60–$80
(570) 836-7257

Union Dale
Stone Bridge Inn , $75–$155
(570) 679-9200; stone-bridge-inn.com

ZONE 11: Central Pennsylvania and Amish Country

Adamstown
Adamstown Inn, $70–$150
(800) 594-4808; adamstown.com
Barnyard Inn, $75–$120
(717) 484-1111
Black Forest Inn, $39–$89
(717) 484-4801

Akron
Boxwood Inn, $95–$185
(888) 594-9697 or (717) 859-3466; www.800padutch.com/boxwood.html

Bird-in-hand
Village Inn of Bird-in-Hand, $69–$149
(800) 914-2473; www.bird-in-hand.com/villageinn

Boyertown
Twin Turrets Inn, $95–$120
(610) 367-4513

Clay
Clearview Farm, $95–$145
(717) 733-6333

Denver
Cocalico Creek, $83–$97
(717) 336-0271

Ephrata
Historic Smithton Country Inn, $75–$150
(717) 733-6094

Lampeter
Australian Walkabout, $99–$225
(717) 464-0707

Lancaster
Flower & Thyme, $85–$115
(717) 393-1460
Gardens of Eden, $95–$130
(717) 393-5179

Marietta
Railroad House, $79–$119
(717) 426-4141

Paradise
Verdant View, $39–$89
(717) 687-7353

Reinholds
Barnyard Inn, $80–$155
(888) 738-6624; barnyardinn.com

Willow Street
Apple Bin Inn, $95–$135
(800) 338-4296; applebininn.com

ZONE 12: Southcentral and Western Pennsylvania

Abbottstown
Inn at the Altland House, $82–$92
(717) 259-9535

Annville
Swatara Creek Inn, $60- $80
(717) 865-3259

Benton
Red Poppy, $65–$85
(570) 925-5823

Bradford
Glendorn-A Lodge in the Country, $425–$625
(814) 362-6511

Bloomsburg
Inn at Turkey Hill, $87–$185
(570) 387-1500; innatturkeyhill.com

Bradford
Glendorn –A Lodge in the Country, $425–$625
(814) 362-6511

Chambersburg
Shultz Victorian Mansion, $70–$87
(717) 263-3371

Donegal
Mountain View, $135–$195
(724) 593-6349

Gettysburg
Baltimore Street, $90–$155
(888) 667-8266 or (717) 334-2454
Brafferton Inn, $90–$135
(717) 337-3423
Brick House, $90–$145
(800) 864-3464 or (717) 338-9337; brickhouseinn.com

Jim Thorpe
Harry Packer Mansion, $125–$595
(570) 325-8566

Mechanicsburg
Ashcombe Mansion, $100–$180
(717) 766-6820

New Berlin
Inn at Olde New Berlin, $99–$169
(800) 797-2350 or (570) 966-0321; newberlin-inn.com

New Oxford
Barker House, $65–$95
(888) 546-1520 or (717) 624-9066; barkerhouse.com
Flaherty House, $65–$120
(800) 217-0618 or (717) 624-9494; www.bbonline.com/pa/flaherty

Orrtanna
Hickory Bridge Farm, $95–$125
(717) 642-5261

Rockwood
Laurel Echo Farm, $40–$75
(888) 655-5335 or (814) 926-2760

Scottdale
Zephyr Glen, $65–$75
(724) 887-6577

Shippensburg
McLean House, $35–$50
(800) 610-0330 or (717) 530-1390

Somerset
Inn at Georgian Place, $95–$185
(814) 443-1043

Warfordsburg
Buck Valley Ranch, $75–$125
(800) 294-3759; buckvalleyranch.com

Maryland

ZONE 13: Western Maryland

Deep Creek
Haley Farm, $130–$195
(888) 231-3276; haleyfarm.com
Red Run Lodge, $79–$135
(800) 898-7786; www.deepcreek times.com/redrun

Grantsville
Elliott House Victorian Inn, $85–$150
(800) 272-4090; elliotthouse.com
Walnut Ridge, $75–$125
(301) 8955-4248

Frederick
Middle Plantation Inn, $90–$110
(301) 898-7128; mpinn.com
Spring Bank Inn, $90–$105
(800) 400-4667

Hagerstown
Beaver Creek House, $75–$95
(301) 797-4764
Sunday's, $79–$159
(800) 221-4828; sundaysbnb.com

New Market
Strawberry Inn
(301) 865-3318

ZONE 14: Baltimore and Central Maryland

Baltimore
Scarborough Fair, $139–$179
(410) 837-0010; scarborough-fair.com

Havre de Grace
Vandiver Inn, $85–$160
(800) 245-1655; vandiverinn.com

Linwood
Wood's Gain, $75–$125
(410) 775-0308; woodsgainbnb.com

Middleburg
Bowling Brook Country Inn, $95–$215
(410) 848-0353

Olney
Thoroughbred, $85–$220
(301) 774-7649

Stevenson
Gramercy Mansion, $175- $295
(410) 486-2405

Westminster
Winchester Country Inn, $85
(410) 848-9343

ZONE 15: Eastern Shore Maryland

Betterton
Lantern Inn, $75–$90
(800) 499-7265;
www.bbonline.com/md/lanterninn

Chestertown
Claddaugh Farm, $85–$95
(410) 778-4894; claddaughbb.com
Lauretum Inn, $65–$140
(800) 742-3236; www.chester town.com/lodging
Parker House, $110–$125
(410) 778-9041; www.chester town.com/parker
Widow's Walk Inn, $95–$120
(888) 778-6455; www.chester town.com/widow

Church Creek
Loblolly Landings & Lodge, $80–$175
(800) 862-7452 or (410) 397-3003;
loblollylandginsbandb.com

Easton
Chaffinch House, $90–$125
(800) 861-5074; chaffinchhouse.com

Galena
Rosehill Farm, $75.60
(410) 648-5334; www.eastern shorelodging.com

Hurlock
North Fork, $75–$160
(800) 636-7522

Ocean City
Lighthouse Club, $185–$285
(410) 524-5400

Oxford
Nichols House, $100–$125
(410) 226-5799;
www.oxfordmd.com/nicholshouse

Ridgely
Chesapeake Inn, $100
(800) 787-4667; chesapeakeclays.com

Rock Hall
Huntington Manor, $90–$130
(410) 639-7779

St. Michaels
Barrett's Bed & Breakfast Inn, $190–$250
(410) 745-3322; barrettbb.com
Kemp House, $100–$110
(410) 745-2243
Parsonage Inn, $140- $160
(800) 394-5519 or (410) 745-5519

Snow Hill
Mansion House, $140–$160
(410) 632-3189; mansionhousebnb.com

Tilghman Island
Black Walnut Point Inn, $120–$150
(410) 886-2452;
www.tilghmanisland.com/blackwalnut
Sinclair House, $75–$105
(888) 859-2147;
www.tilghmanisland.com/sinclair/

Whitehaven
Whitehaven, $75–$100
(888) 205-5921; whitehaven.com
Wingate
Wingate Manor, $75–$150
(888) 397-8717
Wittman
Inn at Christmas Farm, $145–$195
(800) 987-8436; innatchristmas farm.com

ZONE 16: Southern Maryland

Annapolis
Eastport House, $100–$145
(410) 295-9710 ; eastporthouse.com
Harbor View Inn, $145–$195
(410) 626-9802; harborviewinn ofannapolis.com
Inn at Spa Creek , $125–$165
(410) 263-8866; innatspacreek.com
Jonas Green House, $105–$140
(410) 263-5892; www.bbhost.com /jghouse
Prince George Inn, $100–$115
(410) 263-6418
Saltier, $220
(410) 263-8619
Two-O-One
(410) 268-8053; 201bb.com
Huntingtown
Serenity Acres, $99 –$114
(410) 535-3744;
www.bbonline.com/md/serenity
Solomons
Adina's Guest House, $90
(410) 326-4895
By-The-Bay, $90–$125
(410) 326-3428; www.chesapeake.net /~bythebaybandb
Scotland
St Michael's Manor, $75–$80
(301) 872-4025

Virginia

ZONE 17: Capital Suburbs and Northern Virginia

Berryville
Smithfield Farm, $135–$160
(877) 955-4389; smithfieldfarm.com
Culpepper
Fountain Hall, $95–$125
(800) 476-2944
Inn at Meander Plantation, $135–$275
(800) 385-4936; meander.net
Hillsboro
Catoctin House Inn, $85 –$110
(800) 851-3305 or (540) 668-6725
Leesburg
Norris House Inn & Stone House Tea Room, $110–$150
(800) 644-1806 or (703) 777-1806; norrishouse.com
Marshall
Fox Gloves, $135–$150
(540) 364-4499
Middleburg
Inn at Stringfellow Farm, $175–$250
(877) 409-4449; (540) 554-8730; innatstringfellowfarm.com
Longbarn, $115–$125
(540) 687-4137; www.members. aol.com/thlongbarn
Round Hill
Poor House Farm, $115–$155
(540) 554-2511; poorhousefarm.com
Spotsylvania
Littlepage Inn, $119–$164
(800) 248-1803; littlepage.com
Stafford
Courthouse Road, $85–$150
(540) 720-3785 or (800) 720-3784; courthousebandb.com
Upperville
Pizenpeeks Farm, $140
(540) 592-3054; piizenpeeksfarm.com
Washington, D.C.
Dupont at the Circle, $130–$250
(202) 332 - 5251

ZONE 18: Tidewater Virginia

Champlain
Linden House, $85–$135
(800) 622-1202 or (804) 443-1170
Chincoteague
Island Manor, $85–$130
(757) 336-5436

Champlain
Linden House, $85–$135
(800) 622-1202 or (804) 443-1170

Chincoteague
Island Manor, $85–$130
(757) 336-5436
Miss Molly's, $89–$175
(757) 336-6686

Charles City
Colonial Beach, $100–$110
(800) 224-7000
Piney Grove at Southall's Plantation, $130–$170
(804) 829-2480; pineygrove.com

Exmore
Gladstone House, $75–$85
(757) 442-4614
Martha's Inn, $85
(800) 996-2784 or (757) 442-4641

Gloucester
Inn at Warner Hall, $130–$215
(800) 331-2720 or (804) 695-9565; warnerhall.com

Norfolk
Bianca Boat & Breakfast, $250–$400
(800) 599-7659
Page House Inn, $122- $200
(757) 625-5033

Onancock
76 Market Street, $95
(757) 787-7600; 76marketst.com
Spinning Wheel, $75–$95
(757) 787-7311

Montross
Inn at Montross, $110
(804) 493-0573

Williamsburg
Candlewick Inn, $115–$145
(757) 253-8693
War Hill, $80–$150
(757) 565-0248; warhill.com

Yorktown
York River Inn, $110–$130
(757) 887-8800

ZONE 19: Central Virginia/President's Country/The Piedmont

Gordonsville
Sleepy Hollow Farm, $65–$115
(800) 215-4804 or (540) 832-2225; sleepyhollowfarmbnb.com

Petersburg
Folly Castle, $120–$130
(804) 861-3558
La Villa Romaine, $85
(804) 861-2285; www.lavilla.tieranet.com

ZONE 20: Shenandoah Valley/Blue Ridge Highlands

Abingdon
Summerfield Inn, $100–$140
(800) 668-5905 or (540) 628-5905; summerfieldinn.com

Catawba
Cross Trails, $75–$80
(800) 841-8078 or (540) 384-8078

Christiansburg
Oaks Victorian Inn, $135–$170
(800) 336-6257 or (703) 381-1500; www.bbhost.com\theoaksinn

Covington
Milton Hall, $95–$150
(877) 764-5866 or (540) 965-0196

Etlan
Dulaney Hollow , $85 –$135
(540) 923- 4470

Goshen
Hummingbird Inn, $110–$155
(800) 397- 3214

Lexington
Inn at Union Run, $85–$120
(800) 528-6466; unionrun.com
Maple Hall, $55–$180
(877) 463-2044; maplehall.com
Willow Pond Farm Country House, $115–$190
(540) 348-1310; willowpondfarm inn.com

Locust Dale
Inn at Meander Plantation, $95–$185
(800) 385 - 4936; meander.net

Luray
Woodruff Collection of Victorian Inns, $125–$295 MAP
(540) 743-1494; woodruffinn.com

Lynchburg
Lynchburg Mansion, $109–$144
(800) 352-1199; lynchburgmansion inn.com

Millboro
Fort Lewis Lodge, $150–$210
(540) 925-2314; fortlewislodge.com
Nellysford
Mark Addy, $90–$145
(800) 278-2154; mark-addy.com
Stanley
Milton House, $85–$185
(540) 778-2495; miltonhouse-inn.com
White Fence, $135–$160
(540) 778-4680; whitefencebb.com-
Staunton
Ashton Country House, $70–$125
(800) 296-7819 or (540) 885-7819;
www.bbhost.com/ashtonbnb
Thornhouse House at Gypsy Hill, $70–$90
(540) 885-7026; thornrosehouse.ccom
Steeles Tavern
Sugar Tree Inn, $110 –$150
(800) 377-2197; sugartreeinn.com
Warm Springs
Inn at Gristmill Square, $80–$140
(540) 839-2231; www. vainns.com/grist.htm
Meadow Lane Lodge, $105–$125
(540) 839-5959; meadowlanelodge.com
Waynesboro
Iris Inn, $85–$150
(540) 943-1991; irisinn.com
Woodstock
Inn at Narrow Passage, $95–$145
(800) 459-8002; innatnarrowpassage.com
River'd Inn, $95–$325
(800) 637-4561; riverdinn.com

West Virginia

ZONE 21: West Virginia—North

Augusta
Almost Heaven Guest House, $100
(304) 496-1073
Berkeley Springs
Manor Inn, $85–$130
(304) 258-1552; bathmanorinn.com
Charles Town
Cottonwood Inn, $85–$120
(800) 868-1188; cottonwoodbb.com
Gilbert House, $80 –$140
(304) 725-0637
Elkins
Warfield House, $80–$100
(888) 636-4555 or (304) 636-4555;
www.bbonline.com/wv/warfield
Davis
Bear's Den, $45
(304) 259-1245; bearsdenwv.com
Meyer House, $75
(304) 259-5451; meyerhousebandb.com
Gerrardstown
Mill Creek Manor, $85–$105
(304) 229-1617
Hedgesville
Farmhouse on Tomahawk Run, $85–$150
(304) 754-7350; tomahawkrun.com
Martinsburg
Boydville Inn, $125
(304) 263-1448; boydvilleinn.com
Morgantown
Almost Heaven, $75–$150
(304) 296-4007
Thomas
Lady Bug, $45
(304) 463-3362; www.ladybugbandb.bizland.com

ZONE 22: West Virginia—South

Bramwell
River's Bend, $65
(304) 248-8543;
www.geocities.com/riverbend
Charleston
Historic Charleston, $75–$85
(304) 345-8156
Fayetteville
Morris Harvey House, $75–$85
(304) 574-1902
Huttonsville
Cardinal Inn, $55
(800) 335-6149 or (304) 335-6149;
cardinalinnbandbwv.com
Lewisburg
Church Street, $90
(304) 645-7014
General Lewis Inn, $85–$146
(304) 645-2600; generallewisinn.com

Index